European Literary History

This clear and engaging book offers readers an introduction to European literary history from antiquity through to the present day. Each chapter discusses a short extract from a literary text, whilst including a close reading and a longer essay examining other key texts of the period and their place within European Literature. Offering a view of Europe as an evolving cultural space and examining the mobility and travel of literature both within and out of Europe, this guide offers an introduction to the dynamics of major literary genres, international literary networks, publication cultures and debates, and the cultural history of 'Europe' as a region as well as a concept.

Maarten De Pourcq is Professor of European Literature at Radboud University Nijmegen, Netherlands.

Sophie Levie is Professor Emeritus of Literary and Cultural Studies at Radboud University Nijmegen, Netherlands.

European Literary History

An Introduction

**Edited by Maarten De Pourcq and
Sophie Levie**

LONDON AND NEW YORK

First published 2018
by Routledge
2 Park Square, Milton Park, Abingdon, Oxon OX14 4RN

and by Routledge
711 Third Avenue, New York, NY 10017

Routledge is an imprint of the Taylor & Francis Group, an informa business

British Library Cataloguing-in-Publication Data
A catalogue record for this book is available from the British Library

Library of Congress Cataloging-in-Publication Data
A catalog record for this book has been requested

ISBN: 978-1-138-88672-8 (hbk)
ISBN: 978-1-138-88673-5 (pbk)
ISBN: 978-1-315-71462-2 (ebk)

Typeset in Bembo
by Apex CoVantage, LLC

Contents

Contributors

Rebecca Armstrong is Associate Professor in Classical Languages and Literature at St. Hilda's College at the University of Oxford in the United Kingdom.

Helleke van den Braber is Assistant Professor in Literary and Cultural Studies at Radboud University Nijmegen in the Netherlands.

Frank Brandsma is Associate Professor of Comparative Literature (Middle Ages) at the University of Utrecht in the Netherlands.

Bé Breij is Professor in Latin Language and Culture at Radboud University Nijmegen in the Netherlands.

Katherine Clarke is Associate Professor in Ancient History at St. Hilda's College at the University of Oxford in the United Kingdom.

Marguérite Corporaal is Associate Professor in English Literature at Radboud University Nijmegen in the Netherlands.

Theo D'haen is Professor Emeritus of American Literature at the University of Leuven in Belgium.

Maarten De Pourcq is Professor of European Literature at Radboud University Nijmegen in the Netherlands.

Koen De Temmerman is Professor in Classical Literature at Ghent University in Belgium.

Kai Evers is Associate Professor of German at the University of California at Irvine in the United States.

Robert Folger is Professor of Romance Literatures at the University of Heidelberg in Germany.

Nina Geerdink is Assistant Professor of Early Modern Dutch Literature at the University of Utrecht in the Netherlands.

Anke Gilleir is Professor of German Literature at the University of Leuven in Belgium.

Ellen Greene is Professor of Classics and Letters at the University of Oklahoma in the United States.

Raphaël Ingelbien is Associate Professor of English and Comparative Literature at the University of Leuven in Belgium.

Madeleine Jeay is Professor Emerita in Medieval Literature at McMaster University in Ontario, Canada.

Lotte Jensen is Associate Professor of Dutch Literary History at Radboud University Nijmegen in the Netherlands.

Erik Kooper is Assistant Professor in Middle English Literature and Culture at the University of Utrecht in the Netherlands.

Nita Krevans is Associate Professor in Classical and Near Eastern Studies at the University of Minnesota in the United States.

Pedro Lange is Professor of Comparative Literature, Film and Urban Studies at the University of San Francisco in the United States.

André Lardinois is Professor of Ancient Greek Literature at Radboud University Nijmegen in the Netherlands.

Sophie Levie is Professor of European Literature at Radboud University Nijmegen in the Netherlands.

Chris Louttit is Assistant Professor of British Literature and Culture at Radboud University Nijmegen in the Netherlands.

Konstantin Mierau is Assistant Professor of European Literature (Spanish) at the University of Groningen in the Netherlands.

Alicia C. Montoya is Professor of French Literature at Radboud University Nijmegen in the Netherlands.

László Muntéan is Assistant Professor of Cultural Studies and American Studies at Radboud University Nijmegen in the Netherlands.

Roberto Rea is Associate Professor in Italian Philology, Romance Philology, and Italian Literature at the Tor Vergata University of Rome in Italy.

Yolanda Rodríguez Pérez is Associate Professor in the Department of European Studies at the University of Amsterdam in the Netherlands.

Roy Rosenstein is Professor in Comparative Literature and English at the American University of Paris in France.

Mathijs Sanders is Professor in Modern Dutch Literature at the University of Groningen in the Netherlands.

Ruth Scodel is Collegiate Professor of Greek and Latin at the University of Michigan in the United States.

Catriona Seth is Professor of French Literature at All Souls College at the University of Oxford in the United Kingdom.

Claire Stocks is Lecturer in Classics at Newcastle University in the United Kingdom.

Bernhard Zimmermann is Professor of Classics at Albert-Ludwigs-Universität in Freiburg in Germany.

General introduction

Maarten De Pourcq

Travelling literatures

Figure 0.1 Europe city lights

Europe is a continent with numerous languages and diverse literary cultures that have been thriving for at least three millennia. From a geographical point of view, the European land stretches from the Arctic Ocean in the north to the Mediterranean Sea in the south, and from the Atlantic Ocean in the west to the Caucasus and Ural mountain ranges in the east, although this last border is subject to discussion. To define Europe in cultural terms is more difficult and requires even more caution, given the huge time span and the different kinds of cultural exchanges that have taken place across the continent and with other continents. Our starting point, whence the title of this introduction, is that literature has "travelled" in many different fashions and guises throughout Europe, both in time and in space. Literature can be regarded as one of the "international affairs" that binds Europeans, since sharing books is sharing culture. Interestingly, the geography of the European continent has been favourable to the travelling of literature, much more than those of other continents with inhospitable deserts, canyons, swamps or mountain ranges. As George Steiner once noted when discussing the idea of a European culture:

> Europe has been, is walked. This is capital. The cartography of Europe arises from the capacities, the perceived horizons of human feet. European men and women have walked their maps, from hamlet to hamlet, from village to village, from city to city. More often than not, distances are on a human scale, they can be mastered by the traveller on foot, by the pilgrim to Compostela, by the *promeneur*, be he *solitaire* or gregarious.[1]

The relative ease by which communities can come into touch with each other naturally intensifies the exchange of cultural goods, memories, practices, ideas and values, and produces the cultural infrastructure by means of which these exchanges can take place. Think of religious festivals, inns, theatres, coffee houses, universities, book shops and so forth. This handbook endeavours to explore these cultural exchanges, as well as the concomitant cultural conflicts, that have been or still are ongoing, from antiquity to our modern times. To get a sense of what we can learn from a European literary history, let us begin with an anecdote that is replete with cultural contacts and has had resonances even beyond the European continent.

The year is 1816. It is the beginning of a strange summer that would become known as "The Summer That Never Was". A climatic anomaly caused unusually low temperatures in different parts of Europe. It is raining heavily and incessantly over the Lake of Geneva, when a company of anglophone writers gathers around the fireplace of the Villa Diodati, a mansion close to the borders of the Swiss lake. They are reading from the *Fantasmagoriana*, a French anthology of German ghost stories, when their host, the English author Lord Byron, invites them to write a ghost story themselves as an appropriate pastime for these exceptionally gloomy days. It is here that John William Polidori, the son of an Italian father and an English mother, writes *The Vampyre*, a tale that would initiate the popular genre of the vampire story. It is also here that Mary Shelley laid the basis for a book that would become a world classic: *Frankenstein, or the Modern Prometheus*.[2] The protagonist, who creates a monster in this book, was probably named after the mysterious castle *Burg Frankenstein* in Germany where in the seventeenth century an alchemist experimented with an elixir that could give life to dead matter. Shelley equates her modern doctor in the subtitle of her book with the Prometheus of ancient Greek myth, who stole the element of fire from the gods and gave it to men, who used it to create their civilization. Prometheus, however, was severely punished by the gods for his crime: he was chained to a mountain in the Caucasus, on the outskirts of the European continent, where an eagle would peck daily at his liver, only for that liver to regenerate and to be pecked out again the next day. The reader who is familiar with this myth knows, or may expect, that Frankenstein – our modern Prometheus – in his attempt to transgress the limits of human power and become a God-like creator will be punished in his turn. The reader just does not yet know how, and so the classical reference to Prometheus gives zest to the reading experience. Prometheus also connects this book to the revolutionary age in which this book was written and which saw Prometheus as a rebel overturning the established royal powers. A last writer in the Villa Diodati worth mentioning here is Mary Shelley's lover and future husband, the Romantic poet Percy Bysshe Shelley, who was also very much intrigued by the revolutionary potential of the Prometheus myth. Yet, the tale he was working on was inspired by the vampire folk stories that Byron had encountered during his travels through the Balkans, where oral storytelling was still a defining part of literary culture, much more than in the literate West. This literary horror company, writing and reading together in a house threatened by unsettling weather, has become legendary and may remind us of the setting of Boccaccio's *Decameron* (see Chapter 10). In this classic literary work from the Middle Ages, a group of ten youngsters tries to evade "the Black Death", one of the worst plagues in European history, by hiding in a villa outside of the city of Florence and telling each other love stories. Ranging from medieval Florence to modern Geneva, from England to the Balkans, from Germany to the ancient Caucasus, our anecdote is laden with typical examples of cultural exchange and cultural mobility: travel and emigration; exchanges and contests among writers; translations, adaptations and oral transmissions, which keep narratives and cultural memories alive and inspire people to rewrite and create; reading practices, multilingualism and *linguae francae* (in this anecdote, anglophones reading French); references to classical narratives from another language or era; and genres that are practised regardless of languages or eras. These cultural practices transcend the borders of traditional national literatures and their literary histories, and can be brought together under the banner of a European literary history because of their international nature.

To some of this book's readers, the following pages will be their first encounter with such an international literary history, perhaps even with a literary history *tout court*. The purpose of the rest of this introduction is therefore twofold: to address some introductory aspects of the genre of a literary history, and to consider the general principles that underlie this specific European literary history.

The genre of literary history

One of the remarkable things about the genre of a history is that it is always written in the present. Even though its main interest is the past, its narrative and its form are motivated by present-day views, needs, styles and limitations. For example, the present of this literary history differs in at least three important ways from the present of Erich Auerbach's *Mimesis: The Representation of Reality in Western Literature* (1946). Auerbach's study is a history of European literature in its own right, written in Istanbul after his exile from Nazi Germany. The first difference lies in the availability of sources on European literature, which for Auerbach was fairly limited in Turkey. This may have forced him to concentrate on carefully reading single canonical texts, for which his literary history has become a true classic and a point of reference for many authors of this handbook. Unlike Auerbach, the authors of this handbook partake in large international networks and are equipped with comprehensive university libraries and digital collections, which obviously pose entirely different challenges to writing a concise literary history. However, access to scholarship, literature and the internet is not divided equally over the world, or on the European continent. This may already tell us something about the place and function of archives, libraries and, by extension, printed texts in European literary history. Books have become self-evident carriers of literature in most of the Western world but do not necessarily coincide with what literature looks like in each and every culture. In Russia, for instance, it took roughly until the eighteenth century before literature became a written culture; instead, an oral literary culture had been thriving for many centuries, just as in the Balkans in our previous anecdote. Literary history, however, generally concentrates on written texts. This "tyranny of the text", as it is usually called, is one example of a rule that informs many literary histories, including ours. It has become known as a distinctly *European* and *Western* rule. The material availability of written sources makes them accessible for people to collect, to read and to study, which is why European literary history traditionally concentrates on written culture and – especially from the invention of the printing press onwards – on the literary book. Yet, it is important to realize that this rule cannot be applied universally to all sorts of literary histories or to literature in general. Even though the literary book is a Western export that has shaped the face of modern world literature, it can also distort our conception of what literature is or can be; for instance a poem performed for a live audience and streamed on social media, or an ancient philosophical text written in poetic verse. There is neither a single nor a static definition of literature, not even in the realm of European literary history, as this book will show. This becomes even more clear when we look at the term "literature", which in its contemporary use is of a rather recent pedigree. Strictly speaking, if this handbook were to cover only those works that were named "literature" or "literary" in their own time, we should have started with the eighteenth century instead of antiquity (see Chapter 13), although the etymology of the term "literature" goes back to antiquity (sc. the Latin word *literatura*, writing). Yet, in antiquity, people used the term "poetry" rather than literature for aesthetical and fictional writing. This quick glance at the use of the term "literature" already lifts a corner of the veil that covers the tremendous complexity that comes with the phenomenon of literature and with European literary history.

A second difference between Auerbach's *Mimesis* and the present handbook is the historical crisis of World War II (c. 1940–1945). At the time that Auerbach was writing, the war was ripping apart the continent, producing Europe as we know it today, although this new world would scarcely have been imaginable to Auerbach, who back then felt the need to counterbalance the life-changing crisis of a world war by composing his own literary history. Present-day Europe is also going through hard times, with the rise of nationalism of various sorts, all of them telling examples of the deep-seated tension between national and international interests in European cultural politics. This tension recurs in a different guise in the way in which we study literary history. As Pascale Casanova, a leading critic in the field of international literary studies, has argued, "our literary unconscious is largely national. Our instruments of analysis and evaluation are national. Indeed, the study of literature almost everywhere in the world is organized along national lines."[3] Even though the European Union is trying to provide us with a new supranational infrastructure (e.g. through international literary festivals, translation awards, heritage databases, literary tourism, residency programs and academic networks), the language in which literature is – at least "originally" – expressed appears to have geopolitical consequences. The ancient poet Homer, for instance, did not write in Turkish or any of its officially recognized early forms, which means that he has not been included in a recent Turkish literary history,[4] although he is believed to have lived in ancient Ionia on the Turkish West Coast. Homer is celebrated as the first Greek poet (see Chapter 1), even though he possibly never put a single foot on present-day Greek soil. Language, not locale or cultural prestige, provides in this case the main selection criterion for being part of a national literary history.

Literature, then, seems to have belonged to nations ever since these nations, roughly from the nineteenth century onwards (when most of the current nations came into being),[5] have appropriated literature as part of their national cultural politics, which is not unlike what other worldly and religious powers had done before, or the European Union is attempting to do today. Literature was believed to express "the soul of the nation" and meant to create a sense of belonging among the people of that nation, especially when that literature was written in the national language promoted by the state rather than in other local or regional languages. France, for example, promoted from the seventeenth century onwards a standardized form of "French" which marginalised other languages like Occitan (see Chapter 8), Breton and Basque. Nations have good reasons for doing so, for language binds people, offering them not only a means of communication but also the first access to a common culture from childhood stories onwards, even if one is illiterate, like many Europeans were up to the beginning of the twentieth century. Literary writers are generally seen to be gifted with the ability to use their language in such a way that they not only create enticing fictional worlds but also make manifest the very nature and powers of their national language. That is one reason why literary writers can become national heroes and are also involved in the cultural competition between nations or with older literatures (e.g. from classical antiquity). Literary works from the past, even though they were written before the national infrastructure came into being (most modern European countries like Bulgaria, Germany and Italy did not exist before 1850), were appropriated as part of a collective memory process that turned these works into national heritage despite their transnational features (see the example of Homer), or the fact that their authors were not interested in any sort of national cultural politics at all. For literature not necessarily perceives itself from a national perspective – it is the way in which literary history is usually written and conceptualized, invigorated by the cultural and educational infrastructure of a nation, that in the first instance makes literature national.

Hence, there clearly are institutional reasons that may underlie the urge to write a new European literary history. This was certainly the case for that other prime example of twentieth-century philology, next to Auerbach: Ernst Robert Curtius's *European Literature and the Latin Middle Ages* (1953). As the title already suggests, this book argues in favour of the study of a European literature and in so doing runs counter to what Curtius saw happening in academia in his lifetime and what he defined as the "dismemberment" of literary history, both in terms of space – between different countries and languages – and in terms of chronology – between classical, medieval and modern literature. This "dismemberment", so Curtius argues, hinders a synthetic perspective on the historical interconnectedness of European literature. We no longer look at the way in which writers operate in international networks, share aesthetic and societal questions, use transnational cultural repertoires (like genres and their foundational texts; e.g. Homer for epic literature), or are being read and discussed at schools and universities across the continent. Curtius was convinced that European literature could be understood from the perspective of two cultural (chronological-spatial) categories: either they belonged to the Antique-Mediterranean culture, or to the Modern-Western culture. Many university programs in literature today are still organized in the "dismembered" fashion (usually combining the study of literature with that of a language, although this language does not necessarily coincide with one nation). But even if a truly synthetic perspective is hardly feasible for such a vast and diverse corpus of literary texts and practices, there is an ongoing shift in current curricula towards collaborative introductory courses that adopt a diachronic and transnational viewpoint on literary history, bringing together students of different European languages (also classical, medieval and modern) or introducing European literary history to students from more general programs like Literary Studies, Cultural Studies, Media Studies or European Studies. This handbook is meant for this kind of introductory literary history course, as it attempts to bring to light the various international dimensions of European literary history whilst also acknowledging, albeit mostly from a cross-national and cross-regional viewpoint, those tendencies and features that are at variance with this transnational dynamic.

Interestingly, both Auerbach and Curtius were German scholars who specialized in Romance literature, sharing a command of their first-language literature and at least one second-language literature, which means that they were capable of *comparing* two major linguistic as well as cultural European traditions, the Germanic and the Romance, and became interested in looking beyond these frontiers. Comparing is a crucial term here, since their work has become representative of what is called "Comparative Literature", a scholarly discipline that aims to explore connections (such as insightful similarities and differences) between literatures or literary texts of different times and places to improve our understanding of the phenomenon of literature or of specific literary phenomena. It is important to mention this here, since the discipline of Comparative Literature has been the subject of contestation in the past few decades for various reasons, one of them being its narrow focus on European literature (its so-called "Eurocentrism"). This criticism was famously expressed by Gayatri Chakravorty Spivak in a book with the ominous title *Death of a Discipline* (2003), a series of lectures addressed to scholars of Comparative Literature and Critical Theory in the USA. Spivak's main argument is that these scholars have unjustly limited their corpus of study to the European literary canon and in so doing reduced their understanding, definition and appreciation of literature itself. This is a third major difference between our present and that of Auerbach and Curtius, who wrote before the breakthrough of a school of progressive cultural criticism that has thoroughly questioned the central position of – usually male and heterosexual – Westerners in literary history and the writing of history at large. Spivak was born in India and works in the United States, two countries that were once part of the British Empire and hence have Great Britain as their former political and cultural oppressor. During the twentieth century, European countries let go of most of the colonies that had granted them long-standing global political power. Along with economic exploitation, many colonies had to endure a European acculturation process in which literature played an ambivalent role. On the one hand, literature was regarded as a prominent place where the civilized "European mind" had expressed itself in exportable books that could serve in colonial education; on the other, literature was also the place where early criticisms against these colonial practices were vented and where cultural interaction was explored, already in the Early Modern period (see Chapter 16). In Spivak's analysis of the state of affairs of comparative literature, dating from around the turn of the twenty-first century, she detects a "post-colonial" kind of imperialism, a "Eurocentric" state of mind among international scholars in a world of former colonizers and colonized. This mindset makes these scholars adhere to categories inspired by the former European nationalist lines, rather than invent new categories to explore other – especially non-European and less canonized – literatures and the role that (also European) literature plays in the new multicultural and globalized world. The current state of world politics, however, shows us that "nationalist" thinking – also outside of Europe – is persistent and that the idea of a multicultural reality is frowned upon as a progressive ideal or even fantasy. This, of course, makes her criticism of the way in which we deal with and organize the discipline of Comparative Literature all the more pressing, even more so for a new handbook on European literary history. The great benefit of the vast amounts of energy that have been put into the (mostly) post-colonial critique of literary history in the past few decades[6] is that it gives us a better idea of how Eurocentrism works and what it looks like. For it has made explicit a set of categories of thought and presumptions that are underlying the study of European literary history, a set of normative and structuring perspectives that came into being at different points in the course of that history in the past 500 (if one lets the history of European literature begin with the Renaissance, as some do) to 2,800 years (if antiquity is taken as the starting point, as this handbook does). In other words, the critique of European imperialism enables us to make explicit much more than before the standard ways in which literary history in Europe has been written and still is being written, and how this handbook relates to this tradition.

The "European model" of literary history

The starting point in this handbook is the hypothesis that European literature has become a model for how literature is generally conceptualized, understood and evaluated – a model which has been transported to and imposed upon non-European literary cultures, usually in former colonies. Speaking in terms of a European model, however, runs the risk of distorting and even obliterating the diversity of literary practices in Europe itself. This European "colonial model", as some have called it,[7] is made up of at least four perspectives that can be abstracted from the way in which a vast amount of European literature, including various national literatures from (Western) Europe, has been studied:

(1) Literature is defined, especially from the Renaissance onwards, as a text written in alphabetic writing, despite the important role of oral literary culture in several parts of post-Renaissance Europe (e.g. in Russia and the Balkans, as previously mentioned). We see this shift from oral to written culture already taking place in antiquity, when alphabetic writing on the European continent came into being, which is one reason why ancient texts are usually seen as the grounding texts of European literature and ancient rhetoric as the foundation of literary criticism (see Chapter 1 and Chapter 5). Another transnational aspect that should be mentioned here is the emergence of universities across the continent where texts were important study objects from the twelfth century onwards. These universities gave rise to a European intellectual elite equipped with a similar literary education and participating in what can be called a shared European culture, since many generations of these intellectuals revisited the same sets of texts that were deemed culturally important in their days and have written books on or have been inspired by them in their turn.

(2) Literary history is studied along the lines of specific historical periodizations (e.g. antiquity, Middle Ages, Renaissance, modernity). The concept of "Eurochronology"[8] has been coined for this, since this periodization cannot be simply applied to other parts of the world – even not to certain parts of the European continent. Interestingly, antiquity again plays a grounding role in defining these periods, as "the Middle Ages" are conceived as the age between antiquity and the Renaissance (when antiquity is said to be "re-born", hence "re-naissance"). Modernity in its turn is seen to have defined itself at its onset as a quarrel with "the ancients". This type of temporality, including the relationship of one's present and future with the or a (classical) past (cf. the cultural practice of imitation and emulation; see Chapter 1), is a driving force behind the European tradition of literary and cultural history.

(3) Literary history is studied along national lines (from the nineteenth century onwards, when the modern nation states created their respective "literary pasts", based on their national languages and expressed in a selection of canonized works) and in a competition between different nations and periods, with a distinction between major and minor literatures, which explains the cultural hegemony of the French, English and German languages, also at universities and schools elsewhere in Europe and beyond.

(4) The literary book is seen as a commodity, meaning that it not only communicates a narrative and gives an aesthetic or ritual experience, but that it is also a product with an economic value, making literature – both as a practice and as an object – part of Western capitalism, an economic model that has been exported from Western Europe to the rest of the world (cf. our modern expression "the literary market", see Chapter 13 and Chapter 28).

These perspectives are interconnected dimensions of one model: if literature cannot be objectified in a written text (perspective 1), it is less prone to be multiplied, shipped and sold (perspective 4). If texts are not published or distributed, it becomes much harder to date them and thus to allot them a place in the chronology of a literary history (perspective 2) or the canon of a national history (perspective 3). If literature originates in an oral context, in a place without national power claims, in a language from a country that has minor cultural influence or by a writer whose gender, class or ethnicity attracts less cultural prestige, it will most likely fall outside of the records of a literary history, especially when it is a European literary history. Does this mean that these literary phenomena, works or practices are less valuable? Or that they are less exemplary for certain tendencies in, for instance, a European literary history? Certainly not. This handbook, despite its relatively compact size, pays attention to the impact on literature of social class, migration and gender; to themes that are often off the beaten track (such as cultural mobility; e.g. Chapter 2 and Chapter 28) or the modern mystery novel (Chapter 23); and to peculiar instances of reception (such as classical myth in ancient school exercises; Chapter 5) or our decision to take a play from the Dutch playwright Vondel as exemplary for Early Modern drama, rather than Shakespeare, which is explained from a reception perspective (Chapter 14). We do make mention of literature from nearly all European countries, even though the selection of key texts discussed in each chapter does not represent as many different national literatures as possible. The aim of this introductory handbook is not encyclopaedic, contrary to the francophone survey *Lettres européennes* (2007), which covers an admiring range of authors and books from the entire continent, or the still ongoing multi-volume series *Comparative History of Literatures in European Languages*, which started in 1973. We have chosen an approach that explores and discusses a great but limited number of themes, mostly from a canonical and traditional perspective, but not without being critical of or even slightly modifying the standard perspectives, as will be clear from this introduction. Even so, this handbook follows for the greater part the perspectives of the European literary history model outlined previously.

Our approach

To begin with, we have organized this history according to a chronology in which we follow a relatively standard periodization of five eras (antiquity, Middle Ages, Early Modern Period, the Long Nineteenth Century and the Modern Era), with the rationale behind this choice explained in the introductions to each period. We believe that if one wishes to navigate and travel comfortably through European literary history – and certainly if one wishes to continue the journey after this book and immerse oneself into more scholarship so as to become an expert – one needs anchor points and points of orientation, which these periods are and have been for at least two centuries. They also bring along their own scholarship, part of which we have tried to capture in the five different themes that are addressed in each of the five periods in this book. Yet, we also stress the relative nature of this periodization, which already becomes apparent in the fact that we speak of the "Early Modern period", which incorporates the Renaissance, or the "Long Nineteenth Century", which for various reasons can be seen to have its historical beginnings and endings beyond the nineteenth century itself. For sure, there are adventures awaiting as soon as one has become familiar with this "Eurochronological" approach and decides to skip these standard anchor points and enter less charted territories. But that is not the primary goal of this book.

Along with the chronological and thematic approach, this handbook uses short extracts of carefully selected literary texts (our so-called "key texts") in each chapter. Thanks to these extracts, readers cannot only become familiar with reading literary texts from the perspective of a specified theme but also experience the feeling, including the pains and pleasures, of reading a historical literary text. This book thus both discusses and presents bits of European literature and it does so always in English. Nearly all of these texts are easily accessible in their original or another language, either through a library or the internet, but to give an idea of the effect of reading these key texts in their original language, we have included one non-English extract next to the English translation, the Occitan version of a troubadour poem by Jaufre Rudel (in Chapter 14). Our hope is that readers, teachers and students will add more primary literature to these chapters so that they can elaborate, flesh out, contrast or criticize their central themes. This also makes it possible to engage more widely and to enter into a broader discussion with different national or less canonical literatures as well as with other internationally relevant literature.

All chapters have been written by (couples of) specialist authors who have a different disciplinary, linguistic or national background, while all periods have been coordinated by a team of mostly Netherlands-based specialist editors. Both authors and editors have been invited to address in each period, either in the introduction or in the thematic chapters, the following topics in relation to European literary history:

- the different materialities and media of literature;
- the medium of literature as such;
- the dynamics of major literary genres;
- the construction of a literary canon, then and now;
- international literary networks, publication cultures and literary infrastructures;
- the international societal debates in which literature plays a role, and the international debates on literature;
- cultural exchanges and contacts within Europe and with non-European worlds;
- reading and analyzing a selection of literary works, and – again, selectively – discussing their readership, reception or afterlife throughout the ages and across regional borders and media;
- the importance of literature for the cultural history of "Europe" as a region and an idea.

This multi-form approach enables readers to follow the tracks of these topics like running threads throughout the narratives of this handbook.

To conclude, we would like to return to the title of this introduction, "Travelling literatures", as it indicates the direction which this handbook has taken. As said previously, we primordially look at literature as texts and written culture, which is why we have not adopted the term "literary culture" in the title of our handbook, as some recent literary histories do. The idea of travelling helps us to look at the international and transnational dimensions of European literature, since literature usually does not abide by national or linguistic borders. Literature travels, or can travel, in various ways, as the Geneva anecdote in this chapter already indicated: e.g. through intertextuality (texts referring to other texts), translations and adaptations (also in other media than literature, for instance puppetry or Hollywood films), travelling writers and audiences, travelling books (e.g. for colonial use or with migrants), universities, schools and encyclopaedias, and so on. The very fact that specific literary texts have travelled cannot be related solely to their beauty or their message, even though we should not overlook these dimensions, since they make up a great deal of what makes literature important, interesting and special for many people. It must be noted that, just like with human beings, not everyone is free or has the means to travel. In other words, many of these literary texts are in one way or another "empowered" to travel because, for instance, they are or have become part of a culturally influential region, person, publishing house, genre or era. It is no coincidence that canonized literature is most often produced in or near powerful places: think of Horace's poetry in Augustan Rome, Rudel's poetry at the French court, Vondel's drama in Amsterdam during its Golden Age, or Zadie Smith's novels in high capitalist London. Since this handbook takes travelling literatures as its starting point to present and discuss European literary history, cultural influence reasonably is a defining aspect of our narrative and the organisation of this handbook.

Perhaps surprisingly in the light of the criticism of Spivak and others, there are few international handbooks that introduce students to European literary history. It is our hope that this book fills a gap and helps beginners to read beyond national borders, being mindful of the shifting and porous nature of these borders as well as being attentive to the historical nature of literature itself.

Postscript

On a more practical note, a few guidelines may help the reader to navigate through this book. Chapters contain parenthetical cross-references to other chapters. Asterisks indicate important technical terms that are collected in the index of terms at the end of this book so that the reader can find other examples or further explanations for each indicated term. Another index provides the reader with a list of authors and works mentioning the respective dates of birth, death and publication. All chapters end with a section of suggestions for further reading.

Finally, we would like to express our warm gratitude to the people and institutions that have made this book possible, along with our publisher Routledge. The Institute of Historical, Literary and Cultural Studies at Radboud University Nijmegen and the Radboud Internationalisation Fund have financed an international expert meeting which brought together the contributors and editors of this book in Nijmegen. Willy Piron from the Centre of Art Historical Documentation at Radboud University has been a great help in sourcing the illustrations for this book. The Department of Literary and Cultural Studies of Radboud University has been a great support throughout, also thanks to its junior assistants Nikkie Jessen, in the very beginning, and Mannick Wolters, for the greater part of the process, who have been invaluable in turning this project into the book that you are now reading. *Dank jullie wel!*

Notes

1 Georg Steiner, *The Idea of Europe: An Essay* (New York/London: Overlook, 2015). The essay is also available in open access at www.opendemocracy.net/can-europe-make-it/george-steiner-benjamin-ramm/idea-of-europe (last visit: 12 June, 2017).
2 For further information on Shelley's *Frankenstein*, see e.g. Anne K. Mellor, *Mary Shelley: Her Life, Her Fiction, Her Monsters* (London/New York: Routledge, 1988) and Graham Allen, *Shelley's Frankenstein* (London/New York: Continuum, 2008).
3 Pascale Casanova, *The World Republic of Letters*, trans. Malcolm DeBevoise (Cambridge, MA/London: Harvard University Press, 2007), xi.
4 Talat S. Halman, *A Millennium of Turkish Literature: A Concise History*, ed. Jayne L. Warner (New York: Syracuse University Press, 2010).
5 See Joep Leersen, *National Thought in Europe: A Cultural History* (Amsterdam: Amsterdam University Press, 2008).
6 Apart from Gayatri Chakravorty Spivak, *Death of a Discipline* (New York: Columbia University Press, 2003) and Casanova, *The World Republic*, see Frederic Jameson, "Third-World Literature in the Era of Multinational Capitalism," *Social Text* 15 (1986): 65–88, David Perkins, *Is Literary History Possible?* (Baltimore/London: The Johns Hopkins University Press, 1992), Linda Hutcheon and Mario J. Valdés, eds., *Rethinking Literary History: A Dialogue on Theory* (Oxford: Oxford University Press, 2002), Christopher Prendergast, ed., *Debating World Literature* (London/New York: Verso, 2004), Theo D'haen, David Damrosh and Djelal Kadir, eds., *The Routledge Companion to World Literature* (London/New York: Routledge, 2011) and Emily Apter, *Against World Literature: On the Politics of Untranslatability* (London/New York: Verso, 2013).
7 The term comes from Walter Mignolo; see Hutcheon and Valdés, *Rethinking Literary History*, 155-ff.
8 Arjun Appadurai, *Modernity at Large: Cultural Dimensions of Globalization* (Minneapolis: University of Minnesota Press, 2000), 30, and Prendergast, *Debating*, 6.

Further reading

Bemong, Nele, Mirjam Truwant and Pieter Vermeulen, eds. *Re-Thinking Europe: Literature and (Trans) National Identity*. Amsterdam/New York: Rodopi, 2008.
Benoit-Dusausoy, Annick and Guy Fontaine, eds. *Lettres européennes: Manuel d'histoire de la literature européenne*. Brussels: De Boeck, 2007.
Domínguez, César, Haun Sassy and Darío Villanueva. *Introducing Comparative Literature: New Trends and Applications*. London/New York: Routledge, 2015.
Hutcheon, Linda and Mario J. Valdés, eds. *Rethinking Literary History: A Dialogue on Theory*. Oxford: Oxford University Press, 2002.
Prendergast, Christopher, ed. *Debating World Literature*. London/New York: Verso, 2004.

Part I
Antiquity

1 Introduction

André Lardinois and Claire Stocks

Figure 1.1 Virgil, depicted in a manuscript of the *Aeneid*, c. 500 CE, Biblioteca Apostolica Vaticana, Vat. Lat. 3867, f. 104r

"I sing of wars and the man" (*arma uirumque cano*). So begins Virgil's *Aeneid*, a Latin epic written at the height of the Roman Empire when ancient Rome was being governed by its first emperor, Augustus, who came to power in 27 BCE. This epic of some 10,000 lines in Latin by the author Publius Vergilius Maro (Virgil, also spelled Vergil in English) tells the story of "the man" Aeneas, the legendary Trojan warrior who left his home town of Troy, in modern-day Turkey, after it had been destroyed by the Greeks, and came to Italy to found a city from which the future Rome eventually would rise.[1] The Aeneas of Virgil's epic never founds this city (the epic ends with Aeneas killing his local Italian enemy, Turnus, on the battlefield), but no matter. This is the epic that came to define Rome; the successor to the Greek epics of Homer and a work that would come to shape European literature from Virgil's own day up to and including contemporary literature.

In the first part of this book, dealing with classical antiquity,[2] we present some of the major literary works from the ancient world, we discuss what literature means in this period, and we consider the impact of classical literature on European literature and thought. We aim to show how these texts, like Virgil's *Aeneid*, can be viewed as "European" despite being written at a time when Europe as we know it today did not exist. The "ancient world" covered a vast period of time from the beginning of recorded history (several thousand years before the common era) up to the early Middle Ages, although those texts that we typically classify as ancient literature generally date from the eighth century BCE until the fifth century CE. Spanning several hundreds of years, this period of history featured changing geographical landscapes as emerging powers claimed new territory for their empires, which at times incorporated not only European regions like Italy and Greece but also areas in Asia and in Africa.

This was the world that "Europe" was part of and the literature that it produced can be viewed as a reflection of this changing political, cultural and geographical landscape. As power shifted from one empire to another, so did Europe's cultural centres, most notably from Athens (Greece) to Alexandria (Egypt) and to Rome (Italy). As each new cultural centre claimed power and influence over its rivals, the authors within those centres sought to respond to these changes in their literary works. When we study texts from the ancient world, therefore, we can see these authors engaging directly with the literary works of their predecessors and contemporaries. This direct and deliberate engagement with other texts is what is known as "intertextuality"*, and it is an important concept for all European literature. No literary text exists in a vacuum, but it builds on and, consciously or unconsciously, responds to previous texts: the ancient Greeks reacted to earlier Near Eastern genres, the Romans to Greek literature, and later European literature to the texts that survived from Greece and Rome.

Singing of arms and men

Ancient literature can be divided predominantly into two different types: works of prose and works of poetry. Ancient prose works cover genres such as historiography, rhetoric, and the ancient novel (all of which are covered in this section), whilst poetic works include lyric poetry, drama, and epic. For those ancients who wrote poetry, this also meant writing in different metres*: lines of Greek and Latin that contained a set number of syllables that were either "long" or "short" and "heavy" or "light" to create a specific rhythmic effect. Such works were often intended to be read aloud – or even performed – since the *sound* of the text mattered as much as its content. When Virgil claims to "sing" about arms and the man, therefore, he means this literally: it was the epic poet's job to proclaim the deeds of heroes*, and this idea of singing is rooted in the very origins of epic. For before the written word was the spoken, and long before the epics of Homer (our earliest extant epics) acquired written form, they were performed by travelling bards* who entertained the crowds they met on their journeys.

We will return to this idea of "orality" in a moment, but for now let us focus on the hero of Virgil's epic, Aeneas, and his own European journey – from Troy in the East to Rome in the West – as a refugee in search of a new home.

> I sing of wars and the man, fated to be an exile, who long since left the land of Troy and came to Italy to the shores of Lavinium; and a great pounding he took by land and sea at the hands of the heavenly gods because of the fierce and unforgetting anger of Juno. Great too were his sufferings in war before he could found his city and carry his gods into Latium. This was the beginning of the Latin race, the Alban fathers and the high walls of Rome.[3]

In the first few words of this epic, Virgil tells us that he intends to focus on wars (*arma*) and on a man (*uir*), Aeneas. But despite the fact that the emperor Augustus claimed direct lineage from him as the supposed founder of the Roman race, Aeneas was not by any modern definition "European". According to tradition he was the son of the goddess Venus and a mortal man, Anchises, who came from Troy, a city located in modern-day Turkey.

This "fact" already problematizes our understanding of what would have constituted a European identity in the ancient world, but first we need to recognise that at this time there was no concept of a shared European identity beyond the basic and often vague recognition of the continent of Europa (so the term was in use and most probably coined in antiquity), alongside Asia and Libya (also known as Africa), and an equally vague, cultural distinction between East and West, with the "East" being made up of ever-changing peoples from Asia and also Egypt. People in the ancient world, therefore, whilst they would have been culturally and politically aware of other states, would not have viewed themselves as "European", but rather would have identified with the geographical location in which they were born and raised. More often than not this would have been a place rather than a country: thus Athens as opposed to Greece; or Rome as opposed to Italy. Ideologically*, therefore, a person's sense of self in the ancient world was most frequently defined in terms of what it meant to be "Athenian" or "Roman". This process of self-definition was put into practice by comparing oneself to the people with whom one came into contact. A repeated pattern that we see in ancient Athens, for example, was the desire of Athenian citizens to define themselves in relation to their Spartan as well as Persian enemies, viewing themselves as the cultural counterpart to both of them.

When the legendary Aeneas makes his journey from Troy in the East to Italy in the West (the voyage referred to in lines 1–3 previously), therefore, he is not simply traversing his way across what was – to Virgil's audience* – the geographical space of Augustus's empire. His journey was a symbolic one, a statement that Rome had become the cultural hub to which all peoples should gravitate. This claim to cultural superiority is also suggested by the opening lines of Virgil's epic. For in lines 5–7, Virgil tells his audience that the *Aeneid* is an epic about foundation and succession. This idea of foundation and succession operates on two levels. First, Aeneas is presented as the founder of the Roman race, with Augustus as his direct descendent. Second, Virgil presents his epic both as a foundation text for Rome, in its guise as the new cultural and political centre of the world, and as the successor to the much-revered Greek epics of Homer, which stand at the beginning of ancient Greek literature: the *Iliad* and the *Odyssey*. Virgil alludes to both these works in the opening words of his epic: to the "wars" that Aeneas will fight, which recall the battles in Homer's *Iliad*, and to the "man", Aeneas, who will follow in the footsteps of Odysseus, as he voyages across the Mediterranean sea, searching for his home.

Thus "wars and the man" are defining features of Virgil's epic and both are inextricably tied to the idea of foundation. The Latin verb for "to found", *condere*, that Virgil uses in line 5 illustrates this tie well. For as well as meaning "to found", this verb can mean "to compose" – thus also referring to Virgil's composition of the *Aeneid* – and "to strike", referring to the physical act of (e.g.) plunging a sword into the heart of an enemy in battle. This is, in fact, how Virgil uses this verb at the *end* of his epic, when he describes how Aeneas kills his enemy, Turnus. This, then, was foundation, achieved by a man through war and embodied in poetry.

Virgil's epic, at both its start and its end, illustrates the role that war plays in the composition and content of ancient literature. This is especially clear to see in literary genres such as epic* and historiography, which frequently address issues of war, but its presence also extends to love poetry*, where poets could present themselves as soldiers battling for the object of their affections. This obsession with warfare is in part a reflection of the times in which these authors were writing. War was an integral part of people's lives in ancient times and throughout most of European history. War, and by reflex literature, was predominantly the domain of "the man" in the ancient world, but it would be wrong to presume that women played no role in ancient literature. Whilst the position of women in society varied across the ancient world in accordance with different time periods and cultures, not only were women influential in political affairs in, for example, Rome and Egypt, but texts have survived that were written by women in Greece and Rome.[4]

Women also play a prominent role as characters within literary texts of the ancient world. These roles are, of course, most frequently assigned by male writers, with the result that the depictions of these women tend to follow distinct stereotypes: they are depicted as the object of the male gaze; they are cast in the domestic roles of mother, daughter, and wife; or they buck these trends and, as a result, are depicted as "problematic". Nevertheless, ancient literature has created many powerful women, such as Helen, Medea, and Dido, whose longevity and influence are evident throughout European literature.

Nor should it be forgotten that according to Greek mythology*, the personification of Europe was a woman, the princess Europa. Like many a mythological female in the ancient world, Europa's story is one of male aggression followed by divine reward. According to the most common tradition, Europa was the daughter of the king of the Phoenician city of Tyre. She was abducted by the god Zeus, who disguised himself as a bull and tricked her into climbing up onto his back when she was playing with friends by the seashore. Zeus whisked Europa away across the sea to the Greek island of Crete – so completing another mythical journey from East to West – and after raping her he gave her as a "reward" (or rather recompense) semi-divine offspring which would rule over Crete. The irony of an "Eastern" woman from Tyre giving her name to what we now call Europe affirms the malleable nature of boundaries – both geographical and cultural – in the ancient world. And it is a reminder that much ancient literature has the idea of travel and transition at its heart. The myth of Europa as the source for the name "Europe" is one of several aetiological* (that is "origin") stories concerning the origin of this world. Such stories captivated ancient writers for millennia, and the re-workings of these tales* are a key aspect of ancient, especially poetic, works.

The literature produced in the ancient world was, therefore, affected by a number of factors: shifting cultural centres and geographical boundaries, wars, and the literary output of previous generations. Yet despite these shifting boundaries and the long stretch of time, it is possible to chart the progression from one cultural powerhouse to the next, and to see within this complex world the development of distinct literary genres, as well as the transition of literature from orality to the written word, and from poetry to prose.

From singing songs to writing prose

Ancient Greek literature is usually divided into four time periods that coincide with four recognisable periods in ancient history: the archaic Greek period (ca. 800–500 BCE); the classical Greek period (ca. 500–300 BCE); the Hellenistic period (ca. 300–30 BCE), when Greek culture (referred to as "Hellenistic") spread over the whole Mediterranean world; and the Roman Imperial period (ca. 30 BCE to 450 CE). Latin literature, of course, started well before 30 BCE, when Rome conquered the last remaining Hellenistic kingdom, Cleopatra's Egypt. It can be subdivided into three periods: the preliterate period (750–250 BCE); the Republican period (250–30 BCE); and the Imperial period from 30 BCE until the end of the western Roman empire, usually dated around 450 CE. At the transition from the Republican to the Imperial period falls the Golden Age of Latin literature with authors such as Cicero, Horace, Ovid, and Virgil. The first century CE is often referred to as the Silver Age of Latin literature.

This periodization is practical for providing an overview of Greek and Latin literature, but it says little about developments in the literature itself. When we survey Greco-Roman literature as a whole, we can see four distinct trends:

1. The emergence of prose next to poetry.
2. The slow transition from orally delivered poetry to written forms of literature intended to be read.
3. A steady increase in the number of genres.
4. The establishment of Latin literature next to Greek.

These developments we will trace in the following paragraphs.

The archaic Greek period (800–500 BCE)

Classical literature starts with a Big Bang: the Homeric epics, *Iliad* and *Odyssey*, which are usually dated to the eighth century BCE. They are of unusually high quality for such early compositions. The reason for this is that, although the Homeric epics represent* the oldest classical (and with it European) written texts, they are the products of a long process of oral composition. In the 1930s the American classicist Milman Parry compared the composition of these epics with orally performed epics in Serbia and Bosnia-Herzegovina, and concluded that the Homeric epics too were based on a long, oral tradition*.

Orality* is a feature not only of the Homeric epics but of much ancient literature. In order to understand this, one ought to distinguish among three different types of orality: oral delivery, oral transmission, and oral composition. Literature is already considered "oral" when it is primarily intended to be performed*, like modern theatre*. In antiquity this was the case not only with drama, but also with lyric poetry, at least in its earliest form, and even with a number of prose genres. The next step is that compositions can also be orally transmitted*, as is for example the case with nursery rhymes* nowadays. Much of early Greek poetry was transmitted by word of mouth before it was written down in the form we possess today. The highest level of orality is when compositions are not only performed and transmitted through word of mouth, but also orally composed in a process of improvisation* on the spot. Parry demonstrated that this must have been the case with the earliest forms of the Homeric epics.

The same is true for the didactic epics that are preserved under the name of Hesiod and date to roughly the same period as the Homeric epics: the *Theogony* and the *Works and Days*. The difference between didactic epics* and the epics of Homer, which are commonly referred to as narrative epics*, is that they do not tell a single story, but try to instruct the reader (or listener) with precepts and short, edifying tales. The *Theogony* describes the origin of the world and the way in which Zeus acquired supreme power among the gods; the *Works and Days* tells how to farm and lead a righteous life. These two epics are, just like the Homeric ones, composed in a distinct metre, known as the hexameter* (lines consisting of six more or less identical rhythmical units) and were originally intended to be orally performed.

From the seventh century BCE onwards, a number of poets are known who composed lyric poetry. In lyric poetry*, which is much shorter than epic, experiences of a single person, usually the first-person speaker* in the poem, are presented as paradigmatic (that is, exemplary). The name "lyric" refers to the fact that these poems were originally performed as songs to the accompaniment of the *lyra* ('lyre').

Towards the end of the archaic Greek period, a number of thinkers emerged in Ionia, a region that was inhabited by Greeks on the west coast of modern Turkey, who started to question the mythical world as described by Homer and Hesiod, and instead looked for natural elements (earth, water, fire, and air) as possible origins of the world. These so-called natural philosophers are the first authors whom we know to have expressed their ideas in prose, perhaps because they intended their work to be read by equally minded people rather than to be publicly delivered. Some of these early philosophers, however, continued to render their thoughts in verse, such as Parmenides and Empedocles.

The classical Greek period (500–300 BCE)

The beginning of the classical period in Greek literary history is marked by a series of wars which the Greeks fought with the Persian empire and which they, rather unexpectedly, won. The outcome of these wars was that the city of Athens acquired a position of considerable power in the Greek world. It headed an alliance against future threats of Persia and required cities and islands who joined this alliance to pay into its treasury. The Athenians used some of this money for large building projects – for example, the splendid temples on the Acropolis in Athens – but also to stimulate the arts. Thus they organised every year in the spring a dramatic festival* for the god Dionysus. For this festival the famous Greek tragedies* and comedies* were produced.

The emergence of drama* as a genre and the prominence it received in classical Athens has sometimes been attributed to democracy, which the Athenians introduced as their form of government in the fifth century BCE. It provided entertainment for great numbers of citizens. The connection with democracy is even greater in the case of rhetoric, a genre that emerged in classical Athens and was practised both in the courts and in the popular assembly.

Rhetoric* was closely connected to philosophy* in classical Athens. The wealth and fame of this city attracted intellectuals, known as "sophists"* (wise men), from all over the Greek speaking world. They taught philosophy, science, and literary criticism*, besides rhetoric. In part as a reaction to the teachings of these sophists, the two most famous

Greek philosophers, Plato and Aristotle, developed their ideas in the fourth century BCE. Under the name of Plato, twenty-five so-called dialogues have been preserved. These dialogues* are not only important for their philosophical content, but also as literary products in prose, because of the way in which Plato subtly characterises his speakers. In antiquity in general, little distinction was made between literary texts and philosophical or scientific treatises. They were all expected to attain the highest level of stylization and literary competence, which is why they are all commonly regarded as part of classical literature. Scientific prose* was produced in the classical period by a doctor named Hippocrates, who in so doing laid the foundation of modern medicine, and by Aristotle and his pupils.

Besides drama, rhetoric, philosophy, and scientific prose, historiography* developed into a distinct genre in classical Athens. Its origin, like those of philosophy and scientific prose, lies with the Greeks who lived in Ionia on the west coast of Turkey. They were the first who reported their "investigation" (*historia*) into the past in simple prose. In fifth-century Athens, this practice expanded into a literary genre in which a writer developed a political and moral vision of history and presented this in more elegant prose. The development of this genre illustrates well the transition from texts delivered orally to those intended to be read. We are told that Herodotus, who wrote a history of the Persian wars and of the peoples who participated in it, gave public recitations of his work in various Greek cities. Later he joined the different parts together and published the work as a whole. Other historical treatises, however, that were composed after Herodotus by such authors as Thucydides and Xenophon, give the impression that they were intended to be read right from their conception.

The Hellenistic and Roman Republican period (300–30 BCE)

In 338 BCE, King Philip of Macedon, a small state in northern Greece, united mainland Greece under his rule. Four years later, his son Alexander – later known as Alexander the Great – led a Greek army into Asia and conquered the Persian empire, claiming sovereignty over vast territories in Asia and Egypt. No other historical event had such an impact on the development of ancient literature. Because of the conquests of Alexander and the cultural politics of his successors, who divided the conquered territories after his death, Greek culture spread over the whole of the Near East and the Mediterranean basin. Everywhere in the East new cities were founded, populated in part by Greek immigrants who brought with them their language, culture, and literature. The most famous of these towns was Alexandria, named after the conqueror, in Egypt. This period is known as the Hellenistic period after the Greek name for mainland Greece, Hellas; "Hellenisation" is the term for the adoption of Greek culture outside of Greece. The new territories into which the successors of Alexander the Great divided his empire are referred to as the Hellenistic kingdoms, of which Egypt, which was ruled by a Greek dynasty until 30 BCE, was the most prosperous.

This enormous expansion of Greek culture was made possible in part by the shift from an orally performed literature to one that was predominantly read. Of course, choral songs* and tragedies continued to be produced, and men competed with one another in the delivery of speeches* also in this period, but most literature from now on was written to be read. The gradual spread of literacy* in great parts of society enabled this development, although the actual reading of literature was a habit mostly of the elites* throughout antiquity.

Another noteworthy development in this period is the great admiration and canonisation* of authors who were active in the archaic and classical periods. This literature became a common reference point for the elites in the Hellenistic kingdoms and later in the Roman Empire, but also for new authors. They could count on their readers to be familiar with these canonical authors and they reacted to them in their own works from a principle known in Latin as *imitatio et aemulatio* ('imitation* and emulation*'). They copied form and content from these canonical authors, but at the same time deliberately deviated from them. Apollonius of Rhodes, for example, worked in the tradition of Homer by writing a narrative epic about the adventures of Jason and the Argonauts, but at the same time incorporated elements of tragedy and contemporary science and philosophy.

Epic poetry was not the most practised or even admired form of poetry in the Hellenistic period, however. This period developed instead a taste for short and refined poetry, which was much more suitable for being read than listened to. Exemplary of this development was the creation of the genre of the literary epigram*: a short, memorable poem of minimally two (but usually four to eight) lines.

Another, small scale genre that was developed in the Hellenistic period is the epyllion* (literally: 'little epic'). It constitutes a short narrative* usually made up of no more than around 100 lines. Examples are the poems of Theocritus, which are also referred to as idylls*. Most famous are his idylls about shepherds and their peaceful lives in beautiful nature, no doubt appealing to readers who were living in busy cities like Alexandria. They are the origin of bucolic literature* or pastoral literature* and were imitated (and emulated) by Virgil in his *Eclogues*, a series of poems which he wrote before the *Aeneid*.

Although Greek poetry, especially as texts to be read, attained new heights in the Hellenistic period, the advance of prose genres continued. Prose became the sole medium for philosophy, science, and historiography. Science* grew more independent of philosophy and explored a great number of subjects, including geography, linguistics, mathematics, and medicine. As example of historiography, the writings of Polybius may serve. He spent much of his adult life as a Greek hostage in Rome and wrote admiringly about the rise of Roman power in forty volumes, of which only five have completely survived; the rest we only know from summaries made in antiquity.

It is important to remember that only a very small part of literature written in antiquity has survived: according to some estimates only between 5–10 percent. Most of this literature was already lost in antiquity itself, because it was not sufficiently copied, but other texts were lost in the Middle Ages. Luckily the desert sands of Egypt, where Greek culture was introduced in the wake of Alexander's conquest, has sometimes preserved ancient texts, which have been discovered and excavated since the end of the nineteenth century.

When Polybius arrived in Rome in 167 BCE, he found a city at the cusp of becoming a world empire. Rome had by then been a republic for over three centuries. It had defeated its archrival, Carthage in North Africa, and gained control over the Western Mediterranean. Through trade with southern Italy, which had been settled by Greek colonists in the seventh century BCE, Rome had long been in contact with Greek culture. This contact intensified when Rome conquered southern Italy and mainland Greece at the end of the third century and beginning of the second century BCE.

The time before the middle of the third century BCE is referred to in Latin literature as the preliterate period. Of this period, very little survived into later times. From the third century BCE onwards, however, the Romans adopted most of the literary genres developed by the Greeks. The Romans themselves identified the beginning of their literature with the figure of Livius Andronicus, a freed slave from the Greek-speaking town of Tarente in southern Italy who translated Homer's *Odyssey* into Latin. Prominent Latin poets in the Roman Republican period were Plautus and Terence, who introduced Greek-style comedy in Rome; Ennius, who produced narrative epics and tragedies in Latin; Lucretius, who wrote a didactic epic on "the nature of things" (*De Rerum Natura*); and Catullus, who stands at the beginning of Latin lyric poetry.

Prose was from the beginning important in Roman society as well. The *Leges XII tabularum* ('Laws of the Twelve Tables') may serve as an example. These laws, which were allegedly passed after civil unrest in the middle of the fifth century BCE, were originally written down on twelve bronze tables and served as the basis of subsequent Roman law. They were composed in very old and archaic Latin. Latin prose was perfected above all by Marcus Tullius Cicero, who lived at the end of the Roman Republic. Cicero is most famous as an orator*, but he also wrote philosophical and political* treatises, handbooks on oratory, and letters.

The Roman Imperial period (30 BCE to 450 CE)

In the first century BCE, Rome further expanded its power by Caesar's conquest of Gaul (modern France) and Augustus's incorporation of Egypt into the Roman Empire. This time was also marked, however, by terrible civil wars, from which Augustus finally emerged as victor. He managed to consolidate all political and military power in his person and effectively ruled as the first Roman emperor from 27 BCE until 14 CE. The beginning of the Roman Imperial period is a watershed both in Greek and Latin literature. From now on, these two literatures developed side by side and can almost be treated as one. Rome was from this period onwards at the centre of a multi-ethnic and multicultural empire, in which the elite mastered both the Greek and Latin language. The basis of this common culture was the educational* system, in which boys were trained in rhetoric.

Epic poetry was picked up by Latin authors such as Virgil and Ovid, who arranged a whole series of Greek and Roman myths around the theme of bodily change in his *Metamorphoses*. Ovid also made an important contribution to the development of Latin lyric poetry. There were very few Greek authors who composed poetry in the Roman Imperial period. A prominent exception is Nonnus of Panopolis (ca. 450 CE), who wrote an epic in over 20,000 verses (twice as long as the *Aeneid*!) about the adventures of the god Dionysus, but also a literary paraphrase of the gospel of John in verse. He exemplifies the transition from "pagan" poetry (better: poetry with a traditional Greco-Roman subject) to Christian poetry (poetry with a Christian subject) at the end of antiquity. The Gospels, which were written in Greek in the second half of the first century CE, had a growing influence on Greek and Latin literature, especially after 312 CE, when the Roman emperor Constantine recognised Christianity as the state religion.

All prose genres were practised under the empire in abundance. The first and second centuries CE produced a number of Greek historians who spent time in Rome and produced histories in Greek about the Roman empire, such as Dionysius of Halicarnassus, who wrote a treatise called "Roman antiquities" (*Romaikê archaiologia*). Latin historiography in this period is dominated by the works of Livy, who wrote a history of Rome *ab urbe condita* ('from the foundation of the city') and Tacitus, who described the first emperors in his *Annals* and *Historiae*. Stoicism, a philosophical school founded by Zeno at the end of the fourth century BCE, was dominant with authors such as Seneca, who wrote in Latin, and Epictetus, who wrote in Greek. From the second century CE onwards, Christian authors, who regularly took over ideas from the Stoics, started to write theological* treatises, explaining and recommending the new faith both in Greek and in Latin. The most prolific Christian author, who had an enormous influence on subsequent Christian thought, was Augustine, who lived around 400 CE. Another very prolific author and representative of scientific prose is Galen. He was trained as a gladiator physician in Asia Minor, but rose to the rank of court physician under emperor Marcus Aurelius. From his hand more than a hundred treatises on medicine have survived, but, as was quite typical of intellectuals of his time, he also wrote on philosophy, grammar, and literary questions. Rhetoric was ubiquitous under the Roman Empire.

The Roman Imperial period saw the emergence of a number of new literary genres as well. In poetry this was satire*, which had been part of lyric poetry, but which the Romans developed into an independent genre with authors such as Horace and Juvenal. The most important development in literature at this time was that Greek and Latin authors for the first time started using prose to write fiction* rather than "truthful accounts" such as history, philosophy, or science. In this way the novel or romance* emerged, a genre which in antiquity was still rather modest, but from the nineteenth century onwards became the most prominent form of literature. The ancient novel* was a kind of narrative epic in prose, in which love was the most important theme: handsome boy and beautiful girl find one another again, after many wanderings and ordeals, at the end of the story. Five such novels have been preserved in Greek, all dating from the first to the fourth century CE. In Latin literature two adventure novels*, both deviating from the standard pattern described previously, are passed down: the *Satyrica* (also known as *Satyricon*) of Petronius (first century CE) and the *Metamorphoses* of Apuleius (second century CE).

Within historiography, the biography* and autobiography* developed as distinct genres. The Greek historian Xenophon had already written a life of the first Persian king, Cyrus the Great, and he had experimented with the autobiographical form in his *Anabasis*, an expedition he undertook with 10,000 Greek mercenary soldiers into the heartland of the Persian empire in 401 BCE. This work clearly influenced Caesar's account of the wars he undertook in Gaul. The Gospels* can also be considered part of the genre of biography. This genre was perfected by Plutarch, a Greek writer who lived towards the end of the first century CE, and in a series of parallel lives compared famous Greeks with Romans, such as Alexander the Great and Caesar. These biographies were very popular in the sixteenth and seventeenth centuries, and Shakespeare drew on several of them for the plots* of his historical plays*. Augustine, who was also mentioned previously, perfected the form of the autobiography in his *Confessions*, in which he delivers a very personal account of his life until his conversion to Christianity, when he was thirty-two years old.

Another genre that became established in the Roman Imperial period was the fable. Fables* are short narratives, usually with a moral lesson, in which animals or sometimes objects act like human beings. Animal fables are known from ancient Egypt and the Near East and Greek poets such as Hesiod (mentioned previously) already incorporated them in their poetry. Demetrius of Phaleron (fourth century BCE) produced a collection of fables in prose, attributed to a slave named Aesop, but only in the Roman period did the genre attain literary status by being turned into verse by the Greek poet Babrius (second century CE) and the Latin poets Phaedrus (first century CE) and Avianus (ca. 400 CE). Their work was to have an enormous influence on later European writers, such as Jean de La Fontaine in France (1621–1695), who in turn inspired a host of writers in other countries.

Finally the letter*, which from its conception was destined for the page, gained literary status. We first hear of letters of Aristotle being published after his death and seven letters of Plato have survived, but most of these look like they were later imitations. Indeed, it became fashionable, especially in the Roman Imperial period, to write pseudonymous letters of famous historical individuals, such as Plato. But it also became more common to exploit the letter form to express one's own views. The early Christians in particular used the letter form to communicate their teachings, starting with the apostle Paul, who wrote his letters to various Christian communities in stylized Greek. In Latin literature the letter form received a boost from the publication of Cicero's letters – some intended for publication, others more private – after his death, and was used by Seneca and Pliny the Younger, among others. The Romans also developed the poetic epistles* with Horace in his *Epistulae* (also known as *Epistles*) playing on the conventions of everyday letters, while Ovid in his *Heroides* composed imaginary letters of famous mythological figures (mostly women). By developing all these genres and elevating them to a sophisticated level, the Greeks and Romans laid the foundation of European literature.

Classical literature from the epics of Homer until the *Confessions* of Augustine covers more than 1,200 years. It was developed in an area stretching from Spain to Persia and Egypt to Britain, and comprises many genres, which underwent significant changes: from oral delivery to literature intended to be read, from poetry to prose, and from Greek to Latin. In the subsequent chapters of this section, we will examine in more detail some of the themes that stand out in this vast body of literature, starting with travel as a returning theme in classical literature in Chapter 2, as the Greeks and Romans were expanding their own horizons into Europe, Africa and Asia. Chapter 3, Chapter 4, and Chapter 5 focus on the very productive genres of lyric poetry, drama, and rhetoric, including the ways in which they touch on other genres in antiquity. Finally, in Chapter 6, we look at classical literature itself as a form of remembrance of the communal past, of great ideas, and, ultimately, of Greco-Roman antiquity itself.

Notes

1 Rome was said to have been founded ultimately by the legendary twin brothers Romulus and Remus, who were credited with being descendants of Aeneas.
2 The word "classical" is often used, as here, as synonym for "Greek and Roman", or it is used for anything that is old and canonical, but it can also refer to a distinct period in Greek history: the classical period (ca. 500–300 BCE).
3 Virgil, *Aeneid* 1.1–7, translation adapted from David West, *Virgil, The Aeneid: A New Prose Translation* (London: Penguin Books, 2003).
4 For an overview, see Ian M. Plant, *Women Writers of Ancient Greece and Rome: An Anthology* (Norman, OK: University of Oklahoma Press, 2004). She lists fifty-five women writers whom we know of by name.

Further reading

Clayman, Dee and Joseph Farrell. *The Oxford History of Classical Literature*. 3 vols. Oxford: Oxford University Press, forthcoming.
Easterling, Pat E., and Bernard M.W. Knox, eds. *The Cambridge History of Classical Literature*. 2 vols. Cambridge: Cambridge University Press, 1985.
Harrison, Stephen, ed. *A Companion to Latin Literature*. Oxford: Wiley-Blackwell, 2005.
Rutherford, Richard. *Classical Literature: A Concise History*. Oxford: Wiley-Blackwell, 2005.
Whitmarsh, Tim. *Ancient Greek Literature*. Cambridge: Polity Press, 2004.

2 Travelling in Greek and Roman literature

Rebecca Armstrong and Katherine Clarke

Figure 2.1 The Siren Vase, red-figured stamnos, attributed to the Siren-painter, 480–70 BCE, Attica, British Museum, London, museum number: 1843,1103.31

Homer's *Odyssey* stands as the earliest travel literature* of Europe, composed around the eighth to seventh century BCE. Set after the Trojan War (see Chapter 1), this epic* poem, divided into 24 books,[1] tells of the long and eventful journey of one of the Greek commanders, Odysseus, back to his homeland, the Greek island of Ithaca, and his struggle to regain control of his kingdom, which was usurped in his twenty-year absence, and to reunite with his wife, Penelope. In the following passage from Book 14, Odysseus has just returned to Ithaca, but he does not yet know whether it is safe to reveal his true identity. While speaking to his old servant Eumaeus, he claims to be the son of a wealthy Cretan who fell on hard times after his father's death, but survived the Trojan War, after which he was able to indulge his passion for sailing and adventure by leading an expedition to Egypt.

Text: Homer, Odyssey *(ca. 800–700 BCE)*

There for seven years I stayed and gathered together
much substance from the men of Egypt, all gave to me:
but when in the turning of time the eighth year had befallen me,
then came a Phoenician man, well skilled in beguilements,
a gnawer at others' goods, and many were the hurts he inflicted
on men, and by his wits talked me over, so I went with him   290
to Phoenicia, where lay this man's house and possessions.
There for the fulfillment of a year I stayed with him,
but when the months and when the days had come to completion,
with the circling back of the year again, and the seasons came on,
then he took me on his seafaring ship to Libya,
with lying advices, that with him we could win a cargo, but in fact
so he could sell me there and take the immense price for me.
I went with him on his ship, forced to, although I suspected
all, on a North wind that was favorable and fair, above
the middle of Crete, but Zeus was plotting these men's destruction.   300
But after we had left Crete behind us, and there was no more
land in sight, but only the sky and the sea, then Kronian
Zeus drew on a blue-black cloud, and settled it over
the hollow ship, and the open sea was darkened beneath it.
Zeus with thunder and lightning together crashed on our vesel,
and struck by the thunderbolt of Zeus, she spun in a circle,
and all was full of brimstone. The men were thrown in the water,
and bobbing like sea crows they were washed away on the running
waves all around the black ship, and the god took away their homecoming.
But Zeus himself, though I had pain in my heart, then put   310
into my hands the giant mast of the ship with dark prows,
so that I still could escape the evil, and I embracing
was swept along before the destructive stormwinds.
Nine days I was swept along, and on the tenth, in black night,
the great waves rolling washed me up on the shore of Threspotia.
There the king of the Threspotians, the hero Pheidon,
looked after me without price, for his own dear son had come on me
when I was beaten by weariness and cold air, and lifted me
up by the hands, and led me home to the house of his father,
and put a mantle and tunic about me to wear as clothing.   320

It was there that I had word of Odysseus, for this king told me
he had feasted and friended him on his way back to his own country;
and he showed me all the possessions gathered in by Odysseus,
bronze and gold and difficulty wrought iron. Truly,
that would feed a succession of heirs to the tenth generation,
such are the treasures stored for him in the house of the great king.
But he said Odysseus had gone to Dodona, to listen
to the will of Zeus, out of the holy deep-leaved oak tree,
for how he could come back to the rich countryside of Ithaka,
in secret or openly, having been by now long absent.[2]   330

Large portions of the *Odyssey* are devoted to Odysseus's adventures on his journey: there are storms, alluring nymphs, a dangerous encounter with a one-eyed giant known as the Cyclops, and so on. His decision to fabricate this comparatively mundane "back-story" rather than more closely adapt the fabulous themes of his real journeying offers a contrast at once amusing and fascinating. The storm scene is reminiscent of that in which Odysseus loses his men in Book 12, and shares its immediacy of description and reflections on the divine: Zeus sends this storm, which he allows the innocent "Cretan" to survive, just as he sent the earlier storm against Odysseus's companions, who had sinned by eating the cattle of the sun god, but allowed Odysseus to escape. The appearance of Odysseus himself within the "Cretan tale" offers an alternative itinerary, a cross-country way Odysseus might have gone, although he actually came via the fabulous lands of the Cyclops and a mythical people called the Phaeacians.

The story is not without its own excitement – a villain from the exotic land of Phoenicia (modern-day Lebanon), storm and shipwreck, and an abundance of treasure – but the Mediterranean here presented belongs to the realm of the real world. The "Cretan" moves from Egypt to Phoenicia, and is on his way to Libya (North Africa) when the storm hits near Crete and he is washed up in Thesprotia, a region in north-western Greece. These are not fantastical, off-the-map places like the island of the Phaeacians, but real and recognisable lands bordering the Mediterranean Sea. Although the dangers of seafaring are very apparent in this tale, so is the underlying ordinariness of criss-crossing the Mediterranean in a ship in pursuit of wealth.

The Phoenicians are particularly fascinating travellers. They are portrayed in Greek literature as renowned sailors and traders, yet also (as here) notoriously untrustworthy and even piratical. The Greek historian Herodotus will later trace the origins of the Trojan War to a Phoenician trading trip which turns to the abduction of Greek women, including Helen (for whose abduction by the Trojans the Greeks started the famous "Trojan War"), in the opening chapters of his *Histories*, but here the would-be slave-trader's actions chime with the experience of the tale's immediate recipient. Odysseus tells his "Cretan tales" to his old servant, Eumaeus, who suffered at these people's hands: he was kidnapped as a boy by Phoenicians.

The (fictional*) report of Odysseus's inland journey to Dodona to consult Zeus's oracle also has the ring of truth about it, even as we know it to be a lie: here religious reasons for travel coincide with the mercenary, as the oracle is relied on for advice about how best to retain the booty amassed on a different kind of journey. Thus from the very start, ancient literature finds in travel a fascinating intersection of the real and the imaginary.

The ongoing influence of Odysseus as the paradigmatic traveller throughout ancient literature, whether in poetry or in prose, is explored in the first section below. From this fictional literary figure we move on to consider how ancient literature depicts real travel, both by land and by sea, as poised between danger and tantalising adventure. We note the way in which the possibilities for safe travel are enhanced by the relative peace under the Roman Empire, although the great mobility of the ancient Mediterranean is reflected in literature from the earliest period onwards, as we have seen. After examining the various motivations for ancient travel – commercial, religious, recreational, or the pressures of war – we turn finally to the ancient figure of the travelling intellectual for whom journeying is inherently bound up with mental enlightenment and the poets for whom journeys themselves become symbols of literary enterprise.

The literary tradition of Odyssean travel

The example of Odysseus and his journey overshadows many a travel narrative*, and ancient literature abounds in allusions* to the Homeric "original", whether via brief references or more sustained interaction. Indeed, the term "odyssey" has come to refer to any extensive journey of exploration in modern parlance. Accounts of other great seafaring adventures, such as the journey of Aeneas from Troy to Italy, are frequently in dialogue with the Homeric (see the introduction). Apollonius of Rhodes's third-century BCE epic, the *Argonautica* (the voyage of the famous ship, the Argo), self-consciously revels in belonging to an age much later than Homer's, yet tells a myth from a time before the Trojan War. The hero, Jason, is often thrown into relief against the memory* of Odysseus: where the latter is the man of many wiles, Jason is nonplussed and cautious. Yet his concern to build consensus rather than impose his authority results in the majority of his crew surviving their voyage, while Odysseus is the only one of his original band who lives to achieve his long-deferred homecoming (*nostos* in Greek). The exploits of the lone adventurer contrast – even in the realms of fabulous creatures and high epic drama – with the comparatively co-operative, even political, approach to travel among Apollonius's Argonauts.

The hero* of Virgil's *Aeneid* (see the introduction) is also a latter-day Odysseus: Aeneas's journey is similarly prolonged by divine intervention, involves encounters with foreign peoples and even monsters (including an overtly post-Odyssean meeting with the now blinded Cyclops), and has at its centre the longing for home. Its political outlook and concentration on the collective endeavour of reaching Italy and successfully waging war once there identify it as an epic with a perspective similar to that of Apollonius's *Argonautica*. Yet much of the emotional punch of the *Aeneid* is found in the complication of the Odyssean theme of return: Aeneas's actual home, Troy, has been reduced to burning embers, and many Trojans are either dead or enslaved. The hero can never achieve a real *nostos*, but must learn to regard the future site of Rome as his home: his heroic goal functions as his *nostos*.

Although later epic journeys are the natural heir to those of Homer's *Odyssey*, the range of genres influenced is far wider. To take just a few examples, in a fragmentary poem praying for the safe return of her brother Charaxus from a trading voyage, the lyric poet Sappho (see next Chapter 3) uses Homeric turns of phrase alongside broader Odyssean allusion to the role of the gods in ships' safe return, and the relief brought by the restoration of the head of the household to women who had been left to cope without him. A tragedy* by the Athenian playwright Euripides, called the *Helen*, offers an alternative myth of Helen of Troy as innocent victim rather than cause of the Trojan War, mapping the reunion of Odysseus and his wife Penelope at the end of the *Odyssey* onto Helen and her husband, Menelaus, in Egypt. In his elegies from exile, called the *Tristia* and the *Epistulae ex Ponto*, the Roman poet Ovid implies a double "epic journey" by presenting his enforced translocation from Rome to the Black Sea in terms both of a variation on the *Odyssey* and of a latter-day *Argonautica*. Ovid is prevented from making the journey he wishes to undertake, back to Rome, but, in a neat literary conceit, his books are imagined as travelling in his stead in the opening line of the *Tristia*.

The appeal of the Odyssean model is not limited to poets, either. Although the opening to Herodotus's *Histories* alludes more obviously to Homer's *Iliad*, nevertheless the Odyssean framework is never far from Herodotus's mind. Both the eyewitness historian, who frequently refers to his own travels, and characters within his narrative, not least successive Persian kings with their armies on imperialistic expeditions, conduct epic journeys across vast lands and seas. Xerxes's expedition against Greece is reminiscent of the *Iliad*: it reverses the trajectory the Greeks went and makes Xerxes actually visit the site of Troy, narrated in Book 7 of Herodotus's *Histories*. But as the defeated Persian army struggles home across the Aegean, the notion of a subverted Odyssean *nostos* is evident. Tales of turbulent travel are also the stock in trade of the ancient novels*, which often align characters' experiences with those of Odysseus. In Heliodorus's novel* *Aethiopica* (from the third or fourth century CE), Odysseus himself plays the part of Poseidon, the god who persecuted him in the *Odyssey*, to the hero and heroine of the story, Chariclea and Theagenes, threatening them with a repetition of his own sufferings on land and sea because they failed to pay homage to his memory.

The *Odyssey* as the paradigmatic travel text provided a literary framework within which authors could formulate a worldview, either explicitly or implicitly alluding to a geography that had already been delineated. Even when the Homeric or Odyssean mythical* map was subject to sceptical disbelief, being clearly incompatible with the known realities of the Mediterranean world, the world travelled by Odysseus still formed the mental map of all those who had enjoyed a decent education. That this influential geography was defined by a creative work of literature rather than by "real" journeys set the mould for writers of the Hellenistic period and beyond to create "maps" through the fiction of travel. Thus, Agatharchides of Cnidos in his *Periplus of the Erythraean Sea* (second century BCE) used the form of a (probably) fictional journey to map out the peoples of the east coast of Africa according to their respective cuisines. Other authors mapped out the shores of the Mediterranean through the medium of coastal voyages. Strabo, author of the only fully extant geographical* description from the ancient world, who lived in the late first century BCE and early first century CE, acknowledges his debt to Homer in the opening chapters of his *Geography* and constructs his description of the world predominantly as an imaginary journey clockwise around the Mediterranean.

Travel by sea and land

Travel in the ancient Mediterranean was in reality and in the imagination interconnected with the seas beyond, as well as the continents which surrounded it. Nevertheless, it enjoyed a conceptual unity, both through its Homeric heritage and through shared characteristics of peaceful commerce and productivity. The idea, propagated by Strabo in his *Geography* that travelling around the Mediterranean was rendered safe by the Roman suppression of conflict and piracy, contradicts his own observations elsewhere that sea-travel was dangerous. The obsession of the ancient novelists with piracy perhaps reflects the relative safety of the seas in their times, with pirate attack and abduction moving from the realm of the real into that of the deliciously adventurous. Nevertheless, the allure of the sea drove men to overcome their fears, however well-founded. When cataloguing the dangers of treacherous sandbanks on the coast of North Africa, Strabo comments that man's disposition to take risks means that he will try anything, especially coastal voyages. The capacity of the sea to entice the unwary traveller onto its perilous waters affords sea-travel a moral ambiguity that pervades ancient literature.

The archaic Greek poet Hesiod, self-confessedly no great sailor, emphasizes the risks of trading by sea, and very conservatively limits the safe sailing season to July and August, while even that is still subject to the whims of the gods; to set sail in the spring is little more than dicing with death. For the Romans, sailing becomes emblematic of the decline from a time of simple virtue, and mankind's insistence on jumping on board ships illustrates his transgression of natural boundaries established by the gods. As the Roman poet Horace puts it: "In vain in his wise foresight did God cut sever/the lands of the earth by means of the dividing sea/if impious ships yet leap/across waters which they should not touch."[3]

At the same time, and precisely *because* sailing allows man to travel where he otherwise could not, ships are also presented in ancient texts as being paradigmatic of human ingenuity. The Parian Marble, a Greek chronicle* recorded on a stone pillar erected in 264/3 BCE, includes the sailing of the first large ship from Egypt to Greece in its list of key moments of invention, discovery, and change. In the choral ode* on the "wonders of man" from Sophocles's tragedy *Antigone* (see Chapter 3), the list of achievements begins with the crossing of the sea under a stormy wind, while the Roman poet Catullus (84–ca. 50 BCE) styles Jason's ship, the *Argo*, as the very first ship and a source of wonder to the sea-nymphs who witness its first voyage in *Carmen* 64. The moral ambiguity associated with turning to the sea could be turned on its head in other ways too. The city of Pisa was, according to Strabo, famed for its ship-timber, which was formerly used to counter perils on the sea, but now was used for buildings at Rome and the construction of luxury villas, "now that people are devising palaces of Persian magnificence."[4] The subversion of timber from being used to secure Mediterranean mobility to being used for luxurious living is given further negative charge by the mention of Persian despotism. Here, moral decline is associated with turning *away from* rather than *towards* maritime travel.

While travel by sea has a particular prominence in ancient literature, the emergence of road networks – most systematically developed by the Romans, but present from earlier periods, too – also leaves its mark on the literary landscape. Heroic adventure was not the sole preserve of marine travel: the encounters of the Athenian hero Theseus with monstrous bandits as he travels overland from the Greek town of Troezen to Athens, as described, for example, by the Greek lyric poet Bacchylides (ca. 520–450 BCE), illustrate the possibilities for a handy hero who chooses to travel by road. The traveller and geographer Pausanias, who lived in the second century CE, characterises the catalogue of conquered brigands as a clearing of that road: Theseus renders the route safe for generations to come. Not to be out-done, Heracles is even credited with road-building: as he passes through the Alps, he transforms the route into one suitable for use by armies and baggage trains, as well as killing off the local bandit population, as reported by the Greek historian Diodorus Siculus (first century BCE).

The Roman success in road-building offered a similar combination of the practical and symbolic, as roads simultaneously facilitated traffic between the centre and peripheries of empire and presented enduring and visible markers of imperial power: indeed, a panel on the victory column erected by the Roman emperor Trajan in Rome in 113 CE depicts men felling trees and engaging in road-building, reflecting the centrality of this activity to the display of imperial ideology*. For the Roman poet Horace, however, in his *Satires** a road-trip from Rome to Brundisium conjures little patriotic fervour, but rather thoughts of endless mud, rutted roads, and unedifying scenes in shoddy roadside taverns.

The Roman philosopher Seneca (ca. 0–65 CE) describes in one of his letters* (*Epistula* 57) a shorter journey from Baiae to nearby Naples: the land road initially seems preferable to a stormy hop along the coast in a ship, but it turns out to involve wading through mud (again) as well as shuffling claustrophobically through the dark and dusty Naples tunnel.

In spite of problems brought by weather and terrain, the enhanced possibilities under the Roman Empire for travel involving both land and sea are brought out vividly in Strabo's description of the journey from the East to Rome. He outlines the various routes across the Adriatic to Brundisium, from where two land routes open up – one manageable only by mules, and both converging on the Appian Way, the famous road from Rome to southern Italy, for the final stretch of the journey. Elsewhere, Strabo reveals his strong interest in the down-to-earth details of multiple modes of real travel in the Roman empire as he describes the Italian coastline at the head of the Adriatic Sea with its many navigable rivers, its transport of barrels of wine and oil by wagon, and its maritime harbour at Timavum. Meanwhile, he simultaneously stresses the supreme importance of the landscape as defined by travellers from the Homeric epics and the mythical age. In the very next chapter after this strikingly practical account, Strabo explores the mythical presence in the area, through stories of the Greek hero Diomedes, who ruled in this part of Italy, and of the Heliades, daughters of the sun god Helios, turned into alder trees near the river Eridanus (now the Po).

The extraordinary mobility which characterized the ancient world finds its natural reflection in literature. The players in Herodotus's *Histories* are travelling from country to country. The Greek people are described as "exceedingly mobile",[5] and this mobility is by no means confined to the mainland Greeks. The Phocaeans, inhabitants of a Greek city in Asia Minor, were, according to Herodotus, the first to engage in long sea voyages, having opened up the Adriatic and sailed to Italy and all the way to Spain. Their innate mobility comes to the fore under the onslaught of Persian expansion in the sixth century BCE, when they readily pack everything onto ships and sail off to the Greek island of Chios. But, as we have seen previously, it is the Phoenicians, already "famed for their ships" in Homer, who are blamed by the Persians in Herodotus's account for having triggered the Persian wars by abducting Greek women on one of their many long-distance voyages. Herodotus's narrative is punctuated by stories of colonizing missions, such as the foundation of the city of Cyrene in North Africa.

Motives for travel

Economic motivations appear to have prompted the seventh-century BCE lyric poet Archilochus of Paros to join the colonization of Thasos off the coast of Thrace, although the fragments of his poetry imply that he found neither island congenial, complaining about the rough landscape of Thasos and describing his fellow colonizers as the "dregs of all the Greeks."[6] It seems that he returned to Paros later in his life; a colonizing journey did not have to be a one-way trip. Alongside the overtly Odyssean elements of Virgil's *Aeneid* already discussed, there is also a strong narrative of colonization and foundation throughout the poem. The ultimate goal for Aeneas in the *Aeneid* is to lead the Trojan survivors over the sea to found the race of the Romans, but there are a whole series of more minor foundations along the way: for example, Aeneas builds a city in Crete, which soon falls victim to a terrible plague; in Sicily, Acesta (later Roman Segesta) is founded as a refuge for some of the travel-weary members of Aeneas's expedition; meanwhile, in poignant parallel to Aeneas's own narrative of exile and foundation, Dido has established Carthage as a city of Phoenician émigrés in Libya. The pressures of war or tyranny which force departure from the original homeland combine with divine and mythical webs of justification for the settling of different peoples on foreign soil. As the protracted war in the second half of the *Aeneid* illustrates, the moment of colonization can mark the transformation of émigrés from underdogs into forces of occupation.

A good deal of travel in Herodotus is enforced by the imperialist designs of the Persians, who literally push other peoples out of place or "net" the population of whole islands, relocating them elsewhere. In Book 6, he describes how this happened to the inhabitants of the Greek islands of Chios, Lesbos, and Tenedos. As we have seen, however, the positive associations of travel were also manifold. Even imperial expeditions, while tiresome for the victims, were exciting and exotic for those expanding their horizons. The wish to depict new peoples and places encountered in the process of imperial expansion is best exemplified by the commentaries* that Julius Caesar wrote about his military campaigns in Gaul and published in 51 BCE. The Roman poet Catullus regards his time serving on the staff of the governor Memmius in Bithynia, a region in modern Turkey, with a mixture of indignation and ennui, but in *Carmen* 46 he expresses a vivid and infectious enthusiasm for a sight-seeing tour of the famous cities on the Mediterranean shores of Asia Minor once his work is done. Many a well-to-do Roman would have taken similar trips with varying combinations of educational*, recreational, and pecuniary motives in mind. Ovid, in his *Epistula ex Ponto* 2.10, reminisces about a year travelling around Greece and Sicily with his friend Pompeius Macer, drawing close connections between intellectual and poetic development and the vicissitudes of travel made bearable by the company of a good friend. By contrast, the erotic elegiac* poet Propertius (ca. 50–15 BCE) finds reason to complain of the effects of others' mobility on his own love life: in his *Carmen* 2.16, he describes how an otherwise unprepossessing man who has spent time abroad has returned with sufficient wealth and cachet to tempt Propertius's beloved, Cynthia, away from his bed, with the result that Propertius wishes the man could rather have been shipwrecked on the Ceraunian rocks. These cliffs, off the coast of Epirus, were a real danger for passing ships, but Propertius seems here to be longing for an epic-flavoured disaster to befall his rival, rather than the more routine and relatively safe journey of an imperial official. The notion of recreational travel is perhaps most fully illustrated by the *Periegesis* of Pausanias, a prose text in which the ephemeral Grand Tour of Greece is immortalized in a self-consciously literary form which goes far beyond the remit of a practical travel guide, a hybrid of different travel genres.

Intertwined with intellectual reasons for travel come religious and spiritual journeys. In Odysseus's Cretan story, cited at the beginning of this chapter, the invented detail of Odysseus's visit to the oracle of Zeus at Dodona is entirely believable, and the consultation of divine authorities and pilgrimage to sanctuaries and cult centres were prominent reasons for travel in the ancient world. In the Christian era the concept of pilgrimage became a metaphor for the journey to salvation, memorably exemplified by the apostle Paul's conversion on the road to Damascus. The *Peregrinatio* (Pilgrimage) of Egeria (fourth century CE) uses the quintessential travelling form of literature, the epistle, to describe for her female friends at home her journey to the Holy Land. In the ancient world, an idea of the expiation of sin could be attached to a journey: back in the *Odyssey*, the hero is told that even once he has reached home he will need to walk inland carrying an oar, until someone mistakes it for a winnowing fan, when he must plant it in the ground and sacrifice to Poseidon to appease the god's anger. Nevertheless, the idea of pilgrimage as a discrete and distinct form of travel was probably not current in the ancient world before the Christian era. Pausanias's *Periegesis* contains many references to religious centres, and in some ways his work can be read as a pilgrim's handbook, but the spiritual intersects with the touristic and the antiquarian in a manner which resists the distinct modern category of pilgrimage.

Travelling literature

The world of real travel and that of the imagination merge more literally in the form of the travelling intellectual. The travelling sage Solon in the first book of Herodotus's *Histories* offers a classic example of the figure who travels in search of wisdom and whose experience of different places constantly enhances his reputation. This notion of enlightenment* through travel enjoys a long history. The earliest poetry itself was disseminated by wandering bards* in the pre-literate age, and the connection between knowledge, poetry and travel remained strong long after the advent of written forms of commemoration*. Homer himself was often imagined as a wandering poet: Heliodorus in his novel *Aethiopica* even provides him with a distinctive (if unconvincing) biography* as the hairy-thighed illegitimate Egyptian son of the god Hermes, who travelled around the Mediterranean performing his songs. Many of the Greek lyric poets* were genuinely itinerant, making their way around the Greek-speaking Mediterranean to participate in choral festivals* and offer their services (or, indeed, have their services requested) as "praise poets" to local dignitaries. They cultivated an aura of wisdom and desirability through their combination of poetic talent and worldly experience: Simonides, born on Ceos in the sixth century BCE, travelled widely and spent extended periods of his life in Thessaly, Athens, and Sicily, composing a wide range of verse. His younger contemporary, the poet Pindar, appears to have been another great traveller, and his commissions flooded in from all corners of the Greek world. He makes complex and extensive use of travel imagery as a metaphor* for the composition process itself: in one of his poems, *Olympian* 6, he compares his song to a journey along a road; in another, *Nemean* 5, he contrasts his mobile, sea-borne verse with the static creations of sculptors; the Muses may offer a favouring breeze to carry the song and with it the memory of great deeds in *Nemean* 6. This association between the creative process and the journey proves highly influential and is given added impetus in the Hellenistic period when the poet Callimachus presents his new – and unabashedly intellectual – approach to poetry as a journey along an untrodden path, chosen in preference to the common road rutted by wagon wheels in the opening lines of his *Aetia*. It becomes common for poets to imbue travel with intensely metapoetic* connotations: a walk from the town to the country offers the context for an exploration of a new form of pastoral* in Theocritus's *Idylls*; a voyaging ship on the high seas symbolized prestigious genres of poetry-like epic, while a smaller boat unsuitable for such adventurous journeying was a humbler form like elegy or lyric, as in Horace's *Ode* 4.15.

Epilogue

"They bent to their rowing, and with their ears tossed up the sea spray/and upon the eyes of Odysseus there fell asleep, gentle,/the sweetest kind of sleep with no awakening, most like/death."[7] Thus the Phaeacians transport Odysseus back home at last to Ithaca where he awakes from his final wanderings, leaving the reader to wonder how much of this iconic and paradigmatic journey has been the stuff of dreams. Odysseus, the traveller *par excellence*, sets the frame of reference for all future literary travellers. Thus it is fitting that, although Odysseus eventually achieves his goal of returning to his beloved Ithaca, Homer hints that this will not be the end of his travels. As early as Book 11, the seer Tiresias indicates that, after slaying Penelope's suitors, Odysseus, far from settling thankfully back into life at home, will journey on to a land of men who know nothing of the sea, a message reinforced through its repetition by Odysseus to Penelope in Book 23. For the eternal traveller the prospect of another journey never loses its allure. At the same time, the idea of a further *Odyssey* tantalises the imaginations of writers through the centuries, generating a wealth of literary responses such as that of the British poet Tennyson (nineteenth century CE), whose restless Ulysses returns home only to find himself longing for new adventures. The scene is set for the figure of the traveller to roam incessantly through later literature:

> Come, my friends,
> 'Tis not too late to seek a newer world.
> Push off, and sitting well in order smite
> The sounding furrows; for my purpose holds
> To sail beyond the sunset, and the baths
> Of all the western stars, until I die.[8]

Notes

1 Sections in ancient Greek literature are often referred to as "books" after the book scrolls on which they were written (see Chapter 6).
2 Homer, *Odyssey* 14.285–330, translated by Richmond Lattimore, *The Odyssey of Homer* (New York: HarperCollins, 1965).
3 Horace, *Odes* 1.3.21–4, translated by David West, *Horace: The Complete Odes and Epodes*. World's Classics (Oxford: Oxford University Press).
4 Strabo, *Geography* 5.2.5, translated by Horace L. Jones, *Strabo: Geography*, 8 vols. Loeb Classical Library (Cambridge, MA: Harvard University Press, 1917–1932).
5 Herodotus, *Histories* 1.56.3, authors' translation.
6 Archilochus, fragment 102, authors' translation.
7 Homer, *Odyssey* 13.78–80, translated by Lattimore, *The Odyssey of Homer*.
8 Tennyson, *Ulysses* 56–61, edited by Christopher Ricks, *Alfred Lord Tennyson: Selected Poems* (London: Penguin Books, 2007).

Further reading

Adams, Colin and Ray Laurence, eds. *Travel and Geography in the Roman Empire*. London/New York: Routledge, 2001.
Alcock, Susan. E., John F. Cherry and Jas Elsner, eds. *Pausanias: Travel and Memory in Ancient Greece*. Oxford: Oxford University Press, 2001.
Hunter, Richard and Ian Rutherford, eds. *Wandering Poets in Ancient Greek Culture*. Cambridge: Cambridge University Press, 2011.
Montiglio, Silvia. *Wandering in Ancient Greek Culture*. Chicago, IL: University of Chicago Press, 2005.
Romm, James S. *The Edges of the Earth in Ancient Thought: Geography, Exploration, and Fiction*. Princeton, NJ: Princeton University Press, 1992.

3   Experiencing life and love

Ellen Greene and André Lardinois

Figure 3.1 Pappyrus with Sappho's "Brothers Poem" and beginning of "Kypris Poem"

On the Greek island of Lesbos, near the coast of modern-day Turkey, the female poet Sappho composed the following poem around 600 BCE:

Text: Sappho, "Prayer to Aphrodite" /
"Sappho Fragment 1" (ca. 600 BCE)

On the throne of many hues, Immortal Aphrodite,
child of Zeus, weaving wiles: I beg you,
do not break my spirit, O Queen,
with pain or sorrow

but come – if ever before from far away   5
you heard my voice and listened,
and leaving your father's
golden home you came,

your chariot yoked with lovely sparrows
drawing you quickly over the dark earth   10
in a whirling cloud of wings down
the sky through midair,

suddenly here. Blessed One, with a smile
on your deathless face, you ask
what have I suffered again   15
and why do I call again

and what in my wild heart do I most wish
would happen: "Once again who must I
persuade to turn back to your love?
Sappho, who wrongs you?   20

If now she flees, soon she'll chase.
If rejecting gifts, then she'll give.
If not loving, soon she'll love
even against her will."

Come to me now – release me from these   25
troubles, everything my heart longs
to have fulfilled, fulfill, and you
be my ally.[1]

This poem, which is commonly referred to as "Sappho's Prayer to Aphrodite" or "Sappho Fragment 1", takes the form of a typical ancient Greek prayer: it opens with an invocation*, continues with the narration of the help of the god in the past and concludes with a new request. In this prayer the first person asks the Greek goddess of love to leave her seat in the house of her father (Zeus), to come to her in a chariot drawn by sparrows (birds that were sacred to Aphrodite) and to help her with her beloved who does not love her anymore. This is, however, not a prayer, but the lyrics of a song Sappho composed for public performances*. It is written in highly stylized poetic language and metre, which sets it apart from ordinary speech. Of the music that accompanied the words nothing has survived and modern readers, therefore, experience the text as a poem, as readers in later antiquity did as well.

What distinguishes this poem from epic* poetry, discussed in the previous Chapter 2, or drama*, discussed in the next Chapter 4, is that it is composed throughout in the first person*. In this case, the first person even identifies herself as "Sappho", the name of the woman who composed the song. Its content therefore could be based on a real experience the composer had with love, yet it is also fictionalised*, as all literature is. Sappho does not describe a real-time event (a real prayer she once addressed to Aphrodite), but adds to and abstracts from it to make her experience relevant to her audience. What she creates is a *persona**: a look-alike of the poet, who may undergo and react to events differently from the poet herself.

In this case, the fictional element is evident in three different ways. First there is the complexity of the poem, which records three different moments in time: Sappho is praying in the here and now to Aphrodite, reminding her of how in the past she came to her and asked her why she was calling "again", thus showing that her visit in the past was preceded by at least one other time when Aphrodite came to her. These three time frames are marked in the wording of the poem by the repetition of the word "again" in lines 15, 16 and 18. This repetition may also point to the different occasions on which the song could be re-performed: note that Sappho mentions her own name, but not the name of her beloved. She therefore could perform this song every time she wanted to portray herself as being in love *again*.

A second fictional element in the poem is her close encounter with the goddess Aphrodite. It is questionable if the original audience* would have believed that such an encounter really took place and it probably would have reacted to it with amusement. The Greeks in general did not believe that the gods came to earth for such trivial matters, at least not in historical times. Personal encounters between gods and mortals were considered more typical of the mythical* age of heroes, the time described in the epics of Homer. Sappho in a way portrays herself as such a Homeric hero*: note her reference to the goddess of love as her ally (in Greek: *summachos* or fellow-fighter) at the end of the poem. She is, however, a soldier of love, not of war. We encounter here, not for the last time in European literature, the equation of the struggles of love with war.

Finally, we may ask ourselves as readers or listeners of this song what it is that Aphrodite exactly promised Sappho in the past. The object of the woman's chase, gift giving and love, is not expressed (lines 21–3). Aphrodite, therefore, does not necessarily promise that the woman will chase, give gifts to or love Sappho again in the future. Instead the goddess may be saying that the woman will chase, give gifts to and love someone else against her will, just as Sappho loved this woman in vain. This is clearly not what the speaker in the poem hopes for or expects, and we see here a rift between Sappho the composer, who created this ambiguity, and Sappho the *persona* in the poem, who understands the words of the goddess to mean that she will persuade her lover to come back to her. Now we can also better understand what the smile on the deathless face of Aphrodite means (lines 13–14) and why she is described as "weaving wiles" (line 2). What this poem ultimately talks about is the vicissitudes of love, both on the human (the *persona* of Sappho in the poem) and on the divine level (Aphrodite).

What makes this poem further remarkable is that Sappho illustrates these thoughts about love by her feelings for another woman, and there are more poems about the love of women for other women in the surviving corpus of Sappho. The ancient Greeks did not radically distinguish between homo- and heterosexuality in the way in which modern people do. It was probably more acceptable for a female poet to describe her feelings of love for another woman than for another man in the segregated society of archaic Greece, in which women were allowed very little sexual freedom with men. Sappho's poems still mark a memorable* moment in history, describing female homosexuality for the first time in European literature. It is no wonder that when modern Europeans were looking for a word to denote female homosexuals in the nineteenth century, they remembered Sappho's poetry and chose a term derived from the name of the island on which she had lived two and a half thousand years before: lesbian.

The character of Greek and Latin lyric poetry

"Sappho's Prayer to Aphrodite" is an example of the genre of lyric poetry*. In antiquity this term was used only for poems that were performed under accompaniment of a lyre, hence the name, but nowadays it is used for all kinds of short poems that very often, though not exclusively, take the form of a first-person account. In antiquity, the genre already comprised a great variety of poems from folksongs* to officially commissioned hymns* to the gods. Some were performed by soloists, such as presumably "Sappho's Prayer to Aphrodite", others by choruses*, such as the victory songs* which the Greek poet Pindar (ca. 516–440 BCE) composed for victors in the athletic games, or the *carmen saeculare*, a hymn which the Latin poet Horace wrote for a religious festival* celebrated by the Roman emperor Augustus in 17 BCE. The choral odes* in Greek and Roman drama are also seen as lyric elements within the genres of tragedy* and comedy*. They were accompanied not only by music but by dance as well (see Chapter 4). From the Hellenistic period onwards (ca. 300 BCE), it became more common to read lyric poetry in the privacy of one's own home, besides attending performances of it.

In the course of the Hellenistic and Roman periods, more and more poets preferred writing very short poems, known as epigrams*. This type of poetry was originally limited to inscriptions (*epigrammata* in Greek) on grave tombs and on temple dedications, but soon it developed into a literary genre of its own (see Chapter 6). An example of such a literary epigram is the following short poem of the Latin poet Martial (ca. 40–104 CE), who is particularly well known for his epigrams in which he pokes fun at his contemporaries from the elites* down to tradesmen and slaves:

> Diaulus used to be a doctor till recently, now he is an undertaker.
>   What he does as undertaker, he used to do as doctor.[2]

This poem, like most epigrams, is written in a so-called elegiac couplet*, made up of two lines: a six-part verse (hexameter*) followed by a shorter, five-part verse (pentameter*). It also adopts a satirical tone. Satire* was always part of the repertoire of the ancient poets, who could praise or blame old heroes and fellow citizens, but it grew into a distinct genre in Latin poetry. The Latin poet Lucilius (second century BCE) was credited with having invented the genre, but it was perfected by poets such as Horace and Juvenal. Famous is Juvenal's *Satura* 3, a diatribe* against the Greeks who lived and worked in Rome.

Ancient lyric poetry addresses a wide range of themes, including politics, religion, friendship, war, old age, love and drinking. There is hardly any aspect of human life that is not reflected on in Greek and Latin lyric poetry, although love remained one of its most celebrated topics. As an example of a politically motivated poem, we cite a fragment of the Athenian statesman Solon, a contemporary of Sappho (ca. 600 BCE; see also Chapter 2). It is written in elegiac couplets as well:

> The commons I have granted privilege enough,
>   not lessening their estate nor giving more;

> The influential, who were envied for their wealth,
>> I have saved them from all mistreatment too.
> I took my stand with strong shield covering both sides,
>> allowing neither to gain victory unjustly.[3]

Solon seems to reflect in this poem on his role as a mediator in the political conflict between the Athenian aristocracy ("the influential who were envied for their wealth") and the people or commons. It is written, like most lyric poetry, in the first person, but Solon is creating just as much a *persona* as Sappho does in her "Prayer to Aphrodite". He portrays the first-person speaker in this poem as an honest broker who gives both parties their fair share. It therefore could be cited by any politician who had to mediate in a similar conflict. The metaphor* of the shield held above both combatants is poetic and deliberately vague. Is he holding his shield above the two parties at the same time? Will they then not continue to fight with each other under his shield? While Sappho associated love with war, Solon compares political strife with the fight between two combatants. War, both as topic and as metaphor, is as deeply engrained in Greek and Latin literature as love is.

Much of Greek lyric poetry has come down to us only in fragments, either in quotations of other Greek writers, such as the Greek philosopher Aristotle (fourth century BCE), who cites these six lines of Solon in a treatise on the constitution of Athens, or through the discovery of fragments in the desert sands of Egypt (see Chapter 1). Of the archaic and classical Greek lyric poets, only the victory odes* of Pindar (previous) and excerpts from poems of the poet Theognis (sixth century BCE) are directly transmitted to us through medieval manuscripts*. In the case of Latin lyric, we are more fortunate. Here we have substantial portions of the corpus of such poets as Catullus, Horace, Tibullus, Propertius, Ovid, Statius and Martial (previous). A substantial amount of Greek and Latin epigrams have been preserved in the *Anthologia Graeca* and the *Anthologia Latina*, two compilations based on earlier collections.

Greek and Latin lyric poetry is composed in a variety of metres*. Traditionally one distinguishes between the more loose form of melic poetry*, which is composed after the melody of the music by which it was accompanied (from Greek *melos*, meaning "song"), and the fixed metres of elegy (see previous) and *iambos** (based on iambics* or trochees*). Lyric themes could be addressed in all these different metres, but Latin love poetry was typically composed in elegiac couplets, while in Greece *iambos* was regularly used for mockery and jest. Iambics are also used in the spoken parts of Greek and Latin drama and were considered to come closest to the sound of ordinary speech.

Poetry and gender

Because of the form ancient lyric poetry takes – short, first-person accounts – it lends itself well to comment on social norms and practices, as we already saw in the case of Solon's political* or Martial's satirical poem previously. Ancient lyric poetry can both confirm and subvert social stereotypes. This can be seen especially in Latin love lyric, where the relationship between the *persona* of the male lover/speaker and his female mistress figures so prominently. Women in Greek and Roman society were usually relegated to a subservient role and often regarded as ungovernable creatures whose inherent irrationality and dangerous sexuality required them to be under the constant guardianship of males. The Roman love poets, however, appear to elevate women to a singularly exalted stature. This may reflect some of the real power of women behind the scenes, but it is also part of the literary game: the Roman poets create *personae* partly based on their own experiences but also on their imagination.

Latin love poetry* is predicated on clearly defined roles for the poet and his female mistress. The poets, named "elegists" after the metre in which they composed their poetry (see previous), portray the male first person speaker in the traditionally passive and subservient role of women and, at the same time, depict the female beloved as masterful, active and dominant. They often refer to their mistresses as *dominae* (female rulers) who subject their lovers to the torments of abandonment and betrayal. Thus, Latin love poetry, in general, seems to subvert Roman conventions of masculinity by assigning to the male narrator*/lover traits that the Romans typically associated with women: servitude, softness and frivolity. The *persona* of the male lover is portrayed as devoted, dependent and passive, while his female mistress is depicted as powerful and domineering – attributes otherwise associated by the Romans with men.

At the same time, however, the Latin love poets may confirm social norms. They can do this in several ways: by portraying their female beloveds as helpless victims, as commodities of exchange between men, and also by having the elegiac lover/speaker adopt a masculine *persona* consistent with the conventional traits of a Roman male: courage, self-mastery and dominance. We will provide some brief examples of how the Roman elegists depict their female mistresses as victims and commodities and in turn how the male *persona* may appear as stereotypically masculine.

In the elegies of both Propertius and Ovid, the male speaker/lover often compares his mistress to female figures in myth known for their helplessness and dependence on men. More than that, these female mythical figures are often captives of men. In Propertius's elegy 1.3, for example, the *amator* or male lover compares his mistress to the mythical female figure Ariadne as she lies helpless on the shore after being abandoned by the hero Theseus, and the speaker implicitly identifies himself with her rescuer, the god Bacchus (in Greek, Dionysus). Similarly, in Ovid's elegy 1.3 the speaker/lover draws analogies between his mistress and several female mythical figures who are notorious for their positions not only as captives but as victims of male violence.

At other times the elegists portray their amatory relationships as transactions in which women are commodities of exchange between men. These representations not only serve to confirm Roman social norms, but also to provide a vehicle for the male *persona* to assert his masculinity. We can see this phenomenon in Tibullus's elegy 1.6 in which the male speaker/lover is at first represented in the conventional role of a feminized, passive figure, enslaved to his domineering, dishonest and unfaithful mistress Delia. Yet the speaker subsequently undermines this ostensibly servile position. The speaker declares that it is he who is the victor, rather than his rival, his mistress' husband. This emphasis on masculine rivalry is a defining feature of the speaker's identity. We see this throughout Roman elegy: the elegiac lover often focuses more on defeating his rival than on his love for his mistress. The speaker/lover constitutes his identity through an assertion of his dominance in the masculine arena. The woman is thus represented as an article of commerce between her lover and her husband. In Tibullus 1.6, the speaker refers to his mistress as *bona* (good things) when telling her husband he should do a better job of guarding her. The implication in referring to his mistress as *bona* is that it emphasizes that she is simply one of her husband's material goods.

Ovid's love elegies almost completely overturn the nominal position of the male lover's subservience, thus confirming social norms and stereotypes in a much more overt fashion than either Propertius or Tibullus. While, on the surface, the male *persona* in Ovid's elegies takes on the traditional elegiac stance of servitude to his female beloved, he asserts his dominance by perpetrating violence on her (*Amores* 1.3, 1.7). We see this sometimes in Propertius as well. Also, as in Tibullus, the male speaker in Ovid's poems strongly affirms his masculine identity by depicting his female mistress as an object. In *Amores* 2.19 and 3.4, for example, Ovid's *amator* (male speaker/lover) tries to "make deals" with the husband of his mistress in order to manipulate how she will be used as an object of his pleasure and a means of achieving literary fame.

In the context of discussing how Latin lyric engages with societal conventions and norms, we must mention the poet Catullus (84–54 BCE). Much of Latin love elegy can be traced to Catullus's slightly earlier love lyrics. As in elegy, Catullus characterizes the male *persona* in his poems as both confirming and subverting social norms. On the one hand, the Catullan speaker/lover is depicted as feminine, in that he is passively in thrall to his female beloved.[4] On the other hand, the male lover throughout the Catullan corpus tries to reject his passionate devotion to his female beloved. He does so because he recognizes or believes that this devotion, deemed "feminine" according to traditional Roman values, has harmed him in that it has led him to abandon not only his duties to the community but also his reason. Succumbing to private passions was considered by the Romans to be not only "unmanly" but morally weak as well. Throughout Catullus's love poetry we see the male *persona* constantly vacillate between his desires and normative conceptions of Roman masculinity (i.e. duty, rationality, honour).

Like the Latin love poets, the Greek and Roman women poets communicate their stances towards male-dominated culture and society. Being largely excluded from the more public genres of epic and drama, lyric poetry is the one genre in which these female poets could express themselves, from Sappho in the seventh century BCE to the Latin poet Eucheria in the fifth century CE. Here we will discuss briefly the Greek epigrams of Anyte (early third century BCE) and the Latin poetry of Sulpicia (second half of the first century BCE). Our discussion will examine to what extent these two poets exemplify how women poets in antiquity engage with social norms and literary conventions. We will also address how their poetry may be considered feminine or gender*-specific.

In the epigrams of Anyte, as in the work of other Hellenistic poets, we find numerous references to and borrowings from established Greek literary culture, particularly Homeric epic. Anyte transforms traditional epigram through her application of the heroic language of Homeric verse to a context that is often personal and idiosyncratic. Thus, Anyte's poems create a unique interplay between the domesticity, typically associated with women, and established male literary culture. We find this interplay, for example, in Anyte's epitaphs* for young unmarried women, where Anyte's focus on female concerns appears to figure most prominently. An example is the following epigram, which presents itself as an inscription that was written on the grave of a young woman named Antibia:

> I mourn maiden Antibia: desiring her, many
>   bridegrooms came to her father's home, drawn
> by her fame for beauty and wit. But in the end
>   destructive Fate rolled far away the hopes of all.[5]

Expressions of grief (lamentations) in Homer's *Iliad* and in literary epigrams written by men before Anyte typically celebrate the heroism of men slain in battle and, more importantly, the fame (Greek: *kleos**) they will receive (see Chapter 6). Indeed, loss and grief in

Homer are often mitigated by the compensations of fame. Anyte, in this epigram, draws on the Homeric conception and representation of fame, but attaches it to the ordinary life of a young woman who is praised for her beauty and wisdom. This not only expresses an affirmation of the worth of women's lives, but at the same time subverts the idea that fame is predicated only on the martial prowess of men.

The Roman poet Sulpicia (second half of the first century BCE) also engages with dominant male culture and convention. Sulpicia wrote love elegies, like her male contemporaries Propertius, Ovid and Tibullus, mentioned previously. While Sulpicia writes primarily about love and erotic desire as the other Roman elegists do, her poems are very different from them. Most obviously, the speaker/lover in Sulpicia's elegies is female and her beloved is male. More than that, the way in which Sulpicia characterizes the female speaker represents quite a departure from the (male) conventions of elegy. She is not portrayed as passively enslaved to her beloved, but rather as an active agent in attempting to fulfil her desires. This shows not only Sulpicia's departure from the literary norms of her male counterparts, but also her independence from social mores and conventions.

In Elegy 13, for example, the female speaker/lover declares that her desires for the man she loves have been fulfilled: "Won over by the Muses, Venus has answered my prayers and placed him in my arms" (lines 3–4)[6]. Male elegists typically lament their lack of fulfilment in love and present their beloved as someone who has to be conquered. Emphasizing the joys and mutuality of love, Sulpicia presents what may be regarded as a different model of desire. Moreover, the fact that the female speaker in Sulpicia's poems speaks openly about her own desires and her lack of concern for what society thinks of her represents her most subversive flouting of convention. Considering that women were often treated as objects in Roman literature, Sulpicia's depiction of a woman who openly pursues and fulfils her sexual desires is especially striking. At the end of Elegy 13, the speaker declares unequivocally that when it comes to love she will do and say what she pleases and, fittingly, describes a version of *amor* (love, desire) that is unlike any other in extant Greek or Roman lyric: "I love to stray. It is tiresome to wear a mask for the sake of my reputation: let all hear that we have been together, each worthy of the other."

Reception

Both Greek and Latin lyric poetry have a rich afterlife, starting in antiquity itself. As an exemplar of the reception of Greek lyric poetry, we will examine the reception* of Sappho first in ancient Rome and then in modern London. This will give an idea about how this poetry travelled through Europe and acquired new meanings in different times and places.

Based on a good deal of evidence we can reasonably infer that Sappho had already achieved legendary status in ancient Athens by the end of the sixth century BCE. In ancient Athens, Sappho was admired for her skill as a poet and considered an authority in matters of love by such thinkers as Plato. In Hellenistic Alexandria, a couple of centuries later (see Chapter 1), Sappho was celebrated not only as a love poet but also as a divine figure akin to the Muses*, the nine goddesses associated in Greek mythology with the creation of poetry and the arts. Indeed, Sappho is the only woman poet included by Hellenistic scholars in the canon of nine lyric poets, a canon that parallels the nine immortal Muses.[7]

In Augustan Rome we see the full breadth of Sappho's effect on the work of major poets in antiquity. For many Roman male writers, notably Catullus, Horace and Ovid, Sappho represents the paradigmatic poetic voice of feminine desire and sexuality. But

Catullus is the only Roman poet whose literary affiliation with Sappho dominates his work. This is most evident in Catullus's adaptation* of Sappho's Fragment 31. This was one of Sappho's most celebrated poems. Its first four stanzas* are preserved in a treatise called *On the Sublime*, (falsely) attributed to the Greek rhetorician Cassius Longinus (see Chapter 5):

> To me it seems that man has the fortune
> of gods, whoever sits beside you
> and close, who listens to you
> sweetly speaking
>
> and laughing temptingly. My heart
> flutters in my breast whenever
> I even glance at you –
> I can say nothing,
>
> my tongue is broken. A delicate fire
> runs under my skin, my eyes
> see nothing, my ears roar,
> cold sweat
>
> rushes down me, trembling seizes me,
> I am greener than grass.
> To myself I seem
> needing but little to die.[8]

Here the author of the treatise stopped quoting the poem, but one of the manuscripts adds the first line of the following stanza, which probably ended the song: "Yet all can be endured, since even a poor man..."

Sappho does not name the speaker in this poem the way she does in Fragment 1, but later readers, including Catullus, assumed it was Sappho herself. Catullus renders the poem in Latin, while preserving Sappho's metre, and adapts it as follows:

> He seems to me to be the equal to a god,
> he, if it may be, even surpasses the very gods,
> who sitting opposite you again and again
> gazes at you and hears you
>
> sweetly laughing. Such a thing, alas,
> takes away all my senses; for whenever
> I see you, Lesbia, at once no sound of voice
> remains within my mouth,
>
> but my tongue falters, a subtle flame
> steals down through my limbs, my ears ring
> with inward humming, my eyes are shrouded
> in twofold night.
>
> Idleness, Catullus, does you harm.
> In your idleness you run riot and exult too much.
> Idleness ere now has ruined both kings
> and wealthy cities.[9]

Both Sappho and Catullus present opening scenarios in which they are outside observers of their beloved who is seemingly engaged in intimate, though non-sexual, contact with a male rival. Both refer to this rival as "god-like" because he can claim the beloved's attentions, but more importantly because he appears to remain miraculously unmoved in the presence of this extraordinary woman. Catullus, however, gives prominence to the presence of the male rival and the power he seems to have in contrast with himself, and reduces the description of the symptoms he suffers as lover from three to two stanzas. In Sappho's original, the man is a generic figure ("whoever sits beside you") and emphasis is placed on the effect of the sweet sound and laughter of the beloved on the speaker. In Catullus's poem the primary relationship is not between Catullus and his beloved, whom he names Lesbia ("the woman from Lesbos") as a tribute to Sappho, but between the speaker and "that man" – the figure that embodies not only the contingencies of the exterior world for the lover, as in Sappho's poem, but the pressures of male power relations in general. In the context of Roman culture, the fact that "the man" can gaze at the woman without any disruptive effects means that he is free to attend to his duties to the community; thus, his imperviousness to Lesbia's charms attests to his manliness. Catullus, on the other hand, describes himself as breaking down at the sight of his beloved, much like the first-person speaker in Sappho's Fragment 31.

Indeed, Sappho and Catullus are both robbed of their faculties, both experience a sense of bodily dissolution. While Sappho catalogues in detail the devastating effects of the beloved's presence on her, she also reveals her ability to evoke the repetition and regeneration of *eros*. Sappho's emphasis on the general nature of her desire, reflected in her statement about how she feels "whenever" she sees her beloved, suggests the renewal of erotic experience through recollection of the beloved. Moreover, Sappho tells herself at the end that "all must be endured." This implies that Sappho has not only achieved some sort of recovery, but also has reconstituted herself out of the experience of being shattered by love.

Catullus's version ends very differently. After describing the devastating effect of Lesbia on him, and in particular how it seems to separate him from the outside world, Catullus then awakens suddenly as if from a bad dream and warns himself about the dangers of idleness (Latin: *otium*). *Otium* was considered to be in direct opposition to *negotium*: a life devoted to work and public service. More than that, *otium* is associated with the frivolous pursuits of love and poetry. The implication in Catullus's apparent rejection of a life devoted to love and poetry is that *otium* has caused him harm because it has led him to abandon not only his duties to the community but also his reason. Indulgence in *otium* is also an indulgence in the pleasures of love and poetry, pleasures which Catullus associated with the world of beauty and imagination evoked for him in the poems of Sappho.

Catullus implies in the last two lines of his poem that *otium* destroys the lover and poet in the same way that it causes the downfall of kings and wealthy cities. But *otium* or leisure/idleness does not destroy the lover. Rather, it creates the conditions that make love and love poetry possible. Catullus is clearly attracted to the Sapphic ideal, which he identified as a life devoted to love, beauty and the poetic imagination, yet this ideal opposes traditional Roman values associated with the military or political life of a Roman male citizen. Clearly, for Catullus, the attempt to "translate"* Sappho into his own experience results in conflict. The opposition between Sapphic and Roman ideals for Catullus is irreconcilable. At most, Catullus may implicitly be expressing the hope at the end that an adherence to traditional Roman ideals (duty, honour) will enable him not only to get over his indulgence in love but also over his identification with the more private, feminine world epitomized by Sappho.

The poems of Sappho and the other Greek and Latin lyric poets have had a rich afterlife after antiquity as well. The Italian poet Petrarch, for example, modelled his love poetry on those of the Latin elegists. Also, Shakespeare's sonnets* are deeply indebted to

Catullus and Ovid. Sappho continued to stir the imagination, as well. The British poet Robert Chandler, for example, wrote the following poem in 1998. It is called "Poem on the Underground", but its subtitle is "A prayer to Hermes", a reference to Fragment 95 of Sappho, in which she speaks to Hermes as the god who guides the souls to the underworld, the kingdom of Pluto, one of the names given to the ruler of the underworld. Another "intertext"* (an earlier text to which this text refers) of this poem is the story of the descent of the Greek poet Orpheus into the underworld to rescue his wife Eurydice, as narrated, for example, by Virgil in his *Georgics*. In Chandler's poem the underworld is identified with the modern London underground:

> Guide me safely down into Pluto's kingdom,
> Make the escalator run swift and smooth, and
> Spare me never-ending delays beside the
> Banks of the Northern
>
> Line. And find me, swiftly, an empty carriage,
> One that's just been hung with the latest poems;
> May I taste each word between lips and tongue as I
> Jolt towards Hendon.
>
> May some young and heterosexual Sappho
> See me mouthing sensuous rhymes – and catch my
> Eye – and join me whispering verses during
> Stops between stations.
>
> May our two hearts beat to a long-lost measure,
> May immortal goddesses smile from posters,
> As we quietly float up the moving stairs into
> Brightening sunlight.[10]

Like Catullus, Chandler composes his poem in the same metre as Sappho, the so-called Sapphic stanza (a fixed alternation of stressed and unstressed syllables). He does not hesitate to have his sentences run over the end of the stanza (line 5), as both Sappho and Catullus can do as well. His immortal goddesses who "smile" from posters are reminiscent of the smile on Aphrodite's deathless face in Fragment 1 of Sappho, quoted previously. Like Catullus, Chandler sees Sappho primarily as a love poet: he wants her to join him in "whispering verses" composed in "sensuous rhymes", like the Sapphic stanza. But he is concerned about her sexuality: he explicitly wants her to be "young and heterosexual".

Catullus has no problem imitating or naming his beloved after a woman who sings of her love for other women. In antiquity, Sappho was considered a love poet for males and females alike. In modern times, with its more rigid distinction between homo- and heterosexuality, she is primarily considered a "lesbian", and a male poet like Chandler has to turn her into a heterosexual to make her into a lover and effective role model for himself. In this way, every reception tells us as much about the modeller as about the model. This is true both for Catullus and his fear of indulging in the anti-Roman value of "leisure" (*otium*) and for Chandler's concern with the homoeroticism expressed in Sappho's verses. Every age adapts her poetry to its own experiences with life and love.

Notes

1 Sappho, Fragment 1, translated by Diane Rayor in Diane Rayor and André Lardinois, *Sappho: A New Translation of the Complete Works* (Cambridge: Cambridge University Press, 2014).

2 Martial, *Epigram* 1.47, translation adapted from David R. Shackleton Bailey in David R. Shackleton Bailey, *Martial: Epigrams*, 3 vols. Loeb Classical Library (Cambridge, MA: Harvard University Press, 1991/1993).

3 Solon, Fragment 5, translated by Martin L. West, *Greek Lyric Poetry: A New Translation* (Oxford: Oxford University Press, 1993).

4 Especially Catullus, *Carmina* 8, 76, 51.

5 Anyte, *Epigram* 6, translated by Diane Rayor, *Sappho's Lyre: Archaic Lyric and Women Poets of Ancient Greece* (Berkeley: University of California Press, 1991).

6 Translation by Ellen Greene based on the following Latin text edition: Johannes Perceval Postgate (ed.) *Albii Tibulli aliorumque carminum libri tres* (Oxford: Oxford University Press, 1927).

7 The canon consisted of the following Greek lyric poets: Alcaeus, Alcman, Anacreon, Bacchylides, Ibycus, Pindar, Sappho, Simonides and Stesichorus.

8 Sappho, Fragment 31, translated by Diane Rayor in Rayor and Lardinois, *Sappho*.

9 Catullus 51, translation adapted from Francis W. Cornish and George P. Goold, in Francis W. Cornish, John P. Postgate and John W. Mackail, *Catullus, Tibullus, Pervigilium Veneris*, second edition, revised by George P. Goold. Loeb Classical Library (Cambridge, MA: Harvard University Press, 1988).

10 Robert Chandler, "Poem on the Underground," in *The Sappho Companion*, ed. Margaret Reynolds (London: Vintage Publisher, 2000), 378.

Further reading

Budelmann, Felix, ed. *The Cambridge Companion to Greek Lyric*. Cambridge: Cambridge University Press, 2009.

Gold, Barbara K., ed. *A Companion to Roman Love Elegy*. Oxford: Wiley-Blackwell, 2012.

Greene, Ellen. *The Erotics of Domination: Male Desire and the Mistress in Latin Love Poetry*. Baltimore: Johns Hopkins University Press, 1998.

Miller, Paul A. *Lyric Texts and Lyric Consciousness: The Birth of a Genre From Archaic Greece to Augustan Rome*. London/New York: Taylor & Francis, 1994.

Snyder, Jane M. *The Woman and the Lyre: Women Writers in Classical Greece and Rome*. Bristol: Bristol Classical Press, 1989.

Thorsen, Thea, ed. *The Cambridge Companion to Latin Love Elegy*. Cambridge: Cambridge University Press, 2013.

4   Performing culture

Bernhard Zimmermann

Figure 4.1 Mosaic depicting theatrical masks of Tragedy and Comedy, second century CE, Capitoline
Museum, Rome

Source: Centre Art Historical Documentation, Radboud University.

The origin of theatre in Ancient Greece

In the classical period (500–300 BCE), Greek literature was still predominantly orally*
performed in a variety of settings. Festivals for the gods, for example, normally included
not only sacrifices, but also performances of hymns* to the gods and sometimes the recita-
tion of the Homeric epics*. At private parties, called *symposia** ('drinking together'), the
Athenians sang old and new lyric* verses. And then there were the Sophists*, well-known
from Plato's dialogues*: travelling teachers (see Chapter 2) who promised to teach their
disciples the art of good speaking, the basis for a political career, in exchange for handsome compensation. They would advertise their skills through events that took the form
of a public show speech* (*epideixis*). Finally, we know that the historian Herodotus recited
parts of his historical work in public, and philosophers like Empedocles and Xenophanes
presented their doctrines to small or large audiences. It is against this background that we
have to understand the development of the Greek theatre, which showcases genres that
are also orally delivered (see Chapter 1).

Although earlier forms of theatre are known from ancient Greece and from other cultures as well,[1] Greek theatre* with its distinctive genres of tragedy and comedy is a genuinely Athenian invention. It was closely tied to the democracy which was introduced in
the city at the end of the sixth century BCE. Contemporary issues related to the state were
debated on the stage in front of a large number of citizens and the voice of the community
was represented through the chorus*, which plays an important role in the dramas. Of the
more than two thousand plays produced in classical Athens, seven tragedies of Aeschylus
(ca. 525–465 BCE),[2] seven tragedies of Sophocles (ca. 495–04 BCE),[3] seventeen tragedies
and one satyr play (see ahead) of Euripides (ca. 480–04 BCE),[4] and eleven comedies of Aristophanes (ca. 455–385 BCE)[5] have been preserved together with one later tragedy (*Rhesus*,
which was attributed to Euripides), and many fragments, especially of Euripides's plays*,[6]
which remained very popular throughout antiquity.

Starting in Athens, this theatre soon spread over the entire Greek world and, from the
middle of the third century BCE, over the Roman world as well. The performances were
organized by the city of Athens and financed by a form of taxation that wealthy citizens
had to pay. At the same time, Athenian theatre was a religious institution*. Dramatic performances were integrated into two festivals* in honour of Dionysus, the god of wine,
excess and ecstasy: the Lenaia, a festival announcing the arrival of spring, and the Great
Dionysia, also known as the City Dionysia, held in the spring. The religious character
explains a particularly remarkable convention of Athenian theatre: the unique nature of
the performances*. With very few exceptions, the plays could only be performed once in
the Athenian theatre of Dionysus since they served as a form of spiritual sacrifice to the
god. This changed fundamentally in 386 BCE when the people of Athens decided that they
should be allowed to re-perform tragedies that had been presented earlier on the occasion
of the festival of Dionysus. That year therefore can be regarded as the beginning of a new
era in the history of theatre. Greek theatre gradually lost its cultic* dimension and was
transformed into a place of aesthetic* enjoyment where it was possible to watch popular
plays on stage in different dramatic performances more than once.

The original, religious* character of the theatre is obvious from the many ritual* actions
surrounding the festivals for Dionysus in the fifth century BCE. The performances were
taking place in the presence of the god whose idol was solemnly carried from the temple
next to the theatre out of the city and back again in a procession commemorating* the
act of endowment of the festival on the day before the Great Dionysia began. The festival
itself was initiated with a procession in which Athenians from all walks of life participated.

The utensils carried along, such as wineskins, wooden *phalloi* ('penises') and a bull led by young men, underlined the religious, Dionysian character of the dramatic performances.

Besides tragedies and comedies, also satyr plays and dithyrambs were performed at the City Dionysia. The "Dionysian" element is obvious in the satyr play*, humorous* plays that were performed at the end of the day, after the tragedies. Its chorus always consisted of satyrs: naughty, wild and salacious creatures with both human and equine features, who were venerated as companions of Dionysus under the leadership of their father Silenus. Dionysian elements are also evident in fifth-century BCE comedy, especially in its culinary and sexual excesses, but in tragedy they are harder to find. With a few exceptions where the myth* of Dionysus was dramatized for stage, such as in the *Bacchae* of Euripides, Dionysian elements are not obvious, but rather concealed in the language and structure of the plays. Dionysus was a god who was known to blur the boundaries between female-male, old-young, elite-ordinary people, outside-inside, wild-civilized, family (*oikos*)-state (*polis*), men-animal and God-men. The transgression of these boundaries is typical of the plots* of Athenian tragedy and comedy as well. The gender* differences between men and women are abolished, the prohibition of incest weakened, and men abandon their scruples about killing. Such a violation of the rules of "civilised" society was probably also evident in the narratives* performed by choruses in the dithyramb* songs. Other elements of these choral songs may well have referred to Dionysus as well, but so few of these songs have survived that it is impossible to draw any final conclusions.

A further peculiarity distinguishing the Athenian theatre from that of later periods explains why the literary genre of tragedy and comedy could emerge from pre-literary mimetic* performances within just a few decades of the fifth century BCE. The performances were organised as a contest* (*agôn*), divided into various disciplines. The ten administrative units of democratic Athens participated with two choruses each reciting the dithyrambs. Then a contest between three tragedians and five comedians took place. While each comedian brought just one play to the stage, every tragic poet wrote a tetralogy*, consisting of three tragedies and one satyr play. At dithyrambic contests the chorus was awarded a prize*, while at performances of comedies and tragedies it was the poet. This reflects the balance between the collective and individuals which was of central importance to the Athenian democracy. The agonal setting led to a permanent competition* between the poets, who also functioned as producers* and sometimes as actors* in the play. It was this competitive dialogue between poets and genres which provoked innovation*, as you could win the favour of an audience* used to watching theatre performances only by writing something new, not by the repetition of familiar plots.

Without any doubt the attractiveness of drama* in the competition with other poetic genres derives from the fact that the performance of a play was a multimedia* event, a combination of spoken and sung word, dance, music and stage effects. One can find four types of recitation* in ancient drama: the actors communicate with each other or with the chorus leader in the form of spoken words; the chorus sings and dances in distinctive choral songs, accompanied by the *aulos*, a wind instrument resembling the oboe; chorus and actor sing alternating strophes in order to make both groups interact; and finally, in the last quarter of the fifth century BCE, arias* (*monodies*) were introduced, particularly in the tragedies of Euripides. Although the original music accompanying these plays is irrevocably lost, we can trace the variety of the music in the different metrical* forms of the text. Accordingly, an ancient Greek tragedy had more similarities with a musical* than with a modern play.

As is the case with music, the staging of an ancient drama is not transmitted. Unlike modern plays, the ancient texts of drama are lacking stage directions. However, there are some hints in the text which allow us to draw certain conclusions about what would have been happening on stage. As far as the technical facilities are concerned, the Athenian theatre of Dionysus, where the dramatic performances took place, cannot be compared with modern theatres. The background to the theatre originally consisted of a small wooden building (*skene**) – later converted into stone – with one to three doors representing the house or palace in front of which the actors performed on a slightly enhanced stage. The chorus was located in the *orchestra** (dancing place), between the audience and the stage. Indoor scenes were shown by means of a rolling platform, the so-called *ekkyklema**, which was rolled out of the middle door onto the stage. Another technical device unfamiliar to the modern theatre was the crane by which gods could appear flying over the stage and landing on the *skene* building, often at the end of a play to resolve the drama. This is where the Latin expression *deus ex machina** ('the god from the machine') comes from. Greek theatre is a theatre of conventions and above all a theatre of the word. What the insufficient technical possibilities did not permit to be shown was narrated by a messenger* in a kind of "verbal scene painting" in such a way that it would become visible in the mind of the spectator. Other conventions were that not more than three actors could appear on stage at the same time; that one and the same actor could have different roles in the same play; and that female characters, including female choruses, were played by male actors.

Sophocles's *Antigone*

A passage from Sophocles's *Antigone* may illustrate some of these characteristics of Greek tragedy. The plot concerns the children of Oedipus, a man who killed his father and married his mother, Jocasta. The two brothers Eteocles and Polynices, born from Oedipus's and Jocasta's incestuous marriage, agreed, after the death of their father Oedipus, to reign alternatively over the city of Thebes each year. However, after his first year of rule, Eteocles refuses to hand over power to Polynices. Consequently, Polynices enlists the help of his father-in-law Adrastus, the king of Argos, and leads an army against Thebes. The Thebans manage to repel the attack of the Argive army and the two brothers die fighting each other before the city gates, after which the rule of Thebes falls to Creon, Jocasta's brother. As his first act in office, Creon orders Eteocles to be buried with all proper honours, but he forbids Polynices to be buried, because he considers him a traitor who attacked his own city. Antigone, sister of Eteocles and Polynices, is not willing to obey Creon's orders and decides to bury Polynices herself. It is exactly at this moment that Sophocles's tragedy begins. The following passage discusses the reactions of some of the characters to Antigone's disobedience of Creon's decree.

At the beginning of the scene a guard appears whom Creon had appointed to guard the unburied body of Polynices. He has to tell Creon that someone – he does not yet know who – nevertheless has managed to throw dust over the corpse as a form of burial. Creon reprimands the guard, but spares him harsher treatment. He orders him to expose the body again and to resume his watch, because he believes that the attempted burial is the work of men who try to undermine his reign. He suspects them of having bribed the guards. After Creon and the guard both leave the stage, the chorus sings a song about the extraordinary capabilities of humans: gifted with language and reason, they are able to dominate nature, to interact socially, and to overcome all kind of hardship, except for death. Since these abilities can be used for good and evil, only he who respects both human and divine law is worthy of a rightful place in society; whoever violates these rules must be expelled from society and will, therefore, become an outlaw. Here the chorus is clearly thinking of the (unknown) perpetrator of the burial. But barely having finished its song, it is shocked to see whom the guard is bringing in as the perpetrator.

Text: Sophocles, Antigone *(ca. 441 BCE)*

Creon (to the guard): If you do not reveal the doers to me, you shall testify that low desire for profit is the cause of pain!
Exit Creon.
Guard: Why, let him [= the perpetrator of the burial] be found by all means! But whether he is found or not, for that is something that fortune will decide, you will never see me coming here again! Indeed, this time I have got off safely beyond my own hopes and my own judgement [330], and I am deeply grateful to the gods!
Exit Guard.
Chorus: Many things are formidable, and none more formidable than man! He crosses the gray sea beneath the winter wind, passing beneath the surges that surround him; and he wears away the highest of the gods, Earth, immortal and unwearying, as his ploughs go back and forth from year to year, turning the soil [340] with the aid of the breed of horses.
And he captures the tribe of thoughtless birds and the races of wild beasts and the watery brood of the sea, catching them in the woven coils of nets, man the skillful. And he contrives to overcome the beast that roams the mountain, and tames the shaggy-maned horse [350] and the untiring mountain bull, putting a yoke about their necks.
And he has learned speech and wind-swift thought and the temper that rules cities, and how to escape the exposure of the inhospitable hills and the sharp arrows of the rain, [360] all-resourceful; he meets nothing in the future without resource; only from Hades shall he apply no means of flight; and he has contrived escape from desperate maladies.
Skillful beyond hope is the contrivance of his art, and he advances something to evil, at other time to good. When he applies the laws of the earth and the justice the gods have sworn to uphold [370] he is high in the city; outcast from the city is he with whom the ignoble consorts for the sake of gain. May he who does such things never sit by my hearth or share my thoughts!
The Guard leads in Antigone.
I am at loss; is this a god-sent portent? But how shall I deny, since I know it, that this is the young Antigone? Unhappy one and child of an unhappy [380] father, Oedipus, what is this? Surely they do not lead you captive for disobedience to the king's laws, having detected you in folly?
Guard: This is the one that did the deed! We caught her burying the body! But where is Creon?
Chorus: He is here, returning from the house just when he is needed.
Enter Creon.
Creon: What is the matter? What is the event that makes my coming opportune?

Guard: King, there is nothing that mortals can swear is impossible! For second thoughts show one's judgement to be wrong; why, [390] I scarcely would have thought I would come here again because of your threats, which at that time battered me. But since the delight that one has prayed for beyond hope is unlike any other pleasure by a long way, I have come, though I had sworn never to do so, bringing this girl, who was caught adorning the grave.[7]

The way in which the characters are portrayed in this scene is representative of the play as a whole: the guard is portrayed through his speech as an ordinary man, who is afraid of his master's power and cares foremost about saving his own skin. Creon, who has only recently come into power, suspects treason and resistance to his reign. His thoughts are repeatedly plagued by the ideas of overthrow, money and bribery.

The chorus plays a twofold role. On the one hand, it consists of old men who are loyal to the royal family and have been summoned by Creon; when conversing with other characters, it is represented by the chorus leader and takes part in the plot like any regular character. On the other hand, in the choral songs* it clearly transcends the role of an ordinary character in the play. Whilst the actual events taking place on stage act as a starting point for those songs, the chorus broadens the audience's horizon, draws their attention to universal principles and develops possible interpretations of the portrayed events. For example, the choral song printed previously was prompted by the report of the guard that someone had tried to bury the corpse of Polynices. It discusses this event, however, in very broad terms, such as general human behaviour or human and divine law, which prove to be essential for the entire tragedy and will be discussed later in the play from the point of view of the family (Antigone), the city (Creon) and the gods (the seer Tiresias, who appears at the end of the play). Using traditional* myths, the tragedians discuss contemporary social problems as well as the general human condition and put them on stage. In the choral songs, these issues are presented in a more abstract way and therefore lifted out of their immediate context. They function as "bridges", inviting the spectators to apply these abstract ideas not only to the mythical events on stage but also to the contemporary world in which they live.

The political function of the theatre

The great spring festival with which the city of Athens honoured Dionysus might be characterized as a forum where the polis celebrated itself, through a combination of religious and cultural actions, while questioning its identity at the same time. The literary genres performed during this festival each contributed in their own way to a discussion of contemporary society. To judge from the fragments, the dithyrambs connected the present of the performances with the history of the city, both with its prehistoric myths and with the heroic deeds of the Athenians in historical times, like their victory over the Persians in the Persian Wars. These choral songs glorified the city and praised its present constitution.

The affirmative effect of the dithyrambs contrasts with the probing effect of tragedy* and the subversive effect of comedy. The actions of tragedy, set in a remote, mythical past, highlight problems of human interaction, such as the relationship between the individual and the collective, between genders or generations, or between humans and the gods. The human condition is dealt with in all its dangers and fragility. Unlike the dithyrambs, in which only the voice of the chorus is heard, tragedy displays a wide array of voices and forces the audience to decide for itself who is right and who is wrong, to follow the action and to relate it to its own life. Often questions remain and no unambiguous solution to the problems presented on stage can be found. This was true not only for the original spectators in classical Athens, but also for contemporary audiences watching *Antigone* or modern interpreters of the play.

In contrast to tragedy, whose plots are, with very few exceptions, set in mythical times, the plots of comedy* are set in present times, although this present is greatly exaggerated and fantastically portrayed. The eleven preserved comedies of Aristophanes provide us with an insight into the workings of this genre in the late fifth and early fourth centuries BCE. Based on his dissatisfaction with contemporary politics and society, the hero* of comedy concocts an idea of how to improve his lot and tries to fulfil it, often in the face of fierce resistance from the authorities. Representatives of contemporary society, both politicians and intellectuals, are mentioned by name and ridiculed in a way we would nowadays regard as libellous. Conventions and rules of life in the city are challenged and subverted, although at the end of the plays the old order is usually restored. Here the fact that performances of comedy, like those of tragedy, were restricted in time to certain festivals of Dionysus may have diminished their impact. The Dionysian festival offered an occasion in which the order of the state could be challenged, comparable to modern carnival* celebrations. This subversion is restricted, however, to certain periods of the year and has a social-hygienic effect. By identifying with the comic hero on stage, spectators can imagine themselves doing what they are not allowed to do in everyday life.

The post-classical Greek theatre

Whereas the further development of Greek tragedy cannot be traced with any certainty, because very little of post-classical tragedy has survived, the preservation of several comedies of Menander, who lived towards the end of the fourth century BCE, offers an insight into the further development of Greek comedy. Menander's plays differ fundamentally from those of Aristophanes. The comic plots are still set in the contemporary world, but the political aspect of the plays in the broadest sense, that is everything related to the city of Athens, has disappeared and made room for private concerns. Now most plays evolve around love affairs and characters are reduced to stereotypes: the young lover, the stern father, the beloved woman (often a prostitute), the smart slave, the parasite or the boasting soldier. Both plot and characters share characteristics with modern sitcoms*. Because the stern father tries to prevent the young lover from pursuing his affair with the woman he loves, he tries to reach his goal with the support of a smart slave. The solution often comes when, at the end of the play, it is revealed that his beloved really comes from a respectable family, but through adverse circumstances beyond her control she ended up in her current, questionable circumstances. Hence, there are no remaining social obstacles to a marriage between the young man and his beloved and they live happily ever after.

Roman drama

According to the Roman poet Horace, the Romans learned the great value of Greek drama from the Greek colonists in southern Italy in the course of the third century BCE.[8] Here Horace alludes to the fact that, during their expansion, the Romans came in contact with Greek culture and soon realised the tremendous ideological* and political potential of dramatic performances. Not surprisingly, it was a Greek freedman, named Livius

Andronicus, who was credited with the first performance of a Latin play in 240 BCE. This was followed by a great number of Latin tragedies and comedies. Of these comedies, twenty-one by Plautus (ca. 250–184 BCE) and six by Terence (195/185–59 BCE) have survived. Thereafter, two kinds of each dramatic genre developed: one based on Greek originals, either tragic or comic, and another one based on Roman content, again either tragic or comic. Roman poets seem to have based their Latin adaptations* only very loosely on the respective Greek plays. In contrast to Terence's humorous, ironical* and "quietly" comedic plays – which led Julius Caesar to call him a "half-Menander" – Plautus's comedies are rude, loud and colourful and gladly indulge in comic effects that are reminiscent of Aristophanes's comedies. In Plautus's comedies, we find wordplay, puns, slapstick, and most importantly long passages of song and recital* (*cantica**), which we do not find in their Greek counterparts. Plautine comedy also employs the "zooming" and "distancing"* technique Greek drama uses: Plautus's use of Latin and allusions* to comic folk* genres make his plays seem very familiar to the audience; at the same time, Greek setting* and Greek character names make them seem unknown and exotic. This technique shifts the plays to a fictitious* Greco-Roman world, where the problems and complications on stage are distant enough that the audience can laugh at them without worry.

Plautus and Terence mostly use the stereotypical plot elements of Menander's plays: mix-ups, false identities, intrigues and recognition scenes, which bring to light the true identity of a character after numerous entanglements – often by means of an inalterable external feature, a piece of jewellery or another item of personal value. Plautus's comedy *Bacchides* ('Two women called Bacchis') combines these elements in a very confusing manner. As the title already suggests, the play deals with the confusion caused by two prostitutes both called Bacchis. Counterpart to these two women are their suitors, two young men called Mnesilochus and Pistoclerus; in addition, there are the young men's fathers and their two slaves, one honest (Lydus) and one clever (Chrysalus), who either support them or try to sabotage their amorous plans. Mnesilochus, who is in love with Bacchis I, defrauds his father, assisted by his slave Chrysalus (meaning 'gold stealer' in Greek), of some money he was supposed to bring back from his journey to the East. He plans to use the money to pay off a soldier named Cleomachus ('fame in battle') who tries to claim this Bacchis I for himself. In a letter, Mnesilochus tells his friend Pistoclerus to keep an eye on his beloved (Bacchis I), who is now staying with her friend Bacchis II in Athens. At once, Pistoclerus falls in love with Bacchis II. As the girls share the same name, various complications occur.

This comedy's conflict is solved in a rather surprising way. According to the rules of the comic genre, there are two possible ways of solving the constellation "young man loves prostitute": either it is revealed that the prostitute is actually a girl from a good family who innocently came into this unfortunate situation, so that the young man can marry her without too much difficulty; or the young man finally realises that his romance is incompatible with social conventions and overcomes his love for the girl. However, in the *Bacchides*, both girls are prostitutes and come from the lower classes. Curiously though, in the comedy's final scene, the young men do not only fail to recognise their actions to be wrong – obviously contrary to the audience's expectations – but their fathers in turn also fall for the two girls and do not hesitate to throw themselves shamelessly into a love triangle with their sons and the two prostitutes. Although this ending does not conform at all to Roman moral standards, we can still guess what could have attracted Roman spectators to this final scene: in this comic performance the rules and norms of everyday life are blatantly ignored. On stage, the characters dare to do things Roman citizens can only imagine. The scene, furthermore, would be acceptable, because in the theatrical illusion it is not Roman characters who break society's standards, but Greeks, a people whom the Romans often accused of lacking the same moral scruples they had.

Despite the prolific production of tragedies in Rome, only nine tragedies, written by Seneca (ca. 0–65 CE), survive. It is heavily debated whether these plays were written for performance, recital or reading*. They, however, show the typical features of Roman literature in the first century CE: rhetoric* dominates the performance, and descriptions of cruelty and horror are evidently favoured. Senecan tragedies revolve around characters who fail because they are overcome by their emotions. According to the prevailing philosophy at the time, Stoicism (see Chapter 1), emotion was considered a substantial cause of human failure to lead a content, independent life. Seneca practically exemplifies in his tragedies what he theoretically discusses in his philosophical works* such as his treatise *De ira* ('On Anger'). His tragic characters are not only victims of their unrestrained emotions, however, but also of the role imposed upon them by literary tradition. This becomes particularly clear in Seneca's *Medea*: beaten by insatiable anger and hate because, despite all her support, her ungrateful, adulterous husband plans to leave her for another woman, Medea wishes to become Medea as Euripides had portrayed her: the woman who killed her own children. "May I become Medea," she says in line 171 of the play. After she then finally brings herself to punish her husband by killing their children, she emphasises that now, finally, she has found her true nature: "Now I am Medea," she says.[9]

Reception of ancient drama

The rediscovery of Aristotle's *Poetics** during the Renaissance* facilitated the return of Greek tragedy on the European stage. In the 1570s and 1580s, Duke Bardi hosted a group of scholars in his palace, Florence's so-called Camerata, to discuss ancient drama. Strongly influenced by their reading of Aristotle's *Poetics*, they reflected about Greek tragedy as a universal artwork, in which song, dance and music, as well as architecture and the spoken word, were joined together to produce a dramatic effect. The performance of Sophocles's *Oedipus the King* – considered by Aristotle as the most perfect play – on March 3, 1585, in Vicenza followed this interpretation of tragedy as a universal artwork. The performance was in Italian and took place in the Teatro Olimpico, which was especially built by the famous architect Andrea Palladio for this purpose. Early modern opera* has its roots in similar attempts to revive Greek drama.

Despite *Oedipus's* successful performance in Vicenza, Greek tragedy soon disappeared, if not from public interest, at least from public stages. Public theatres* preferred to produce plays that were influenced by Seneca's tragedies: Seneca was, as was said, a Stoic philosopher, and Stoic philosophy became very popular again in the sixteenth and seventeenth centuries ("Neo-Stoicism"). An important French tragic poet at the time was Jean Racine (1639–1699), who engaged with Seneca in his *Phédre* (1677), as well as Pierre Corneille (1606–1684), who did so in his *Médée* (1635) and *Œdipe* (1658/9). Tragedy becomes, as the German poet Martin Opitz (1597–1639) states in his version of Seneca's *Troades*, a didactic play about Stoic stability of character (*constantia*) and at the same time offers a welcome distraction and consolation (*consolatio*) from one's own misery in times of war.[10] The malleability of myth and its application to diverse contexts contributed to Greek tragedy's second return, first in German literature, as exemplified by Johann Wolfgang von Goethe's *Iphigenie auf Tauris* (1779/86), and, from the second half of the nineteenth century, more broadly to the modern stage. Ancient comedy's return to the stage has been hindered by its close association with political and social circumstances of the age in which it was first performed, which are not always known to us, although some of Plautus's plays and Aristophanes's *Lysistrata* (a play about Athenian women who stage a sex strike to end the war) have occasionally been adapted and reperformed. Ancient comedy, however, continues to influence comic theatre, films* and TV sitcoms to this day, mostly through its stereotypical characters and recognisable features such as mistaken identities.

A short glance at twentieth-century reception* and reinterpretations of Greek tragedy shows very clearly how an era's preference for certain plays tends to be closely connected with contemporary social and political circumstances. Modern productions of Aeschylean plays are often dominated by a very archaic, primal atmosphere and juxtapose bright, human Hellas, as portrayed by Goethe in his *Iphigenie auf Tauris*, with a more obscure and cruel version of Greece. Euripides's war plays, especially his *Troades*, are frequently turned to in order to criticise modern warfare. Some modern authors see Euripides virtually as a soul mate who anticipated present catastrophes in his tragedies, for example the German playwright Franz Werfel, who produced his *Troerinnen* (1915) in the middle of the First World War.

When adapting Sophocles's tragedies, modern directors and playwrights seem to be most interested in his abnormal and psychologically manifold characters. The Austrian playwright Hugo von Hofmannsthal in his *Elektra* (1903, as opera orchestrated by the German composer Richard Strauss in 1909), which is highly influenced by Sigmund Freud's *Studien über Hysterie* ('Studies on Hysteria', 1895), stages an Electra whose only purpose in life exists in her hate for her mother; after her brother Orestes kills their mother in an act of revenge, she collapses dead whilst triumphing over her mother's death. While Sophocles's Electra is mostly interpreted negatively in modern adaptions, his Antigone becomes a champion of freedom against despotic oppression. The German playwright Walter Hasenclever composes his *Antigone* (1917) as an appeal to peace and as a "protest against war and rape cloaked in ancient robes," as the author says about his play.[11] The French playwright Jean Anouilh in his *Antigone* (1942, debut performance 1944) contrasts Antigone's strict rejection of life with Creon's love of life. As in Sophocles's original, Anouilh's Antigone cannot tolerate the compromises of everyday life and sees death as her only escape from this absurd world. Polynices's funeral, in Sophocles seen as a religious duty, becomes an act of courage against a regime of injustice. In *The Island* (debut performance 1973), written by the South African playwrights Athol Fugard, John Kani and Winston Ntshona in protest against the contemporary Apartheid's regime, Sophocles's original is featured as a "play within a play"* and therein as a manifesto* against political oppression. At night after their day of abasing and pointless forced labour, clearly referencing the ancient myth of Sisyphus, two cellmates rehearse for a performance of Sophocles's tragedy in front of the other captives, John as Antigone and Winston as Creon. Sophocles's play is here reduced to the confrontation between Creon, representing the oppressive state, and Antigone, defending the eternal divine laws. "Gods of Our Fathers! My Land! My Home! Time waits no longer. I go now to my living death, because I honoured those things to which honour belongs," are the last words of John-Antigone.[12]

Fugard's technique in this play is the same as the one used by the Greek playwrights of the fifth century BCE. By building "bridges", the audience can grasp the relationship between the mythical events portrayed on stage and the present. For every theatregoer at the time could recognise in *The Island* Robben Island, the prison camp for the coast of South Africa where Nelson Mandela and other opponents of the Apartheid regime were held captive. This "play within a play"* opens up – just as choral songs do in Greek tragedy – a whole new level of interpretation, which enriches the present plot with more general meaning and impact. In the same way as fifth-century BCE Athenians reflected on the formative elements of their democratic society by watching dramatic performances in the Theatre of Dionysus, Greek tragedy remains until this day, whether it be in reproduction or in adaption, an artistic medium of criticising and analysing our contemporary world.

Notes

1 See Eric Csapo and Margaret C. Miller, *The Origins of Theater in Ancient Greece and Beyond: From Ritual to Drama* (Cambridge: Cambridge University Press, 2007).
2 Alan H. Sommerstein, ed., trans., *Aeschylus*, 3 vols. Loeb Classical Library (Cambridge, MA: Harvard University Press, 2008).
3 Hugh Lloyd-Jones, ed., trans., *Sophocles*, 3 vols. Loeb Classical Library (Cambridge, MA: Harvard University Press, 1994–1996).
4 David Kovacs, ed., trans., *Euripides*, 6 vols. Loeb Classical Library (Cambridge, MA: Harvard University Press, 1994–2002).
5 Jeffrey Henderson, ed., trans., *Aristophanes*, 4 vols. Loeb Classical Library (Cambridge, MA: Harvard University Press, 1998–2002).
6 Christopher Collard and Martin Cropp, eds., trans., *Euripides: Fragments*, 2 vols. Loeb Classical Library (Cambridge, MA: Harvard University Press, 2008).
7 Sophocles, *Antigone* 324–96, translated by Lloyd-Jones, *Sophocles*.
8 Horace, *Epistles* 2.1.156–63, translated by H. Rushton Fairclough, *Horace: Satires, Epistles and Ars Poetica*, revised edition. Loeb Classical Library (Cambridge, MA: Harvard University Press, 1929).
9 Seneca, *Medea* 910, translated by John G. Fitch, *Seneca: Tragedies*, 2 vols. Loeb Classical Library (Cambridge, MA: Harvard University Press, 2002–2004).
10 Martin Opitz, *Gesammelte Werke*, vol. 2 (Stuttgart: Hiersemann, 1979), 430.
11 Walter Hasenclever, *Gedichte, Dramen, Prosa* (Reinbek bei Hamburg: Rowolt Verlag, 1963), 502.
12 Athol Fugard, *The Township Plays* (Oxford: Oxford University Press, 1993), 227.

Further reading

Csapo, Eric and William J. Slater. *The Context of Ancient Drama*. Ann Arbor: The University of Michigan Press, 1994.
Flashar, Hellmut. *Inszenierung der Antike: Das griechische Drama auf der Bühne*. Second edition. München: Verlag C.H. Beck, 2009.
Manuwald, Gesine. *Roman Republic Theatre*. Cambridge: Cambridge University Press, 2011.
Zimmermann, Bernhard. *Greek Tragedy: An Introduction*. Baltimore/London: The Johns Hopkins University Press, 1991.
Zimmermann, Bernhard. *Die griechische Komödie*. Second edition. Frankfurt am Main: Verlag Antike, 2006.

5   Making literature

Koen De Temmerman and Bé Breij

Figure 5.1 Matham, Theodor, "Cicero and discussing figures", engraving on paper, 1661, 20.8 x 15 cm, Rijksmuseum Amsterdam

Text: Horace, "Ars Poetica" (ca. 19 BCE)

You[1] who write, choose a subject that's matched by   38
Your powers, consider deeply what your shoulders
Can and cannot bear. Whoever chooses rightly,
Eloquence, and clear construction, won't fail him.
Charm and excellence in construction, if I'm right,
Is to say here and now, what's to be said here and now,
Retaining, and omitting, much, for the present.
Moreover as the author of the promised work,
Liking this, rejecting that, cautious and precise,
Weaving words together, you'll speak most happily
When skilled juxtaposition renews a common word.

. . .

It's not enough for poems to have beauty: they must have   99
Charm, leading their hearer's heart wherever they wish.
As the human face smiles at a smile, so it echoes
Those who weep: if you want to move me to tears
You must first grieve yourself: then Peleus or Telephus
Your troubles might pain me: speak inappropriately
And I'll laugh or fall asleep. Sad words suit a face
Full of sorrow, threats fit the face full of anger,
Jests suit the playful, serious speech the solemn.
Nature first alters us within, to respond to each
Situation: brings delight or goads us to anger,
Or weighs us to the ground, tormented by grief:
Then, with tongue interpreting, show heart's emotion.
If the speaker's words don't harmonise with his state,
The Romans will bellow with laughter, knights and all.
Much depends on whether a god or man is speaking,
A mature old man, or one still flush with first youth,
A powerful lady, or perhaps a diligent nurse,
A wandering merchant, or tiller of fertile fields,
Colchian or Assyrian, from Argos or Thebes.
Either follow tradition, or invent consistently.
If you happen to portray Achilles, honoured,
Pen him as energetic, irascible, ruthless,
Fierce, above the law, never downing weapons.
Make Medea wild, untameable, Ino tearful,
Ixion treacherous, Io wandering, Orestes sad.
If you're staging something untried, and dare
To attempt fresh characters, keep them as first
Introduced, from start to end self-consistent.[2]

This passage is taken from a poem on how to write poetry. It was written ca. 19 BCE by Quintus Horatius Flaccus ("Horace"), one of the greatest Roman poets. Formally, the poem is part of a collection of letters* addressed to a variety of recipients. It takes its name from its addressees, *Epistle to the Pisones*, but is better known as the *Ars Poetica* (or also:

'The Art of Poetry', see Chapter 4), a name first given to it by Quintilian in his work on rhetoric in the first century CE and commonly used ever since.[3]

As we will show presently, Horace's passage resonates with key concepts underlying this chapter. It is not just that Horace in this poem does what our title says this chapter also does: to discuss how literature (in Horace's case, poetry) is "made" (both "poetics/poetica" and "poetry" derive from the Greek word *poiein*, 'to make'). It is also that the way in which he addresses his material inscribes itself in a broad conceptual tradition of thinking about writing and reading that takes centre stage in this chapter: ancient rhetoric*. This discipline is arguably common to much of ancient literature (and literary criticism alike), written in different languages (Latin and Greek), in different historical eras (from Homer to late antiquity) and different geographical regions (from Spain and Gaul to Egypt and the Near East). Our starting point is that rhetoric, originally the art of speaking skilfully and therefore persuasively, gradually developed into a comprehensive theory of language and literature that is crucial to understanding how texts were written in antiquity. It was ubiquitous in ancient education and it was inextricably bound up with poetics* (the theory of poetry) and literary criticism*, two disciplines that interacted with and cross-fertilized it.[4] Although the importance of ancient rhetoric for European literary history stretches far beyond the temporal boundaries of antiquity (see e.g. Chapter 7, Chapter 13 and Chapter 14), our chapter examines its relevance for creating and assessing ancient literature.

In order to explore these issues, we must first make a few introductory remarks about ancient rhetoric. While people have, of course, always used persuasive speech, the first theoretical reflections on rhetoric emerged with the rise of direct democracy in fifth-century BCE Greece. This form of government made it necessary for (male) citizens to speak persuasively, not just in popular assemblies (of which every free, male citizen could become a member), but also in courtrooms (there were no lawyers or public prosecutors). In this context, rhetorical guidelines began to be taught, first by travelling teachers (called "Sophists"*, literally 'teachers of wisdom'), and later as part of school curricula. Rhetoric was conceptually divided in three genres, according to the three main societal contexts in which it was used: forensic or judicial (prosecution and defence speeches; *genus iudiciale**), political (speeches in support of or against particular policies; *genus deliberativum**) and ceremonial (speeches held at specific civic occasions such as funerals, commemorations*, etc.; *genus demonstrativum**). In the course of some three centuries, a detailed system was developed that theorized the composition of speeches in these three genres (with a strong emphasis on forensic rhetoric, which was regarded as the most complicated and challenging genre). The system was adopted by the Romans and remained essentially the same throughout antiquity; in fact, we still see it operative in modern-day public speeches.

By far the most significant figure in ancient rhetoric is the Roman orator and statesman Marcus Tullius Cicero, who lived in the first century BCE. He wrote an impressive number of handbooks on rhetorical theory. Some of these bear clear educational characteristics. *De Inventione* ('Invention'), for example, is compiled of lecture notes Cicero took when he was only in his teens; *De Partitione Oratoria* ('Divisions of Oratory') reads like a catechism that faithfully reels off the articles of rhetoric. But other works go far beyond book learning. So *De Oratore* ('The Orator') is of paramount importance. As a philosophical* and literary dialogue* responding to the dialogues in which Plato had attacked rhetoric, it is rightly famous for its rehabilitation of rhetoric. But what makes Cicero truly special is that he is the only ancient orator who unites theory and practice. Not only do we have his *Brutus*, in which he gives a survey of Roman oratory up to his own day; also, and much more importantly, we have a large number of his speeches. These are not only valuable historical documents: Cicero was, after all, a major political player and the final symbol of the Roman Republic who was murdered during the onset of the Principate. At least as importantly, they are the works of a brilliant orator* and rhetorician, who finds his material with consummate skill and arranges the results into a cohesive whole, of which he couches each part in a fitting style. In other words, he is the one ancient author we can witness putting his own rhetorical precepts into practice. The most comprehensive ancient handbook, however, is the *Institutio Oratoria* ('The Orator's Education'), written in the late first century CE by Quintilian, who was the first state-appointed professor of Roman rhetoric. This work has rightly been dubbed the *status quaestionis* of rhetoric: it offers an all-out treatment of five hundred years of rhetorical theory and oratorical practice, and dispenses precepts for the life and works of the good orator from the cradle to the grave.

Why is this relevant for the study of literature? Different aspects of an answer will be provided in the following sections of this chapter. For now, the first observation is that the fields of literature and rhetoric have been closely intertwined since time immemorial. In fact, ancient literature was replete with rhetorical patterns from the beginning. The two oldest epics* in ancient literature, Homer's *Iliad* and *Odyssey*, each begin with a rhetorical figure known as *apostrophe**, the direct address not of the actual audience* of the poems (presumably listeners) but of a third party, in this case the Muse*, with a request for inspiration: "Sing about the wrath of Achilles, Goddess" and "Tell me about the man, Muse." Both passages are in a sense emblematic of this chapter, not just because they emphatically thematize the question of how literature is made (i.e. through divine inspiration; see Chapter 6) but also because they aptly point to the rhetorical qualities of ancient literature from the very beginning. Other examples are elaborated speeches in Homer and Greek drama*, rhetorical figures in Sappho and other archaic lyric*, and reports of speeches in historiography* ever since Herodotus and Thucydides.

This rhetorical wealth of ancient literature made it an appealing body of sources for rhetorical theorists, who often drew examples from it to illustrate rhetorical concepts and phenomena. At the same time, however, oratory was treated more and more as a literary genre. Oratorical, originally oral*, material was increasingly recuperated and adapted in literary contexts aimed at readers rather than listeners from the fourth century BCE onwards (e.g. speeches of famous orators such as Demosthenes being revised and published after delivery). And Isocrates, a Greek rhetorician from the fourth century BCE, wrote and published speeches that were never publicly delivered. The same trend persists into the Hellenistic and Roman periods: famous rhetoricians from these periods were Demetrius of Phalerum, under whose name a treatise *On Style* has come down to us, Dionysius of Halicarnassus, the author of a number of rhetorical treatises among other things, and Longinus, to whom a treatise *On the Sublime* has traditionally been ascribed. All these rhetoricians were concerned first and foremost "with literary composition, with imitation of literary models, and with the development of rhetorical criticism."[5]

The pervasive fusion of rhetorical theory and literary praxis is also illustrated by another important development: that of the relative importance in ancient rhetorical theory of diction and stylistic refinement (*elocutio*). Whereas rhetorical treatises from the fifth and fourth centuries BCE treat the field of rhetoric first and foremost as a discipline of argumentation, rhetorical treatises from late antiquity deal primarily with stylistic* concepts. This development suggests that rhetoric was by then perceived more as the art of speaking/writing beautifully than that of developing persuasive, logically coherent discourse.

Concomitant to such a gradual "literaturization" of rhetoric, scholars have identified a so-called "rhetorization" of literature: a growing presence in literary works of rhetorical characteristics such as the use of topics, tropes*, aphorisms*, patterns of arrangement, etc. that becomes particularly visible from the first century BCE onwards and throughout late antiquity (and beyond).

Rhetoric and poetics

Let us now return to our introductory passage of Horace on poetry. Why and how does ancient rhetoric provide instruments helpful for reading it? To answer this question, we turn to the basis of the rhetorical toolkit: the so-called 'tasks of the orator' (*officia oratoris*).[6] These are five consecutive steps detailing how speeches* are written: *inventio** ('invention' or finding relevant material: the ability to take stock of and access everything that makes a given case persuasive), *ordo** or *dispositio** (the 'arrangement' or structure of the material throughout the speech), *elocutio** (diction and stylistic refinement), *memoria** (memorizing* the speech), and *actio** (the actual performance* in front of an audience). The first three tasks in particular (*inventio*, *dispositio* and *elocutio*) form common ground with poetics. In fact, they are relevant to any kind of textual communication.

The relevance of these three tasks for the creation of literature is illustrated by the fact that they are all three covered by Horace. The current passage is (partly) taken from a section discussing the writer's aims. Horace first dedicates a few verses to the clear ordering of material (42–4). He even uses the word *ordo*, which is a standard term in rhetorical theory designating textual structure. He then turns to poetic language and the importance of adopting an appropriate *style** (45–118; *elocutio*). He underlines, for example, that both comedy* and tragedy* have their own *style* and that it is inappropriate to convey comic content with tragic diction, or vice versa. At the same time, he stipulates, *style* should be appropriate to context and circumstances: sorrow and anger require different styles; the merry and the grave speak differently. Here Horace follows a fundamental rhetorical precept, which dictates that appropriateness (*aptum**) is the main stylistic virtue, both eclipsing and encompassing correctness, clarity and even elegance. Finally, he discusses the choice of material (119–27; *inventio*), which either follows tradition or constitutes something new. The passage gives advice on which topics to cover in either case and pays particular attention to the importance of literary tradition as a model (a guideline prominent in rhetorical theory, too).

But Horace's indebtedness to the rhetorical tradition* runs deeper. A more detailed look at the task of *inventio* will show this. In rhetorical theory, the whole of *inventio* is covered by the three means of persuasion that were first conceptualized by Aristotle in his *Rhetoric* (fourth century BCE): as he pointed out, persuasive communication depends not only on *logos** ('argument') but also on *ēthos** ('character'), and *pathos** ('emotion'). Like the *officia oratoris* themselves, these three means of persuasion naturally apply to textual communication at large. It is telling, for instance, that the examples adduced in ancient treatises to clarify (aspects of) *logos* or argument are often taken not from orations but from poetry, especially drama and epic. Aristotle himself cites a (now-lost) tragedy of Euripides, the *Thyestes*, to illustrate one specific type of logical argumentation; and Quintilian discusses the use of examples in fables*. These instances illustrate not just that poets too complied with the rules of logic but first and foremost that reasoning, which forms the basis of our thoughts, naturally informs both rhetoric and poetics – and that ancient rhetoricians were aware of this.

For the other two means of persuasion, *ēthos* ('character') and *pathos* ('emotion'), the link between rhetoric and poetics is even more obvious. *Ēthos* is concerned with representing both the character of the speaker (and/or those for whom he speaks) and that of his opponents. A speaker must display practical wisdom, virtue and good will (and portray his opponents as lacking these qualities). This means that rhetoric, like philosophy, studies human nature, and, like literature, strives to represent it. Horace in our passage carefully takes on board this notion when pointing to the necessity of adapting a person's speech to his/her character, social status, age, gender*, mental qualities and geographical provenance (93–117) – a point developed at greater length later in the poem in a section on characterization (vv. 153–88). This guideline is prominent throughout rhetorical theory, too (for example in the school exercises discussed ahead) and goes back all the way to Aristotle's conceptualization of poetry as a form of representation of reality (*mimesis**), which ought to capture characters in a probable way.

Emotion (*pathos*) too, Horace points out, is relevant to the creation of poetry. In rhetorical theory, it focuses on the audience, whose decisions are impacted not only by reason but also by their emotional dispositions. Speeches, in other words, cannot be persuasive without arousing in the audience the emotions that are most useful (to the speaker's purposes) in a specific situation. From Aristotle onwards, ancient rhetoric therefore offers psychological* guidelines on how to arouse pity (for victims), anger (with defendants), hatred, indignation, envy and fear among other emotions. Horace, for his part, is explicit about the importance of appropriately addressing the emotions of one's audience (108–13). His guidelines recycle some of the emotions that since Aristotle have taken centre stage in discussions of *pathos* (joy, anger, grief).

Finding material, arranging it, and giving it an appropriate shape: as Horace shows, these three tasks occupy not just orators, but also poets (and perhaps creators of any work of art, for that matter). Indeed, the insight that literature is fruitfully approached as a rhetorical construct is one of the broad tenets held in today's literary theory. But its ancient roots ultimately go back to Aristotle. He describes more explicitly than Horace how poetics and rhetoric occupy common ground and complement each other. On tragedy, for example, he writes:

> it remains for me to discuss *style* and thought. The details of thought can be left to my discourses on rhetoric, since they belong more integrally to that subject. Thought pertains to all those effects which must be produced by the spoken language; its functions are demonstration, refutation, the arousal of emotions such as pity, fear, anger, and such like, and arguing for the importance or unimportance of things . . . [i]n matters of verbal style, one kind of study concerns figures of speech. Knowledge of these (for instance, the difference between a command, a prayer, a narrative, a threat, a question, an answer, and so on) belongs to the art of rhetorical delivery and to anyone with such expertise.[7]

Aristotle is explicit that these two important constituents of tragedy (*style* and thought) essentially belong not only to poetics but also to rhetoric. His development of each of these points is replete with technical terms prominent in rhetorical theory (demonstration, refutation, emotions, figures of speech*). Similar conceptual overlaps between poetry and rhetoric are also implied in his *Rhetoric*, where he refers back to his *Poetics* when discussing constituents of speech: poetical *style* and choice of words, metaphors* and comic elements.

The number of ancient literary critics and theorists articulating their views on literature through key concepts of rhetorical theory could easily be multiplied. We give only one further example here: the anonymous author of the famous (and, from the late seventeenth century onwards, very influential) treatise *On the Sublime* (first century CE), written in Greek but long (erroneously) ascribed to a Roman author called Cassius Longinus and now commonly referred to as Pseudo-Longinus. He discusses the qualities of thought and *style* that mark writing as "sublime"* (*hypsēlon*, literally 'high, lofty'). In his opening paragraphs, the author is explicit that the effect of sublime writing is *not* to persuade the audience but rather to bring them into a mental state "out of themselves" (*ekstasis*). Consequently, he continues, it exercises an irresistible power over its audience, while persuasion is usually under the audience's control; and whereas one's experience in *inventio* ('invention') and *dispositio* ('arrangement') emerges only from the totality of a composition, the sublime can be visible in one brilliant word or passage.[8] The underlying dynamic of this passage is significant: in order to connect sublime writing with greatness of mind, the author positions himself as breaking free from the rhetorical tradition in which he writes. At the same time, however, he can only use this tradition in order to define his own position and thus inevitably testifies to its importance as a concept fundamental to thinking and writing about literature.

Rhetorical education: *progymnasmata* . . .

The intertwinement of rhetoric and literature is tangible in ancient education* more than anywhere else. Rhetorical schools provided the dominant form of education for the elite* from Hellenistic times onwards throughout the Roman imperial period and late antiquity. After students had been taught for a few years how to read and write with a so-called *magister* ('teacher'), the curriculum was divided into two stages. First, students (mainly boys) aged between 11/12 and 15/16 years old were taught preliminary exercises in writing and composition by a *grammaticus*. These exercises were called *progymnasmata*, a name that aptly captures their place and function within the curriculum: they were exercises (*gymnasmata*) that preceded (*pro*) "real" rhetoric. After these exercises, indeed, students studied the composition and delivery of entire speeches (declamations) with a *rhetor* (at the age of ca. 15/16 to 18/20). Both stages essentially focused on the same rhetorical patterns, tropes and figures that we find so prominently in literature.

Both in antiquity and later, *progymnasmata* have been at the basis of teaching composition for centuries, not just in Western Europe but also in Egypt and the Near East. They offer a dynamic training in textual composition with the focus moving gradually from reading to writing, and with exercises being ordered from easy (such as the creation or paraphrase of a fable or short story) to more complex, such as vivid descriptions of persons, animals or buildings (*ecphrasis**); the writing of refutations and confirmations (*anasceue, catasceue*), blame and praise (*vituperatio**, *encomium**); impersonations through speech of mythological* or historical persons (*ethopoeia**); and the defense of and elaboration on a law proposal. In all these exercises students, through the use of standard guidelines and prescriptions, were gradually trained in writing, rewriting, paraphrasing and distributing textual material efficiently. Nicolaus, an author of a *progymnasmata* handbook from the fifth century CE, draws attention to the importance of these exercises as building blocks first taught individually and later made operative in a wider system ("we do not practise ourselves in the whole of rhetoric but in each part individually").[9] As he also points out, some of these building blocks are particularly relevant to specific rhetorical genres or to specific parts of orations.

They are also relevant to literature. Like all rhetorical theory, they take their material from existing literature, especially the epics of Homer and tragedy. Another author of a *progymnasmata* handbook, Aelius Theon, insists that teachers should collect good examples of each exercise from ancient prose works and assign them to the students to be learned by heart.[10] Heroes who fought at Troy, like Achilles and Hector, or Hector's wife, Andromache, are prominent figures in the exercises. "What words would Andromache say over the dead Hector," for example, is an exercise in impersonation or *ethopoeia* preserved in a collection of *progymnasmata* by the fourth-century CE rhetorician Libanius.[11] Often, progymnasmatic rewritings challenged well-established literary and/or mythological traditions: for example, students had to write a speech in praise of a character who was usually depicted negatively in the literary tradition, or a speech blaming a hero* traditionally depicted in a favourable light. The exercises built on known material, and the whole point was to rephrase, rehearse, transform and/or adapt it. The *progymnasmata* thus consciously inscribed themselves in a long literary tradition through processes of imitation* and adaptation*, in which literature offered models for new creations by the students.

Not only do the *progymnasmata* draw heavily on traditional literary genres and types of discourse, they also contribute themselves to literary composition. Given the prevalence of rhetoric in ancient education, the concepts and writing patterns taught in *progymnasmata* became part of the conceptual toolkit of virtually every writer. Theon is explicit about the usefulness of *progymnasmata* for future writers:

> training in exercises is absolutely useful not only to those who are going to practice rhetoric but also if one wishes to undertake the function of poets or historians or any other writers. These things are, as it were, the foundation of every kind of discourse.[12]

Broadly speaking, the *progymnasmata* conceptualize their own relevance to literary production in two ways. First, *progymnasmata* themselves can be developed into independent literary creations. Ovid's *Heroides*, for example, is a collection of *ethopoeiae* ('impersonations'): it contains epistolary* poems that present themselves as written by famous heroines from Greek and Roman mythology and are addressed to their lovers who have either left, mistreated or neglected them. Given the unhappy plot underlying their love stories, these poems profoundly resonate with progymnasmatic guidelines on *ethopoeia*, which themselves were based largely on lamenting monologues in Greek tragedies from the classical period and detailed that lamentations ought to establish contrasts between a happy past, an unhappy present and a possibly even worse future.

Second, *progymnasmata* are also employed as parts of texts. Examples in ancient literature are legion. One of these, both instructive and amusing, is an episode in Longus's ancient Greek novel* *Daphnis and Chloe* (ca. 200 CE) that relates a rhetorical contest* between Daphnis (the novel's hero, exposed after birth, suckled by a goat and subsequently raised by a goatherd) and Dorcon, who aims to seduce the heroine, Chloe (a foundling too, and suckled by a sheep). The winner of the contest will receive a kiss from Chloe. The episode (like Longus's entire novel) is clearly inscribed in the tradition of bucolic* (or pastoral*) literature, a genre founded by the Sicilian poet Theocritus in the third century BCE and thematizing rural life using a number of stock characters, such as shepherds and goatherds. Dorcon speaks first[13]:

> I am bigger than Daphnis, miss; I am a cowherd and he is a goatherd. <So> I am as much better than him as cows are better than goats. I am as white as milk, and fire-fair

like a field of corn waiting to be cut. I was nursed by a mother, not a wild animal. But this fellow is little, beardless like a woman, and black like a wolf. He tends billy-goats and stinks of them, and is too poor even to keep a dog. If, as they say, he is the nursling of a nanny-goat, then he is no different from a kid.

Daphnis replies:

A goat did nurse me, just like Zeus, and I tend billy-goats bigger than his cows. And I do not smell of them at all, because not even Pan does, despite being more than half goat. All I need is cheese, and bread baked on the spit, and white wine, which are what rich countrymen have. I am beardless, but so is Dionysus; I am black but so is the hyacinth. But Dionysus is better than Satyrs and the hyacinth is better than lilies. But this fellow is fire-fair like a fox, bearded like a goat and white like a woman from the town. And if you have to give a kiss, you will kiss my lips but the whiskers on his chin. Do not forget, miss, that you were nursed by a sheep, but you are beautiful.

These passages playfully rework a number of the standard elements of praise (*encomium*) and blame (*vituperatio*) as prescribed by the *progymnasmata* authors. One of these prescriptions is that praise and blame should pay attention to (social) origin, a point picked up by Dorcon's emphasis on the fact that he himself has been brought up by a (human) mother, whereas Daphnis has been suckled by a goat. Similarly, his emphasis on the contrast between his own occupation as cowherd and that of Daphnis, who is only a goatherd, recalls the topos* of official office, another aspect that *progymnasmata* treatises advertise as an essential part of any blame/praise. A third such topos is that of physical beauty, addressed by Dorcon at length in a number of comparisons that contrast Daphnis's physical appearance with his own. Daphnis, in turn, replies with a refutation (or *anasceue*, another *progymnasma*) of each of these *topoi*, which he uses to align himself with divine paradigms. In the beauty contest, then, the standard *topoi* usually adopted to blame and/or praise in ancient rhetoric are humorously* adapted to the pastoral setting both in Dorcon's speech and in Daphnis's refutation.

The relevance of *progymnasmata* does not stop at rhetorical and literary composition. The *progymnasmata* handbooks also present themselves as relevant to literary criticism. Theon explains, for example, that knowledge of *ethopoeia* ('impersonation') is useful for the study of ancient literature: "we praise Homer first because of his ability to attribute the right words to each of the characters he introduces, but we find fault with Euripides because his Hecuba philosophizes inopportunely."[14] With this reference to the character of Hecuba (the legendary queen of Troy at the time of its capture by the Greeks) in Euripides's tragedy *Trojan Women*, Theon is explicit that guidelines from the *progymnasmata* can be (and are) used to evaluate and assess traditional literature. In this case, it concerns a guideline from the exercise of *ethopoeia* explaining that impersonations through speech should as plausibly as possible take into account the gender of the impersonated person, among other aspects. The implication of Theon's criticism is that philosophical, rational discourse is not suitable for a female character (an idea also present elsewhere in ancient rhetorical theory, where female voices are associated first and foremost with emotional rather than rational discourse). As Theon's criticism illustrates, the *progymnasmata* incorporate the broad idea that rhetoric profoundly shapes not just literary composition but also the understanding and evaluation of literature by its readers.

. . . and declamations

In the final stage of their rhetorical education, students wrote so-called declamations, fully fledged speeches for which the *progymnasmata* prepared, and of which there are two types.[15] The mock-deliberative speech (*suasoria**) came first in the curriculum, because it was felt to be the easier exercise. It involved giving advice to a famous historical or mythological character in a political context – for example, to Agamemnon (not) to sacrifice his daughter Iphigenia in order to procure a favorable wind, or to Cicero (not) to burn his writings in order to have Mark Antony spare his life. The mock-forensic speech (*controversia**) was more difficult, but also more popular. For this exercise, the *rhetor* set his students a civil or criminal case combined with a contractual stipulation or law. Some of the laws used were genuine (for example those against murder or treason) but others were fictitious, like the decree that "a girl who has been raped may choose either marriage to her ravisher without a dowry or his death."[16] The cases were fictitious too, and usually quite dramatic and adventurous. This made them attractive material for students of rhetoric and their teachers for purposes of education and advertisement, but they were also used by orators for public showpieces and even became a favorite pastime of the male elite. This observation itself is another indication of the close intertwining of rhetoric and poetics: these speeches were being enjoyed by an audience as performed literature, comparable to theatre* performances (see Chapter 4).

Offering material for higher education, *suasoriae* and *controversiae* integrate several *progymnasmata* into a coherent whole according to the guidelines of the *dispositio* (arrangement). As detailed in rhetorical theory, speeches should follow a more or less fixed sequence of sections (the so-called "parts"), each of which has specific functions. An introduction or *exordium*, for example, aims to secure the audience's attention, benevolence and receptivity; a survey of the facts (*narratio**) should present preceding events in an orderly, brief, clear, and probable form; a statement of what the orator wants to prove (*propositio**) should then precede the actual argumentation, which supports the *propositio* and refutes the fictitious opponent's view; and finally, each conclusion (*peroratio**) should not only recapitulate (*enumeratio**) but also contain an emotional appeal (*adfectus**). All these guidelines (and many more) were put into practice in the declamations, with attention being paid to the relevance of specific *progymnasmata* for specific parts. Comparisons (*syncrisis**), for example, were particularly useful in the development of an *argumentatio**; basic principles of storytelling, taught in the exercises of fable and short story, were put into practice in a *narratio*; guidelines on how to persuasively blame or praise someone were useful to provide as part of the *argumentatio* a convincing character sketch of either a supporter or an opponent; and progymnasmatic prescriptions concerning descriptions (*ecphrasis*), highlighting vividness and clarity, were useful throughout the declamations.

Like *progymnasmata*, declamations interact with literature on different levels: they are useful for assessing the literary (and persuasive) qualities of literary genres and they are influenced by, and at the same time influence those genres. In the case of declamations, this influence is usually situated on the level of literary (and often intertextual*) borrowings: the speeches repeatedly adopt* literary motifs* and themes, make allusions* to myths and often cite canonical* writers. It was the delight of Roman declaimers to pepper their speeches with (more or less) hidden quotes from especially Cicero, Virgil, Ovid and Seneca; and it was the audience's delight to recognize these references. But again, this was by no means a one-way process: since, as we have pointed out, authors were usually educated in rhetoric, we also find declamatory elements in their works. Frequently it is impossible to determine whether a particular expression made its way from the work of a famous author into the schools or the other way around. In addition, declamations share a broad pool of motifs and themes with fictional literary genres such as New Comedy* and ancient novels. As in these genres, the declamations are organized around well-known character types such as pirates, prostitutes, young girls in brothels trying to protect their chastity, generals, war heroes, rich despots and their poor victims, tyrannical fathers, downtrodden mothers and wicked stepmothers. They would be involved in lawsuits over borders, loans, damages and legacies, but also adoption, divorce, rape, abduction, torture, murder, incest, cannibalism and suicide. The outlandishness of such cases, which usually prompted a matching theatrical style, was not without its critics. In the opening scene of what we have left of Petronius's *Satyrica* (also known as *Satyricon*), a Latin novel from the mid first century CE, one of the characters vigorously attacks (with a speech, appropriately) the farfetched and absurd character of declamations.[17] But for all the criticism that it encountered, the declamatory system underwent no real changes throughout antiquity.

What was the secret of declamation's success? It must have lain precisely in its hybrid character: like all convincing speeches it was required to accommodate a well-proportioned mix of Aristotle's three technical means of persuasion (*logos*, *ēthos* and *pathos*) – but at the same time to display all the characteristics of exciting stories. Obviously, bizarre cases require valid and persuasive arguments just like mundane ones, but they have the advantage that they afford opportunities for originality* and creativity, as well as technical prowess. Further, the necessity of casting oneself in the role of litigant or defendant, of taking on the persona* of, say, a war hero, tyrant or frustrated son being confronted with a terrible dilemma in outrageous circumstances, made for situational ethics which provided not just an exercise in persuasion, but also social and philosophical training.[18] Living through and describing the persona's extreme experiences was an excellent opportunity for conveying *ēthos* ('character') and *pathos* ('emotion'). Moreover, every declaimer had to put himself in the position not just of his own persona, but also in that of his fictitious opponent, so that he would always have to master all possible facts and arguments – and all ethical and emotional aspects – of any given case. And of course, just like authors of literature, declaimers were then required to put all their findings into a well-ordered and coherent whole, and adorn it with styles fitting the various parts and aspects.

Conclusion

The bottom line of this chapter is that ancient rhetoric throughout antiquity provided a conceptual toolkit indispensable for literary production and that for us today it consequently provides the central tools to appreciate the intellectual dynamics underlying ancient literature at different levels of its conceptualization (*inventio*, *dispositio*, *elocutio*). We have aimed to show that ancient rhetoric, originally the art of speaking persuasively, throughout antiquity developed into a broad conceptual tradition of thinking about reading* and writing that fundamentally impacted both literary production and literary criticism. We have explained that ancient rhetoric and poetics basically adopted the same conceptual language in order to describe and prescribe discourse, and that this language pervaded ancient literature at large. Special attention was drawn to the crucial role that education played both in incorporating and in stimulating the intertwinement of rhetoric and literature. Both *progymnasmata* and declamations engaged with literary traditions at various levels and in turn contributed themselves to creating literature.[19]

Notes

1 Taken from Tony Kline, "Horace," accessed December 16, 2016, www.poetryintranslation.com/PITBR/Latin/Horacehome.htm.
2 Horace, *Epistles* 2.3.
3 Quintilian, *Institutio Oratoria* 8.60.
4 David A. Russell and Michael Winterbottom, *Ancient Literary Criticism: The Principal Texts in New Translations* (Oxford: Oxford University Press, 1972) and Jeffrey Walker, *Rhetoric and Poetics in Antiquity* (Oxford: Oxford University Press, 2000) still belong to the best overviews.
5 George A. Kennedy, *Classical Rhetoric and Its Christian and Secular Tradition From Ancient to Modern Times* (Chapel Hill: The University of North Carolina Press, 1999), 130. See also Françoise Desbordes, *La rhétorique antique* (Paris: Hachette, 1996), 113–30, who conceptualizes the development of rhetorical theory as a change of emphasis ("déplacement d'accent") towards literary criticism.
6 The most important ancient sources are: *Rhetorica ad Alexandrum*; Aristotle's *Rhetoric*; *Rhetorica ad Herennium*; Cicero's *De Inventione, De Oratore,* and *Orator*; and Quintilian's *Institutio Oratoria*. Good modern overviews are, among others, Josef Martin, *Antike Rhetorik: Technik und Methode* (München: Beck, 1974) and Heinrich Lausberg, David E. Orton and R. Dean Anderson, *Handbook of Literary Rhetoric: A Foundation for Literary Study* (Leiden: Brill, 1998).
7 Aristotle, *Poetics* 1456a.33-b.14, translated by Stephen Halliwell in Stephen Halliwell, W. Hamilton Fyfe and Doreen C. Innes, *Aristotle: Poetics, Longinus: On the Sublime, and Demetrius: On Style*, Corrected edition. Loeb Classical Library (Cambridge, MA: Harvard University Press, 1999).
8 Pseudo-Longinus, *On the Sublime* 1.4, translated by W. Hamilton Fyfe and David A. Russell in Halliwell, Fyfe and Innes, *Longinus: On the Sublime.*
9 Nicolaus, *Prog* 449, Leonhard Spengel, ed. *Rhetores Graeci*, 3 vols (Leipzig: Teubner, 1854). Translations of the *progymnasmata* treatises are taken from George A. Kennedy, *Progymnasmata: Greek Textbooks of Prose Composition and Rhetoric* (Atlanta: Society of Biblical Literature, 2003).
10 Theon, *Prog* 65–6; Spengel, *Rhetores Graeci*, 2 vol.
11 Libanius, Speech in Character 2, translated by Craig A. Gibson, *Libanius's Progymnasmata: Model Exercises in Greek Prose Composition and Rhetoric* (Atlanta: Society of Biblical Literature, 2008).
12 Theon *Prog* 70.24–8; Spengel, *Rhetores Graeci*, 2 vol.
13 Longus 1.16.1–5. The translation is taken from John R. Morgan, Longus, *Daphnis and Chloe* (Oxford: Aris & Phillips, 2004). The point that we make about this passage is developed at greater length in Koen De Temmerman, *Crafting Characters: Heroes and Heroines in the Ancient Greek Novel* (Oxford: Oxford University Press, 2014), 234–36, with further reference to the *progymnasmata* treatises.
14 Theon, *Prog* 60.25–30 Spengel, *Rhetores Graeci*, 2 vol.
15 The most important Latin collections are those by Seneca the Elder: Michael Winterbottom ed., *Seneca the Elder: Declamations.* Loeb Classical Library (Cambridge, MA: Harvard University Press, 1999 [1974]); Ps.-Quintilian both minor and major declamations, edited by David R. Shackleton Bailey and Quintilian. *The Lesser Declamations.* Loeb Classical Library (Cambridge, MA: Harvard University Press, 2006) and Lennart Håkanson, *Declamationes XIX Maiores Quintiliano Falso Ascriptae* (Stuttgart: Teubner, 1982), respectively; Lewis Sussman, *The Major Declamations Ascribed to Quintilian* (Frankfurt am Main: Peter Lang translates the major declamations, 1987); and Calpurnius Flaccus: Lewis Sussman, ed., trans., comm., *The Declamations of Calpurnius Flaccus* (Leiden: Brill, 1994). The most important Greek collections are those of Libanius (David A. Russell and Libanius, *Imaginary Speeches: A Selection of Declamations* (London: Duckworth, 1996)) and Choricius of Gaza (Robert J. Penella, *Rhetorical Exercises From Late Antiquity: A Translation of Choricius of Gaza's "Preliminary Talks" and "Declamations"* (Cambridge: Cambridge University Press, 2009)). Good introductions to the genre are Stanley F. Bonner, *Roman Declamation in the Late Republic and Early Empire* (Liverpool: University Press of Liverpool, 1969) and David A. Russell, *Greek Declamation* (Cambridge: Cambridge University Press, 1983). Declamation's literary properties are discussed in Danielle van Mal-Maeder, *La fiction des Declamations* (Leiden: Brill, 2007), while the ways it evokes socio-cultural issues are the subject of Erik Gunderson, *Declamation, Paternity and Roman Identity: Authority and the Rhetorical Self* (Cambridge: Cambridge University Press, 2003) and Neil Bernstein, *Ethos, Identity, and Community in Later Roman Declamation* (Oxford: Oxford University Press, 2013).
16 Among others, Seneca the Elder, *Controversia* 1.5 (trans. Winterbottom, *Seneca the Elder*).
17 Petronius, *Satyrica* 1–2. Edition and English translation: Michael Heseltine and William Henry Denham Rouse, *Petronius: Seneca: Apocolocyntosis.* Loeb Classical Library (Cambridge, MA: Harvard University Press, 1969).

18 See e.g. W. Martin Bloomer, "Schooling in Persona: Imagination and Subordination in Roman Antiquity," *Classical Antiquity* 16 (1997): 57–78 and Bé Breij, "Dilemmas of *Pietas* in Roman Declamation," in *Sacred Words: Orality, Literacy and Religion: Orality and Literacy in the Ancient World*, vol. 8, ed. André P.M.H. Lardinois, Josine H. Blok and Marc G.M. van der Poel, 329–51 (Leiden: Brill, 2011).
19 This chapter was written with the support, for Koen De Temmerman, of the European Research Council Starting Grant *Novel Saints* (grant agreement 337344).

Further reading

Cizek, Alexandru N. *Imitatio et tractatio: Die literarisch-rhetorischen Grundlagen der Nachahmung in Antike und Mittelalter.* Tübingen: Max Niemeyer Verlag, 1994.
Lausberg, Heinrich, David E. Orton and R. Dean Anderson. *Handbook of Literary Rhetoric: A Foundation for Literary Study.* Leiden: Brill, 1998.
Martin, Josef. *Antike Rhetorik: Technik und Methode.* München: Beck, 1974.
Russell, Donald A. and Michael Winterbottom. *Ancient Literary Criticism: The Principal Texts in New Translations.* Oxford: Oxford University Press, 1972.
Walker, Jeffrey. *Rhetoric and Poetics in Antiquity.* Oxford: Oxford University Press, 2000.

6 Remembering the past

Nita Krevans and Ruth Scodel

Figure 6.1 Poussin, Nicolas, "Et in Arcadia ego", 1637–1638, oil on canvas, 87 x 120 cm, Musée du Louvre, Paris

Source: Centre Art Historical Documentation, Radboud University.

Literature from antiquity has survived until the present day ultimately because it was written down and later copied. This literature was meant to be read – and remembered – by posterity, as illustrated by the Latin poet Horace, who in 23 BCE published a book of lyric poems in three papyrus rolls, a collection arranged with utmost care. The final poem in the collection serves as a "seal", a metaphorical* stamp of authorship and authority, and addresses the promise of its survival:

Text: Horace, "Ode 3.30" (23 BCE)

I have built a monument more lasting than bronze
and set higher than the pyramids of kings.
It cannot be destroyed by gnawing rain
or wild north wind, by the procession
of unnumbered years or by the flight of time.
I shall not wholly die. A great part of me
will escape Libitina [i.e. death]. My fame will grow,
ever-renewed in time to come, as long as
the priest climbs the Capitol with the silent Virgin.
I shall be spoken of where fierce Aufidus thunders
and where Daunus, poor in water,
rules the country people.[1] From humble beginnings
I was able to be the first to bring Aeolian song
to Italian measures. Take the proud honour
well-deserved, Melpomene, and be pleased
to circle my hair with the laurel of Delphi.[2]

Poetry had long claimed the power to preserve the past, and it was an old theme that a poem could outlast a physical monument. Horace's ode, though, gives this familiar ambition to defeat time new force, precisely because the poet is also boasting about a material object, the scrolls* that constitute the book. Poetry, for Horace, is especially able to guarantee memory* because the book is a material object with distinct boundaries, yet it can easily be copied or read aloud. The poems in the book will do more than merely sustain the memory of the poet: in his glory, he will actually be alive ("I shall not wholly die"). Still, Horace does not name himself. Instead he either trusts that the book will carry his name as paratext,[3] or boldly assumes that his reader knows who he is. He reminds the reader of his biography* by saying that he will be spoken of in southern Italy (where he was born) as being "the first to bring Aeolian song to Italian measures" (that is, the first to adapt the meter* and style* of the sixth-century poets Sappho and Alcaeus, who composed in the Aeolic Greek dialect, into Latin). The poem not only says that the poet will be remembered, but it actively controls memory's content.

Horace's lyric poetry* does not grant memory only to the poet, however. Many poems of this book celebrate important contemporary Romans. The first word of the collection is the name of Horace's patron, Maecenas, a close associate of the emperor Augustus, and the last word of the next poem contains a reference to Augustus himself. The book mixes the political and personal, myth*, remote history, and recent events, so that all are committed to what is known as cultural memory*: the collective, shared notion of the (Roman) past. Here, at his book's close, Horace not only evokes the long history of Egypt (he claims that his book is higher than the pyramids, line 2), but refers to rituals* that defined Roman identity and celebrated continuity with the past: Horace will grow in renown "as long as the priest climbs the Capitol with the silent virgin" (lines 8–9). The *pontifex maximus* (high priest), the Vestal Virgin (a Roman priestess), and the Capitoline hill with its temples at the centre of Rome combine to identify the poet's time with the entire span of Roman history. They literally embody Rome and its traditions. Yet the silent Vestal Virgin stands in contrast to Horace's fame, which is preserved in the book, can be read aloud, and has long outlasted imperial Rome.

This single poem reveals the complexities of memory and its role in Greek and Roman literature. As we will see in this chapter, memory is inextricably associated with poetry from the very first, oral compositions of the Greek bards*. But as writing becomes the dominant mode of composing and preserving literature, words become an even more powerful tool for preserving the past, both in books and in inscriptions on stone. Once books became ubiquitous, libraries* were built to store them and scholars employed to preserve and to comment on older texts, so they remained accessible. With the growing possibilities of preserving memory in writing, reflections on the forms memory can take – and the uses to which it could be put – also increased. Horace's poem moves back and forth between a physical notion of memory (the book, a monument, bronze, pyramids) and a more spiritual notion (his own immortality as he is "spoken of" in the future).

Poets and muses: from oral to written

The earliest extant Greek texts, the Homeric epics*, do not identify their composers or their patrons. They preserve the memory only of a legendary past and are acutely conscious of the difficulty of this task. The epics are set in the late Bronze Age, but they were composed centuries later, about 700 BCE. Since there were no written records in the intervening period, only oral* tradition* preserved the memory of this past, and the "literary" form of oral tradition was sung heroic* poetry. Long before Greek culture had written texts, it had a tradition of songs about heroic deeds and specialists who performed them. In an oral culture, Horace's text-as-monument was not imaginable. Indeed, until the Greeks adapted the Phoenician script around 800 BCE, even monuments had to depend on the human voice to maintain the stories they commemorated*. Within the world depicted in Homeric poetry, monuments are merely prompts to memory – memory can be transmitted only by the living voice. In the *Iliad*, Nestor describes a mound on the Trojan plain as either the tomb of someone who died long ago or as a turn marker for chariot racing. Nestor knows the monument should prompt memory, but cannot be certain what that memory is.[4] It was the function of the poet to preserve the memory of famous individuals.

Homeric heroes seek fame, *kleos** (literally "what is heard"), and are desperate for that fame to last long after them. The plural, *klea andrôn* ("famous deeds of men") is epic's term for its own content. Oral poetry, however, is by nature unstable, since performers* constantly adapt* and recreate stories. To supplement *kleos*, Greek literature had a unique source of memory: the Muse or Muses. The Muses* are the daughters of Memory, a goddess, and the supreme god Zeus. They guarantee that poetic* performances provide true memory. The epic poet selects a topic and asks the Muse to tell it "to us also",[5] so that they repeatedly renew the chain of transmission*.

By the sixth century BCE, poets claimed that they could memorialize individuals and would themselves be remembered. Sappho of Lesbos says of another woman that she will be forgotten after her death because she does not share in the "Pierian roses" (Pieria was a haunt of the Muses).[6] Sappho's poems, which circulated individually as songs, preserved the social relationships of her family, the political events of her city, and her name along with those of the young women around her. Ibycus, a Greek poet of the second half of the sixth century BCE, makes the same promise of poetic immortality. In one fragment, he sings about the legendary heroes of Troy – but ends by promising the addressee, Polycrates, that he, like those heroes, will have unfading glory "as song and my fame can give it."[7]

The term "seal" for self-labelling passages comes from the sixth-century poet Theognis, who imagines stamping his poetry with an identifying mark:

> For me, a skilled and wise poet, let a seal, Cyrnus, be placed on these verses. Their theft will never pass unnoticed, nor will anyone take something worse in exchange when that which is good is at hand, but everyone will say, "These are the verses of Theognis of Megara, and he is famous among all men."[8]

Like Ibycus, Theognis claims to be a famous poet, whose fame guarantees the quality and durability of the poems. However, if Theognis hoped to ensure that his seal would preserve and differentiate his poems, he failed. Theognis composed short poems for performance at drinking parties. Inevitably they were adapted and appropriated in circulation. So the surviving collection of "Theognis" includes poems that are clearly not his, while some poems appear elsewhere, in different versions, attributed to other poets. Theognis may have made a written copy that he hoped would preserve its seal, but until books and their materiality came to be a significant (and more stable) form of transmission, the seal could protect only the unit in which it was contained, a mere eight lines of Theognis's poetry.

The rise of the book

Books and emerging institutions* for performance, however, changed the relationship between poetry and memory. The poems of Theognis were performed on social occasions, where nobody controlled them. At the Athenian festival* for its patron goddess Athena, referred to as the Great Panathenaea, every fourth year there was a competition* for the professional performers of Homer called "rhapsodes"* from sometime in the second half of the sixth century BCE onwards. We do not know whether the rules went back to the origin of the competition, but later rhapsodes were required to begin their segments precisely where the previous competitor ended (rather than to jump to especially dramatic parts that would sway judges). This implies a written text for reference, but it also means that the text itself is canonized*, repeated almost identically in reperformance over time under the control of public officials. The Homeric poems are now an official "past" and are themselves an object of public, ritualized memory. Even though the book is not the medium of transmission, it authorizes the performance.

In other cases, however, books were becoming a medium of transmission. The philosopher*/mythographer Pherecydes of Syros in the sixth century BCE wrote the first prose book known to later authors. Before writing, all "literature" was poetry – ordinary speech was not special or memorable enough to be preserved in oral tradition. But writing led to literary prose. While much later Greek and Latin prose writing is truly technical, much also claims literary status: the philosophical dialogues* of Plato and Cicero; the historical* works of Herodotus and Thucydides, Livy and Tacitus. Even orations given in assemblies and law courts were afterwards edited and published (see Chapter 4). Prose writers, too, claim literary authority. The historian and geographer Hecataeus of Miletus, who lived around 500 BCE, began his *Genealogies* with the words: "Hekataios of Miletos speaks as follows: I write these things, as they seem to me to be true."[9] "Sealing" the book in its opening words, he evokes his voice in a distancing* third person*, just as Theognis invents future performers to say his name, while in the first person* he says that he writes. In the fifth century BCE, both Herodotus and Thucydides similarly begin their prose histories by announcing their names as a "seal" of authenticity.

Reading both poetry and prose became a source of pleasure as well as instruction. A lost tragedy* of Euripides, *Erechtheus*, has a chorus* sing about the pleasure of opening a tablet to read, and in the Aristophanes comedy* *Frogs* of 405 BCE, Dionysus says that he was on a ship reading Euripides's *Andromeda*, produced in 412 BCE. The play* has become a book, potentially readable anytime, anywhere. The reader does not need to memorize it in order to preserve the text.

By the late fifth century, Athens had a book trade*. Books, consisting of papyrus scrolls (see ahead), were material objects. They added new possibilities to literature; they could be produced with paratext* (e.g. labels giving author and title), and individuals could write notes on them. They also rendered it possible to maintain a written version of performances. Homeric epics already had this status, but in the fourth century BCE, the Athenians added a reperformance of an old tragedy to the programme of their most important dramatic festival, the Great Dionysia (see Chapter 4); the plays of the three great tragedians Aeschylus, Euripides, and Sophocles had become a significant part of civic heritage. These reperformances required a (relatively) stable, written version of the text. In the late fourth century BCE, the Athenians created an official archive of the works of the three canonical tragedians. These official copies monumentalized the text, and statues of the tragedians were also erected in the theatre*. And the Athenians, fanatical inscribers of their public records, commemorated the dramatic performances at the Great Dionysia by inscribing, for each year, which poets had produced which plays, how they placed in the competition, and who paid for the chorus. Only fragments of these inscriptions survive, but Aristotle's students collected the information, which was subsequently used by ancient scholars of literary history.

As scripts for performances of epics or tragedies became books and an important form of cultural memory in themselves, they needed to be kept accessible to readers unfamiliar with their original context and vocabulary. Already in the fifth century BCE, schoolboys had to learn "glosses"*, explanations of strange, old words that appeared in the epics of Homer. A secondary literary industry developed, producing commentaries*, dictionaries, anthologies*, and summaries that made the old canonical texts available and meaningful for a variety of purposes. An orator who needed a lofty quotation could go directly to a collection arranged by topic. Medieval manuscripts* of plays sometimes offer one or more "hypotheses"* in front of the play itself. Some of these are learned, presenting information about the original production that goes back to the Aristotelian inscription-based records, while others are plot* summaries that derive from a now lost book known to modern scholars as the "Tales from Euripides".[10]

Inscription: words on stone

The inscriptional habit is also part of the story of literature and memory. As soon as the Greeks acquired the alphabet, they began writing on durable objects, sometimes in verse. Dedications in sanctuaries and epitaphs* on tombs aimed at preserving the memory of the donors and the dead: one of the regular Greek words for "tomb" is *mnêma*, "memorial". Tombs often had relief or free-standing sculpture: an inscription helped ensure that the purpose of the monument would not be forgotten. Both statues and inscriptions were effective memorials, as the Athenian commemoration of the tragedians and their plays shows, and tombs often combined them.

Verse inscriptions could be particularly effective. Tombs were often placed along roads, and the funerary epitaph is frequently addressed to the passer-by, who needed to be persuaded to stop and read. Since the sound of poetry is pleasing to the ear, such inscriptions invited reading aloud. However, they do not usually ask overtly for the reader to remember, but rather to respond in the present. A sixth-century epitaph from outside Athens, for example, says:

> Let everyone, whether townsman or stranger from abroad,
>   before he pass, mourn Tettichus, valorous man
> who died in battle and yielded up his tender youth:
>   lamenting this, proceed to worthy tasks.[11]

Epic fame made important characters like Achilles an enduring presence in the lives of the epic audience*, and the poet Theognis hoped that his songs and his name would survive; this epitaph seeks to preserve the name of Tettichus every time the stone is being read. Other epitaphs give advice (from Smyrna, second/first century BCE: "seeing this image, reckon your end, and use your lifetime not as if you were able to live for ages, and not as if you were fated to a short life"). Advice, of course, has no purpose if it is immediately forgotten.

A monument's very materiality can demand attention, but it also links the poem's fate to that of the material. A famous epitaph attributed to Cleobulus, one of the legendary wise men called "Seven Sages" as well as a poet who lived in the sixth century BCE, claimed to be spoken to by the bronze statue of a girl on the tomb of King Midas. She promised to declare to passers-by that Midas was buried there as long as the sun and moon shone, the rivers ran, and waves rose in the sea. The Greek poet Simonides criticized Cleobulus for claiming eternity for such a mortal object as a statue.[12] Yet the criticism itself implies that the epitaph has become familiar. Assuming that it was an actual inscription, it has escaped its monument and entered a different kind of memory, where Midas's monument itself has become an object of commemoration.

Publicly erected tombs for groups of war dead may claim everlasting fame for their valour, but do not provide their names; the soldiers are collectively held in honoured memory. If their names were given, it was in a separate inscription. These verse epitaphs show yet another irony* in poetic memory: a man from outside the elite who died in battle might be remembered in a poem, but only as part of the group. In our era, many nations have a "Tomb of the Unknown Soldier", a monument that symbolically commemorates those who are in a more literal way deprived of commemoration.

The inscribed poem, then, creates new possibilities of poetic memory, opening poetic memory to a much wider social group. A funeral monument was expensive, but epitaphs – short, metrically simple poems – could be composed by amateurs, and some surviving inscribed poems evidently were. When poets began writing short poems that imitated epitaphs, these poems may have pretended to be epitaphs for famous people of the past, but they also often commemorated people (it is often impossible to know whether real or fictitious*) who would never have been given poetic memory in other genres. Leonidas of Tarentum (early third century BCE), for example, has a ten-line epitaph for a fisherman who died in his reed hut, ending: "This tomb was not set up by his children or wife, but by the guild of his fellow fishermen."[13] Such organizations have ensured that epitaphs survive for people of all classes from the Roman world. An epitaph by the Greek poet Callimachus honours a Phrygian slave-nurse Aeschra; Miccus put up a statue for her "that future generations may see how he rewarded the old woman for her milk."[14] Callimachus's contemporary Posidippus also has a nurse-epitaph:

> I, an old workwoman, grew old in charge of new-born babies,
>   I, Batis, hired by Phocean Athenodice,
> teaching how to take care of wool and the many-colored threads
>   for headbands and the plaiting of perforated hair-nets.
> And now, as the girls go the threshold of their bridal chambers,
>   they have buried me, the old rod-bearer.[15]

Writing could therefore preserve memory in a wide range of less or more permanent physical forms. Most temporary are notes, receipts, and election ballots scratched on potsherds or on the back of discarded documents. One step up would be the wood-framed wax tablets* used by school children for exercises and by literate Greek and Roman adults for quick messages, drafts of serious work, or memos; the wax could be smoothed over and reused many times. Next would be writing in ink on papyrus* sheets (a form of paper); thousands of papyrus scraps from Greco-Roman Egypt have survived in the desert sand, offering glimpses of private letters, contracts, census returns, petitions, and magic spells. More enduring still are the books; the earliest were book rolls* (scrolls made of continuously glued papyrus sheets), but gradually, from the first to the fourth centuries CE, the codex* (bound pages, like our modern book) largely replaced the book roll, and parchment offered an alternative to papyrus. The codex format and the option of parchment meant that books became sturdier and could survive handling and reading far longer. Also, long papyrus rolls were unwieldy; with a codex, the reader can easily skip forward or backward. Many scrolls could be copied into a single codex. The codex is still in use today, although electronic texts*, ironically, are returning us to the era of the scroll. Finally, inscription on stone (or occasionally on metal) promised a memory that could be preserved for centuries.

Libraries and scholar-poets

From the archive created by the Athenians for tragedies, it is a short but not a trivial step to libraries. After the conquests of Alexander, as Greeks and Macedonians flooded east to the courts of the Hellenistic kings and settled in territories formerly held by Persia, anxieties about memory took on a new and compelling form. On the one hand, writing had now fully emerged as a technology capable of recording and transmitting thought and language – even language primarily intended to be performed (drama*) or sung/recited (poetry). On the other hand, writing fixes the past, reifies it, and walls it off.

Ptolemy the First, called Soter, a general of Alexander who seized Egypt after Alexander's death in 323 BCE, founded a dynasty that ruled until Cleopatra's death in 31 BCE. He and his heirs were energetic patrons of art and literature, and they created and supported the great library at Alexandria. The library staked a claim for Alexandria as the new centre of Greek culture and an indispensable repository of the Greek past. Books had become a source of prestige. This was not the first or the only such library in the ancient world. Wealthy individuals could have impressive private libraries as well: the Villa of the Papyri in the Roman town of Herculaneum, destroyed by the eruption of Vesuvius in 79 CE, held an extensive collection of Greek books, probably from the library of Lucius Calpurnius Piso, the father-in-law of Julius Caesar.

There is a story that Ptolemy III, who ruled over Egypt from 246–222 BCE, paid the Athenians a huge sum as a security deposit for the right to copy the official texts of the tragedians, but kept the originals and returned the copies, forfeiting the money. There are similar stories about how the library came to own Aristotle's books. These anecdotes are meaningful even if they are not true – they show how particular copies of books could be imagined as carriers of cultural memory of value in themselves, but also suggest that giving so much value to the literary artefacts of the past could make it hard to imagine what contemporary authors might contribute.

Aiming to copy and store all of Greek literature, the library embodied both the promise and the threat of such preservation. The library was part of a larger complex for the promotion of literature and science*, the Mouseion, which collected not only books, but writers and scholars as well. For the scholars associated with the library, the accumulated literature of the past was a resource for literature of the present, but also a burden: there was more memory than anyone could readily manage. Since many of the Hellenistic scholars were also poets, they found themselves torn between their responsibilities as curators and their calling as poets. Poets in Alexandria, confronted with the collected masterpieces of their forebears, found composing new work daunting and almost presumptuous.

When, halfway between Theognis (sixth century BCE) and Horace (first century BCE) we find another seal poem, the Seal of Posidippus (third century BCE), it therefore plays with many kinds of memory: written, oral, and spiritual. Originally from Pella, in Macedon, Posidippus was, at least for a time, one of the court poets in Alexandria under the Ptolemies. The poem opens with an address to the Muses: "If, O Muses of my city, you have heard with ears attuned/Phoebus playing on his golden lyre."[16] So far, so traditional. The poet invokes the Muses, daughters of Memory. But, we discover, instead of speaking/ singing to the poet (as they do in Homer), they themselves are listening – to Apollo. And when they transmit Apollo's song, they will use writing: "take up with Posidippus now the theme of grim old age,/writing in your golden tablets, line by line." The poet then prays to Apollo not for a song, but for "an oracle." Such oracles commanding honours to poets were already found in Greek tradition. An inscription in the shrine to the Greek poet Archilochus on his native island of Paros told how the Delphic oracle ordered the Parians to honour him. Posidippus imagines his oracle to be the living voice of the god Apollo, who asks the Macedonians to grant honour to the poet in the future:

> proclaim and cry aloud from your sanctuary, O Lord,
>   a like immortal directive [voice] in my behalf,
> that the Macedonians – those on [the islands] and those
>   along the coast of Asia, end to end – may honour me.
> I hail from Pella. There, in the busy market place,
>   let there be a statue of me, a book in both [hands], reading.[17]

Memory here becomes even more physical and visual: the "immortal voice" is now the voice of Apollo as prophet*, not musician, and he will ensure the preservation of Posidippus as an object (a statue) holding another object (a book). While poets are often depicted holding writing implements or scrolls, the statue of Posidippus reading invites onlookers to remember the poems they have read. The seal poem concludes with a prayer by Posidippus for inclusion in the happy afterlife of an initiate after death ("may I make my way along the mystical path to Rhadamanthus" [a judge in the underworld]) and in its final couplets turns to the most fundamental type of memory humans desire as they approach death: praise from those around them ("missed by the people, missed by them all") and children to succeed them ("my children, heirs to my home and wealth").

What begins as a conventional invocation* to the Muses, then, moves through many different types of speech, writing, and commemoration in its quest for immortality. The Muses record Apollo's song on tablets; Apollo himself offers everlasting fame through a prophecy manifested in statue form; Posidippus envisions how mystical initiation will give his soul eternal happiness after death while in the world above his fellow-citizens mourn and his children inherit. Thus while the poem has all the expected ingredients of a "seal" (the poet's name, his birthplace, and claims of immortality), the seal undercuts its own authority by vacillating between oral and written memory and between physical and spiritual immortality.

This poem was probably placed at the beginning or end of a book of Posidippus's poems; we have similar poems framing other poetry collections. But even in its artificially isolated state, the Seal of Posidippus aggressively promotes the new world of the library and the book roll. In this world, memory can take a new, written form, which can preserve entire collections of a poet's work and stamp them, as Horace does, with a celebration of his own written achievements as a poet.

Poetry and the science of the memory

Poetry is also linked to practical techniques of memorization. The legendary inventor of mnemonic techniques was the poet Simonides of Ceos, who lived around 500 BCE. The Roman author Cicero gives the clearest version of the tale*.[18] Simonides composed a poem of praise for Scopas, ruler of Thessaly. When it was performed at a banquet, however, Scopas, annoyed because the poem also praised the divine twins Castor and Pollux, paid only half the fee, instructing Simonides to collect the rest from the two gods. Shortly afterwards, Simonides was told that two young men were asking for him at the door, and just as he went out to meet them, the roof collapsed, killing everyone else and crushing them beyond recognition. By recalling where each guest had been sitting at the banquet, Simonides was able to identify the dead. Thus, Simonides discovered the science of memory* by recognizing that "order" (spatial order, or arrangement) is the key to clear and accurate memory. Specifically, Cicero attributes to Simonides a mnemonic technique still taught today, the method of *loci** (places), which recommends mentally linking items to be remembered – for example, a list of names – with images of objects and then placing those objects in different rooms of an imaginary house.

At the beginning of this story, in a typical exchange of patronage* for poetic immortality, Scopas has hired Simonides to create lasting favourable memory through his lyric* compositions. Unfortunately, Scopas is *sordidus* (the word means both "filthy" and "cheapskate") and fails to acknowledge that the gods must always be praised. The two youths at the door are, of course, the divine twins Castor and Pollux, who preserve the poet and punish the arrogant patron (along with his guests). Scopas gains infamy instead of fame (the wrong kind of memory), while Simonides receives divine protection and becomes the "inventor" of the science of memory. Simonides's importance as a legendary figure associated with memory is further signalled by the first use he makes of mnemonic techniques, the correct assignment of corpses to mourners. The "memory" that surviving kin owe to the dead, proper funeral ritual and mourning, is only possible because of

Simonides's mnemonic feat. His piety to the divine twins in the poem enables the commemorative piety of the banqueters' heirs.

The technique of *loci* is designed for remembering lists or the order of arguments in a speech*, not for memorizing and performing verse. For the Roman elite, the ability to give extended speeches without notes was essential (see Chapter 4). It is interesting, then, that the technique is closely associated with poetry, which from the beginning of Greek literature boasts of its ability to remember long lists, like the Homeric Catalogue of Ships: a 250-line roster of the Greek commanders at Troy, preserved in Book 2 of the *Iliad*. The invention of four letters of the Greek alphabet that improved its readability was also attributed to Simonides. Cicero directly compares the *loci* to a writing tablet, "we shall employ the *loci* and images as a wax writing tablet and the letters written upon it."[19] The technology of writing and techniques of memory (mnemonics*), in other words, are closely parallel to one another, and both trace their origins to a poet.

In other anecdotes, however, Simonides originates a less noble tradition: he was said to be the first poet who directly traded praise for cash. In one story, he did not like the fee he was offered for praising the winner of the mule-race, and addressed the winning team as the children of donkeys. With more money, the mules were transformed into the "daughters of storm-footed horses." This anecdote reflects a wider anxiety about the exchange of money for poetic immortality. The Greek poet Pindar in one of his poems composed ca. 470 BCE, imagines a happy past when poets simply praised beauty, but now "money is the man."[20] Ancient scholars interpreted this passage as covert criticism of Simonides. In another anecdote, when asked to compose a praise poem in return for "thanks" (*charis*), Simonides said that he had a thanks-box and a money-box, but only the second was of any use. The Hellenistic poet Theocritus imagines his own poems as Graces, called *Charites* in Greek, who come home barefoot and complaining from an unsuccessful begging excursion. Being written scrolls*, they sit unhappily in their box. The poet acknowledges that few potential patrons want to invest, and some think "Homer is enough for all."[21] Once poetic memory is a simple commodity, those who can afford it may no longer want it, particularly because the materiality of literary texts makes it obvious that there is an abundance of poetry already. Just as poets were anxious about competing for attention in an already crowded market, so might patrons worry that even a superior poem of praise might not ensure eternal fame among text-saturated readers.

Cynicism about memory as a commodity is not inevitable, however. Towards the end of the Roman literary tradition we find one of the most extensive and influential discussions of memory. The Christian bishop Augustine (see Chapter 1) devotes an entire book of his *Confessions* to a loving examination of *memoria**. Like Cicero, he envisions memory as a space ("halls", "palaces") where items are deposited into "receptacles".[22] But Augustine's view of memory goes far beyond the practical mnemonic organizational techniques of the method of *loci* described previously. Memory operates across all forms of perception; anticipating the twentieth-century French author Marcel Proust (see Chapter 26) by 1,600 years, Augustine asserts that memory stores not only words and images but all sensory impressions – sound, smell, taste, touch. Nor is memory envisioned only as a limited, constructed mental space (a house with rooms): Augustine also describes it as "fields", or as a vast and abstract "force", a "capacious and infinite recess", which, paradoxically, can never be fully known by the mind which houses it. The infinite nature of memory allows Augustine to see it as a means to achieve understanding of oneself, as a platform for examining past, present, and future, and – most crucially – as the dwelling place of God in the human mind. When Augustine ascends towards his creator, he arrives at memory:

"climbing by stages towards him who made me, I come to the fields and wide palaces of memory." Memory is, like God, an infinite space that connects mortal man with the immortal divinity. It is no coincidence that the final word of the *Confessions* describes a door opening to communion with God: *aperietur* ('it is opened').

Conclusion

From its origins, literature, which can be characterised as language specially designed to be aesthetically* pleasing and relevant outside an immediate context, has served cultural memory. The earliest Greek poets, however, were limited by the nature of oral composition. Epic songs changed with each performance, and although some content was stable, it could not be entirely fixed. The epic narrative style did not encourage the poets to insert themselves, making authorial identity less secure. And the repertory of an oral culture can be large, but must be finite. Typically, in oral cultures, the memory of the past falls into three categories. A remote time of ancestors is stable in memory. Recent events, those personally remembered by the elders, are recounted. In between, time is telescoped and only a few significant events are retold. As new events enter memory and elders die, there is relentless winnowing of what will earn a place in the available space of memory.[23]

The technology of writing expanded that space. The book in the library will still be there, even if nobody reads it this year or next. Writing also means that not only does the text itself remain, but that the author's name is likely to be attached to it. Authors write to preserve their own memory as well as memory of the past or of their patrons, and literature itself acquires a history. A famous inscription of 264/3 BCE, the Marmor Parium, sets major historical events and the lives of famous authors side by side; the death of Sophocles (406/5 BCE) and the rebellion of Cyrus the Younger of Persia against his brother Artaxerxes are listed together. Moderns take such timelines for granted, but it was not inevitable that the history of literature should become part of public memory.

Purely functional writing could simply preserve facts about the past, but for the Greeks and Romans literature was essential for a memory that was meaningful, moving, a spur to action in the present. Poetry in particular never lost its role as guardian of memory (even though history, the genre we now consider the primary recorder of the past, was written largely in prose) and in ancient education* students learned a great deal of it by heart. Literature was also closely connected to the personal, practical memories of readers. While moderns have notes or teleprompters for public speaking, the ancients relied on memory, and it was not an accident that they ascribed their mnemonic technique to a poet. Finally, poetry was the preferred mechanism for communal memory. It could give special meaning to places, which in turn would then evoke the poetry that celebrated them, whether the place was small and personal (a burial site) or a city-state like Athens or Rome. Poetry and memory were in constant, reciprocal interaction. The Muses, after all, are the daughters of Memory.

Notes

1 These are places in southern Italy, where Horace came from.
2 Horace, *Odes* 3.30, translated by David West in David West, *Horace: The Complete Odes and Epodes* (Oxford World's Classics: Oxford University Press, 1997).
3 Paratext refers to material such as titles, subscriptions, etc. supplied by editors or scribes and not part of the original literary composition.
4 Homer, *Iliad* 23.326–34.

5 Homer, *Odyssey* 1.10. Authors' translation.

6 Sappho, *Fragment* 55. For more on Sappho, see Chapter 3.

7 Ibycus, *Fragment* 282, line 48, translated by David A. Campbell, ed., *Greek Lyric* (Cambridge, MA: Harvard University Press, 1982–1993).

8 Theognis lines 19–23, translated by Douglas E. Gerber, ed., *Greek Elegiac Poetry From the Seventh to the Fifth Centuries BC* (Cambridge, MA: Harvard University Press, 1999).

9 Hecataeus, Fragment 1, translated in Ian Worthington, ed., *Brill's New Jacoby: Fragments of the Greek Historians* (Leiden: Brill, 2006–2017).

10 Although the "Tales" themselves do not survive, we infer their existence from these hypotheses and from papyrus fragments preserving similar plot summaries.

11 Paul Friedländer, *Epigrammata: Greek Inscriptions in Verse From the Beginnings to the Persian Wars* (Chicago: Ares, 1948 [1987]), nr. 135.

12 Both the poem of Cleobulus and Simonides's response are quoted by Diogenes Laertius 1.89, translated by Robert D. Hicks, ed., *Diogenes Laertius: Lives of Eminent Philosophers* (Cambridge, MA: Harvard University Press, 1972).

13 *Anthologia Palatina* 7.295, translated by William R. Paton, ed., *The Greek Anthology*, 5 vols. (Cambridge, MA: Harvard University Press, 1916–1918).

14 *Anthologia Palatina* 7.458, translated by Paton, *The Greek Anthology*.

15 Posidippus, Epigram 46 Austin-Bastianini, translation by Colin Austin in Colin Austin and Guido Bastianini, eds., *Posidippi Pellaei Quae Supersunt Ominia* (Milan: LED, 2002).

16 Posidippus, *Epigram* 118.1–2 Austin-Bastianini, translated by C. Austin in Austin and Bastianini, *Posidippi Pellaei*.

17 Posidippus, *Epigram* 118.12–18.

18 Cicero, *De Oratore* 2.86, translated by James M. May and Jakob Wisse, *Cicero: On the Ideal Orator* (Oxford: Oxford University Press, 2001).

19 Cicero, *De Oratore* 2.354.

20 Pindar, *Isthmian* 2.11, translated by Race (1997).

21 Theocritus, *Idyll* 16.20, translated by Andrew S.F. Gow, *The Greek Bucolic Poets* (Cambridge: Cambridge University Press, 1953).

22 Augustine, *Confessions* 10.8, translated by Maria Boulding, *Saint Augustine, The Confessions* (New York: New York City, 2012).

23 Jan Vansina, *Oral Tradition as History* (Madison, WI: University of Wisconsin Press, 1985).

Further reading

Kenyon, Frederic G. *Books and Readers in Ancient Greece and Rome*. Oxford: Clarendon Press, 1951.

Klooster, Jacqueline. "Persona, Alias and Alter-Ego in *Sphragis*-Poetry." In *Poetry as Window and Mirror: Positioning the Poet in Hellenistic Poetry*, 175–208. Leiden: Brill, 2011.

König, Jason, Katerina Oikonomopoulou and Greg Woolf, eds. *Ancient Libraries*. Cambridge: Cambridge University Press, 2013.

Small, Jocelyn Penny. *Wax Tablets of the Mind: Cognitive Studies of Memory and Literacy in Classical Antiquity*. London: Routledge, 1997.

Woodman, Tony. "*Exegi monumentum*: Horace, Odes 3.30." In *Quality and Pleasure in Latin Poetry*, edited by Tony Woodman and David West, 115–28. Cambridge: Cambridge University Press, 1974.

Part II
Middle Ages

7 Introduction

Frank Brandsma

Figure 7.1 A round map of the world, set in a square ornamental frame, Jerusalem being in the centre, England, thirteenth–fifteenth century, The British Library, London, dd. 28681, f.9

Source: Centre Art Historical Documentation, Radboud University.

History has turned the years between 500 and 1500, our so-called "Middle Ages", into an in-between time, ten centuries between antiquity and the renewed interest in Classical literature, ideas, and ideals in the Renaissance*. This suggests that nothing significant happened during this long period, yet the opposite is true. It is a time of many great changes and innovations*. The theme of literary love as we know it today was developed in the Middle Ages, as was the university, to give just two examples. This introduction will go into some of these innovations, especially those relevant to literature in the vernacular, and their historical and cultural context. In this period, literature was also written in Latin, the language of the Church and of the universities. But the group among whose members these Latin texts circulated was limited, and the language was an insurmountable barrier for most people, including the upper classes.

Periodization

The period is usually divided into three main parts: the Early, High, and Late Middle Ages. The Early Middle Ages (sixth to tenth centuries) are deeply rooted in the Latin culture of late antiquity (third to fifth centuries). Three of the four church fathers (Ambrosius, Augustine, and Jerome) lived and worked in the fourth century, when Christianity became the official Roman religion*. They built up its main tenets and texts, as did the fourth church father, Gregory, who lived in the sixth century. The preservation and development of Latin Christian culture is characterised by looking to the past as a golden age and seeing the present, and especially the future, as lesser times. In science*, the authority of the wisdom of the ancients was undisputed and leading. For medieval scholars, knowledge was to be found in books like the *Etymologiae* by Isidore of Seville (ca. 560–636), not in experiments or empirical research. There were no open questions, since the ultimate answer to everything was: God. The Bible explained how the world was made and why, and the natural world testified to God's omnipotence and benevolence.

In the High Middle Ages (eleventh to thirteenth centuries), the religious focus shifted from the Father to the Son, and to love as the key element in the relationship between man and God. From obedient subject, man emancipates to a creative being with a divine spark ("created in His image," as it says in Genesis) and begins to manifest his creativity, for instance in the introduction of fiction* in storytelling in the medieval vernaculars. The cultural elite in the emerging courts thinks highly of itself and uses literature to project a positive self-image. Noble patrons invite and reward court clerics to write romances that demonstrate the new ideals of courtliness and courtly love.

In the Late Middle Ages (fourteenth and fifteenth centuries), the cities become more important as centres of cultural activity. This is where the audience* and money is, so new forms of literature cater to the interest of the city-dwellers. Drama, which had completely disappeared in the Early Middle Ages, now re-emerges and soon becomes a crowd magnet. By this time, literature in the vernacular is everywhere, yet as long as every single book is written by hand (this is the age of the manuscript), it lacks a medium to reach many readers. The printing press*, developed as a commercially valid enterprise by Johannes Gutenberg in Mainz around 1455, is the answer to this problem, as the introduction to the early modern period will explain. There is much continuity from this period to the next one, even when Renaissance authors like to suggest a clean break with the medieval past.

Europe: historical and cultural context

As in antiquity, in the Middle Ages the concept of Europe as a whole was still in the making, even when in some periods large parts of the area were in the hands of one ruler, like Charlemagne or the emperor of Byzantium. The gradual withdrawal of the Roman armies and the fall of the Western Roman Empire in 476 resulted in a fragmented world of small kingdoms and tribes. In the fifth and sixth centuries, most tribes were on the move, as the people in Eastern and Central Europe fled westward to escape the invasion of the Huns, led by Attila. This mass migration (the Wandering of Nations) brought German tribes of Saxons, Angles, and Jutes from Northern Germany and Denmark to the shores of Britain, where they at first settled in areas like Sussex, Essex, and Kent. The language they spoke would develop into English (the language of the Angles). The earliest sources regarding the literary hero King Arthur refer to this era: the historical Arthur may have been a kind of general uniting the local British kings against the Saxon invaders. The invasion also brought the story of Beowulf to England from the south of Sweden. The orally transmitted song of this heathen hero's* battles against the monster Grendel, Grendel's mother, and a dragon was eventually written down in Old English by a Christian scribe who Christianised the tale*, giving Beowulf God's support and describing Grendel as Cain's kin. Then as now, people on the move took their stories with them, in their mother tongue and preserved in their heads and hearts rather than in writing. It is remarkable that *Beowulf* found its way onto parchment in the vernacular, rather than in the Latin that was commonly used by the parchment and quill specialists, the clergy. This demonstrates the process of assimilation that characterises the early medieval period: the power of Roman rule was waning already as the Romans intermingled with the Germanic tribes that they had fought, but also had enlisted as soldiers. The tribes, on their side, were influenced by Roman ideas, used Latin as a common language especially for writing, and were eventually Christianised. It was a time of constant change and instability, with Christian monasteries as the only stable safe houses for the cultural and religious legacy of the Roman era, and the plundering Vikings in their fast ships as a constant danger. In the Early Middle Ages, the monasteries were the centres of culture. After 1100, the courts and castles of the nobility also took that role, whereas in the thirteenth to fifteenth centuries the growing cities became more and more important.

From the turmoil of the migrations slowly new centres of power emerged, especially in the West, in what now is France; whereas in the East, the Eastern Roman Empire in Byzantium remained in power until the Ottomans conquered it in 1453. Charlemagne (ruled 768–814) brought most of Europe (except Britain) under his rule in the decades around 800. As was usual in this time, Charles was an itinerant ruler, moving from palace to palace, yet he also saw the value of communicating by writing (in the *lingua franca* Latin) with his subjects in his widespread realm, and for that purpose developed the chancery as the court's writing centre. As a secular ruler, he employed clergymen as his advisors and made use of the church's stable network of bishoprics to enforce his power. The cultural revival in his time has been characterised as the "Carolingian Renaissance*", since Charles stimulated learning and the formation of schools. Manuscripts from antiquity were collected, studied, and copied. The Carolingian *scolae* are seen as the starting point for the institutionalisation* of knowledge and learning which in later centuries will lead to the establishment of universities* in cities like Bologna (started in 1088), Paris (founded in 1257 by Robert of Sorbon), and Oxford, where some of the colleges also date back to the thirteenth century. As a powerful ruler, Charlemagne even became a literary hero: throughout the Middle Ages, "chansons de geste" like the *Song of Roland* celebrated Charles's deeds. In the thirteenth to fifteenth centuries, translations* and adaptations of these texts are found in most European vernaculars, from Scandinavia to southern Italy.

In 800, the pope crowned Charles as emperor, demonstrating that medieval rulers saw themselves as the inheritors of the Romans. When the Carolingian empire fell apart, the eastern region (containing modern Germany and its neighbours, as well as Italy down to Rome) became the Holy Roman Empire. The idea of continuing in the Romans' footsteps goes by the name of *translatio imperii**. In the twelfth century, the romance writer Chrétien de Troyes describes it in a prologue:

> Our books have taught us that chivalry and learning first flourished in Greece; then to Rome came chivalry and the sum of knowledge, which now has come to France. May God grant that they be maintained here and may He be pleased enough with this land that the glory now in France may never leave.[1]

With regard to learning, the line from antiquity to the Middle Ages is carried by the Latin language, but chivalry is a new and typically medieval element. For Chrétien, it does not just refer to fighters on horses, but more in general to the secular courtly culture that emerged in the eleventh and twelfth centuries. France has had a leading role in this development, in which literature was an important agent for cultural change. This introduction will therefore focus mainly on the areas where French was the language for literature. After the Norman Conquest in 1066, Britain was part of that area too, since the Anglo-Norman nobility spoke French. As the chapter on the *Canterbury Tales* will explain, the English language slowly became a literary medium in its own right in the fourteenth century.

Although Charlemagne's empire, which covered most of modern Europe, soon lost its cohesion, the continent found more stability in the subsequent ages. By the year 1000, most of Europe had been Christianised. The Catholic Church provided a hierarchical structure to society with the small village parish as the basic unit, by building chapels, churches, and even cathedrals, around which cities arose. It preached peacefulness, rather than aggression, even when the Crusades revealed a violent attitude towards Muslims. The eleventh and twelfth centuries saw slow yet persistent economic growth, due to better agricultural methods and an improvement in the climate. The feudal structure of society, with labourers, farmers, and slaves working for minor nobles, who in turn were vassals of the higher nobility who held their lands from a count or king, led to increased wealth in the highest circles and to the emergence of a new elite* lay culture. Freed from the constant concerns of surviving harsh winters after failing crops or floods, the nobility, and more particularly the high nobility, now had leisure time and began to spend that time together in the castles they were building and improving. Perhaps inspired by cultural contact with the more sophisticated Muslim world in Spain and the Eastern Mediterranean, the European nobility began to develop new rules of conduct, characterised by respect for others, especially for women. This process of civilisation was necessary to avoid conflict during the court meetings, when every noble man and lady was sensitive with regard to rank and social standing.[2] Table manners, respectful behaviour, generosity, and politeness now became more important than the strength of one's arm. Since the court was the place to be, these new rules of conduct are called "courtliness". Our words "courtesy" and "courteous" still refer to this concept.

There was one aspect of human behaviour in particular that the new courtliness spoke to: love*. In a time of arranged, politically motivated marriages, often at an early age, the relationship between husband and wife was not the place to find love, yet the contact between the sexes was of course one of the attractions of life at court. The poetry of the troubadours, discussed in Chapter 8, is an eloquent testimony of the feelings of joy and sorrow this contact entailed. Love became the central issue in the cultural image of an ideal society, where an amorous knight is the loyal and obedient servant of his lady, serving her by means of his prowess and sensitive to her every whim. There is a remarkable parallel to themes in Sappho's work here (see Chapter 3), yet the medieval poets had no knowledge of her work. The – often adulterous – love relationships were topic number one on the social agenda at court. Like the troubadours, the authors of romances* and "lais"* (see Chapter 8) told their audiences (first mostly noble ladies and later also men) tales of exemplary lovers, like Tristan and Lancelot. These new heroes excelled in courtliness and in their absolute dedication to their ladies, even though these women were married to kings. The literary characters were role models, yet their stories were invitations to discuss love matters and the dilemmas of the characters, rather than rigid rule books on how to do things in love. Listening to a book being read aloud thus became a social activity for a small group, like watching a favourite TV show or series together, and it remained like this well into the eighteenth century. Enjoying a medieval romance required a certain audience competence: knowledge of the rules and sentiments of the courtly love game, and a willingness to suspend disbelief and to engage emotionally with the story.

Courtly poems* and stories* were created by the troubadours* in the twelfth and thirteenth centuries. The poems celebrate the emotional turmoil in the lover's heart, and were probably sung to a congenial audience of young people who knew these feelings from experience and could share them. It was a kind of role-playing with a very specific, codified language and behaviour. The poets in southern France were successful and their ideas moved north, to the area around Paris and to the Anglo-Norman regions, including Britain. Here, the courtly poets often were court clerics, rather than noble men or women like many of the troubadours. They chose longer narrative forms for their stories, where the troubadours favoured lyric poetry*. Chrétien de Troyes created rhymed* romances of 6,000–7,000 lines and had many followers. The prose format* we now associate with this kind of romantic storytelling (in novels*) was also developed as a literary form in the decades just after 1200.

The new vernacular texts, describing a new way of (ideal) courtly life, soon found their way into other regions and languages. The noblemen, and the poets in their employ, travelled around Europe and took their entertainment along. From France, the stories travelled to the neighbouring countries and also farther afield, to, for instance, Scandinavia (see Chapter 9). The Tristan story, to give another example, came to Bohemia and the Slav countries by way of the German and Italian courts, as *Povest o Tristanu o Izoti* (in Serbo-Russian) and *Tristram a Isalde* (in Czech) testify. Images from the courtly stories are used in decorative arts all over Europe; there are images of Arthur and his knights as early as the eleventh century (in Modena, Italy) and as far east as Poland.

Writing for the high nobility, the poets all over Europe used their proper vernacular, yet they had been trained to write in Latin, since that was what one learned in school. The seven *artes liberales* (modern liberal arts colleges go back to this concept) consisted of grammar, logic, and rhetoric* (together called the three-way, *trivium**), and, at a more advanced level, geometry, arithmetic, astronomy, and music. For writing in the vernacular, the rhetorical tradition* and its handbooks were very influential: what was learned for composing a speech* or text in Latin (see Chapter 5) was also used when writing in French, German, Italian, or Dutch, just like the same type of letters and the same abbreviations were employed. The Latin handbooks for giving good speeches thus became "How to write" manuals for the new courtly texts. The rhetorical models are often recognisable. Since the handbooks give the "how" and "what" of describing, for instance, a beautiful woman, by starting at her golden hair and ending with her tiny feet, the romance poets tend to follow this lead and present rather similar looking heroines: blond babes with rosy cheeks, pearly white teeth, long necks, and so on.

Latin culture is inseparable from the Christian faith, the strongest unifying factor in medieval Europe in the West, whereas the Orthodox Church and its old Slavonic language played a similar role in Eastern Europe and Russia. The term Christendom covers both the Western worldview and the lands, with the exception of Spain, where the Muslim caliphs of Cordoba ruled well into the thirteenth century. As a power structure, Christendom was so successful that it began to expand to the south and east. The Crusades started just before 1100 and led to the conquest, and later again loss, of the Holy Land and Jerusalem. Focussing aggression outward onto a common enemy often is a good recipe for peace at home, but that does not quite go for Europe in the thirteenth and fourteenth centuries. Apart from all kinds of smaller conflicts and wars, a central point of contention was the relationship between France and England. After 1066, a strange situation arose, where the Anglo-Norman king of England held lands in France (Normandy, but also Aquitaine and other regions in the South of France) as vassal of his French counterpart. When after 1200 the power of the French kings increased, they claimed these continental regions and a long war was the result. The Hundred Years' War (1337–1453; two long truces account for the sixteen years that seem to be extra in the dates) was an economic disaster, yet the French victory (due to, among others, Joan of Arc) brought us closer to Europe as we now know it, with England and France as two quite separate entities. The war also was one of the factors in the emancipation of the English language.

The minor conflicts mentioned previously were of course each in their own right disasters as the – often mercenary – troops of every army lived off the land, burning and looting. It was a time of calamities, famine, and epidemics. The Black Death, the Bubonic Plague transmitted through flea bites, swept through the medieval cities like wildfire, killing off a large percentage of the European population. Some twenty million casualties is the standard estimate. The first epidemic ran from Genoa to Iceland from 1347–1351, and there were several further waves in the fourteenth and fifteenth centuries. Boccaccio's *Decameron* is set against the backdrop of the Plague in Florence, describing how ten young people flee from the disease-ridden city to the countryside and the comfort of storytelling. In literature, the Plague left its mark: afterwards there is a sense of disillusion (especially regarding the clergy), quite similar to the sentiments after the Great War of 1914–1918. *Memento mori* becomes an important theme.

Dante Alighieri had already shown his contemporaries what to expect after death in his *Commedia* (1321), the *Divine Comedy*. Where the twelfth century saw the invention of Purgatory as an in-between place where the soul could do time to atone for sins and still find a way to Heaven, Dante gives a detailed eyewitness account of a trip to Hell and its wickedly creative devils, the mountain of Purgatory and the luminous spheres of Heaven (see Chapter 10). The fact that Dante includes several popes and high clerics in the souls punished in the different circles of Hell shows that the bad habits of the church (bribery, forging documents, and so on) were in the public eye. Papal power was far from uncontested throughout the ages, and there were at times two or even three popes in play. Around 1400, for instance, there was a pope in Rome, and also one in Avignon. The idea that the official church was on the wrong path led to heretical movements (like the Cathars in the South of France), which were forcefully repressed, and to more moderate reforms from within by establishing new orders for monks and nuns, like the Franciscan order. A common element here is the wish to follow in Christ's footsteps, to come as close as humanly possible to the Divine. In the twelfth and thirteenth centuries, mystic poets like the celebrated Hadewych focused on the connection between God and man/woman, created in His image. They experienced contact with the Divine in the form of visions, made possible by their love for Christ. In their metaphors* and literary formats, these mystics used the models of courtly love poetry. In later centuries, the idea that God was only accessible to the faithful through the intermediary of the priests, preachers, and bishops (mass was celebrated in Latin, for instance) became more and more problematic. The Bible was translated into the vernacular and, especially when the printing press became accessible and productive, was read by the believers themselves. This led to the Reformation of 1517, but that is the province of the next part of this book.

Literature

One of the key issues in the medieval literary world is the co-existence of an oral* sphere of storytelling in the vernacular and a sphere of writing in Latin, Old Slavonic, or in the vernacular languages. Since we only have manuscripts*, texts written down on parchment, we tend to focus on what became fixed in writing, while for medieval people the oral information channel was just as important, perhaps even more so. In some parts of Eastern Europe, like the Serbo-Croatian region, medieval style orality persisted until the twentieth century, allowing modern scholars to study this way of storytelling and transfer in live action. In medieval Ireland, laws were considered too valuable to be written down. They were to be remembered, embodied in memory* and voice by lawmen. The manuscripts of Old Irish legal texts therefore have only the first words of the law, accompanied by commentaries* on its interpretation and by jurisprudence, written down by the practitioners, who knew the actual law text by heart.

Medieval poets were well aware that stories existed both in writing and in spoken words. In an aside* to his audience, Thomas of Britain says in his *Tristan* (ca. 1175):

> My lords, this tale is told in many ways, so I shall keep to one version in my rhymes, saying as much as is needed and passing over the remainder. But the matter diverges at this point and I do not wish to keep too much to one account. Those who narrate and tell the tale of Tristan tell it differently – I have heard various people do so. I know well enough what each says and what they have put into writing, but to judge by what I have heard, they do not follow Breri, who knew all the deeds and stories of all the kings and all the counts that had lived in Britain.[3]

Thomas has heard the story several times and remembers the contents of these performances* well enough to be aware of variants. Each performance of the tale in fact brings into existence a new version, which fades away with the sound of the spoken words and is retained only in the memory of the listeners, some of whom (like Thomas) may be able to retell the story to another audience. Some storytellers have also written it down, however, and so did Thomas. Although he is well aware that he does not own the story, he claims that his version is better by referring to an authorative source, a person with reliable knowledge.

There are two more elements in Thomas's words that help us understand how medieval writers work: he uses the word "matter" to refer to the story, and right at the beginning he speaks to his audience, addressing them as "My lords." The creative process and the reception*/patronage situation define how the texts came into being, for whom they were made, and how they were enjoyed.

Thomas's colleague Chrétien de Troyes provides us with more insight in the creative process. He was active as a writer and court cleric (a member of the court with religious and cultural functions: he would also be responsible for reading texts aloud to a mostly female audience) from around 1170–1191, maybe first in England, but later certainly in Champagne (France) and Flanders. He discusses his ideas about writing stories in the prologues to his romances. This may seem somewhat out of place, but in this period authors do not write separate theoretical essays about literature (cf. Aristotle's *Poetics**, see Chapter 5). That kind of reflective texts arises in the vernacular only in the first half of the fourteenth century, although there were rhetorical manuals like Geoffrey of Vinsauf's *Poetria Nova* (ca. 1200). As Chrétien begins his story and prepares the audience for what is to come, he introduces three technical terms: *matière**, *conjointure*, and *san*. The first term stands for the source material, the story matter, to which meaning (*san**, sense) is given by means of a new structure (*conjointure**, the joining of the parts). Like Thomas, Chrétien positions himself vis-à-vis other storytellers: he states, for instance, that he will tell the story of the knight Erec better than "those who try to live by storytelling" who "customarily mangle and corrupt [it] before kings and counts." His tale is better, because "from a tale of adventure he draws a beautifully ordered composition."[4] The final word translates *conjointure*, whereas the "tale of adventure" is the *matière*. The oral performers use the same material, but make a mess of it; only Chrétien knows how to structure the narrative* properly. He even claims that his story will live as long as Christianity lasts, and his claim has come true, since we still read Chrétien's romances about King Arthur, Erec, Lancelot, and the Grail.

In the prologue to his *Lancelot* tale, Chrétien speaks about *san* and *matière* in connection to the patronage* issue, the second element mentioned previously. He has written this romance because a noble lady, Marie de Champagne, has asked him to do so. She is his patron, he is in her service, and his prologue shows that he knows how to flatter her. Her influence on the book goes quite far. Chrétien explains that "the subject matter and meaning are furnished and given him by the countess, and he strives carefully to add nothing but his effort and careful attention."[5] Here Chrétien presents himself as the competent craftsman, rather than designer of the tale. What the story is about and which message it is to convey is decided by his patroness. Although often the exact nature of the patronage is not as clearly described as in this situation, the relationship is an important and remarkable factor in the development of courtly romance and medieval literature in general.

Nowadays financial resources for writing, printing, and distributing a book are provided by the eventual buyers, but no such system existed before the printing press was invented. A medieval author could only afford the time and the expensive parchment* (the skin of one sheep, calf, or goat yields no more than eight or ten pages) if he was employed by a wealthy nobleman or rewarded for his work by a patron afterwards. Chrétien needed Marie, and she needed him to produce the text for her, according to her wishes and containing the courtly ideals she wished to propagate. She is mentioned as an authority in matters of courtly love by another contemporary writer, Andreas Capellanus ('André the chaplain'), when he describes how these things were discussed by courtly ladies like Marie and her mother, Eleanor of Aquitaine, Queen of England. The discussions Andreas describes involve problematic romantic situations (a young lady must choose between two lovers, a young and uncivilized man or an older, experienced lover, etc.) that often sound like love stories in a nutshell. It is impossible to ascertain in how far Andreas reports about real events, people, and situations, but it was not done at this time to just make up things like this. Fiction still required a specific construction, like the setting of a dream. The famous *Roman de la Rose* ('Romance of the Rose'), begun around 1230 by Guillaume de Lorris and rounded off by Jean de Meun between 1268–1285, presents itself as a lover's dream in order to describe all kinds of fictional allegorical* figures (like Jealousy, Poverty, Sadness, and Amor) that oppose and help the lover in his quest to be united with his ladylove, the Rose.

With regard to the *matière*, there were three main topics in medieval literature: the matter of Rome (classical stories about Troy or the travels of Aeneas, see Chapter 1 and Chapter 2), the matter of France (*chansons de geste** describing the deeds of the Franks, especially Charlemagne) and the matter of Britain (tales of King Arthur and his knights, and of the Grail [see Chapter 9]). Especially the latter material became the vehicle for the new ideas about courtliness and courtly love. The mutual interest of court clerics and their noble patrons lay in the civilization process, in creating new social roles for men and women. Since for medieval people the past provided good examples for the present, the new ideals were projected onto characters and situations of long ago. Thus, the Greeks and Trojans are presented as taking some time off from the siege to engage in courteous conversation with lovely ladies, Aeneas behaves as a love-struck courtly knight, and King Arthur's court is the hallmark of courtliness. This creative anachronism obviously helped to bring the message across to the contemporary audiences, since the romances were quite popular, as the number of manuscripts and adaptations* into other vernaculars indicates. Old stories pack meaning, also in the later Middle Ages, when an author like Christine de Pizan uses the deeds of classical heroines to demonstrate the importance of women in the development of human civilization. Stories about good women form the building blocks of the city she builds in her *Le Livre de la Cité des dames* ('The Book of the City of Ladies') (see Chapter 12).

The poems and songs of the troubadours, epics* like *Beowulf*, the romance narratives in verse* and prose, funny short stories* like the *fabliaux*, allegorical texts like Christine's *Le Livre de la Cité des dames* or the *Roman de la Rose*, and religious works like Dante's *Commedia*: medieval literature takes many forms. Yet one kind of text is absent for a long time: drama*. Where classical tragedy* and comedy* provided highlights of world literature and Shakespeare is on the Renaissance horizon, medieval drama is slow to emerge. In a way, it is re-invented, since the Greek models were unavailable to medieval writers. From performances in church (especially around Easter, when the scene of finding the empty grave of the resurrected Christ is played out) and in Latin, drama moves into the town square and the vernacular. The themes at first are biblical (about Adam and Eve, or Noah's ark). In cities like York and Arras, but also in Croatia, religious pageants are organised, with plays* on Biblical themes on every street corner, and the audience walking from scene to scene. The plays soon have secular topics as well as religious ones, and begin to relate to current debates in society (e.g. lovers from different classes or of different ages and the problems these relationships cause). The Dutch so-called *abele spelen** are the first sophisticated plays on worldly themes, like love between a prince and a less noble girl. These serious plays were followed by comic relief for the audience in the form of a short comical play (a farce*), often about shrewd adulterous women and their stupid husbands and ending in a big verbal or physical fight on stage. The cities provided new and large audiences for the plays, and on many occasions (Carnival*/Mardi Gras, Easter, Christmas) festivals* were organized where theatre* clubs competed in putting on the best play. In the castles and especially the cities, medieval people knew how to party big time.

In the Middle Ages, literature is for the ears and hearts, something you do together and share rather than enjoy quietly, alone by yourself in a corner with a book. Manuscripts were rare and expensive, and not many people were able to read, much less to perform a written text properly before an audience. So, when a story was read aloud, it was something special, a social event, which provided important lessons (and probably also discussions) on how to live and love. From the monastery and Latin religious texts, vernacular literature develops in the courts of the high nobility into an agent for cultural change, a means to bring courtly civilization to the lay elite, and insightful entertainment for the nobles at court and more and more also for the common people in the towns. Cloister, court, and city were the consecutive centres for literary activity, where the Latin and oral circuits mingled and met to bring onto parchment the multiform literature in the vernacular, spreading from France all over Europe, at first only for an elite audience, yet more and more for everyman. The next five chapters discuss medieval texts in the vernacular that later ages have come to consider masterpieces of world literature.

Notes

1 Chrétien de Troyes, *Cligés*, ll 30–9, in *Arthurian Romances*, trans. William Kibler (Harmondsworth: Penguin, 1991): 123.
2 For this process, see Norbert Elias, *The Civilizing Process: Sociogenetic and Psychogenetic Investigations*, trans. Edmund Jephcott, ed. Eric Dunning (Malden, MA: Wiley-Blackwell, 2000).
3 Thomas of Britain, *Tristan*, trans. Arthur Thomas Hatto (Harmondsworth: Penguin, 1960): 338.
4 All three quotations: Chrétien de Troyes, *Arthurian Romances*, trans. William Kibler (Harmondsworth: Penguin, 1991): *Erec and Enide* (trans. Carleton Carroll): 37.
5 Chrétien de Troyes, *Arthurian Romances* (cf. note 1), 207.

Further reading

Bumke, Joachim. *Courtly Culture: Literature and Society in the High Middle Ages.* Translated by Thomas Dunlap. Berkeley: University of California Press, 1991.
Damrosch, David, David L. Pike, April Alliston, Marshall Brown, Sabry Hafez, Djelal Kadir, Sheldon Pollock, Bruce Robbins, Haruo Shirane, Jane Tyles and Pauline Yu, eds. *The Longman Anthology to World Literature. Vol. B: The Medieval Era.* New York/London: Longman, 2012.
Jackson, William T.H. *Medieval Literature: A History and a Guide.* New York: Collier Books, 1966.
Krueger, Roberta L., ed. *The Cambridge Companion to Medieval Romance.* Cambridge: Cambridge University Press, 2000.
Rosenwein, Barbara H. *A Short History of the Middle Ages.* Toronto: University of Toronto Press, 2014.

8 Desiring

Roy Rosenstein

Figure 8.1 Veldeke, Hendrik, "Codex Manesse", ca. 1300, Univeristätsbibliothek Heidelberg, Heidelberg,
Cod. Pal. germ. 848

Like the rhapsodes* in antiquity (see Chapter 2 and Chapter 3), the Middle Ages also had travelling poets. This chapter will look into the love poetry of Jaufre Rudel, one of the most influential troubadours*. In the manuscripts of Jaufre's lyrics, a biography*, quoted here in full, sometimes precedes the poems:

Text: Jaufre Rudel, "Vida" followed by his "Lanquan li jorn" (original poem ca. 1140)

Jaufre Rudel of Blaye was a very noble man, Lord of Blaye. He fell in love with the Countess of Tripoli, without ever seeing her, because of the good he heard tell of her from pilgrims coming back from Antioch. He made many songs about her with good melodies and poor words. And from desire to see her he took the cross and set out to sea. But he fell ill on the ship and was carried almost dead to an inn in Tripoli. The Countess was notified and she came to him, to his bed, and took him in her arms. He knew she was the Countess and recovered his hearing and sense of smell. And he praised God for having sustained his life until he had seen her. And thus he died in her arms. She had him buried with great honour in the Temple. And then, that very day, she became a nun, for the grief that she had in his death. And here is written one of his songs:

Lanquan li jorn son lonc en mai
m'es bels doutz chans d'auzels de lonh.
E quan mi sui partitz de lai
remembra'm d'un amor de lonh:
vau de talan embroncs e clis,
si que chans ni flors d'albespis
no'm platz plus que l'inverns gelatz.

When the days are long in May
I love the sweet song of birds from afar.
And since I am far away from there
I keep in mind a love from afar.
I go about bowed and bent with desire,
so that neither songs nor hawthorn flowers
please me more than wintry frost.

Ben tenc lo Seignor per verai
per qu'ieu veirai l'amor de lonh.
Mas per un ben que m'en eschai
n'ai dos mals, car tant m'es de lonh. . .

I believe the Lord to be true:
through Him I shall see the love from afar.
But for one good fortune that befalls me,
I have two misfortunes, for She is afar. . .

Be'm parra jois quan li querrai,
per amor Dieu, l'alberc de lonh.
E s'a lieis platz, albergarai
pres de lieis, si be'm sui de lonh. . .

Joy will come to me when I ask of Her,
for the love of God, the sanctuary from afar.
And if it please Her, I will lodge
near to Her, so much am I from afar. . .

Iratz e jauzens m'en partrai,
quan veirai cest'amor de lonh.
Mas non sai coras la veirai,
car trop son nostras terras lonh. . .

Sad and joyful I shall part
when I shall see this love from afar.
But I do not know when I shall see Her
for our lands are much too afar. . .

Ja mais d'amor no.m jauzirai
si no.m jau d'est'amor de lonh.
Que gensor ni meillor non sai
vas nuilla part, ni pres ni lonh. . .

Never again shall I enjoy love
if I do not enjoy this love from afar.
For none nobler or better do I know
anywhere, neither near nor afar. . .

Dieus qui fetz tot quant ve ni vai,
e formet cest'amor de lonh,
mi don poder – que'l cor eu n'ai –
qu'en breu veia l'amor de lonh. . .

God who made everything that comes and
goes and created this love from afar,
give me the strength – for the heart I have –
that I might soon see this love from afar. . .

Ver ditz qui m'apella lechai	Truth speaks he who calls me hungry
ni desiron d'amor de lonh.	and desirous of this love from afar.
Quar nuills autre jois tant no'm plai	For no other joy pleases me so much
cum jauzimens d'amor de lonh. . .	as the enjoyment of a love from afar. . .
Mas so qu'ieu vuoill m'es ataïs.	But what I desire is forbidden me.
Toz sia mauditz lo pairis	Damned be the godfather
Que'm fadet qu'ieu non fos amatz.	who cursed me with being unloved.[1]

Just as they do in medieval manuscripts*, the above two passages strikingly juxtapose prose and poetry, biography* and song, in introducing the twelfth-century troubadour Jaufre Rudel by first telling a thirteenth-century idealized version of his life story, called a *vida**, and only then providing a sampling of his poetic production.

This double transmission* represents a later stage in the presentation of troubadour poetry* in the various manuscripts. First came the songs, composed and performed* by Jaufre in the twelfth century, at that point perhaps not even written down. Only later, in the thirteenth century, was the *vida* composed and combined with the songs. The two were then codified together on parchment*. Because songs like this one were a resounding success, the making and singing of such love songs became an exportable cultural phenomenon, characteristic of the South of France and spreading from there to all of Europe. Hundreds of such poets composed and performed in Occitania (a region in Southern Europe, covering parts of Southern France, Italy, and Spain as well as Monaco) and across Europe, both noble and lower-class, both male and female.

The song as presented and the story ostensibly behind it show a thematic and interpretive overlap between the two genres of biography and poetry. Here the two texts together evoke the mesmerizing allure of an enigmatic love for the troubadour and a hesitant understanding of the mysterious song for the reader. First come the geographical and other obstacles blocking the poet's love, according to his romanticized life. These anticipate and attempt to resolve for readers the challenge we face in penetrating the nature of the distant and unidentified love interest evoked in his complex song. The long song, abbreviated here, is short on any explicit context to Jaufre's life work: the love object is never identified, much less named, not even stated to be a lady. That role is transparently undertaken by the *vida*: namely, to fill in the blanks in our grasp of the poet and his song together, not separately. The two faces of the troubadour, as narrative subject and as poetic voice, are thereby mutually enriched, making the two even more compelling in an exemplary story and in a powerful poem, yet each still tantalizingly elusive.

Biography

We know little about the historical Jaufre Rudel and even less about his distant love. In all likelihood, we will never discover more. No doubt the poet cultivated that ambiguity in his songs just as much as the biographer attempted to dissipate it in his *vida*. Our uncertainty not only fuels debate about both texts but also contributes to their enduring fascination across the centuries. In this case, any grasp of the poet's songs is influenced by our knowledge of the *vida*, which was, among other functions, the earliest known attempt at a critical reading of the poems. The *vida* defines an all-consuming love for the far-off Countess of Tripoli based on the melding of several documented elements incorporated into the prose text. Her stellar reputation in the Holy Land and in Europe is coupled with three then widely known and today accepted facts: Jaufre's defining poetic motif of an ill-defined distant love, his departure on the Second Crusade in 1147, and his final illness on the journey to the Holy Land. The would-be biographer and critic creatively connected the dots in imagining how the poet may have sought a dream lady, to whom the *vida* attributes a historical identity. But above all, the *vida*'s innovation is to make Jaufre Rudel give up the ghost in her arms on arrival on a mission abroad, presented here as more sentimental and personal than political* or religious*, as had been the Second Crusade (1147–1149). Whether the troubadour's* departure was inspired by the collective movement or had a private purpose remains unclear: probably both, in that in his personal song he also gave voice to a widespread desire among his fellows to go to the Holy Land. His sailing off on crusade and his broken health *en route* are indeed independently confirmed historical events; only the intent of his journey and the circumstances of his death are expanded imaginatively in interpreting the quest evoked in his lyrics.

The song versus the legend

Perhaps by as much as a century, the poetry predates the legend: the latter developed gradually, partly around the historical figure and partly from the poet's thematics. This process is difficult for us to unravel. In the medieval manuscripts and on the modern printed page, as well as in literary history, the legend always comes first in previewing the poetry for us, prejudging its mystery and explicating it for us, whether we want this or not. For we must not forget that the song does not presuppose the story or our knowledge of it even when they have become difficult to separate, all the more because the secondary legend invariably is read before the primary text. Today, as in the Middle Ages, few if any will come to Jaufre's poetry without a previous encounter with his legend, for better or worse.

All that we can affirm about the author from the song is that he is Jaufre Rudel. Not only are the medieval manuscripts unanimous in attributing the song to him: it and his other surviving lyrics are defined by his signature notion of distant love, inscribed in his lyrics, particularly this one. In addition, the grammatical variation on forms of the verb *jauzir* 'to enjoy' (*jauzens, jauzirai, jau*), related as in English to the noun 'joy' (*jois, jauzimens*), recurs frequently in this and other songs by the same poet. In echoing the first syllable of Jaufre's name, *jauzir* is indeed a second signature: like his preferred motif, the play on his name authenticates his authorship.

What then does his song say about the nature and direction of his desire, if we try to abstract it from the preceding narrative* on the page and peel off the overlay of a later interpretation? What or whom did Jaufre Rudel desire? We must for a moment distance ourselves from the historical and legendary figure of the author and focus instead on the voice of the lover in the poem (see Chapter 3 for a similar case with the *persona** of Sappho).

The lyric language of desire here is alternately carnal ("love"; "Her") and spiritual ("the Lord"; "Him"), both earthly ("enjoy love") and transcendent ("none nobler"), at once mournful yet somehow rejoicing too ("sad and joyful"). The leitmotif* of *amor de lonh* ('love from afar'), recurring twice at the rhyme* in the second and fourth lines of each stanza* (here shortened after the first), expresses the pressing human need for reaching a faraway partner. Since Plato's allegory* of the hermaphrodite, according to which an originally sexually self-sufficient human was split into two different sexes, each of us is more or less ardently seeking the lost other half. The repeated word-rhyme of Jaufre Rudel's song on *amor de lonh* resonated in the medieval and post-medieval imagination like a refrain, echoing from stanza to stanza, from generation to generation.

Therein lies the eerie fascination of this song, which the *vida* helped perpetuate instead of laying it to rest, as its creator perhaps intended in biographizing the historical poet and his distant love.

Trobador and *trobairitz*

The future development of troubadour love lyric was prefigured with considerable clarity by Jaufre Rudel, the first of these poets after their great forerunner, the Count of Poitiers, active some twenty years earlier, ca. 1100. It has been proposed that this Count of Poitiers (Count William IX of Aquitaine) is labelled the "godfather" at the end of Jaufre's song, because he had set the standard for not only vernacular love poetry in general but specifically for the inaccessibility topos* that Jaufre popularized with his distant love. That distance for subsequent generations of poets is not exclusively geographical, but also cultural and social, and of course sexual. In another song, "Pro ai del chan essenhadors," Jaufre says "far off is the castle where she sleeps with her husband."[2] The idealized Lady, when Jaufre and his successors sing her praise, is at least nominally beyond their grasp, on whatever plane or at whatever distance. Theirs is a poetry of unrequited love, in which the poets express their yearnings and much less often their satisfactions. Love poetry* is in majority a poetry of desire: those whose wishes are fulfilled do not so much sing love as they make it. A poetry of desire does not preclude fulfilment, but that satisfaction is achieved beyond the realm of the lyric proper. Desire is here cultivated and promoted as an ennobling end in itself, prompting the lovers to think and act apart from the satisfaction of their private desires in refining their personal discourse and public interactions. In this way, love is represented as the noblest of sentiments, leading to socialization through the integration and refinement of interpersonal attractions crucial to the development of courtliness.

Hundreds of troubadours in the South of France wrote in the same vein, voicing their unresolved desire for a love object usually assimilated to an untouchable noble woman. Political, moral, and satirical song is also present, but in less stylized* forms. These poets' influence was prodigious because their pursuit of love was intrinsically new and attractive, no doubt, but also because another crusade, the Albigensian Crusade, early in the thirteenth century and called by Saint Louis (the French King Louis IX), would lead to the annexation of Occitania to (Northern) France and to the dispersal of the Southern courts and courtiers. The same poets continued to perform in Sicily and across Northern Italy as well as in far-off Galicia, in Northern Spain. The same strains may be heard in the Middle High German and Middle Dutch lyrical poetry of the Middle Ages, but less if at all in the British Isles.

Who were these troubadours* of the twelfth and thirteenth centuries composing in the Occitan language of the South of France, and how then did their role in the development of modern European lyric poetry* come to be so decisive? According to legend, these poets were simply wandering minstrels*. Yet the earliest and most renowned were aristocratic men . . . and women: there were among them not only male *trobadors* but also female *trobairitz*. The earliest song by a *trobairitz*, or woman troubadour, is attributed to Na Tibors. Her *vida* says that:

> Na Tibors was a lady from Provence, from a castle of Lord Blacatz called Sarenom. She was courtly and educated, attractive and very learned, and she knew how to compose songs. She was loving and was much loved: she was much honoured by all the

worthy men of the region, also well respected and obeyed by the noble ladies. And she wrote these stanzas and sent them to her lover:

Bels dous amics, ben vos puosc en ver dir	Fair, sweet friend, I can truly tell you
qe anc no fo q'eu estes ses desir	that never have I been without desire
pos vos conosc ni'us pris per fin aman.	since I met and took you as a true love.
Ni anc no fo q'eu non agues talan,	Nor ever was I without desire,
bels dous amics, q'eu soven no'us veses,	fair, sweet friend, to see you often,
ni anc no fo sasons qe m'en pentes.	nor ever was there a time I repented.
Ni anc no fo si vos n'anes iratz	Nor ever did you go away angry
q'eu agues joi tro qe fosetz tornatz,	that I knew joy until you had returned,
ni anc. . .	nor ever. . . (the song is incomplete)[3]

We know enough about the individual identities and careers of many troubadours and a few *trobairitz* to affirm that several well-travelled poets from the South of France carried or exported their spirited love poetry to all of Europe, including Spain and Portugal to the West and Italy, Germany, and even Hungary to the East. But their presence is mostly immediately discernible throughout France, and in the principal vernacular language of Northern France, namely French (or *langue d'oïl*, as opposed to the *langue d'oc*, the language of Occitania in the South).

A cultural divergence between the North and the South is well attested beyond their different languages, French and Occitan. It was proverbial in the Latin Middle Ages to say that *Francigeni ad bellum, Provinciales ad amorem*. That is, before the troubadour influence from the early twelfth century, the descendants of Charlemagne's Franks in the North devoted themselves entirely to making war (*ad bellum*). But the troubadours and *trobairitz* of the South, the Provençals, from Provence and other Mediterranean provinces, preferred to make love (*ad amorem*) . . . and sing its virtues, soon to be so influential on the international scene far beyond just Southern and Northern France.

For the troubadours, yearning drives love and the literary love vision. Poetry extols the perfection of earthly beauty. But when the natural human desire for love is frustrated, it may channel into the objectification of the beloved, either disparaged in satire* or idealized in a love song. A geographical, social, or other separation does not necessarily impede and may instead breed a sentimental closeness: "absence makes the heart grow fonder," as the proverb has it. The medieval poets sang a stylized unrequited desire for a lady of high rank and the lover's stubborn determination in the face of her detachment or rejection. Love poetry has always been concerned more with impatient anticipation than past or even present satisfaction. The medievals' persistent love service and their polished poetry, both anchored in a state of ritualized* frustration, are offered in hopes of the Lady's accepting the poet-lover and his courtship. In the romantic love traceable to the troubadours, desire entails emotional, even bodily, pain before it can achieve physical pleasure. Delayed love in contrast to urgent desire thus socializes men and women as it ennobles them. In so doing, it also legitimizes obsessive passion outside of wedlock.

The reception of troubadour songs and ideas

Long before Wagner's opera *Tristan und Isolde* (1860), the tragic fortunes of iconic mid-twelfth-century lovers Tristan and Iseut became an exemplary narrative for the Middle Ages.

The tale* of these two unmarried lovers, passionate and inseparable in their shared end, anticipates that of Romeo and Juliet and countless other such "star-crossed lovers" before and since Shakespeare. With love, death has long been the other great literary theme. In the legend* as in the poetry of Jaufre Rudel, love and death, Eros and Thanatos, are united. The partly biographical legend lent seriousness to his love songs, solidifying his reputation and guaranteeing their diffusion. Jaufre Rudel in his poetry is prepared to brave death in a laudable and enduring passion for an unnamed idealized love whose universal admiration had stirred him. He became a model of death for love, like Tristan and Iseut, in a romantic fable* developed around his end across the seas. The poet and his legend became fused.

For post-medieval readers too, the same troubadour has remained ever the powerful poet, literary legend, or both. In fourteenth-century Florence, when composing the most famous of all love sonnet* sequences, the *Canzoniere*, to his beloved Laura, Petrarch (1304–1374) did not expressly refer to the songs of Jaufre Rudel. Instead, he forefronted his life and legend in his own "Triumph of Love", where he cites the case of Jaufre Rudel, who, he recalls, used sail and oar to seek his death. Petrarch's treatment of desire in his sonnets echoes the spirit of our troubadour, who had sensed a closeness across distance, who felt some imagined or real reciprocation across time and space, always keeping his beloved close to his heart even while still beyond his embrace: "ni pres ni lonh" ('neither close nor far off'), said Jaufre Rudel in the song quoted previously. For Petrarch as well, his Laura in life as in death – for she died prematurely, like Dante's Beatrice (see Chapter 10) – would always be at once near to and far from him: "sempre m'è si presso e si lontano" ('always to me [she] is so close and so distant').[4]

Writing in sixteenth-century Provence, Jean de Nostredame was the first to publish both the legendary *vidas* of the troubadours and some of their authentic lyrics. In his *Lives of the Old Provençal Poets* (1575), he placed Jaufre Rudel at the outset of the troubadour tradition, not simply by elevating the poet to the head of a broadly chronological presentation and by recounting the already famous legend yet again, but by synthesizing his best-known song in sixteen lines that would be translated into all major European languages. Since this version becomes an important source for post-medieval reception*, it is given here in Nostredame's original and in the free English translation by Thomas Rymer, published in 1693:

Irat & dolent m'en partray,
s'yeu non vey est'amour de luench.
E non say qu'ouras la veyray,
car son trop nostras terras luench.

Dieu que fes tout quant van, e vay,
e form' aquest'Amour luench,
my don poder al cor, car hay
esper, vezer l'Amour luench.

Segnour, tenés my per veray
l'Amour qu'ay vers ella de luench.
Car per un ben que m'en esbay,
hay mille mals, tant soy de luench.

Ia d'autr'Amours non iauziray
s'yeu non iau d'est'Amour de luench,
qu'na plus bella non en say
en luec que sia, ny pres, ny luench.

Sad and heavy should I part
but for this Love so far away;
not knowing what my ways may thwart,
my Native Land so far away.

Thou that of all things Maker art,
and form'st this Love so far away;
give body's strength, then shan't I start,
from seeing her so far away.

How true a Love to pure desert,
my Love to her so far away!
eas'd once, a thousand times I smart,
whilst, ah! she is so far away.

None other Love, none other Dart
I feel, but hers so far away,
but fairer never touch'd an heart,
than hers that is so far away.[5]

In the seventeenth century, when Rymer's translation* appeared in England, Jaufre's legend had been cited in France as a case history by rationalist doctor of medicine Jacques Ferrand in his book on lovesickness: the tale of love and death became a caution against the fatal disease of all-consuming passion. That unshakable devotion, read as life-threatening by Enlightenment* physicians, would by the nineteenth century be admired as a worthy model for romantic dreamers. Henceforth, the matchless legend of the poet's death for love and the enduring life of his poems in translation could inspire new generations of writers. It would take centuries before anyone after Jean de Nostredame considered the much neglected original lyrics, which continued to sleep in the medieval manuscripts.

Among the earliest modern writers who admired Jaufre's poetry more than his legend, Robert Burns in 1796 naturalized the same Occitan love song, borrowed via Rymer's translation of Nostredame and transformed into a typical Burns song of separation. Burns left us many such lyrics in which the protagonist parts ways with a lady love. Jaufre Rudel's song had expressed joyful expectation, but for readers of Burns his words seem just another "fare thee well" to a beloved he would never see again – nor sought to. Glaswegian patriots and Burnsian scholars still believe this song to be fully a part of their Scottish heritage and have attempted to identify the Highlands lass it refers to before dating it and posting it on the city website under the title "My Native Land So Far Away".[6] But Burns never left his native Scotland and Glasgow residents are evidently unaware of this song's origins, to be found not at home but in far-away Occitania, although re-"written for this work by Robert Burns" in Scots to accompany an old Scottish tune:

O sad and heavy should I part,
but for her sake sae far awa;
unknowing what my way may thwart,
my native land sae far awa.

Thou that of a' things Maker art,
that form'd this Fair sae far awa,
gin body strength, then I'll ne'er start,
at this my way sae far awa.

How true is love to pure desert,
so love to her, sae far awa:
and nocht can heal my bosom's smart,
while, oh, she is sae far awa.

Nane other love, nane other dart,
I feel, but hers sae far awa:
but fairer never touch'd a heart
than hers, the Fair sae far awa.[7]

While some readers today are still moved by the probably apocryphal story of Jaufre's death in his lady's embrace, others continue to update his signature motif in their poetry. These include American and French translators like poet Paul Blackburn, who freely modernized the same song of distant love in his anthology* *Proensa*, and the late poetess Jacqueline Risset, who reprised its thematics in her own collection entitled *Amour de loin*. In a similar if lighter vein, Dame Isobel Wren, pen name of a graduate in medieval literature making her living as a practising sex counsellor and striptease artist, posted her own take on Jaufre Rudel's most famous song. It staged her tongue-in-cheek separation anxiety from a distant partner back in the days (1995) before smartphones, Facetime, and Skype:

> When now the days are long in June
> I love to hear the dial tone distant,
> and when the sound must die – too soon –,
> I dream about a love as distant;
> deep in my worst debts I am drowned.
> Adverts for calling cards abound,
> and warm me no more than winter snow.[8]

Lastly, medieval legend and authentic lyrics have finally been reunited on stage in the successful 2000 opera* *L'amour de loin*, co-authored in French by two Paris residents, Finnish composer Kaija Saariaho and Lebanese novelist and historian Amin Maalouf. Performed at the Metropolitan Opera House of New York during its 2016–2017 season for a first appearance there, this opera continues to sell out to standing-room-only audiences* in France and the United States. The two authors' close collaboration has given Jaufre Rudel's lyrics and legend yet another moment of celebrity. The birth of the opera was itself a product of distant love, in that the authors residing in Paris worked together by correspondence*, the imposing, outspoken Saariaho having at that point never yet met the shy, retiring Maalouf.

The cross-fertilization of the lyrics and the legend of one troubadour have assured more than the triumph of a Western vernacular romantic love ethic. Jaufre Rudel's genuine poetry and his fantasy biography conflate love and death while affirming the parity of a historical poet and his poetic identity. In courting a distant beloved, Jaufre enacted a desire for an idealized love which has inspired Western poets from the troubadours to Petrarch to the present.

Notes

1 Text in Roy Rosenstein and Yves Leclerc, eds., trans., *Jaufre Rudel: Chansons pour un amour lointain* (Gardonne: Fédérop, 2011), 56–63; the poem and its translation are abridged here.

2 Rosenstein and Leclerc, *Jaufre Rudel*, 24–5.

3 *Vida* in Jean Boutière and Alexander H. Schutz, eds., trans., *Biographies des troubadours* (Paris: Nizet, 1973), 498–9; text in Matilda Tomaryn Bruckner, Laurie Shepard and Sarah White, eds., trans., *Songs of the Women Troubadours* (New York: Garland, 2000), 138–9.

4 Robert M. Durling, ed., trans., *Petrarch's Lyric Poems* (Cambridge, MA: Harvard University Press, 1976), 264–7, line 61.

5 Jean de Nostredame, *Vies des plus celebres et anciens poetes provensaux* (Lyons: Marsilii, 1575), 23–7; Thomas Rymer, *A Short View of Tragedy* (London: Baldwin, 1693), 70–2.

6 "My Native Land Sae Far Awa," accessed May 2016, www.glasgowguide.co.uk/wjmc/mynative.shtml

7 Robert Burns and James Johnson, eds., *The Scots Musical Museum*, vol. 5 (Edinburgh: Johnson, 1796), 461.

8 Dame Isobel Wren, "Miscellaneous Structured Poems," accessed May 2016, http://webspace.webring.com/people/ul/ladyisobelwren/miscpoems.html

Further reading

Akehurst, Frank R.P. and Judith M. Davis, eds. *A Handbook of the Troubadours*. Berkeley: University of California Press, 1995.

Bruckner, Matilda Tomaryn, Laurie Shepard and Sarah White, eds./trans. *Songs of the Women Troubadours*. New York: Garland, 2000.

Haines, John. *Eight Centuries of Troubadours and Trouvères: The Changing Face of Medieval Music*. Cambridge: Cambridge University Press, 2004.

Paden, William D. and Frances Freeman Paden, eds./trans. *Troubadour Poems From the South of France*. Cambridge: D.S. Brewer, 2007.

Rosenstein, Roy and Yves Leclair, eds./trans. *Jaufre Rudel: Chansons pour un amour lointain*. Gardonne: Fédérop, 2011.

9 Searching for the Grail

Frank Brandsma

Figure 9.1 Perceval witnesses the Grail procession at the table of the Fisher King (detail). From a 1330 manuscript of *Perceval ou Le Conte du Graal* by Chrétien de Troyes, Biblithèque nationale de France, 12577, fol. 74v

Source: Centre Art Historical Documentation, Radboud University.

After describing, in his first Arthurian romances, how knights find a balance between courtly love and their chivalric ambitions, Chrétien de Troyes introduces in his fifth work a new element, the Grail, in the Arthurian world. The text's naïve hero Perceval does not quite know what to make of this object when he encounters it in the castle of the Fisher King, and his behaviour has consequences when he returns to King Arthur's court.

Text: Chrétien de Troyes, Le Conte du Graal *('the Story of the Grail') (ca. 1190)*

Great was the joy that the king, the queen, and all the barons made over Perceval the Welshman, as they returned with him that night to Caerleon. And all night they revelled, and the whole of the next day, until on the third day they saw a damsel approaching on a tawny mule, holding a whip in her right hand. The damsel had her hair twisted into two tight black braids and, if the words given in the book are true, there was never a creature so ugly even in the bowels of Hell. . . . She greeted the king and all the assembled barons except Perceval alone, to whom she spoke from her tawny mule: "Ah, Perceval! . . . Cursed be anyone who'd greet you or who'd wish you well, for you didn't catch hold of Fortune when you met her! You entered the castle of the Fisher King and saw the bleeding lance, but it was so much effort for you to open your mouth and speak that you couldn't ask why that drop of blood flowed from the tip of the white shaft! And you didn't ask or inquire what rich man was served from the grail you saw. Wretched is the man who sees that the propitious hour has come but waits for a still better one. And you are that wretched man, for you saw that it was the time and place to speak yet kept your silence! You had plenty of time to ask! Cursed be the hour you kept silent since, if you had asked, the rich king who is suffering so would already be healed of his wound and would be ruling in peace over the land he shall now never again command. And do you know the consequence of the king not ruling and not being healed of his wounds? Ladies will lose their husbands, lands will be laid waste, and maidens will remain helpless as orphans; many a knight will die. All these troubles will occur because of you."

(In reaction to the damsel's words, Perceval stated) that he would not spend two nights in the same lodgings as long as he lived . . . until he had learned who was served from the grail and had found the bleeding lance and been told the reason why it bled. He would not abandon his quest for any hardship.[1]

Bad news indeed! After the lovely ladies in the troubadour poems and in earlier courtly romances, the hideous and mysterious damsel is a nasty surprise. She may not come straight from Hell, like Dante's demons and souls in the next chapter (Chapter 10), yet she is the ugliest woman in vernacular literature so far. And impolite as well: her courtly greetings are only extended to the king and courtiers; Perceval does not even merit "Hello." He has done something seriously wrong, when confronted with the Grail and Lance in the castle of the rich and wounded Fisher King. What exactly occurred there will be discussed later in this chapter, but he obviously failed to do a good deed. Perceval had the opportunity to ask who was served from the Grail (a priceless dish) and why the Lance bled, yet kept silent. Just asking these questions would have cured the wounded king. The health of the king and the wellbeing of the lands he rules are somehow connected, so Perceval's silence will lead to disaster. The waste land motif* of T.S. Eliot's famous 1922 poem is born in this scene.

Perceval's reaction to the damsel's message is striking and typical for knightly conduct in Arthurian romance, the genre created by Chrétien de Troyes in the decades 1170–1190. He does not protest against the damsel's accusations. The narrator* does not describe any thoughts or emotions (shock? shame? embarrassment? anger?) on his part. Perceval does what Arthurian knights do: he undertakes a quest. Riding away seems the logical answer to personal problems in medieval romance: to set things right, the character gets going, rather than start thinking or talking. Venturing into the dangerous world outside the court will bring Perceval the insights he sorely lacks now. In his classic work *Mimesis: The Representation of Reality in Western Literature* (see also the general introduction), Erich Auerbach has described how this works:

> The world of knightly proving is a world of adventure. It not only contains a practically uninterrupted series of adventures; more specifically, it contains nothing but the requisites of adventure. Nothing is found in it which is not either accessory or preparatory to an adventure. It is a world specifically created and designed to give the knight opportunity to prove himself.[2]

Perceval will eventually learn the reason why he did not ask the required questions, and so will the audience* of Chrétien's tale*. The listener's curiosity is piqued and will remain so for quite a while, since the story will first focus on the adventures of Gawain rather than Perceval, as will be explained in the second part of this chapter ("What happens next?"). However, diving into the Perceval story *in medias res*, as we have done here, first necessitates a discussion of what came before in the romance, and of what came before in Chrétien's oeuvre and in vernacular French literature in the twelfth century.

What came before?

How did Perceval end up in this fix? At the start of the romance, he is a rather clueless young man, raised by his noble mother in the isolation of the Waste Forest. She has kept him far from knightly society, since her husband and two other sons died in combat. Out hunting in the forest, Perceval meets five of Arthur's knights and first assumes they are angels, in their bright and colourful armour. When they have explained who and what they are, Perceval decides to become a knight and go to Arthur's court. Nothing his mother says or does can hold him back. She does give him some advice on how to deal with other people, especially ladies (help maidens in distress; they may want to kiss you or give you a ring: accept that). As he rides away a few days later, he looks back and sees his mother has collapsed, yet does not turn his horse around to see if she is all right.

On his way to Arthur, Perceval's social ineptness becomes evident when he kisses a damsel against her will and jerks a ring from her finger. He enters the court on horseback and accidentally knocks the king's hat off. Having met a red knight nearby, Perceval wants this knight's red armour, even more so when Sir Kay mocks him and challenges him to go fight the knight, who has insulted the queen and stolen the king's wine cup. Kay even slaps a damsel, who laughs for the first time in years and then tells Perceval that he will become the best knight in the world. Armed with only his hunting spears, Perceval manages to defeat his mighty opponent by throwing a javelin through the visor of his helmet. He dons the red armour, but does not return to court. After sending back the cup with a message to the damsel that he will avenge Kay's slap, he rides off again.

Fortunately, he soon encounters a gentleman, Gornemant, who gives him important advice on all kinds of chivalric behaviour and, among other things, tells him not to be too talkative or to gossip. Perceval's further adventures will show his growing accomplishments, especially when he meets the beautiful Blancheflor. She considers him very handsome and comes to his bedroom in the night, weeping copiously. Her tears wet his face and he wakes up, courteously taking her in his arms. She explains that she is upset because an evil knight is besieging her castle in the hope of capturing her. Perceval promises to help her and holds her tightly in his arms all night. Although he manages to defeat Blancheflor's enemies, there is no continuation to this amorous (and possibly sexual) encounter, as Perceval soon leaves again, since he now remembers that his mother collapsed when he left her.

Once more on the road, Perceval meets a gentleman fishing from a boat in a river and is invited to spend the night at his nearby castle. Welcomed by an elderly, wounded king, Perceval witnesses a mysterious procession. First a squire comes in bearing a white lance. A drop of blood runs from the tip of the lance down to the squire's hand. Then big candelabras are brought in, followed by a beautiful maiden. She is carrying "a grail", which lights up the room.[3] It "was of pure gold. Set in the grail were precious stones of many kinds, the best and costliest to be found in earth or sea: the grail's stones were finer than any others in the world."[4] When seeing the lance and again when looking at the grail, Perceval remembers Gornemant's admonition not to speak too much and refrains from asking questions. After the procession an excellent meal is served, during which the grail comes by once more, then the beds are prepared and Perceval sleeps the night away. In the morning, he is all alone in the castle. Finding no one, he leaves; as soon as he has passed the drawbridge, it is drawn up. The events on "the morning after" are the first signs that something went not quite right in the grail castle. Perceval will receive further hints regarding his failure from people he meets on his way back to Arthur's court, yet he also has successful adventures. One morning, he sees how three drops of blood from a wounded goose fall in the white snow and becomes completely absorbed by this image, as the red and white remind him of Blancheflor. He is found by Arthur's knights, but lost in thought does not react to their invitations to come with them. As Kay tries to use force to get Perceval's attention, Perceval defends himself with his lance and manages to hit Kay so hard that he breaks his opponent's upper arm and dislocates his collarbone, thus avenging the slapping of the damsel. Finally, Gawain is able to break Perceval's trance by means of courteous words rather than threats. With the dissolving of the drops of blood on the snow, Blancheflor and love disappear from Perceval's mind and life, especially after the hideous damsel comes to court and accuses him of negligence.

The Lance and Grail are remarkable new story elements, and especially the latter will dominate Arthurian romance in the decades to come. Yet, here it still is "a grail", not "the Grail": an expensive golden dish, decorated with priceless jewels, but without a hint of holiness or special powers. There are lists of household goods from the twelfth century which also mention grails, referring to shallow serving platters. Somehow Chrétien managed to upgrade a piece of medieval dishware to one of the most powerful and enduring symbols in European culture. In part, this is due to his brilliant storytelling: he keeps his audience mystified and curious by not revealing things. The German scholar Walter Haug has called this technique *Verrätselung**, mystification.[5] Like Perceval, the medieval listeners will have burned with questions about Lance and Grail, yet no answers are forthcoming at this point in the tale. After five years of questing, Perceval will meet a hermit who will explain that God made him tongue-tied because he left his mother for dead. His sin caused his silence, rather than too strict an interpretation of Gornemant's advice. More about this and the religious connotations of the Grail are to come in the second part of this chapter.

Did Chrétien invent the Grail? No and yes. In the prologue, he dedicates his work to his patron, count Philip of Flanders, and explains that the count commanded him to put to rhyme this tale, the best story ever told in royal courts. In the original French, the text then states: "Ce est li contes do greal/Don li cuens li bailla lo livre" ('It is the Story of the Grail, the book of which was given to him by the count').[6] In the medieval making of literature, patrons* are very important, since they provide the means (parchment*, housing, money, and so on) that the poet needs to be able to spend his time and effort on making a text in manuscript*. This also means that the patron has a say in what is to be written and sometimes even provides the story matter. Count Philip gave Chrétien a Grail book, which he used as his source; at least, that is what he claims in the prologue. So, the answer is "No"; it would seem that Chrétien found the Grail in this book. However, it is also quite common for medieval poets to invent a source, in order to lend authority and authenticity to a subject which actually is their own original idea. Old and traditional things work for the medieval audience, in contrast to the modern demands for new and original* work. Because no trace has been found of the count's Grail book, and since it is also not mentioned or used by poets following in Chrétien's footsteps, it is quite possible that the source book never existed, that Chrétien himself is responsible for the upgrading of the Grail, and that the answer should be "Yes". It most certainly was his tale that got Grail-things going in medieval literature.

With prologue and patron, the other subjects of this first part come to the fore: Chrétien's oeuvre and its literary context. In contrast to an author like Chaucer, very few facts are available about the man himself. What we know is gleaned from Chrétien's own prologues, which sometimes mention his other works and reveal his poetical ideas. He calls himself "Crestïens de Troies" in the prologue of his *Erec et Enide*, and most of his work was made in Troyes (some 100 miles to the east of Paris) around 1170–1180, at the court of the widowed countess of Champagne, Marie, the explicitly named patroness of Chrétien's Lancelot romance. The Chrétien manuscripts that have come down to us contain the texts of five romances, a few poems, and a shorter tale (*Philomena*, based on Ovid's *Metamorphoses*). He may have written more texts, since not all the titles that he mentions as his "past performance" in the *Cligés* prologue have survived. The five romances that were preserved are named after their protagonists and/or subject:

- *Erec et Enide* (Erec and his wife Enide find a balance in courtly love and chivalric responsibility)
- *Cligés* (true love conquers all for Cligés and Fénice, in a Greek/Arthurian setting)
- *Le chevalier de la charrette (Lancelot)* ('The Knight of the Cart'; Arthur's abducted queen is liberated by her lover Lancelot)
- *Le chevalier au lion (Yvain)* ('The Knight of the Lion'; with a rescued lion as his companion, Yvain finds a balance of knighthood and marital love)
- *Le conte du Graal (Perceval)* ('The Story of the Grail'; unfinished, the tale of the Grail and chivalry)

As discussed in the introduction to this part of the book (Chapter 7), Chrétien presents his stories not as new material, but as familiar *matière**, old and therefore good in the opinion of the medieval audience. In some form, the story of Erec and Enide already existed, yet

Chrétien claims he will tell it in a better way, because he provides "a beautifully ordered composition" (*une moult bele conjointure**), which the earlier, most probably oral*, versions/ performances* of the tale lacked.[7] For the Lancelot romance, his patroness Marie provided both the *matière* and what Chrétien calls the *san** ('meaning'): she told him what the story should be about and which lesson it was to present to the audience. Marie's requests, like count Philip's in the *Perceval* prologue, indicate that noble patrons saw Chrétien's stories as a means to an end, as a way to bring about cultural changes in courtly society by showing the audience models of ideal chivalric behaviour. Chrétien himself gives a similar message in his *Yvain* prologue: the would-be courtly lovers in his audience should take the lovers in Arthur's long-gone days as their examples.

For the first time in medieval vernacular literature, stories are credited with "agency" and this is even more remarkable since the stories are the first examples of what we now see as fiction*. Chrétien makes things up – he invents adventures and other plot* elements to bring the message of his tales across, even when he pretends to have used an old tale as his source (*Erec et Enide*) or to have used a book (*Cligés*; *Perceval*). Like his contemporary Marie de France, the author of beautiful short love stories* called *Lais**, Chrétien teaches his audience lessons in courtly behaviour by means of the hot new ideas about love, introduced by the troubadours* who in his time have travelled to the north of France and to French-speaking England (see Chapter 8). In the northern parts of France and in England, in the cultural and political sphere where the *langue d'oïl* and its variants (e.g. Anglo-Norman) were spoken, the literary concepts of *fin amor* and courtliness developed in new directions.

The so-called *trouvères* wrote love poetry* like the troubadours, but other literary forms became popular as well: short rhymed* tales (lais) and romances*, written in octosyllabic verse (verses consisting of eight [*octo-*] syllables). For these texts, a new story matter became popular: the *matière de Bretagne* now provided the heroes and adventures, where the *matière de France* had provided these for the *chansons de geste** (Charlemagne epics*) in the eleventh and twelfth centuries. Around 1136, a Welsh cleric called Geoffrey of Monmouth produced his Latin *History of the Kings of Britain* for the Anglo-Norman nobility, providing them with an illustrious predecessor: King Arthur. Arthur is the ideal king in this work, and his court excels in courtliness. Geoffrey's Latin text was soon translated* into Anglo-Norman verse by a poet named Wace, who offered his book in 1154 to the newly wedded queen of England, Eleanor of Aquitaine. Wace says of the courtly love* life at King Arthur's court:

> No knight, however highborn, even found love or had a courtly lady as lover, if he had not proven himself three times in chivalric endeavours. This made the knights more brave, and they did better in battle, and the ladies also were more courteous and lived more chastely.[8]

The connection between love and chivalric prowess, already made by Geoffrey and taken over by Wace, proved to be very influential in Arthurian romance: being in love makes a knight courageous, his deeds make him more desirable for his lady, her greater love makes him even more brave, and so on. Love has an ennobling effect: it makes a man a better knight and person. Chrétien's hero Erec, for instance, finds the extra fighting power he needs to defeat an opponent by looking at his beloved Enide, who is in tears for his sake as she watches him fight. In the *Prose Lancelot*, to be discussed in the second part of this chapter, the love for Queen Guinevere makes Lancelot the best knight in the world.

Love inspires. Quite often in Arthurian romance, as in the troubadour lyric*, the love relationship has no connection to marriage. The lady may well be married already – think of Queen Guinevere or Tristan's lover Isolde – but that does not preclude an affair. Chrétien's fellow author at the court of Champagne, chaplain Andreas, has explained in his *De amore libri tres* ('Three books about love') that love and marriage are two completely different things. Quite an understandable idea in a time of politically motivated marriages, when often the bride and groom were promised to each other at a very young age. The concept of courtly love thus did by no means preclude adultery, which makes Chrétien's position in these issues all the more remarkable. Apart from his Lancelot romance, which he did not finish himself and where the *matière* and *san* came from countess Marie, and his Perceval story, also left unfinished, Chrétien brings the lovers in his texts together in a "happy ever after" marriage. Erec and Enide, Cligés and Fénice, Yvain and Laudine all have to overcome many obstacles to find happiness, but they do so either as a married couple or with their marriage as the happy ending. The balance between individuality (whether in total dedication to love or to building a reputation as knight) and society is each time resolved in marriage, as the beloved wife keeps on inspiring the knight to do good deeds.

What the stories make clear time and again is how difficult it is to behave properly as a knight and lover. In Chrétien's romances, the heroes* are often placed in difficult situations and usually make serious mistakes, which take a lot of adventures, long quests, and good deeds to correct. He does not give a straightforward set of rules for courtly behaviour, but demonstrates how to do things by means of trial and error on the character's part. The texts pose questions (what should X do in this dilemma?) and then provide one or more possible answers. As in the scene of the hideous damsel and her accusations, the audience of these "problem romances" (as Douglas Kelly has called them) may, in the small groups of the reading-aloud sessions, have been invited to think about the questions and come up with possible solutions.[9] The pondering of alternatives invites discussion among the listeners, and that may well have been one of the charms of Chrétien's texts. The aforementioned mystification technique (*Verrätselung*) keeps the medieval listeners on their toes, just like we, as modern readers, in fact still are curious with regard to the question of what will happen to Perceval after the damsel's message.

What happens next?

As in the previous part, the analysis of the events in the story will precede a discussion of the developments in Chrétien's oeuvre and in the French and European literary context. In line with his mystification technique, Chrétien makes his listeners wait for news of Perceval, as he first describes Gawain's adventures. This splitting up of the narrative* into two separate narrative threads ("Gawain" and "Perceval") is an early example of 'interlace'* or *entrelacement*: several simultaneous storylines are followed by alternating the narration of sections of the different threads in such a way that the simultaneity is suggested, even though the events are narrated one after the other. The *Prose Lancelot* will take this technique, which is not unlike the storytelling in modern soap* series and fantasy* books, to a new level, interlacing the threads of up to twenty characters. In Chrétien's *Conte du Graal*, five years of Gawain adventures are described in some 1,500 lines before the story returns to Perceval who "had lost his memory so totally that he no longer remembered God."[10] His Godless-ness is soon remedied when he meets a hermit, who turns out to be his uncle and who knows exactly what happened when Perceval saw the Grail, which he calls a "sainte chose" ('holy object').[11] He explains that God withheld him from speaking in the Grail Castle because Perceval committed a severe sin: he left his mother for dead as he departed for King Arthur's court. Perceval feels extreme remorse – a flood of tears runs from his eyes down to his chin – and the hermit lays a regime of penance on him: he has to fast for two days and to learn a special, secret prayer. From now on, he must attend mass every day and behave as a Christian knight should, protect and help widows, orphans, and maidens, and so on. Truly repentant, Perceval receives communion the next Sunday, and then the tale shifts to Gawain again.

Chrétien's audience now knows why Perceval's Grail Castle visit was such a disaster, yet is left with the question of how the "new" Perceval will find the Grail. As far as Chrétien himself is concerned, this mystification* will remain unresolved, since after some more Gawain adventures, his tale breaks off. No more is said about Perceval, and the Gawain thread is also far from closure. When Chrétien left his Lancelot story unfinished, a second poet called Godefroi de Leigny stepped in and provided the happy ending. For the Grail story, the "gap" left by Chrétien also functioned as an invitation: over the next decades, four consecutive continuations were created, by four different poets. The anonymous *First Continuation* describes further Gawain adventures, whereas the *Second Continuation* by Wauchier de Denain returns to Perceval, yet stops before the Fisher King can describe the Grail mysteries. These wonders (the Grail contained Christ's blood; the Lance was used to pierce Christ's side on the Cross) are given in the *Third Continuation* by Manessier, who also describes how Perceval heals the Fisher King, becomes his successor and restores the Grail wasteland, until he retires to become a hermit, sustained only by the Grail. Upon his death, the Grail and Lance go with Perceval's soul to Heaven. In some manuscripts, an extra, fourth, continuation (made by Gerbert) is inserted between the second and third. Since each of these poets wrote at least 10,000 lines, the augmented story ends up being four to five times longer than Chretien's original.

The Grail story develops rapidly, in the previously described continuations, and also in new texts. Robert de Boron gives the Grail a far stronger religious* background by describing it as the dish of the Last Supper, that was later used by Joseph of Arimathea to collect the blood of Jesus after taking him down from the cross. As a blood relic, the Grail has mysterious healing and feeding powers. Joseph and his followers take the Grail into the desert and thence it comes to Britain. Around 1200, Robert used verse to write his *Joseph d'Arimathie* and *Merlin*, but almost immediately his works were put into prose and the prose versions became far more popular than the original texts. Around this time, the prologues of chronicles* and other works indicate that prose came to be considered more prestigious and truthful than verse*, since in verse the poet had to add words of his own to the straightforward narrative in order to create rhyming couplets*. Prose, the language of chronicles and the Bible, was considered a more suitable vehicle for serious topics like the Grail, so gradually the Grail prose texts come to eclipse the verse romances. Where before the so-called "*integumentum* argument" (that is: a fictional text may contain a deeper truth and therefore is worth telling) was a sufficient defence for the use of fiction in verse romances, the suggestion of veracity that the prose form brings to the fictitious tales now is considered the better option. The new prose narratives may look like chronicles, yet they are made up stories, just like Chrétien's romances. Fiction rules, even when it hides behind the mask of a "realistic"* chronicle.

Around 1220–1230, the champion of Old French prose romances is created: the so-called *Vulgate Cycle** or *Prose Lancelot Cycle*, of which over 200 manuscripts have come down to us, complete or in fragments. This five-book cycle starts off with the *History of* *the Holy Grail*, then describes how Arthur became king with the help of Merlin, and how Lancelot came to court and became the best knight in the world, inspired by his love for Queen Guinevere. He becomes the father of Galahad, the new, chaste Grail hero, who in this cycle replaces the perhaps not so chaste (Blancheflor!) Perceval and finds the Holy Grail in the *Quest of the Holy Grail*. When the Grail has left the earthly plane, this time with Galahad's soul, the end of Arthur's world soon comes, when the relationship between Lancelot and the queen is exposed. This leads to war and to Mordred's treason, and thus to a final battle in which Mordred, Arthur, and the knights of the Round Table are killed. Lancelot dies as a hermit and goes to Heaven.

As a separate story or enclosed in this huge "Arthurian history*" in prose, the Grail story soon becomes popular outside the French-speaking areas, as well. Chrétien wrote his romance for the Count of Flanders, whereas Manessier's *Third Continuation* was made for Countess Johanna of Flanders. In this region, French as well as Dutch (Flemish) was spoken, and one of the first Arthurian romances translated into Middle Dutch was Chrétien's *Perceval*. Of this translation, a few fragments and a special adaptation* have come down to us. Even more remarkable than this neighbourly cultural transfer* is the way three of Chrétien's romances travelled to Scandinavia in the first half of the thirteenth century.

Two men play important roles in this northward voyage: a king and a monk. The monk was called Brother Robert. His non-Scandinavian name indicates that he may have come from Britain or Normandy originally, which would also explain his ability to translate French romances into Old Norse. The king is Hákon Hákonarson, who ruled from 1217–1263. In 1226, Robert translated the story of Tristan and Isolde "at the behest and decree of King Hákon."[12] In the next decades, on the basis of Chrétien's last two romances, *Ívens saga** and *Parcevals saga* were also created, most probably by the same Robert or people in his circle, and for the same king and court. These works were followed by an adaptation of Chrétien's *Erec et Enide*. The story of Perceval actually is divided in two: in *Parcevals saga* the story is concluded after Perceval's meeting with the hermit, whereas *Valvens þáttr* ('Gawain's tale') presents Gawain's adventures as Chrétien describes them after the Perceval interlude.

The translator of *Parcevals saga* has closely followed his French source, so he must have worked on the basis of a manuscript, rather than on, for instance, his recollection of having heard the story told or read aloud. Although the prose form of the Scandinavian saga literature is used, at some points the rhyming couplets of Chrétien's text show through when the prose lines have internal rhyme. The text is much shorter (a reduction by 40 percent), but the storyline is the same. Episodes like Perceval's encounter with Gornemant (here: Gormanz) and his crash course in courtly chivalry are given in full, and much attention is given to the love theme. This indicates that the text provided the Scandinavian audience with role models of courtly behaviour. It functioned as a "mirror of knighthood" in King Hákon's plan to educate as well as entertain his courtiers. As a kind of *Bildungsroman** *avant la lettre*, Chrétien's story of young Perceval and his (amorous) adventures suits this purpose perfectly, since the audience learns what the hero learns as the tale unfolds. The best example of how the French texts functioned in the new context is found in *Ívens saga*, where the hero's companion, a lion he has saved from a serpent, is said to behave courteously and not to act like a berserker (the Scandinavian bearlike warriors, famous for their battle rage). Even the Arthurian animals are courtly examples, set against their uncouth Scandinavian counterparts.

There were some elements in the French text that the translator obviously struggled with. He added a prologue explaining why Parceval is living in the forest with his mother, thus undoing some of Chrétien's mystifications, and seems to have valued the courtly love between Parceval and Blankiflúr more than the Grail theme. Much attention is given to Parceval's correct and courteous behaviour towards Blankiflúr, whom he could have married, as the saga says, after defeating her enemies, but for his wish to see his mother again. Again, this fits well in the idea that King Hákon wanted the text to show his people how to do things courteously. The translator does mention the Lance and the Grail, albeit in a rather muddled way, and only very briefly speaks of the hideous damsel and her message. Although he tones down the tearfulness, he describes Parceval's remorse and repentance in the hermit episode. The hermit mentions Parceval's mother and explains how Parceval's sin of leaving her kept him from asking the proper questions, but does not reveal that she has died. Still, this episode seems to have been considered as some kind of closure, since after this *Parcevals saga* is wrapped up in a few lines: Parceval returns to Blankiflúr, marries her, and rules her territory as an ideal and victorious knight for ever after. The sudden, but happy, ending leaves the Grail and Lance unfound and Gawain/Valven's adventures unfinished. The continuation of the story in *Valvens þattr* breaks off at the same point as Chrétien's text. This indicates that the translator used a manuscript of just Chrétien's work, without any of the four continuations. How the manuscript (and those of the other translated French sources) came north is as yet unknown; perhaps the monk Robert brought them to King Hákon, after travelling to France or Britain?

With the stories, the new concepts of courtliness, new story matter, and new narrative scenarios travelled all over Europe. Via Latin and French texts, the legendary British King Arthur became part of the European cultural narrative, with all kinds of versions of his tale, based on Geoffrey of Monmouth, on Chrétien, on the *Prose Lancelot Cycle*, or on other sources, in almost every vernacular language. Images of Arthurian knights like Lancelot are found in castles as far east as Poland (Siedlecin Castle, southern Poland).[13] Arthur's court and knights reflect the contemporary ideals of civilization, and provide models for courtly behaviour and demonstrations of courage and compassion, of refined emotions, of loyalty and of dedication to love, or, as in the Grail stories, dedication to a religiously motivated kind of chivalry. Adventures and quests become stock motifs, that still are alive and kicking – for instance in role-playing games* and fantasy novels. The Holy Grail has become an omnipresent metaphor* for ultimate goals and ideals: on the internet, the Garnicia fruit may be labelled "the Holy Grail of weight loss" and a certain business model may be called "the Holy Grail of marketing", to give just two examples. Not quite what Perceval was looking for . . . yet the adaptability of the Arthurian material is the ultimate explanation for its enduring popularity.

Notes

1   Chrétien de Troyes, "The Story of the Grail (Perceval)," in *Arthurian Romances*, trans. William W. Kibler (Harmondsworth: Penguin, 1991), 437–8 (l. 4579 ff.). The line numbers for the original French text refer to Chrétien de Troyes, "'Le Conte du Graal' or 'Le Roman de Perceval," in *Romans*, ed., trans. Charles Mela, according to the manuscript Berne 354 (Paris: Pochotèque, 1994), 937–1211.
2   Erich Auerbach, *Mimesis: The Representaion of Reality in Western Literature*, trans. from the German by Willard Trask (Princeton, NJ and Oxford: Princeton University Press, 1957), 119.
3   Chrétien de Troyes, "The Story of the Grail (Perceval)," 420.
4   Chrétien de Troyes, "The Story of the Grail (Perceval)," 421.
5   Walter Haug, *Das Land, von welchem niemand wiederkehrt* (Tübingen: Max Niemeyer Verlag, 1978), 45.
6   Chrétien de Troyes, "Le Conte du Graal," ed. Méla, ll. 64–5; Chrétien de Troyes, "The Story of the Grail (Perceval)," trans. Kibler, 382.

7 Chrétien de Troyes, *Erec et Enide*, ed. Méla l. 14; trans. Carleton Carroll in *Arthurian Romances* (Harmondsworth: Penguin, 1991), (cf. note 1), 37.

8 Wace, *La partie arthurienne du Roman de Brut*, ed. Ivor Arnold and Margaret Pelan (Paris: Klincksieck, 1962), ll. 1965–74; translation FB.

9 Douglas Kelly, "Chrétien de Troyes," in *The Arthur of the French*, ed. Glynn Burgess and Karen Pratt (Cardiff: University of Wales Press, 2006), 135–85, quote 144.

10 Chrétien de Troyes, "The Story of the Grail (Perceval)," trans. Kibler, 457.

11 Chrétien de Troyes, "Le Conte du Graal," ed. Méla, l. 6351; Chrétien de Troyes, "The Story of the Grail (Perceval)," trans. Kibler, 460.

12 For the section on the Scandinavian versions, see Geraldine Barnes, "The Tristan Legend," (quote on p. 61) and Claudia Bornholdt, "The Old Norse-Icelandic Transmission of Chrétien de Troyes's Romances: *Ívens Saga*, *Erex Saga*, *Parcevals Saga* With *Valvens þáttr*,", both in *The Arthur of the North: The Arthurian Legend in the Norse and Rus' Realms*, ed. Marianne E. Kalinke (Cardiff: University of Wales Press, 2011), 61–76 and 98–122.

13 Przemyslaw Nocun, "Wall Paintings in Siedlecin Castle, Poland. Fourteenth-Century Pictoral Representations of Lancelot's Story," *Bibliographical Bulletin of the Arthurian Society* LVI (2004): 403–22.

Further reading

Archibald, Elisabeth and Ad Putter, eds. *The Cambridge Companion to the Arthurian Legend*. Cambridge: Cambridge University Press, 2009.

Barber, Richard. *The Holy Grail: Imagination and Belief*. Cambridge, MA: Harvard University Press, 2004.

Burgess, Glynn and Karen Pratt, eds. *The Arthur of the French: The Arthurian Legend in Medieval French and Occitan Literature*. Cardiff: University of Wales Press, 2006.

Haug, Walter. *Vernacular Literary Theory in the Middle Ages: The German Tradition, 800–1300, in Its European Context*. Translated by Joanna M. Catling. Cambridge: Cambridge University Press, 2006.

Rikhardsdottir, Sif and Stefka G. Eriksen. "État présent: Arthurian Literature in the North." *Journal of the International Arthurian Society* 1 (2013): 3–28.

10 Reaching salvation

Roberto Rea

Figure 10.1 Michelino, Domenico de, "La Commedia Illumina Firenze" (portrait of Dante, in the background Florence and Purgatory), 1465, Santa Maria del Fiore, Florence

Source: Centre Art Historical Documentation, Radboud University.

Text: Dante Alighieri, Commedia *('The Divine Comedy') (1321),* Inferno
('Hell'), canto 1, ll. 1–60

Midway along the journey of our life
I woke to find myself in a dark wood,
for I had wandered off from the straight path.

How hard it is to tell what it was like,
this wood of wilderness, savage and stubborn
(the thought of it brings back all my old fears),

a bitter place! Death could scarce be bitterer.
But if I would show the good that came of it
I must talk about things other than the good.

How I entered there I cannot truly say,
I had become so sleepy at the moment
when I first strayed, leaving the path of truth;

but when I found myself at the foot of a hill,
at the edge of the wood's beginning, down in the valley,
where I first felt my heart plunged deep in fear,

I raised my head and saw the hilltop shawled
in morning rays of light send from the planet
that leads men straight ahead on every road.

And then only did terror start subsiding
in my heart's lake, which rose to heights of fear
that night I spent in deepest desperation.

Just as a swimmer, still with panting breath,
now safe upon the shore, out of the deep,
might turn for one last look at the dangerous waters,

so I, although my mind was turned to flee,
turned round to gaze once more upon the pass
that never let a living soul escape.

I rested my tired body there awhile
and then began to climb the barren slope
(I dragged my stronger foot and limped along).

Beyond the point the slope begins to rise
sprang up a leopard, trim and very swift!
It was covered by a pelt of many spots.

And, everywhere I looked, the beast was there
blocking my way, so time and time again
I was about to turn and go back down.

The hour was early in the morning then,
the sun was climbing up with those same stars
that had accompanied it on the world's first day,

the day the Divine Love set the beauty turning;
so the hour and sweet season of creation
encouraged me to think I could get past

that gaudy beast, wild in its spotted pelt,
but then good hope gave way and fear returned
when the figure of a lion loomed up before me,

and he was coming straight toward me, it seemed,
with head raised high, and furious with hunger
the air around him seemed to fear his presence.

And now a she-wolf came, that in her leanness
seemed racked with every kind of greediness
(how many people she has brought to grief!).

This last beast brought my spirit down so low
with fear that seized me at the sight of her,
I lost all hope of going up the hill.

As a man who, rejoicing in his gains,
suddenly seeing his gain turn into loss,
will grieve as he compares his then and now

so she made me do, that relentless beast;
coming towards me, slowly, step by step,
she forced me back to where the sun is mute.[1]

In this world-famous opening passage of the *Comedy*, Dante, who is the author and the protagonist of the poem, describes the beginning of his otherworldly journey. "Midway in the
journey of his life," when he was thirty-five years old, Dante finds himself in a "dark wood",
after having lost the "straight path" (lines 1–12). In the grip of anxiety, he sees the top of a
hill illuminated by the sun, in which he recognizes a chance of salvation (13–30). But his
ascent is obstructed by three beasts: a leopard, a lion, and a she-wolf. The latter prevents him
from going up any further and sends him back into the darkness of the valley (31–60). In
what follows, we learn that Dante will be rescued by Virgil, the ancient Roman poet, who
will tell him that he needs to undertake a journey through the otherworldly realms.

The text might be disorienting for the reader, as it is not entirely clear whether what Dante
presents here is the description of a real experience or a mystical vision. At line 11, Dante
says that he felt "so sleepy" when he entered the wood. It remains to be seen if this is, metaphorically*, the sleep of reason, as modern commentators* think, or that Dante was actually
sleeping, as some medieval commentators thought. In the latter case, the voyage would be a
*visio in somnis**, 'a truthful dream'. Despite the direct style of writing, which makes the text
still enjoyable for modern readers and helps to draw us into the experience of the I-narra-
tor*, the description of the landscape lacks concreteness, as it is brought back to essentials
and evanescent elements: a forest, a hill, darkness, light, the three beasts. Spatial and temporal
coordinates, as well as information about Dante's situation, are minimal. To understand this
scene we have to grasp its symbolic meanings in contemporary religious* culture. The forest stands for the condition of bewilderment in sin; the "straight path" is that of Christ; the
illuminated hill is an image of salvation, the happiness towards which we should strive; the
three beasts blocking the way represent the three diabolical temptations that threaten mankind: lust, pride, and cupidity; the poet Virgil represents human reason. In this opening scene,

the symbolical dimension can be seen to prevail over the literal and "realistic"* level, almost jeopardizing it. In the eyes of the medieval reader, the scene would appear full of meaning, much more than it may appear to us. Dante's narration is in fact rich in allusions* and inter-textual* references to the Bible and classical literature. These references convey to the reader basic meanings and models for the interpretation of the work. The image of the dark wood, for instance, comes from Augustine's *Confessions*, where "this immense forest full of dangers" is mentioned.[2] That of the "straight path" draws on the *Gospel* of John*, where Christ says "I am the way, the truth, and the life."[3] The three beasts recall the three beasts sent by God to punish men in the *Book of Jeremiah*: "a lion out of the forest shall slay them, [and] a wolf of the evenings shall spoil them, a leopard shall watch over their cities,"[4] and also refer to the three worldly vices damned in the *Letters* of John*: "For all that [is] in the world, the lust of the flesh, and the lust of the eyes, and the pride of life."[5] These and other biblical references enable the medieval reader to recognize Dante's text as prophetic.

Structure and meaning of the *Comedy*

The *Comedy*, written roughly between 1307 and 1321 (the year of Dante's death), is the tale* of an extraordinary experience: a voyage by the living human protagonist Dante in the afterworld, from Hell through Purgatory to Heaven. The 14,233 lines of the poem present a symbolic structure based on the number three. It is divided into three parts: *Inferno* ('Hell', 1 + 33 cantos), *Purgatorio* ('Purgatory', 33 cantos), and *Paradiso* ('Heaven', 33 cantos). If we consider that the first canto* of *Inferno* works as a prologue to the entire poem, every part devoted to a region of the afterworld has 33 cantos (a multiple of three, the symbolic number of the Holy Trinity). The poem is composed of verses in *terza rima**, an interlocking three-line rhyme* scheme: aba, bcb, cdc, ded, etc. It is called *Commedia* because the story starts badly (Dante has fallen into sin) and ends well (he achieves salvation), which, according to classical rhetoric*, was a typical feature of the genre of comedy*. This established genre also allowed Dante to use a multiform instead of a highly stylised* language. The poem's main theme, however, goes far beyond the merely literary or aesthetic*. Based on the moral and historical experience of the protagonist, the poem aims to spread a universal message.

This universal meaning is expressed by means of allegory*, a very common technique in medieval culture. It consists in recognizing "other" meanings than those expressed by the letter of the text. In this way the Scriptures were interpreted as well as the events of one's everyday life: the world had an allegorical meaning that a faithful person had to recognize in order to understand the signs of God's will. Dante believed that his mission, like that of the biblical prophets, was to offer his testimony to all Christians, showing them, through the letter of his text and its powerful allegories, the way to restore moral and political order in a world full of strife and disorder, and to reach salvation, the unique and perfect fulfilment of human life. What the *Comedy* offers, however, is not an exemplary life but the representation of a unique personal experience. All Dante's previous works are characterized by this unusual autobiographical* element. By featuring his personal experience, Dante innovates vernacular literature in this period and paves the way for many important authors, including Chaucer and Christine de Pizan (see Chapter 11 and Chapter 12).

Dante before the *Comedy:* the autobiographical element

Dante begins his career as a lyric poet. Love poetry*, from its courtly* origins (see Chapter 8), is in itself a subjective genre: speaking in the first person*, the poet declares his love for a lady. Nevertheless, troubadour poetry* has a level of linguistic and thematic codification so high that, with few exceptions, the individuality of the poet tends to become formalized in a sort of impersonal Self (a *persona**, as the next chapter will explain, see also Chapter 3), quite remote from his historical identity. Despite the strong awareness of their role and the constant claims of sincerity, courtly poets* perform a limited number of codified motifs*, leaving in the background their biographical* experience. In the context of Florence at the end of the thirteenth century, Dante's poetry, like that of his friend and master Guido Cavalcanti (1250–1300), overcomes this courtly, troubadour model by focusing on new spiritual and intellectual values.[6] Dante, from the beginning of his career, turns out to be a poet of outstanding personality and autobiographical vocation. In his first sonnet*, *A ciascun alma presa e gentil core* ('To every captive soul and noble heart'), written when he was eighteen, he invites the most famous troubadours* of the time to interpret his love dream*. In so doing, he establishes a circle of poet friends, lending his lyric persona a strong social consistency.[7] Even more surprising is the self-confidence with which Dante assigns objective values and meaning to his personal experiences. In the song *E' m'incresce di me sì duramente* ('I feel such deep compassion for myself'), he explains how on the day when his beloved Beatrice was born, he, as an infant, suffered a shock, a sort of epileptic seizure, which he interprets as the objective sign of predestination for his love for Beatrice.

This autobiographical trend reaches its fulfilment in the *Vita nuova* ('The new life'). In this narration in prose, Dante inserts and reinterprets his early poems. He reconstructs the story of his love for Beatrice, from their first meeting to her early death at the age of twenty-four, up to the acknowledgment of her heavenly nature, which he sees as the discovery of a new life. His memories, as he presented them in the fragmentary format of lyric poetry*, are in the *Vita nuova* reinterpreted into a coherent story and enriched with an overall meaning. Unlike Petrarch (1304–1374) in his *Canzoniere* ('Songbook'), which will become the reference model for European lyric poetry of the following centuries, Dante in the *Vita nuova* does not tell an exemplary story so that every man can identify himself with the poet, but he describes the exceptional experience of his love for Beatrice. Such a sublimation of Beatrice implies also the celebration of Dante himself as a poet. His innovation* is both spiritual and artistic. The discovery of *love-caritas*, an unselfish and spiritual love, which replaces the topical *love-passion* of lyric poetry, leads him to the creation of a new idea of poetry, focused not on the request for a love reward or on complaints of his own pain, but on the disinterested praise of the beloved.[8]

After the *Vita nuova* and before dedicating himself to the *Comedy*, Dante begins to compose two treatises, which will remain unfinished. His *De vulgari eloquentia* ('On Eloquence in the vernacular') promotes writing in the vernacular, at a time when the use of Latin was still widespread. In the *Convivio* ('The Banquet'), Dante approaches philosophical and moral topics starting from the interpretation of his own songs. These works belong to a tradition* and a genre that do not usually have an autobiographical dimension. Yet again Dante adopts an autobiographical perspective. In *De vulgari eloquentia*, he makes continual reference to his poems and to himself as a poet. In the *Convivio* the frame story is autobiographical.

Dante became a famous poet and influential figure in his hometown Florence, and he was deeply involved in its political struggles, in the context of the larger Italian, and even European, conflict between the emperor and the pope, who also claimed worldly power. In 1302, when his party lost power, he was exiled from Florence and never returned to his city. The historical and political passion that runs through the *Comedy* reflects the indignation of an *exul inmeritus*, a 'guiltless exile', as Dante considered himself. The *Inferno* presents a number of his political opponents, as well as corrupt popes and emperors, receiving their punishment in the afterlife in Hell.

Models for the *Comedy* as a journey to salvation

In the second canto of the *Inferno*, Dante is about to descend into the abyss of Hell when he shares his feelings of anxiety with his guide Virgil. Dante does not consider himself worthy of such an undertaking. Up to then only a few men have had the privilege of visiting the world of the dead while alive: among them a hero, Aeneas, and a saint, Paul ("But why am I to go? Who allows me to?/I am not Aeneas, I am not Paul,/neither I nor any man would think me worthy").[9] Notwithstanding the apparent modesty, Dante is placing himself on the same level as his predecessors, by taking over their historical and spiritual mission. He wants to be both the "new Aeneas" and the "new Paul".

The *Aeneid* (see Chapter 1) is the most active model for the *Comedy*. Its author, Virgil, is chosen as a guide to Hell and Purgatory and called *saggio* 'wise', *maestro* 'master', *duca* 'leader', and finally, when he takes his leave, *dolcissimo padre* 'most sweet father'. The *Aeneid* is a model that works on different levels. As a literary masterpiece, it provides endless inspiration for Dante's poetic* imagery. Many demons (such as Charon, Cerberus, Geryon, the Harpies) and various elements of the geography* of the underworld (e.g. the rivers Styx, Acheron, Cocytus) come from Book VI of the *Aeneid*, which describes Aeneas's descent into Hades. In addition, Dante draws from the *Aeneid* countless, more or less explicit, citations. To give one example: when he sees Beatrice on the top of Purgatory, Dante pronounces the words uttered by Dido at the sight of Aeneas with whom she instantly fell in love: "I recognize signs of the ancient flame."[10] Finally, the *Aeneid*, which describes the foundation of Rome and celebrates the empire of Augustus, assumes a precise historical and political meaning for an exile like Dante, who feels the urgent need for a new empire to renew the moral, social, and political order in Christendom. In short, Dante considered the *Aeneid*, as well as his *Comedy*, a sacred poem.

Dante's mention of St Paul, already given above, refers to the *Second Epistle to the Corinthians*, where the Apostle says that he was abducted to Heaven. Dante likely also has in mind the *Visio Pauli* ('The Vision of Paul'), an apocryphal text in which the saint visits Hell, where souls are punished in accordance with their sins, and then comes to Eden and attends a sacred procession of patriarchs and prophets. Another *visio** that Dante may have known is that of the monk Alberico from Montecassino (first half of the twelfth century), where the protagonist travels to the afterlife guided by St Peter. These works are part of a religiuos tradition of visionary texts* that spread particularly in the twelfth and thirteenth centuries. Another kind of visions, which had didactic or purely literary purposes, were those of allegorical poems. In these poems, the protagonist narrates in the first person an allegorical journey as a dream or fantasy. The most famous example of such a dream allegory is the French *Roman de la Rose* ('Romance* of the Rose'). Another influential work is the *Tesoretto* ('Treasury'), by Dante's master Brunetto Latini, who also begins his allegorical journey after being lost in a forest.

The medieval philosophical* tradition also was an important source for the *Comedy*. Not only does Dante work out the hierarchy of sins and merits, he deals with all the fundamental issues related to salvation: the role of grace and free will, the nature of the human soul, and the limits of rational knowledge. Like the medieval philosophers, such as Albertus Magnus and Thomas Aquinas, Dante seeks to integrate, on a rational basis, the Christian conceptions with the ideas of the ancient Greek philosopher Aristotle, who at this time was considered the greatest philosophical authority.

Overall, the *Comedy* goes far beyond the Latin *visiones* and the vernacular poems, far beyond the emulation* of the classical epics*, and far beyond the speculations* of philosophical treatises. Dante sets out to create a sacred poem that reproduces the salvific message of the Scriptures by adopting a similar sort of "polysemy"*: the multiplicity of meanings from the letter of the text to all kinds of allegorical meanings. Dante's synthesis appears as an unprecedented novelty, with a message of salvation that comes across the more strongly since it is personal as well as universal.

Dante as protagonist and narrator

From the outset, it is important to differentiate between the author Dante and the character Dante in the *Comedy*. The first is the poet, who describes as an omniscient narrator* his journey in hindsight. The second is the protagonist, the *viator* ('traveller'), whose perspective is entirely internal to the story and changes with the development of the narration. This distinction is very useful to modern criticism*, but it would have been unacceptable for Dante himself, who in the poem strives to consolidate his identity with that of the protagonist to affirm the idea that he really experienced what he describes.

Unlike Aeneas, the protagonist of the *Comedy* is not a classical hero* but a Christian self, who tells in the first person his own story. As a description of an inner experience, the great precedent is Augustine, whose *Confessions* were the archetype of every Christian autobiography. The *Confessions* tell a story about moral failing and ultimate conversion as actually experienced by the protagonist. As such the story is charged with a strong exemplary value for the reader. Augustine is in fact mentioned in Dante's *Convivio* to justify the intention of talking of himself, which was allowed to a medieval author only when it was "extremely useful to others because of doctrine."[11]

The autobiographical dimension is invoked right from the first verse (*"I* woke to find *myself"*) and figures and facts belonging to Dante's biography are part and parcel of the story. The privilege of visiting alive the otherworldly realms is granted thanks to the woman he loved, Beatrice, whom Dante believes to be blessed in the Heaven of the Virgin Mary. She leads him through Paradise, after having obtained a full confession of the sinful life Dante led after her death. Among the souls encountered along the way, there are many friends, fellow citizens, and political rivals. Examples are master Brunetto, in front of whom Dante is not able to hide his emotions, although Brunetto is damned among the sodomites[12]; the musician Casella, who sings, as he used to do in life, a song composed by Dante himself[13]; Farinata degli Uberti, famous leader of the political faction Dante opposed; and the father of his friend Guido, Cavalcante Cavalcanti, who desperately asks for news about his son.[14] The poem includes precise references to Dante's life, from the prophecy of his exile[15] to the memory of his participation in a battle[16] and other minor anecdotes. The exile's controversial feelings for Florence are present throughout the poem: he misses the "sweet fold" of his childhood and curses the city fiercely for its present corruption and decadence.

The otherworldly journey is inevitably also a literary journey, and not only for the intense use of intertextual references. Dante meets the souls of many poets. In the area called Limbo (the first circle of Hell, where the unbaptized and the virtuous pagans are found), among the "mighty shades", he presents himself explicitly as a successor of five great classical poets (Homer, Virgil, Horace, Ovid, and Lucan), calling himself "sixth among such minds."[17] Moreover, Dante does not forget his beginnings as a love poet. In the afterlife, he speaks with other vernacular poets, like Bonagiunta Lucca, Guido Guinizzelli, and Arnaut Daniel.[18]

The autobiographical component plays a key role in the search for salvation. Although scholars often tend to neglect this aspect, the *Comedy* enacts a story of salvation based on an individual biography*. Thus, for example, as was quite clear to medieval commentators, the three beasts that Dante meets in the first canto represent his own sins as well as the three great vices of mankind. The emotions, like fear, pain, or pity, which Dante experiences in front of some sinners in Hell and Purgatory, reflect his inner feelings and reveal his personal need for expiation. So, Dante's often discussed compassion for some damned souls, such as those of the lustful Paolo and Francesca in the fifth canto of the *Inferno*, expresses his sense of remorse and contrition for having fallen into the same vice.

It all begins with the fear experienced in the forest. For Dante, narrating his extraordinary experience means, first of all, reliving that anguish (see lines 4–6). Dante does not remember anything else of the bewilderment in the forest: he does not say how he got there, nor how he came out. He insists instead on his terrible fear, how it tormented his heart (14–15); how, once outside, it was a little calmed by the sight of a hill (17–19); how it was still alive when looking at the danger he just escaped (23–5); how a new invincible fear was aroused by the sight of the three beasts (44–54). It can be said that in the opening scene the action of the protagonist, who will speak his first words only at line 65, consists only of his reactions to fear. Fear lends truthfulness to Dante's story by obliterating the distance between Dante the character and Dante the narrator, who claims to relive that anguish. Fear, like every element of the prologue scene, has a precise moral meaning. It evokes a basic notion of the theology of repentance: the so-called *compunctio timoris*, 'the compunction of fear', quoted by Dante in the image of his heart "compunto di paura" ("plunged deep in fear"; 15), which, according to Christian philosophers, is the starting point of the redemption of a believer.

Dante as a prophet

Scholars like Charles Singleton have recognized that Dante the character is "Everyman": every man, as a sinner, can recognize himself in the protagonist.[19] But this perspective is not entirely correct. Unlike Petrarch, who in the *Secretum* ('My Secret Book') and in the *Canzoniere* ('Songbook'), by representing his own story of backsliding and salvation, explicitly proposes himself as a model for the reader, Dante in the *Comedy* does not require a real identification. As already in the *Vita Nuova*, Dante presents his experience as unique and unrepeatable. His mission is to transmit to mankind what he has seen, so that every human being can find his or her own way to reach salvation.

We do not know if Dante really considered himself a prophetic* spirit, but it is undeniable that he assumes a prophetic attitude. Besides numerous prophecies *post eventum*, i.e. regarding biographical or historical events that had already occurred at the time of the composition of the poem, Dante formulates enigmatic prophecies on the advent of a "Greyhound"[20] and of a "Five Hundred, Ten, and Five,"[21] which will come in a near future as redemption for mankind that has fallen into sin. But, above all, in a series of crucial meetings, Dante presents himself as invested with a prophetic mission. Beatrice, his ancestor Cacciaguida, and finally St Peter in Heaven urge him to reveal his salvific vision to the corrupt world. It is difficult to say to what extent Dante believed this himself, but it is certain that, as it has been observed by Giorgio Padoan:

> [A] Christian, and not only from the fourteenth century, who has Alighieri's deep and sincere faith, does not gamble away his soul by declaring that St Peter ordered him to report his words to the men (and what words!) just to make "poetry."[22]

For this reason, Dante considered his *Comedy* not a *fictio*, a 'literary fiction*', but a *visio*, a 'truthful vision'. This possibility is less remote than it may seem. In the Middle Ages, truthful imaginations, dreams, visions, and mystical experiences in the waking state were accepted as truthful, not only in religious culture but also in the philosophical tradition.

In sum, it is not unlikely that Dante considered his words to be inspired by the Holy Spirit, like those of the biblical prophets. Just like he says in *Purgatory*, where, questioned about his experience as a vernacular poet, he declares that he only writes down what the God of Love dictates in his heart.[23] Guido da Pisa, a medieval commentator, said: "Dante was the pen of the Holy Spirit, by whose pen the Spirit describes the pains of the damned and the glory of the blessed."[24] After all, Dante himself claims a divine involvement in his creative act when he speaks of his "sacred poem/to which both Heaven and Earth have set their hand."[25]

The *Comedy*'s popularity in later times

All of these levels of meaning, transmitted by a linguistic and literary construction without precedent, explain the success of the *Comedy* in the Middle Ages, but there is one feature which, more than any other, explains its success in ages distant from medieval culture, including the present one. It is the human and down-to-earth nature of Dante's representation. Despite their function as *exempla**, Dante's characters, unlike the personifications* of medieval poetry, are humanly alive. In a place without time and actual presence, thanks to an outstanding realism, the shadows in the hereafter retain their full historical individuality as human beings of flesh and blood. Such as they were at the height of their lives, so they are forever fixed in death, as the blasphemer Capaneus says to Dante: "What I was once, alive, I still am, dead."[26] Their earthly life is a *figura*, a 'prefiguration' of their otherworldly condition. By describing the "status of souls after-death," Dante also describes the world of the living, a great representation of humanity, with its passions, dilemmas, and errors.

In Italy, Dante's *Comedy* became immediately extremely popular. Almost eight hundred manuscripts* have come down to us, and the book was among the first texts produced on the printing press* (after Gutenberg's Bible): in 1472, Johann Neumeister produced the first printed edition of Dante's *Comedy* in the city of Foligno. In France and Spain, Dante's work is already well known in the fourteenth and fifteenth century. In England, after Chaucer, it was rediscovered in the seventeenth century, especially thanks to the poet John Milton. But it is in the eighteenth and nineteenth century that Dante becomes a "European" and even "world" author, when translations* appear all over Europe and in the United States. In 1865, the American poet Henry Wadsworth Longfellow set up the Dante Club in Harvard, with the purpose of discussing his translation of the *Comedy* with fellow poets. Even today many important American universities* offer courses entirely dedicated to the work of Dante. The *Comedy* also strongly influenced some of the most important poets of the twentieth century, such as Ezra Pound and T.S. Eliot.

Today the figure and work of Dante continues to fascinate, also in popular culture. Just think of the twelve million viewers who watched the lecture of the last canto of Paradise by the actor and director Roberto Benigni on Italian television, not to mention the many novels, movies, and videogames that, in a more or less imaginative way, appeal to Dante's extraordinary representation of the afterlife.

Notes

1 Dante Alighieri, *The Divine Comedy, I: Inferno*, trans. Mark Musa (New York: Penguin Books, 2003), 67–9.
2 Augustine, *Confessions* (Book 10, section 35).

3 *Gospel of John* (14:6).
4 *Book of Jeremiah* (5:6).
5 *Letters of John* (2:16).
6 Guido Cavalcanti, *Rime*, ed. Roberto Rea and Giorgio Inglese (Rome: Carocci, 2011).
7 Modern criticism refers to this circle of friends and poets, which includes Guido Cavalcanti, Lapo Gianni, Cino da Pistoia, and other followers, by the name "*stilnovisti*", on the basis of the definition of "*dolce stil novo*" ('sweet new style') given by the same Dante in *Purgatory* canto 24. About Dante's poetry see *Dante's Lyric Poetry: Poems of Youth and of the* "Vita Nuova", ed. Teodolinda Barolini, with new verse translations by Richard Lansing (Toronto/Buffalo, NY/London: University of Toronto Press, 2014).
8 See Pirovano's introduction to Dante Alighieri, *Vita nuova e Rime*, ed. Donato Pirovano and Marco Grimaldi, vol. I (Rome: Salerno Editrice, 2015).
9 Alighieri, *Inferno*, canto 2, lines 31–3.
10 Alighieri, *Purgatory*, canto 30, l. 48; cf. *Aeneis*, 4.48 "Adgnosco veteris vestiges flammae,"
11 Alighieri, *Convivio*, I, ii, 14.
12 Alighieri, *Inferno*, canto 15.
13 Alighieri, *Purgatory*, canto 2.
14 Alighieri, *Inferno*, canto 10.
15 Alighieri, *Inferno*, canto 10.
16 Alighieri, *Inferno*, canto 21.
17 Alighieri, *Inferno*, canto 4, l. 102.
18 Alighieri, *Purgatory*, cantos 24 and 26.
19 This famous definition was formulated in Charles S. Singleton, *Commedia: Elements of Structure* (Cambridge, MA: Harvard University Press, 1957).
20 Alighieri, *Inferno*, canto 1, l. 101.
21 Alighieri, *Purgatory*, canto 33, l. 43.
22 See Giorgio Padoan, *Introduzione a Dante* (Firenze: Sansoni, 1975).
23 Alighieri, *Purgatory*, canto 24.
24 Pisa, Guido da. *Expositiones et Glose super Comediam Dantis, or Commentary on Dante's Inferno. Edited with Notes and an Introduction by Vincenzo Cioffari*. Albany, N.Y., State University of New York Press, 1974.
25 Alighieri, *Paradise*, canto 25, l. 1–2.
26 Alighieri, *Inferno*, canto 14, l. 50.

Further reading

Alighieri, Dante. *Commedia*. Edited by A. Chiavacci-Leonardi. Bologna: Zanichelli, 2001.

Alighieri, Dante. *The Divine Comedy of Dante Alighieri*. Edited and Translated by Robert Durling, introduction and notes by Ronald Martinez. Oxford: Oxford University Press, 2001.

Barolini, Teodolinda. *Dante and the Origins of Italian Literary Culture*. New York: Fordham University Press, 2006.

Jakoff, Rachel, ed. *The Cambridge Companion to Dante*. Cambridge: Cambridge University Press, 1997.

Commentaries and translations of Dante's *Comedy* are available at http://dantelab.dartmouth.edu/reader

A full bibliography is available at http://dantesca.ntc.it/dnt-fo-catalog/pages/material-search.jsf

11 Telling tales

Erik Kooper

Figure 11.1 Chaucer, Geoffrey, *The Canterbury Tales*, "The Miller", 1400–1425, Huntington Library, San Marino, California, EL 26 C 9 "Ellesmere Chaucer", f.34v

Source: Centre Art Historical Documentation, Radboud University.

Although unfinished, Geoffrey Chaucer's *Canterbury Tales* is one of the most famous texts of the Middle Ages. Set in the framework of a pilgrimage, the "tales"* are told by the characters that accompany the narrator on his way to Canterbury, like the slightly drunken miller.

Text: Geoffrey Chaucer, Canterbury Tales *(1390–95), "The Miller's Prologue"*

Here follows the argument between the Host and the Miller:

And when at last the knight's tale had been told,
There was not one among us, young or old,   3110
Who did not say it was a noble story,
Well worth remembering; especially
All of the better sort. Laughing, our host
Swore, "As I live, we're now on the right track!
A good beginning; we've unstrapped the pack.
And now let's see who'll tell another tale,
For there's no doubt the game is well begun.
Now tell me, Mister Monk, that's if you can,
Something to cap the knight's, and pay him out."
The miller, half-seas over, was so pale   3120
With drink that he could barely keep his seat
Upon his horse; his manners were quite lost,
He'd not doff hood nor hat, and wouldn't wait,
But, ranting like a Pilate on the stage,
Began to swear: "Christ's arms and blood and bones,
I've got a splendid tale for the occasion
To pay the knight out with, and cap his tale."
Our host could see that he was drunk with ale,
And said, "Hold hard, Robin! Watch it, brother!
Some better man must first tell us another,   3130
So pipe down now; let's make a go of it."
"By all that's holy, that I won't," said he,
"I mean to speak, or I'll be on my way."
Answered our host, "In Satan's name, say on!
You're nothing but a fool, your wits are drowned."
"Now listen,' said the miller, 'one and all!
But first I make a public avowal
That I am drunk; I can tell by the sound."   3138
. . .
In short, the miller would not curb his tongue   3166
Or language for the sake of anyone,
But told his vulgar tale in his own way.
I'm sorry that I must repeat it here.
And therefore, I entreat all decent folk   3170
For God's sake don't imagine that I speak
With any evil motive, but because
I'm bound to tell, for better or for worse,
All of their stories, or else falsify
My subject-matter as you have it here;

And so, should anyone not wish to hear,
Turn the page over, choose another tale.
There's plenty of all kinds, to please you all:
True tales that touch on manners and on morals,
As well as piety and saintliness;   3180
I'm not responsible if you choose amiss.[1]

At the crack of dawn one morning in the early spring a group of pilgrims make ready to begin their journey to Canterbury, where they will visit the shrine of England's most popular saint, Thomas Becket. They have met the night before, and at the instigation of Harry Bailey, the host of their inn, they have decided to travel together.

Who are these people that we meet with here? The text in which they make their appearance is the *Canterbury Tales*, written towards the end of the fourteenth century by Geoffrey Chaucer. In its opening lines we have heard how the day before the narrator*, Chaucer himself, arrived at "The Tabard", an inn on the south bank of the Thames and a well-known London starting point for a pilgrimage to Canterbury. In the inn he soon gets acquainted with a number of other guests, all with the same intention, and they decide to make the pilgrimage together. The narrator continues with a detailed presentation of practically all the pilgrims, describing their outward appearance, their good and bad habits, their social status and often even their horses.

When the evening draws to an end, the Host of the inn, Harry Bailey, who has been watching them with pleasure, addresses the group: "The road to Canterbury is long," he says, "and without much comfort or distraction."[2] He therefore proposes a game to shorten the time: each of them should tell two stories on the way to Canterbury, and two on the way back. And then Harry shows to be a keen businessman: he himself will join the group and act as their referee, and upon their return the winner will have a free meal at his inn, at the expense of the others. And anyone who disagrees with his decisions, he adds in a jocular manner, will have to pay for whatever they spend on the road. The next morning it soon appears that he takes this role seriously, for he invites all the pilgrims to gather around him, so that they can draw straws to decide who will tell the first tale. And, as the text says, "whether it was luck, or chance, or fate/The truth is the lot fell to the knight,/Much to the content of the company."[3]

The Knight starts the game with a rather drawn-out romance* about two young noblemen in love with the same lady, and when he has concluded it he is praised by all, and in particular by the members of the gentry (see the opening quotation). But when the Host invites the Monk to take the next turn, something unexpected happens, both for the pilgrims themselves and for us, Chaucer's readers and listeners. The Miller protests loudly and in plain terms that the story of the Knight has nothing to do with real life, and in spite of the initial objections of the Host he insists that he will tell a tale about a carpenter and his pretty young wife, and how the old man was cuckolded by a young student. Before he begins his tale the Miller himself as well as the narrator give out some explicit warnings: that the Miller is drunk and that the subject of his tale, and the way it is told, are highly improper. But since the narrator has promised that he will recount all the stories he hears, he should not be blamed for the churlish words of the Miller. All he can do is to advise his audience* to skip the Miller's tale, and seek one of a more edifying nature, of which there are plenty.

The unprecedented contrast between the first two storytellers, and in general the innovative* opening of the *Canterbury Tales* with its introduction of such a mixed group of pilgrims, is exemplary of the entire work, and in fact of Chaucer's entire oeuvre. However, before going into the intricacies of the *Canterbury Tales*, something should be said about their author.

Geoffrey Chaucer was born and bred in London. As the son of a well-to-do wine merchant he went to school, where he learnt reading, writing and arithmetic, and of course Latin. With a father who was a member of the successful and influential London merchant class, Chaucer grew up in a milieu that held a middle position both socially and linguistically between the French-speaking nobility and the working classes whose language was English. It meant that he learnt French at an early age, and in 1357 he obtained a position as a page in the household of the wife of one of the sons of King Edward III. It was to be the beginning of a lifelong service to the crown, directly or indirectly.

In 1359, he had already accompanied Prince Lionel on a campaign into France (it was the age of the Hundred Years War with France, 1337–1453), and since he had apparently acquired a good knowledge of Italian as well, he was also sent to Italy on several occasions, the first in 1372. It seems likely that he lived in Greenwich in Kent for most of the time between 1385 and 1398, and he represented the shire in Parliament in 1386. In 1399, Chaucer rented a place for himself in a house in the garden of Westminster Abbey, and when he died in 1400 he was buried in the Abbey. Only much later, in 1556, were his remains moved to a tomb in what is now known as "Poets' Corner".

Thanks to the circumstance that most of his working life Chaucer was employed at or by the royal court, his public career is fairly well documented, so well indeed that we know more about his life than about Shakespeare's.

Chaucer as a poet

Although we have no certainty, it is probable that, like many other young men (and women) of his generation, Chaucer tried his hand at writing poetry in the fashionable style of the time, and in the only language thought suitable for that, French. In a later poem he acknowledges that he translated the French *Roman de la Rose*, the thirteenth-century love allegory by Guillaume de Lorris and Jean de Meun of over 24,000 lines.[4] In this poem, a first-person narrator tells us how he had a love dream* which later came true. In this dream he entered the garden of love, where he fell in love with a rosebud. The rest of the poem is an account of the difficulties he had to overcome to see, meet, kiss, and finally pick the rose. Chaucer's reputation as a translator of French poetry spread across the Channel and around 1380 the French poet Eustache Deschamps addressed him in a *ballade** as the "grant translateur" who planted the rose tree in England, no doubt a reference to Chaucer's translation* of the *Roman de la Rose*. Also English poets refer to him as a poet already during his lifetime.

Chaucer's breakthrough as a poet occurred around 1370 with his first long narrative poem in English. In 1368, Blanche, Duchess of Lancaster and wife of John of Gaunt, died while she was in Normandy. Probably at the request of John of Gaunt, Chaucer produced a commemorative poem, *The Book of the Duchess*, which betrayed its French sources in practically all of its lines and yet constituted an entirely original, new poem in the English language, the language that was up to then thought to be too ungainly, too clumpy to emulate* the elegant French type of poetry.

The *Canterbury Tales*, Chaucer's unrivalled masterpiece and the one for which he was best known both in his own days and in the centuries thereafter, dates from his later life.

He probably started to pay serious attention to it after 1385, while he was living in Kent, and he continued to work on it until his death in 1400. And to this we must now return.

The *Canterbury Tales*

The company of pilgrims that sets off for Canterbury consists of representatives of practically all layers of society: there are a knight and his son (the Squire), both members of the gentry (the lowest echelon of the nobility); for the middle class, a merchant and a ship's captain; for the commons, a number of craftsmen; for the clergy, a monk, a friar, a parson, a priest, a pardoner and a student of divinity; and then a mixed group who are a little more difficult to categorize: a miller, a manager of an estate (the Reeve), a buying agent for one of the London inns of court (the Manciple) and a servant of a court of justice (the Summoner), but also a prominent lawyer (the Sergeant of the Law), a doctor and a landowner (the Franklin). In addition to these men there are three women: a prioress, a nun and a clothmaker from Bath.

As we have seen, the poet Chaucer has arranged it that the Knight, the pilgrim of the highest social rank, must begin. From the narrator's description, we know that he is a pious, honest and modest person who has fought the enemies of Christianity in such remote corners of Europe as the Baltic states and Spain, and in the Holy Land. But because of that we also know that he represents an ideal of knighthood that has outlived itself: in the late fourteenth century, there were few pagans to fight in the Baltic lands, and the *Reconquista* of Spain had left the Muslim kings only a small territory in the south, while hopes to regain the Holy Land had been given up entirely. And the story he tells is in keeping with that: it is a slightly old-fashioned, longwinded tale of a friendship between two young men that would have been destroyed by their love for the same woman, were it not that in the end, thanks to the noble unselfish character of the dying victor of the duel they fought, his friend is united with the lady. Members of the Knight's social group, like the Monk, react with enthusiasm, as does the Host, who then invites the Monk to take the next turn. But at that moment the Miller butts in: he thinks the tale absolute rubbish, and he promises that he will "requite" it with a tale that is based on life as he knows it. And in spite of the Host's initial protestations the Miller has his way, and he recounts a story which is beyond doubt the funniest in the whole of Middle English literature, but in fact as unrealistic as that of the Knight: the way in which the student and the carpenter's young wife betray her husband is as ingenious as it is incredible. And on top of that it is obscene as well. The contrast between these two tales could not have been greater.

The kind of story the Miller tells is called a *fabliau**. This was a genre that originated in France where it had enjoyed a great popularity since the twelfth century. It is a humorous tale, usually in verse, often obscene, whose main characters belong to the middle and lower social classes or lower clergy, and which often deals with the sexual adventures of dissatisfied wives, cunning youngsters and stupid husbands. Curious it is, however, that the genre had long lost its appeal in France while it had never become an established genre in England. Of course it was known there, as we know from the many French manuscripts copied in England in which they occur, but there were no precursors of the genre in English. This explains why Chaucer has the Miller apologize so profusely beforehand for his rudeness, and why he himself, as the narrator of the story, does exactly the same at the end of the General Prologue. It is clear that, as the first author to present a *fabliau* in English, he wants to avoid possible accusations of indecent language.

So far, we have only just dipped into the work, and already the conclusion must be that what Chaucer does here is completely new:

1. The group of pilgrims consists of people of all layers of society.
2. The leader of the group is a self-promoted member of the London middle class, not the Knight, although his social status is high above that of the Host.
3. The Knight is an atypical member of his class, and certainly not the kind of nobleman that the audience would be familiar with.
4. The Miller not only acts counter to the proposed order of the Host, he also breaks his promise to obey him, and, even worse, he gets his way.
5. Not new is a first-person narrator*, but unusual is that this narrator, once he has set the story going, recedes into the background. The active part in connecting the tales is played by Harry Bailey, the Host, who chooses the tellers, is the first to comment on a tale and "chairs" discussions among the pilgrims.

The first two conclusions reflect major changes in England's society that had taken place during Chaucer's life. As a result of the devastating impact of the Plague on the population, the ongoing transition from an economy based on exchange of services to one based on money had been accelerated. London wool merchants profited from the flourishing Flemish cloth industry, and had acquired enormous riches, and consequently status and political power. In the House of Commons, representatives of the shires and of the London merchants sat side by side with members of the nobility, while its Speaker was not necessarily a nobleman (Chaucer's son Thomas would hold this position five times). It had become a force to be reckoned with, but also a place where the different classes would meet.

In the years in which he was working on his *Canterbury Tales*, Chaucer will have realised that his initial plan was too ambitious. Just before the group arrives in Canterbury, the Host invites the Parson to tell a tale, "For," he says, "every man except you has told a tale" (fragment X, line 25). This is the last tale of the collection, and it shows that Chaucer had apparently reduced the number of tales to one per pilgrim, and moreover decided to limit his account of the pilgrimage to the way out from London to Canterbury. This may have been a very late decision, for he never brought the text of the General Prologue in line with this new setup for the storytelling contest*. As a result of this change, the number of tales would have gone down from 120 to 30. But even in this shortened form the work is still incomplete with its 24 stories for 30 people, and not only that, the tales do not constitute one continuous narrative*. There are ten fragments, which vary in length from a single tale to a series of six. Internally, the fragments are held together by links which connect the tales and in which we return to the frame narrative*. It is here that we see the Host in his role as the stage director who oversees what happens between the tales.

In comparison to Chaucer's original intentions, 24 may seem a small number, but his motley assembly of pilgrims show a wide variety of genres in their tales: they encompass romances, saint's lives*, sermons*, *fabliaux*, parodies*, a fable*, a folk tale and some of a mixed genre. As many as six of these are adaptations* from a story in Boccaccio's *Decameron* (see next section), attesting to the enormous influence of this work on Chaucer's. Often the teller presents the audience with a message, a moral lesson or a warning: the Knight, for instance, makes a plea for male friendship which may be destroyed by foolish love, and the Wife of Bath for equality in marriage. The Nun's Priest warns of the dangers of overestimating oneself, both the Miller and the Merchant of marrying out of purely selfish calculations, and the Pardoner of the vile practices of people like himself. But we should do well not to take these as the views of Chaucer the poet, as there is often a recognisable connection between a teller and his own tale (as with the Pardoner) or someone else's, as with the Miller, whose tale about an old carpenter offends the Reeve, himself a former carpenter (as the Miller knew very well). In other cases, it would be inadvisable to try and find Chaucer's opinions in them simply because these tales are highly controversial, to say the least. Thus, the snobbish Prioress tells a sanctimonious story illustrating her idolizing worship of Mary, and the student of divinity (the Clerk of Oxford) retorts to the Wife of Bath's tale with a story in which a marquis tests the love of his devoted, virtuous wife Griselda, the daughter of a pauper, to such excess that the story would have become unpalatable but for its happy ending.

Chaucer and Boccaccio: famous frame stories

From this brief sketch of the setup of the *Canterbury Tales*, it is clear that it is constructed as a frame story*. The framework for the narrative consists of the account of the pilgrimage to Canterbury as told by the narrator, the pilgrim Chaucer, and it provides the setting* for the stories told by his companions. This setup is not new, for Chaucer had a famous precursor, Giovanni Boccaccio (1313–1375). Once again, as with the *Roman de la Rose*, we see how stories and genres did not exist in isolation, and how poets were inspired by their colleagues in other countries. In the *Decameron* seven young women and three young men of the Florentine upper class flee the city which has been struck by an outbreak of the Plague. They spend the time at their country houses with singing and dancing and the telling of tales. Every evening one of them is made the queen or king for the following day and in that capacity she or he sets the theme for the stories to be told. Thus, after ten days (*Decameron* means 'ten days'), we have a collection of one hundred stories.

In the Prologue to his *Decameron*, Boccaccio describes what life in the city of Florence was like during the Plague, and a gruesome picture it is. The Bubonic Plague, which ravaged Europe in 1348–1349 (and again in 1360–1361 and 1368–1369), caused the death of millions of people. It is estimated that at least a quarter of the entire population died, but in many places numbers were much higher, running to 50 percent and up. Since people had no idea about the cause of the disease, they could not protect themselves against it and especially those who took care of others could hardly avoid being contaminated. The streets were full of bodies which were no longer buried, the stench was unbearable, and life was utter chaos. No wonder that those who could afford it left the cities and fled to the country.

Boccaccio probably finished the *Decameron* around 1351, and it was an immediate success. Over 30 manuscripts survive, and its first printed edition (Naples, 1470) was soon followed by dozens of others. Both the book and the individual stories crossed the Italian borders and conquered Europe. The *Decameron* was translated, whole or in part, into French in 1414, Catalan in 1429, German in 1473 and Dutch in 1564, with the first (expurgated) English translation appearing only in 1620. It also inspired a whole range of authors to produce similar collections. In Italy there is the *Novelliere*, by Giovanni Sercambi, which has the same plot* as the *Decameron*, be it that the tellers now escape the Plague from the city of Lucca (unfinished at Sercambi's death in 1424), while in France there are the *Cent nouvelles nouvelles* ('One Hundred New Stories'), supposedly told at the court of Philip the Good, to whom the stories are dedicated (ca. 1460). In addition to this, we have another work in French, the *Heptameron*, written by the French princess Marguerite, queen of Navarre (1558), and in Spanish, the *Novelas ejemplares* ('Exemplary Stories', 1613) by Miguel de Cervantes, the famous author of *Don Quixote*. Separate stories were translated and adapted already during Boccaccio's lifetime. Petrarch translated the very last story, that of 'Patient Griselda', into Latin (which is the version that was used by Chaucer for the Clerk's Tale), and the *Decameron* also influenced much later authors, like Jean de la Fontaine in his collection of fables (1668–94), or Shakespeare (the plot of *All's Well That Ends Well* ultimately goes back to the ninth story of the third day).

Returning now to Chaucer's *Canterbury Tales*, we cannot fail to notice that in spite of the resemblances, Chaucer's work is of a completely different order than Boccaccio's *Decameron*. Apart from the obvious fact that the work is incomplete with no more than a meagre 24 tales (four of which are unfinished), a major difference is in the composition of the group: in the *Decameron* they are all members of the same elite* social class, whereas Chaucer's pilgrims are from all ranks and files of English fourteenth-century society. Another difference arises from this social inequality of the tellers. Both collections contain tales of all kinds of genres, but just as in the *Decameron* the tellers are of one and the same social category, their tales are couched in a single form, that of the *novella**, a short story* in prose, while in the *Canterbury Tales* Chaucer attempts to fit the genre to the teller: a romance for the Knight, a *fabliau* for the Miller.

But the difference that will immediately catch the eye or ear of those among Chaucer's audience who know the *Decameron*'s opening is that of the setting. Horrifying as the description of Plague-stricken Florence may be, as soon as the young persons have left the city its misery is completely out of sight and out of mind, and we are drawn into a world of luxury, leisure and carefree entertainment. In contrast to Boccaccio's "real life" introduction, Chaucer's opening uses a topos* quite common in love poetry*, that of the *reverdie** ('re-greening'), a genre celebrating the arrival of spring. But instead of continuing with a description of a young man in search of love (as in the *Roman de la Rose*), the narrator informs us that he intends to go on a pilgrimage. Do we have to conclude from this opening that the *Canterbury Tales* is a religious* poem? The question cannot be answered unequivocally. Chaucer is not a religious author, none of his works is primarily religious in content, and by far the majority of the tales that are presented in the *Canterbury Tales* are of a secular nature. But the last tale, just before the company arrives in Canterbury, is told by the Parson, and is a treatise on the seven deadly sins and how to avoid or overcome them. Therefore the religious aspect is definitely present, even though the pilgrims, like all other humans, move in a world that shows a very recognisable everyday reality. Salvation of the soul is usually not the first of their concerns, yet one to which they can be alerted by unsettling circumstances in their personal lives, like sickness, the example used by Chaucer at the end of the opening section of the General Prologue:

> [In the spring] people long to go on pilgrimages...
> And most especially, from all the shires
> Of England, to Canterbury they come,
> The holy blessed martyr there to seek,
> Who gave his help to them when they were sick.[5]

What Chaucer seems to imply then is that we must see interpersonal love as part of the human existence on earth, but also that we must be aware that there is more to life than just that.

Chaucer's poetic innovations

Especially in the early part of his career, we see that Chaucer is experimenting with both form and metre*. His first narrative poem, *The Book of the Duchess*, was not only greatly indebted to contemporary French poems for its ideas and its language; also, the metre had been adapted from the French. But Chaucer soon discovered that the octosyllabic verse (see Chapter 9) did not work well in English and limited his possibilities. After one more attempt he changed to the decasyllabic line (consisting of ten syllables) which he would continue to use for the rest of his life. What these two early poems also had in common was that they were written in rhyming* couplets*: aa, bb, cc, etc. But in some of his shorter lyrical poetry*, Chaucer tested other verse forms, in particular various types of stanza*. We find stanzas with seven, eight, nine and even ten lines, sometimes combined in the same poem. In this way he developed what would become his favourite form, the so-called "rhyme royal", a seven-line stanza rhyming ababbcc, which he employed for many of the tales in the *Canterbury Tales*. By the time he was composing these, he had achieved complete control over the form of his verse, as becomes clear when the Host invites the pilgrim Chaucer to tell a tale. The poet Chaucer makes his narrator present the story of Sir Thopas, a romance of his own making and a parody* of both the contents and the form of a popular type of romance (of the B-category, we would now say), for which he uses two characteristic types of stanza, one of which has six lines. In Chaucer's version this six-line stanza consists of two lines with four beats, followed by one with three beats, and this twice over. But the metre is of such a deadly regularity that it effectively kills all interest in the audience, as can be experienced by reading aloud the opening stanza:

> Listen, lords, with good intent,
> And I will tell a true event
> Of joy and of solace;
> About a knight, quite fair and bent
> To shine in fight and tournament.
> His name was Sir Thopas.[6]

After little more than 200 lines this self-mockery culminates in the abrupt interruption of the Host, who swears that he has never heard anything as bad as this, and orders Chaucer to tell something different or hold his tongue.

The *Canterbury Tales* in manuscript and print

Chaucer's *Canterbury Tales* survives in more than 80 manuscripts*, 55 of which preserve, or were intended to preserve, complete texts. The oldest two of these possibly date to Chaucer's last years or just after 1400. When William Caxton had set up his printing press* in Westminster, one of the first texts he took on was the *Canterbury Tales*, which appeared in 1478. Since then the work has never gone out of print, the only book in the whole of English printing history about which this can be said. The first edition by Caxton was followed by a second in 1484; soon two more incunabula* appeared, one by Richard Pynson, in 1492, and one by Caxton's successor Wynkyn de Worde, in 1498. Six early prints in the sixteenth century attest to the work's continued popularity. In 1894, Walter Skeat presented the first scholarly edition of *The Complete Works of Geoffrey Chaucer*, in six volumes, with explanatory notes and a full glossary. This standard edition was only superseded in 1957 by the first edition of what is now, with the third edition, known as *The Riverside Chaucer.*

Chaucer's fame at home . . .

Towards the end of his life Chaucer had become a celebrated poet, acknowledged as such by his contemporaries. The monk and poet John Lydgate (ca. 1370–1449), who wrote a sequel to the *Canterbury Tales* around 1420, *The Siege of Thebes*, praised him as the "flower of poets in Britain" in its Prologue. Another near-contemporary, Thomas Hoccleve (1366/7–1426), goes a step further. In his *Regiment of Princes* (1412), he claims to have known Chaucer personally, and not only salutes him as "maister deere, and fadir reverend," but has a portrait of him painted in the margin next to these lines, in order that later generations "By this peynture may ageyn hym fynde" (line 4998). We must assume therefore that the portrait really shows a likeness of Chaucer. This is an absolute novelty in medieval culture, and marks the beginning of a tradition* of Chaucer portraits.[7]

. . . and abroad

When William the Conqueror defeated Harold at the Battle of Hastings in 1066, he became the first of a long line of French-speaking kings of England. In the fourteenth century, this variant of French, Anglo-Norman, was still the native language of the nobility and the standard for the country's administration, and therefore a prerequisite for anyone who aspired to a public career. But this was true not only for England. At least since the twelfth century, France had been the centre of civilised society and French the language of its courts and culture. As a side effect, it had become the language of trade as well, whereas English had no function in international contacts, and was known to only a few outside England. When in 1436 Jacqueline, Countess of Holland, died, she left six manuscripts with texts in English, probably a wedding gift from her husband Humphrey, Duke of Gloucester, the youngest son of Henry IV and a great collector of manuscripts (he donated over 280 manuscripts to the University of Oxford). Because no one close to the Countess appeared to have any interest in them, the executor (as we know from his report) eventually sold them to an English merchant, who no doubt realised that he had made the bargain of his life, for among them was a beautifully illustrated manuscript that not only contained the *Canterbury Tales*, but that appears to be one of the first attempts to collect Chaucer's complete works.[8] Modern readers may find this anecdote difficult to believe, but it reveals unequivocally the insignificance of the English language outside the British Isles. Thanks to his personal contacts in England and on the continent, Chaucer's activities as a translator and a poet were known there, but this does not mean that his English works were read. In her monumental survey *Five Hundred Years of Chaucer Criticism and Allusion*, Caroline Spurgeon concluded that "from the time that Deschamps wrote his ballad to the beginning of the 18th century, for . . . the whole French nation English literature simply did not exist."[9] This situation begins to change around the middle of the eighteenth century, when one of Chaucer's tales was translated into French, but for the first reliable translation, into prose, the French had to wait until 1908. The situation in Germany is slightly better, and a small number of writers show a first-hand knowledge of Chaucer's works from the seventeenth century onwards.[10] It is only after World War II that reliable translations began to appear in practically all modern languages, and not only of Western Europe, but also, for instance, in Japanese. These translations in turn resulted in adaptations for the stage and film, or in a new life as the basis for a novel*. And of course the availability on the internet of the original text in Middle English, with explanatory notes and a translation into Modern English, has made the *Canterbury Tales* accessible to a wider audience than ever before.[11]

Notes

1 All quotations are from Geoffrey Chaucer, *The Canterbury Tales*, trans. David Wright (Oxford: Oxford University Press, 1985), here 79–81. All references to the Middle English text are to *The Riverside Chaucer*, third edition, ed. Larry D. Benson (Boston: Houghton Mifflin, 1987). Since the work has survived in ten fragments, the Roman numbers refer to the fragment from which the quotation was taken (here: fragment I, lines 3109–81).
2 Chaucer, *The Canterbury Tales*, trans. Wright, 20; I, lines 769–76.
3 Chaucer, *The Canterbury Tales*, trans. Wright, 22; I, lines 844–46.
4 Of Chaucer's *Romaunt of the Rose* only one manuscript, with three fragments, survives; together these amount to some 10,000 lines. The first of these, Fragment A, "is almost certainly by Chaucer, B certainly not by him, and C probably by him"; see Derek Pearsall, *The Life of Geoffrey Chaucer*, Blackwell Critical Biographies (Oxford: Wiley-Blackwell, 1992), 82.
5 Chaucer, *The Canterbury Tales*, trans. Wright, 1; I, lines 12, 15–18.
6 To achieve the required effect the words "solace" and "Thopas" should be stressed on the last syllable, as they were in Middle English. The translation of the lines is mine and based on the text in Chaucer, *The Riverside Chaucer*, VII, lines 712–17.
7 For an extensive treatment of the portraits, see Pearsall, *The Life of Geoffrey Chaucer*, 285–305.
8 The manuscript is now in Cambridge University Library (MS Gg.4.27); for a facsimile edition, see Malcolm Beckwith Parkes and Richard Beadle, eds., *The Poetical Works of Geoffrey Chaucer: A Facsimile of Cambridge University Library MS Gg. 4.27* (Norman, OK: Pilgrim Books, 1980).
9 Caroline F. E. Spurgeon, *Five Hundred Years of Chaucer Criticism and Allusion* (London: Cambridge University Press, 1908–1917), Part V, Appendix B, 2.
10 Spurgeon, *Five Hundred Years of Chaucer Criticism and Allusion*, Part V, Appendix C, 126–27, 140.
11 See: "The Canterbury Tales," accessed February, 2017, http://sites.fas.harvard.edu/~chaucer/CTlist.html

Further reading

Lorris, de, Guillaume and Jean de Meun. *The Romance of the Rose*. Translated by Charles Dahlberg. Princeton, NJ: Princeton University Press, 1971.
Cooper, Helen. *The Canterbury Tales*. Second edition. Oxford: Oxford University Press, 1996.
Wallace, David. *Giovanni Boccaccio*. Decameron: *Landmarks of World Literature*. Cambridge: Cambridge University Press, 1991.

12 Self-fashioning

Madeleine Jeay

Figure 12.1 Various works (also known as "The Book of the Queen"), including "Cent balades",
c. 1410–1414, French, Christine de Pizan in her study, British Library, London, Ms. Harley
4431, f° 4

Source: Centre Art Historical Documentation, Radboud University.

Male authors predominate in medieval literature. This makes it all the more special to encounter in Christine de Pizan a confident, learned, and productive writer taking up the pen to show the world how brilliant and important women are. Her *Le Livre de la Cité des dames* ('The Book of the City of Ladies'), made in 1405, begins with a personal prologue:

Text: Christine de Pizan, Le Livre de la Cité des dames *('The Book of the City of Ladies') (1405)*

One day, I was sitting in my study surrounded by many books of different kinds, for it has long been my habit to engage in the pursuit of knowledge. My mind had grown weary as I had spent the day struggling with the weighty tomes of various authors whom I had been studying for some time. I looked up from my book and decided that, for once, I would put aside these difficult texts and find instead something amusing and easy to read from the works of the poets. As I searched around for some little book, I happened to chance upon a work which did not belong to me but was amongst a pile of others that had been placed in my safekeeping. I opened it and saw from the title that it was by Matheolus. . . . I had scarcely begun to read it up when my dear mother called me down to supper, for it was time to eat. I put the book to one side, resolving to go back to it the following day. The next morning, seated once more in my study as is my usual custom, I remembered my previous desire to have a look at this book by Matheolus. I picked it up again and read on a little. But, seeing the kind of immoral language and ideas it contained, the content seemed to me likely to appeal only to those who enjoy reading works of slander and to be of no use whatsoever to anyone who wished to pursue virtue or to improve their moral standards. I therefore leafed through it, read the ending, and decided to switch to some more worthy and profitable work. Yet, . . . an extraordinary thought became planted in my mind which made me wonder why on earth it was that so many men, both clerks and others, have said and continue to say and write such awful, damning things about women and their ways. I was at a loss as to how to explain it. It is not just a handful of writers who do this, nor only this Matheolus whose book is neither regarded as authoritative nor intended to be taken seriously. It is all manner of philosophers, poets and orators too numerous to mention, who all seem to speak with one voice and are unanimous in their view that female nature is wholly given up to vice.[1]

These opening lines give a striking picture of what it meant to be a female writer in the Middle Ages. The way in which Christine is describing herself, surrounded by books, is a scene that can be seen in the manuscripts* of her works, which contain images of her in her study, sitting at her desk writing or reading. The book she has begun to read in order to clear her mind, *Liber lamentationum Matheoluli* ('The Lamentations of Matheolus') by Mathieu de Boulogne, is a collection of satirical antifeminist observations on the vices of women, which has the opposite effect of depressing her deeply. Full of self-doubt and, as she says, despising herself and the whole of her sex "as an aberration in nature," she begins by internalizing Matheolus's view of women as vile creatures, thus experiencing what happens emotionally to a woman confronted with an antifeminist tradition going back to antiquity.[2] Then, relying on her womanly experience, she decides to refute this legacy with the demonstration that it is riddled with slander and unfounded affirmations. These authors claim that women are "unstable and fickle, frivolous, flighty and weak-minded, as impressionable as children and completely lacking in resolution."[3] Her main target for her demonstration is Jean de Meun's *Roman de la Rose* ('Romance* of the Rose') and the sexist opinions conveyed by its characters. Her opposition to the ideas put forward in this book proved to be instrumental in her career. Christine's *Le Livre de la Cité des dames* will be a response to the works that defame and disrespect women.

Her reply is based not only on her own judgment as a learned scholar, but on her first-hand knowledge of femaleness. Christine puts in parallel the homeliness of the scene with her devotion to literary studies. The mother providing her physical needs becomes herself a figure of authority who gives dignity to all aspects of Christine's experience of womanhood. To the demeaning statements she reads in too many treatises, Christine opposes the totality of her experience, not only what she has learned from books, but what life has taught her. Her credibility comes from the unique blend she offers in her texts: she is a learned woman who can rely on her knowledge of the major ancient works, but also provide firsthand evidence of women's reality. This is why she stages herself at the centre of her work, reflecting on her intellectual progress and her writing while concerned with the ordinary problems of the widowed mother she is.

She will be inspired and guided in this journey by female allegorical* figures with whom she speaks and identifies. In *Le Livre de la Cité des dames*, the personifications* of three virtues – Reason, Rectitude, and Justice – appear to her and comfort her in the despair produced by the reading of Matheolus's book. They will construct a city for ladies, in which the stones are illustrious women who have distinguished themselves, from pagan women to those of her present time, each allegorical figure being responsible for one of the three sections of the book. Christine's self-construction, however, transcends her own situation, presenting herself as a model to other women and, most significantly, to offer lessons to be learned by the whole human community. Speaking in the first person*, she offers a self-portrait which evolved during her career, using events of her life for their exemplary* value. Throughout her work, which is not strictly speaking an autobiography*, Christine inscribes in her texts the process of self-construction by which she has developed into a professional writer. It is precisely this author's progress that we will follow, how she evolved from a young widow mother of three children without formal education into a respected figure among scholars and among the princely patrons* who sponsored her works.

Constructing an exemplary *persona* as author

Constructing an image of an author – a process which is referred to by critics as building up an author's *persona** – supported by a proper name and autobiographical details told in the first person, is far from unique among medieval authors. This self-fashioning process can already be observed since the first troubadours* (see Chapter 8), mostly in the debate genres, like the *tensos** or *jeux-partis** in which two poets argue about issues related to courtly love*. It also characterizes Christine's predecessors and contemporaries such as Guillaume de Machaut, Jean Froissart and François Villon, who play with the image of themselves as inexpert lovers. After looking first at the process and intentions of Christine's self-fashioning as an example for other women as well as for humankind, it will be necessary to understand her endeavour in the light of this tradition* of self-representation. More generally, we will focus on a process of self-construction which plays with the fiction that it is based on real facts, whether they correspond to a documented truth or not.

Christine de Pizan's intellectual and literary achievements are all the more striking in that she was marginal in a number of ways, as a foreigner, an Italian in France, and as a woman committed to scholarship. Born around 1365 in Venice, she moved to Paris with her family to join her father Thommaso da Pizzano, who had been appointed astrologer and physician of Charles V, King of France. With her father's encouragement, she had the opportunity to access the king's rich library* and was able to pursue her intellectual interests. However, married at fifteen to Étienne du Castel, a royal secretary, and mother of three children, she had to wait until Étienne's death ten years later to devote herself entirely to learning. The greatest tragedy in her life proved to be her greatest chance in allowing her to dedicate her life to study. Now a widow supporting a family and plagued by financial problems, she first succeeded in being recognized in courtly circles for her poems. A turning point for asserting herself as a legitimate intellectual was what is known as the "Débat sur le *Roman de la Rose*" ('The Debate of the *Romance of the Rose*'): she published and dedicated to Queen Isabeau on February 1, 1402, the letters she exchanged with three eminent scholars: Jean de Montreuil, royal notary, and Pierre Col and his brother Gontier, both royal secretaries and ambassadors. Referring to herself as "a woman of untrained intellect and uncomplicated sensibility," she had dared to confront these clercs "subtle in philosophical* understanding, accomplished in the sciences*, nimble in polished rhetoric and refined poetic skill," by attacking misogynist assertions voiced by Jean de Meun in the *Romance of the Rose*.[4] As a woman without formal university training, she was bold enough to challenge the authority of one of the most prestigious works of the time, thus assessing her own interpretative skills. The publicity given to a dispute in which such distinguished intellectuals were involved established her own credentials not only as a writer of courtly poetry but also as a scholar in her own right.

From then on, Christine's writing would be supported and sometimes commissioned by important French and English patrons. Without totally giving up courtly poetry, she devoted herself mostly to allegorical and didactic treatises in prose in which she advocated respect for women and reflected on the conditions required for good governance, a crucial issue in the context of the Hundred Years war. In twenty years, from 1399–1418, she produced a total of forty pieces (of which fifteen are substantial works), a corpus to which a poem in honour of Joan of Arc composed in 1429 must be added. In all these works, she transcends her first-person womanly experience in order to reflect on the situation of women in society and on the impact of their contribution to human development and culture in general.

If the reader wants to get a sense of the range and amplitude of Christine's production, a good way is to look at the manuscript collections of her works she supervised or edited herself for publication and presentation to noble patrons. Accessible on the internet, the "Book of the Queen", copied in her own hand and assembled for Isabeau of Bavaria, and the manuscripts of the Bibliothèque Nationale in Paris,[5] give an excellent idea of how these works contributed to legitimizing her as an authoritative auctorial figure.[6] The way in which she portrays herself in her study works as a signature in the same way as the mention of her name or the characteristic features by which she defines herself.

A recurring keyword by which Christine defines herself from her first collection of poems, *Les Cent ballades* ('One Hundred Ballads*'), to the end of her career is *seulette*, 'alone'. In Ballad XI, the word, obsessively repeated at the beginning of each line, translates her sorrow on the death of her husband and her decision to embrace solitude for devoting herself to learning: "Seulete suy et seulete vueil estre" ('Alone am I, alone I wish to be'). She may have felt surrounded by enemies when her widowhood confronted her with trials and tribulations. She describes in *L'Advision Christine* ('Christine's Vision*') how she was bothered by lawsuits and legal actions. However, as always, she gives a universal quality to her own situation, for example in *Les Lamentations sur les maux de la France* ('Lamentation on the Troubles of France'). She opens this appeal for peace made to princes and to women who risk losing their loved ones because of the war, with a reference to her own isolation, "seulette a part" ('alone and aside'), rising above her distress to show compassion for human suffering.

As the critic Kevin Brownlee says, Christine frames a universal history in her personal history in a text centred on the "mutation", the metamorphosis she experienced at her husband's death.[7] The change she suffered is an image of the instability governing the world. Her sudden widowhood transformed her from a woman into a man: "How I, a woman, became a man/by a flick of Fortune's hand/How she changed my body's form/ To the perfect masculine norm" (*Le Livre de la mutacion de fortune*, 'The Book of the Mutation of Fortune', v. 142–5). She describes the process in terms of physical transformations, with the hardening of her body and the deepening of her voice. This gender change induced by Fortune means that, now head of the ship, as she says, she will have to enter the public world in order to support her family with her writing. Brownlee explains that she fashions herself as "virtuous widow, caring mother and female author."[8] Christine will from now on build her public authority on her choice not to remarry and to dissociate what pertains to her sexuality from her gender*, which is the way in which she assumes her femininity. There will, however, be an evolution between *Le Livre de la mutacion de fortune* written in 1402–1403 and *Le Livre de la Cité des dames* from 1405, in which, guided by the allegorical figures of Lady Reason, Lady Rectitude, and Lady Justice, she will learn that she does not have to deny her female nature in order to be a respected writer.

Allegories as sources of comfort and guidance

In *Le Livre de la Cité des dames*, Christine finds comfort in her exchange with the three allegories, inspired by the model of the sixth-century philosopher Boethius, who is for her not just a classical reference worth quoting for asserting her authority, but a constant source of reassurance. Boethius describes in his *De consolatione philosophiae* ('Consolation of Philosophy'), how, awaiting his execution in prison, he found support in his conversation with Lady Philosophy. Christine sees the three crowned ladies, Reason, Rectitude, and Justice, standing before her, announcing that because of her studies she will be asked to build the City of Ladies. They will erect with her a place of refuge for protecting women from antifeminist attacks, in which their achievements will be celebrated. Inspired by Saint Augustine's *City of God*, Christine reinterprets Boccaccio's *De Mulieribus Claris* ('On Famous Women', a catalogue of illustrious women) in order to demonstrate that women, as well as men, can be successful in all areas, whether military, political, cultural, or religious. She lists as many as 189 women worthy to be praised for their accomplishments.

In the first part of the book, Reason – who is responsible for laying the foundations of the city walls – presents warriors, rulers, and sovereigns, from mythological* figures like the Amazons to contemporary queens such as Blanche de Castille, mother of the French king known as Saint Louis. She continues with women remarkable for their intellect, for example Minerva, who "invented countless sciences, including the art of making arms" (p. 66), or Anastasia, the illuminator of Christine's manuscripts. In the second part, Rectitude speaks about the houses within the city, which are formed by the stories of the ten sibyls and other prophetesses*, and by examples of women's love for their parents, children, and husbands. Finally, in the third part, Justice explains how the construction of the city is completed with the turrets of the towers. She brings Mary, the Queen of Heaven, to live in the City of Ladies with a number of saints, among whom her patron saint, Christine, holds a significant place.

The first important text in which Christine displays her love of learning is *Épître d'Othéa* ('The Letter of Othea to Hector', 1399), an instruction book intended for a young man about to become a knight. With the role of the young prince of Troy's mentor given to the goddess Othea, she feminizes the mythological background provided by her main sources: Virgil's *Aeneid*, Ovid's *Metamorphoses* (certainly through its French translation, the *Ovide moralisé*), and Boccaccio's compilation, *On the Genealogy of the Gods*. Another source of inspiration is Dante's *Comedy*. In *Le Livre de la Cité des dames*, her meeting with Reason is a reference to the encounter between Dante and his guide Virgil. In *Christine's Vision*, she echoes the opening lines of Dante's *Inferno*, "Midway along the journey of our life/I woke to find myself in some dark woods" (see Chapter 10),[9] by saying: "I had already passed halfway through the journey of my pilgrimage when one day at eventide I found myself fatigued by the long road and desirous of shelter."[10]

Christine's allegorical works can be seen as female, re-gendered versions of the relationship between Philosophy and Boethius or Dante and Virgil, with feminine figures showing the way ahead. In *The Long Road of Learning*, it is a prophetess from ancient mythology, the Sibyl of Cumae, who appears to Christine in her sleep to reassure her about the capacity for a woman to be recognized as a legitimate author and to play herself the role of mentor, especially in the troubled times France is experiencing. This is precisely what she does in *Le Livre des trois vertus à l'enseignement des dames* ('The Book of the Three Virtues'). Also called *Le Trésor de la cité des dames* ('The Treasure of the City of Ladies'), this text complements *Le Livre de la Cité des dames*. The three same allegorical figures urge Christine to provide advice to women of all ages and from all levels of medieval society, from princesses and ladies in court to poor women and prostitutes, in the hope that they will become themselves worthy inhabitants of the City. This manual of education* written for the eleven-year-old Margaret of Burgundy, on the occasion of her marriage with the dauphin Louis de Guyenne, was disseminated throughout Europe by the dedicatee's sisters who made prestigious marriages. Worldly Prudence, who provides much of the instruction, can be seen as impersonating Christine herself.

Establishing oneself as a feminine figure of authority in courtly circles

In fact, the tension between the erudition she has acquired and her experience as a woman, whether through the needs of her body or the necessities of her domestic life, becomes an asset for establishing her authority. This is particularly true when, faced with the mere textual tradition of misogynist authors who rely just on books, she opposes the testimony of her life. It was because of her reputation as a learned person, and the personal circumstances of her father's function at the court, that she could benefit from the support necessary to her writing. Having to rely, like most artists, on the generosity of patrons, she managed to capture the interest of highly placed people willing to protect a woman. Her two main sources of patronage were the French royal court at the beginning of her career, especially the queen, Isabeau of Bavaria, and the king's uncle Louis d'Orléans, and later the Dukes of Burgundy, Phillip the Bold and John the Fearless.

The attention she received from the Burgundian court reinforced her interest in issues related to history, education, and political reform, issues particularly important in a time of war. Christine's early concern for education can be seen in the two pieces intended for her son in 1400–1401, *Les Enseignemens moraux* ('Moral Teachings') and *Les Proverbes moraux* ('Moral Proverbs'), then in the advice offered to a young princess in *Le Livre des trois vertus*. In two works dedicated to the dauphin, Louis de Guyenne, *Le Livre du Corps de Policie* ('The Book of the Body Politics', a "mirror* for Princes") and *Le Livre de la Paix* ('The Book for Peace'), she insists on the virtues that should be developed from child-hood in order for a prince to properly rule a country. One of the models which Christine proposes to the dauphin is his grandfather, Charles V. In 1404, she had been commissioned by Philip the Bold to write a biography* of his brother, *Le Livre des Fais et bonnes meurs du sage roy Charles V* ('The Deeds and Good Customs of the Wise King Charles V'). She gives the dimension of a political lesson to the king's actions, since his wisdom and virtues offer an example of how to govern a state. As in her other works, Christine interweaves learned sources and the personal experience of someone who had first-hand knowledge of his reign and could also rely on the testimony of people who had known the king. Christine's views on the social and political role that women should play are consistent: urging them to intervene in public affairs, she assumes more and more openly her mission to provide guidance to her readers. This is especially true for *Le Livre des Faits d'armes et de chevalerie* ('The Feats of Arms and of Chivalry') (ca. 1410), a manual on warfare for those who are engaged in military action and don't have access to treatises on the subject.

The medieval tradition of auctorial self-representation

By displaying her name in the texts, Christine follows in the footsteps of her two major fourteenth-century predecessors, Guillaume de Machaut and Jean Froissart. They both use their plain name or play with anagrams* and the readers' ability to decipher the enigma of their signature, inviting them in fact to confirm an identity that was already known in the context of the diffusion of manuscripts in the relatively small circle of their patrons. As we have seen with Christine's works, the name identifies an author who speaks in the first person, playing therefore a role of protagonist in texts which include an autobio-graphic component. This pseudo-autobiographic trend, as critics have labelled it, raises several questions which deserve attention, since it is a new element in the development of vernacular literature in Europe. Does the fact that it is particularly flourishing in the late Middle Ages mean that it is characteristic of the period? Or, following Michel Zink's study on the invention of literary subjectivity, should we see in the thirteenth century a turning point with the construction of a *roman du moi*, a romance of the "I"?[11] Or rather, should we go back to the first vernacular poets and see already in the lyrics* of the trou-badours a staging of the self which is presented as real life experience?

All of these issues are topics for further research, as is another set of questions connected with the relationship between the "real" individual and the literary *persona* fashioned by the text. The fact that it is illusory to differentiate between fact and fiction* and, espe-cially in the Middle Ages, to unearth the real individual behind the auctorial figure, does not mean that the poetic "I" is a pure textual construct without connection to empirical reality. It is true that, in spite of their autobiographic dimension, medieval works cannot be read as autobiographies, chiefly because personal experience is transcended into the expression of a general truth. It is precisely this quest for exemplarity, which we have seen to be so central in Christine de Pizan's approach of her work, that requires to be supported by what is given by the author as real life facts. This is the lesson given by Saint Augustine, demonstrating in his *Confessions* the necessity of conversion from his own experience. The reader must be aware, however, that transposed into literature, the author's life becomes an autobiographical fiction. First, facts can be distorted or misrepresented. Second, in the highly conventional and stylized* conception of literature of the Middle Ages, the author's self-representation is filtered by a set of conventional features.

The process of the author's self-fashioning evolves through a series of variants and recurrent patterns since the twelfth century and the very first troubadours. The wide variety of the troubadours' social backgrounds, from great lords and kings to the lower nobility and the bourgeoisie as well as clerks and wandering minstrels*, is a manifestation of the cultural diversity of the noble courts of Southern France, Northern Spain, and Italy. In these small-scale courtly settings, the poetic "I"* cannot just be a purely textual device: it refers necessarily to an individual who is usually well known by an audience* familiar with his repertoire. In the *canso**, the love-song, the composer stages himself as the first-person voice of the lover, in a situation of live performance* which implies the confusion of these two instances (lover and composer) with the performer of the song. The image exhibited by the poet is a paradoxical combination of humility as the long-suffering and adoring vassal of the beloved lady and of pride in his poetic mastery. The poems often express a sense of competitive* rivalry. This emulation* finds its expression in debating contests that could be compared to modern slam poetry: the *tensos* and *partimens* give an unflattering image of the poets. They are targeted for their physical appearance, their ugli-ness, or the hoarseness of their voice, and satirized for their moral misconduct and sexual debauchery with hints at their possible homosexuality. Even if such invectives should be interpreted as pure jest in the context of a rhetoric of praise and blame, the personal details constituting the portrait were recycled in the biographic pieces written about the troubadours. In some manuscripts, the songs are accompanied by little stories, the *razos**, explaining the circumstances of their composition, and by *vidas**, narrating anecdotes about the poet's life.

Throughout the medieval period, the characteristic features that can be observed in the practices of troubadour self-fashioning are carried out by later authors. Constants are the playful de-valorisation of their personality and life experience, associated with a strong sense of their literary achievements and responsibility, often hidden behind a posture of humility. Another means is the authors' self-identification, either by their real name or by a pseudonym, functioning as a signature and a statement of authorship. Among the trouvères, the poets of Northern France, Rutebeuf plays on his name and the paradox of a skilful writer pretending to be just a *rude bœuf*, literally a clumsy ox, an exhibition of ineptitude which in fact underlines his artistic craftsmanship. He adopts the character of the wandering poet always in need because of his addiction to dice and drinking, and quarrelling with his wife when he returns home without money. The moral and satirical purpose is manifest in his works: debauchery should lead to repentance, poverty can be transcended into austerity.

This mix of laughter and seriousness defines satire* that uses sarcasm and derision to expose and possibly remedy the flaws of people and society. It can be found among the thirteenth-century authors identified with the town of Arras in Northern France, who satirized its elite*, especially in Adam de la Halle's play *Le Jeu de la feuillée* ('The Play of the Greensward'). Adam stages himself in the role of an unhappily married resident of the city, too poor to study in Paris, complaining about his father's avarice and ridiculing the other inhabitants' greed and folly. Also known under his surname of Adam le Bossu, Adam the hunchback, he expresses his mixed feelings towards a town which he is about to leave in his *Congé* ('Leave Taking'). Once again, one can see a correspondence between the author's self-identification and the substance of his work: his physical features are not unrelated to the distortions of the city life in Arras. As the previous chapter has shown, Geoffrey Chaucer also contributes to this tradition of self-fashioning, especially in his portrait and actions as pilgrim/narrator* in the *Canterbury Tales* (see Chapter 11).

In many respects, Christine's predecessors, Guillaume de Machaut and Jean Froissart, adhered to this tradition of presenting in their works a multifaceted identity. In their case, this identity can be subsumed under the tension between the *personas* of lover and poet, which is resolved, most of the time, with the affirmation of their literary craftsmanship. With Machaut this tension goes hand in hand with that of a clerk posing as a knight who traditionally assumes the role of lover. One consequence in his *dits*, his narrative* and didactic* poems, is that he will intervene in the narration as a character speaking for himself or as a protagonist, as witness and advisor of another character's personal issues. In his last work, the *Voir Dit* ('The True Tale'), the poet portrays himself as an elderly man suffering from lack of inspiration, but personally and poetically re-energized by the loving admiration of a young aristocratic woman. The autobiographical allusions present in all Machaut's works culminate in the *Voir Dit* with the details of what is presented as an authentic love affair plagued by the sense of inadequacy of an old man afflicted by melancholia and physically impaired by gouty attacks. We should, however, be aware of the symbolic dimension of this self-portrait contrasting with the youth of the loved one. Such a description corresponds too well to the self-demeaning portrait of the poet since the twelfth century to be taken at face value. The same can be said about Jean Froissart's self-representations in his poetic works: within an autobiographical framework, his unsuccessful love relationships contrast with his ability as a poet.

Finally, let us jump to fifteenth-century Paris and François Villon, a direct heir of these poets exhibiting their misfortune. Maybe even more than in their case, it may seem that we encounter the individual under the first-person protagonist*, who is the victim of many unjust treatments, the marginal outcast condemned to jail and about to be hanged. In his two main pieces, the *Lais** and the *Testament*, the bequest of imaginary or valueless possessions to legatees chosen among his Parisian contemporaries is based on biographical facts. They provide a host of details about his student life, his consorting with thieves, and the subsequent offences that led to a wandering life, about his destitute family and his gratitude to his stepfather Guillaume de Villon who had been more than a father for him. The autobiographical aspect of Villon's work must be taken into account as an integral part of its literary significance. Inscribed in the long tradition of the poet's self-defamation and combined with the conventional figure of the martyr of love he pretends to be, it contributes to its ironic* and parodic* twist, to its ambiguity. Villon is at the same time wisdom and folly, the irresponsible student who regrets his lack of seriousness and the highly educated scholar who speaks to his peers, the victim of courtly love and the pimp of "La Grosse Margot" ('Fat Margot').

Christine's self-representation and reception*

The difference is striking between the procedures of auctorial self-representation developed by Christine de Pizan and those which are displayed by her male counterparts. In their case, the recurrence of similar motifs from the twelfth century stresses the codified nature of their self-portrait. The global picture is an ambivalent one in which physical and often moral deficiencies go together with the sense of their artistic achievement. This rhetorical* dimension, however, must not obscure the subjectivity of authors who play with aspects of their empirical reality and biography to provide exemplarity to their personal experience. In Christine's case, the recourse to her life is not mediated by the characteristic *topoi** depicting male authors. The validity of her messages, either for the rehabilitation and guidance of women or the instruction of princes, is based on the reliability of her testimony. The whole foundation on which she built her work depends on the reader's conviction that what she reports about her life is true: her father's prestige and mother's love, the blessings of her marriage and anguish of her widowhood, her concern for her children, and her enthusiasm for learning. Her work also forms a great example of the interplay between literature and life, fiction and reality, which is of course a recurring theme in the history of literature, as this book will show time and again.

Another important reason for Christine's peculiar way of presenting herself comes from her marginality. Even when she wrote her first courtly pieces, she was not totally fitting in. As a distressed widow she had to hide her pain in order to sing about love, while as a prudent counsellor she was trying to warn against love's dangers. More generally, as a woman she had to find her personal way through, on the one hand, the counterexamples for women's dignity offered by the literary tradition, and, on the other hand, through the works of authors whom she recognised as models. Her systematic way of quoting herself throughout her production, of constantly referring to her previous pieces, is a clear indication that she positioned herself among these authorities.

It is no surprise that her works benefited from the advent of printing, not only in France, but also with a translation* in Dutch (produced in manuscript for the wealthy citizen Jan de Baenst of Bruges in 1475) and several ones in English published by William Caxton, the first printer in England. Sets of tapestries* with scenes taken from *Le Livre de la Cité des dames*, listed among Henry VIII and Elizabeth I's possessions and owned by the ruling families in Europe, are another indication of a continued interest in Christine de Pizan's work. She even deserved to be included among fifteenth- and sixteenth-century catalogues of women worthy of praise, thus becoming herself one of the stones of the City of Ladies.

Notes

1 Christine de Pizan, *Le Livre de la Cité des dames*, trans. Rosalind Brown-Grant (London: Penguin, 1999), 5.
2 The quotation is from Pizan, *Livre de la Cité*, tr. Brown-Grant, 7.
3 Pizan, *Livre de la Cité*, tr. Brown-Grant, 150.
4 For the quotations, see Christine de Pizan, *Debate of the Romance of the Rose*, ed., trans. David F. Hult (Chicago: The University of Chicago Press, 2010), 50 and 96.
5 Paris, Bibliothèque nationale de France, manuscripts fr. 835 and 836; both available online via the BnF Gallica database http://gallica.bnf.fr/accueil/?mode=desktop
6 For the "Book of the Queen," see "Christine de Pizan," accessed May, 2016, www.pizan.lib.ed.ac.uk/
7 Kevin Brownlee, "The Image of History in Christine de Pizan's *Livre de la Mutacion de Fortune*," in *Contexts: Style and Values in Medieval Art and Literature*, ed. Daniel Poirion and Nancy Freeman Regalado, *Yale French Studies*, special issue (New Haven, CT: Yale University Press, 1991), 44–56.
8 Kevin Brownlee, "Widowhood, Sexuality, and Gender in Christine de Pizan," in *Romanic Review* 86 (1995): 339–53, quote on 340.
9 Dante Alighieri, *Inferno*, canto I, 1–2.
10 Christine de Pizan, *The Vision of Christine de Pizan*, trans. Glenda McLeod and Charity Cannon Willard (Woodbridge: Brewer, 2005), 18.
11 Michel Zink, *The Invention of Literary Subjectivity* (Baltimore: Johns Hopkins University Press, 1999).

Further reading

Blumenfeld-Kosinski, Renate and Kevin Brownlee, trans. *The Selected Writings of Christine de Pizan: New Translations, Criticism*. New York/London: Norton, 1997.

Brabant, Margaret, ed. *Politics, Gender, and Genre: The Political Thought of Christine de Pizan*. Boulder: Westview Press, 1992.

Brown-Grant, Rosalind. *Christine de Pizan and the Moral Defence of Women: Reading Beyond Gender*. Cambridge: Cambridge University Press, 2000.

Margolis, Nadia. *An Introduction to Christine de Pizan*. Gainesville: University Press of Florida, 2011.

Willard, Charity Cannon. *Christine de Pizan: Her Life and Works*. New York: Persea Books, 1990.

Part III
Early modern period

13 Introduction

Nina Geerdink and Alicia C. Montoya

Figure 13.1 Carracks of the India Armada of 1507, Livro de Lisuarte de Abreu, 1565, Pierpont Morgan
Library, New York

In a famous letter to his son in his burlesque novel* *Pantagruel* (1532), François Rabelais's fictional giant Gargantua recalled his youth:

> The times were not fit or favourable for learning as is the present day; and I did not have the abundance of instructors that you do. The times were still dark, and reflected the misery and calamity caused by the Goths, who had destroyed all good scholarship. But, through divine grace, during my life light and dignity have been restored to learning; and we have witnessed so much improvement that I would have trouble now being accepted into an elementary children's schoolclass, I who in my maturity was reputed (and not wrongly) the most learned man of the age. . . . Now all disciplines have been restored, languages revived: Greek, without which it is shameful for a person to call himself learned, Hebrew, Chaldean, and Latin. Elegant and correct printed editions are available, the result of a divinely-inspired invention of my time, as by contrast guns are the product of diabolical suggestion.[1]

This letter is paradigmatic: it reflects a consciousness on Gargantua's part – and, by implication, on the part of the author Rabelais, writing in 1532 – that a new epoch, described as an era of "light and dignity," had dawned. This new epoch was tellingly contrasted to the "dark times" of the Goths, or the Middle Ages. It was further marked by its learning, the "revival" of the languages of classical antiquity – Greek, Hebrew, Chaldean, Latin – and a new invention that made knowledge widely available: the printing press*. Gargantua also mentions the military revolution brought about by the invention of "guns".

This, then, was "modernity". Presenting itself as a break with the medieval, modernity's self-definition was, from the beginning, founded on the opposing images of light and darkness, equated respectively with the present-day age and the medieval past. The metaphor* had originated in Italy, with the movement of humanism* and in the writings of Petrarch, an author who – like Rabelais – stood at the crossroads of the medieval and early modern era. Like Rabelais, Petrarch and the Italian humanists presented antiquity as a source of light for modernity, and the Middle Ages as a period of darkness and ignorance. Later on, in the seventeenth and eighteenth centuries, the metaphor of modern light acquired new meanings with the movement known as the Enlightenment*. But as Gargantua's letter made clear, the legacy of modernity was double-edged, as indicated by the two modern inventions he cited: the printing press, that made learning widely available and allowed literature to bloom, but also guns, that made war, death and destruction an inescapable part of daily life for many early modern Europeans. It is this many-faceted nature of "modernity" that we will discuss in this introductory chapter to the early modern age.

Chronological boundaries and features of modernity

While Gargantua's letter expressed the author's feeling that a clear break with the past had taken place, the Middle Ages did not end overnight. Rabelais himself drew inspiration from medieval chapbooks* and legendary characters. So the idea of a "modernity" completely distinct from the medieval past has to be nuanced, and it is impossible to mark a specific turning point. Nonetheless, historians commonly use the term "early modern" to denote a period distinct from and following the Middle Ages. Beginning with the various European Renaissances in the fifteenth and sixteenth centuries, the period extended through the seventeenth and eighteenth centuries. When this period ended has equally been subject of debate. There is some agreement, however, that early modernity came to an end with the age of revolutions, that marked the end of centuries-old political regimes in Europe and its overseas possessions: the American Revolution in 1776, the French Revolution in 1789, and the Haitian Revolution in 1791. These revolutions, and the Napoleonic Wars that followed, announced the dissolution of "old" Europe and ushered in new political entities.

If historians continue to discuss the start and end dates of the early modern period, they similarly debate what modernity encompassed exactly. Scholars do agree, however, about several components that both shaped and characterized modernity. Some were named in Gargantua's letter, such as the invention of the printing press. Others included religious differentiation (Reformation* and Counter-Reformation*), secularisation, individualisation and European expansion overseas.

A series of media revolutions

As Gargantua pointed out, one of the distinguishing features of the new era was the invention of the printing press, that made the spread of knowledge possible among a broad public. While at the end of the Middle Ages the biggest library in Europe, at the University of Paris, possessed only about a thousand volumes, the invention of the printing press made books widely available and accessible even to private citizens. By the middle of the eighteenth century, not only did libraries possessing many times that number of books exist throughout Europe; several also opened their doors to the public at large, so that readers now had many different ways to come in contact with the written word.

The printing press led to the first of several "media revolutions"* that marked the early modern period. While the technique of printing was older than 1453, the real innovation of Johannes Gutenberg, the "inventor" of the printing press, was that he managed to make printing commercially attractive. By improving the technique, he quickened the process, and found shareholders to diminish the financial risks. In Gutenberg's day, a printer could produce about twenty Bibles in the same time a scribe needed to make a single one. And the speed of printing would only increase. Possibilities of distribution* for these printed books also grew. There was an enormous diffusion of the printed word: like the mighty fleet of warships, the Spanish Armada, a veritable fleet of books travelled to new readers through routes both official and unofficial. When European ships sailed to the New World*, they carried not only guns and diseases, but also printed books – Bibles, catechisms, chapbooks, novels and much more. Books crossed borders more easily than did people, and the early modern period was one during which books travelled far and wide.

The importance of the invention of the printing press is evident, but it did not mean that manuscript culture* disappeared altogether. Manuscript circulation of texts remained important until the end of the early modern period. Manuscript transmission was a logical choice in some contexts. Women writers, for example, often preferred to spread their works in manuscript form only, since openly printing their work collided with the modest attitude expected of them. Authors critical of existing powers might also opt for manuscript distribution, in order to avoid censorship* or spread their ideas quickly.

As the manuscript circulation of literature shows, a second aspect of the early modern media revolution was the improved means of communication available to writers and readers. These made possible the creation of what contemporaries called the "Republic of Letters*", an international network of intellectuals who communicated by writing letters. The participants could be professional scholars or scientists, or amateurs. In the correspondences*, they discussed new insights and discoveries as well as issues like academic or scientific institutions, politics and religion, or family life. Alongside the letters, the correspondents sent each other books or pamphlets and material objects of study, like exotic flowers. It was, in a sense, a worldwide web before the invention of the World Wide Web.

The Republic of Letters originated within circles of humanists, corresponding in Latin within a relatively small group, but gradually evolved with the help of universities, academic life and other institutions into a bigger and more organized group of networks in the eighteenth century, communicating primarily in French. Out of this Republic of Letters grew also a new kind of text, uniquely modern, further diffused by means of the printing press: journals and periodicals*. The birth of journalism* in the late seventeenth century was another important event in the early modern media revolution: it announced the separation of authors from the courts and aristocratic patronage networks that had supported them previously – in other words: the advent of free speech.

All the people engaged in making and consuming literature – authors, but also printers, booksellers, hawkers, critics, translators, salon hostesses – collectively gave value to texts, and constituted the literary field*. In the early modern period, this literary field expanded and came to include many new players. Literary criticism* came into being as the increased supply of books led readers to seek advice to guide them in making reading choices. Authors found new ways to profit financially from their writing, with the growth of the book market* and the commercialization of patronage. The increase in reading matter led to new kinds of books, that sought to reach larger numbers of readers. The concept of the modern best-seller* was an invention of this period, made possible by the printing press and improved means of distribution (see also Chapter 11).

Because of all these factors – the growth in number of available texts, new networks of distribution, an expanded literary field – there were also changes in reading practices. Europeans during the early modern period were surrounded by writing: books were widely available in bookstores and libraries, and posters on walls, graffiti, chapbooks and brochures sold by peddlers were everywhere. It has been hypothesized that this early modern information overload led to a "reading revolution" as Europeans moved from intensive to extensive forms of reading, from a literary culture based on the intensive perusal of a single text (the model of Biblical reading) to the more superficial consumption of increasing numbers of texts produced primarily for readers' entertainment – although, as with most generalisations, there were exceptions, and it is best to speak of a diversification and variety of reading experiences than a univocal move towards extensive reading practices.

Religious differentiation and individualisation

Another important historical development was the Reformation and Counter-Reformation. With the Reformation, the Church split into several new groups, one that defined itself as traditionally Catholic, and other Protestant groups that claimed to be truer to the spirit of primitive Christianity than the established Roman Church. This split was spiritual, but also geographic, as Europe split into northern (Protestant) and southern (Catholic), but also eastern (Orthodox) and western units. Europe was torn apart by a series of bloody and immensely destructive wars of religion, and even after, when the dust had settled, religion* continued to play a central role in strengthening or forging political allegiances. The Reformation in turn provoked the Catholic Counter-Reformation, or an attempt to formulate the basic tenets of Catholicism. In this battle for souls, among the means used to reformulate and strengthen faith were printed books – Bibles, prayer books and catechisms* – that enabled ecclesiastic authorities to broadcast their message widely.

One major byproduct of the Reformation and Counter-Reformation was secularisation*. The power of the Catholic Church as an institution diminished, and during the wars of religion secular authorities came to play an important role. The dominance of Catholicism before the Reformation had brought a sense of community. Most people were involved in collective rituals around the church, to which their individual identity was subsumed. During the Reformation, people were forced to make their own choices. Moreover, within the new Protestant and reformed Catholic confessions, individual religiosity was foregrounded, also outside religious institutions. Thus, the influence of religion on society and daily life changed, in a process that is called secularisation.

Secularisation and individualisation emerged in important publications of the time such as the Italian author Pico della Mirandola's *Oratio de hominis dignitate* ('Oration on the dignity of the human being', 1486), which presents the human being as the centre of the universe, between the divine and material spheres, or his fellow countryman Niccolò Machiavelli's *Il principe* ('The Prince', 1513), in which rulers are advised to act morally, thereby implying they also could act immorally – an impossibility from the perspective of the older concept of divine kingship that regarded rulers as ambassadors of God.

Individualisation was not only related to religion. Modernity also saw the birth of the modern self. Although this is a much-debated notion, scholars agree that during early modernity, ideas about individuals changed. Early modern individuals were part of collectives (regional, family, religious) like their medieval counterparts, but during this period self-consciousness about their individual possibilities grew. Authors like Petrarch and Montaigne took individual experiences as a starting point for their writings. Montaigne in his *Essais* ('Essays', 1580) wrote one of the first autobiographical texts in which the individual's private feelings and outlook and not political or military achievements took centre stage. At the same time, his radical subjectivity was marked by scepticism about the possibilities of the individual to know oneself or one's own real inner motives.

Europe and (early) modernity

Most importantly, perhaps, early modernity was a period during which Europe turned outward, in an era of increased cultural and geographical mobility, starting with the Portuguese and Spanish voyages of discovery and leading to the establishment of the first European (plantation) colonies overseas. Modernity had a particular relation to Europe's "others". Historically speaking, a major event often used to mark the beginning of the early modern period is the so-called "fall" of Constantinople, or actually the capture of Constantinople – until 1453, the easternmost outpost of the (Byzantine) Roman Empire – by the Ottoman Turks. This event led to an exodus of intellectuals from Constantinople to mainland Europe, first Italy and then beyond. These intellectuals brought with them knowledge and books from the eastern reaches of the Roman Empire, infusing mainland Europe with new ideas and new inspiration. But the name given to this event reveals the politics at work in early modern definitions of "Europe". What Europeans called the "fall" of the last outpost of the Roman Empire, others viewed as an event to be celebrated: Turks refer to the "conquest of Istanbul", Istanbul being the new name of Constantinople after the "fall". The new ideas that inspired European modernity, then, emerged from this changing relationship between Europe and the world beyond.

Similar remarks could be made about the other major relationship with the world beyond that Europe forged during the early modern period: the voyages of "discovery" and the opening up of "the New World". The "discovery" of America was a discovery only from the European point of view, as native Americans witnessed the cataclysmic destruction of their own world and age-old civilizations like the Aztec and Inca empires. Another European contact with the non-European world was a direct consequence of the settlement of the New World, as several million Africans were enslaved and transported to the Americas to work the land, with a million more killed during their brutal voyage overseas. With the slave trade, Europe's population also changed: by 1600, about 10 percent of the population of Lisbon was African, and throughout Europe, a new urban, multi-ethnic culture took shape that, in many ways, can be regarded as producing the first "modern", geographically displaced European subjects.

European contacts with the world beyond led to a new consciousness of something that was not yet called "European"-ness, but that was nonetheless clearly taking shape. New notions of collective identity were emerging, even if there was as yet no political sense of Europe as such. Articulations of this new, collective self can be found, for example, in Montaigne's essay "Des Cannibales" ('Of Cannibals') in his *Essais*, possibly inspired by his meeting with a group of Tupi-speaking native Americans who had been brought from Brazil to France. In this essay, Montaigne concludes his comparison of Europe with the New World by adopting the first-person "I" and then the plural "we". It is not entirely clear, however, to whom this "we" refers: Montaigne and his French readers? French people in general? Europeans? The so-called civilized world? Such articulations of the collective self, while ethnocentrically never explicitly referring to a specifically "European" identity, were yet preparing the ground for this notion. At their most extreme, however, such hesitations could also lead to a new relativism regarding the cultural primacy of Europe – as is the case in "Des Cannibales", where Montaigne ends up condemning the destruction of the Inca and Aztec empires by the conquistadors.

At the same time, there was a continuous struggle for power between European states, fighting over trade, territory, religion and the relationship with the other outside of Europe. So while, on the one hand, contacts with the non-European world led to the first iterations of a "European" identity, on the other the cultural relativism and hybridization this produced, as well as centrifugal forces redrawing the political map of Europe, led to continuously shifting boundaries in contemporaries' definition of "Europe".

Literary periodizations: three defining metaphors

The different historical periods within early modernity have been described using a series of significant metaphors: Renaissance*, Golden Age* and Enlightenment. Metaphors are a particularly significant figure of speech, because in replacing one term for another, speakers who use metaphors express their own difficulty describing a new phenomenon.

The first defining metaphor used to describe the early modern period was that of Renaissance, literally "rebirth". This points at an element Gargantua's letter underlines, the rediscovery of classical texts and other aspects of antiquity, suggesting that this influence was absent during the Middle Ages. The Renaissance metaphor owes much to nineteenth-century scholarship and Swiss historian Jacob Burckhardt's *Die Kultur der Renaissance in Italien* ('The Culture of the Renaissance in Italy', 1860). This much-debated work has permanently influenced our ideas about the Renaissance. Burckhardt distinguished three crucial transformations in this period: individualism, the rediscovery of antiquity, and the discovery of the world and humankind. These are still the transformations that historians consider crucial.

The poet Petrarch, although he lived before the period we now call the Renaissance, was the founding father of "humanism". In contrast to medieval scholars, he considered it essential to read and study Latin and Greek texts in the original language, following the motto *ad fontes*, back to the sources. Other humanists followed Petrarch's example. Generally speaking, the Renaissance started in southern Europe in the fifteenth century and spread across the continent during the sixteenth century. The medieval idea of *translatio imperii**, the succession of political power from one emperor to the other, was now applied to the new era. This idea described how political and cultural pre-eminence, knowledge and books travelled from antiquity to modernity, first to Renaissance Italy and from there to France and to northern Europe. In some northern regions, such as the Low Countries, important Renaissance developments only really took off at the end of the sixteenth century. At the same time, there was not one universal Renaissance. Every European country had its own Renaissance developments.

A second metaphor, referring to the sixteenth and seventeenth centuries, was that of the Golden Age. During the early modern period, Europe witnessed a succession of "Golden Ages": periods of remarkable prosperity, both economic and cultural. In Spain and England, this Golden Age started in the sixteenth century, whereas the Dutch Republic located its Golden Age in the seventeenth century. The concept of a Golden Age was derived from antiquity, especially Hesiod and Ovid's *Metamorphoses*, in which he described the history of the world, interspersed with classical myths. Ovid organized world history as a sequence: a golden, a silver, a bronze and an iron period. The utopian golden period had known only harmony and prosperity, whereas the iron period was the opposite and the silver and bronze were in between. The economic and cultural prosperity of the early modern period was thereby linked to the classical concept of the Golden Age. Like the term Renaissance, it was fully developed and linked to the creation of national literary canons* only in the nineteenth century.

A third defining metaphor was that of the Enlightenment. Light or enlightenment was a common metaphor to denote knowledge, truth or the use of reason to attain knowledge. During the eighteenth century, throughout Europe, Europeans started using similar terms to describe their age and its ideals: in the English-speaking world, they spoke of "Enlightenment"; in France intellectuals referred to *Lumières*; in Germany to *Aufklärung*; in Hungary men and women spoke of *felvilágosodás*; in Spain they spoke of *Ilustración*; in Denmark of *oplysningstiden*; and in Italy of *illuminismo*. Because the term "Enlightenment" was a metaphor and its meaning was not clearly defined, it could refer to very different worldviews or traditions. Thus, rather than a coherent set of ideas and approaches, the Enlightenment should rather be viewed as a continuing, Europe-wide debate on the means to reach reliable knowledge and to build an ideal society. In this debate, the objects and terms of discussion were continually shifting, and the instruments of the early modern media revolution – printed books, periodicals, the Republic of Letters – played a crucial role in furthering the debate.

The concept of literature

A fundamental continuity during the early modern era was the importance of classicism*. Although the ways in which they were referred to, used and reworked changed over time, the works of classical antiquity remained a crucial literary model. A striking example was the prevailing genre hierarchy. In early modern Europe, literature – like society – was ordered according to a strict hierarchy. At the summit of the genre hierarchy were the most prestigious genres, epic* and tragedy*. Their prestige rested firstly on their relation to history and therefore to the state. Tragedies often recounted the dilemmas of famous rulers, while epics told of the founding of states. Most importantly, epic and tragedy went back to the oldest known literary texts in Europe, the epics of Homer and his later imitator Virgil, and the tragedies of Aeschylus, Sophocles, Euripides and Seneca. Since age equalled prestige in the early modern period, this gave tragedy and epic particular value. Midway along the genre hierarchy was lyric poetry*, a much practised genre, especially in contexts of literary sociability. At the bottom of the genre pyramid was the modern novel*, that began to be accepted as a literary genre only during the eighteenth century.

Dialogue genres* were perhaps most characteristic of the early modern period. The prominence of theatre is only one aspect of this dominance. Among the books used in the cause of religious (re)education in the Reformation and Counter-Reformation was a new genre: the catechism, used first by Protestant leaders such as Martin Luther, whose Large Catechism dates from 1529, and imitated by Catholic authors. The typical question-and-answer format of the catechism made it a genre accessible to many kinds of readers, not only those who had enjoyed advanced schooling but also newly or barely literate readers. Often, indeed, the catechism was – alongside the Bible – the only book owned by early modern readers. But dialogue forms were just as typical of communication among intellectuals, in the correspondences that characterised the Republic of Letters, and in real conversations. Conversation was an important element of humanism, which held that participants best displayed their rhetorical skills, wit and intellect in conversation. Dialogue* was also central to seventeenth- and eighteenth-century salons*, where authors discussed various literary topics under the eye of the presiding salon host or hostess, as well as during the Enlightenment with its focus on debate. In a dialogue, viewpoints shifted, and it was possible to bring together opposing views within one framework. In the eighteenth century, the influence of dialogue forms could be felt in the rise of the epistolary novel*, or a novel made up of letters exchanged between two or more correspondents, and therefore again reflecting a diversity of opinions.

While all of these genres, from tragedy to conversation and from lyric to the novel, made up the literature of the early modern period, the term "literature" itself did not yet exist as such. In French, *littérature* referred simply to all written texts, including such diverse genres as theological works and scientific treatises. In other European countries, the term did not exist at all. Literature as we know it today was most commonly referred to by the term poetry – not unreasonably, since literary genres such as drama were often in verse form, and prose genres, especially the novel, were often excluded from the literary value system*. Authors moved easily between genres: Rabelais for example was trained as a medical doctor, and his first published texts were translations of medical texts. Only at the end of the eighteenth century did terms such as *belles-lettres** begin to be used to distinguish literary texts, or texts with a primarily aesthetic purpose, from other texts.

If the concept of literature was as yet ill-defined, the language of literature was also changing. Whereas, in the Middle Ages, the most prestigious texts were written in Latin, during the early modern period the vernacular languages* of Europe – including English, French, Spanish and German – rose to prominence. In some cases, one particular variety gained dominance: thus, thanks to the influence of Petrarch and other Tuscan humanists, Tuscan, one of the many dialects spoken on the Italian peninsula, came to be considered the standard form of Italian. In other cases, vernacularization was state-driven. Thus, in

France, the ordinance of Villers-Cottêrets, issued in 1539 by the French king, proclaimed French henceforth to be the official language of the kingdom, to be used in all legal and official documents. In northern Europe, Protestantism had an impact on vernacularization and language systematization, since readers were encouraged to read the Bible for themselves. In the Dutch Republic, for example, the so-called States Bible (1637) was the recommended Bible translation for all Protestants and greatly influenced the systematization of Dutch and its use in literary texts. In general, Latin became less important as a literary language, although many authors still continued to write in it, often alongside texts in their own vernacular. Increasingly, translations enabled readers to gain knowledge of texts otherwise inaccessible to them, and naturally gained importance with the decreasing use of Latin as Europe's *lingua franca**. Latin's demise was finally sealed in the course of the eighteenth century, when a new, vernacular *lingua franca*, gained widespread acceptance in Europe, French – not coincidentally, perhaps, at the same time as the new concept of *belles-lettres*, modern "literature", also rose to prominence.

From media revolution to political revolution

Despite the generally inclusive definitions given by contemporaries of "literature", a last important difference between literature now and in the early modern period is the fact that literature was one of fewer media available to the public, and therefore a very powerful one. Since classical rhetoric remained the backbone of literary education, literature was conceived in utilitarian terms, as the art of using language persuasively, in a number of specific contexts: in courts of law, in state councils, to praise or censure great men. Literature played an important role in societal, political and intellectual contexts, and this influence was increased by the media revolutions that made possible the large-scale diffusion of texts among a broad reading public.

During most of the early modern period, literature was closely bound to power. Patronage* was provided by ruling royal families, by powerful aristocrats vying for political influence or by the Church. Literary texts were important means of propaganda and were crucial in preserving power. At the same time, literary texts were the means for individuals or collectives to show their criticism and, in some cases, to enforce changes. The critical role of literature increased during the early modern period since authors began to emancipate themselves from existing power structures, creating what has been called the "public sphere", or an intermediate space between state institutions and the private domain where open debate could flourish. The increasingly autonomous role of literature and authors can therefore also be considered one of the defining features of early modernity. This reached its apex in the eighteenth century.

In fact, the metaphor of the Republic of Letters used by early modern authors also had a political dimension. As an idealized expression of the harmony and cooperation within the community of learned people, the term "republic" denoted a political ideal and expressed the increasingly critical function of literature. While most early modern Europeans lived under monarchic regimes, which were often repressive and had systems of censorship in place to prevent overly critical stances, the metaphor of a Republic of Letters expressed authors' political ideals. A republic, after all, was a state-form that granted its citizens some form of representation and freedom of expression. In addition, republics were more egalitarian than other kinds of state, so what counted in a "republic" of letters was not one's birth, but one's erudition and style. Finally, in a "republic" of letters, knowledge was allowed to circulate freely, crossing linguistic and national borders, and thereby creating a supra-national, virtual entity to replace the harsh political restrictions with which most authors had to deal in their daily life.

The enormous political influence of literature was brought to the fore by a series of publishing events – books banned, burned or censored, and authors exiled or imprisoned for their critical writings – that culminated, finally, in the revolutions that marked the end of the early modern period. Indeed, according to a famous thesis, the French revolution had not only a political but also an intellectual origin, that can be traced back to the new ideas being expressed and circulated in the writings of the period's most prominent authors. If books did not directly cause revolutions, they at least laid the cultural ground-work for them, and the new ideals first expressed in the realm of literature – the birth of the modern self, ideals of political self-determination – eventually found their way into political reality, with the French Revolution, the Napoleonic Wars and the redrawing of the political map of Europe that they set in motion. As Rabelais had intimated in 1532, books and guns would prove to be powerful allies indeed.

Note

1 François Rabelais, "Pantagruel," in *Œuvres Completes*, ed. Mireille Hutchon (Paris: Gallimard [La Pléiade], 1994) (1532), chapter 8, our translation.

Further reading

Bots, Hans and Françoise Wacquet. *La République des Lettres*. Paris/Brussels: Belin/De Boeck, 1997.

Burke, Peter. *The European Renaissance: Centres and Peripheries*. London: Wiley-Blackwell, 1998.

Chartier, Roger. *The Cultural Origins of the French Revolution*. Ithaca: Duke University Press, 1991.

Febvre, Lucien and Henri-Jean Martin. *The Coming of the Book: The Impact of Printing, 1450–1800*. London: Verso, 2010.

Pettegree, Andrew. *Europe in the Sixteenth Century*. Oxford: Wiley-Blackwell, 2002.

14 Staging

Nina Geerdink and Yolanda Rodríguez Pérez

Figure 14.1 Salomon Savery, Stage and hall with boxes in the first public theatre in Amsterdam (1637), engraving on paper, 1658, 51.3 x 72.1 cm

Source: Rijksmuseum, Amsterdam.

When thinking about theatre* in early modern Europe, the figure of William Shakespeare and The Globe theatre in London come almost immediately to mind. We imagine the theatre company of the Lord Chamberlain's Men producing Shakespeare's unforgettable plays that would become a cultural reference for many of us. However, the world of early modern theatre comprises much more than this one association. Our historical perceptions of the past are strongly determined by the late eighteenth- and nineteenth-century discourses that forged literary and historical canons*, both national and European. Shakespeare has since then become a European cultural myth: everyone in Europe feels he or she "owns" a bit of Shakespeare. It is difficult to realize nowadays that Shakespeare was hardly known outside England in the sixteenth and seventeenth centuries and that English was not an international language. Shakespeare's works only started being seriously translated halfway through the eighteenth century.

Nonetheless, we will start this chapter in a non-traditional way with a short overview of Shakespeare's reception during the early modern period.[1] Because so much research has been done on his work during the last century, taking the European reception* of his plays as a starting point can help us to reconstruct important aspects of early modern theatre, such as the power of theatre as a vehicle for the preoccupations in a certain period, or how commercial and ideological motives were instrumental in the cultural transfer* of theatrical texts throughout Europe. Another essential point we will focus on in the following is the practice of staging at a time when theatre was developing into a new form commanding the attention of a cross-section of the population. The key text of this chapter is the Dutch political allegory* *Palamedes* (1625) by Joost van den Vondel.

In the late sixteenth and seventeenth centuries, there were occasional performances of Shakespeare on the continent. There is some scanty evidence of these. Shakespeare performances in Germany, for example, have been mapped systematically.[2] Between 1586 and 1693, only nine possible Shakespeare plays have been identified among plays performed in Germany. An important problem in such an enterprise is that Shakespeare's name was not important at all in this period, and the circulation of his plays across Europe was not only marginal but also anonymous. The content of the plays was more often than not derived from another source than Shakespeare's plays themselves, and often differed fundamentally from the *First Folio*, the 1623 compilation of Shakespeare's works that is the basis of most editions nowadays.

Shakespeare's atrocious revenge tragedy* *Titus Andronicus* (composed around 1590), for example, found an afterlife on the Continent through a German adaptation* that was part of a playbook for English strolling players touring through the German countries. This German adaptation was the source for a now lost Dutch play about Titus Andronicus, which probably was the source for another Dutch adaptation, by the Amsterdam poet Jan Vos, which was very successful and in its turn the source for the English 1678 version by Edward Ravenscroft.[3] It could thus happen that an English author at the end of the seventeenth century used a Dutch play rather than Shakespeare's in order to deal with the same theme on stage as his fellow countryman had done an age earlier.

One of the first published critical opinions on Shakespeare outside of England was the Italian Antonio Conti's in 1726, in the preface of his play *Il Cesare* ('Caesar').[4] It perfectly illustrates the hierarchy at that time: whereas nowadays everybody except the French themselves would probably say Pierre Corneille is France's Shakespeare, Conti wrote that Shakespeare was the Corneille of the English. Some decades later (1761), Voltaire would famously make the same comparison, in his case however with the aim of criticizing Shakespeare. At that time, Shakespeare had started to gain fame outside of England and Voltaire's criticism was rebutted firmly by continental playwrights and other important actors in the field of theatre.

It has been suggested that it was in the first place Shakespeare's *persona*, not his oeuvre, which caused the rise of his fame in the eighteenth century. Shakespeare's presence in Europe developed from marginal and anonymous into monumental and heroic under the influence of the first romantic writers. Before most of his works were read, translated and adapted in other European countries, he had become a hero as the representative of the romantic individual genius, writing against the odds as the son of a glover. The creation of this romantic hero* took place in Germany, the cradle of romanticism, first, but soon enough it became a European topos*. Writers all over Europe used Shakespeare in poetical debates about the strictness of literary rules, the elitist character of literature and the importance of it for the nation-state. The works of Shakespeare fit perfectly well into this discourse, elevating romantic ideals such as lifelikeness and identification, and thematically focusing on the coming into being and the organization of nations. During the eighteenth and nineteenth centuries, many European plays* that aimed at national self-definition show Shakespearean influences. To mention just one example: the Swedish historic opera *Gustaf Wasa* (1786), written by the poet-king Gustav III and his librarian and secretary Johan Henrik Kellgren, was influenced by *Richard III*. Since the end of the eighteenth century, Shakespeare has become the ultimate European representative of early modern theatre, in many countries one of few authors from the period whose plays are still performed now, in the twenty-first century.

Nonetheless, we do have to reset our minds if we are to understand European theatre from the sixteenth and seventeenth centuries. The Spanish monarchy was the leading power at that time, at least until halfway through the seventeenth century, and Spanish hegemony was also strong in the cultural field. Spain provided the world with what we could describe as "the first global drama". Influenced by the Italian *commedia dell'arte**, a tradition of improvised, masked plays, Spanish playwrights such as Félix Lope de Vega y Carpio and Pedro Calderón de la Barca produced plays whose plots and characters would be followed, adapted and further elaborated on European stages. By the 1640s, France would take up the theatrical torch with gifted playwrights such as Pierre Corneille, Jean Racine and Molière (pseud. Jean-Baptiste Poquelin). The Comédie Francaise, Europe's first official national theatre, was founded in 1680, not coincidentally around the time that France became Europe's theatrical capital.

Plays were translated, imitated and emulated within Europe, profiting from the new medium of print, while playwrights, actors, proto-directors and theatre designers travelled and worked internationally. The cross-fertilization between all these different "national" traditions is part of European theatre. Political conflicts and rivalries did not seem to hamper cultural traffic. In this way, Spain and the Dutch Republic could be at war for a seemingly endless period (The Eighty Years' War), but when, in the 1630s, the municipal Theatre of Amsterdam (founded in 1638) needed to be provided with a steady flow of plays for performance, it was not a problem to translate, adapt and freely rework a wide array of Spanish plays.

The power of staging

Whereas a visit to the theatre nowadays is one of many possibilities people have to entertain and educate themselves and learn about public debates, theatre in the early modern period was one of fewer possibilities and, from the sixteenth century onwards, the most important one. Theatre was part of everyday life. It was a window onto the world.

The importance of staging in early modern European culture appears from politics, poetics and the commercial success of drama*. Theatre had become an extremely popular genre during the second half of the sixteenth century. Unlike other literary genres, its social reach was much wider, attracting the attention not just of literate minorities or social elites. Moreover, plays managed to catch the imagination of the public, and their power grew stronger and stronger. The influential poetics of famous Greek and Roman writers such as Aristotle and Horace underlined the power of staging by foregrounding drama, and especially tragedy, as one of the most worthy genres – only epic* was held in higher esteem (see Chapter 1). According to the Dutch playwright Joost van den Vondel in the dedication of his 1654 tragedy *Lucifer*: "Tragedy alone beats them all."[5] At the same time, comedy was one of the most successful genres among the wider swaths of the population who longed for thrilling plots full of surprise, action and strong emotions.

Literature in general, now as then, can be considered as an alternative vehicle for contemporary perceptions and preoccupations and theatre revealed itself, as a consequence of both its high esteem and its commercial possibilities, not only a provider of entertainment but also a highly effective medium to ventilate ideological messages. Like any early modern text, this happened by means of (ancient) rhetoric* (see Chapter 5). But there was more to the power of theatre. A play offered authors the possibility to discuss different aspects of a problem while subtly presenting audiences with the most desirable solution. This could be expressed by reliable and sympathetic characters. Many performative techniques, such as choral hymns, meaningful costumes and decors, or *tableaux vivants*, could be used to underline the messages of the play. The fact that a theatre performance is always seen in company gives it the power to unite an audience and strengthen its opinion in line with the messages of the play. The rich array of performative possibilities provided through staging had been elaborated on in poetical treatises from the classical period onwards (see Chapter 4).

It comes as no surprise, then, that in most European countries there existed a close relationship between the theatre and the court, courtly and aristocratic patronage* being a frequent way of financing and supporting playwrights. This patronage facilitated the use of the stage in a top-down manner as a vehicle for certain views, such as defending political decisions or conflicts with neighbouring countries. But theatre was also a medium to voice dissident perspectives and critique within one's own society. Plays reflect a social order that can be contested or put into question.

A case in point is the Dutch play *Palamedes* by Joost van den Vondel, published in 1625. The plot* deals with the betrayal of the Greek army commander Palamedes, but was immediately recognized as an allegory for the execution of the former Advocate (Grand Pensionary) of Holland Johan van Oldenbarnevelt in 1619. The execution of Oldenbarnevelt was the climax of heated religious and political debate and uproar in the Dutch Republic. His death had caused a great shock. Oldenbarnevelt had been the opponent of stadholder prince Maurits van Nassau who became, after the 1619 execution, the most important leader of the country. The theme of *Palamedes* remained topical during the whole seventeenth century since it reflected the tension between two political factions: the supporters of the Nassaus and the republicans who did not want this or any dynasty in power.

As appears from several handwritten keys that revealed the allegorical layers of the play, for example by identifying characters from the play with real persons, it was in vogue to decode *Palamedes* as a narration of the real-life drama of Oldenbarnevelt during the whole seventeenth century.[6] The play itself motivated this decoding, as is clearly shown in the description of the execution of Palamedes at the start of the fifth act. As was usual in those days, something as horrifying as an execution, a stoning in this case, was not performed, but visually recounted by a messenger. In the below quotation, in which we emphasized words related to our argument in this chapter, the messenger recounts the execution at Palamedes's brother's request.

> *Text: Joost van den Vondel,* Palamedes, oft vermoorde onnooselheyd
> *('Palamedes, or Killed Innocence', 1625)*
>
> The prince of the Euboeans rose then from his seat
> And spoke: O men, so stirred to frenzy that you seek
> To pounce upon my innocence! Is this the way

My forty years of loyal service you'd repay?
Must all my slaving end in blood-soaked infamy?
Traitor, they screamed, may Jove avenge your perjury!
You have been judged! He spoke no more and left the hall.
. . .
With courage then he walked, his bearing dignified;
Pushed onward by the guards and townsfolk thronging close,
He slowly made his way towards Ida's wooded slopes.
A hill that rises at the mountain's foot had grown
Aslant, much like a **theatre** – its summit crowned
In splendor with a temple to the sun, whose gifts
Of costly ornaments sent out, when mighty ships
Still anchored there, a beacon in the sea. The god
It was, who at the eastern gable proudly stood
With flaming torch of gold, that in its natural way
Illumined human faces with the light of day.
Now this majestic building lies there devastated,
Reduced to here and there a heap of desecrated
Stones, all its former glory mourned in long laments.
Our soldiers' malice feasted on that sacredness,
Devouring it in flames. No word came from the priest,
Who laughed as human scum laid Phoebus' shrine to waste,
And grinned at how they mocked the lofty Phrygian god
With the unholy **spectacle** they **staged**. This spot –
Revered as hallowed ground by generations past,
But since the soldiers' rampage, spat upon and cursed
And by appalling verdict doomed to **patricide** –
Now **swarms with people**. Streaming in from far and wide,
They gather on the mountainside till Ida crawls
With life, for there they've found an **open view** across
To this hilltop. Unnumbered souls climb cypresses,
Bend branches, shake the foliage. What turmoil this!
Each has his motive: This one's calm and cool and knows
Not what he hopes for in these world affairs, but goes
To **see** it all unfold, just following the throng.
Another spews his gall and whets his deadly tongue
To arrow-sharpness; imitating priestly style,
He fulminates against his fellow man in vile
Words, driven to a pitch by his benighted zeal
That thirsts for noble blood. A third has made a pale
Attempt to speak against the action on that stage,
But, fearing he'll incur the rabble's growing rage,
Now holds his tongue, and comes with rueful heart to see
This prologue to a **European tragedy**.[7]

In this gripping passage, the messenger describes the moment when Palamedes is ordered to leave his imprisonment to be executed. He tells the public what is happening from a high viewpoint on a hill. This was a frequent technique used since classical times ("tei-choscopy"*) and it was used for dramatic effect or in cases when certain scenes were difficult to stage, such as battles or, as in this case, an execution with a witnessing mob. The messenger presents Palamedes, who in Greek mythology was the son of Nauplius, king of Euboea, in the first line of the quoted fragment as a Euboean prince. The words of Palamedes, however, do not at all correspond to the mythological figure: he pleads innocent and shows disappointment about the fact that he is to be put to death in return for forty years of loyal service. The young warrior Palamedes was not even forty years of age when he was executed, whereas Oldenbarnevelt in 1619 was an old man who famously walked to the scaffold leaning on his cane. (The collection of the Dutch Rijksmuseum still has a cane that is said to have been Oldenbarnevelt's.) He had worked in the service of the Dutch Republic for more than forty years. After this evident deviation from the original myth, the resemblances between the description of Palamedes walking to the temple of Themis, the goddess of Justice, where he will be lapidated, and what was known about the context of Oldenbarnevelt's beheading cannot go unnoticed. Oldenbarnevelt was said to have walked from the courtroom to the scaffold steadily and holding his head high, which corresponds to the words "brave and with an apt attitude" (verse 1,892). Oldenbarnevelt had to make a way for himself through an immense crowd of soldiers and burghers. Palamedes too, can barely walk through the crowd.

The words the messenger uses to describe the death of Palamedes are pervaded with the critical perspective Palamedes's brother logically represented. This perspective corresponds with the harsh criticism of the persecution and death of Oldenbarnevelt that was (anonymously and in disguise) uttered by Vondel and others in 1619 and the following years. The messenger expands on the wrongful situation, and his argumentation is filled with persuasive stylistic figures, to describe the event as a very sad and unnecessary one. He uses words such as patricide (verse 1,913), referring to Oldenbarnevelt's nickname as *pater patriae* ('father of the country'), and elaborates on the opposition between the holiness, beauty and importance of the place where the sentence will be executed, a mountain that is regarded as a holy place since it houses the oracle of Themis,[8] and its ugliness afterwards, when it is cursed by the cruel execution. Palamedes's death is presented in the last line of the quote as a danger for peace and harmony in the whole of Europe. Indeed, the death of Oldenbarnevelt was an event of great importance not only for the Dutch Republic itself, but also for many other European countries, with which the Dutch Republic was at war (e.g. Spain), or which were experiencing comparable religious and political troubles.

It thus comes as no surprise that the theme also reached the English stage in Philip Massinger and John Fletcher's *The Tragedy of Sir John van Olden Barnavalt*, an English play that was published in 1619 only a couple of months after the execution of the Advocate of Holland. The play by Massinger and Fletcher portrayed, remarkably, both Maurits and Oldenbarnevelt as leading figures with serious shortcomings. It was suspected of criticizing the monarchy of James I. *The Tragedy* thus offers an interesting analogy with *Palamedes*: the narrative of the execution of Oldenbarnevelt is the surface level in this English play, whereas in *Palamedes*, it is the allegorical level.

As one could expect, these kinds of critical plays could encounter censorship because of their controversial contents. The same holds for examples of immorality. Censorship* was applied in both Catholic and Protestant countries for reasons of both religious and political origin. The way to handle censorship, its character, approach and focus, differed within Europe and even within countries. Vondel's *Palamedes*, for example, was forbidden immediately after it was published and the central government in The Hague was ready to condemn its author to death, but the city council of Amsterdam, where the play was published, was more lenient and after prosecuting him at the town hall, they let him go with a fine. The fact that the play was forbidden made it impossible to perform it, but it sold very well under the counter. The English topicality of *The Tragedy of Sir John van Olden Barnavalt*, however, was noticed in a preventive action of censorship, which was common in England, but after a postponement and some revisions, Massinger and Fletcher were able to perform the play nonetheless.

One of the main actors in the censorship "game" were the church and ecclesiastical authorities. They could have a major impact on the freedom of movement within theatres. Protestant preachers were critical about theatre in general and seized their chances every time something that had to do with theatre plays caused any disturbance. It led to many polemics and often also to the prohibition of plays or forced revisions and interventions. The fact that theatre was regarded as a serious threat to Calvinist morality, and to peace and order in general, reveals the importance of this literary genre in early modern society.

Theatres could be closed for years because of religious complaints or for example because of mourning following a death within a royal family (as in Spain when Philip II died in 1598, or when his grandson Philip IV passed away in 1665, after which theatres were closed for five years). Other reasons were of political character, like the closure in England in 1642 with the outbreak of the Civil War (1642–1649) and the ensuing Commonwealth under the Puritan Oliver Cromwell. Public theatres were only reopened after 1660, when the monarchy was restored and Charles II came to power.

In the cultural transfer of theatrical texts, both commercial and ideological motives are visible. The decision of the Amsterdam Theatre directors to stage Spanish plays from the moment of the creation of this institution in 1638 onwards was mainly due to economic reasons, since they knew these plays were much liked among the public and could easily be box-office successes. Surprisingly for some, in a period when the Dutch Republic still was at war with Spain, the plays by the Spanish "Phoenix of Wits" Lope de Vega were more popular than those by the great Dutch author Joost van den Vondel.[9]

At the same time, ideological motives could explain the appeal of certain plays. Thomas Kyd's famous *Spanish Tragedy* (1582–92), with its cruel main character Jeronimo, enjoyed great popularity in the Dutch Republic, and was also freely adapted in Dutch with the title *Ieronimo* by Adriaen van den Bergh. The play was performed in Utrecht in 1621, the year when war with Spain was resumed after the Twelve Years' Truce. It could not be a sheer coincidence that a vengeful and bloodthirsty Spaniard was brought to the stage at such a bellicose historical moment.[10]

The practice of staging

As both a cause and a consequence of the power of staging in early modern European societies, theatre became, at the end of the sixteenth century, a very visible practice. This in contrast to previous forms of staging such as the French medieval dramatic societies (*puys**) or the Dutch and Flemish ones (*rederijkerskamers**) with their more limited reach and static presentation. Drama had passed from the hands of the clergy into those of the laity by then. Plays were first performed in private homes as well as in religious and political buildings, and on streets and squares during carnivals, fairs or other festivities (see also Chapter 7). In Spain, charitable brotherhoods built hospitals for the needy in the city and were licensed to erect a temporary stage in certain yards between houses in order to raise funds for their institutions. From the second half of the sixteenth century onwards, theatre plays were performed more and more often in buildings that were especially designed and built for them. These playhouses were designed as palaces with a representative function and the possibility to accommodate sometimes up to thousands of people. The progressive establishment of theatres had far-reaching consequences for the stability of the theatrical profession and for the development of stage effects.

With the theatres a new profession was born: professional acting troupes. Where did these actors* perform, and what means did they have to perform? The architecture of the first early modern playhouses was inspired by Italian examples, relying on the ancient Roman *theatrum**. They were partially open-air buildings of a rectangular shape (France, Spain) or polygonal (England), with a plain curtain as a backdrop and consisting of different tiers with galleries and an open central yard where the noisy and boisterous "groundlings" or *mosqueteros* stood (the *parterre*). The audience was socially mixed; about a third of the play-goers stood, and the remaining two-thirds sat. The nobility sat in lateral boxes. Women and men were seated apart in some countries. The unruly groundlings could make or break a play with their interventions. In the Dutch Republic, the first theatre was only built in the 1630s, following examples from Spain and France (and thus showing the relevance of these countries for seventeenth-century theatre in Europe), but without an open-air part.

Theatre buildings in most European cities were more than just a building where plays could be performed. They were moveable props in the power contest between European countries during the sixteenth and seventeenth centuries. The architecture of the buildings, on the inside as well as the outside, was developed in order to showcase the significance of the town or the country. It was magnificent and contained many references to the wealth of the city or the country and the importance of theatre. Rulers always took their international visitors to the theatre to show off their country's might. When visiting Amsterdam in October 1648 (the year of the signing of the Peace with Spain), the Prince of Wales, the future Charles II, also visited the city theatre and saw a play by Isaac Vos, actually an adaptation of Lope de Vega's *Fuerza Lastimosa* ('Painful Force').[11] This example reveals the international nature of theatre. There was nothing odd in an English king seeing an adaptation of a Spanish play on Dutch soil.

Performance practices were relatively simple until the beginning of the seventeenth century. The stage, with a curtain as a backdrop and some objects on stage, had to be enough to conjure an imaginary world for the public. As theatre became more popular, playwrights started to think about the possible ways to meet their public's expectations and as the century proceeded, spectacular stage effects became more and more frequent, since baroque style focused on effect and surprise. Lope de Vega ridiculed this exaggerated obsession with "special effects" in a dialogue between the personified "Theatre" and a "Visitor": the former complains about the way he is perforated and tampered with for the installation of those over-the-top stage tricks and flying systems.[12] Sophisticated techniques were developed for royal theatres like the one in the Buen Retiro Palace in Madrid, where the stage was placed close to an artificial lake so that naval battles could be re-enacted and a wide variety of special effects like fireworks could be integrated into the play. Also, European theatres began to look more like the theatres we know now, with changeable decors that could be richly decorated. The extended possibilities of the theatres, as much as their architecture and programme, played an important role in the international competition between countries. The fact that Amsterdam did not have any of the modern facilities at its disposal that other countries did have was a decisive factor in the renovation of the theatre in 1665.

As far as performance* practices are concerned, it is interesting to remark that the way plays or scripts were used differs greatly from its functioning nowadays. The idea of copyright* had not been invented yet. Plays belonged to theatrical companies or theatres, and playwrights had no rights over them. This fact reveals the instability of the written script in this historical period. A play could be altered by the director of the company or theatre if it was deemed necessary. Scenes could be changed or added, and dialogues altered. Theatre was a fluid art. When the intellectual poet Joost van den Vondel, who had written *Palamedes* in his younger years, wrote his ambitious tragedy *Lucifer* about the angel's revolt in Heaven, boosting philosophical, theological and political deliberations and debates reaching from questions of political sovereignty and individual free will to God's election, the directors of the Amsterdam theatre did everything in their power to make the intellectually challenging play a visual spectacle too, creating a wooden "Heaven" on stage which allowed the angels to fly, and adding some spectacular *tableaux vivants*.[13] Around the turn of the century, performances of *Palamedes* were made into an attractive visual spectacle by adding *tableaux vivants* too, one of which represented Palamedes's lapidation.

The current practice at the time of keeping original manuscripts* by the poets among the company's papers (in a chest) contributed to the survival of many autographs*. At the same time, early modern theatre plays were printed very often. This has to do with the essential role the theatre public played in the staging. Whereas the public in theatres nowadays is a quiet listener, absorbing without disturbing, the early modern public was expected to react. When they saw something awful, they were expected to scream, when they saw the villain running away, they would give the hero instructions to catch him, and so forth. Since this led to chaos and noise among the public, one could read what was actually said on stage in printed leaflets that could be bought in the theatre. The printed theatre texts were also sold at bookstores and read at home, sometimes long after a play was performed. Or, in a case such as *Palamedes*, where staging was impossible, long before it was performed. *Palamedes*, written in 1625, was not performed for the first time until 1664.

In European theatres, plays were performed by the theatre's own professional acting troupe, but there were also visiting troupes that performed outside of theatre buildings too, during carnivals and at fairs and other festivities. Strolling players were travelling around Europe long before the first static theatres were built, from the second half of the fifteenth century onwards, and they were pivotal for the European circulation of theatre plays.[14] This was also the circuit in which some of Shakespeare's plays were performed outside of England. The second life of a Spanish play like Calderón's *La vida es sueño* ('Life is a dream', 1635), about the Polish prince Segismundo and with the central themes of free will and fate, is a case in point. Spanish companies performed with some regularity at the court of the Archdukes in Brussels, where they coincided with English and French companies. The Spanish Archduchess introduced performances of Spanish plays at court, staged in Spanish by her own ladies-in-waiting and servants. The southern Netherlands thus had an intermediary function in the circulation of Spanish plays in Northern Europe. Calderón's play was performed at the Amsterdam theatre in the 1647 translation of a minor poet from Brussels called Schouwenbergh. The same translation* was performed all over Europe by a Dutch itinerant troupe. This group travelled in the southern Netherlands, in some German countries, in Scandinavia and in Poland. The Dutch acting group had a good reputation in Northern Europe and was often invited to play at royal courts or on the occasion of local festivities. We know for sure that the troupe performed Calderón in Hamburg in 1654 and at the royal court in Stockholm between 1664 and 1667, but since they had the costumes for the play (Polish clothes) in their possession, they must have performed the play at many other places, too.[15]

Strolling players, and thus the circulation of plays throughout Europe, met with difficulties of all kinds during their travels. In the first place, there were the practical difficulties that came with travelling from, for example, Madrid to Amsterdam or Amsterdam to Stockholm in a world without planes, trains or cars. The actors had to move themselves and their costumes and decor in mule- or horse-drawn carts and wagons. Moreover, the different acting traditions in European countries sometimes caused problems for itinerant troupes: whereas in France and Spain women could perform on stage since the end of the sixteenth century, boys took the female parts in London and Amsterdam. In the Dutch Republic, the first female known to have performed on stage was acting in 1655, whereas in England, women were allowed to act in 1660. Although some long-living prejudices link the Catholic south with a certain narrow-mindedness, the possibilities for female actors were certainly better there than in the northern Protestant countries. Cross-dressing, women disguised as men, was a successful dramatic resource in early modern theatres where female actors were allowed, but a certain sexual *decorum* still had to be followed: these female actors wore male clothing above the waist and a skirt below, not provocative tight clothes.

The travelling acting groups performing everywhere are but one example demonstrating that staging was not restricted to theatre buildings, courts and official open-air playgrounds. Many events could be strongly theatrical. In some households, during parties or among gatherings of family or friends, stagings could be a social event, taking the form of informal role-playing, theatrical games and also scripted drama. Staging also played an important role on the occasion of communal festivities, such as royal entries. When a city welcomed a ruler – its own or a guest from another country – the central streets and squares were crowded with people and performances, both looking at the ruler and the performers in his parade, and showing their own. This theatrical decor was held to be very important, something that is evident from the amount of money that was involved: the entry of the future King Philip II in Antwerp in 1549 was more expensive than the building of the town hall slightly over a decade later.[16] But of course, Philip was travelling with his father Charles V for the first time to the Low Countries to meet his future subjects and the northerners wanted to be magnificent and lavish in showing their loyalty and affection. This entry involved, among other things, the staging of many *tableaux vivants*, a processional parade and a presentation in battle array.

Theatrum mundi

Since theatre was literally everywhere in early modern Europe, people often compared the real world with a stage. The so-called *theatrum mundi** metaphor, the idea that the world can be seen as a stage where individuals play roles and wear masks, finds its origins in classical antiquity (Seneca, among others). It was very popular in early modern culture, in the world of theatre itself in the first place. Shakespeare voiced it in his famous verses "All the world's a stage,/And all the men and women merely players" (from *As You Like It*, 1599 or 1600[17]) and like him, many other playwrights made use of this metaphor: Joost van den Vondel did so, as did Pierre Corneille, as did Calderón de la Barca.

The metaphor* helped people to understand the society they lived in, but at the same time problematised it, showing how life is in fact as unreliable as the world shown on stage. In the context of the brevity of human existence, life was seen like a play, with a beginning, middle and end. This basic idea was further elaborated, stressing that it did not matter how long life took, as long as one lived in the right way before death came. Worldly riches and merits were just like a disguise that one takes off at the end of one's life, just like an actor does with his clothes at the end of the play.

This vision connects with another long European tradition: the "dances of death*", *danse macabre* or the *danzas de la muerte*, a medieval allegorical concept that underlines the all-conquering and equalizing power of death. It also reveals a certain determinist fatalism, since man is presented as a passive toy of Fortune or of God, that cannot bend his destiny (the script) that has been written for him in advance. We see here the conflict between theories of predestination against the possibility of a free will, which were so essential in the theological debates of the time. Calderón de la Barca in his religious play, *El gran teatro del mundo* ('The great theatre of the world', staged in 1659), reflects in a Christian key on these existential questions. Actors in his play (mankind) are judged by the playwright (God), their moral conduct is weighed, and at the end the author underlies the fugacity and futility of life: *vanitas vanitatis*.[18]

Parallel to the prominence of the *theatrum mundi* metaphor within theatre plays and debates about theatre, we see the same ideas appearing in the rest of early modern society. Comparisons to theatre were part of daily life, in which people tended to model their behaviour after the roles they thought fit for certain settings. Famous philosophers such as Erasmus, Thomas More and Montaigne refer to the world as a stage, and the map-maker and geographer Abraham Ortelius named his famous atlas of the world in 1570 *Theatrum orbis terrarum*.

Such comparisons and references are both a sign of the power of staging, and a reinforcement of it. The power of staging increased as a consequence of the dominance of the topos: a play such as Vondel's *Palamedes*, an allegory referring to an actual political situation, can be read as a powerful statement about that particular situation, even more so because the borders between stage and reality were perceived to be crossed so easily.[19] The play itself underlines this interconnection between stage and reality by referring to events on stage with theatrical terms, which is very clear in the fragment cited above. When describing the future execution from his high vantage point, the messenger compares what he sees with a "theatre" (verse 1,896). He alludes to the gathering of the people and their attitude is described in terms that could also be used in the description of a theatre public eager to have a good view, some of them self-contained, some ready to react heatedly. The execution itself is called a "tragedy" (verse 1,929). Vondel's intention with his tragedy about the unjust death of such an exemplary political figure was probably crystal clear for the alert public of the time, who would grasp the implicit criticism. Thanks to plays like these we can reconstruct nowadays the importance of the role of literature, and specifically theatre as a mass medium, as a vehicle for contemporary reflection.

Notes

1 Our overview is primarily based on Luis A. Pujante and Ton Hoenselaars, *Four Hundred Years of Shakespeare* (London: Rosemont Publishing, 2003).
2 Albert Cohn, *Shakespeare in Germany in the Sixteenth and Seventeenth Centuries* (London: Asher & Co, 1865).

3 Helmer Helmers, "The Politics of Mobility: Shakespeare's *Titus Andronicus*, Jan Vos's *Aran en Titus* and the Poetics of Empire," in *Politics and Aesthetics in European Baroque and Classicist Tragedy*, ed. Jan Bloemendal and Nigel Smith (Leiden: Brill, 2016), 344–72.

4 Alberto Conti, *Il Cesare* (Faenza: G.A. Archi, 1726), 54–5. Quoted in Balz Engler, "Constructing Shakespeares in Europe," in *Four Hundred Years of Shakespeare in Europe* (Newark: University of Delaware Press, 2003), 26–39, 27.

5 Joost van den Vondel, *Lucifer*, ed. J.F.M. Sterck (Amsterdam: Wereldbibliotheek, 1931), 604.

6 Nina Geerdink, "Politics and Aesthetics – Decoding Allegory in *Palamedes* (1625)," in *Joost van den Vondel: Dutch Playwright of the Golden Age*, ed. Jan Bloemendal and Frans-Willem Korsten (Leiden: Brill, 2012), 225–48.

7 Joost van den Vondel, *Palamedes, oft vermoorde onnooselheyd*, ed. J.F.M. Sterck (Amsterdam: Wereldbibliotheek, 1929), v. 1881–1887, 1892–1930, translation by Myra Scholz. Emphasis added.

8 It appears from Vondel's foreword to the play that he had meant the execution of Palamedes to take place at Delphi's oracle, that used to be Themis's before it became Apollo's. Vondel situates the oracle on a hill in Beotia, however, which was not the region in ancient Greece where Delphi was situated.

9 Leonor Álvarez, Frans Blom and Kim Jautze, "Spaans Theater in de Amsterdamse Schouwburg (1638–1672)," *De Zeventiende Eeuw* 32 (2016): 12–39.

10 See Ton Hoenselaars and Helmer Helmers, "*The Spanish Tragedy* and the Tragedy of Revenge in the Low Countries," in *Doing Kyd: A Collection of Articles on the Spanish Tragedy*, ed. N. Cinpoes (Manchester: Manchester University Press, 2016), 144–67.

11 Andries van Praag, *La comedia espagnole aux Pays-Bas au XVIIe et au XVIIIe siècle* (Amsterdam: A.H. Paris, 1922), 50–2, 84.

12 José María Ruano de la Haza, "Lope de Vega and the theatre in Madrid," in *A Companion to Lope de Vega*, ed. Alexander Samson and Jonathan Thacker (Woodbridge: Tamesis, 2008), 45.

13 Mieke B. Smits-Veldt, "Vertoningen in opvoeringen van Vondels Tragedies 1638–1720," *De Zeventiende Eeuw* 11 (1995): 214–15.

14 See Robert Henke and Eric Nicholson, eds., *Transnational Mobilities in Early Modern Theater* (Farnham/Burlington: Ashgate, 2014).

15 About the travels of the Dutch troupe and their performances of De Vega's play, see Ben Albach, *Langs kermissen en hoven* (Zutphen: De Walburg Pers, 1977).

16 Stijn Bussels, *Spectacle, Rhetoric and Power* (Amsterdam/New York: Rodopi, 2012), 10–11.

17 William Shakespeare, *As You Like It*, ed. Alan Brissenden (Oxford: Oxford UP, 1998), 2.7.139–140.

18 John J. Allen and Domingo Ynduráin, *El gran teatro del mundo* (Barcelona: Crítica, 1997).

19 René van Stipriaan, "Het *theatrum mundi* als ludiek labyrint," *De Zeventiende Eeuw* 15 (1999): 12–23.

Further reading

Bloemendal, Jan and Frans-Willem Korsten, eds. *Joost van den Vondel: Dutch Playwright of the Golden Age*. Leiden: Brill, 2012.

Henke, Robert and M.A. Katritzky, eds. *European Theatre Performance Practice, 1580–1750*. Farnham/Burlington: Ashgate, 2014.

Henke, Robert and Eric Nicholson, eds. *Transnational Mobilities in Early Modern Theatre*. Farnham/Burlington: Ashgate, 2014.

Pujante, A. Luis and Ton Hoenselaars, eds. *Four Hundred Years of Shakespeare in Europe*. London: Rosemont Publishing, 2003.

Samson, Alexander and Jonathan Thacker, eds. *A Companion to Lope de Vega*. Woodbridge: Tamesis, 2008.

15 Reading

Robert Folger and Konstantin Mierau

Figure 15.1 Gustave Doré adapted by W. Piron

Today, *Don Quixote* is *the* classic of Golden Age Spanish literature; yet Miguel de Cervantes's masterpiece can hardly be considered typical of its time, a time in which literary quality was still very much considered in the light of received classical precepts. However, the model authors of Greco-Roman antiquity and authoritative poetics* had not provided a paradigm for longer fictional prose texts, and in the Middle Ages, literature was essentially poetry. Prose was used for historiography and "practical" texts in the broad sense of the term, ranging from administration to science and theology. Even in Cervantes's time, in treatises on literature such as *Philosophia antigua poetica* (1596) by Alonso López ("El Pinciano"), fictional prose texts were considered suspect as "lies" unless they could claim to offer moral reform, indoctrination or edification. One of the great projects – and achievements – of Spanish Golden Age literature was exploring the literary potential of prose texts for the representation of lived reality. Ironically, works like *Don Quixote* became classics precisely because they were groundbreaking in their own time.

Don Quixote has a complex structure and a broad, heterogeneous content, bound together by the theme of reading*. This central theme connects the knight errant's adventures and his phantasmagoric world, the life of many of the characters he encounters and, not least, the narrators' preoccupations. The humble squire Alonso Quijano loses his mind and becomes the "heroic knight" Don Quixote as a consequence of his imprudent and excessive reading. The episodic sequence of chivalric adventures is gradually transformed into a novelistic plot by characters who are also readers of chivalric romance*, which allows them to play along with and manipulate Don Quixote and his peasant-turned-squire Sancho Panza, whose initial oafishness, colloquial language and interest in material well-being make him the perfect side-kick to the "Ingenious Gentleman". We find readers of literature at all social levels (judges, soldiers, shepherds, innkeepers, women) and in the most unlikely places (homes, inns, the wilderness), and their reading practices become the starting point for reflections on the "art of reading". The narrator* is yet another reader; rather than narrate a story he conceives himself, he turns out to be basing his narrative on an Arabic chronicle*, which he reads in translation* into Castilian. Reading characterizes every fibre of this unique literary universe. In the second part, to add yet more complexity, many of the characters have actually read the first part and react to Don Quixote as one would react to a crazed actor who appears to have assimilated the identity of his character. What is more, some have even read an "apocryphal" second part, a sequel by another author, making the web of readings even more complex.

Don Quixote is a novel of novels and melting-pot of literary tradition*. An undisputed inspiration for *Don Quixote* and other innovative prose fiction throughout Europe was Fernando de Rojas's *Celestina* (1499–1502), a prose drama in imitation of Roman comedy*, which promised remedies against the perils of passionate love. This work, set in brothels and inns and featuring a go-between as a central character, opened the path for one of the great contributions of Spanish letters to world literature: the picaresque novel*, first-person narrations of low-born rogues recounting episodes of failed social ascent. The depiction of "low-life heroes", called *pícaros*, is the counterpoint to lofty pastoral* romance, which drew on the prestige of classical bucolic* models (see Chapter 5) in terms of topics, style and setting. In the pastoral novel, universal themes such as love and death are contemplated in an idealized nature: a fiction with an undoubtedly escapist function in an increasingly urban culture. Chivalric romance, another important prose genre, had a medieval pedigree. The first manifestations presented themselves as chronicles*, and told the adventures of heroic knights errant (see Chapter 9). These texts enjoyed substantial popularity in the sixteenth century, but they were also vilified by the learned elites* because they could not claim to be "useful". Cervantes, however, who shared the erudition of the learned elites yet had a profound understanding of the reading public's taste, succeeded in utilizing the literary potential of the chivalric novel*. As an avid reader and connoisseur of literary traditions and trends, he would integrate all of the major prose genres of his time into the narrative frame of chivalric romance. In doing so, he created a text that, rather than following a genre, reflected on the notion of genre itself, thus creating a milestone in literature: the first modern novel, *El ingenioso hidalgo don Quijote de la Mancha* ('The Ingenious Hidalgo Don Quixote De La Mancha').

Reading as a mode of characterization

Most if not all characters in Cervantes's novel are characterized through what they read. This principle has its hyperbolic manifestation in the protagonist; excessive reading of chivalric romances is the cause of his insanity.

> *Text: Miguel de Cervantes,* Don Quixote *(1605, 1615)*
>
> Now you must understand that during his idle moments (which accounted for most of the year) this hidalgo took to reading *books of chivalry*. . . . [H]is foolish curiosity reached such extremes that he sold acres of arable land to buy these books of chivalry, . . . he liked none of them so much as those by the famous Feliciano de Silva, because the brilliance of the prose and all that intricate language seemed a treasure to him, never more so than when he was reading those amorous compliments and challenges delivered by letter, in which he often found: "The reason for the unreason to which my reason is subjected, so weakens my reason that I have reason to complain of your beauty." . . . Such subtleties used to drive the poor gentleman to distraction, and he would rack his brain trying to understand it all and unravel its meaning[1]

The undisputed foundational classic of the chivalric romance in Spain is Garci Rodríguez de Montalvo's *Amadís de Gaula* (1508), a compilation and revision of older medieval texts. It spawned a host of translations into the major European languages, as well as sequels* and imitations*. *Amadís* inspired several operas in the seventeenth and eighteenth centuries, and the considerable number of Renaissance and Baroque tapestries preserved in European museums indicates that the novel and its cast also had a visual presence in the palaces and homes of European aristocrats. When Cervantes wrote his *Don Quixote*, the heyday of the chivalric novel had passed, although it was still popular with readers.

Feliciano de Silva – Don Quixote's personal favourite, as we learn in the fragment previously – was a prolific and successful sixteenth-century author of chivalric romances (*Lisuarte de Grecia, Amadís de Grecia, Florisel de Niquea, Rogel de Grecia*), some of them "sequels" to the famed *Amadís de Gaula*. The popularity of the genre, and its wide diffusion among all layers of Spanish society, was a matter of concern for "serious writers" and moralists. Chivalric romance is indebted to medieval epics*, presenting a heroic knight who embarks, often unaware of his own noble lineage, on a quest of honour through adventure. This quest is presented to the reader as a chronicle that artfully combines and alternates several subplots*.

A reader of these and other chivalric novels, the lowly *hidalgo*, or squire, Alonso Quijano goes mad and reinvents himself as Don Quixote. Inspired by the *razones* or 'reasons' ridiculed in the quote opening this section, he sets out in the make-shift attire of a knight to restore the halcyon days of the knights errant, who save damsels in distress and champion the disenfranchised. The narrator juxtaposes Don Quixote's reading-induced projection of chivalric imagery* onto the world (e.g. regarding prostitutes as fair virgins), with minute descriptions of everyday life in sixteenth-century Castile. The reader is aware that

Don Quixote's damsels in distress are actually prostitutes, his disenfranchised nobles canny criminals; this constant contrast is one of the major sources of the book's timeless humour.

In the sixteenth century, the chivalric novel was successful, but by no means universally praised. There was fierce criticism, mostly of its profane content, which was not considered conducive to moral improvement. Chivalric romance contains elements of courtly love, but also mundane eroticism. In *Amadís de Gaula*, for example, there is a rather explicit love scene involving Amadís and his beloved Oriana. The two, after a morning of horse-riding, find themselves in a valley with a lovely little brook and fresh green grass, at which point Amadís dismounts, helps Oriana off her horse and lays her on a cloak so that she may rest. Amadís takes of his armour, and, overcome with rapture for the recumbent damsel, he makes "a woman of the fairest maiden of the world."[2] This manifestation of passionate, carnal love with no hint of spiritual redemption worried contemporary moralists. The celebrated humanist Antonio de Guevara, for example, saw in chivalric romance a danger to spiritual welfare and social peace.[3]

This critique is echoed in Cervantes's characterization of Dorotea, another avid reader of chivalric romance. This young woman has lost her virginity to the treacherous Don Fernando, who, after having his way with her, abandons her for another woman. Dorotea escapes the dishonour and flees to the Sierra Morena, where Don Quixote and his party find her. When Don Quixote's friends concoct a ploy to lure him back to his home, Dorotea is able to apply her knowledge of chivalric romances to act out the part of the Princess Micomicona, the classical damsel in distress in search of a knight in shining armour.[4] Her excessive reading of chivalric romances explains the imprudent behaviour. By reading the wrong books wrongly, she has, like Don Quixote, contracted a "madness" of sorts that makes her a social outcast.

This mode of characterization* through reading extends to most, if not all, characters in the work. One of the innkeepers, who appears repeatedly in the first part, is also a connoisseur of chivalric romance, indicating the social reach of this type of literature. When Dorotea (whom we have met earlier) hears the innkeeper recount the feats of several of the literary knights errant with such detail and passionate enthusiasm, she whispers to a bystander: "Our host could almost make the second part of Don Quixote."[5] As in Dorotea's case, the innkeeper's knowledge of chivalric romances allows him to join in Don Quixote's projection of chivalric romance onto the world.

In both parts of the novel, we find characters who are well-versed in the tales and vocabulary of chivalric romance. Not only Don Quixote, but also other characters are shaped by their reading experiences in ways mostly detrimental to morality, judgment and behaviour. From this angle, Don Quixote's madness – caused by his reading – is but a hyperbole of the perils of reading. The effects of overly exciting reading on the mental faculties, imagination and judgment in particular, were a real, scientifically backed concern at the time when Cervantes wrote his novel. Not only moralists but also physicians warned against excessive reading – not unlike today's warnings against the presumably noxious effects of new media*.

In the 1640s, a young English gentleman fell into a grave melancholic state. Several attempts to alleviate his condition failed and it was suggested to him, as he himself recalled, that to "divert his Melancholy," he should "read the stale Adventures [of] Amadis de Gaule; & other Raving Bookes Fabulous & wandring Storys." Our English patient later testified that the stories "prejudic'd him by unsettling Thoughts." His noxious readings "accustom'd his Thoughts to such a Habitude of Raving, that he has scarce ever been their quiet Master since." By means of constant mental exercise, algebra in particular, he finally managed to "fixe his Volatile Fancy."[6] Yet until his death in 1691, he would occasionally fall back into a state of mental perturbation caused by the reading of chivalric romances. The part-time lunatic who suffered this fate, so similar to that of Don Quixote, was Robert Boyle, one of the founding figures of the Royal Society, inventor of the "machina Boyleana" (vacuum pump), propagator of a ground-breaking atomic-mechanical theory, the "father of chemistry" – in short, one of the great heroes of modern science. If even the most advanced minds of the time could fall victim to dangerous reading, is this not an ingenious leitmotiv* for a book about reading?

In Cervantes's *Don Quixote*, the characters are more or less what they read, and the author uses these characters to shape a narrative about reading. Hence his work is a strong comment on the uses and abuses of literature: the fact that excessive reading of chivalric romances turns Don Quixote into an at times aggressive, socially dysfunctional madman is more than a condemnation of chivalric romance. The suggestion arises that his behaviour might have been different had his library only contained devotional literature – or at least better fictional texts, like *Don Quixote*.

The *mise-en-scène* of reading and its effects on readers in *Don Quixote* is also a comment on literature and fiction. In literary criticism*, the reflection of fiction on fiction is called metafiction*. Metafiction calls the reader's attention to the fact that they are reading fiction, and consequently that there is nothing "natural" about the narration, that it could be told differently, as Cervantes shows with his own text. Thus metafictionality contributes to the denaturalization of the narrative and causes a "defamiliarization"* (see Chapter 26). In the first half of the twentieth century, the Russian formalists put forward the notion that the literariness* of a text is a function of its rupture with "familiar", conventionalized language and the conventions* of literary genres. In this sense, *Don Quixote* is the quintessentially literary text because it defamiliarises its readers with the conventions of the genres he parodies (picaresque, pastoral and, most of all, chivalric novels), and he achieves this by making reading and readers (good ones and bad ones) the protagonists of his novel.

The narrator as reader

The famous prologue* of *Don Quixote* is a prologue about not being able to write a prologue. "Cervantes" tells us he is pondering how to introduce the "son of his brain,"[7] Don Quixote de la Mancha. His problem is that, unlike the learned authors, he is not versed enough in the classics to be able to refer to Cicero in his prologue and add laudatory poetry from famous fellow poets. A friend enters his study and advises him to simply make up the usual quotes from authorities, write them himself, and ascribe them to famous authors. The reader soon realizes that even these authors are fictitious: the narrator has introduced himself as a reader of texts and authors that do not exist. The doubts he casts on himself as a reliable chronicler of the adventures of Don Quixote resurface in chapter eight of the first part, when we hear about Don Quixote's battle with a Basque. The narration is interrupted when both combatants have raised their swords to deliver blows:

> [A]t this very point the author of this history leaves the battle unfinished, excusing himself on the ground that he hasn't found anything more written about these exploits of Don Quixote than what he has narrated. It is true, though, that the second author of this work refused to believe that such a fascinating history had been abandoned to the laws of oblivion.[8]

"Cervantes," the narrator we meet in the prologue, reveals that he is actually the reader of another text. If the "second author" is not himself, as the logic of the narration suggests, then he is the reader of a reader. In the next chapter, the narrator, a man who would "read anything,"[9] finds an Arabic manuscript in Toledo about the adventures of Don Quixote, which he has translated. Only with the help of this translation is he able to continue the story where he left off "with his sword aloft."[10] Cervantes presents his original text as the result of a *mise en abyme** (literally 'falling into the abyss') of reading and writing processes: a writer is a reader of a writer who is a reader, and so forth. An Arabic chronicler reads documents in the archive, referring to the exploits of Don Quixote de la Mancha; an unknown "second author" reads this chronicle, or, more likely, the translation made by another reader; "Cervantes" reads the second author's text, and, when this text ends abruptly, he has a Moor read and translate the "original" text, which enables him to continue his own text without indicating how faithful he is to the texts of the preceding authors. *Don Quixote* is, therefore, a text about reading, that uses this theme to reflect on itself. Ironically, this complex narrative structure* had its embryonic precedent in the ridiculed model *Amadís de Gaula*, which passes itself off as a manuscript that was found in a tomb in a hermitage near Constantinople. While in medieval literature the topos* of the found manuscript had the function to bolster the tale's authority (for instance in Chrétien de Troyes's *Cligès*), Cervantes uses it for a dazzling display of narrative art that questions the very notion of narrative authority.

One of Cervantes's narrative ploys is a recurring reference to the first author, a certain "Cide Hamete Benengeli, an Arab historian."[11] The relationship between "Cervantes" the narrator and Cide Hamete is, however, highly ambiguous: within the space of a few paragraphs he both praises this author as a diligent chronicler and casts doubt on his credibility because he is an Arab. The references to Cide Hamete become more frequent in the second part, published in 1615, and increasingly undermine the credibility of the tale. At one point the translator in fact expresses his doubt concerning the veracity of the tale, because Sancho Panza is speaking in language so out of character. Yet he decides, for reasons of professional pride, "not to leave it untranslated."[12]

The translator casts doubt on the authenticity of the text he is reading (the manuscript found in Toledo, supposedly authored by Cide Hamete). He does this in the vein of a humanist scholar or literary critic, referring to idiosyncrasies in style and content. Does he question the reliability of Cide Hamete, or do we have to assume yet another (Arabic) author/reader, who has worked on the original manuscripts or written a sequel to Cide Hamete's text? The dazzling narrative architecture of *Don Quixote*, the *mise en abyme* of the reading processes, and the literary technique of reading apocryphal or imaginary texts are other features of the modernity of the *Don Quixote*. They have become the hallmark of sophisticated modern writing, showing that all of today's writers are, consciously or unconsciously, readers of Cervantes's *Don Quixote*.

Cervantes was not pleased with all of the readers and readings of the first part of *Don Quixote*. In 1614, a certain Alonso Fernández de Avellaneda had published a second part of *Quixote* in which the errant knight is a ridiculous dimwit who finds himself in a madhouse in Toledo at the end of the novel. Cervantes was not amused when he read this sequel, and it stands to reason that he would not have published his own second part only a year later without the incentive provided by the "apocryphal" *Quixote*. Moreover, his second part would have taken a different shape without his having read Avellaneda, because with this plot twist all of the characters of the second part are readers of the unauthorized sequel. In a comparative reading of sorts, they associate this reading of Avellaneda with Cervantes's first part, making the latter a pervasive frame of reference for the narrator and the characters.

Cervantes's library

It is a commonplace in scholarship that *Don Quixote* is an "archive" of the most important literary models and currents of this time (Italian novellas, humanist, picaresque, sentimental, pastoral novels, etc.). In other words, *Don Quixote* is a mirror of "Cervantes's library". One of the primary targets of Cervantes's parody* – and admiration – is the picaresque novel. The prototype of this genre is the *Lazarillo de Tormes* (1554), a novel of unknown authorship that recounts the life of a small boy who manages to rise from abject poverty to the position of town crier in Toledo, possibly compromising his honour with a seedy *ménage à trois* between himself, his wife and his benefactor, the Archpriest of Toledo. The genre was consolidated by Mateo Alemán's *Guzmán de Alfarache*, published in two parts in 1599 and 1604, shortly before *Don Quixote*. Guzmán de Alfarache tells us of his career as a rogue, which brings him to the galley where he awaits royal pardon after having blown the whistle on a mutiny. It is an arduous text for the modern reader, because the life story of the *pícaro* is interspersed with rambling moral disquisitions which the former *pícaro* can insert due to his newly gained authority as a reformed man. The novel was considered by contemporaries as the pinnacle of literature because of its exuberant baroque style and the moralizing which the modern reader finds so tedious. The success of Alemán's text was apparently a thorn in the side of Cervantes, who struggled throughout his life for recognition. The picaresque novel is represented in *Don Quixote* by the figure of Ginés de Pasamonte, a *pícaro* who is dragged by the authorities to the galleys. Don Quixote and his squire meet a chain gang and inquire about the prisoners. One of them is Ginés de Pasamonte, who purports to have written his life's tale in a book he pawned in prison:

> "It's so good," replied Ginés "that I wouldn't give a fig for *Lazarillo de Tormes* and all the others of that kind that have been or ever will be written. What I can tell is that it deals with facts, and that they are such fine and funny facts no lies could ever match them."
> "And what is the title of your book?" asked Don Quixote.
> "*The Life of Ginés de Pasamonte,*" replied the man of that name.
> "And have you finished it?" asked Don Quixote.
> "How can I have finished it," he replied, "if my life hasn't finished yet?"[13]

Cervantes shows himself here as a literary critic. Portraying the *pícaro* as a rogue without any remorse, he undermines the moral authority that Guzmán de Alfarache had usurped. More importantly, he points out the essential constraint of the picaresque genre: A first-person (pseudo)autobiographical narration has a limited scope, epitomized by the fact that Ginés cannot give an account of the totality of his life. In freeing the *galeotes* (galley slaves) and Ginés de Pasamonte, Cervantes literally frees the *pícaro*. The subaltern was not part of the cast of traditional literature and the lofty world of the nobility. In the picaresque novel he is, as it were, a prisoner of his own world, in spite of his repeated efforts to become an honourable man, condemned to make public his miserable and abject position. Cervantes's *pícaro*, Ginés de Pasamonte, is free to roam in the world evoked by the novel, appearing on several occasions and several guises in *Don Quixote*.

Readers in *Don Quixote* and early modern readers

In the second part, while Don Quixote is in bed, recuperating from the adventures in the first part, Sancho Panza arrives with disturbing news. Apparently, the son of one of the villagers, Bartolomé Carrasco, had returned from Salamanca University and told him that a book had been published with the title *The Ingenious Hidalgo Don Quixote de la Mancha*, a book about *their* adventures. Sancho is rather vexed by the fact that in the book the narrator talks of events that happened when he and Don Quixote were alone. Sancho simply cannot grasp how a writer could have come to know these things.[14]

This comic scene addresses a serious issue. Don Quixote and Sancho can only imagine an account of their story as a *historia*, a chronicle of their adventures. Logic dictates that this chronicle can only be based on observation of the events, or on information from eyewitnesses. They are quite reasonably puzzled that this chronicler has information on what happened when nobody else was present. They conclude that supernatural forces, a sorcerer, must be responsible. The scene mirrors Don Quixote's original predicament: he does not understand that the world of the knights errant in his books is not his own but fiction.

This confusion of narrative planes (the narrator/reader outside of the narrated world of the narrative, and the narrated world), or different levels of existence, is called a metalepsis*. Don Quixote is metaleptically challenged because he repeatedly meshes fiction with reality. The irony of the scene previously referred to is that Cervantes consciously creates a metalepsis. The *historia* of Don Quixote is not a chronicle, but a novel, which creates a likeness of reality but is distinct from it. Confronting knight and squire with a fictional text that they do not recognize as fiction (because it is congruent with their memories) makes an important comment on literature in the modern sense. Don Quixote is a premodern reader who still operates with the distinction between truth and lie, while his illiterate squire is not familiar with the conventions of reading. *Don Quixote* is not only a book about the perils of reading, but also a manual on how to read modern literature, a mode of fiction that is modelled on "reality" yet draws a sharp line between "reality" and a narrated universe that has its own logic. In a sense, it presents an empirical test of the real-world applicability of a worldview inspired by a form of literature deemed "useless".

Don Quixote arrived on the scene when literature and reading practices were undergoing profound changes. These changes were discussed by intellectuals like the previously mentioned moralists; they were primarily negotiated in fiction itself, establishing a sort of dialogue with the reader. In the Middle Ages, when few could read, what we call now literature was a collective experience. One person would read aloud and many others would listen. In monasteries, for instance, a designated reader would read edifying stories aloud during meals; epic tales were actually more like public performances, based on a written text or recorded after the fact. Individual silent reading of poetry was considered unusual. "Literature", then, had a different place in life: it was part of everyday experience, not a world apart.

The sixteenth century saw the rise of the industrially operated printing press*, large print runs and relatively affordable editions, in Spain and in Europe as a whole; the authorities favoured this development and tried to control it through a complex bureaucratic apparatus of licensing and censorship*. The necessity of controlling the production of books was essentially related to the fact that reading now reached sectors of society that had been excluded from the circulation of books in the past (women such as Dorotea, the poor and marginal such as the innkeeper and Sancho), and that reading gradually became a solitary experience. Don Quixote, who reads his chivalric romance in the solitude of his reading room, is a medieval reader who cannot adjust to modern times. He is literate, even a voracious reader, but he is a reader fallen out of time, similar to present-day computer illiterates. *Don Quixote* is, among many things, also a book about media change, and the ensuing possibilities and dangers.

The effects of this change are not only reflected in Alonso Quijano's mental affliction, but also shown in its economic dimension. At the beginning of part two, knight and squire are confronted with the publication of their adventures; later they learn that there is also an apocryphal second part. They see this novel and its protagonist in a metaleptic perspective as their competitors, but fail to understand that this competition is also one on the book market*. Cervantes fleshes this out when Don Quixote tours a printing shop while he is in Barcelona, to find that several of the employees are correcting the proofs for a book titled *The Second Part of the Ingenious Hidalgo Don Quixote de la Mancha*, apparently authored by somebody from Tordesillas.

This is almost certainly a reference to the second part of the *Don Quixote* by Avellaneda. It shows that literary creativity in the seventeenth century was part and parcel of a competition for economic resources, and that Don Quixote, character and book, had become a commodity. The first print-run of Cervantes's *Don Quixote* in Madrid (by the publisher Juan de la Cuesta) consisted of 1,200 volumes, and was sold at price of 290 *maravedís*, which amounted to roughly half a month's wage for a typical craftsman. A second run was issued soon after. This indicates that a considerable proportion of Madrid's inhabitants could have access to Cervantes's work. The population of Madrid was characterized by a higher percentage of readers, as it was the administrative centre of the empire, and thus home to many scribes, clerks and other literate officials, in addition to the traditional elites.

In the beginning of the second part, Don Quixote and Sancho discuss the popular appraisal of the first part with the *bachiller* ('bachelor') Sansón Carrasco:

> "About that," the young graduate replied, "opinions differ, as tastes do: some prefer the adventure of the windmills, which you thought were Briareuses and giants; others, the description of the two armies that turned out to be two flocks of sheep; one man praises the adventure of the corpse being taken to Segovia to be buried; another says that the best one of them all is the freeing of the convicts; yet another that none of them equals the adventure of the two Benedictine giants and the fight with the brave Basque."[15]

Don Quixote, then, like the "Cervantes" of the prologue, takes a genuine interest in the readers' comments on the tale of the first part. Through these comments we can construct the persona of the reader, now as a literary character. Apparently, opinions on the text differ ("opinions differ, as tastes do"), yet they coincide in two aspects: first, the rejection of too many interpolated stories, and second, popular preferences for all scenes involving Don Quixote and Sancho. The extent to which these opinions appear to have determined the writing of the second part is striking. Gone are the long interpolated narratives of the first part (for instance, the story of the "Captive's tale"), which dominate roughly half of the book. The scenes involving Sancho are much more elaborate, and he even takes centre stage in one episode as governor of an island. Don Quixote, moreover, becomes the involuntary protagonist of a spoof of a courtly love story, staged by the court of a rather bored duke. This duke is yet another reader of chivalric romance in general, and of the first part of *Don Quixote* in particular. In an elaborate scheme, the duke and his wife abuse their own superior "reading skills", and the knight's anachronistic understanding of literature, in order to entertain themselves. The duke's main flaw is an excess of leisure, a perceived problem of early modern Spanish aristocrats (among them the humble nobleman Alonso Quijano). Here, too, we find a critique of the absurd behaviour caused by excessive leisure spent in reading and enacting literature.

Don Quixote represents both premodern and modern reading practices when humble illiterates such as Sancho (who claims not to know even the first letters of the alphabet) and modern solitary and media-savvy readers like Sansón Carrasco and the duke coincide. Arguably, the involvement of the readers' opinions, or, more precisely, consumer demand (the avoidance of intercalated novellas, or the "upgrading" of the popular Sancho in part two), in the confection of the literary work is one of the most modern aspects of Don Quixote, because it reflects the commodification of literature* and shows the world of literature as a marketplace. If readers want more of Don Quixote and Sancho, the writer shall supply it. If readers are tired of the interpolated novels inspired by Renaissance authorities like Boccaccio, the writer will suppress them. In the case of *Don Quixote*, the amused or displeased reader as consumer was instrumental in shaping the modern novel. Much of Cervantes's celebrated genius lies in his capacity to respond to the expectations of a modern reader.

Don Quixote's afterlife

In his prologue, Cervantes labels his protagonist as an "ugly son" who does not deserve his father's undivided love. He had invested all his hope for literary fame into his last project, the *Trabajos de Persiles y Sigismunda* (1616), an adventure novel in the vein of fourth-century writer Heliodorus's *Aethiopica* (see Chapter 2). The book failed to garner the appreciation he had hoped for, but his *Don Quixote* was a considerable success in its time. Readers particularly liked the humorous aspect of the novel; they read it, as P.E. Russell has aptly remarked, as a "funny book."[16] Funny books are rarely the material for world literature*. The potential of a book is, however, never exhausted by the intention of the author, and it is never determined by the "original" interpretations of the contemporaries. Every generation involves its own horizons, interests and preoccupation in the reading of literature. Later generations of writers and readers could add layers of new meaning to this ingenious text. Authors of the Enlightenment more or less freely adapted *Don Quix-ote*; for instance, Christoph Martin Wieland in his *Der Sieg der Natur über die Schwärmerei oder die Abenteuer des Don Sylvio von Rosalva* ('The Adventures of Don Sylvio de Rosalva', 1764), or Goethe in his *Wilhelm Meisters Lehrjahre* ('Wilhelm Meister's Apprenticeship', 1795–6). *Don Quixote*'s career as a masterpiece of world literature gained momentum with nineteenth-century Romanticism*. Spain fascinated romantics in Germany and England, and *Don Quixote* was their favourite book. They did not deny that *Don Quixote* was a humorous work, but they understood that this was a highly complex, metafictional narration which allowed for a wide variety of interpretations. They appreciated the book's total vision of reality, and as representatives of an age that cherished imagination and worshipped the individual, they identified with the errant knight and his squire.

From then on, *Don Quixote* would be enshrined in the pantheon of great works – and inspired great works like Gustave Flaubert's *Madame Bovary* (1856), a "Don Quijote in skirts," in the words of Spanish philosopher José Ortega y Gasset.[17] It is hard to imagine that any piece of literature has attracted more readers and comments. Arguably the most Cervantine reader of the *Don Quixote* was the Argentine writer Jorge Luis Borges, who, in 1939, authored a curious short story* with the title "Pierre Menard, author of the *Quixote*". The story takes the shape of an homage to the works of fictitious French symbolist author Pierre Menard. Among Menard's greatest achievements was a rewriting of two chapters of the first part of the *Quixote*. These chapters are, word for word, identical to Cervantes's text. Borges's narrator has learned from Menard that he had striven to *become* Cervantes, living his life in seventeenth-century Spain, but abandoned the project. The narrator says that he considers Menard's work infinitely subtler and richer than Cervantes's. Pierre Menard is the reader as writer, who, in the reading process, reproduces the author's work but adds meaning to it, drawing on his own experiences and the layers of meaning supplied by previous readings. Cervantes might have seen him as the ideal reader of his masterpiece.

Notes

1 Miguel de Cervantes, *Don Quixote*, I, I, 26, italics added.
2 Garci Rodríguez de Montalvo, *Amadis de Gaula*, XXXV.
3 Barry W. Ife, *Reading and Fiction in Golden-Age Spain: A Platonist Critique and Some Picaresque Replies* (Cambridge: Cambridge University Press, 1985), 34.
4 Cervantes, *Don Quixote*, I, XXIX.
5 Cervantes, *Don Quixote*, I, XXXII, Translation is ours. The Spanish *hacer* could be read as both 'to make' i.e. write or 'to do' i.e. enact.
6 Quoted in Adrian Johns, *Nature of the Book: Print and Knowledge in the Making* (Chicago: University of Chicago Press, 1998), 380–81.
7 Cervantes, *Don Quixote*, I, prologue, 11.
8 Cervantes, *Don Quixote*, I, VIII, 70.
9 Cervantes, *Don Quixote*, I, IX, 74.
10 Cervantes, *Don Quixote*, I, VIII, 70.
11 Cervantes, *Don Quixote*, I, IX, 75.
12 Cervantes, *Don Quixote*, II, V, 514.
13 Cervantes, *Don Quixote*, I, XXII, 182.
14 Cervantes, *Don Quixote*, II, II, 501.
15 Cervantes, *Don Quixote*, II, III, 504.
16 Peter E. Russell, "Don Quijote As a Funny Book." *Modern Language Review* 64 (1969): 312–26.
17 José Ortega y Gasset. "Flaubert, Cervantes, Darwin." Antología de la crítica sobre el Quijote en el siglo XX. Cervantes Virtual. Accessed 25.11.2017. https://cvc.cervantes.es/literatura/quijote_antologia/ortega.htm

Further reading

Auerbach, Erich. "The Enchanted Dulcinea [1949]." In *Mimesis: The Representation of Reality in Western Literature* [1953]. Princeton Classics Edition. Princeton, NJ/Oxford: Princeton University Press, 2013.
Close, Anthony J. *Miguel de Cervantes: Don Quixote – (Landmarks of World Literature)*. Cambridge: Cambridge University Press, 1990.
D'haen, Theo and Reindert Dhondt, eds. *International Don Quixote*. Amsterdam: Rodopi, 2009.
Gónzalez Echevarría, Roberto. *Cervantes's Don Quixote: A Casebook*. Oxford: Oxford University Press, 2005.
Quint, David. *Cervantes's Novel of Modern Times: A New Reading of Don Quixote*. Princeton, NJ: Princeton University Press, 2003.

16 Exploring new worlds

Konstantin Mierau, Alicia C. Montoya and Catriona Seth

Figure 16.1 Novae Insulae XXVI Nova Tabula by Sebastian Munster, 1540

In his sixteenth-century epic* *Os Lusíadas* ('The Lusiads', 1572), the Portuguese sailor-turned-author Luís Vaz de Camões described the voyages of discovery undertaken by Portuguese and Spanish sailors starting in the fifteenth century. He announced his subject in the epic's opening strophes.

Text: *Luís Vaz de Camões,* Os Lusíadas *('The Lusiads') (1572)*

Arms, and the Barons signally renowned   1
Who from the western Lusitanian shore,
Far beyond Taprobane a passage found

By seas none ever sailed across before:
In perils great, fierce wars on unknown ground,   5
Meeting all adverse human strength with more:
To found midst people of a different sky,
A new realm that raised their names so high.
Likewise those Kings whose memorable deeds
Gloriously spread our holy faith and nation,   10
And to the wicked lands of sinful creeds
In Africa and Asia, devastation;
And those achieving by their valour's deeds
From the dread law of death their liberation;
Singing I will proclaim, both far and wide,   15
If art and genius be not me denied.
No more of the sage Greek, nor the Dardanian,
About their great and perilous navigation;
Cease about Alexander; wars Trajanian;
Of all their victories cease the long narration!   20
I sing the illustrious valour Lusitanian;
Neptune and Mars alike obeyed that nation;
Cease all that ancient Muse could sing or praise,
Another valour loftier still to raise.
. . .
Listen, and never with those exploits vain,   25
Fantastical, vainglorious, pretending,
Shalt thou see thine joined in heroic strain,
By Muses thus themselves to raise intending:
Those veritably thine so great remain,
The dreamy and fabulous so far transcending,   30
That they exceed Rhodamonte, even if true,
Roger, Orlando, and all they were said to do.
For these I will produce a Nuno fierce,
Who to the King and realm such service wrought;
An Egas, a Dom Fuas, – worthy of verse   35
For which great Homer's lyre I could have sought.
Then to the twelve Peers I set in obverse
Magriços twelve, who nobly in England fought:
I give you besides Gama's illustrious name,
Who to himself takes all En[e]as' fame.[1]   40

From the start, Camões makes it clear that he is setting out to "sing the illustrious valour Lusitanian" (l.21) – "Lusitania" being the Roman name given to the part of the Iberian peninsula known today as Portugal. To do so, he naturally chose epic, the most prestigious literary genre* of the early modern period. Epic's importance was strengthened by its link to the past, particularly to the foundational poems of Homer and Virgil that recounted the noble deeds of Odysseus (*The Iliad* and *The Odyssey*) and of Aeneas (*The Aeneid*) (see Chapter 1). Camões's opening stanzas position the sixteenth-century poet and his poem in an illustrious classical lineage. The poem's very first words, "Arms, and the Barons," refer to the opening words of Virgil's *Aeneid*, "I sing of wars and the man," which in turn was an allusion* to the opening of Homer's *Iliad*, the founding text of European literature.

Right from the outset, Camões was inviting a comparison between his hero and the great heroes of antiquity, the Greek Odysseus/Ulysses and the mythical founder of Rome, Æneas (1.40).

The reference to antiquity served as much to assert the originality of the modern text as its indebtedness to its antique models. It is an instance of intertextuality*, the phenomenon whereby one text references others, and thus derives significance from its relation to other texts. The development of literature consists to a great extent in this dialogue between texts within a changing context. In this example, Camões referred to Virgil to suggest that civilisation had passed from classical antiquity to modern Western Europe (the *translatio imperii** topos*). In his poem, civilisation moved first from Greece to Italy (evoked in the reference to the Renaissance* Italian epics in the phrase "Roger, Orlando, and all they were said to do," 1.32) and subsequently to Portugal.

Virgil referred to "the man" (singular). Camões, however, emphasized his own originality by referring to "Barons" (plural). The celebration of the singular hero's exploits in the Latin tradition became a communal, national endeavour in *The Lusiads*. More importantly, the opening reference to antiquity was preparing the ground for an opposition, as the poet went on to explain that his readers should no longer wonder at the "great and perilous navigation" (1.18) of Odysseus, "the sage Greek" (1.17), since a new race of heroes whose deeds far surpassed those of the heroes of old had appeared. These included Nuno Alvares Pereira (1.33), a general who helped establish Portuguese independence against Spain; Dom Fuas or Puas Roupinho (1.35), the legendary first admiral of the Portuguese fleet; and above all Vasco da Gama (1.39), the Portuguese explorer who was the first European to round the Cape of Good Hope and reach India by sea in 1497–1499, thereby ushering in a new era of European exploration, conquest and colonisation.

With this long series of comparisons, Camões evoked men renowned for their military prowess as a prelude to praising the feats of his modern-day heroes who fought "fierce wars on unknown ground" (1.5) and "in Africa and Asia [brought] devastation" (1.12). It is worth noting that Camões did not distinguish between historical figures and fictional characters – a point to which we shall return shortly. The subject of the poem was to be Portugal's conquests overseas; its aim was to glorify Camões's native country. But through his use of intertextuality, Camões was also telling readers that the deeds of his modern heroes surpassed those of past heroes, i.e. that modernity might define itself by turning away from antiquity and moving towards new and as yet undocumented worlds and experiences. This crucial role of literature as an instrument to help explore and understand new worlds is central to our discussion in this chapter.

Camões's aim to contribute to the glory of his country was singularly successful. *The Lusiads* was recognised as an instant classic, and is universally hailed today as Portugal's national epic, with Camões himself firmly ensconced in literary history as the country's national poet. This status, we suggest, can be explained not only by the poem's intrinsic literary merits, but also by its subject matter – European expansion overseas – that played a central role in the European continent's self-definition at the dawn of the modern age.

The beginnings of European expansion overseas: between fact and fiction

Camões's *Lusiads* offered both a reflection on literary history, and a reflection on a series of historical events: the Portuguese voyages of discovery that started after 1400 and led to an unprecedented series of encounters between Europeans and the many peoples beyond. These voyages of exploration were, in the beginning, an extension of the battles fought on the Iberian peninsula, as local Christian kings sought to capture Muslim strongholds in Spain and Portugal and drive away the Muslim occupiers, whom they called "Moors".

Since 711, the largest part of the Iberian peninsula, known as al-Andalus, had come under Muslim rule. At its height, Muslim Iberia was under the control of the Caliphate of Córdoba (929–1031) under which culture flourished, with Córdoba as the intellectual centre not only of al-Andalus, but of a large region beyond. During the Caliphate, al-Andalus was the culturally and politically most diverse and developed part of Europe. This cultural flourishing was, however, contested by the Christian kingdoms in the north of the Iberian peninsula, which launched a war of so-called "reconquest", or Reconquista, against their Muslim neighbours. The Reconquista advanced substantially with the conquests of Córdoba (1236) and Seville (1248), leaving Granada as the last Muslim state on the Iberian Peninsula. Then, perpetuating the wars of Reconquista, the Portuguese set their eyes beyond Europe, and in 1415 captured Ceuta in Morocco, thus gaining a first foothold on the African continent. In *The Lusiads*, Camões underlined this historical link between the Christian Reconquest and overseas exploration when he evoked "those Kings whose memorable deeds/Gloriously spread our holy faith and nation,/And to the wicked lands of sinful creeds" (1.9–11). Conceived in these terms, European expansion overseas was part and parcel of a wider religious campaign, continuing a culture of conflict glorified in such medieval epics of religious strife as the French *Chanson de Roland* ('The Song of Roland', eleventh-twelfth century) and the Spanish *Cantar de mio Cid* ('Song of my Cid', ca. 1200).

The Portuguese victory at Ceuta opened the way to maritime exploration further along the African coast. By 1497, a squadron headed by the aristocrat Vasco da Gama rounded the Cape of Good Hope and sailed up the East African coast, continuing to western India: the feat that Camões was to celebrate at greatest length in his *Lusiads*. Within a decade of rounding the Cape, the Portuguese had reached China. Along this route, Portuguese sailors established a network of trading posts that enabled them to do business with local potentates, and to grow rich as middlemen over the following century.

If Portugal's voyages of exploration were astounding for the speed with which they gave Europe access to the East and its fabled riches, its neighbour on the Iberian peninsula, Spain, was just as speedy in its conquest of the Americas. Spain's start in its expansion overseas was delayed by the survival of Muslim states in Spanish Iberia, with Granada falling to the Spanish kings as late as 1492. Initially, Spain too sought a new route to the Indies, i.e. India and China, but – hindered by Portuguese progress along the African coast – instead sought it by sailing westward. Supposedly heading for China, in 1492 Christopher Columbus set foot in the Bahamas, thereby "discovering" the "New World". Shortly after, in 1522, with a force of only four hundred men, the obscure but ambitious soldier Hernán Cortés overthrew the centuries-old Aztec empire in Mexico, aided by enemies and disaffected subjects of the Aztecs, by the European diseases the conquerors carried and to which the Americans had no immunity, and by tactical advantages like the use of horses and dogs against the Aztec foot-soldiers. In Peru, Francisco Pizarro and Diego Almagro overthrew the already war-torn, disease-ravaged Inca Empire, so that by the 1550s, Spanish government had been established throughout much of Central and South America.

It is hard to imagine the political and psychological effects brought about, both in the "new" worlds and in Europe itself, by this lightning-quick colonisation of vast portions of the non-European world. The "discovery" and subsequent conquest of America was, of course, a discovery only from the European point of view: Native Americans viewed this event as the destruction of their own way of life and age-old civilisations. At the same time, the voyages of exploration and the encounter with other cultures led to profound self-questioning in the West, as Europe's centrality in the world was no longer evident faced with the complex political systems and advanced cultures in the Far East and the Americas.

This self-questioning inevitably also focused on the Western intellectual canon* and its beliefs. If the celebrated geographers of antiquity such as Ptolemy (100–168 CE), whose treatises inspired most medieval maps, the so-called "mapa mundi", and sources such as Pliny the Elder (23–79 CE), who provided knowledge of far-off peoples, were proved wrong by the discovery of a continent that was missing from the maps, and if peoples in sub-Saharan Africa did not have one giant foot with which to protect themselves from the sun's heat, as Pliny had contended in his *Natural History*, then what else had the established authorities got wrong? The "discovery" of Africa, India and the Americas required a complete re-writing of the Western library, and forcefully made Europeans enter a new, modern age in which the old certainties no longer held.

Literature not only offered a reflection on current events, but also provided the explorers and conquistadors with a recognisable language to describe their experiences in the "new" worlds. Right from the beginning, exploration and conquest were conceived of in terms borrowed from literary tradition, and fact and fiction were sometimes difficult to separate. Thus, when the first conquistadors headed for the Americas, they did so in search of the legendary "El Dorado" (literally 'the golden one'), a mythical city or realm of untold wealth. More powerful still was the influence of the medieval romances* of chivalry* that the conquistadors, like many of their compatriots, so avidly consumed. As G.L. Scammell has noted:

> [T]he sixteenth century was the heyday of the romance of chivalry in Iberia, read alike by princes, scholars, soldiers and even future saints . . . Explorers, as besotted with these fantasies as was the hapless Don Quixote himself, and consciously modelling their behaviour on that of the improbable paladins of fiction, sought in the Americas for the land of the Amazons, mythical female warriors from antiquity, and searched the coast of Florida for that fountain whose waters brought the joys of everlasting youth and virility.[2]

Thus, when the Spanish conquistadors first sighted California, they named it after a mythical land described in one of the sixteenth century's best-selling chivalric fictions. In *Amadís de Gaula* (1508), Garci Rodríguez de Montalvo described a remote land overflowing with riches, inhabited by griffins and other marvellous beasts, named *California*. This fictional paradise was peopled by black Amazons and ruled by Queen Calafia, a military leader whose name might refer to the title taken on the Iberian peninsula by its Muslim leaders, caliph, and who herself had Muslim allies – thereby implying, according to some readings, that California was itself a new Caliphate. In *The Adventures of Esplandián* (1510), a sequel to *Amadís*, the author explained to his readers:

> Know ye that at the right hand of the Indies there is an island called California, very close to that part of the Terrestrial Paradise, which was inhabited by black women without a single man among them, and they lived in the manner of Amazons. They were robust of body with strong passionate hearts and great virtue. The island itself is one of the wildest in the world on account of the bold and craggy rocks.[3]

It was not entirely surprising, then, that when the Spanish conquistadors first beheld the western coast of North America, they thought they had found the wondrous region described in the novels they read so eagerly. Similarly, when Bernal Díaz del Castillo, accompanying Hernán Cortés on his conquest expedition, described the conquistadors' approach to Tenochticlán, the capital of the Aztec empire, he wrote that "we were amazed and said it was like the enchantments they tell of in the legend of *Amadis*."[4] Fact and fiction ran into one another, as literature provided the images and vocabulary Europeans needed when seeking to explain unseen regions of the world. In this sense, literature acted as virtual space or laboratory in which Europeans could imagine new worlds, with fictional and non-fictional texts as powerful tools to explore and think through new ideas and experiences.

Literary reflections on European expansion and conquest overseas

Epics such as *The Lusiads* and the chronicles* of the conquistadors were by no means the only genres inspired by the voyages of discovery. The literature celebrating Europe's arrival in the Americas and the evangelical drive of the missionaries is substantial and diverse. Epics and historical chronicles remained a natural choice of genre for these texts throughout the early modern period. Drawing on the model of Camões's *Lusiads*, Anne-Marie Du Boccage's eighteenth-century epic *La Colombiade ou La Foi portée au nouveau monde* ('The Columbiad or Faith brought to the New World', 1758), for example, was typical in that it continued to trumpet Europe's gift of Catholicism but also, *Amadis*-style, basked in the beauties of the exotic world across the oceans. (It was also doubly unique: it is a rare case of a French epic, and it was written by a woman.)

Some authors, however, adopted a more critical stance. Inca Garcilaso de la Vega, born in Cuzco, Peru, to a Spanish conquistador and an Inca princess, wrote in Spanish and is considered the first major Peruvian author. After moving to Spain in his early forties, Garcilaso wrote about his homeland in an influential work, the *Comentarios Reales de los Incas* ('Royal Commentaries of the Incas', 1609), which deals at once with his Inca ancestors and with the European conquest of Peru. His personal experience and history mean that his vision is much less Eurocentric than most early literature about Latin America. In an even more polemical vein, in Spain, Bartolomé de Las Casas wrote sermons* and official letters* demanding an end to forced labour and better working conditions for the indigenous population of the Americas. Las Casas was a Spanish missionary known as "the friend of the Indians" who advocated native peoples' rights and tirelessly crossed the oceans between Europe and the Americas seeking to improve the fate of the Amerindians. He attempted – and, by most accounts, succeeded in – changing laws and attitudes, not least because his letters, sermons and histories reached a wide audience throughout Europe. His *Brevisima relación de la destrucción de las Indias* ('Very Short Account of the Destruction of the Indies', 1552), is a clear denunciation of the excesses of colonialism*. It is a polemical text which often relies on exaggeration or hyperbole*, and would go on to fuel much of the so-called "black legend" about the cruelty of the Spaniards. However, as a self-critical analysis, it provides a remarkable counterpoint to the often bombastic nationalism with which authors like Camões, Cortés and Du Boccage chose to celebrate the explorers, barely stopping to consider the viewpoint of the "discovered".

Moving beyond the genres of epic and historical chronicles, the voyages of discovery also inspired new forms of writing, including the quintessentially early modern genre of the essay*, that served as a vehicle to critically examine new phenomena. The essay (literally 'attempt') was an innovation by Michel de Montaigne, an erudite Frenchman who, rather than follow pre-established models, chose to use texts of varying length to let his thoughts on various topics meander. He habitually juxtaposed observations of human behaviour and classical authority, often reaching ground-breaking interpretations. In his essay "Des Cannibales" ('On Cannibals'), Montaigne reflected on the West from the point of view of the Brazilian Tupinambi "cannibals" said to have visited the French town of Rouen in 1562. This led him to a new relativism regarding the cultural primacy of Europe and to an explicit condemnation of the destruction of the Inca and Aztec empires by the Spanish conquistadors, not unlike Las Casas's earlier denunciation.

In the eighteenth century, or age of Enlightenment*, the relative values of different civilisations and the possibility of looking at things from the point of view of the colonised rather than the coloniser became increasingly prominent. This is visible, for example, in the implicit dialogue between two works, a document and a fictional exchange. The first is Louis-Antoine de Bougainville's *Description d'un Voyage autour du monde* ('A Description of a Voyage round the World', 1771) in which he narrates his 1766–1769 circumnavigation of the globe. During this voyage, the seafarer visited many foreign lands, including Brazil, Tahiti and Samoa, shaping an enduring European conception of exoticism linked to tropical islands, white sands and turquoise seas. The other text is the purported addition by Denis Diderot, his *Supplément au Voyage de Bougainville* ('Supplement to Bougainville's Voyage', 1772), which only circulated in manuscript* during his lifetime. While the *Voyage* gave ethnographical observations and dealt with botany and geography as observed by the French sailors, the *Supplément* purports to recount an old Tahitian's remarks on the Europeans' departure. The old man tells his compatriots that they should be weeping not at the Westerners sailing away from "Otahiti" but at the fact that their arrival heralded the death of a traditional way of life. Europeans had claimed the land even though the Tahitians had been there since time immemorial, they took advantage of local customs and they brought jealousy and disease. The old Tahitian further denounces the Christian vision of marriage and condemnation of illegitimacy as unnatural, compared with the free unions and celebration of all children in Tahiti. In this response to Bougainville, Diderot used his contemporaries' fascination for tales of voyage and discoveries to question an accepted way of life – that of the Europeans – and attempted to guide the reader towards an understanding of cultural relativism. Similarly, Westerners were observed in fictional travel accounts like Montesquieu's *Lettres persanes* ('Persian Letters', 1721), Cadalso's *Cartas marruecas* ('Moroccan Letters', 1789) and texts by genuine voyagers like Nikolay Karamzin, whose *Letters of a Russian Traveller* (1791–1792), modelled on Irishman Laurence Sterne's semi-fictional *Sentimental Journey through England and France* (1768), met with huge success in his homeland.

Knowledge production and the realism of the novel

While the early accounts of the conquistadors drew on a framework that did not distinguish between fact and fiction, or between imaginative and historical literature in the modern sense, this kind of writing quickly ran up against limitations. In the early modern period, the explorers and conquistadors increasingly had to deal with the uneasy recognition that the new worlds they were encountering had been unknown to ancient authorities (see Chapter 2). Thus, the literature on the voyages of discovery came to be characterised by a sense that the ancient authorities were true only in a metaphysical sense, that is in providing models of heroism, empire and identity, rather than being true in the physical sense of providing empirical knowledge for navigation and interaction with native peoples. The discoveries spawned a plethora of travel narratives, which were increasingly cross-examined with other narratives and thus held accountable against new standards of empirically verifiable veracity. Bernal Díaz del Castillo, treasurer to Cortés's mission, reflected in his *Historia verdadera* ('True history') on the conquest of Mexico, knowing that his account would have to compete with many other accounts, such as Cortés's own dispatches. He may have used references to literary texts to embellish his descriptions of the splendor of Tenochtitlán, but they were no longer considered a reliable source for historical truth about the mission itself.

Thus, beyond their interaction with fiction, travel narratives also produced much new geographical, anthropological and scientific knowledge in response to European readers' growing curiosity about other worlds. Early accounts of Asia and the customs and political organization of its people were sent back to Europe by Dutch travellers. Jesuits' letters, which were published, spoke in detail about Chinese culture, from music to medicine. Tradesmen looking to bring jewels and silks to Europe left accounts of what they discovered. Part of the attraction of the new travel literature* lay in its documentary value, and authors underlined this aspect of their work. Bernardin de Saint-Pierre's travel narrative *Voyage à l'Île de France* ('Voyage to the Île de France', 1773), despite its condemnation of slavery, was first and foremost a travel narrative, whose catalogue of Mauritian flora and description of the island would have been appreciated for their documentary value. Englishwoman Mary Wortley Montagu's *Turkish Letters* (1763), one of the first documents on the Ottoman Empire by a Western woman, are likewise full of historically valuable facts about costume and customs, social and political practices.

The discovery of other worlds led to attempts to rationalise and organise knowledge in numerous fields. In France, Richelieu promoted the foundation of the Académie Française in 1635 part because he thought the French language could be used to commercial and political ends – it remained the diplomatic and court language of choice in many countries until well into the nineteenth century. The Académie undertook to create a dictionary of French as a way of controlling and normalising its use throughout France, including its colonial possessions. Spain, which also had a vast colonial empire – as is still evidenced by the prevalence of Spanish as a language through much of Latin America – likewise went down the route of academic control of vocabulary and grammar. Other means of organising knowledge can be found in enterprises like the Swede Linnaeus's taxonomy or classification of plants – which was promoted by his compatriot Solander, who travelled to England and then to Australia and New Zealand with Captain James Cook. In other fields, the Italo-French Cassini family attempted to map both land and sky, while the Frenchman Buffon's multivolume *Histoire naturelle* ('Natural History', 1749–1789) set out to describe all known animals, whether native European or exotic species, and also included chapters on the biological differences between the various human races.

Scientific interest in the voyages of discovery interacted with another development in the literary field: the rise of the novel* during the eighteenth century and its use of realism* and the naturalistic, exact description of things as they are in the real world. One of the early masters of realistic description, Daniel Defoe, also dealt repeatedly with colonial topics. Defoe's most famous novel is *Robinson Crusoe* (1719), based in part on the real adventures of Alexander Selkirk, and considered by many early readers to be a true account of a shipwrecked Briton. As Edward Said has written:

> [T]he novel is inaugurated in England by *Robinson Crusoe*, a work whose protagonist is the founder of a new world, which he rules and reclaims for Christianity and England . . . Crusoe is explicitly enabled by an ideology of overseas expansion – directly connected in style and form to the narratives of sixteenth- and seventeenth-century exploration voyages that laid the foundations of the great colonial empires.[5]

Robinson Crusoe was an enormous success in its own time, and has continued to inspire contemporary writers like Michel Tournier in France, Patrick Chamoiseau in Martinique and Kamel Daoud in Algeria. Another of Defoe's novels, *Fortunes and Misfortunes of the Famous Moll Flanders* (1722), published anonymously, was taken by early readers to be the autobiography* of the narrator, Moll, born to an inmate of Newgate prison in London, whose loose life and adventures led her to Virginia – with a husband whom she later discovered to be her half-brother – and back to Europe through a succession of events in which her artful deceit often came in handy. Shipped off to the colonies as a felon, she returned to England and her family thanks to her repentance and good qualities. The novel struck a chord because it is replete with concrete details – like the cost of giving birth according to one's class. Readers could vicariously experience thrilling and dangerous events like being transported as a criminal. At the same time, the novel's description of the colonies and its many realistic aspects fired readers' imagination.

The slave trade and the beginnings of modernity

European expansion overseas also ushered in the modern age in other ways, as the colonisation of the New World laid the groundwork for the advent of the modern individual. Expansion overseas brought Europeans into contact with distant peoples and civilizations, but it also created a new class of rootless, displaced subjects. When Columbus sailed to the Americas, his crew was comprised not only of sailors who had joined the voyage of their free will, but also of others, including indentured labourers and Africans, whose loyalties were the product of necessity. Travel and adventure overseas was, to some, a means of escaping the social and economic constraints of Europe, while to others it was not the result of free will but of gross coercion.

   Indeed, one of the consequences of the settlement of the New World was the enslavement of several million Africans who were transported to the Americas to work the land, after the European powers – influenced in part by Las Casas's polemic in favour of the aboriginal populations – had deemed the native Americans unsuited to hard labour. In order to work the plantations and mines they established in the New World, Europeans drew on a practice that predated the voyages of discovery in al-Andalus – the enslavement of sub-Saharan Africans – but now applied it on a new, transatlantic scale. Between the Atlantic slave trade's beginning in the sixteenth century and its end in the nineteenth century, over ten million Africans were enslaved and transported to the Americas, primarily to Brazil and to British, French, Dutch and Danish colonies in the Caribbean. The slave trade reached its climax during the so-called age of Enlightenment. Between 1725 and 1825, English, Dutch and French ships transported more than 7.2 million people to the New World, with several million more dying during the brutal voyage to the Americas.

   With the slave trade, the population of Europe also changed: by 1600, about 10 percent of the population of cities like Lisbon, Cadiz and Seville was made up of Africans. Throughout Europe, a new urban*, multi-ethnic* culture took shape that, in many ways, can be regarded as producing the first "modern" European subjects, or people who faced the challenges of living in non-homogenous, socially and economically complex societies. As Achille Mbembe has argued, African slavery was the crucible in which European modernity was forged. It was with the system of plantation slavery that, for the first time, the capitalistic organization of labour was attempted on a large scale. As for the labourer himself, reduced to the status of a material thing – the "Negro" or *pieza de India* ('piece of India', i.e. slave) of official documents – he was forcefully torn away from his original socio-cultural context in Africa. As such, the slave came to represent the model of the modern, alienated worker, displaced both physically and psychologically from his own needs, and of value only in economic terms.

The African resurfaced as a character in fiction in early modern European literature. William Shakespeare's play *The Tempest* (ca. 1610), for example, showed how the protagonist Prospero used magic to establish rule over a far-away island, including mastery over its original inhabitant, Caliban (an obvious anagram for "cannibal"). The parallels with the European colonisation of the New World were clear, yet the role of Caliban remains sufficiently ambiguous to allow a subtle questioning of European dominance overseas. Other texts describing real and imaginary travels provided an occasion for a critical interrogation of slavery. In one of the earliest works of fiction devoted to this topic, *Oroonoko, or the Royal Slave* (1688), Englishwoman Aphra Behn condemned slavery by recounting a tale of doomed love between two slaves set in the Dutch colony of Surinam. While the evils of slavery could also be denounced in theoretical texts like Montesquieu's *Esprit des Lois* ('Spirit of Laws', 1748), the impact of such denunciations was far greater when they figured in fictional texts. In Voltaire's 1759 bestseller *Candide*, one of the most memorable scenes shows the hero arriving in Surinam and meeting a slave who lacks an arm and a leg. His cruel owner, Mr Vanderdendur (the name's harsh sonorities are an indication of his mindset) punished slaves who had accidents at work, like trapping their finger in millstones, by chopping off their arm, and hacked off the leg of anyone who tried to escape. Both punishments had been meted out to the man Candide encounters, which explains his parlous condition. When the hero expresses his horror at the situation, the unfortunate "Surinam negro" states in a matter-of-fact way: "It is the price we pay for the sugar you eat in Europe."[6] Ironically, despite his denunciation of slavery, the author of this book, Voltaire, owed some of his own wealth to ethically dubious investments, and eighteenth-century contemporaries saw no discrepancy in naming a slave-trading ship after Voltaire – illustrating reality's struggle at times to catch up with the ideals or alternative worlds first described in literary texts.

In a different literary genre, Bernardin de Saint-Pierre's travel narrative *Voyage à l'Île de France* ('Voyage to the Île de France', 1773) – the old name for Mauritius – has two frontispieces. One shows a shackled African. In the second, a naked prostrate slave is being whipped by a fully dressed white man while, in the foreground, a naked black woman, in chains, one child on her back, another clinging to her, is close to another naked black man who appears to be eating a banana. The caption reads "What you use for your pleasure is soaked in our tears." This is an indictment of Westerners who were happy to close their eyes to the unethical provenance of their luxury goods – rather like contemporary consumers who buy cheap clothes without considering that they were probably made in sweat-shops on the other side of the world. Bernardin de Saint-Pierre was writing in the years preceding the French Revolution, at a time when his readers would have been ready to hear the denunciation of European hypocrisy. The tendency to use informative texts for polemical purposes was particularly widespread in eighteenth-century Europe as it entered the age of revolutions – including the 1791 slave revolt in the French colony of Saint-Domingue (present-day Haiti) – that marked the end of the early modern period.

Finally, in a few rare cases, slaves themselves took up the pen as authors. Phillis Wheatley was an African, probably from The Gambia or Senegal, brought to America as a slave. The Bostonian family that purchased the eight-year-old, the Wheatleys, gave her a thorough education. She visited England where, at the age of twenty, with their support, she published her *Poems on Various Subjects, Religious and Moral* (1773), which were widely read on both sides of the Atlantic and are considered to be the first volume published by an African-American. The Wheatleys eventually emancipated Phillis, who was then free to marry. Wheatley's poems often show conventional inspiration but in her letters and exchanges she defended slaves' natural rights. Her poem "On being brought from Africa to America"[7] was ambiguous, for despite criticizing slavery, Wheatley presented her lot as a fortunate one: she had discovered God thanks to her Christian masters.

Voyages of discovery and the post-colonial critique of modernity

Authors such as Las Casas and Montaigne, who criticized the new world being brought about by European expansion overseas, were the first to engage in what was later to become a full-fledged critique of modernity. Critiques of modernity gained ground in the twentieth century, and played an important part in the creation of the academic field of post-colonial studies, or the study of the representation by Europeans of the non-European world, as well as critical responses to these representations. One of the most fruitful approaches to the European literature of colonial exploration was formulated by Edward Said in *Orientalism: Western Conceptions of the Orient* (1978). According to Said, the non-European world evoked a complex mix of responses on the part of European authors: fascination with exotic landscapes (the white sands and turquoise seas of Bougainville), and escape fantasies, but also processes of "othering" (such as the reduction of Africans to the status of object).

Out of the recognition of this distorted nature of representation of the non-European world grew various attempts by authors from the former colonies to set the picture straight. One of the key strategies in this process was that of intertextuality, or critically rewriting the canonical texts of old – the same strategy Camões had used in his 1572 *Lusiads*. During the course of the twentieth century, canonical texts such as Shakespeare's *The Tempest* (and Defoe's *Robinson Crusoe*, as mentioned previously) became the object of post-colonial rewritings. Among the first was *Une tempête* ('A Storm', 1969) by the Martiniquais poet Aimé Césaire. Césaire, one of the founders of the *négritude* movement, sought to replace the negative stereotypes of black people, born of the trauma of Atlantic slavery, by a cultural reawakening. In *Une tempête*, he gave pride of place to Caliban, presented as a hero rebelling against foreign rule, and set out to "de-mythify" Prospero's magic, showing that it was merely the result of superior technology. Césaire's relation to *The Tempest* was therefore ambivalent: while on one hand, by re-writing it, he placed himself in the literary tradition Shakespeare represented, on the other hand his version was a critical revision, proclaiming the need to use literature to imagine new realities. Thus, where Camões in his *Lusiads* celebrated modernity by opposing it to antiquity, taking European expansion overseas as paradigmatic of European modernity, in the twentieth century other authors sought to celebrate their own world, that had been created by that same European expansion overseas, by opposing it to the early modern Western literary canon born of that expansion.

Notes

1 Luis de Camões, *The Lusiads*, trans. Thomas Livingston Mitchell (London: T. & W. Boone, 1854), 1, 3–4.
2 Geoffrey L. Scammel, *The First Imperial Age: European Overseas Expansion c. 1400–1715* (London: Routledge, 1989), 59.
3 Robert Southey, trans., cited in Seymour I. Schwartz, *The Mismapping of America* (Rochester, NY: The University of Rochester Press, 2003), 128.

4 Cited in Schwartz, *The Mismapping of America*, 129–30.
5 Edward Said, *Culture and Imperialism* (London:Vintage, 1993), 83.
6 Voltaire, *Candide, or Optimism*. trans.Theo Cuffe (London: Penguin Classics, 2005), 52.
7 www.encyclopedia.com/arts/educational-magazines/being-brought-africa-america   (Accessed 28.11.2017).

Further reading

Aravamudan, Srinivas. *Enlightenment Orientalism: Resisting the Rise of the Novel*. Chicago, IL: University of Chicago Press, 2011.
Mbembe,Achille. *Critique de la raison nègre*. Paris: La Découverte, 2013.
Said, Edward. *Orientalism:Western Conceptions of the Orient*. London: Routledge & Kegan Paul, 1978.
Scamell, Geoffrey V. *The First Imperial Age: European Overseas Expansion c. 1400–1715*. London: Routledge, 1989.

17 Corresponding

Catriona Seth

Figure 17.1 "Woman Writing a Letter", Gerard Ter Borch, Oil on panel, 38.3 x 27.9 cm. c. 1655, Mauritshuis, The Hague

Numerous seventeenth- and eighteenth-century paintings show the sitter engaged with some form of correspondence*: poring over a letter*, writing a message with a quill, slipping a note to a servant . . . The early modern period saw a considerable rise in literacy*. There was a development of reading* for leisure as opposed to straightforward information or instruction and a notable increase in the number of women readers*. Letter-writing became more frequent, partly thanks to improved roads and mail coach timetables which made it possible to exchange missives regularly within cities (towns like London or Paris set up courier services), but also from province to province or indeed across borders – there were no postage stamps like the ones we use: the recipient paid a fee according to the letter or parcel's size and the distance it had travelled. Intellectuals throughout Europe traded ideas and corresponded as members of the "Republic of Letters"*, an informal transnational virtual network of researchers and writers with varying fields of expertise. Publications like the Royal Society's *Philosophical Transactions*, launched in 1665, included information which had circulated in correspondence from remote cities like Constantinople or Stockholm and not just cities close to London like Edinburgh or Amsterdam. Newspapers printed letters from readers who were reacting to published articles or current events, or who had sent information useful to the community at large. Practical guides – including French *Secrétaires* which were reprinted, translated, revised and plagiarised, from Madrid to Berlin or Amsterdam, gave models of letters for all occasions and were often aimed at young men who were entering the world, at the countryman or woman who was not at ease with urban culture, or at the upwardly mobile who might have to acquire epistolary (from the Latin *epistola*, meaning 'epistle' or 'letter') talents analogous to those fostered in the upper classes from an early age. They were an equivalent to domestic conduct-books, but rather than simply setting out rules, they functioned through written examples of letters which could be copied or imitated. Unsurprisingly, English writer Samuel Richardson's first foray into the epistolary genre, before his success as a novelist, was through his renowned manual of *Familiar Letters on Important Occasions* (1741) which was translated (notably into French and Dutch) and went through several print runs.

Except when addressed, for instance, to an academy or a journal, letters were private exchanges, generally sealed with wax by the sender to ensure confidentiality. To read someone else's correspondence without his or her permission was considered by the Church to be a sin. Letters of exceptional individuals were sometimes collected and published after their death, like the seventeenth-century French noblewoman, Marie de Rabutin-Chantal, marquise de Sévigné's delightful and whimsical addresses to her married daughter, first printed clandestinely in 1725, or the English aristocrat and poetess Lady Mary Wortley Montagu's witty and lively missives from Constantinople where her husband was the British ambassador. These *Turkish Letters*, published posthumously in 1763, constitute an early presentation of life in the Ottoman Empire through a Western woman's eyes. As such examples indicate, whilst letter-writing could be the stuff of erudite discussions, it could also be a pastime for ladies of leisure and was seen as a written equivalent to conversations. This led to a frequent association of women with the epistolary genre, as both authors and readers.

Letters from far and near

In their different forms, letters afforded a means of organising a society which still relied greatly on oral exchanges. Letters patent from monarchs allowed their subjects to do various things, from adding a title to their name to printing books. Pastoral letters helped religious leaders ensure their message filtered down to ordinary parishioners. Letters were a way of abolishing distance whether in hierarchical terms or in geographical ones. Jesuits setting out to convert the Chinese wrote back to Europe about their experiences and gave accounts of Oriental music or traditional healthcare. Eminent physicians, like Samuel-Auguste Tissot in Lausanne, offered medical diagnoses, advice and prescriptions by letter to German princes, the Italian nobility or Scottish merchants whom they had not examined, but who had given an account of their symptoms by correspondence. The Enlightenment* was in many ways the golden age of letter writing.

Building on exchanges between academies and individuals based on models which often stretched back to the Renaissance*, networks of correspondence united scholars across Europe who might never meet but would discuss discoveries and ideas. An author like Voltaire, celebrated as a playwright, poet and philosopher, who spent much of his time far from Paris, sent missives practically every day to publishers, friends, relatives and potentates as well as open letters for periodicals to print. In the latter part of his life, when engaged in defending victims of unjust trials, like Jean Calas, wrongly executed in 1762 for his son's murder, Voltaire, by now an internationally renowned public intellectual, mobilised an impressive web of contacts throughout Europe whilst not leaving his home in Ferney (now Ferney-Voltaire), near Geneva. Several hundred letters were instrumental in obtaining a posthumous royal pardon for the unfortunate Calas. These, along with Voltaire's other correspondence, were included in his complete works published by the playwright Beaumarchais and the philosopher Condorcet between 1785 and 1790. Their edition of Voltaire gave the same treatment to 4,500 rediscovered letters addressed to some three hundred correspondents as to major canonical texts like his tragedy *Zaïre* or his epic *La Henriade*. This set in motion a process of collection which culminated in the middle of the twentieth century with Englishman Theodore Besterman's edition of Voltaire's correspondence, published first in Geneva, then in Oxford and Paris. Like that of other early-modern and Enlightenment luminaries, from Pierre Bayle to Jean-Jacques Rousseau and Benjamin Franklin, Voltaire's correspondence is still considered to be a treasure trove, and, in modern electronic editions, their fully searchable form means academics can find new ways in which to examine them.

Travel journals, when published, often took the form of letters to friends or relatives. A book like Voltaire's *Lettres philosophiques* ('Philosophical Letters'), containing short pieces on religion*, literature, commerce, politics, etc., written by the Frenchman whilst in exile in England, draws on such a tradition to showcase what the author saw as exciting modern developments. We are all, in a sense, to consider ourselves as being addressed by the author. This conceit was used by other writers across Europe (like Denis Diderot and Johann Gottfried von Herder) all through the century. In their texts, which are often closer to the essay form than to a personal letter, people in whom no specific socio-political authority is vested expounded their ideas on questions important to all. Such publications accompanied the emergence of public opinion by drawing private individuals into contemporary debates, if only by making them implicit recipients of open letters.

A time-honoured tradition

In colleges and schools, Latin letters like Cicero's or Seneca's served as translation exercises and as the basis for philosophical or literary discussions. They would have been known to any well-educated intellectual of the early-modern age. Ovid's *Heroids*, fictional verse letters purporting to be from famous lovers – e.g. Dido to Aeneas or Penelope to Ulysses –

were often read and imitated. Pope penned his celebrated poem, *Eloisa to Abelard* (1717), on this model. It inspired imitations and parodies in English, French and Spanish. The verse form referred to as "Héroïdes" was popular in France in the mid-eighteenth century (and subsequently in Spanish translations). It included letters supposedly exchanged between mythological but also more recent historical characters.

Letters had long been inserted in novels or plays as plot devices before becoming a stand-alone literary genre. Whilst there are early expressions of the epistolary form like Diego de San Pedro's late sixteenth-century *Cárcel de Amor* ('Prison of Love'), the genre as such belongs to a later period. Englishwoman Aphra Behn, with her *Love-Letters between a Nobleman and his Sister* (1684–1687), was among the early authors to see the possibilities of epistolary fiction*. As the titles indicate, the genre served originally to showcase love letters. Long thought of as authentic, Gabriel-Joseph de Lavergne, comte de Guilleragues's *Lettres portugaises traduites en français* ('Portuguese letters translated into French', 1669) began a tradition of sentimental fiction (see Chapter 19) in which a spurned woman gives an elegiac account of her destiny: five passionate letters, ostensibly from a Portuguese nun to the French officer who has abandoned her, deplore her fate and express her love and despair in lyrical tones. The slim volume was published anonymously and was widely believed, until the last century, to be a series of historical documents, rather than a fictional text.

Because private letters were considered confidential, there was a particular thrill in reading them. The letters included in epistolary novels are frequently prefaced by someone claiming to have found them in a trunk in the attic or an abandoned satchel, or by an "editor" who claims to have known the protagonists. By such artifices, epistolary fiction plays on verisimilitude and presents itself as authentic both to avoid criticisms often levelled at novels for their lack of gravity and to intensify the reader's experience.

The epistolary genre has a long history which is still being written. It reached its height of popularity – and became a mainstream form – from the 1750s to the turn of the eighteenth and nineteenth centuries. Whilst its popularity diminished subsequently, it never disappeared completely. There are epistolary drafts in Jane Austen's papers, though not for books published during her lifetime. Mary Wollstonecraft Shelley's world-famous *Frankenstein* (1818) uses letters as a framing device. Honoré de Balzac's *Mémoires de deux jeunes mariées* ('Letters of Two Young Brides', 1841) takes the convention of girls meeting when pupils in a convent as the basis for a long friendship during which they exchange letters. There are many notable nineteenth-century examples of texts in which correspondence plays a part. Bram Stoker's hugely popular 1897 *Dracula*, the celebrated gothic horror story which continues to exert huge influence in vampire fiction and cinema, includes telegrams, extracts from diaries and newspaper clippings as a way of renewing the genre. Hugo von Hofmannsthal's 1902 *Ein Brief* ('A Letter') and Stefan Zweig's 1922 *Der Brief einer Unbekannten* ('The Letter from an Unknown') are a couple of early twentieth-century German-language fictional letters. Jean Webster's epistolary coming-of-age fiction *Daddy-Long-Legs* (1912) remains popular to this day. C.S. Lewis's 1942 exchanges on matters theological between a Senior Demon and his nephew, a Junior Tempter, *The Screwtape Letters*, and Lionel Shriver's powerful 2003 *We Need to Talk about Kevin* – letters from a distraught mother to her presumably estranged husband as she attempts to come to terms with the fact that their son is an assassin – are other instances of successful epistolary texts. When the form is chosen by contemporary authors, they often add modern messaging technologies like emails to traditional letter-writing.

Points of view

An Italian called Giovanni Paolo Marana (1642–1693) who lived a colourful life and spent periods in prison published an influential novel *L'Esploratore Turco e le di lui pratiche segrete con la Porta Ottomana* ('Letters writ by a Turkish spy . . . giving an impartial account of the Divan of Constantinople . . . and discovering several intrigues and secrets of the Christian courts') in 1684. Rapidly translated into French, it purported to be the letters of a Turk at the French court. Building on this idea, political and legal theorist Montesquieu's very popular polyphonic *Lettres persanes* ('Persian letters'), first published in 1721, showed that epistolary fiction had considerable satirical potential: writing home to their friends, his Persian visitors make apparently innocent but scathing remarks about religion, society and politics in France. The book renewed the genre by choosing foreign observers and also pandered to Europe's taste for exotica by having letters sent from the seraglio by the wives and eunuchs of one of the main characters. George Lyttelton's *Letters from a Persian in England to his friend at Ispahan* (1735), Françoise de Graffigny's *Lettres d'une Péruvienne* ('Letters by a Peruvian woman', 1747) and José Cadalso's *Cartas Marruecas* ('Moroccan letters', 1789) are examples of works in three literary traditions (English, French and Spanish), which were direct heirs of Montesquieu's text and bear witness to its success. They hint at the vitality of the conceit whereby an exotic gaze was used as a means of criticising contemporary society. The reader is drawn to look anew, and without prejudice, at what he or she takes for granted. For instance, the use of foreign terms draws an analogy between something usual and something exotic – as when Montesquieu's Persians refer to churches as "mosques". The characters' incomprehension of how the pope – a magician greater than the king, in their words – manages to get away with trading in apparently empty promises, means that to judge whether their interpretation is legitimate or not, we must imagine ourselves in their position. The novel with its travelling heroes is thus suggesting we change places mentally with the Persians. A dinner guest's silly question on meeting one of them – *Comment peut-on être persan?* ('How can one be Persian?') – is a way of prompting us to wonder how we can be Europeans. Cultural relativity is thus the order of the day.

The taste for all things foreign – in literature as in the decorative arts – led to sets of fictional letters being penned by characters supposedly from the four corners of the earth – including Iroquois or Turks. Oliver Goldsmith's satirical *Citizen of the World*, subtitled *Letters from a Chinese Philosopher Residing in London to his Friends in the East* (1760–1761), is in part a variation on this theme.

When the fictional letters are those of a single correspondent – like in the *Lettres portugaises* or in Claude Crébillon's 1732 *Lettres de la marquise de M*** au comte de R**** ('Letters of the Marchioness de M*** to the Count de R***') – our knowledge remains one-sided: we are forced to build up our appreciation of the letter-writer and his or her fate without external elements. Montesquieu boasted that his *Lettres persanes* had taught his contemporaries to compose epistolary fiction. In formal terms, he shows real mastery with the inclusion of distinct letter writers in Europe and in Persia. This means we can read questions and answers or listen to dissenting voices on a single subject. Since each correspondent gives his or her own reaction, it is subjective, but eminently believable. The reader discovers it without having to take the word of an omniscient narrator*. Scotsman Tobias Smollett's 1771 mock-epic *Expedition of Humphry Clinker* uses the technique to great effect by giving us six characters' takes on events as they travel from southwest England to Edinburgh via a series of spa towns where Matthew Bramble attempts to cure his melancholy. By giving contrasting views, the letter-writers reveal their faults, their pretensions, their self-deception and their misunderstandings, but also their deep humanity.

"Polylogic" epistolary fiction – which has several letter-writers – also encourages variety in pace and tone. Both tragic and comic effects can be achieved by the order in which events unfold. Expectations can be met or defeated. Fanny Burney's first book, *Evelina* (1768), has scenes with humorous overtones. The heroine discovers the minutiae of etiquette and conventions through the *faux pas* she recounts as she makes her début in fashionable circles – rather like Cécile Volanges, at the start of Frenchman Pierre-Ambroise-François Choderlos de Laclos's *Les liaisons dangereuses* ('Dangerous Acquaintances', 1782), who tells her convent friend Sophie Carnay how she mistook the cobbler for a suitor or how she fell asleep during a society dinner.

By ensuring very different characters take up their pens and allowing for multiple voices, epistolary fiction also made it easier to introduce the discussion of important societal ideas (the role of commerce in *Lettres persanes*, the education of women in *Lettres d'une Péruvienne*, the future of republican ideals after the French Revolution in *Ultime Lettere di Jacopo Ortis* ['Last Letters of Jacopo Ortis'], etc.). In a case like Laclos's *Les Liaisons dangereuses*, which raises implicit questions about the status of women in Ancien Régime society or the basis of relationships, etc., the reader ends up not knowing what the author's overall intentions really are: prefatory remarks attributed to the editor and publisher – as well as to the bookseller in the 1787 edition – give contradictory explanations, and the open-ended tale, which, an editorial note indicates, could be continued, does not impose an overarching view.

Epistolary fiction also allowed educated servants to play a part alongside their masters or for young professionals like Julianne, the seamstress in Dutch-Swiss authoress Isabelle de Charrière's 1784 *Lettres neuchâteloises* ('Letters from Neuchâtel'), to write to friends and family. This bears witness to increased literacy among the working classes but also allows such characters to express opinions and become fully fledged protagonists of the plot*. By having one or several main female characters in their books (like *Clarissa* or *Lettres d'une Péruvienne*) authors could give women a voice – even if it was sometimes just for them to denounce their oppression or their unfaithful lovers – and developed the idea (which the publication of authentic correspondences had tended to suggest) that they were in a sense "natural" letter-writers. It is therefore unsurprising that many women authors undertook to write epistolary fiction – they include Frances Brooke who, with her 1769 *History of Emily Montague*, penned the first North American novel whilst living in Quebec.

At a time of considerable developments in the field of pedagogy, some epistolary fiction was specifically aimed at children and used them as characters. An imitation of Richardson's 1753 *History of Sir Charles Grandison*, with its virtuous male hero, Maria Gertruida Decambon van der Werken's 1782 *De kleine Grandison* ('Little Grandison') was to enjoy particular renown among junior readers in Arnaud Berquin's 1787 French translation (*Le Petit Grandisson*). Félicité de Genlis's *Les Petits émigrés* ('The Young Emigrants', 1798) went so far as to include badly phrased letters from a dunce whose prose is mocked by his correspondents which leads him to make greater efforts and tends to suggest an example to be followed by the young reader.

Unmediated feelings

Tragic relationships were at the centre of several important works which use the epistolary form as an appropriate vehicle for sentimental fiction*. The reader could, as it were, look over the writer's shoulder and into his or her soul. By considering the letters presented as real, he or she has unmediated access to the character's feelings and vision of events. In addition, there is an apparent simultaneity of the time of writing and reading. The narrative technique means that the text appears to unfold before the reader's eyes.

Sentiment, as Richardson's heroines make clear, was all the rage. Times were changing. Arranged marriages, often between a young virgin and an older experienced man, which were the norm among the upper classes and led to a widespread tolerance of extra-marital affairs, were being contested by younger generations anxious to find love and happiness with a soulmate, rather than a mere financial partnership. This major societal change is perceptible in plotlines with their discussion of female morality, consideration of feelings and reason, inclusion of characters with differing backgrounds and prejudices, etc.

As an expression of sentiment, tears are widespread in eighteenth-century literature. Just as plays invited spectators to behave as though the scene being acted out before their eyes was real, epistolary fiction led one to shed tears over the protagonists' sad tales. A virtual circle of communication was set up in which the protagonists' often overblown reactions drew readers to feel the same way, and there are accounts of them identifying with the heroes and crying, laughing or sighing with them. Readers of *La Nouvelle Héloïse* ('The New Heloise'), Rousseau's hugely successful 1761 tragic love story which was a bestseller* throughout Europe, believed in the characters. They wrote the author fan letters and went on tours of Lake Geneva to search for the sites where the story took place, demonstrating how far their "willing suspension of disbelief"[1] could go.

Another contemporary epistolary novel, Goethe's *Die Leiden des jungen Werthers* ('The Sorrows of Young Werther', 1774), (see also Chapter 19), was so popular that readers dressed up as Charlotte and Werther and compared its effect to a sickness: reading-madness (*Lesewut*). The eponymous character falls hopelessly in love with a charming upright married woman. Incapable of facing the prospect of life without her, Werther blows his brains out having written a heartfelt farewell note, asking to be buried with a pink ribbon once worn by his adored Charlotte. The work was widely imitated, parodied and translated – Senancour's Oberman, Constant's Adolphe and Foscolo's Jacopo Ortis all inherited some of the hero's traits. It is also said, although historians agree this is excessive, to have led to a wave of suicides by young men, initiating what sociologists call the "Werther effect."

The "pursuit of happiness" included as an inalienable right in the American Declaration of Independence (1776) could take on personal or political overtones. The rise of an educated middle class led to its members aspiring to some of the privileges of the nobility. The problem of politics interfering with passion took on a particular acuity after the storming of the Bastille in Paris on July 14, 1789. Such concerns are reflected in fiction whether it is set in contemporary Europe, in faraway lands or in the more-or-less distant past. François Vernes of Geneva's *Adélaïde de Clarencé ou les Malheurs et les délices du sentiment* ('Adélaïde de Clarencé or the Misfortunes and Delights of Sentiment', 1796) shows a heroine torn between her reactionary father and her revolutionary lover and committing suicide because there is no simple solution to her fate, as she admits in a testamentary letter. Germaine de Staël's 1802 *Delphine* also allows characters to express their differing political options as Europe is in turmoil: personal feelings struggle to be heard when warfare is the order of the day. The heroine takes her own life when her beloved is sent to his death after being tried for military offences. *Ultime lettere di Jacopo Ortis*, the first Italian epistolary novel, appeared in various stages and versions between 1798 and 1817. It is by Ugo Foscolo, a poet and consummate letter-writer – as his published *Epistolario* ('Collected Letters') demonstrates. It is based in part on the author's own experience. Like Werther, the hero Jacopo takes his own life – he cannot marry his cherished Teresa and feels he has no future as a young patriot, stateless in a divided Italy threatened by French imperial expansion.

A pan-European culture of the novel

Eighteenth-century readers appreciated epistolary fiction. Books like *Clarissa* or *La Nouvelle Héloïse*, to name two prime examples, were well received not only in the countries in which they were published, but also gained wide acclaim throughout Europe. This was partly helped, in the case of texts written in French, by the fact that many people, particularly in the upper echelons of society, had some fluency in the language – it was the court tongue in Vienna and Parma, for instance. Russians and Poles often read French, just like Spaniards or Bavarians. In addition, the market for fiction was such that translations were popular – there was every expectation that a blockbuster which had been a success in one European country would do well in another language. Translations were sometimes unfaithful and often undertaken without the original author and editor being contacted. Commercial arguments often prevailed in the choice of what to translate as well as in the selection of titles for original fiction – for instance *La Nouvelle Clarice* ('The New Clarissa', 1767), by Frenchwoman Marie Leprince de Beaumont, was meant to attract readers who had already enjoyed *Clarissa*.

Richardson's *Clarissa: Or the History of a Young Lady* (1748) was translated into French by an author who had lived in England and the Netherlands. It was read across Europe. It served as a template for other authors and was taken as the yardstick for great fiction by Diderot, among others. The novel included a wide cast of letter-writers, some drawn from lowlier walks of life, and one, the rake Lovelace, who would be a model for future literary villains and libertines. The English author's other bestseller, *Pamela: Or, Virtue Rewarded* (1740), stunned many contemporaries by taking a teenage maidservant as its heroine. She resists attempts to seduce and corrupt her and, through her integrity, is finally treated as an equal by her master, a rich landowner, who ends up proposing marriage to her. Whilst certain contemporaries dismissed it as licentious, there are accounts of the story being read aloud in villages to great popular acclaim. Turned into Italian plays by Goldoni, and illustrated by Highmore, it was mercilessly parodied by another talented contemporary, Henry Fielding, in *Shamela* (1741). Richardson's influence was extensive: Laclos quotes him in *Les liaisons dangereuses* and the first Dutch novel in prose, Wolff and Deken's 1782 *De Historie van mejuffrouw Sara Burgerhart* ('The Story of Miss Sara Burgerhart'), is a witty tale defending bourgeois values, and which owes much to the authors' reading of *Clarissa* and *Pamela*.

Rousseau's 1761 *Julie ou La Nouvelle Héloïse* – its subtitle illustrates the vogue for mediæval lover and letter writer Eloisa – is, the preface explains, intended as a form of inoculation against the worst kind of contemporary fiction. The idea is that by reading it a young woman will be protected against the moral assaults of inferior tales which set bad examples of giving in to one's passions and thus pervert innocent young minds. The letters, written by a small cast of characters, include a discussion of themes such as suicide, popular traditions, hygiene, etc. whilst presenting a compelling love story set against the fashionable backdrop of Switzerland's idyllic scenery. Like many novels of sentiment, *La Nouvelle Héloïse* – to give it the title by which it is generally known – ends tragically: Julie dies from an illness contracted when she casts herself into the lake to rescue her son from drowning, an illustration of the importance of motherhood and family ties. Along the way, many tears are shed as the heroine attempts to resist her illicit passion for her tutor Saint-Preux, and suffers from her father's intransigent position, from committing what she understands to be a grave sin by having a full-blown affair with her lover, from their separation and from knowing, once she marries, that her husband will only ever be second-best. Throughout Europe, thanks to his fictional letters, which were widely read in the original and in various foreign languages, Rousseau was renowned as a master of sensibility.

Translations* and imitations* crossed borders. They fostered a modern pan-European culture, promoted the circulation of common values like a respect for learning or a defence of the individual and opened up debates on questions like the relative importance of nature and nurture.

An unrivalled masterpiece

More than *Clarissa*, *La Nouvelle Héloïse* or even *Werther*, the best-known epistolary novel of all time nowadays is probably the only one written by a French artilleryman: Laclos's *Les liaisons dangereuses*, which paradoxically owes much of its current fame to cinematic adaptations*. An instant *succès de scandale*, it was discussed in European salons but on the whole the serious press ignored it. Multiple pirated editions came out. It was rapidly translated into English and German, as well as Russian. Readers tried to identify models for the characters who illustrate the almost unlimited power of letters – after all, madame de Tourvel is in effect wounded to death by the "epistolary model" (letter CXLI) the marquise de Merteuil gets the vicomte de Valmont to send her. Considered to have quite a risqué storyline, though not remotely explicit in its language, the book fell out of favour after the French Revolution and for much of the nineteenth century, though the poet Charles Baudelaire drafted notes for a preface to an edition which never came out. "Decadents"* like Arthur Symons, Aubrey Beardsley or Remy de Gourmont – who prized artifice more than nature and looked beyond Romanticism* to the eighteenth century for literary and artistic models – praised it at the turn of the nineteenth and twentieth centuries, and multiple editions and translations (into English, German, Italian and others) were published at the time. In the mid-twentieth century, the novel became the object of serious critical interest which has continued ever since. It was turned into a film in 1959 (Roger Vadim and Roger Vaillant, *Les liaisons dangereuses 1960*, which updates the plot and sets it in jazz age France with characters using telegrams, telephones and tape recorders rather than letters to further their devices) and several times subsequently – most notably by Stephen Frears in 1989 after Christopher Hampton's renowned 1985 stage adaptation. Further films have been made in the United States, France and Korea in particular. Significantly, some descriptions in the original epistolary version already had a theatrical quality (e.g. when the vicomte de Valmont sets out for Cécile how she is to hand over the key to her room or when the présidente de Tourvel tells of being laughed at by a loose woman when her carriage gets stuck in traffic by the opera house).

Whilst deeply rooted in Ancien Régime aristocratic society with its conventions and prejudices, Laclos's text handles a variety of timeless themes (manipulation, social reputations, secrecy etc.) which probably explains why it has stood the test of time better than many works of the period and has, sometimes with references to the author's biography, spawned various imitations or responses. To give some instances over the past half century, we could mention books published in the Netherlands (*Een gevaarlijke verhouding of Daalen Bergse brieven* ['A dangerous Affair or Daal-en-Bergisch Letters', 1976] by renowned author Hella Haasse), the United Kingdom (most recently *A Factory of Cunning/Murderous Liaisons* [2005] by Philippa Stockley), Russia (Leonid Filatov's play *Dangerous, dangerous, very dangerous*, 2001), Italy (Hélène-Claude Frances, *Il fantasma di Laclos. Lettere da Taranto* ['Laclos's Ghost. Letters from Taranto', 2006]) or France, where barely a year goes by without some writer or another using *Les liaisons dangereuses* as a direct inspiration for a modern text often at least partly in epistolary form.

Les liaisions dangereuses

Les liaisons dangereuses has two libertine characters, the wicked marquise de Merteuil and her erstwhile lover, the debauched vicomte de Valmont. She sets him the task of perverting Cécile, an innocent teenager, fresh out of her convent, and who is due to be married off to a nobleman they both despise. Whilst taking up the challenge, Valmont also undertakes to seduce a virtuous married woman, the présidente de Tourvel. He triumphs in that he gets both Cécile – who is in love with her young music master, Danceny – and Tourvel to sleep with him, but the relationships have disastrous consequences: Cécile has a miscarriage, her affair is discovered by Danceny and she runs off to become a nun in order to hide her shame; Valmont is killed whilst duelling with Danceny, and Tourvel lets herself die having been first spurned by her libertine lover and then learnt of his demise. Merteuil loses an inheritance and is horribly disfigured when she catches the smallpox. Socially ruined, she flees to Holland.

This letter is part of Valmont's seduction of Tourvel. He writes it during a "stormy night" of passion with an old flame, Emilie, a dancer and prostitute whose body serves as a "table" to write to the présidente. It reads like a declaration of love but is full of innuendo – the blank line between the paragraphs is the interruption during which he has sex with his partner. It is based on *double-entendre**, as is made clear by Valmont's explanation in the previous letter to Merteuil, whom he entrusts with the responsibility of sending the missive from Paris to avoid betraying where he is.

Text: Choderlos de Laclos, Les liaisons dangereuses
('Dangerous Acquaintances') (1782)

The Vicomte de Valmont to the Présidente de Tourvel (Bearing the postmark of Paris):

It is after a stormy night, during which I have not closed my eyes; it is after having been ceaselessly either in the agitation of a devouring ardour, or in utter annihilation of all the faculties of my soul, that I come to seek with you, Madame, the calm of which I have need, and which, however, I have as yet no hope to enjoy. In truth, the situation in which I am, whilst writing to you, makes me realise more than ever the irresistible power of love; I can hardly preserve sufficient control over myself to put some order into my ideas; and I foresee already that I shall not finish this letter without being forced to interrupt it. What! Am I never to hope then that you will some day share with me the trouble which overcomes me at this moment? I dare believe, notwithstanding, that if you were well acquainted with it you would not be entirely insensible. Believe me, Madame, a cold tranquillity, the soul's slumber, the imitation of death do not conduce to happiness; the active passions alone can lead us thither; and, in spite of the torments which you make me suffer, I think I can assure you without risk that at this moment I am happier than you. In vain do you overwhelm me with your terrible severities; they do not prevent me from abandoning myself utterly to love, and forgetting, in the delirium which it causes me, the despair into which you cast me. It is so that I would avenge myself for the exile to which you condemn me. Never had I so much pleasure in writing to you; never have I experienced, during such an occupation, an emotion so sweet and, at the same time, so lively. Everything seems to enhance my transports; the air I breathe is laden with pleasure; the very table upon which I write to you, consecrated for the first time to this office, becomes love's sacred altar to me; how much it will be beautified in my eyes! I shall have traced upon it the vow to love you for ever! Pardon, I beseech you, the disorder of my senses. Perhaps, I ought to abandon myself less to transports which you do not share: I must leave you for a moment to dispel an intoxication which increases each moment, and which becomes stronger than myself.

I return to you, Madame, and doubtless, I return always with the same eagerness. However, the sentiment of happiness has fled far away from me; it has given place to that of cruel privation. What does it avail me to speak of my sentiments, if I seek in vain the means to convince you of them? After so many efforts, I am equally bereft of strength and confidence. If I still tell over to myself the pleasures of love, it is only to feel more keenly my sorrow at being deprived of them. I see no other resource, save in your indulgence; and I am too sensible at this moment of how greatly I need it, to hope to obtain it. Never, however, has my love been more respectful, never could it be less likely to offend you; it is of such a kind, I dare say, as the most severe virtue need not fear: but I am myself afraid of describing to you, at greater length, the sorrow which I experience. Assured as I am that the object which causes it does not partici-pate in it, I must at any rate not abuse your kindness; and it would be to do that, were I to spend more time in retracing for you that dolorous picture. I take only enough to beg you to reply to me, and never to doubt of the sincerity of my sentiments.

Written at P. . .; dated from Paris, 30th August, 17**.[2]

Notes

1 The term 'willing suspension of disbelief' has entered into common usage. In 1817 the English writer Samuel Taylor Coleridge coined it to explain the fact that a reader or audience member is happy to enter into the spirit of a text and believe in characters or events which he or she knows to be imagi-nary and might normally condemn as unrealistic or impossible. It is part of our enjoyment of fiction, whether we are reading novels or poems or watching plays.
2 Choderlos de Laclos, *Les liaisons dangereuses*, trans. Ernest Dowson (London: The Nonesuch Press, 1940), 92–4.

Further reading

Altman, Janet Gurkin. *Epistolarity: Approaches to a Form*. Columbus: Ohio State University Press, 1982.
Beebee, Thomas O. *Epistolary Fiction in Europe, 1500–1850*. Cambridge: Cambridge University Press, 1999.
Brant, Clare. *Eighteenth-Century Letters and British Culture*. New York: Palgrave Macmillan, 2006.
Herman, Jan. *Le Mensonge romanesque: paradigmes pour l'étude du roman épistolaire en France*. Louvain/Amsterdam: Rodopi, 1989.
Kany, Charles E. *The Beginnings of the Epistolary Novel in France, Italy, and Spain*. Berkeley: University of California Press, 1937.

18 Educating

Alicia C. Montoya

Figure 18.1 Textbook by M van Heyningen Bosch, "Vader Jakob en zijne kindertjes", Amsterdam, c. 1805

Source: Den Haag Koninklijke Bibliotheek.

In the *Magasin des enfants* by French author Marie Leprince de Beaumont, a governess named Mademoiselle Bonne/Mrs. Affable tells her pupils the well-known fairy tale "Beauty and the Beast". The following excerpt starts at the end of the fairy tale*.

Text: Marie Leprince de Beaumont, Magasin des enfants
('Children's Warehouse') (1756)

[Beauty] turned to her dear Beast, for whom she trembled with fear; but how great was her surprise! Beast was disappeared, and she saw, at her feet, one of the loveliest princes that eye ever beheld; who returned her thanks for having put an end to the charm, under which he had so long resembled a Beast. . . . He married Beauty, and lived with her many years, and their happiness – as it was founded on virtue – was complete.

   Lady Charlotte. And were her two sisters always statues?

   Mrs. Affable. Yes, my dear, because their hearts were never changed.

   Lady Witty. I could hear you a whole week without being tired; I love this Beauty prodigiously, yet, methinks, had I been in her place, I could never have consented to marry so frightful a monster.

   Lady Sensible. But, lady, he was so good-natured, that sure you would never let him die with grief, especially after he had behaved so kindly to you.

   Lady Witty. I should have just said as Beauty did in the beginning, I will be your friend, but I cannot be your wife.

   Lady Mary. And I should have been so frighted at him, that I should always have thought he was going to eat me.

   Miss Molly. I believe that, like Beauty, by often seeing him, his ugliness would have grown familiar to me. When papa first took a little black to be his foot-boy, I was afraid of him, and hid myself when he came in, but by little and little I grew used to him, and now he lifts me into the coach when I go abroad: I never so much as think of his face.

   Mrs. Affable. Miss Molly is in the right; for ugliness, by being used to it, grows familiar, and affects one less, but vice is always shocking. We must not be concerned, if we are not handsome, but endeavor to behave so as to make full amends for the want of personal advantages.[1]

Beaumont was not the inventor of the fairy tale "Beauty and the Beast". Before her, another French author, Gabrielle de Villeneuve, had published a first version of the story in her novel *La Jeune Américaine et les contes marins* ('The Young American Heiress and the Sea Tales', 1740). However, Beaumont's "Beauty and the Beast" is remarkable because of its educational setting, and is one of several fairy tales she included in her best-selling pedagogical *Magasin des enfants*.

   The *Magasin des enfants* was structured as a series of dialogues* in which the reader followed a governess, Mrs. Affable (Mademoiselle Bonne in the French original) in her daily lessons with her pupils, seven girls aged five to thirteen. Beaumont's purpose in this book was to provide educators with a model to structure their own lessons. The best way to teach students, she thought, was to create situations in which they would reach new insights by reflecting on their own experiences and on material provided by their teacher. Thus, stories and fairy tales could be used as a starting point to encourage personal reflection. In a Socratic dialogue, teachers and students engaged in conversation, critically examining different viewpoints that did not necessarily lead to one clear conclusion. That is why, in this excerpt, the dialogue between the governess and her pupils is as important as the fairy tale itself.

   The setting for Mrs. Affable's telling of "Beauty and the Beast" was a garden. This garden setting – that figured in many other eighteenth-century texts, most famously Voltaire's

Candide – referred to the original state of innocence in which mankind lived in the Garden of Eden, and which childhood still recalled. But the garden also allowed for reflection on the natural world. As soon as the tale was over, Mrs. Affable's pupils broke into animated discussion about the theme central to the fairy tale, the metamorphosis of the beast into a charming prince. The pupils realized that metamorphoses were common in the natural world, and the fairy tale became a pretext for a biology lesson. Having observed some butterflies during their walk in the garden, Mrs. Affable described the metamorphosis these creatures underwent in nature. The governess promised her pupils that she would save some butterflies for them, so they could see for themselves how the butterflies produced caterpillars that built cocoons, out of which would emerge new butterflies.

This observation of the natural world was in turn linked to another insight, that of God's role in shaping the natural world. In his infinite goodness, God had provided the butterflies with "a storehouse in which the caterpillars can find all they need to spin the thread to build their houses."[2] This was the key insight of physico-theology, or the view that by observing the perfection of nature, one saw God's infinite power at work. The title image of the warehouse or store (*magasin*) thereby became a metaphor* for God's omniscience.

Beaumont thus not only included a fairy tale or work of fiction within a schoolbook, but she also instructed her pupils in the proper way to use fiction*. One of the recurring scenes in her works was that of reading or storytelling. Mrs. Affable was shown telling the fairy tale to her pupils, and other characters – including Beauty – were often portrayed reading. Reading* was presented as a collective act, and reflected a conception of human beings as fundamentally sociable, destined to live together with others in society, and therefore requiring some form of political organization. This collective, political dimension of literature and reading, as activities performed together with other people, was important during the period known as the Enlightenment*. Reading and acquiring knowledge were not ends in themselves, but had a social purpose, as literature's aim was to help readers become better citizens and construct a better society.

What was the Enlightenment?

Beaumont's version of "Beauty and the Beast" was in many ways typical of the Enlightenment. Chronologically, the term Enlightenment is used to designate a movement that took place in the long eighteenth century (1660–1815), during which Europeans supposedly became "modern". Thus, the terms Enlightenment and "modernity" are also often used as synonyms. As we saw in the introduction to this section (Chapter 13), the term Enlightenment was a metaphor that referred to various ideas. The metaphor of light could, first, refer to classical antiquity and the sun god Apollo, who was also the god of knowledge and science. Drawing on religious tradition, light could alternatively reference the Biblical notion of light as emanating from God, or Jesus as the "light of the world". In Christian theology, the Church Father Augustine of Hippo (fourth–fifth century CE) referred to light as divine knowledge that came from above. Announcing the Enlightenment, however, the French philosopher René Descartes invoked a new notion, that of "lumen naturale" (natural light) or human reason, perceived as the surest way to gain knowledge. Nature was ordered by the precepts of reason, and so it was possible to use reason to study, understand and ultimately control the natural world.

All these definitions of the term "Enlightenment" emphasized knowledge. The age of Enlightenment was a period during which men and women sought new or more reliable ways of knowing the world. Most often knowledge was held to bear a special relation to the use of human reason, even if this reason could itself be God-inspired. Not for nothing did the German philosopher Immanuel Kant formulate the slogan of the Enlightenment in a famous essay "Was ist Aufklärung?" ('What is Enlightenment?', 1784), as "Sapere aude!" ('Dare to Know!'). Using reason as a weapon, Enlightenment authors sought to combat "ignorance" and "superstition". This went together with the rise of a scientific worldview, as the Enlightenment began in the late seventeenth century with the scientific revolution brought about by Descartes's new, rationalistic philosophy.

The fact that so many different contents were given to the term "Enlightenment" demonstrates that no single definition can be given of this movement. Rather than a coherent set of ideas, the Enlightenment was a debate – a debate in which the objects and terms of discussion were continually shifting. This is why the dialogue was the form Enlightenment texts so often took. In a dialogue, viewpoints shift, and it is possible to bring together opposing views within one text. Apart from pedagogical dialogues such as Beaumont's, the eighteenth century was the period during which the epistolary novel*, or novels made up of letters exchanged between two or more correspondents, rose to prominence, therefore again reflecting a diversity of opinions. The literary works of the Enlightenment also included real correspondences*, or letters* exchanged between authors in different parts of Europe, such as those of the French philosopher Voltaire, the Dutch-Swiss novelist Isabelle de Charrière, and the American statesman Benjamin Franklin.

Another feature of the Enlightenment was that it was an international movement. The intellectuals who held "Enlightened" ideals valued cosmopolitanism*. Cosmopolitanism was visible in another metaphor often used during this period, the Republic of Letters*. Contemporaries described the European-wide exchange of ideas, using a term drawn from economics, as a "commerce" of ideas. Although the Republic of Letters was a European phenomenon, in the eighteenth century many felt its centre was in France, as the French language, French authors, and French books played a defining role in political and literary exchanges.

How, then, were these Enlightenment ideals translated into literary practice? An important aspect of this answer lies in the new role literature came to play in daily life during the eighteenth century. This role was related to two other developments: the creation of what has been called "the public sphere", and the rise of new literary genres, including the novel* and pedagogical literature.

The creation of the public sphere

As literature came to play a more prominent role in public life, new spaces were created where men and women could meet to discuss literature and, more generally, their views on society. The German philosopher Jürgen Habermas has described these new spaces as constituting a "public sphere", or a new space situated midway between typically private spaces (the home, the family) and the spaces of official decision-making (palace and parliament).[3] It was here, in the public sphere, that public opinion was born, and it was thanks to the public sphere that public opinion became a force rulers had to contend with. Even in non-democratic states, after all, governments sought legitimacy, and by looking towards public opinion, rulers could gauge their subjects' acceptance (or not) of their policies.

In order to have a free and open discussion about politics and society, people needed places where they could meet away from the watchful eye of their rulers. Such spaces were provided by the new cultural institutions* that took shape during the eighteenth century. These included state-sponsored learned societies and academies, such as the Royal Society in London (Royal Society of London for improving natural knowledge), presided by the famous physicist Isaac Newton, or the Académie royale des sciences in Paris. These new societies offered scientists a platform to discuss the newest scientific advances, opposing them to the universities that still persisted in teaching the natural sciences within an Aristotelian framework. Other societies, even less tied to rulers, were created to bring together Freemasons, amateur artists or writers, or other interest groups. For the literary-minded, several new spaces emerged for discussion. In the course of the century, libraries* opened up to a more socially diverse readership: whereas they had been closed institutions, the domain only of scholars, in previous centuries, new kinds of libraries – especially commercial lending libraries – opened their doors to a broader public. Literary salons* became important places where men and women with literary ambitions could meet to discuss both literature and society.

Another important site for discussing and reflecting on society was the theatre. The enduring popularity of the theatre during the eighteenth century has often been noted. At no time in history did European men and women go more often to the theatre, often several times a week, and sometimes to several theatres in the same day. Some of the most popular works of literature during this period were plays*, such as those of John Gay in England, Gotthold Ephraim Lessing in Germany, and Voltaire in France. But many of these plays were not terribly modern. Voltaire, for example, wrote mostly classicist tragedies*, very similar in style and approach to those written a century earlier by Corneille and Racine. In Germany, Johann Christoph Gottsched's *Critischen Dichtkunst* ('Critical Art of Poetry', 1730) proposed a modernisation of the French classicist* ideals rather than a new approach. So it was not only the content of the plays so much as the theatre itself – a large, public space in which people from different walks of life could gather – that provided an impetus for public debate.

But above all, a new commercial space took shape during the eighteenth century that decisively influenced public opinion: the coffeehouse or café. After the first coffeehouse in Europe had opened in London in 1652, the innovation spread to the continent. One of the most famous was the coffeehouse founded in 1686 in Paris (and still standing today) by Francesco Procopio dei Coltelli, known as "le Procope" after the owner's name. Originally designed as a place where people could consume an exotic new drink, coffee, the coffeehouse quickly gained a role as a unique space where ideas could be freely exchanged away from the courts and parliament, and where everyone, in theory, could gain admittance for the price – literally – of a cup of coffee. Here, social classes could mingle, visitors could hear the latest gossip or read the newspapers often available along with the drinks sold, and they could observe the comings and goings of modern city life. In coffeehouses, a new social class, the bourgeoisie or middle class, came into its own, thereby underlining the important link between the new consumer society and the "commerce" of ideas. As the century wore on, the role of coffeehouses as hotbeds of new political ideas grew, as this new institution would play an important role in the years leading up to and during the French Revolution.

Not surprisingly, coffeehouses also inspired new kinds of literature and art, ranging from Voltaire's comedy, *L'Ecossaise ou le café* ('The Scottish Girl or the Coffeehouse', 1760) to Johann Sebastian Bach's so-called coffee cantata (c. 1735). The coffeehouse especially came to be identified with one genre: the spectator, the most famous of which was Joseph Addison and Richard Steele's *The Spectator* (1711–1714). This was a periodical publication that appeared three times a week and relayed amusing pieces of gossip gleaned in the London coffeehouses. The central figure was the spectator who observed and reported on the various goings-on around him. The genre of the spectator contributed to the growth of a new kind of writing in the eighteenth century, journalism*, that eventually led to the invention of the modern newspaper. Many authors practised these periodical genres. Beaumont, before embarking on her career as an educator, had also published a periodical*, the *Nouveau magasin français*, in which she participated in public debate on a variety of topics. Thus, the public sphere was intimately connected to the new media* that took shape during the eighteenth century, foremost among them newspapers and periodicals produced by writers and journalists not in the pay of the state.

With the rise of the public sphere, finally, another new figure emerged in the literary field: the public intellectual. The most well-known of these was François-Marie Arouet, known by his pen-name Voltaire. Voltaire took up his pen in the defence of various oppressed groups, from slaves to protestants, had an opinion on every matter of public interest, and was regarded (and reviled) by many as an authority in matters regarding the running of society. Besides Voltaire, other recognisable groups of intellectuals emerged who actively sought to influence public opinion through their sophisticated use of the new media. One of the most well-known of these groups were the so-called *philosophes*, or a group of intellectuals that included, besides Voltaire, the political theorist Montesquieu, the maverick philosopher Jean-Jacques Rousseau, and the art critic and editor of the *Encyclopédie*, Denis Diderot. These men were not philosophers in the modern sense of the word, i.e. builders of systems or abstract thinkers, but intellectuals who sought to popularize and spread the newest ideas about society, science, and the arts among a broad public. They viewed literature – and all of them were authors of popular novels as well as more theoretical writings – as a prime means to influence public opinion and, ultimately, to change society and its institutions. The ideals they sought to popularize were greater equality among people, individual human rights, the use of reason to understand the world, toleration of other opinions, and cosmopolitanism, or an openness to traditions and views from other parts of Europe and, indeed, the world. Their job, in other words, was not to provide a new set of ready-made ideas to replace those of previous eras, but to question traditional practices and common opinion, and to bring about a public dialogue about the means to improve society.

From the public sphere to the novel

With the emergence of the public sphere, public opinion, and public intellectuals, a new literary genre gained prominence that incarnated many of the epoch's ideals: the novel. It was not in the traditional realms of theatre and poetry that innovations made themselves felt in the Enlightenment, but in the novel. Eighteenth-century theatre, as we saw, largely stuck to classicist norms, especially in the prestigious genre of tragedy. In the realm of poetry, a successful English author like Alexander Pope became well-known for his so-called Augustan poetry (e.g. Horatius, see also Chapter 3), following classical norms. These authors, in other words, continued to follow ideals and models formulated already during the various European Renaissances*. This is the reason that the Enlightenment can also be considered a kind of late humanism*. Both theatre and poetry, in addition, continued to reflect an essentially aristocratic worldview, transmitting the values of the ruling classes.

The novel, by contrast, has been described as a typically "bourgeois" or "middle-class" genre. During the eighteenth century this previously despised genre began to be appreciated in its own right – much as the middle classes themselves began to play a prominent role in political discussion during the same time. While the novel had never been considered a "literary" genre before 1700, and as such had had no place in literary canons*, during the eighteenth century authors and readers increasingly came to value it.

The novel was a "bourgeois" genre for several reasons. First of all, the characters portrayed in novels were often neither aristocrats, nor kings and queens (as in the genre of tragedy), nor lowborn (as in picaresque narrative, see Chapter 15), but represented a new, in-between class. Second, novelistic plots typically revolved around love and marriage, private or domestic happiness rather than the public good. Frequently, novels told stories of protagonists who, through their own hard work, succeeded in making a place for themselves in the world, attaining economic success in the process. In this sense, Daniel Defoe's *Robinson Crusoe* (1719) can be considered the archetypical eighteenth-century novel. Shipwrecked on a deserted island, the protagonist, Robinson Crusoe, must manage to survive in an initially hostile environment and find his own means of subsistence. Through hard work and cleverness, he eventually manages to make a home and a comfortable life for himself, becoming the ultimate representative of the self-made man. Like the bourgeois, who prided himself on reaching material comfort by dint of his labour, Crusoe owed nothing to either birth or inherited wealth.

At the same time, novels often concentrated on the life and growth of a single protagonist, as evident by the titles of the most successful eighteenth-century novels in France and England: Abbé Prévost, *Manon Lescaut* (1731); Samuel Richardson, *Clarissa* (1748); Henry Fielding, *Tom Jones* (1749); Jean-Jacques Rousseau, *Julie ou la Nouvelle Héloïse* ('Julie, or the New Heloise', 1761, see also Chapter 17). (Until the end of the century, the novel remained a largely Franco-British affair: Gotthold Ephrasim Lessing's *Geschichte des Agathon* ('History of Agathon'), the earliest German novel, appeared in 1766, and in many countries, novels only started to appear in the last decades of the eighteenth century.) All the elements typical of novels – domestic happiness, economic success, emphasis on self-made men and women, individualism – were also elements that defined the emerging class of the bourgeois, or a new, urban class of self-employed small businesspeople (artisans, shopkeepers, merchants) who during the course of the century succeeded in attaining new levels of material comfort due to their industry. The idealization of a new set of values associated with the bourgeois is present, too, in Beaumont's *Magasin des enfants*. Not only does the title reference the store (*magasin*) and thus the commercial values identified with the new middle classes. The protagonist Beauty, too, belongs to the middle classes, and her father is portrayed as a virtuous merchant or working man, as opposed to an aristocrat such as one would find in classicist tragedy.

Educating the new citizen

Given the social aspirations of the new middle classes, there was one concern that, above all, dominated the eighteenth-century novel: education. Many novels were so-called novels of education (in German: *Bildungsroman*), and told the story of a protagonist who gradually gained knowledge about the world and made a place for him- or herself in the world as a respectable member of society. So, although novels ostensibly focused on domestic and economic fulfilment, they often carried a larger social, even political dimension, as they reflected on the forming of the citizen.

There were various forms of pedagogical literature, many of which took as their starting point, in some form or another, the concept of nature and the ideas of the British philosopher John Locke. John Locke had theorized, in his *Essay Concerning Human Understanding* (1689), that children at birth were a kind of *tabula rasa*, or blank slate. Because they were born with no previous ideas or knowledge of the world, education was crucial in shaping them into good citizens. In addition, because of their blank-slate quality, children were judged to be closer to nature than corrupted adults, so it became essential to preserve in them the presumed innocence of the state of nature. A key to providing such an education was to develop new teaching guidelines, as well as (reading) material to be used by teachers and students. Not surprisingly, the eighteenth century witnessed an explosion of pedagogical texts and literary genres, all of which aimed to produce ideal citizens.

The oldest form of pedagogical literature were treatises – such as Locke's *Essay Concerning Human Understanding* (1689) – and books that adapted the centuries-old genre of the "mirror of princes". The mirror of princes was a text that described the adventures that befell a young protagonist, and thereby held up a fictional mirror to the reader – often a highborn aristocrat or prince, destined to rule – instructing him how to behave in his future life as a sovereign. To this genre belonged one of the most widely read works of fiction of the eighteenth century, Fénelon's *Les Aventures de Télémaque* ('The Adventures of Telemachus', 1699). Penned by a prominent French archbishop, François de Salignac de la Motte-Fénelon, as an educational book destined for his royal pupil, this novel recounted the adventures of Ulysses's son Telemachus, as he travelled across the ancient world in search of his father. It continued to be read and praised throughout the eighteenth century, most notably by Jean-Jacques Rousseau, who was to become the most influential educationalist of the century.

In addition to traditional genres such as the treatise and "mirror of princes", new genres were also invented. The most lastingly influential of these was the fairy tale. While many readers today think of fairy tales as stories that have been transmitted orally for centuries by peasants and tellers belonging to the "folk" (hence the nineteenth-century term "folklore"), fairy tales also had literary origins. Their present-day form goes back to the work of one author, Charles Perrault, who in 1697 published a collection of eight tales, *Contes de ma mère l'Oye* ('Mother Goose Tales') containing classics such as "Little Red Riding Hood", "Sleeping Beauty", "Puss in Boots", and other well-known tales. These tales were a response to another author, Jean de La Fontaine, who had shortly before published a series of very popular *Fables*, or short animal tales, that were often given to children as educational reading material. Perrault, however, claimed these fables* were immoral and would teach children pernicious lessons, and therefore proposed a new genre, the fairy tale, that according to him would be better suited to young minds. Perrault had intended his fairy tales to be read by both adults and children, but very quickly it became clear that he had hit upon a best-selling formula for young readers (see also Chapter 21). In the following decades, fairy tale authors (many of them women) increasingly targeted an audience made up exclusively of children. Eventually, thanks also to the intervention of the brothers Grimm in the nineteenth century, fairy tales became what they are today – a quintessential children's genre, known throughout the world, in adaptations ranging from novels and video games to Disney blockbusters – so widely known, in fact, that most readers have forgotten that fairy tales originally had authors and had been conceived as part of the Enlightenment pedagogical project.

Another new pedagogical genre was that of the educational dialogue-novel. In 1749, English author Sarah Fielding published a book, *The Governess, or the Little Female Academy*, which was one of the first English novels written specifically for children. In it, the author transcribed a series of dialogues* between a governess, Mrs. Teachum, and her young pupils, as the pupils learned to acquire the virtues they would need for their future life in society. This book inspired other authors, among them Beaumont, who in her *Magasin des enfants* adopted the same basic structure of a series of conversations between a governess and her pupils. It was from Sarah Fielding, too, that Beaumont took the idea of interspersing the conversations with a series of fairy tales, which became part of the young pupils' education.

By the 1760s, the stream of publications on education had grown into a veritable flood, and so it was not surprising that the new pedagogical insights were brought together and made the object of renewed debate by one of the century's most important and controversial intellectuals, Jean-Jacques Rousseau. A Swiss-born autodidact, Rousseau was something of an outsider in Enlightenment debate, although at the beginning of his career he had been befriended by the Parisian *philosophes*. In his major work of pedagogy, the novelistic *Emile, ou de l'éducation* ('Emile, or on Education', 1762), he completely overturned many ideas that had by then become commonly accepted.

In *Emile*, Rousseau followed Locke in his idea that children were born as blank slates, and that education was crucial in forming future citizens. However, rather than actively teaching them about the world through a series of lessons or readings, Rousseau felt children should be given what he termed a "negative education". Recalling Beaumont's Edenic garden, he wrote that his pupil should be moved away from the dangerous influence of the city and brought up in the countryside. There, he (education was for boys only) was to discover the workings of the world through his own observation of the natural world, unfettered by any encounter with book-knowledge. Banishing all books from the schoolroom, Rousseau made an exception only for Defoe's *Robinson Crusoe*, since it described the experiences of a man cut off from corrupt European society. At a later stage, his pupil Emile was to learn a useful trade to be able to earn his own living in the future – a bourgeois stance that, once again, recalls Beaumont's earlier defence of middle-class values.

However, Rousseau went much farther than his predecessors. While Beaumont believed in combining religious faith with Enlightenment science and reason, Rousseau criticized the use of reason. Reason was an instrument that men and women used instrumentally to deny or override their own human instincts, Rousseau believed, and therefore educators should be wary of it. In particular, the use of reason was to be discouraged in female pupils – the original subject of Beaumont's *Magasin*, at which Rousseau now took aim. Likewise, where previous Enlightenment educators had insisted on humankind's social nature (for example, in the scenes of collective reading in Beaumont's *Magasin*), Rousseau now regarded society as a necessary evil, a human construct that distanced men and women from their own true nature. Rousseau's *Emile* was thus a milestone in debates on Enlightenment and education, but at the same time it also announced a new era, that of Romanticism*. Following Rousseau, Europeans gradually turned away from the rational, societal ideals of the Enlightenment, and adopted a more subjective, emotionally inflected worldview. With him, we have arrived at a turning point and a new chapter in European literary history.

Spreading the new pedagogical ideals in Europe

As the discussion on education demonstrates, books and ideas circulated widely in eighteenth-century Europe, moving between England, France, Switzerland, and other countries. The Enlightenment was a transnational debate, best understood when viewed not only from the viewpoint of the production* of literature, but also its reception*. This can be illustrated by the reception in one region of Europe, Russia, of the text with which we started this chapter, Beaumont's *Magasin des enfants*.

Beaumont's works enjoyed widespread success and spawned numerous imitations*, from Spain to Denmark, from the Dutch Republic to the newly independent United States and Mexico, and were translated into over a dozen European languages. This fame lasted well into the nineteenth century. In nineteenth-century Poland, for example, the novelist Clementine Hoffmann Tanska evocatively described in one of her novels how at the family castle of her protagonist count Krasinski, the young girls at their morning toilette listened to the *Magasin des enfants* being read aloud while their lady's maid did their hair.

The *Magasin des enfants* was originally published by subscription, thanks to the financial support of the imperial court of Russia and its ruler, Catherine the Great. Among its original readers were the empress Elizabeth and the future Peter III. Subscribers included the most influential families and individuals at court, among them the curator of the University of Moscow, the president of the Saint Petersburg Academy of Sciences, and the Russian ambassador in London. Thus, this work was integrated into the new public sphere being created in Enlightenment Russia. When the children of the Russian subscribers of the *Magasin* embarked on the *grand tour* that was a standard component of their aristocratic education, many of them stayed with the families of the English subscribers, and vice versa, so that this subscription list reflects cosmopolitan relations between English and Russian elites* during the Enlightenment. Yet it is also remarkable that the middle-class values Beaumont transmitted were so well received by aristocratic readers. This is an indication of the profound change in mentalities the Enlightenment brought about.

Russian aristocrats' interest was related to the influence and prestige of French culture throughout Europe during the eighteenth century. Russian elites – like elites elsewhere in Europe – sought to speak French, and were eager to find books accessible to French language learners. Catherine the Great's personal copy of the *Magasin* shows her son Paul Petrovich, the future Paul I, used it to learn French. Not only was the work dedicated to him, the copy in her library also carries material traces of a child's reading, including ink stains and French-language notations in Paul's handwriting.

Read both in French and translated into Russian, a dozen different editions of the *Magasin* were published in Russia. The first appeared in 1761 under the title *Children's School*, at the Infantry Cadets Corps School for the lower nobility where the translator Peter Svistunov had been a student. This school was a breeding ground for a new, self-styled class of literati that saw its calling as enlightening the Russian public at large. Svistunov viewed his translation* in the context of the Enlightenment and the "new Russia". Alluding to the present growth of knowledge in Russia, he substantially expanded the encyclopedic information contained in the *Magasin*, and praised Peter the Great and his enlightened successors for their campaign against "the previous ignorance". It was clear that for him, as for Beaumont, literature was primarily an instrument to improve society.

Shortly after Svistunov's translation, the philosopher Andrey Bolotov began work on an imitation entitled *Children's Philosophy*. Bolotov, too, belonged to the Russian elite, and was closely connected to court circles. He had developed as a thinker while stationed in Königsberg – the city where Kant had written his essay "What is Enlightenment?" (1784) – as secretary under the governor-general of Prussia. Like many Europeans following Rousseau's critique of corrupt city life, Bolotov sought renewal in the countryside, and withdrew to his country estate in 1762. From there, he aimed to enlighten the public at large by writing works popularizing practical scientific and moral knowledge. His *Children's Philosophy* distinguished itself from its model by its more extended treatment of the natural sciences, including cosmology, physics, mineralogy, and botany.

Like the *Magasin des enfants*, *Children's Philosophy* was made up of a series of lively dialogues that appealed to children's own experience. These dialogues took place between a mother, Mrs. C** – not, as in Beaumont, a governess – and her two children, Feona (aged fourteen) and Cleon (aged thirteen). Mostly the dialogues took place in the garden, where Feona and Cleon took walks between their lessons. As in the *Magasin*, the garden setting provided the occasion for several lessons on nature. And just as in the *Magasin*, these lessons were exercises in natural theology, since in *Children's Philosophy* knowledge of God was based on personal exploration and experience of nature. As Mrs. C** explained, the Creator had created everything with infinite wisdom, for everything had a special purpose and there was nothing without use. God looked after his creatures and his providence could be detected by observing the natural world.

Bolotov continued to use Beaumont's dialogue format in his other works, written after *Children's Philosophy*. He went on to create the first children's theatre in Russia, in Bogorodice, and wrote several pedagogical plays for it. His debt to Beaumont is clear in his re-use of the characters of Cleon and Feona in some of these plays. In Bogorodice, Bolotov also founded a boarding school, where he used his *Children's Philosophy* as teaching material.

The Russian reception of Beaumont's *Magasin des enfants* was probably so extensive because it was a useful tool in Catherine the Great's drive to educate Russia's children in the rationalist ideas of the Enlightenment, combined with the necessary religious instruction. The moralistic yet open-ended character of the education provided by the *Magasin* also reflected the increasingly "bourgeois", practical-minded views of Russia's elites, of which Svistunov and Bolotov were two prominent members. The Russian reception of this text finally illustrates how the Enlightenment itself was a vast cosmopolitan commerce of ideas, extending across decades and across different regions of Europe, and reaching audiences from different social classes and walks of life. Education, far from being a matter confined to schools and governesses, was central to this European-wide dialogue.

Notes

1 Marie Leprince de Beaumont, *Magasin des enfants* (London: J. Nourse, 1756), vol. 1, 109.
2 Beaumont, *Magasin des enfants*, vol. 1, 109.
3 Jürgen Habermas, *The Structural Transformation of the Public Sphere: An Inquiry into a Category of Bourgeois Society*, trans. Thomas Burger (Cambridge, MA: MIT Press, 1989).

Further reading

Edelstein, Dan. *The Enlightenment: A Genealogy*. Chicago, IL: University of Chicago Press, 2010.
Fumaroli, Marc. *When the World Spoke French*. Trans. Richard Howard. New York: NYRB Classics, 2011.
Gill, Natasha. *Educational Philosophy in the French Enlightenment*. London: Routledge, 2010.
Moretti, Franco. *The Bourgeois: Between History and Literature*. London: Verso, 2013.
Outram, Dorinda. *The Enlightenment*. Third edition. Cambridge: Cambridge University Press, 2013.

Part IV

The long nineteenth century

19 Introduction

Marguérite Corporaal and Lotte Jensen

Figure 19.1 Eugène Delacroix, "Liberty Leading the People", 1830, oil on canvas, 260 x 325 cm, Museé
du Louvre, Paris

Source: Centre Art Historical Documentation, Radboud University.

In 1829 the Italian writer and political activist Giuseppe Mazzini (1805–1872) published a survey of European literatures, in which he reflected upon the distinct nature of national literatures:

> If I open the history of the various literatures of different nations, I observe an alterna-tion of glory and decay, of reciprocal influence, of transfusion from one to another, as well as a continual mutability of taste, now national, now servile, now corrupt. The liter-ature of no country is so entirely original as to have received no intermixture of foreign mutability, either through tradition in its early days, or through conquest at a later date.[1]

Mazzini's observations are quite valid. Although nationality became the primary organiz-ing principle of the European landscape and national traditions and pasts were celebrated in culture and literature, there were also many transnational developments in the literary field*. Similar modes, genres and characters emerged in literature across Europe. While the growing attention for national pasts made writers such as Sir Walter Scott turn to local legends*, histories and traditions, the genre of the historical novel* became prominent in various European countries as a transnational* genre, ranging from Sweden to Spain, and from England to Russia.[2] Furthermore, the historical novel was transnational in that writers like Allessandro Manzoni in Italy and Jacob van Lennep in the Netherlands were greatly inspired by the Scottish author's style and themes. In Van Lennep's case, this earned him the nickname of the Dutch Walter Scott.

European literatures during the long nineteenth century were also essentially transna-tional in several other respects. The development of new printing techniques* which ena-bled more rapid and cheaper production* of books, in combination with modern forms of transport which facilitated the dissemination of texts, meant that literary works were read more widely, and even "travelled" across national borders, either in their original lan-guage or in translation*. The increasing market of periodicals* also offered significant new platforms for literature: not only on a national level, through their serialization* of novels, for example; but also transnationally, as foreign writers and their work would often be dis-cussed. Thus, "Portrait of an Author, Painted by his Publisher", an article which appeared in Charles Dickens's journal *All the Year Round* on 18 June 1859, praises the writings of Honoré de Balzac, an author who most English readers "unaccustomed to study French literature in its native language" would be unfamiliar with,[3] and recommends that more novels by French writers should be translated into English.

The long nineteenth century was certainly the age of "travelling" authors. The Danish fairy tale* writer Hans Christian Andersen and British novelist Charles Dickens would tour across and even beyond Europe, in order to meet foreign writers and give public readings. Readers in turn also undertook journeys to visit the homes of their favourite authors and locations they knew from their works, leading to a growing fashionability of literary tourism*. The residence of the German poet Johann Wolfgang Goethe (Goethe-haus Frankfurt) attracted admirers from all over Europe. The improved modes of transport which increased authors' and readers' opportunities to travel led to a wider impact of texts and notions of literature across national boundaries.

In this introductory chapter to the long nineteenth century, we will focus on these "travelling" aspects of European literatures while, at the same time, emphasizing the role literature played in shaping national cultures. For despite the transnational nature of many cultural trends and developments, literature was also perceived as the ultimate expression of national values and traditions.

Time frame

When we speak of the "long nineteenth century", we roughly mean the period between 1770 and 1914. From a cultural and literary perspective, 1770 appears to be an unexpected but logical starting date. The 1770s saw the rise of a cult of sensibility, which centralized the expression of (excessive) emotions. Heroines who are prone to fainting and blushing, and heroes sobbing convulsively, are no exception in literature which transmitted this cult, as becomes clear from Henry Mackenzie's Scottish novel *The Man of Feeling* (1771), a text which according to its 1886 editor "caught the tone of the French sentiment of his time, has, of course, pleased French critics, and has been translated into French."[4] This transeuropean cult of feeling* can be seen as a response to the Enlightenment* (see Chapter 13), which centred on reason as the primary source of knowledge and authority. Authors put more emphasis on the role which authentic feelings played in everyday experiences. On the other hand, it was precisely enlightened thought that paved the way for more individualistic perceptions of the world and its surroundings. By questioning old dogmatic schemes and attaching more value to people's own authority, space was created for the individual and his or her emotional life.

This transitional period between the Enlightenment and Romanticism* is often labelled as "Sturm und Drang"*, referring to a group of German intellectuals and poets who resided in Weimar and placed emotions at the heart of their artistic activities. Authors like Christoph Martin Wieland, Johann Gottfried Herder, Johann Wolfgang von Goethe and Friedrich Schiller cultivated the idea of the poetic genius* and saw literature as a means of expressing authentic emotions and connecting to primitive natural instincts. Goethe's epistolary novel* *Die Leiden des jungen Werthers* ('The Sorrows of Young Werther', 1774) is one of the best known examples of this new cult of feeling. The unrequited love of the passionate protagonist for the married Charlotte eventually leads him to shoot himself. This suicide was perceived as highly shocking at the time: when the novel inspired copy-cat suicides across Europe, it was banned in Denmark and Italy.[5] However, the novel had a wide transeuropean impact: it was translated into many European languages, including French (1774), Danish (1776), Dutch (1776), English (1779), Russian (1781) and Swedish (1783).[6]

From a literary perspective the 1770s marked a new era, but the same can be argued from a political perspective. The 1770s, marked by the American War of Independence, the rise of the abolitionist movement in Britain and the growing awareness of civil rights on a global scale, can be viewed as leading up to one of the most influential events in European history: the French Revolution. On 14 July 1789, civilians stormed the Bastille, supported by their democratic motto *Liberté, egalité, fraternité*. The French King Louis XVII was beheaded, and new forms of parliamentary rule were introduced. Eulogised in Eugène Delacroix's history painting "La Liberté Guidant le Peuple" ('Liberty Leading the People', 1830), this was a watershed event, which changed the political landscape of Europe drastically and irreversibly.

The revolt quickly ended in internal bloodshed between rival groups, and resulted in the autocracy of Napoleon Bonaparte. He initially supported the ideals of the French Revolution, but gradually started to assume supreme power and crowned himself emperor of the French in 1804. The massive and destructive battles that were fought during the years 1792–1815 had an immense transeuropean impact, as Napoleon waged war with England, the Low Countries, Spain, Italy, Sweden, Russia and Austria. The French hegemony became one of the driving forces behind the rise of nationalism in Europe, and deeply affected the literature of those days. It is by no means coincidental that satirical prints and poems flourished in these days of oppression, in particular in England. One of the major novels of the long nineteenth century, Lev Tolstoy's *War and Peace* (1869), furthermore demonstrates that this time of upheaval during the Napoleonic wars signified a shared, transeuropean past. While primarily set in Moscow and St Petersburg, this novel neverthe-less suggests a broader European vista by including French soldiers and even Napoleon himself as speaking characters in the narrative.

Literature and politics were often intertwined, which makes it difficult to demarcate the boundaries of "the long nineteenth century". This is also the case when trying to deter-mine where the "long nineteenth century" ends. From a cultural point of view, one could consider the rise of Modernism* in the 1910s as a starting point of a new era. Author Virginia Woolf saw the first post-impressionist exhibition in London, which opened in December 1910, as an important watershed, observing that "human character changed."[7] From a political perspective, however, there is a clear cut in 1914, when the first World War broke out. This total war was of an unprecedented scale and caused the loss of millions lives. Life before and after would never be the same, a sentiment retrospectively reflected by the famous stanza in T.S. Eliot's "The Hollow Men" (1925): "This is the way the world ends."[8]

Europe

What was nineteenth-century Europe, and which countries were considered to be European? Marking off geographical boundaries is difficult, for European nations had expanded their territories considerably by means of colonial expansion. By the end of the nineteenth century, Great Britain had become the largest colonial empire* in the world. Its rule stretched from large parts in North America and Africa to India and Australia. Although these parts of the British Empire were not part of Europe in a strict continen-tal use of the word, they partook in European culture values in many ways. In 1866, the first transatlantic telegraph cable was completed, which literally connected Europe and America. It sparked off a vast infrastructure of electrical communication between both continents. Other nations with considerable colonial possessions were France, Spain and the Netherlands.

European emigrants made these parts of the world their new homes, introducing Euro-pean educational values and cultural traditions overseas. Books, newspapers and illustrated magazines travelled across the globe, informing emigrants about the latest developments in their homeland. Some authors contributed literature to magazines* both in the colo-nial world and at the imperial centre, in the "motherland". This is the case for Rudyard Kipling, who between 1885 and 1886 wrote short stories* for the British-Indian news-papers *The Civil and Military Gazette* and *The Pioneer*, but later also became successful as a writer for London magazines.

This raises the question of where to draw the borders of nineteenth-century Europe: if colonial possessions are to be included, then Europe covers many different parts of the world. If one focuses on Europe itself, then its territory and constellation was under per-manent change. During the Napoleonic wars (1792–1815) a process of European integra-tion was incited by Napoleon, who implemented his ideology and centralized system in large parts of his rule. However, the protests against his regime also ignited strong feelings of patriotism and inspired nationalist movements. In 1815, after the defeat of Napoleon at the Battle of Waterloo, the Great Powers (the Russian Empire, the United Kingdom, Prussia and Austria) gathered together to negotiate the future of Europe. Their aim was to ensure the security of Europe by creating a so-called "balance of power" which would prevent nations – in particular France – from once again threatening Europe's stability. The map of Europe was redrawn, creating new national states and confederations, and restoring old monarchies such as France and Spain.

The post-Napoleonic era can be characterized as a period in which nationalist and internationalist interests were often at odds. Nationalism pervaded politics throughout Europe, and also had a cultural component: the press, the arts and literature were filled with patriotic ideology, trying to persuade people to see their nation as the best of all possible worlds. Cultural nationalism became manifest in language emancipation movements across Europe, for instance in Ireland, Hungary, Belgium and Finland. At the same time, transnational bonds were shaped in combating the archenemy of Christian Europe, the Ottoman Turks. Many Europeans joined the Greek War of Independence (1821–1832), during which the Greeks successfully revolted against the Ottoman rulers. Among the volunteers was the famous poet George Gordon Byron, better known as Lord Byron. Before he could partake in the fighting, he fell ill and died; in the eyes of the Greeks, he was perceived as a martyr who had been willing to die for their liberty. In 1853, a new war broke out, but now the Ottoman Turks joined forces with France, Britain and Sardinia in order to defend themselves against the Russians at the Crimean Peninsula. This war brought to an end the "balance of power" created in 1815, and is often considered the first "media war". The press played a prominent role in creating anti-Russian feelings and shaping transnational bonds between their opponents.

Context

Europe during the long nineteenth century was in constant flux, due to the forces of war that changed power constellations, the expansion of colonies on other continents and tides of emigration and immigration. Severe economic crises, such as Ireland's Great Famine (1845–1849), as well as oppressive political regimes, such as Tsar Alexander II's pogroms of the Jewish population in the southwestern parts of the Russian Empire (today's Poland and Ukraine), resulted in the relocation of population both within and outside Europe. Many of these emigrants settled in suburbs of European cities, and the growing sense of urban cultural diversity to which they contributed left its traces on literature as well. Thus, George Eliot's *Daniel Deronda* (1876) contains lively descriptions of the London Jewish scene, as well as reflections upon the Jewish diaspora by the fiery Jewish nationalist in the novel, Mordechai Cohen, who pleas for the creation of a Jewish nation in Israel. Emile Zola portrayed a provincial French Jewish milieu in his last novel *Vérité* ('Truth', 1903), pointing out the growing antisemitism in society. The novel was clearly inspired by the trial of Jewish Captain Alfred Dreyfus, who was accused of treason in 1894, and whose cause Zola had taken up, as well as his criticism of the growing intolerance towards Jews that he had previously voiced in 'Pour les Juifs' ('For the Jews', 1896), an article published in *Le Figaro*.

The expanding European cities became transnational sites, due to the influx of inhabitants from different nationalities: by 1877, Vienna was inhabited by – among others – Serbians, Croatians and Hungarians. Cities were also sites of mobility in that great numbers of unskilled manual workers from the countryside had moved to the city to find alternative labour. Oliver Goldsmith's poem "The Deserted Village" (1770) laments the depopulation of the persona's childhood village, showing that the big migration of farmers to the cities has often implicated them in severe destitution and even prostitution. The First Industrial Revolution (1760–1840) and its mechanization of work had not only led to the creation of a factory system, but had also greatly impacted agricultural life. The rural population's hatred of labour displacing machinery instigated revolt, such as the swing riots in the south of England, during which farmers destroyed threshing machines. At the same time, those looking for employment moved away from their native regions to centres of industrialization and urbanization.

The industrialization and urbanization of Europe in the long nineteenth century triggered tensions which on the one hand led to an idealization of simple country life, and on the other to a fascination with and concern for conditions in the city. Romanticism* (1770–1850), a cultural movement which not only centred on feeling, but also on the past and the sensations that the natural landscape inspired as well as the simple people and their traditions, sparked off an interest in folklore*, local languages and legends*. While Romanticism was therefore enthralled by the region and its past, its engagement with old and local languages and traditions also came to be the foundation for the formation of national identities and nationalist ideologies in, most notably, Germany, Italy, Ireland and Scandinavia.

The veneration of traditions and the past also informed the visual and decorative arts, which were marked by medievalism*: a fascination with medieval histories and legends as subject matter, medieval sculpture and architecture and artisan traditions that often expressed nationalist sentiments. One such neomedieval movement in England was the Pre-Raphaelite Brotherhood (1848), which sought to reproduce the colour schemes of medieval paintings, and which addressed Arthurian legends as well as medieval pastoral scenes with shepherds. The Pre-Raphaelites in turn were affiliated with William Morris, whose Arts and Crafts movement advocated craftsmanship in response to the celebration of industrial achievement at the 1851 Great Exhibition in London. The German-Austrian Nazarenes were a comparable movement: founded in 1810, these artists moved from Vienna to Rome, with the aim of bringing back sincerity and spirituality in art, seeking inspiration from Italian medieval and early Renaissance artists and reviving fresco painting. The local, picturesque landscape, unspoilt by modernization or even human intervention, also became a favourite subject for European artists in the early nineteenth century, such as John Constable in England and Johan Christian Dahl in Norway.

The rural traditions were central to Romantic art, but the countryside and its people were also represented in the early Realist paintings of, for example, the French Barbizon school (1830–1870), which drew inspiration from Constable's work and sought to represent nature and rural life as it really was. Jean-François Millet's "Des Glaneuses" ('The Gleaners', 1857) is an example of a less idyllic and more realistic focus on the toil of agricultural labourers. Realism* as a cultural movement is, however, more often identified with the urban middle classes who had experienced social mobility, and, as a leisure class, engaged with city life at theatres, music halls, bars and the newly introduced department stores, such as Harrods in London (1834), Au Bon Marché in Paris (1838) and the St. Petersburg Passage (1846). Charles Baudelaire's "Le Peintre de la Vie Moderne" ('The Painter of Modern Life'), published in *Le Figaro* in 1864, represented the well-to-do, educated *flâneur* as a man who is at ease in the urban crowd, the spectator of city life who confidently interprets its scenes and dynamics.

Celebrating modernity, paintings such as Gustave Caillebotte's "Rue de Paris; temps de pluie" ('Paris Street on a Rainy Day', 1877), and Edgar Degas's "Place de La Concorde" (1875) give expression to that modern city experience, and Degas's painting, with its suggestion of a snapshot composition, moreover betrays the influence of the new medium of photography. After the development of the daguerreotype in 1839, photography became available commercially. While the illustrated press across Europe did not resort to this new medium until the end of the century, the engravings and lithographs that were used to accompany news items demonstrate the increasing demand for visual documentary of life in its many forms. This focus on realism was also increasingly directed to the underbelly of society, the poor and those living at its margins. Attention for the plight of those living in the slums was especially prominent in journalistic reports, such as Henry Mayhew's *London Labour and the London Poor* (1851), and in *How the Other Half Lives* (1890), an impressive account with photographs of the slums in New York City created by Danish immigrant Jacob Riis.

The long nineteenth century is the age of class conflict and reform. Ironically, while the ideals of the French Revolution had been equality and liberty for all, urbanization and industrialization greatly aggravated the conditions of the working classes who were facing long working hours, low payment and bad housing. Legal reform to improve the situation of the working classes was slow, and by the middle of the nineteenth century several movements across Europe, such as the Chartists in Britain and Fourierists in France, propagated socialist ideals. The publication of *The Communist Manifesto* (1848) by Karl Marx and Friedrich Engels at the behest of the Communist League was followed by the March insurrection of workers in Berlin. During this turbulent year of revolutions, France was the centre of a rebellion that ended the constitutional monarchy of Louis-Philippe and established the French Second Republic, and the International Workingmen's Association (IWA), also known as the First International, founded in London in 1864, had its first congress in Geneva in 1866.

The call for equality and independence that inspired the socialist and nationalist movements and revolutions – such as the Hungarian revolt against the Habsburg regime in 1848 – also extended to the position of women. Olympe Gouge's *Déclaration des droits de la Femme et de la Citoyenne* ('Declaration of the Rights of Woman and the Female Citizen', 1791) and Mary Wollstonecraft's *Vindication of the Rights of Woman* (1792) emphasised the necessity for woman's education and engagement in public life. Legislation to improve women's position in marriage was enacted in various European countries, and issues such as the plight of working class women and enfranchisement were addressed by various European women's movements such as the suffragettes in France and England and the Bund Deutscher Frauenvereine in Germany.

Literature

The developments that marked European nineteenth-century society also left their traces on the medium of literature. It can be argued that during the long nineteenth century, literary production was characterized by four major trends: a growing fascination with the individual's emotions, the dynamics between tradition and modernity, commercialization and emancipation.

The cult of feeling that emerged in the 1770s (see Chapter 20) inspired a new kind of poetry that focused on the expression of personal emotions. Poets would emphasize emotions, often in connection to an unspoilt natural landscape. As Wordsworth described it in the 1800 preface to *Lyrical Ballads* (1798), poetry should be the "spontaneous overflow of powerful feelings . . . recollected in tranquility."[9] In Lamartine's poem "Le Lac" ('The Lake', 1816), Lake Bourget indeed functions as a site which evokes the deepest feelings and thoughts about the flow of time and loss. Often the landscapes that trigger the persona's feelings are what Immanuel Kant and Edmund Burke would classify as sublime: these are overwhelming scenes that demonstrate the power of nature and divine creation and that may inspire awe as well as fear. Thus, Percy Bysshe Shelley's "Mont Blanc" (1817) suggests that the "unfathomable deeps" of the Alps bring the persona in a "trance sublime and strange/ To muse on my own separate phantasy."[10] As Shelley's line indicates, imagination played an important role in Romantic poetry: Wordsworth saw poets as the legislators of the people, in that they, through their poetic imagination, could point the way to truth and justice.

In its focus on feeling, European Romantic literature also addressed darker emotions, such as fear and immoral passions like revenge and lust. This spectrum of the Romantic literary imagination mainly found its expression in the Gothic: a literature that explores the sensations of terror; is often set in an exotic setting, preferably a medieval castle or abbey in southern Europe; is imbued with the supernatural; and, through a plot which features a villain or monster, deals with issues that are taboo or macabre and morbid emotions that are normally swept under the carpet. As the Marquis de Sade, who used a Gothic framework in *Justine* (1791) and *Eugénie de Franval* (1800), observed, the Gothic can be interpreted as a response to the shock of the French Revolution. The genre became especially prominent in Britain, through early Gothic novels*, such as *The Italian* (1797) by Ann Radcliffe, which were strongly pervaded by anti-Catholic sentiments. The genre was, however, also intensely popular in Germany, in the form of the *Gespensterroman* and *Schauerroman* ('ghost novel' and 'shudder novel') in which Friedrich von Schiller and Karl Grosse excelled. While the mode was even adopted in Russia by Nikolay Karamzin, it did not gain much ground in southern Europe, possibly through the ethnic and religious bias in which the Gothic was rooted.

Walpole had a neo-medieval Gothic castle, Strawberry Hill, built for himself, but the fascination with the past and its traditions was not restricted to Gothic literature. As we saw, and as will be discussed in Chapter 21, the historical novel as a transeuropean genre often went back to legends from the Dark Ages, and was inspired by oral traditions*, the local languages (vernacular) and folklore, both as a counterweight against the rapid progression of modernity and as the foundation for a collective sense of national identity. It was not just the genre of the historical novel, however, that played a central role in the mediation of a national identity by looking at traditions. The epic national poem, which not only recollected heroic events from the nation's past, but was also infused by its mythology and traditions, had a similar function. Thus, Adam Mickiewicz's poem *Pan Tadeusz* ('Sir Thaddeus', 1834), set in 1811–1812, is an ode to Poland at a time when Poland–Lithuania had been divided by Russia, Austria and Prussia and was no longer existing.

The tensions between tradition and modernity are described in Chapter 22. The brothers Grimm in Germany started to collect these folk tales, looking for those that were essentially of German origin, and elsewhere in Europe, the Russian Alexander Afanasyev and the Norwegians Peter Christen Asbjørnsen and Jørgen Moe undertook similar projects. While these genres were infused with the supernatural, regional literature* had a similar function in crystallizing traditions in a time when indigenous cultures were vastly disappearing. Focusing on the customs and traditions of the rural population, and stressing the opposition between country and city in favour of the former, this local colour literature often helped produce national cohesion. Published in magazines, these regional narratives circulated among groups of readers at geographical distances from one another, thereby creating mutual understanding beyond cultural boundaries. These local colour stories were sometimes also translated into other languages and made it across European borders, thereby contributing to the rise of a transnational genre that negotiated traditional identities in a modernizing and globalizing world.

The cheaper methods of printing, and the fact that literature was published in widely disseminated weeklies and monthlies, contributed to a growing commercialization* of literature during the long nineteenth century. Periodicals such as Charles Dickens's *Household Words* (1850–59) and *Die Gartenlaube* ('The Bower', 1853–1944) in Germany were widely read, and the format of serialized fiction in instalments meant that people were encouraged to buy the following issues. As the literature published in such periodicals had to appeal to broad audiences, it meant that genres that were attractive to various classes, such as the novel of sensation (Chapter 4), the detective story and the ghost story, gained popularity. In fact, the long nineteenth century in general can be considered the age of the democratization of literature: the focus on the common people and their folklore in Romanticism also signified a more inclusive gesture towards potential readers of lower classes, while the eighteenth century had been the age of the middle-class novel.

The middle of the nineteenth century saw a shift towards realism in literature that ran parallel to the one in the visual arts. The origins of literary realism are attributed to French writers Honoré de Balzac and Gustave Flaubert, who aimed for a detailed, almost photographic representation of reality which resulted in lengthy descriptions of clothes and interiors, and elaborate studies of character. Flaubert set out to present an analytical narrative of life, and based his novel *Madame Bovary* (1857) on a story that made the papers in 1848: the suicide of Delphine Delamare, a provincial doctor's wife and adulteress. As this reveals, realism often walked a thin line between journalism* and fiction, and many authors of realist fiction* in the United States had careers in journalism: Stephen Crane and Ambrose Bierce are examples in case.[11] Realism was not only a transeuropean but also a transatlantic movement, and authors of realist fiction such as Henry James and Edith Wharton lived in Europe for considerable parts of their lives.

As the example of *Madame Bovary* makes clear, realist fiction became a mode to explore the conditions of women, and while novels such as Flaubert's examined the effect of restrictions on a woman's life, the so-called New Woman* novel*, a genre that became popular across Europe during the 1880s and 1890s, focused on the modern, well-educated woman who defied gender conventions (see Chapter 24). In addressing the interplay between character and environment, *Madame Bovary*, which sketches a woman whose inherent longing for romantic passion is stifled in married life in a provincial town, is often also regarded as a forerunner of the naturalist genre.

Naturalism in literature viewed the human being as determined by genetics as well as its environment, and often looked at the inhabitants of the slums or those who had dwindled into poverty, alcoholism or prostitution. The Goncourt brothers defined naturalism in the preface to *Germinie Lacerteux* (1865), a novel which centres on a poor country girl who, upon coming to Paris, cannot resist the city's many temptations, has sexual affairs with many men and dies in loneliness. They saw it as a genre which would bring the realism of suffering on the streets, "la souffrance humaine", to readers,[12] even if that truth would be upsetting or hard to digest. Shifting its attention away from what American author Frank Norris would call "teacup tragedies"[13] to the harsh conditions of the urban poor, naturalism in literature underscored the need for social reform. While these texts played an important role in creating social awareness, a novel like Émile Zola's *Germinal* (1894–95) suggests the future potential of the labouring classes to escape their fate by joining forces. Even if the miner's strike in the novel is unsuccessful, the narrative expresses the hope that one day there will be a major breakthrough. Nineteenth-century literature became a platform for rhetoric supporting the emancipation of various social groups.

This emancipatory aspect of the novel once again illustrates the transnational nature of European literature in the long nineteenth century. While each nation had its own political, social and moral preoccupations, literatures travelled in a transnational context, transferring genres, modes and trending topics to new national contexts. This rendered an international community of readers, who were connected across borders through the books, poems, magazines and stories they consumed.

Notes

1 Cited in Alex Drace-Francis, *European Identity: A Historical Reader* (Amsterdam: Amsterdam University Press, 2013), 115.
2 Brian Hamnett, *The Historical Novel in Nineteenth-Century Europe: Representations of Reality in History and Fiction* (Oxford: Oxford University Press, 2011).
3 Wilkie Collins, "Portrait of an Author, Painted by His Publisher," *All the Year Round* (18 June, 1859): 184.
4 Henry MacKenzie, *The Man of Feeling* (London: Cassell & Co., 1886), v.
5 See Frank Furedi, "The Media's First Moral Panic," *History Today* 65.11 (2015).
6 Stephen Prickett, "General Introduction: Of Fragments, Monsters and Translations," in *European Romanticism: A Reader*, ed. Stephen Prickett (general editor) and Simon Haines (London: Bloomsbury, 2014), 17.
7 Virginia Woolf, *Mr Bennett and Mrs Brown* (London: L. and V. Woolf, 1924), 2.
8 *The Poems of T.S. Eliot*, Volume 1: *Collected and Uncollected Poems*, ed. Christopher Ricks and Jim McCue (London: Faber & Faber, 2015), 84.
9 William Wordsworth, "Preface," in *Lyrical Ballads: With Other Poems* (1800), accessed October 1, 2016, www.online-literature.com/wordsworth/lyrical-ballads-vol1/0/
10 Percy Bysshe Shelley, "Mont Blanc," (1817), accessed October 1, 2016, www.mtholyoke.edu/courses/rschwart/hist256/alps/mont_blanc.htm
11 Richard Daniel Lehan, *Realism and Naturalism: The Novel in an Age of Transition* (Madison, WI: University of Wisconsin Press, 2005), 5–6.
12 Edmond and Jules de Goncourt, *Germinie Lacerteux* (Paris: Belenus, 2008), 8.
13 Joseph R. McElrath and Douglas K. Burgess, eds., *The Apprenticeship Writings of Frank Norris, 1896–1898*, vol. 1 (Philadelphia, PA: The American Philosophical Society, 1996), 86.

Further reading

Hamnett, Brian. *The Historical Novel in Nineteenth-Century Europe: Representations of Reality in History and Fiction*. Oxford: Oxford University Press, 2011.
Hill, David, ed. *Literature of the Sturm und Drang: History of German Literature*. Vol. 6. New York: Camden House, 2003.
Langford, Rachael, ed. *Textual Intersections: Literature, History and the Arts in Nineteenth-Century Europe*. Amsterdam/New York: Rodopi, 2009.
Offord, Derek. "Nineteenth-Century in Russian Thought and Literature." In *The Routledge Companion to Russian Literature*, edited by Neil Cornwell, 123–35. London/New York: Routledge, 2001.

20 Feeling

Anke Gilleir

Figure 20.1: Unknown artist, "Die Leiden des Jungen Werther", print

Source: Centre Art Historical Documentation, Radboud University.

In November 1772 the Swiss philosopher Johann Lavater wrote a letter to his colleague, the German theologian and cultural philosopher Johann Gottfried Herder, which contained the following lines:

> Never in my life have I felt what I feel now, as I sit down to write to you, my most favorite friend. O, how you have taken care of me, judge of the heart, creator of bliss! providence! Too little I have believed in you with absolute faith! I cannot reply to you now, my friend, but write I must – and I would rather weep – wander towards you – melt away – lie against your chest.[1]

The two men had never met before. Their acquaintance consisted of a mutual appreciation of each other's work and one single other letter which Lavater had written and which took Herder four years to answer.[2] From a present-day perspective, the outpour of emotions in the correspondence* between two eminent scholars who were strangers to one another is surprising. The affirmations of empathy up to the point that the writing threatens to break up (but does not) appear too excessive to be credible, let alone be "authentic". But as the history of emotions has revealed, emotional dispositions and expressions can be understood only properly within their cultural context. Feelings* may be a universal human characteristic, but they are also always part of what sociology calls a *habitus**, i.e. the way in which a person thinks and acts according to the rules of a social group. In the case of Herder and Lavater, this meant that they were part of the culture of emotions* that was spread by the literature and philosophy of their time.

Emotions and the language to shape and express them became colloquial in European culture during the eighteenth century. Of course, people had had feelings before and the power of affects was a major theme in a variety of treatises and literary texts in premodern times.[3] Yet, it was in the age of reason, the historical period during which man was defined as a free and self-conscious subject, that emotions became part of a person's self-awareness and her/his awareness of others. As the influential British literary theorist and critic Terry Eagleton has pointed out, the rising significance of emotions was allied with the emergence of the middle class. It was the bourgeoisie, who, as a social group, began to cultivate personal affiliations in opposition to the aristocracy and its "impersonal system of traditional kinship."[4] The political position of the bourgeoisie was different throughout Europe, yet due to its rising economic power and its intellectual and moral self-assurance, the dissemination of its values became indeed "universal". These values, which could roughly be summarized as professional success and emotional satisfaction, are still largely ours today, yet its rhetoric and role patterns changed in the course of time.

The American historian and anthropologist William M. Reddy offers some of the most interesting theories of feeling and emotional expressions. In his analyses, he reveals that emotions are neither a purely natural thing nor entirely determined by social life. In other words, expressions of emotions are never pure descriptions of a non-verbal (universal) affective state, but they cannot be reduced to mere social conventions either. Though a culture does not simply create emotions, conventions* do promote certain emotional spheres that "strongly influence individual emotion in a manner that allows for a certain stability and ideological comprehensibility in a community's life."[5] In terms of European history, this means that the rise of a new social group across the continent came with an image of man that did not only imply the challenge to think. "Saupere aude" ('dare to know') is indeed what the German philosopher Immanuel Kant said in his famous 1784 essay "Was ist Aufklärung?" ('What Is Enlightenment?') (see also Chapter 13). Equally strong was the prerequisite to foster empathy and affective sensibility. Social relations involved personal emotions.

In her novel* *Corinne ou l'Italie* ('Corinne, or Italy', 1807), Germaine de Staël offers an example of the conflict between the older formal and the modern personal mode of communication in the encounter of two protagonists, Lord Nelvil and the count d'Erfeuil. Both men have the same age and social rank. They get acquainted in order to cross the Alps on their journey to Italy. The French count appears as a pleasant fellow traveller, never at a loss for witty remarks, full of gay stories and always polite. Yet Nelvil is irritated to find that his companion only talks about the perceptible world, never about personal feelings. The man simply does not seem to possess any form of deep affection which Nelvil could appeal to in order to relieve some of his own pressing hopes and fears. The contrast between these fictional characters has been explained mainly in terms of cultural difference: French frivolity versus British gravity. Yet the difference can also be read as a *generational* one, in which d'Erfeuil, who has an unfailing sense of social conduct, belongs to an era that did not cultivate the disposition for fostering and confessing personal emotions. Although the novel is clearly in sympathy with the tormented Nelvil, his antagonist is equally confused by the "unpredictable" behaviour of his peer. Yet d'Erfeuil belongs to the past and the modern subject now set out to sail by the compass of his/her affections, which, as literature was to reveal amply, did not make life easier.

Inflamed feelings

Literature played a major role in the articulation and dissemination of the modern emotional *habitus* throughout the Western world. It did not just *represent* the affections that started to characterize modern culture, it also *moulded* them. In her seminal dissertation on literature and society, *De la littérature* ('On Literature', 1800), Madame de Staël acknowledges how literature put feeling on the map:

> When I talk about modern literature, and in particular about that of the eighteenth century, in which love was painted in Tancrède, la nouvelle Héloise, Werther and in the English poets etc. I will show how this talent expresses sensitive affections with much more strength and warmth than theoretical reflections or philosophy have ever managed at their highest level.[6]

Literature provided the default language of feeling, the role patterns in the game of self and other, and a spectrum of passions unleashed by it, ranging from absolute bliss to the black pitch of despair. Even before the reading audience was well absorbed in this (fathomless) world of feeling, literature also already revealed how narcissist, ludicrous or even life-threatening excessive emotion could be. A survey of the literature of sensibility as it developed, from the late eighteenth century on, would have to be quite extensive, since feeling became somehow synonymous with humanness. Yet looking at some figures and texts that were if not representative then at least of major importance to their own time may give some understanding as to why two philosophers like Herder and Lavater wrote to each other in the dramatic tone they did. Some literary figures became, as Eagleton states so aptly about Samuel Richardson's first novel *Pamela* (1740), "public mythologies, coordinates of a mighty moral debate, symbolic spaces."[7] So, although they were products of the imagination, they became a real part of the eighteenth-century world of experience.

Samuel Richardson can indeed be considered as a first major landmark in the history of feeling in literature. The voices of his eponymous heroines in *Pamela* (1740) and *Clarissa* (1748) echoed through the imagination of the following generations and became figures of discussion in literary and non-literary texts throughout Europe. Johann Gottfried Herder's happy exclamation in a letter to his fiancée, "You are reading *Clarissa*? Have I told you I started reading her too this autumn?" more than twenty years after the novel was first published is indicative of this.[8] The appeal had to do with the genre: *Pamela* and *Clarissa* are epistolary novels*. Fiction* disguised as letters provided a sense of familiarity with the world they evoked and made it sound authentic. Richardson's novels relate the story of two young middle-class women who defend their personal and moral integrity against a ruthless pursuer. In contrast to the deeply rooted Lutheran prejudice of women as weak and susceptible to seduction, the letters of Pamela and Clarissa opened a spectrum of both high sensitivity and steadfastness. It inspired many women writers to continue this fictional universe from their perspective. The Dutch writing duo Aagje Deken and Betje Wolff, who are said to have written the first modern novel in the Netherlands, *Historie van mejuffrouw Sara Burgerhart* ('The History of Ms. Sara Burgerhart', 1782), have their protagonist refer to "de godlyke clarisse" ('the divine Clarisse'), as does Sophie la Roche's heroine in *Geschichte des Fräuleins von Sternheim* ('The History of Ms. Sternheim', 1771). Yet sensibility also affected the other sex. Until well into the nineteenth century, masculinity was not associated with the muting of emotions, as gender stereotype* has it today. Men as well as women were allowed – expected, even – to reveal their deep inner feelings and shed tears. The work of Jean-Jacques Rousseau and (the young) Johann Wolfgang von Goethe offered excellent examples of this.

Rousseau, who, as Madame de Staël said, invented nothing but inflamed everything, became the embodiment of the *âme sensible* ('sensitive soul') through his extensive autobiographical writings. His *Confessions* (published in 1782) are usually considered as the archetype of modern autobiographical writing*, shifting from objective chronicle to a narrative of personal revelations.[9] But it was his 1761 epistolary novel *Julie, ou la nouvelle Héloise* ('Julie or the New Héloise') that spread his rhetoric of sensitivity through Europe. *Julie* relates the – eventually – tragic love story between a young aristocratic woman and her teacher Saint-Preux. Julie is forced to renounce her beloved in order to marry one of her father's peers and succumbs to the social pressure. Yet she does not merely obey, she is determined to be a faithful wife and repudiates the idea of adultery. When she communicates her decision to Saint-Preux, he is left devastated, but can but respect her strength: "No, no, in spite of my torment in feeling and saying this, you will be never more my Julie than in the moment you renounced me. Alas, it is in losing you that I found you."[10] After years of separation, on seeing Saint-Preux again, Julie realizes that her love for him has not changed. Yet every possible dilemma to yield to her feelings is resolved by her sudden death after saving her child from drowning. Her last words to Saint-Preux recall both her love and honour:

> Would my soul have existed without you? What bliss would I have experienced without you? No, I do not leave you, I will wait for you. The virtue that separated us on earth will unite us in the eternal hereafter. I will die with this sweet expectation: how happy that I can buy the right to love you forever without guilt at the price of my life and that I should be able to tell you this one last time.[11]

Rousseau was inspired by the twelfth-century story of Abelard and Héloise (hence the subtitle "*nouvelle* Héloise"), and some echoes of the spiritual tone of its historical predecessor remained. But the detailed intensity with which his protagonists describe and reflect their affections, up to the point that it inflicts a sense of voyeurism on the reader, was in key with the emotional culture of his time. The affective role play was expanded by also making the male protagonist a full partner in despair.

"The sorrows of young werther"

We do not know what happens to Saint-Preux after Julie's death, but it is suggested that he will continue with his life after a process of intense mourning. This potential redemption was withheld from the greatest hero of emotions, Goethe's Werther, whose story was an apex and also turning point in the era of sensibility. *Die Leiden des jungen Werthers* ('The Sorrows of Young Werther') was first published in 1774, when Goethe was barely twenty-five years old. It is, again, an epistolary novel that consists of the letters of a young man called Werther (his first name is never mentioned) to his friend Wilhelm, written between May 1771 and December 1772. Although we do not get to read Wilhelm's replies, the profound emotional acquaintance of both men is underscored at the outset: "My dear! Do I need to tell this to you, who has so often carried the burden of seeing me pass from sorrow to excess and from sweet melancholia to destructive passion?"[12]

Werther is a solicitor. His story, or rather his letters, start with his arrival in a small town, where he has to settle a legacy matter and where he meets Lotte, a young woman with whom he falls in love, but who is already engaged to be married. Werther also gets acquainted with her future husband and spends much time with the couple. Yet a growing sense of frustration incites him to take on a position elsewhere and leave. After a minor social incident in his new working environment, Werther returns to Lotte, who meanwhile has become married. His hope to be able to lead a content life merely by being in her vicinity proves an illusion. Growing more desperate every day, he decides to put an end to his sorrow and commits suicide by shooting himself through the head with her husband's pistol. The story ends with a final letter which Werther writes to Lotte just before his death and the description of his death scene and funeral by the anonymous editor of his letters.

Werther can be read as a love story and indeed has been since its first publication. The protagonists, the title hero in particular, became in their time the embodiment of tragic love. While the reader gets to know very little about Lotte, there is no doubt as to Werther's overwhelming passion for her, both in terms of empathy and erotic attraction. He is tormented. He desperately longs for something that is forbidden, while trying not to do so. His being in love with her makes him restless and frustrated up to the point that he fears losing his sanity.

Text: Johann Wolfgang von Goethe, Die Leiden des jungen Werther *('The Sorrows of Young Werther') (1774)*

What is this, my friend? I am frightened by myself. Is my love for her not the holiest, purest, brotherly love? Have I ever felt a punishable wish in my soul? – I do not want to swear – and now, dreams! O how right people were who believed strange powers to have such contradictory effects. Last night! I tremble at confessing it, I held her in my arms, pressed her close to my chest and covered her love whispering mouth with endless kisses; I drowned in the bliss of her eyes! God, I am guilty about the happiness I still feel now, that I should recall these glowing delights with ardour. Lotte! Lotte!

I am finished. I lose my senses, since eight days I have not come to my senses, my eyes are full of tears. I feel nowhere well, and well everywhere. There is nothing I wish or long for. It would be better if I would go. . . . Her presence, her fortune, her sympathy with mine, it forces the last tears from my scorched brain. To pull the curtain up and step behind it. That is everything! And why doubt and delay? Because one does not know what it looks like behind there? and one does not return? and because it is a property of our mind to suppose chaos and darkness in places of which we know nothing certain. . . . Thank you, my dear Wilhelm, that you have understood the word well. Yes, you are right, it would be better for me to go. But your proposal to return to you does not convince me entirely, as least I should like to take a roundabout route, because it has been freezing for quite some time and we can hope for good roads. Also, it is very kind of you come and pick me up, but do postpone it for a fortnight and wait for another letter I will write you. Nothing should be harvested that has not ripened.[13]

Though Werther's letters leave no doubt as to the honesty and depth of his feelings, it does not take much to see that the novel also deals with a man caught in an imaginary world ruled by unrestrained emotions. The very first line he writes indicates that his move to a new location is already an escape from another situation of emotional compromise caused by his lack of restraint:

How glad I am to be gone! . . . that poor Leonore. And yet I was innocent. It was not my fault that, while her sister's peculiar appeal amused me a great deal, a strong passion arose in her poor heart? And yet, am I totally innocent?[14]

So before Werther has even met Lotte, his rhetoric reveals a highly strung character for whom the outside world functions as a mirror of his own feelings. He realizes that he is different from other people, but his spiritual and emotional "freedom" is to him a gift that sets him apart from his dulled and blinkered fellow men:

When I look at the limitations that imprison the busy and investigating forces of man, when I see how everything man does is aimed at satisfying certain needs that have no other aim than to prolong our pitiful life, and then, all reassurance about certain elements of investigation is nothing but a dreamful resignation, man happily decorates the walls he is caught between with colorful drawings and bright views − all that, Wilhelm, leaves me speechless. I return to myself and find a whole world![15]

He concludes the same letter with the reassurance that at least he possesses the "sweet sense of freedom to be able to leave this prison whenever he wants to." Or: "Yes, I am but a wanderer, a pilgrim on this earth! Are you more?"[16] Wandering is what many romantic heroes* after Werther would do, often, as in Wordsworth's poem "I Wandered Lonely As a Cloud" (1807), but rarely heading so straight to death. Werther's encounter with Lotte is initially described in familiar emotional terms, yet soon his language is intertwined with death metaphors that reveal the fatal nature of his "whole world." Lotte may literally be the love of his life, as others have experienced it before him, but she also functions as a trigger in his complete abandonment of the outside world. As he passionately defends passion, he seems to perform his own fate. In his second letter to his friend, he tries to evoke the − again extreme − feeling of happiness that has seized him in his new surroundings:

"[if I] could breathe onto paper what lives so full, so warm in me, so that it would become the mirror of my soul."[17]

Expressing his feelings in an authentic manner is only one side of the story, because Werther does not merely try to describe his feelings. The constant re-enactment of his affective state through the hyperbolic language of his letters accelerates his nervousness, which leads to another important aspect of Werther's sorrows, namely literature. From his first letters until the description of his death, Werther's story is permeated with names of authors, literary texts, plots, fictional characters* and quotes that make up the literary universe of Goethe's time. Werther's problem, however, is that he does not seem to be able to tell fiction from reality. Not only does he have a vivid imagination, his entire disposition has been modelled by literature. In that sense, as Rüdiger Safranski remarks, Werther is comparable to Don Quixote (see Chapter 15).[18] The catalyst of the process towards his tragic death is *Ossian*, another key text that enhanced the culture of sentiment of late eighteenth-century Europe. Werther's deteriorating state of mind is reflected by his changing literary preference. He starts as an eager reader of Homer, symbol of natural simplicity, but increasingly he is attracted and eventually totally absorbed by *Ossian*:

> Ossian has pushed Homer out of my heart. What a world, this glorious creature leads me to! To wander over the moors, driven by the stormy winds that lead one through the fuming fog to the ghosts of the fathers in the dawning light of the moon. To hear coming down from the mountains, through the roaring sound of the rivers, the windswept lamentations of the ghosts in the caverns.[19]

The *Works of Ossian* (1765) were published by the Scottish writer and philologist James Macpherson and consisted of ancient epic poems that he had translated from Gaelic. Ossian tells the story of ancient warriors, evoking rugged landscapes, heroic deeds and, equally, deep emotions. The success of *Ossian* was great, and can be explained by the rising interest in national culture and ancient languages at that time. From the point of view of *feeling*, it also becomes clear why Macpherson's work was so eagerly read, for the ancient protagonists are as tearful and melancholic as their modern readers. Goethe translated parts of *Ossian* into German after Herder had brought the Scottish epic* to his attention. He inserted several pages of the translation* into his novel and attributed them to Werther, who makes it a present for Lotte. The text has a strong impact on both protagonists and reading *Ossian* together leads to a climax in their tense relationship.

> A flood of tears that flowed from Lotte's eyes and relieved her feelings stopped Werther from reading. He threw down the paper, took her hand and wept the bitterest tears. . . . The world around them disappeared. He flung his arms around her, pulled her to his chest and covered her shivering, stammering lips with violent kisses. – "Werther!" she cried with a suffocated voice, trying to avert him, "Werther!", and with her weak and tried to push his chest from hers. "Werther" she cried in the resolute tone of the noblest feeling. – He did not resist, let her go out of his arms and threw himself frenzied before her. – She pulled herself together, and in anxious confusion, shivering between love and anger said: "This is the last time! Werther! You will never see me again!"[20]

The success of Goethe's *Werther* in European culture surpassed everything that had been written until then. The author became a star and wild rumours spread through the continent: Werther was none but Goethe himself, and that Werther even inspired people to commit suicide. Though none of this is historically verifiable, it is symptomatic of the impact of a novel that pushed the culture of feeling to its ultimate conclusion. It was to pursue Goethe for the rest of his life, though he distanced himself from both the novel and its extreme cult of feelings already a few years after its first publication. Until his death in 1832, he was the defender of a humanist aesthetics*, a theory that believed that the beauty of art could redeem the harsh reality of history and even improve mankind.

Romanticism and beyond

It is often claimed that the cult of feeling was an invention of romanticism*. Yet as we have just shown, it was in the course of the eighteenth century that personal affection came to be considered an essential aspect of the modern subject. One of the greatest writers of the Enlightenment*, Gotthold Ephraim Lessing, summarized this aptly in his play *Emilia Galotti* (1772), in which one of the protagonists claims: "If a person does not lose his mind over certain things, he does not have a mind to lose."[21] Werther, who died with *Emilia Galotti* open next to him, literally lost his mind: "Above his right eye he had shot himself through the head, his brain had been driven out."[22] He was the literary embodiment of feeling, yet also revealed that literature did not provide the guide to a happy life.

This is what the narrator of *Don Juan*, Lord Byron's last major epic poem that was first published in 1819, seems to express ironically when he looks back upon the unfortunate adventures of Don Juan:

> But let me change this theme, which grows too sad
> And lay this sheet of sorrows on the shelf;
> I don't like much describing people mad,
> For fear of seeming rather touch'd myself.[23]

Romanticism both inherited and claimed feeling as the vortex of life, but it shifted the problem of "virtue versus passion" towards a preoccupation with the self that transcended the sphere of social (mis)communication. Feeling received a philosophical profundity in the romantic definition of man. In spite of its diversity, European romanticism was generally characterized by a deep sense of subjectivity and emotional sensitivity. Yet as feeling had become a colloquial aspect of the human condition that no longer needed justification as such, it could be pursued in diverse and profoundly particular ways. The British poet Lord Byron and his melancholic protagonists, the so-called "Byronic heroes", are and in indeed *were* the most well-known representatives of this changing direction of emotional energy.

Byron and his heroes, Childe Harold, Manfred and Don Juan, became iconic of the romantic persona* – tempestuous, wayward, strong-willed and both passionate and ironic – whom generations of writers throughout Europe looked up to.[24] Byron himself was an admirer of Goethe, whom he called "his liege lord, the first of existing writers,"[25] yet his fascination was less inspired by *Werther* as it was by *Faust*. More than a personal preference, this is characteristic of the new patterns of identification. Faust is not a victim of an overstrung sensitivity, nor does his passion concern one particular person. It is the entire universe which he desires. Instead of being crushed by the world, as Werther was, he is angered and challenged by its limitations, wants to discover all its dimensions and strives to transcend it with the help of the devil. Byron's Childe Harold and Manfred are gloomy and repelled by society, they flee and wander through Europe. Harold defies being virtuous and delights in sensual pleasures, but it becomes clear that his excesses are attempts to escape from melan-cholia. In other words, the sardonic mask hides an impressionable soul. The fact that Harold is not at all without feeling in spite of his self-declared indifference ("I have not loved the world, nor the world me") is revealed during his journey and his sensitivity for the sublime: nature, ancient cities, political struggles. Looking at Lake Leman in Geneva, Harold confesses that he once loved the roaring ocean, "but thy soft murmuring/Sounds sweet as if a sister's voice reproved/That I with stern delights should e'er have been so moved."[26]

Harold gnashes his teeth instead of letting his tears flow, and as such he embodies a masculine model of emotion that increasingly left the weeping to the women. Symp-tomatic of this gendered suppression of emotion is a small scene in Charles Dickens's famous novel *Oliver Twist* (1837). When the orphan Oliver gets wounded during a rob-bery and is taken into the care of Miss Rose and her guardian Mrs. Maylie, he recounts to them some of the misery of his (indeed extremely miserable) life. Whereas the mere sight of the young boy moves both women to tears, the family doctor, who is present at the scene, does not yield to their expression of emotion: "Oliver composed to rest again, then the doctor, after wiping his eyes and condemning for being weak all at once, betook himself downstairs."[27]

Feeling did not evaporate, but the articulation of emotions changed and it became less violently explicit. Yet, whereas revealing feeling became inalienable with womanhood in general, the expression of emotions by men reveals some interesting cultural gradations. The French romantic writer François-René de Chateaubriand allows the male protago-nists of his famous novels *Attala* (1801) and *René* (1802), which greatly impressed Byron, to weep amply. In the introduction to his famous autobiography* *Mémoires d'outre-tombe* ('Memoirs from Beyond the Grave', published after his death), Chateaubriand underscores the importance of fiction for the acknowledgment and expression of feeling. He states:

> Most of my feelings remain buried deep in my heart, or have only been revealed in my works as if applied to imaginary beings. Now that I miss my chimeras, without pursuing them, I want to revive the inclinations of my best years.[28]

The "spleen" of later generations of poets such as Charles Baudelaire and Paul Verlaine – "O triste, triste était mon âme" ('How sad, sad was my soul', 1844–96) – continues the consen-sus of emotion as the core of subjectivity and aesthetic creation. The German poet Heinrich Heine did so in a comparable manner and gave throughout his oeuvre voice to his sense of "Weltschmerz" ('world-weariness') fuelled both by personal and political sensitivity. "Him-melhoch jauchzend zu Tode betrübt" ('on top of the world or in the depths of despair') was how Goethe coined this roller coaster of feeling (in love) in his drama "Egmont".[29] One of Heine's most well-known poems, "Heimkehr" ('Coming home', 1827), summarizes this moment, opening with a speaker expressing sadness in spite of a beautiful day and ending with wishing he would be killed by a soldier, whose rifle shimmers in the sunlight:

> *Er spielt mit seiner Flinte,*
> *die funkelt im Sonnenrot,*
> *er präsentiert und schultert –*
> ich wollt, er schösse mich tot.

> (He plays with his rifle/
> That shines in the sunny red/
> he presents it and shoulders/
> I wish he'd shoot me dead)

Chateaubriand, Baudelaire and Verlaine became part of the cultural canon* in France. Heine, however, whose poetry was among the most popular of the nineteenth century, became marginalized in the German canon as a Jewish intellectual and a writer with "the total lack of restraint that makes women complete and language deficient."[30]

Notes

1 Julius Zeitler, ed., *Deutsche Freundesbriefe aus sechs Jahrhunderten* (Leipzig: Julius Zeitler, 1909), 62.
2 See Johann Gottfried Herder, *Briefe*. Gesamtausgabe, vol. 2 (Mai 1771–April 1773), ed. Wilhelm Dobbek and Günter Arnold (Weimar: Hermann Böhlaus Nachfolger, 1984), 252.
3 As the American medievalist Sarah McNamer argues, literary texts have always served "as affective scripts, capable of generating complex emotional effects in those who engage with them." Sarah McNamer, "The Literariness of Literature and the History of Emotion," *Publications of the Modern Language Association* 130.5 (2015): 1436.
4 Terry Eagleton, *The Rape of Clarissa: Writing, Sexuality and Class Struggle in Samuel Richardson* (Oxford: Wiley-Blackwell, 1982), 14.
5 William M. Reddy, "Against Constructionism: The Historical Ethnography of Emotions," *Current Anthropology* 38.3 (1997): 334.
6 Madame [Germaine] de Staël, *De la littérature considérée dans ses rapports avec les institutions sociales*, ed. Axel Blaeschke (Paris: Garnier, 1998), 116. William Reddy explicitly points out the importance of Germaine de Staël in the process of emotionality in European history: "Two centuries ago, Germaine de Staël anticipated and fully understood . . . words and ideas enriched and educated feelings," William M. Reddy, *The Navigation of Feeling: A Framework for the History of Emotions* (Cambridge: Cambridge University Press, 2001), 144.
7 Eagleton, *Clarissa*, 5.
8 Herder, *Briefe*, vol. 2, 111.
9 "I have revealed myself as I was; despicable and evil as I have been, good, generous, sublime, as I have been: I have unmasked my inner self as you have seen yourself," Jean-Jacques Rousseau, *Les Confessions* (Paris: Pocket, 1996), 33.
10 Jean-Jacques Rousseau, *Julie, ou la nouvelle Héloise* (Paris: Garnier-Flammaration, 1967), 270.
11 Rousseau, *Julie*, 566.
12 Johann Wolfgang von Goethe, "Die Leiden des jungen Werther," in *Goethe Werke: Hamburger Ausgabe*, vol. 6. *Romane und Novellen*, ed. by Erich Trunz (München: DTV, 1986), 10.
13 Goethe, "Die Leiden des jungen Werther," 100.
14 Goethe, "Die Leiden des jungen Werther," 7.
15 Goethe, "Die Leiden des jungen Werther," 13.
16 Goethe, "Die Leiden des jungen Werther," 7, 75.
17 Goethe, "Die Leiden des jungen Werther," 9.
18 Rüdiger Safranski, *Goethe: Kunstwerk des Lebens* (München: Carl Hanser, 2013), 161 f.
19 Goethe, "Die Leiden des jungen Werther," 82.
20 Goethe, "Die Leiden des jungen Werther," 114–15.
21 Gotthold Ephraim Lessing, "Emilia Galotti" (IV, 7), *Werke*, vol. 2, (München: Hanser Verlag 1970 ff.), 187.
22 Goethe, "Die Leiden des jungen Werther," 124.
23 Lord Byron, *Don Juan: A New Edition* (Boston: Phillips, Sampson, and Company, 1854), 165.
24 See Richard A. Cardwell, ed., *The Reception of Byron in Europe*. 2 vols (London/New York: Thoemmes, 2004).
25 Lord Byron, "Sardanapalus: A Tragedy," accessed March 30, 2016, www.gutenberg.org/files/23475/23475-h/23475-h.htm
26 Lord Byron, "Childe Harold's Pilgrimage," in *The Norton Anthology of English Literature*, ed. Stephen Greenblatt and Meyer Howard Abrams (New York: Norton, 1999), 528.
27 Charles Dickens, *Oliver Twist* (Ware: Wordsworth Classics, 1992), 265.
28 François de Chateaubriand, "Mémoires d'Outre-Tombe," trans. A.S. Kline, accessed April 18, 2016, www.poetryintranslation.com/klineaschateaubriand.htm

29 Johann Wolfgang von Goethe, "Egmont," in *Goethe Werke: Hamburger Ausgabe*, vol. 4 *Dramatische Dichtungen* II, ed. by Erich Trunz (München: DTV 1988), 411.
30 Karl Kraus, "Heine und die Folgen," (1910), accessed April 18, 2016, www.uni-due.de/lyriktheorie/texte/1910_kraus.html

Further reading

Buffault, Anne-Vincent. *Histoire des Larmes*. Paris: Rivages, 2001.
Jensen, Katherine Ann and Mirjam L. Wallace, eds. *Emotions*, special issue of *Publications of the Modern Language Association* 130.5 (2015).
Reddy, William M. *The Making of Romantic Love: Longing and Sexuality in Europe, South Asia, and Japan, 900–1200 CE*. Chicago, IL: University of Chicago Press, 2012.
Safranski, Rüdiger. *Romantik: Eine deutsche Affäre*. Frankfurt am Main: Fischer, 2007.
Thoma, Heinz, ed. *Handbuch europäische Aufklärung: Begriffe. Konzepte. Wirkung*. Stuttgart: J.B. Metzler, 2015.

21 Defining the nation

Lotte Jensen

Figure 21.1 Motion picture poster for the 1913 film *Ivanhoe*, featuring actor King Baggot as Ivanhoe, London, Middlesbrough: Jordison & Co., Ltd.

The blasts of trumpets, the clashing of swords, breezing horses and bleeding knights: these phenomena abound in the historical novel* *Ivanhoe* by Sir Walter Scott.

Text: Sir Walter Scott, Ivanhoe (1819)

Laisser aller! The trumpets sounded as he spoke – the spears of the champions were at once lowered and placed in the rests – the spurs were dashed into the flanks of the horses, and the two foremost ranks of either party rushed upon each other in full gallop, and met in the middle of the lists with a shock, the sound of which was heard at a mile's distance.

The consequences of the encounter were not instantly seen, for the dust raised by the trampling of so many darkened the air, and it was a minute ere the anxious spectators could see the fate of the encounter. When the fight became visible, half of the knights on each side were dismounted, some by dexterity of their adversary's lance, – some by the superior weight, which had broken down both horse and man, – some lay stretched on earth as if never more to rise – some had already gained their feet, and were closing hand to hand with those of the enemy who were in the same predicament – and two or three, who had received wounds by which they were disabled, were stopping their blood by their scarfs, and endeavouring to extricate themselves from the tumult. The mounted knights, whose lances had been almost all broken by the fury of the encounter, were now closely engaged with their swords, shouting war-cries, and exchanging buffets, as if honour and life depended on the issue of the combat.

The tumult was presently increased by the advance of the second rank on either side, which, acting as reserve, now rushed on to aid their companions. The followers of Brian de Bois-Guilbert shouted: "Ha! Beau-seant! Beau seant! – for the Temple – for the Temple." The opposite party shouted in answer – "Desdichado! Desdichado!" – Which watch-word they took from the motto upon their leader's shield.

The champions thus encountering each other with the utmost fury, and with alternate success, the tide of battle seemed to flow now toward the southern, now toward the northern extremity of lists, as the one or the other party prevailed. Meantime the clang of the blows, and the shouts of the combatants, mixed fearfully with the sound of the trumpets, and drowned the groans of those who fell, and lay rolling defenceless beneath the feet of the horses. The splendid armour of the combatants was now defaced with dust and blood, and gave way at every stroke of the sword and battle-axe. The gay plumage, shorn from the crests, drifted upon the breeze like snow-flakes. All that was beautiful and graceful in the martial array had disappeared, and what was now visible was only calculated to awake terror or compassion.[1]

Ivanhoe, set in England during the reign of King Richard the Lionheart in the late twelfth century, was one of the most popular novels of the nineteenth century. It travelled across European in countless editions, translations* and adaptations*, and inspired many authors to write novels in a similar vein.

This chapter aims to show that Ivanhoe is illustrative of several literary trends of the first half of the nineteenth century. The most important two are Romanticism* and nationalism*. Romanticism refers to the fact that works of art often became an expression of the inner life of the individual artist and that imagination became a primary criterion in the creation of literature. Novelists and poets became highly interested in the past, ranging from medieval topics to the Enlightenment*. Nationalism points to the use of literature as an instrument of nation-building: by evoking heroic episodes from the nation's history and by representing and inventing national heroes who were willing to sacrifice their lives for the nation's welfare, authors contributed to the rise of national sentiments in their countries. At the same time, another type of hero emerged who can, to some extent, be considered as quite the opposite type: the Byronic hero. This figure was a product of Romanticism as well, but represented feelings of loneliness and despair, which ultimately led to his downfall.

Ivanhoe: martial heroism

Ivanhoe was both the product of romantic and nationalist tendencies. In this work, the author Sir Walter Scott sketches a lively image of chivalry and courtly manners. War and knight fights played a central role in the novel, which celebrated martial heroism. Descriptions of the horrors of the battlefields were not held back, as the previously quoted fragment shows, but they only added to the sublime of warfare and the grandeur of the victors. One of the most well-known excerpts is the tournament at Ashby-de-la-Zouche which ends in a duel between the good-hearted disinherited knight Ivanhoe, here referred to as "Desdichado", and the savagely violent Norman knight Brian de Bois-Guilbert. Ivanhoe is about to lose until a knight in black dress, later revealed to be King Richard, comes to his rescue. Ivanhoe is proclaimed the winner, and honoured with a chaplet by the Queen of the tournament, the Saxon Lady Rowena.

  Ivanhoe deals with the ongoing strife between the Normans and Saxons, and their attempts to establish power over England. Ivanhoe's father, the Saxon leader Cedric, tries to arrange a marriage between the noble Athelstane of Coningsburgh and Rowena, in order to make Athelstane heir to the English throne. To avoid any further contact between Ivanhoe and his lover Rowena, Cedric has abandoned and disinherited his son, who then joins the crusade under the command of King Richard.

  The narrative starts with the return of Ivanhoe from the tournament at Ashby-de-la-Zouche. He is severely injured and treated for his wounds by Rebecca, a beautiful Jewish woman. She is impressed with Ivanhoe, but the social codes prohibit them to have any further contact. Later on, Rebecca is kidnapped by the Normans and accused of witchcraft. Bois-Guilbert, who is in love with Rebecca, has to defend the honour of the Templars against Ivanhoe, who wins the duel and saves Rebecca's life. Meanwhile, Athelstane dies in a fight against the Normans, but after his funeral he returns from death – a highly unlikely event in the novel. Athelstane withdraws his claims to the throne, which clears the way for the marriage of Ivanhoe and Rowena. Rebecca decides to leave the country to continue her life in Spain, under the protection of Mohammed Boabdil, the king of Grenada. This ending affirms the position of Jews as outsiders, and stands in sharp contrast with the marital happiness of Rowena and Ivanhoe.

  The key motives in *Ivanhoe* are exclusion and deracination versus integration and reconciliation. Exclusion is in particular thematized in the portrayal of the Jewish characters, Rebecca and her father Isaac. On the one hand, Scott offers a very negative, stereotypical image of the Jews; especially Isaac is portrayed as an avaricious and opportunistic man. On the other hand, the caring and beautiful Rebecca is a sympathetic character, who is liberated by the hero of the story, Ivanhoe. The message of harmony and unity is embodied by Ivanhoe, who strives for justice and stands above the mutually hostile parties. It is significant that his wedding is attended by high representatives both from the Saxon and Norman sides. Consequently, Ivanhoe symbolizes the later merging of Saxon and Norman traditions into one single, united English identity.

Romanticism and medievalism

Sir Walter Scott is undoubtedly one of the most influential writers of the nineteenth century. He is not only considered to be the founding father of the historical novel, but he was also famous for his ballads*, in which he wrote about old Scottish customs and manners. He cultivated the medieval past in poems like the *Lay of the Last Minstrel* (1805), *Marmion* (1808) and *The Lady of the Lake* (1810), and introduced a new type of historical writing with novels such as *Waverley* (1814), *Guy Mannering* (1815), *Ivanhoe* and *Quentin Durward* (1823).

Scott's poems were an instant success. His historical tales, which portrayed ethnic strife, were published during the heyday of the Napoleonic wars. They appealed to a broad audience, as they propagated patriotism and loyalty in times of warfare. *Lay of the Last Minstrel*, which dealt with the sixteenth-century rivalry between Scotland and England, sold 12,500 copies in two years. It was followed by *Marmion*, a tale about the armed conflict between England and Scotland in 1513, which reached a selling figure of twenty-five thousand copies in four years. An absolute record was set by *The Lady of Lake*, a tale about the armed conflict between James V and the Clan Alpine: twenty thousand copies were disseminated in only a few months.[2] Scott's novels were even more successful. At the start his books were mainly popular in England and Scotland, but soon they travelled all over Europe in the form of translations and adaptations. Scott's engaging way of historical storytelling, the combination of fact and fiction*, love and warfare, strife and harmony, appealed to the readers on the continent, as well. With his publications, Scott laid the foundations of two genres which would become immensely popular in the first half of the nineteenth century: narrative poetry* and the historical novel. This chapter concentrates on these two genres and their transnational* character.

Scott's work fits in a European pattern: between 1780 and 1850, the past was re-invoked in literature throughout Europe, and successful writers of that period increasingly resorted to historical topics. Literature became one of the most important gateways to history, since it made the past accessible to a broad audience: by lowering the prices, sales figures quickly went up, developing the historical novel gradually into a mass medium*. It opened up new horizons and created new historical sensations of long-forgotten worlds. The illusion of authenticity was increased by long and detailed descriptions of ancient customs, manners, clothing and natural surroundings (the so-called *couleur locale*). Some authors even used old dialects to suggest historical accurateness in speech. Nevertheless, the representation of historical characters and the nation's past was very much influenced by contemporary elements as well: present-day ideals were projected upon the main characters, and historical subject matter was often used to comment upon actual social and political issues. *Ivanhoe* could, for instance, also be interpreted as a political commentary on the demonstrations in Manchester in favour of parliamentary reform in 1819. Scott supported the interventions of the authorities, and was firmly opposed to an escalation of the conflict. He made this clear in a letter in the *Edinburgh Weekly Journal*, which he signed with the initials "L.T." It is not a coincidence the dedicatory epistle of *Ivanhoe* was signed by "Laurence Templeton". By using the same initials, Scott made a connection between both writings. The borders between fact and fiction, and past and present, were fluid.

The heightened interest in the past was closely linked to the rise of Romanticism in the last quarter of the eighteenth century. Romantic thought was strongly influenced by the German philosopher Johann Gottfried von Herder, who adhered to the idea that each nation had its own unique culture, which was rooted in a long historical and linguistic tradition. To lay bare the roots of their national cultures, historians and philologists started searching for old manuscripts in archives* and libraries*. Their aim was to find long-forgotten medieval sources*, such as songs, old folk tales*, myths*, ballads and poems. These antiquarian explorations led to important discoveries. In Germany, manuscripts* were found of the *Nibelungenlied*, a heroic epic* from the thirteenth century. The story about the brave *Beowulf*, written in ancient English, was transcribed and published for the first time by an Icelandic scholar. In France and Spain, the original manuscripts of the *Chanson de Roland* and *El Cantar de mio Cid* were rediscovered. These medieval epics were seen as foundational texts in the nation's history and became pivotal in the construction of national self-images by intellectuals, poets and novelists.

Medievalism not only became visible in the rise of antiquarian and philological activities, but also in the literary production* of that period. New genres emerged – such as the narrative poem and the historical novel – while older genres, such as the romance*, were revitalized. From 1770 onwards, it became fashionable to write ballads and romances. One of the trendsetters was the English bishop, antiquarian and poet Thomas Percy. In 1765, he published a collection of old folk tales and legends, *Reliques of Ancient Poetry*, which had a great impact on later Romantic poets. The Arthurian ballad about "The Boy and the Mantle" is illustrative for the style and form. It begins as follows:

> In Carleile dwelt King Arthur,
> A prince of passing might,
> And there maintain'd his table round,
> Beset with many a knight.
> And there he kept his Christmas
> With mirth and princely chear
> When lo! A strange and cauning boy
> Before him did appear.[3]

Percy's collection of ancient ballads was an instant success, and was translated into German by Gottfried August Bürger, who was equally interested in ancient folk poetry*. It also inspired Bürger to write ballads himself, in which he tried to create an authentic medieval atmosphere. His poems were widely read in Germany, and his best-known ballad, *Lenore* (1773), was translated into French and English. Walter Scott used both Percy and Bürger as sources of inspiration. After having published a collection of ancient Scottish ballads in 1802–1803, he started writing original ballads on medieval topics. By then, however, the political climate in Europe had changed drastically.

Nationalism

In 1799, Napoleon had taken over power in France, and gradually his true ambitions to conquer the whole of Europe became evident. He managed to occupy large parts of Europe, and appointed several of his brothers on European thrones: Joseph-Napoléon was made king of Naples and Sicily (1806–1808), Louis of Holland (1806) and Jérôme of Westphalia (1807). As a reaction to the French regime, a vast corpus of extremely patriotic resistance literature* emerged. Moreover, a heightened interest in the nation's past can be witnessed, because the nation's history came to be seen as an important instrument to raise national awareness and express resistance against the French. The literary scholar Joep

Leerssen has aptly described the general spirit of that period as "political Romanticism": many European authors were inspired by Romantic attitudes as well as political ideals.[4]

According to some critics, Scott's romances can be read as a form of resistance literature, as well.[5] Some fragments of the *Lay of the Last Minstrel* and *The Lady of the Lake* invoked the contemporary war with France, and the celebration of heroic war deeds of medieval knights could also be seen as celebrations of the British soldiers resisting the Napoleonic regime. The admiral Horatio Nelson and the British prime minister William Pitt, who had both played key roles in the fight against Napoleon, were extensively praised in the introduction of *Marmion*, and Napoleon was referred to as "the dragon".

In Germany, such poets as Heinrich von Kleist, Theodor Körner and Ernst Moritz Arndt joined the common cause of rebellion to Napoleonic tyranny. Kleist, for instance, published a political-historical play*, entitled *Die Hermannsschlacht* ('The battle of Herman', 1808), in which he called for military action against the foreign aggressors. The play was about the first king of the Germanic tribe the Cheruski, Arminius or Hermann, who won the battle against the Romans at the Teutoburg Forrest in 9 CE. This historical figure would become one of the most important symbols of German national identity during the course of the nineteenth century. He was celebrated as one of the founding fathers of the nation.

Körner incorporated his own experiences as a soldier in his patriotic songs. He died in battle against Napoleon in 1813, and left his readers a volume of *Zwölf freie deutsche Gedichte* ('Twelve free German poems', 1813). Arndt became known for his song *Was ist des Deutschen Vaterland* ('What is the German Fatherland', 1813), in which the fatherland stretched beyond the borders of the regional states: it was the sum of states which made up Germany. The first strophe reads:

> What is the German Fatherland?
> Is it the land of Prussia, is it the land of Schwaben?
> Is it at the Rhine, where the grapevine grows?
> Is it at the Belt, where the seagull flies?
> Oh no! no! no!
> His fatherland must be bigger![6]

Arndt's song, which envisions a German nation that is the sum of all regions, became very popular and functioned as an (unofficial) national anthem until approximately 1870.

Resistance literature also flourished in the Netherlands. Jan Frederik Helmers wrote one of the most nationalistic poems ever written in Dutch literature: *De Hollandsche natie* ('The Dutch Nation', 1812). In this national epic, which comprised more than three thousand stanzas, Helmers gave an extensive overview of Dutch history. In contrast with the German poets, Helmers did not look to the medieval past for his main inspiration, but directed his attention to the "golden age" of the Dutch Republic: the sixteenth and seventeenth centuries. Admiral Michiel de Ruyter is, for instance, honoured for his many victories in naval battles, while the poet Joost van den Vondel is celebrated for his qualities as a poet. The point Helmers tried to make was clear: there had been no greater nation than the Dutch in the past, and ultimately, this would lead to a new victory over the French. The provocative undertone did not go unnoticed by the French censors*: Helmers had to delete many passages before he received the permission to publish the poem. After Napoleon had been defeated, the original poem was published and soon became one of the classics of Dutch literature.

The cult of the great national past was a reaction to the overwhelming innovations Napoleon had imposed on the territories he had conquered. The French domination was an important driving force behind the nascent ideology of nationalism, which would culminate in the second half of the nineteenth century. Literature played an important role in cultivating national cultures. Through literature, a shared national self-image and a sense of collective togetherness were constructed, which implied the exclusion of others, especially the French. On the one hand, this type of literature was made instrumental to evoking national sentiments; on the other, the rise of genres such as historical narrative poetry, the romance and the historical novel were transnational from the start: the national past was integrated into the production of literature throughout nineteenth-century Europe, and works reached international audiences by means of translations.

The Byronic hero

Since its rediscovery as a literary genre in 1765, the medieval romance had undergone different generic transformations. At first it was mainly used to write fictitious medieval love stories, then it became a political means to express resistance against the Napoleonic regime by portraying national heroes from the past. A third type was introduced by one of the most influential poets of the early nineteenth century: George Gordon Byron. In 1812, he published the first two cantos of *Childe Harold's Pilgrimage*, a poem which has been considered the romance *par excellence*. By the time the fourth and final canto was published in 1818, Byron had become a true literary celebrity.

Childe Harold's Pilgrimage is about an aristocratic young man who is unsatisfied with his current life, leaves home and starts a quest for higher ideals in an exotic Mediterranean environment. He is the modern version of the wandering medieval knight. His departure is emotional:

> Adieu, adieu! my native shore
> Fades o'er the waters blue;
> The night-winds sigh, the breakers roar,
> And shrieks the wild sea-mew.
> You sun that sets upon the sea
> We follow in his flight;
> Farewell awhile to him mand thee,
> My native Land – Good Night![7]

Harold's quest brings him to many countries, such as Portugal, Spain, Albania and Greece. Interestingly enough, the third canto, which was published in 1816, also includes a stay at the fields of Waterloo in Belgium, where Napoleon was defeated in 1815. The protagonist shivers at the thought of all the soldiers killed and mourns the loss of so many beloved ones. This episode emphasises the main difference with the medieval quest, as it entails a critique of martial heroism. Harold's travels end in Venice and Rome, where the protagonist experiences the beauty of ancient cultures.

With his narrative poems, Byron introduced a new kind of protagonist, the so-called "Byronic hero." This hero is of a pensive and melancholic nature, and tormented by unrequited love. He wanders around in search for higher ideals, revolts against social conventions and turns away from religious beliefs. Byron was admired by many for his uncompromising and unconventional verses, which were highly influenced by his personal experiences. His eccentric personality, the many scandals and his self-chosen exile only added to this. He participated as a volunteer in the Greek insurrection against the Ottoman Empire in 1823, and died there at the age of thirty-six from a fever. As such he became the role model of the true Romantic poet, who struggled with the outer world both in real life as well as in his poems. He inspired many authors all over Europe.

At the same time, he was criticised by just as many for his immoral behaviour and the atheistic tendencies in his work. In the Netherlands, for instance, his poetry did not find a fertile soil. Only a few poets followed his style, but it was generally felt that this type of exotism and extremism did not fit in with the dominant discourse on Dutch national character.

At first sight, the Byronic hero does not seem to fit in the wave of nationalism which spread across post-Napoleonic Europe, as he was the personification of individualism, solitude and isolation from the outer world. Nevertheless, this heroic type also functioned as the ultimate embodiment of liberty and freedom: he also represented the people's right to stand up against foreign oppression and tyranny. Byron's own participation in the Greek war of independence was the ultimate consequence of this political ideal and was, as such, an act of true (Greek) nationalism.

Every nation has its own Walter Scott

From 1820 onwards, the historical novel would become the most important medium for telling stories about the past. Walter Scott's influence on the spread and development of this genre can hardly be overestimated. In the first half of the nineteenth century his novels were translated into Danish, Swedish, Dutch, French, Italian, Spanish, German, Russian, Polish, Dutch, Czech, Hungarian, Portuguese and Greek. What is more, nearly every European nation had a Walter Scott of its own. It is worth making a (selective) tour around the European nations: tracing Scott's influence automatically brings up the names of the most well-known novelists of these days. They have in common that they all wrote about their nation's past, and contributed to the rise of national thought and nationalism.

In the Scandinavian countries, for instance, Hans Christian Andersen (1805–1875) used elements of Scott's work in his novels *O. T.* (1836) and *De to Baronesser* ('The two baronesses', 1848). Both novels are set in Denmark, and pay ample attention to the social and historical circumstances of those days. In his diaries, he revealed that reading Scott's novels opened up new worlds for him. He also visited the monument of Walter Scott in Edinburgh and the Highlands to see some of the scenery where Scott's work was set. During his journey, he was greeted with the name "the Danish Walter Scott."

The Dutch politician and author Jacob van Lennep was soon given the name "Dutch Walter Scott". He emulated the Scottish author by writing a series of ballads about the Dutch medieval past, *Nederlandsche legenden* ('Dutch legends', 1828–1847), and also published several historical novels that were modelled after Scott's narratives. One of his most well-known novels, *De Roos van Dekama* ('The Rose of Dekama', 1836), deals with the strife between the Count of Holland and the Frisian people in the fourteenth century. It opens with a vivid description of a tournament in the city of Haarlem, a scene which was clearly based upon the passage about Ashby-de-la Zouch in *Ivanhoe*. Van Lennep was criticized for having adopted too many elements of Scott's work, and some critics even accused him of plagiarism*. Van Lennep refuted the accusations by stating that he had enriched Dutch historical literary writing by choosing typically Dutch surroundings and habits.

The other great nineteenth-century Dutch historical novelist was Anna Louisa Geertruida Toussaint. In contrast with Van Lennep, she situated her novels in the sixteenth and seventeenth centuries, because she felt that the true awakening of the Dutch people had started with the reformation. One of her best-known novels, *Het huis Lauernesse* ('The house of Lauernesse', 1840) tells the love story of two young people who have converted to Lutheranism. The couple ends up in Wittenberg, the home of Martin Luther, where they devote the rest of their lives to their religious conviction. Several scenes are clearly inspired by *Ivanhoe*. At a certain point the female protagonist Ottelijne appears to die, but in the next chapter the narrator reassures the readers that she was only playing a trick. Another scene which can be traced back to *Ivanhoe* is the burning of Ottelijne's family castle by Catholics; it reminds one of the lunatic Ulrica, who sets the castle of Front-de Boeuf on fire.

In Belgium, the most popular novelist was Henrik Conscience. His historical novel, *De Leeuw van Vlaanderen* ('The Lion of Flanders', 1838), went back to the Battle of the Golden Spurs of 1302, which was fought between the County of Flanders and the Kingdom of France. Conscience offered a romantic account of the historical event, and included a love story between a daughter of the count of Flanders and a brave knight. The historical novel had a large impact on the Flemish national movement in the nineteenth century. Nationalists considered the Battle of the Golden Spurs, as told by Conscience, as the starting point of Flemish emancipation from the French-speaking elite*.

In France, Victor Hugo was one of the most prominent Romantic novelists who took Scott as a role model. Many elements of *Notre-Dame de Paris* (1831) were inspired by *Ivanhoe*. The story was set in Paris in 1482 and deals with the unrequited love of the hunchback Quasimodo for the gypsy Esmeralda. Quasimodo is an ugly outcast who is raised by the deacon Frollo. Both of them have feelings for Esmeralda, but she is enamoured with the handsome soldier Phoebus. Frollo's jealousy makes him accuse Esmeralda of witchcraft. Quasimodo tries to save her from hanging, but in the end she is captured and brought to death. Quasimodo murders the deacon and then commits suicide. Just as Scott did, Hugo used the medieval past to comment upon contemporary issues. In contrast with Scott, however, Hugo clearly sympathized with the less privileged and criticized the social inequalities of contemporary society.

In some cases, the admiration of Scott went so far that authors crossed the line of the acceptable. Such was the case with the Spanish novelist Ramón López Soler. For a long time, he was regarded as one of the great inventors of the Spanish historical novel, but his reputation changed when it became clear how much he had copied and pasted from Scott's work. His most well-known novel, *Los bandos de Castilla o el caballero del Cisne* ('The gangs of Castilla or the knight of Cisne', 1830) was, in fact, a compilation of translated fragments from *Waverley*, *Ivanhoe* and *Quentin Durward*, while many characters were exact copies of those of Scott. He also included a translation of a poem by Byron and pretended this to be an authentic Catalan song. Another Spanish follower of Scott, whose reputation is less disputable, was Francisco Navarro Villoslada (1818–1895). This author, who was often called "el Walter Scott español", published several historical novels between 1840 and 1850, but his work soon fell into oblivion. The works of Benito Pérez Galdós, who tackled more recent history in his *Episodios Nacionales* ('National episodes', 1873–1912), became canonical, however. This collection of forty-six historical novels started with the Battle of Trafalgar of 1805 and continued to the early years of the Restoration in the 1880s. His use of "average Spaniards" and the addition of characteristic fictional characters were inspired by Scott's works. The series was very successful and is generally acknowledged as an important expression of Spanish national identity in those days.

Finally, Scott's influence can also be witnessed in the Eastern European countries. Two of the greatest Russian writers, Alexander Pushkin and Lev Tolstoy, were possibly influenced by the Waverley novels. The former published a historical novel in 1836, *The Captain's Daughter*, which bore many traces of Ivanhoe. The Russian readers were taken back to the years 1773–1775, when Pugachev led a revolt during the reign of Catherine II. Against this background a love story unfolds between Pyotr and Masha. At first Pyotr does not receive his father's permission to marry her, but after having rescued her from a fortress the two are wedded.

This tour makes clear that Scott had a huge impact on the European literary landscape. His influence cannot only be traced back to the level of the plot or specific characters in works of other novelists, but he also contributed to the generic features of the nineteenth-century novel in general. In a similar manner, European writers presented their readers with vivid descriptions of the local costumes, landscapes and manners in the past while *supplanting* political messages about the present at the same time.

Remediation and collective memory

Although Walter Scott wrote many poems and novels, one particular work became an all-pervasive point of reference up until today: *Ivanhoe*. No other nineteenth-century novel has been disseminated so widely and reprinted, remediated and re-enacted so many times. Adaptations include theatre plays, operas, paintings, board games, children's books, comic books and computer games. A major Hollywood movie (1952) and two television series (1958, 1997) have added significantly to its popularity.

The character of the Jewish woman Rebecca especially captured the imagination of novelists, playwrights and artists. Many engravings and painters were made of the beautiful and slightly mysterious woman; for instance by Eugène Delacroix, who painted her abduction twice. Her position as an outcast and the open ending also gave rise to various interpretations. In 1832, the English sociologist and writer Harriet Martineau, for instance, took Rebecca as a role model for the cause of women:

> Yes, women may choose Rebecca as representative of their capabilities: first despised, then wondered at, and involuntarily admired; tempted, made use of, then persecuted, and finally banished – not by a formal decree, but by being refused honourable occupation, and a safe abiding place. Let women not only take her for their model, but make her speak for them to society, till they have obtained the educational discipline which beseems them; the rights, political and social, which are their due.[8]

For Martineau, the marginal position of Rebecca was symbolical for the subordinate position of women in general.

One of the most remarkable reactions to *Ivanhoe* was a satiric story by William Makepeace Thackeray, *Rebecca and Rowena: A Romance upon Romance* (1850). Thackeray offers a sequel* to the story out of dissatisfaction with the ending. He imagines how their life continues after the wedding: Ivanhoe is extremely bored sitting at home, while Rowena is unable to cope with her jealousy of Rebecca. The restless knight leaves home to go fighting again but is killed on the battlefield. Rowena quickly remarries Athelstane, but later it appears that Ivanhoe is not dead at all. When both Athelstane and Rowena have passed away, Ivanhoe remarries Rebecca, who has converted to Christianity.

Thackeray mocks many elements of the original novel, such as the unlikely resurrection of Athelstane, Ivanhoe's ongoing successes as a warrior, the continuous narrative interventions and the intermittent singing of medieval ballads by the characters. Thackeray exaggerates Ivanhoe's bravery to the extreme, repeatedly mentioning the number of enemies he has killed during the fights:

> The valour displayed by Ivanhoe, in all these contests, was prodigious; and the way in which he escaped from death from the discharges of mangonels, catapults, battering-rams, twenty-four pounders, boiling-oil, and other artillery, with the besieged received their enemies was remarkable . . . . he would kill you off a couple of hundred of them of Chalus, whilst the strongest champions of the King's host could not finish more than their two dozen a day.[9]

Ivanhoe's heroic deeds are so many that the author gets bored by his own story:

> The account of all the battles, storms, and scaladoes in which Sir Wilfrid took part, would only weary the reader, for the chopping off one heathen's head with an axe must be very like the decapitation of any other unbeliever.[10]

The many cartoons in the volume, which portray Ivanhoe as a saint whilst chopping off heads, reinforce the satiric character of the novel.

Thackeray's satire*, however, reaches further than Scott's novel: it can also be read as a general critique on the historical novel, which offered too many unrealistic events and offered a highly idealistic world. When Thackeray published his parody*, the historical novel had already started to decline in popularity and been replaced by a new form: the realistic novel*.

Today, the durable legacy of *Ivanhoe* probably has more to do with the recycling of the protagonist's name on a various range of objects – ranging from street names and metro stations to bicycles and walking trails – then with literacy*. Nevertheless, mentioning *Ivanhoe* immediately recalls associations with medieval England, fighting knights and bravery. As such, *Ivanhoe* still occupies a firm position in Europe's cultural memory*.

Notes

1   Walter Scott, *Ivanhoe*, ed. with an introduction by Graham Tuloch (London: Penguin Books, 2000), 111–12.
2   Simon Bainbridge, *British Poetry and the Revolutionary Wars: Visions of Conflict* (Oxford: Oxford University Press, 2003), 120–1.
3   Thomas Percy, *Reliques of Ancient English Poetry*, vol. 3 (London: J. Dodsley, 1765), 314.
4   Joep Leerssen, *National Thought in Europe: A Cultural History*, second edition (Amsterdam: Amsterdam University Press, 2008), 105–26, 118.
5   Bainbridge, *British Poetry*, 120–39.
6   "Was ist des Deutschen Vaterland?/ Ist's Preussenland, ist's Schwabenland?/ Ist's, wo am Rhein die Rebe blüht?/ Ist's, wo am Belt die Möwe zieht?/ O nein! nein! nein! /Sein Vaterland muss grösser sein!" In Ernst Moritz Arndt, *Gedichte: Vollständige Sammlung* (Berlin: Weidmansche Buchhandlung, 1860), 233.
7   Georg Gordon Byron, *The Works of Lord Byron, Including the Suppressed Poems* (Paris: A. and W. Galignani, 1831), 40.
8   Harriet Martineau, "The Achievements of the Genius of Scott," *Tait's Edinburgh Magazine* 9.7 (1832): 457.

9 Mr. M.A. Titmarsh [William Makepeace Thackeray], *Rebecca and Rowena: A Romance Upon Romance*, with illustrations by Richard Doyle (London: Chapman and Hall, 1850), 26–7.

10 Titmarsh, *Rebecca and Rowena*, 77.

Further reading

Bainbridge, Simon, ed. *Romanticism: A Source Book*. Houndmills: Palgrave Macmillan, 2008.

Hamnett, Brian. *The Historical Novel in Nineteenth-Century Europe: Representations of Reality and Fiction*. Oxford: Oxford University Press, 2011.

Leerssen, Joep. *National Thought in Europe: A Cultural History*. Second edition. Amsterdam: Amsterdam University Press, 2008.

Pittock, Murray, ed. *The Reception of Sir Walter Scott in Europe*. New York: Continuum, 2006.

Robertson, Fiona, ed. *The Edinburgh Companion to Sir Walter Scott*. Edinburgh: Edinburgh University Press, 2012.

22 Circulating traditions

Marguérite Corporaal and Raphaël Ingelbien

Figure 22.1 Henry Justice Ford, "The Snow Queen Takes Kay in Her Sledge". Drawing by Henry J. Ford
for the fairy tale by Hans Christian Andersen, 1886–1920

Collections of folk tales* are one of the most representative creations of nineteenth-century European literary culture. The folk tale presents itself as a short narrative that has been transmitted orally among a local community, and reflects beliefs that prevail in certain regions or countries. It often revolves around the adventures of children or lower-class individuals who must overcome obstacles in life. When they are helped or thwarted by supernatural agents, the narrative can be called a fairy tale. In due course, nineteenth-century writers would not just collect such tales, but would model both shorter and longer narratives of their own invention on the folk tale.

Early modern writers like the Frenchman Charles Perrault had also collected fairy tales, but the Enlightenment* saw the genre as a pedagogical tool that would teach moral sense to educated children. By contrast, nineteenth-century collectors saw their work as a way of preserving stories that belonged to popular culture* – the very word "folk-lore"* was, after all, coined in the nineteenth century. In their seminal collection of *Kinder und Hausmärchen* ('Children's and Household Tales', 1812), the German brothers Grimm sought to apply scientific principles drawn from the emerging disciplines of philology and textual scholarship to the rendering in print of oral stories whose origins seemed lost in timeless popular tradition.

The popularity of the folk tale was partly a nostalgic response to the encroachments of a modern, industrial and urban world on traditional, rural lifestyles, and partly a result of the rise of national consciousness in various European countries. The growing interest in oral traditions* of the common people was a central feature of the cultural nationalism* promoted by German Romantic intellectuals and movements such as the Celtic Renaissance in Ireland, the *Risorgimento* in Italy and *La Renaixença* in Catalonia – movements that frequently found inspiration in each other's tactics. The French Revolution of 1789 and the Napoleonic invasions that followed brought new ideas of statehood to Europe, while they also crystallised national forms of resistance to French aggression. If the old order had seemed restored after Napoleon's defeat in 1815, the Revolution's legacy still inspired the various uprisings that swept the continent around 1848: nations were increasingly no longer defined through dynastic power, but through the people, whose cultural identity became a source of political legitimacy. In that context, many Romantic intellectuals saw it as their task to help map and express that identity. But whereas they often viewed the folk cultures of their respective countries as repositories of pre-modern, immemorial traits that defined the national psyche, collections of folk tales frequently ended up borrowing material from other cultures.

The transnational character of folk tales

The Grimms' work as philologists was central to the emergence of German Romanticism*, yet their first collection of tales included material from Charles Perrault's *Contes* ('Tales'), even though some of these (e.g. "Sleeping Beauty") may have owed more to literary tradition* than to popular folklore (see also Chapter 18). Other supposedly "Germanic" tales could turn out to have equivalents in many different European folk traditions. Such crossovers do not just point to fundamental similarities between comparable European folk cultures, they also attest to the porousness of popular traditions: instead of preserving the ancestral purity of national traditions, oral folk cultures were in fact quite responsive to influences from abroad and from the world of print. While they saw their interest in fairy tales as part of a wider effort to map a German folk culture, the Grimms actually stopped short of calling their collections "German". Others often branded their collections with names of nations or regions, despite the inclusion of material whose origins remained elusive. Such branding could serve explicitly nationalist purposes at home: in the late nineteenth century, the Irish poet W.B.Yeats published collections such as *Fairy and Folk Tales of the Irish Peasantry* and *Irish Fairy Tales* which, originating from different parts of Ireland, transcended the more strictly local scope of earlier collections like the antiquarian Thomas Crofton Croker's *Fairy Legends and Traditions of the South of Ireland* (1825). Even so, Irish nationalist reviewers of Yeats's collections of Irish stories balked at the inclusion of "un-Irish" stories that appeared to be variants of "Teutonic" tales: thus, Samuel Lover's "The Legend of the Little Weaver of Duleek Gate" seemed modelled on the Grimms' "Das tapfere Schneiderlein" ('The Brave Little Tailor').[1]

If folk and fairy tales could be made to serve nationalist purposes for a "home" readership, they also had a clear transnational* appeal, as the genres inspired countless translations* and helped propel authors to international fame well beyond their own countries. Translations thus helped the Danish writer Hans Christian Andersen gain many more readers than he had in his own country. Such fame did not always make him a transnational author: indeed, national or regional labels were also used to brand collections that circulated in translation. Even though Andersen's tales are partly rooted in Scandinavian folklore, his original collections did not explicitly define themselves in national terms. However, translations of his work sometimes appeared bearing a national label, as in French editions of *Contes Danois d'Andersen* ('Danish Tales by Andersen', 1873). Beyond the exotic appeal of such titles, the transnational circulation of popular narratives could also serve a quasi-ethnographic function, as translations of folk tales of a particular country were offered as sources of insight into foreign national character – thus reinforcing national stereotypes* about the country or region that they were supposed to typify. Some collectors put the genre to more boldly transnational uses: Joseph Jacobs, a prolific Australian-born British folklorist with Jewish roots, produced collections of *English Fairy Tales* (1890), *Celtic Fairy Tales* (1892), and *Indian Fairy Tales* (1912), spanning different parts of the multi-ethnic British Empire, as well as an edition of the Arabic classic *One Thousand and One Nights* (1896) and a collection of *European Folk and Fairy Tales* (1916). For Jacobs, folklore was a global phenomenon, even if he often fitted its various expressions into national moulds.

The folk tale and "high culture"

The written folk tale is a typically Romantic* form in that authors claimed literary value for texts that fell short of the classical standards of taste that had dominated European literature. In the eighteenth century, "literature" largely reflected a cosmopolitan* elite* culture of sophisticated writers engaged in a rational conversation with polite, educated society. An interest in folk tales went radically against that definition. Nowhere was this more obvious than in French literary culture, whose classicism* had set the tone in European letters throughout the eighteenth century. The French Romantic novelist George Sand's turn to the rustic tale was of a piece with her reputation for political radicalism and moral unconventionality; in her prefaces, she boldly extolled the virtues of folk narratives and chastised the social prejudices of "educated" readers. Set in a French countryside where old, quasi-pagan traditions still persist, her controversial novella *La Mare au Diable* ('The Devil's Pool', 1846) purports to be the transcription of a tale told by a homely, childlike peasant to a narrator*. The latter actually apologizes for not being able to render the peasant's "antiquated and naïve" speech more successfully, even though she preserved some words of his local dialect in her tale. The transcription of folk tales faced collectors and regionalist authors with a conundrum, as the translation to print and the inevitable standardization of language that it involved could always imply a betrayal of the popular storytelling art for which they claimed aesthetic legitimacy.

In advanced societies such as England, the interest in folk stories went hand in hand with the nostalgic perception that such beliefs had vanished from modern life. A keen reader of fairy tales, the protagonist of Charlotte Brontë's *Jane Eyre* (1847) laments that elves are "all gone out of England to some savage country where the woods were wilder and thicker, and the population more scant."[2] At the same time, folk tale elements were also recycled in archetypal stories set in modern environments, which resulted in types of fiction characterised by a blend of realism* and Romanticism*. Jane Eyre may think that the fairies have vanished from England, but Brontë's romance sees the protagonist, a little governess, married to the dark, mysterious aristocrat she secretly loved: Brontë's novel* frequently echoes fairy tales like "Cinderella" and "Bluebeard". Through its international popularity and countless film adaptations, a novel like *Jane Eyre* has itself fed back into a global popular culture, taking its place alongside the folk and fairy tales whose passing it mourned.

The folk tale's entry into modern print culture* was further marked by complex inter-actions with "high" culture. Some authors suggested daring comparisons between the folk material they were presenting and more elevated forms of art. George Sand thus boldly invoked Virgil's Latin poem *Georgics* and the German Renaissance painter Holbein's etchings of *Images of Death* to introduce the simple peasant tale that makes up *La Mare au Diable*, simultaneously inserting the narrative within a transnational and transmedial* frame of artistic references. Other writers suggested parallels with canonical literature* through the use of epigraphs*: the title page of some editions of Croker's *Fairy Legends and Traditions of the South of Ireland* bore a quotation from Shakespeare's *A Midsummer Night's Dream*, thus establishing a kinship between Irish folklore and the towering figure of English literature. High culture itself was in its turn responsive to the folk tale. Although Yeats's highbrow, modernist poetry* seems to be far removed from his interest in local fairy lore, he clearly did not see those two dimensions of his work as incompatible. Neither was his interest in the genre limited by an Irish perspective: in a sophisticated, modernist poem like "Sailing to Byzantium" (1928), Yeats uses imagery that would remain obscure without a knowledge of "The Nightingale", a tale by Hans Christian Andersen to which some of Yeats's lines allude.

Within and beyond the local: regionalist literature

Folk tales mostly belonged to a pre-modern rural culture that was fast disappearing in the very countries where antiquarians set about collecting such stories, and its traces mostly persisted in backward or peripheral regions. Nineteenth-century European literatures not only show an interest in folk traditions, but also in the region, often in the form of (a collection of) local colour stories and novellas*, or through regional novels which wove local stories, beliefs and customs into the texture of realist fiction set in rural circumstances. An example is Serafín Estébanez Calderón's *Escenas Andaluzas* ('Andalusian scenes', 1847), a collection of anecdotes, essays and stories that present provincial life in the South of Spain and includes scenes of bull fighting as well as references to traditional *caña* and *polo* flamenco music. This regionalist literature*, that often reads like an anthropological inventory, depicted the local customs, vernacular and landscape of specific regions – in particular rural communities which were regarded as more traditional or even backward. The Italian Giovanni Verga's Sicily, the Frenchman Alphonse Daudet's Rhône Valley and Provence, and the Swedish Selma Lagerlöf's Värmland were depicted as places where indigenous dialects and folk memories still survived despite the rapid modernisation and urbanisation of European societies. Influenced on the one hand by the emerging genre of realism in its minute documentation of local colour, and on the other by Romanticism in its nostalgia for a world that is gradually disappearing, regionalist literature expresses a strong ambivalence towards the wider world and towards modernity.

One example of a character that rejects modern city life is Pauli Lohner, the wood-carver in Ludwig Ganghofer's *Heimatroman, Der Herrgottschnitzer von Ammergau: Eine Hoch-landsgeschichte* ('The Crucifix Carver of Ammergau: A History of the Highlands', 1890). He has strong artistic abilities but declines an offer to leave his native village in order to go to art school in Munich. As an "Ammegauer" by birth, Pauli feels he belongs to the region of his birth, for people born there have a natural calling to become *Herrgottschnitzler*, i.e. a carver of religious wood work. In one of the novels that made the rural West of Eng-land famous as the fictional county of "Wessex", the protagonist of Thomas Hardy's *The Return of the Native* (1878) gave up a successful business career in Paris to come back to his native village and become a schoolteacher for the poor – an ambition that disappoints his new wife, who hopes to escape with him to the continent. Alphonse's Daudet story "Le Secret de Maître Cornille" ('The Secret of Master Cornille'), included in his collection *Lettres de mon moulin* ('Letters from My Mill', 1869), shows the devastating effects of mod-ernisation on the local community. It relates the resistance of a local miller to the newly opened steam flour mill, an initiative of some Parisians, which has led to the closure of all wind-mills. Convinced that the steam mill will produce meal that will poison the villag-ers, Cornille keeps his wind-mill running without grinding anything in it. While Selma Lagerlöf's *Gosta Berlings Saga* (1890) does not depict a similar clash between an old and a new world, it evokes the idea of a closed-off oral cultural community at the Ekeby estate in the imaginary Lake Löven region (based on Lake Frykken), as the deposed minister Gosta and his fellow cavaliers spend the evening playing musical instruments and telling each other traditional sayings, fancies and songs.

Although European regionalist literatures display an inward-looking, anti-modern, anti-urban perspective, they simultaneously reach out on a transregional level in several respects. For one thing, regionalist narratives often incorporate a plot about the arrival of an outsider to the community, who, coming from a different (urban) region or country, fails to fit in and often becomes a source of communal conflict. Thus, in "The Minister of Dour" from the collection *Bog-Myrtle and Peat* (1895) by Scottish writer Samuel Ruther-ford Crockett, the villagers turn against their new minister Abraham Liggartwood, who is foreign to the region and who chastises the fishermen's "black, solemn, evil-hearted drinking."[3] Liggartwood is ostracised by the community to the point that children are no longer baptised in the parish church, but relations improve when the minister goes out of his way to care for the fishermen and their families once there is an outbreak of the "White Death". After this episode, the minister becomes incorporated into village society, and his final resting place in the churchyard even becomes a monument to the indigenous people. A travelling foreigner in Jane Barlow's *Irish Idylls* (1892), "a hapless Neapolitan organ-grinder ... with his monkey clinging round his neck" who strayed into the region, does not survive "in the vast, murky, sunless world" of Ireland's West to which only natives of the region can adjust.[4] He and his monkey die and, generations later, his grave is mistaken for that of a Frenchman, as all foreigners are indistinctively classified as "French" by the local community.

The foreigner is thus included in regionalist literature as the means to underscore the values and boundaries of the local community, leading to his or her expulsion from or eventual successful inclusion into the regional community. At the same time, regionalist fiction often consciously moves beyond the borders of the regional community that is represented, by inviting identification with the region from a readership* that is geographically and culturally removed from it. Daudet's *Lettres de mon moulin* are presented as letters* written from a mill that is inhabited by the author, a former citizen of Paris, to a Parisian readership, assuring them that he does not miss black and bustling Paris as he is very content in his sweet-smelling spot in the Provence. The narrator thus writes back from the peripheral region of the nation to its centre.

Several scholars on regionalist literature and culture of the nineteenth century have argued that regionalism functioned as a tool in nation-building. The stories set in different parts of a country or even empire serve to make readers from different geographical parts aware of and able to identify with the diversity of their nation and to stimulate a sense of cohesion. They connected bourgeois readers in urban centres with the popular traditions of underdeveloped regions that were sometimes politically marginalised, and thus invested the nation's peripheries with symbolic significance. Often, regionalist fiction found its way to nationwide audiences through publication in widely disseminated periodicals*, thereby familiarising readers across the country with the traditional, regional subcultures* within its geographical boundaries. Thus, Lagerlöf's *Gosta Berlings Saga* had originally been written for the Swedish popular magazine* *Idun*. Several of Daudet's stories included in *Lettres de mon moulin* had first appeared in *Le Figaro* and *L'Événement*.

From the 1830s, nationalism was often rooted in identification with the rural land, and this is a tendency we see reflected in art: in paintings by Ettore Tito in Italy, by Ketty Gilsoul-Hoppe in Belgium, by Jacek Malczewski in Poland and by Akseli Gallen-Kallela in Finland, the rural region functions as an expression of national authenticity. Pietro Mascagni's opera *Cavalleria Rusticana*, which was based on Giovanni Verga's novella of the same title ('Rustic Chivalry', 1880), premiered in Milan on 17 May 1890 and was interpreted through its political resonances in an Italian context, because Verga's protagonist Turiddu was a soldier in the king's army. European regionalist fiction bears witness to a similar tendency to portray the region as the microcosmic nation. William Carleton, in his *Traits and Stories of the Irish Peasantry* (1836), sketches the traditions and vernacular of the rural labourers in his native County Tyrone, such as matchmaking rituals, wakes, cooking traditions and superstitions. Simultaneously, the preface frames the regional characters that feature in the collected tales as national types, stating that the readers will be acquainted with "the condition and character of the peasantry of Ireland." Drawing such a national character of the Irish, Carleton specifically addresses English audiences, seeking to sketch the brighter and "darker shades of the Irish character."[5]

Likewise, Berthold Auerbach presents his stories of the Black Forest region, *Schwarzwälder Dorfgeschichte* ('Village Stories from the Black Forest', 1843) as expressions of a provincial life that will generate a consciousness of "Vereinigung und Einheit" ('community and unity') that underscores the process of German unification.[6] Furthermore, a focus on the region could also question the national narrative that folk tales would normally be made to serve. Writing from Milan, one of the cultural centres of a newly unified Italy, Giovanni Verga set the dour, naturalistic regional tales of *Vita dei Campi* ('Life in the Fields' 1880) in his native Sicily, calling attention to the endemic poverty of the southern regions that had not benefited from the *Risorgimento*, but where Italian life was still to be met with in more authentic forms than in the modernising cities of the north.

The politics of regionalist literature

Regionalist literatures flourished during a rather long time span, ranging from the early nineteenth to the early twentieth century; the phenomenon can be attributed to the fact that nationalist movements in Europe took place across different decades and regionalist literature was specifically popular in geographical areas that sought to claim political or cultural autonomy. Emerging nations, such as Germany and Italy, witnessed a strong output of regionalist writing that fitted in with the ideologies of the *Bürgertum* and *Risorgimento* (1850–1870) movements. Flemish nationalism, which followed upon the Belgian revolution of 1830, sought to establish a distinct Flemish identity and, after 1880, strove for greater political autonomy. This led to an outpouring of sociohistorical publications on Flanders regional cultures by Alfons de Cock and Pol de Mont, who co-founded the journal* *Volkskunde* ('Knowledge of the People') in 1888; and in 1893 supporters of the Vlaamse Beweging such as August Vermeylen and the poet Karel van de Woestijne, who set up the magazine *Van Nu en Straks* ('Of the Present and Future'), saw literary aspirations as the vanguard of a struggle for the broader cultural recognition of the Flemish language. In Ireland, the fetishisation of the Western regions by the Celtic Renaissance in the 1880s and 1890s was similarly rooted in ideologies of cultural nationalism; that is, the dissemination of nationalist ideas through the arts and literature. It inspired a rich tradition of regionalist writing set in Connemara by, among others, Jane Barlow and Katharine Tynan.

Regionalist literatures of the nineteenth century also wrote back to political and social elite groups, in order to criticise the marginalisation of specific areas or the conditions of certain classes. Daudet's *Lettres de mon Moulin* show that the once flourishing artisan community in the Provence has suffered from the mechanization brought by the elite industrialists from Paris. In *Traits and Stories of the Irish Peasantry*, Carleton writes back to the heart of the British Empire by subverting common colonial stereotypes* about the Irish as backward people who lack cultural sophistication: "That the Irish either were or are a people remarkable for making bulls or blunders, is an imputation utterly unfounded, and in every sense untrue."[7] The harsh circumstances under which the Irish peasants labour also form a central theme in his stories, and regional tales like "Owen McCarthy or the Landlord and Tenant", published in *Alley Sheridan and Other Stories* (1858) depict the deprivations of the rural population who face starvation and eviction from their cottages by the landed class. Similar themes are addressed by Verga in "Don Licciu Papa" from *Novelle Rusticane* (1883): bailiffs are ushered in to seize the cattle of farmers such as Vito who are in arrears of payment. Farmers who can no longer pay the rent and are therefore cast out of their cottages also feature in works by other European regionalist writers like Flemish Hendrik Conscience. In *De Plaag der Dorpen* ('The Scourge of Villages', 1875), Boer Staers will be evicted from his farm. His plight is a result of his alcoholism, but Conscience's narrative also foregrounds the relative poverty of hardworking, morally upright agricultural labourers such as tenant Torfs.

The circulation of folk tales and regionalist writing

Because European regionalist literatures became immensely popular during the second half of the nineteenth century, one can speak of a transnational genre. The transnational nature of regionalist fiction is also revealed by its audiences. Immigrant communities in especially North America would often write and read regional stories about the country of origin as a way to cement transatlantic cultural ties. Thus, Alice Nolan's novel *The Byrnes of Glengoulah* (1868) aims to acquaint second generations of Irish Americans who "never saw the old historic land of their fathers" with the "beautiful County of Wicklow, in Ireland."[8] Furthermore, many European works of regional fiction were translated and published in other European countries, thereby reaching readerships across Europe. Giovanni Verga's *Vita dei Campi* was translated in French by Edouard Rod and in English by D.H. Lawrence; Lagerlöf's novel was translated as *Gösta Berling's Saga* by Lillie Tudeer in 1894; and William Carleton's *Traits and Stories of the Irish Peasantry* went through editions in German (1837) and French (1861).

Folk tales would equally travel across national borders. Their growing international circulation was sometimes accompanied by a shift in the reception* of folklore: from being seen as an expression of national consciousness, folk narratives were increasingly turned into "household tales" meant for consumption by children within the middle-class home. In contrast to the philological rigour of the brothers Grimm, Hans Christian Andersen produced stories that freely mixed oral traditions* with his own fertile imagination, and liked to cast himself as a somewhat naïve man who, because he thought like a child, naturally spoke to children. Some of his work could still be seen as a form of (Danish) Romanticism, as in tales that glorified national heroes ('Holger Danske') or that used childish innocence as a means of exposing the hypocrisy and self-delusions of the powerful. In a context where absolute monarchies (including the Danish one) were rocked by the revolutions of the early nineteenth century, a tale like "The Emperor's New Clothes" could obviously be seen as subversive: it takes a small, innocent child to point out the truth that the lackeys of the court dare not speak, i.e. that the emperor is actually naked – and, symbolically, no different from anyone else. Andersen, however, often stressed the universal Christian moralism of his work. Some tales thus extol the virtues of silent suffering and self-sacrifice. "The Little Mermaid", in which a siren falls in love with a human prince, is also a warning against impossible aspirations: despite all her efforts and her painful transformation into a human being, the mermaid will never be able to win the prince's heart; she eventually dies reconciled to her fate and gains salvation as she blesses the prince's marriage to another woman. "The Snow Queen", of which an extract is analysed in the next section, mixes a very Romantic message about the superiority of popular wisdom and childish innocence to rational learning with an explicit reference to Christian teaching, as its ending quotes the Biblical warning that the kingdom of God is only accessible to those who "become as little children".[9]

"The Snow Queen" relates the story of Gerda and Kay, two children from a big town. Since splinters of glass from a magic mirror entered his heart and eye, Kay has been under the spell of the Snow Queen, who has abducted him into her icy, wandering realm dominated by cold reason. Gerda embarks on a search for her best friend that takes her through many adventures across Scandinavia. In the sixth story, she meets two women who will help her rescue Kay from the Snow Queen.

Text: Hans Christian Andersen, Snedronningen *('The Snow Queen') (1844)*

"Oh, you poor things," said the Lapland woman; "you've a long way to run yet! You must go more than a hundred miles into Finmark, for the Snow Queen is there, staying in the country, and burning Bengal Lights every evening. I'll write a few words on a dried cod, for I have no paper, and I'll give you that as a letter to the Finland woman; she can give you better information than I."

And when Gerda had been warmed and refreshed with food and drink, the Lapland woman wrote a few words on a dried codfish, and telling Gerda to take care of these, tied her again on the Reindeer, and the Reindeer sprang away. Flash! flash! The whole night long the most beautiful blue Northern Lights were burning.

And then they got to Finmark, and knocked at the chimney of the Finland woman; for she had not even a hut. There was such a heat in the chimney that the woman herself went about almost naked. She at once loosened little Gerda's dress and took off the child's muffles and boots; otherwise it would have been too hot for her to bear. Then she laid a piece of ice on the Reindeer's head, and read what was written on the codfish; she read it three times, and when she knew it by heart, she popped the fish into the soup-cauldron, for it was eatable, and she never wasted anything...

And she went to a bed and brought out a great rolled-up fur, and unrolled it; wonderful characters were written upon it, and the Finland woman read until the perspiration ran down her forehead.

But the Reindeer again begged so hard for little Gerda, and Gerda looked at the Finland woman with such beseeching eyes, full of tears, that she began to blink again with her own, and drew the Reindeer into a corner, and whispered to him, while she laid fresh ice upon his head.

"Little Kay is certainly at the Snow Queen's, and finds everything there to his taste and thinks it is the best place in the world; but that is because he has a splinter of glass in his eye, and a little fragment in his heart; but these must be got out, or he will never be a human being again, and the Snow Queen will keep her power over him."

"But cannot you give something to little Gerda, so as to give her power over all this?"

"I can give her no greater power than she possesses already; don't you see how great that is? Don't you see how men and animals are obliged to serve her, and how she gets on so well in the world, with her naked feet? She cannot receive her power from us; it consists in this – that she is a dear, innocent child. If she herself cannot penetrate to the Snow Queen and get the glass out of little Kay, we can be of no use!"[10]

Both the Lapland woman and the Finland woman are noticeably poor: in contrast to the Snow Queen's palace, their interiors are homely but also very warm. As repositories of popular lore, the old women are opposed to the enlightened, elitist intellect symbolized by the Snow Queen and her Bengal lights. They represent an alternative culture that relies on other modes of transmission* than the world of print: the Lapland woman does not have paper, but writes a message on a dried fish, which the Finland woman commits to memory. The Finland woman herself reads strange characters written on a piece of fur. The figure of the wise old woman who tells stories around the fire is a key feature of the oral traditions that collections of folk tales paradoxically preserve in printed form.

The two old women are rooted in, and indeed defined by, their local identity. Lapland and Finland embody the outer, peripheral and rural regions of Europe, as opposed to the nameless town that Gerda and Kay grew up in, and to the cosmopolitan, rootless realm of the Snow Queen, who moves with the weather and is only "staying" in the country. Gerda's search for Kay is thus an initiatic journey for the urban child, who discovers the potential that lies in herself through an immersion in the immemorial wisdom that has been preserved in outlying rural regions.

The Finland woman's lesson is that the rationality incarnated by the Snow Queen can only be defeated if Gerda trusts her own childish innocence – etymologically, the absence of knowledge. Andersen's cultivation of folklore is here thoroughly Romantic, as it values spontaneous emotion at the expense of reason. Kay will not be a human being again until the splinters of glass are removed from his heart and eye: the glass is associated with the icy surfaces of the Snow Queen's palace and with the intellectual reflection symbolized by the magic mirror.

As an apology for the childhood realm of pure feeling and for the wisdom of local, oral, popular traditions, Andersen's story paradoxically came to resemble the Snow Queen herself in some respects: its dissemination through countless editions in different languages and the many travels of its author show how the transition to the world of nineteenth-century print made folklore part of the very cosmopolitan cultural networks* that the story implicitly criticised.

The travels of European fairy tales

The work of the brothers Grimm quickly found an echo among other antiquarians and philologists across Europe. Their mutual contacts gave rise to various forms of exchanges: for instance, the Grimms produced German translations of *Fairy Legends and Traditions of the South of Ireland* (1825) by Thomas Crofton Croker, who in turn included an English translation of the Grimms' accompanying introductory essay "Über die Elfen" ('About the Fairies') in later editions of his collection. In the Romantic era, the collection and edition of fairy tales was an intellectual pursuit that drew increased prestige from its ability to cross borders.

The brothers Grimm's collections of fairy tales were not originally intended for children: their work reflected serious scholarship and the spirit of German cultural nationalism. Re-editions and translations would change this. As the nineteenth century developed, publishers increasingly pitched such collections at young readers. The Romantic genre became commodified, as lavishly illustrated editions of folk tales became gifts for the children of affluent middle-class families. Those illustrations also contributed to the hybridisation of the folk tale, as different "national" illustrators helped frame the way each translation would be received. For instance, the English artist George Cruikshank's illustrations to the English translations of Grimms' *Kinder und Hausmärchen* ('Children's and Household Tales') often focused on humorous characters or episodes, ensuring that the English reception of the Grimms' work played down the darker aspects of the German tales. The fact that Cruikshank also illustrated some of Charles Dickens's novels further helped make the Grimms' work familiar to English readers.

The transnational reinvention of the folk tale was also partly a result of the self-fashioning of authors such as Andersen. Andersen played an active role in advancing his international reputation and increasing the popularity of his work by travelling extensively to, among other countries, Germany, Italy, France, Switzerland, the Netherlands, Belgium and England in order to initiate personal ties with literary celebrities. In June 1847, Andersen visited the London salon of Irish novelist Marguerite Gardiner, Countess of Blessington, where he was thrilled to become acquainted with the novelist Dickens. Admiring Andersen's fairy tales which had appeared in Mary Howitt's translation, *Wonderful Stories for Children*, in the preceding year, Dickens left a parcel containing twelve presentation copies of his books at Andersen's lodgings in the city. Over the next ten years, the two writers would write to each other intensively. Andersen would establish a lasting friendship with the Dutch poet Jan Jacob Lodewijk ten Kate, whom he had met during his travels to the Netherlands in 1868. Ten Kate was greatly influenced by the nationalist, folkloristic poetry of Scottish and Irish writers such as Robert Burns and Thomas Moore, and he had written free adaptations* in Dutch of Andersen's stories, published as *Winteravond Sprookjes* ('Winter Evening's Fairy Tales') in 1862.

The French critic Xavier Marmier, who was invited to Andersen's home in Denmark in 1836, was known for his collections of folk literature and songs, such as *Souvenirs de voyages et traditions populaires* ('Reminiscences of Travels and Popular Traditions', 1841) and *Chants populaires du Nord* ('Popular songs of the North', 1841). This Xavier Marmier played a significant role in the public reputation that Andersen acquired and in the reception of his stories. His biographical sketch of Andersen, published as "Vie d'un Poète" in 1837 in the *Revue de Paris*, together with a translation of Andersen's poem "The Dying Child", was frequently reprinted; for instance, as an introduction to David Soldi's popular French translation, *Contes D'Andersen* (1876). "Vie d'un Poète" represents Andersen as a self-made man who was born in poverty and denied elementary schooling, but who through perseverance and education later in life managed to attain success as a writer. Suggesting that Andersen's later fame was foretold by a local, old clairvoyant in his birth town Odense, Marmier frames Andersen's career in the manner of some of his fairy tales in which usually lowly placed and lonely characters, such as the Ugly Duckling and the Tin Soldier, overcome hardship and find their hopes realized.

Andersen would himself enhance this sense of magical redemption in the account he gave to his friend B.S. Ingemann of his visit to the Bavarian King Maximilian II at Hohenschwangau: "it was like a chapter in a fairy tale that I, the poor shoemaker's son, was traversing the mountains by the side of a king."[11] Furthermore, the ways in which Andersen underscored Marmier's interpretation of his life as a fairy tale is illustrated by his autobiography*, aptly entitled *Das Märchen meines Lebens* ('The Fairy Tale of My Life'), which had been commissioned in 1847 by the publisher Carl B. Lorck in Leipzig, as a companion to a German edition of Andersen's collected works.

Translated into English as *The True Story of My Life* (1847), the autobiography not only bears witness to Andersen's active involvement in the construction of his image as a writer, but also to his transnational reception. The fact that a Danish version of this autobiography only appeared in 1855 shows that, while Andersen tapped into and rewrote Danish folk tales, paradoxically he received more recognition for his work outside his native country. As Gilbert K. Chesterton maintained in 1916, Andersen's stories were so popular as to have "become English."[12] The strong popularity of Andersen's stories outside Denmark suggests that folk tales do not necessarily function in an exclusively regional or national context as ways to engage the people in processes of identity construction. Rather, the transeuropean interest in folklore and local colour in the nineteenth century may explain the appeal of Andersen's fairy tales across Europe. Andersen's position as a writer of folk tales is surrounded by additional paradoxes: while his stories advocate innocence and a simple, rural life, he embraced the inventions of the modern age as ways to disseminate his fame: he would not only make use of modern modes of transport to seek connections and audiences throughout Europe; he also made use of the new medium of photography to enhance his popularity in and outside Europe: over 150 photographs were made of him over the years. Andersen was the epitome of the modern author who literally and symbolically travelled through Europe.

Notes

1   Anon., "Irish Fairy Tales. Edited, with an introduction, by W.B. Yeats," *Freeman's Journal* (16 November, 1900): 3.

2 Charlotte Brontë, *Jane Eyre* (London: Penguin, 1996), 28–9.
3 Samuel Rutherford Crockett, "The Minister of Dour," in *Bog-Myrtle and Peat Tales Chiefly of Galloway* (London: Bliss, Sands and Foster, 1889), 18.
4 Jane Barlow, *Irish Idylls* (New York: Dodd, Mead and Company, 1893), 3.
5 William Carleton, *Traits and Stories of the Irish Peasantry* (Dublin: William Frederick Wakeman, 1833), vol. 1, viii.
6 Berthold Auerbach, *Schwarzwälder Dorfgeschichte* (Stuttgart: Cotta, 1869), vol. 1, ix.
7 Carleton, *Traits and Stories of the Irish Peasantry*, vol. 1, v.
8 Alice Nolan, *The Byrnes of Glengoulah* (New York: P. O'Shea, 1868), iv.
9 Matthew 18:3–4.
10 Hans Christian Andersen, "The Lapland Woman and the Finland Woman," in *The Snow Queen*, trans. Henry William Dulcken (London: George Routledge and Sons, 1895).
11 Royal Danish Ministry of Foreign Affairs, *Hans Christian Andersen* (Copenhagen: Royal Danish Ministry of Foreign Affairs, 1997), 2.
12 Gilbert K. Chesterton, *The Crimes of England* (New York: John Lane, 1916), 106.

Further reading

Bancroft, Timothy and David Hopkin, eds. *Folklore and Nationalism in Europe During the Long Nineteenth Century*. Leiden: Brill, 2012.
Koch, Arne. *Between National Fantasies and Regional Realities: The Paradox of Identity in Nineteenth-Century German Literature*. Oxford/New York: Peter Lang, 2006.
Markey, Anne. "The Discovery of Irish Folklore." *New Hibernia Review* 10.4 (2006): 21–43.
Schacker, Jennifer. *National Dreams: The Remaking of Fairy Tales in Nineteenth-Century England*. Philadelphia, PA: University of Pennsylvania Press, 2005.
Zipes, Jack. *Grimm Legacies: The Magic Spell of the Grimms' Folk and Fairy Tales*. Princeton, NJ: Princeton University Press, 2014.

23 Selling literature

Chris Louttit

Figure 23.1 Les Mystères de Paris, by Eugene Süe, Jules Rouff ed., 1891, Bibliothèque nationale de France, Paris

In 1870, the English novelist Anthony Trollope observed that "novels* are in the hands of us all." His comment acknowledged the fact that in the middle decades of the nineteenth century, social, cultural, and economic forces had created a mass market* for fiction*, making the novel form accessible, as Trollope put it, not only to "the Prime Minister" but also "to the last-appointed scullery maid."[1] This rapid commercialization* of literature between the late-1830s and mid-1850s has not gone unnoticed in critical and historical accounts of the period. The subject has, though, been approached less often from a comparative perspective. This chapter therefore sets out to move beyond the limiting frame of individual national literatures to consider some of the pan-European dimensions of these significant changes to the literary marketplace in the nineteenth century. That the phenomenon was described as "la littérature industrielle" in France and as "economic literature" by British critics is no coincidence. Literary markets* across Western Europe were affected by similar commercializing forces that radically altered how print was produced and consumed.

This chapter begins with a brief account of those radical changes that both expanded the readership* for literature and also provided the means to produce reading matter for this new public. It then considers the effect of these developments on the form of literature itself, exploring how the rise of the serial novel* not only affected the style of fiction in this period, but also realigned the relationship between authors and readers, and readers and texts. In its subsequent sections, the chapter moves beyond institutional and infrastructural questions to discuss how the commercialized literary market of the era helped shape its popular genres. Close study of the cross-cultural influence and reception* of genres such as the mysteries novel and sensation fiction* confirms, finally, that their popularity and influence extended beyond the confines of national boundaries.

The rise of a new reading public

As the century progressed, rates of literacy* steadily improved across much of Western Europe. This democratization of reading inevitably took subtly different forms in the continent's various nations. With the Loi Guizot ('Guizot law') of 1833, for instance, France established a state system of primary education. In Britain, by contrast, reforms were more haphazard and localized; nonetheless, after the Reform Act of 1832, improving educational provision and a strong culture of working-class self-improvement meant that literacy steadily increased. In both countries, marriage register records were taken as a basic measure of the ability to read and write. They showed, in the case of Great Britain that in 1841, 67 percent of men and 51 percent of women could sign their name in the register; by 1901, both figures had jumped to 97 percent. A new, much expanded, European reading public was therefore formed in the early decades of the nineteenth century. It was a public rather different from the one that had existed in the seventeenth and even eighteenth centuries. Lacking in many cases a rigorous, classical education, these new readers were predominantly city dwellers and from the working class, often with limited leisure time. They were, nevertheless, hungry for stimulating reading matter, and represented an expanding market in the 1830s and 1840s.

Significant technological advances in the production* and distribution* of print coincided with these deep changes in the make-up of the reading public. The steam printing press* was first used by the German Friedrich Koenig in 1814; its creation meant that printed pages could be produced at an increasingly rapid rate, and further developments in print technology, such as the rotary press, followed later in the century. Other crucial innovations included the substitution of old rags with wood pulp in the production of paper. This was not only cheaper than the old method; it also led to a more efficient, mechanized system, helping to produce cheap newspapers and popular editions. The continuing expansion of the railways across much of Western Europe, finally, provided a reliable and fast distribution network for the proliferation of printed matter. The reading revolution, in other words, was accompanied by a technological one.

Given such rapid social and technological change, it is understandable that many at the time responded with some concern. To middle-class commentators, the new reading public was alien and mysterious, and categorized as "the unknown public" or "the million." The products churned out by an expanded fiction industry for that public were, moreover, seen in some quarters as evidence of cultural decline, and described in heated and strongly critical terms. Such pronouncements, though, did little to stem the irresistible, rising tide of "economic literature." In the coming decades, the experience of all sorts of fiction would be significantly altered as a result of these commercializing forces.

The serial revolution

1836 is an important turning point in the history of European fiction. It was the year in which serial novels, those works of fiction appearing in instalments in newspapers* and magazines*, gained a strong foothold in the literary marketplace. In France, this year saw the rise, more specifically, of the *roman-feuilleton**, or newspaper novel. Its origins lie with Émile de Girardin, who founded a new popular newspaper, *La Presse*, and offered it at half the price of existing publications. Girardin wanted to increase the circulation of his paper to make up for the loss of subscription revenue; one of his innovations in attracting a broader readership was the creation of the feuilleton. Starting with Honoré de Balzac's *La Vieille Fille* ('The Old Maid', 1836), an instalment of fiction appeared on the bottom half of the front page every day. Other popular novelists of the period, such as Eugène Sue and Alexandre Dumas, produced their fiction to match the rhythms of the appearance of the feuilleton, and the serialized form persisted into the second half of the nineteenth century.

Across the Channel that same year, the serial novel took its British form with the overnight success of Charles Dickens's *The Pickwick Papers* (1836–7). Dickens had initially been hired to write copy to appear alongside illustrations by the then better-known Robert Seymour. When Seymour committed suicide, Dickens took control and shaped a hugely popular episodic novel rather than just a series of sporting sketches. Dickens subsequently released many of his novels in this format, and other authors adopted it too in an attempt to match his great success. As the century progressed, almost all of the period's significant novelists had published in serial form.

There are some differences in the ways in which serialization developed in Britain and France. In the latter, the usual serial frequency was daily; in the former, the weekly or monthly appearance of new fiction was common. In Britain, the marketplace was broader, stretching from the so-called weekly "penny bloods" – cheap magazines packed with thrilling fictions – to weightier novels published monthly in family journals; in France, the focus was on the middle-class fiction of the daily press. Beyond these contrasts, however, the rise of serialization* broadly conceived had a significant and comparable influence on the production and reception of the novel across Europe.

One effect of serialization was to alter the position of the novelist. The idea of the author as artist working for a patron* was gradually replaced by the conception of a professional man or woman of letters writing for a broad audience of readers. If a writer was regularly to meet the demands of eager readers, writing would have to become an industrialized mode of production, with serial instalments created at a weekly and even daily rate. In this context, it is perhaps unsurprising that prolific authors like Anthony Trollope confessed to machine-like work habits, and privileged hard work over inspiration. Really successful authors, moreover, tended to create a strong sense of sympathy between themselves and their audience. This expressed itself, in many cases, in enthusiastic statements about being welcomed by the reading public; in the opening number of his magazine* *Household Words*, for instance, Charles Dickens wrote of his great "ambition . . . to be admitted into many homes with affection and confidence." On some occasions, hugely popular authors such as Dickens and Eugène Sue even wrote personally to readers and changed the course of narratives in response to their comments.[2]

That Dickens and Sue had enough time to revise their work after receiving reader feedback underlines another important feature of serialization: its extension of the duration of the reading experience. Readers had to wait months or even years to find out the climax of a serial; in this regard, the serialized novel is more like modern long-running television series or soap operas than one-volume literary fiction that can be devoured in a few sittings. This elongated appearance of popular novels affected their consumption* in two main ways. The production of relatively affordable instalments – whether in newspapers, magazines, or serial parts – had the effect of spreading the cost of expensive books, and therefore brought the fiction of the day to a larger audience than had been the case before the rise of serialization. It significantly changed, too, how readers responded to and interacted with their reading; as Matthew Rubery has recently explained, since they appeared over a period of months or even years, serial texts "intertwined the fictional narrative with the reader's life" to produce a form of extended "long reading."[3] Those following the serialized work would be forced to speculate about and discuss plot developments and possible conclusions that were many months away, thus becoming more actively involved in the unfolding of the narrative.

This extension of reading time also had a strong influence on elements of the form and content of the period's fiction. The serial rhythm, for instance, encouraged authors to save exciting scenes or climaxes for the end of a particular part, thus leaving the reader wanting more. Serial novels, moreover, tended to situate themselves in the world of the expanding reading public, and described in detail surface features of contemporary situations and people. In doing so, they drew on the panoramic literature of the 1830s and 1840s, such as Dickens's *Sketches by Boz* (1833–6), which documented the changed realities of urban experience. This realist attitude was blended with the important influence of melodrama*. Social issues and the sufferings of the poor were dealt with, but in many cases an idealized solution was found to deal with such difficulties, and good inevitably (and sometimes implausibly) triumphed over evil.

The serial novel's typical combination of social realism with melodrama arose in part as a result of the demands of the new reading public for plausible but escapist fiction. The form's adoption of melodramatic elements can be explained, too, by the close relationship of the novel and the stage in this period. Major novelists like Balzac and Dickens deployed theatrical conventions* by including vivid scenes and making obvious the difference between good and bad characters, and dramatists also drew liberally on the fiction of the day in their plays. The novelists were not always entirely satisfied with the results of the theatrical adaptation* of their work, but these stage versions of popular novels expanded interest in an author and brought renewed attention to the original text. In some cases, moreover, novelists themselves adapted their own fiction for commercial benefit; one notable example was Alexandre Dumas, who staged his already phenomenally successful works of fiction *Les Trois Mousquetaires* ('The Three Musketeers', 1844) and *La Reine Margot* ('Queen Margot', 1845) at his own theatre in Paris.

What emerged, then, in this period is what Julia Thomas has labelled a "rich multimedia culture*" in which "different art forms coincided."[4] The theatricality and adaptability of the era's serial fiction was but one significant part of this development, which also saw the rise of a "pictorial" culture that both stressed the narrative elements of illustrations and painting and also very often saw images placed alongside words. The novel–feuilleton and serial–part fiction, in fact, were regularly published with one or two illustrations in each instalment. It has been assumed that these pictures gave the semi-literate an entry point into the experience of fiction; while this may be true, it should also be noted that such illustrated popular novels were part of a broader culture that was particularly sensitive to the relationship between the verbal and the visual.

Channel crossings

The rise of popular genres* is another significant feature of the "industrialization" of fiction. Genres of fiction, in the first instance, allowed authors, often writing at speed, to follow formulas and patterns. Publishers could then effectively market and promote particular types of fiction to specific sections of the reading public. Popular genres including the crime novel, supernatural stories, and adventure fiction came in and out of fashion, and were often short-lived phenomena. As the century wore on, however, genre fictions became increasingly well defined and were produced on an industrial scale. They also often had a strong impact on the literary world* beyond their own national boundaries, influencing other works of fiction written in the same style, and being printed, translated, and adapted in numerous forms.

Another watershed cultural moment provides a more focused means of beginning to explore these broad cultural trends. Between June 1842 and October 1843, Eugène Sue's *Les Mystères de Paris* ('The Mysteries of Paris') appeared serially in the *Journal des Débats*. Sue's text may be rather neglected now, but when it first appeared, it caused a literary sensation. One of the century's most popular and influential novels, it attracted a huge readership and spawned a range of spin-offs, adaptations, and imitations*. This "mystery-mania" gripped French culture in the first instance, with reading rooms rationing the time readers were allowed for the latest instalment, and a rival newspaper, *Le Courier Français*, bringing out a similarly themed serial, Paul Féval's *Les Mystères de Londres* ('The Mysteries of London', 1844). The influence of Sue's novel soon spread further. Versions of the urban mysteries novel inaugurated by Sue appeared in Germany, Spain, and the United States; Sue's followers included August Brass's *Die Mysterien von Berlin* ('The Mysteries of Berlin', 1844), E.Z.C. Judson's *The Mysteries and Miseries of New York* (1848), and Juan Martínez Villergas's *Los misterios de Madrid* ('The Mysteries of Madrid', 1844–5). The fame of *Les Mystères* also extended to the Paris and London stage, with adaptations such as *Les Bohémiens de Paris* ('The Bohemians of Paris') and *The Scamps of London* among the several that appeared in 1843 to take advantage of the great popularity of the text.

Perhaps the most significant product of this "mysterymania" beyond Sue's novel was the work of another hugely successful but now rather neglected nineteenth-century author: George W.M. Reynolds's *The Mysteries of London* (1844–8). Reynolds had lived in France for six years between 1830 and 1836, and after his return to London maintained an interest in French culture and politics. Reynolds was also an enthusiastic recycler of the ideas

of other writers; before *The Mysteries of London*, he had produced a series of plagiarisms*
of the novels of Charles Dickens. It is unsurprising, then, that he looked to imitate Sue's
great success in Paris with his own series of urban mysteries. The serialization of Reynolds's *The Mysteries* began in October 1844, a year and half after the conclusion of Sue's
Les Mystères. Its popularity exceeded that of even Sue: the serial continued to be published
in weekly numbers for the next four years and reached a mass audience around the world,
often selling forty thousand copies a week.

As critics such as Berry Chevasco and Anne Humpherys have noted, there are a number of similarities between these mystery narratives by Sue and Reynolds. Both respond
sympathetically and in detail to the plight of the working poor in the dangerous urban
environments of Paris and London. Both are built, moreover, on melodramatic foundations, stressing the contrast between the wealthy and the destitute and depending on
coincidental plotting and stock characters. Yet there are also differences in approach. These
differences arise because Reynolds's *The Mysteries of London* adapts the urban mystery
novel form to reflect the political preferences of its author and suit the demands of the
literary market for which it was created. Thus, while both authors were progressive in
their politics, Reynolds's serial novel is much more confrontational in its attacks on the
aristocracy and the injustice of their treatment of the poor; by contrast, Sue calls calmly
for the situation to be reformed more slowly. Reynolds's *Mysteries of London* is also more
explicit and direct than Sue's *Mystères* in its representation of the degradations of slum life;
this has much to do with the fact that it was published in penny weekly numbers at the
least respectable end of the print culture* of the period.

This account of the "mysterymania" of the 1840s shows that this particular popular
fictional genre was a culturally mobile one. Its cross-cultural popularity, moreover, was
far from unique. Generic trends and influences travelled around Europe. At the time
of its publication, for instance, Gustav Freytag's popular novel *Soll und Haben* ('Debit
and Credit', 1855) was viewed, both in Britain and Germany, as a German imitation
of elements of British social realism. Other Anglophone authors working in particular
generic traditions also exerted an influence on German writing. As Charlotte Woodford
has recently explained:

> Charlotte Brontë's *Jane Eyre* (1847) gave rise to a long line of governess novels in
> German by authors such as Amelie Boelte . . . [and] The American James Fenimore
> Cooper's . . . novel *The Last of the Mohicans* (1826) provided a model for many [Ger-
> man] authors [including the adventure writer Karl May].[5]

Those examples provide evidence of the strong influence of fictional genres across cultures. Popular genres also developed through time in response to the types of fiction that
preceded them. One pertinent case of these processes at work is provided by the rise of
what in the 1860s came to be called sensation fiction.

Novel sensations

In 1860s Britain, sensationalism was a cultural as well as a literary phenomenon. The term
referred to the population's growing appetite for excitement and thrills. These thrilling
experiences could be found in a number of different contexts. In the world of the theatre and popular entertainment, plays wowed audiences with shocking sensation scenes

(including heroic rescues from burning buildings or treacherous lakes) and spectators' nerves were tested by the ingenuity of famed acrobatic performers like Charles Blondin, the French tight-rope walker. The press turned increasingly to sensational modes of journalism*, which focused, in lurid detail, on high-profile divorce, bigamy, and murder trials. The fashion for the sensational was such that the theme was even satirized in well-known music hall songs and in cartoons in *Punch* magazine.

The sensation novel, brought to prominence by authors such as Mary Elizabeth Braddon, Wilkie Collins, and Mrs. Henry Wood, draws a great deal of inspiration from this cultural moment. Murder, bigamy, and spectacular plots all play an important role in the most characteristic works of sensation fiction, which also often relied closely on the reporting of actual criminal cases in the newspapers. Critics of the genre agree, however, that the influences that shaped it go beyond the period's fascination with the sensational. Sensation fiction is typically defined, in fact, as a hybrid form, one that shows a clear debt not only to journalism but also to a number of different elements of European popular culture and literature from preceding decades. There are, as Anne Humpherys has shown, important points of influence between the urban mysteries novel of the 1840s, surveyed earlier, and 1860s sensationalism.[6] The sensation genre also draws upon the influential Gothic* tradition (see Chapter 19) that developed in a number of different literary contexts from the eighteenth century onwards.

What was particularly revolutionary about sensation fiction was the way in which it brought those elements of cheap, generic literature into the world of the middle-class novel. As the nineteenth-century reviewer W. Fraser Rae memorably put it about Mary Elizabeth Braddon, perhaps the most notorious of the sensationalists:

> Others before [Braddon] have written stories of blood and lust, of atrocious crimes and hardened criminals, and these have excited the interest of a very wide circle of readers. But the class that welcomed them was the lowest in the social scale. . . . To Miss Braddon belongs the credit of having . . . published them in three volumes in place of issuing them in penny numbers. She may boast, without fear of contradiction, of having temporarily succeeded in making the literature of the Kitchen the favourite reading of the Drawing room.[7]

Literary sensationalism, in other words, succeeded in bringing what was previously published only in ephemeral "penny numbers" to the attention of the middle-class, respectable audience who read fiction primarily in more expensive, three-volume form. The sensational content found within the covers of those volumes also transposed the often foreign and exotic dangers of the Gothic romance and of crime fiction into supposedly safe domestic settings. The threat to respectable domesticity was therefore no longer a foreign or criminal other, but rather secrets and lies lurking behind closed doors.

Given such challenges to middle-class values, it is perhaps unsurprising that sensation fiction was viewed by Victorian reviewers and cultural pundits as a dangerous form. It was seen, on the one hand, as a superficial sort of writing lacking in literary merit; as fiction, it placed too much emphasis on thrilling plots and neglected careful character development and moral instruction. On the other hand, deep concerns were raised about its actual physiological effect on readers. Some commentators worried that this exciting form would encourage a nervous reaction in inexperienced female readers*, overstimulating them and making their hearts beat faster. Others were concerned that the novelistic transgressions of sensational female heroines* would be recreated in real life and encourage women to go beyond the bounds of what was considered respectable. As the novelist and critic Margaret Oliphant wrote in a contemporary review, even if women readers of sensation fiction did not "marry their grooms in fits of passion," they would nonetheless "at the very least of it . . . give and receive burning kisses and frantic embraces, and live in a voluptuous dream."[8]

The genre's transgressiveness, then, meant that it was subjected to critical attack in its own time. This very quality, however, has also led to a period of critical recovery for sensationalism since the 1970s. As a result of the rise of feminist scholarship and a cultural studies approach willing to attend to popular as well as canonical literatures, attitudes to the sensation novel have changed. The genre is no longer seen as it was in the 1860s, as mere literary trash that poses a threat to the morals of its readers. Instead, its focus on familial secrets and dangerous heroines has been given a more positive spin, and is now interpreted as a protest against the restricted nature of domesticity and feminine roles such as the "Angel in the House" in the Victorian period.

Mary Elizabeth Braddon's *Lady Audley's Secret* was one of the most influential of the first wave of sensation novels. It includes many of the typical sensational ingredients, from bigamy and attempted murder to blackmail and madness. As the following extended extract from Chapter Eight shows, the novel is also notable for containing Lucy Audley, perhaps the archetypal mad, bad, and dangerous sensation heroine. This excerpt depicts the visit of Robert Audley, the nephew of Lord Audley, and George Talboys, Lucy's estranged husband, to Audley Court, where Lucy has bigamously married Sir Michael Audley. With her secret under threat, Lucy and Sir Michael have left for London. Robert and George pay a visit to the Court nonetheless, and manage to gain access to Lucy Audley's boudoir through a secret passage, keen to catch a glimpse of Lucy's portrait.

Text: Mary Elizabeth Braddon, Lady Audley's Secret *(1862)*

By this time it was dark, the one candle carried by Robert only making one bright nucleus of light as he moved about holding it before the pictures one by one. The broad bare window looked out upon the pale sky, tinged with the last cold flicker of the dead twilight. The ivy rustled against the glass with the same ominous shiver as that which agitated every leaf in the garden, prophetic of the storm that was to come. . . .

"George Talboys," he said, "we have between us only one wax candle, a very inadequate light with which to look at a painting. Let me, therefore, request that you will suffer us to look at it one at a time: if there is one thing more disagreeable than another, it is to have a person dodging behind your back and peering over your shoulder, when you're trying to see what a picture's made of."

George fell back immediately. He took no more interest in my lady's picture than in all the other wearinesses of this troublesome world. He fell back, and leaning his forehead against the window-panes, looked out at the night.

When he turned round he saw that Robert had arranged the easel very conveniently, and that he had seated himself on a chair before it for the purpose of contemplating the painting at his leisure.

He rose as George turned round.

"Now, then, for your turn, Talboys," he said. "It's an extraordinary picture."

He took George's place at the window, and George seated himself in the chair before the easel. . . .

It was so like and yet so unlike; it was as if you had burned strange-coloured fires before my lady's face, and by their influence brought out new lines and new expressions never seen in it before. The perfection of feature, the brilliancy of colouring, were there; but I suppose the painter had copied quaint mediæval monstrosities until his brain had grown bewildered, for my lady, in his portrait of her, had something of the aspect of a beautiful fiend.[9]

The atmosphere in this scene, much like other moments in the novel's early chapters, is one of gloomy mysteriousness. Its mood is very much influenced by some of the defining features of the Gothic romance. Robert and George, after all, enter the chamber with some difficulty after crawling through a secret passage and entering via a trap door. Once inside, they view the pictures by the light of a single candle as some ivy "rustles" against the window pane. All of the trappings of the chilling Gothic tale are here, but significantly these effects are experienced, not in a far-away or long-ago Gothic setting, but in the staunchly English Audley Court in the here and now of the 1860s. A lurking sense of danger is, in other words, brought close to home.

What makes this sense of danger even more disturbing is the fact that it is also partly embodied in the strikingly contemporary, Pre-Raphaelite image of our heroine, Lucy Audley. The Pre-Raphaelites were a controversial group of Victorian artists who turned to the bright colours and flattened perspective of late-medieval art to breathe new life into the painting of the time. A Pre-Raphaelite style is obvious in the way the painting captures the "perfection of feature" and "brilliancy of colouring" in Lady Audley's face. More disturbingly, the statement that she "had something of the aspect of a beautiful fiend" evokes the many wicked women painted by Pre-Raphaelite artists like Dante Gabriel Rossetti and William Holman Hunt. Since elsewhere in the early stages of *Lady Audley's Secret* Lucy is portrayed as a doll-like and angelic figure, doting in her attention to her husband and to children, the portrait effectively begins to reveal that dark secrets lurk beneath this apparently tranquil surface. Much like this novel and others of its kind, the portrait provides a clever, meta-textual warning that appearances can be deceptive.

Yet Lucy Audley is far more than a stock stage villainess or wicked woman. Her portrayal here as a "beautiful fiend" can be read in more general terms as a provocative peeling back of the idea of female purity as a cultural value: if a woman as apparently gentle and innocent as Lucy Audley is actually a scheming, murderous "fiend", then what might lie within the hearts and minds of real Victorian women forced to uphold the cultural image of the domestic angel? In compressed form, then, the portrait raises the idea that conventional forms of feminine behaviour are but a performance to be judged by the measured assessment of men. The fact that elsewhere in the novel Lucy is described as an actress playing a part underlines the point further.

Reception

With its emphasis on thrilling plot lines, domestic secrets, and the transgression of mainstream values, it is easy to see why sensation fiction was so successful as a popular genre. The sensation novel also experienced a rich afterlife in translated popular editions in countries such as France, Germany, and the Netherlands. Mary Elizabeth Braddon and Wilkie Collins were extremely popular with readers in a number of different cultures, often going through several printings; one indication of their success is provided by the fact that forty-six of Braddon's novels and twenty-six of Collins's were translated into German. Intriguingly, as Margaret Rubik has revealed in her study of the reception of sensation fiction in Germany, sensationalism was approached slightly differently by German translators, reviewers, and readers. The genre was positioned as one that foregrounded thrilling crime narratives rather than social commentary on the position of women.[10] In more general terms, Rubik's research on the German reception of the sensation novel confirms that, even if a genre is popular in a number of cultures, the nature of that popularity often changes to fit the new context.

Novels by Braddon, Collins, and Wood did not maintain their popularity much beyond the start of the next century, and with the rise of high Modernism* their reputations sank even further. The cultural influence of the genre, though, persisted. Sensation fiction is now commonly seen, for instance, as a forerunner of the detective* novel, one of the most fertile popular genres of the twentieth century. The spirit of the critical panic that maligned the genre as aesthetically impoverished and morally corrupting, moreover, has been replayed on multiple occasions in response to concerns about the possibly malign influence of subsequent popular literary and cultural crazes. More significant for our purposes here, however, is the historical importance of sensation fiction in the context of nineteenth-century literature itself. It can be said to represent a turning point at which the popular novel was finally, as Anthony Trollope memorably put it, "in the hands of us all," from "the Prime Minister" down to the "last-appointed scullery maid." No longer luxury items only for the wealthy, novels had now become disposable household goods that could be read and enjoyed by the masses.

Notes

1 Anthony Trollope, "On English Prose Fiction as a Rational Amusement," in *Four Lectures*, ed. Morris L. Parrish (London: Constable: 1938), 108.
2 Dickens's comments are taken from Charles Dickens, "A Preliminary Word," *Household Words* 1 (1850): 1. A discussion of Eugène Sue's correspondence with some of his readers during the serialization of *Les Mystères de Paris* is provided in Peter Brooks, *Reading for the Plot: Design and Intention in Narrative* (Oxford: Clarendon Press, 1984), 163–6.
3 Matthew Rubery, "*Bleak House* in Real Time," *English Language Notes* 46 (2008): 113.
4 Julia Thomas, *Pictorial Victorians: The Inscription of Values in Word and Image* (Athens, OH: Ohio University Press, 2004), 3–4.
5 Charlotte Woodford, "Introduction: German Fiction and the Marketplace in the Nineteenth Century," in *The German Bestseller in the Late Nineteenth Century*, ed. Charlotte Woodford and Benedict Schofield (Rochester, NY: Camden House, 2012), 8.
6 Anne Humpherys, "Generic Strands and Urban Twists: The Victorian Mysteries Novel," *Victorian Studies* 34 (1991): 455.
7 W. Fraser Rae, "Sensation Novelists: Miss Braddon," *North British Review* 43 (1865): 204.
8 Margaret Oliphant, "Novels," *Blackwood's Edinburgh Magazine* 102 (1867): 259.
9 Mary Elizabeth Braddon, *Lady Audley's Secret* (Oxford: Oxford University Press, 1998), 69–71.
10 Margaret Rubik, "Die Furcht der Kritiker vor der Revolution: Der Englische Sensationsroman im Spiegel Deutscher Rezensionen in den *Blättern für Literarische Unterhaltung* und im *Magazin für Literatur des Auslandes*," in *Beiträge zur Rezeption der Britischen und Irischen Literatur des 19: Jahrhunderts im Deutschsprachigen Raum*, ed. Norbert Bachleitner (Amsterdam: Rodopi, 2000), 119–36.

Further reading

Cachin, Marie-Françoise, Diana Cooper-Richet, Jean-Yves Mollier and Claire Parfait, eds. *Au Bonheur du Feuilleton*. Paris: Creaphis Éditions, 2007.

Gilbert, Pamela K., ed. *A Companion to Sensation Fiction*. Oxford: Wiley-Blackwell, 2011.

Hughes, Linda K. and Michael Lund. *The Victorian Serial*. Charlottesville, VA: The University Press of Virginia, 1991.

Law, Graham. *Serializing Fiction in the Victorian Press*. Basingstoke: Palgrave Macmillan, 2000.

Lyons, Martyn. *Readers and Society in Nineteenth-Century France: Workers, Women, Peasants*. Basingstoke: Palgrave Macmillan, 2001.

24 Emancipating

Marguérite Corporaal and Sophie Levie

Figure 24.1 Samuel Begg, "Lady Cyclists in Battersea Park", London. Original Publication: Illustrated London news, 1895

Source: Centre Art Historical Documentation, Radboud University.

During the nineteenth century, longstanding religious beliefs were challenged by new ideas about the origins of the human species, as expressed by the works of Charles Darwin. Other existing social structures and traditions also came to be seen as confining. In his 1844 essay *The Conditions of the Working Class in England*, Friedrich Engels decried the inhuman conditions of the factory workers in Manchester and Salford. Twenty-five years later, John Stuart Mill would draw attention to another similarly appalling oppression in *The Subjection of Women* (1869): although male slavery had been abolished throughout Christian Europe, women continued to be legally subordinated. This chapter examines how literary texts from the nineteenth century reflect on these forms of confinement in terms of class* and gender* and how they attempt to imagine forms of liberation.

The cult of domesticity

Across Europe in the nineteenth century, legislation such as the Marriage Property Acts in Britain and the Napoleonic Code in France restricted women's agency and ownership of property. The period also saw the rise of the middle-class ideal of the self-effacing, nurturing mother and spouse. This ideal, which was epitomized in Austria by Friedrich von Amerling's Biedermeier family portraits, in England by Coventry Patmore's bestselling poem 'The Angel in the House' (1854) and in Spain by María del Pilar Sinués de Marco's popular domestic novel* *El ángel del hogar* ('The angel of the home', 1859), has been called the "cult of domesticity."[1]

In the second half of the century, many writers tapped into the emerging current of realism* to question this ideal of domestic femininity. This repudiation of idealizing traditions and closer examination of social roles led many realist writers to reject the cult of domesticity, to represent marriage as confinement rather than fulfilment and to expose the restricted scope of both married and unmarried women's intellectual lives. George Eliot's novel *Middlemarch* (1871–1872), for example, reveals how Dorothea Brooke's energy and talents are stifled when she marries the elderly scholar Casaubon, hoping to contribute to his research. Casaubon thwarts her aspirations to learn and uses her merely as his amanuensis. Even in her second, more fulfilling marriage to the rising politician Will Ladislaw, Dorothea's role is limited to giving "wifely help"; her friends regret "that so substantive and rare a creature should have been absorbed into the life of another, and be only known in a certain circle as a wife and mother."[2]

The adultery novel

The genre of the adultery novel*, which became popular in Europe in the middle of the century, also offered a reflection on women's position in marriage. The best-known example is Gustave Flaubert's *Madame Bovary* (1856), which centres on a physician's wife who is bored by life as a mother and spouse in a small village. Emma throws herself into affairs first with the aristocratic rake Rodolphe and later with the law clerk Léon. Ultimately, however, she never experiences the bliss and passion she has read about in the romantic fiction of her youth; the novel* ends with her suicide through arsenic poisoning. *Madame Bovary* debunks the idealizing sentimental literature of the early decades of the century, which failed to prepare women for adulthood.

Flaubert's novel was highly influential and inspired many imitations abroad. Lev Tolstoy, who arrived in Paris in February 1857, one month after the obscenity trial concerning *Madame Bovary*, may possibly have been inspired by its heroine in his portrayal of Anna

Karenina, who also commits adultery with a notorious womanizer. Unlike Emma, Anna leaves her husband to start a life with Vronsky, but their happiness is marred by the intransigence of her husband, who insists on his marital rights and denies her contact with her child, and by the social stigma of her position as an adulteress. In the end, Anna too commits suicide, jumping in front of an approaching train. *Madame Bovary* was certainly an important source for the Spanish novel *La Regenta* ('The regent', 1884–1885) by Leopoldo Alas (pseudonym, "Clarín") whose heroine, Ana Ozores, is in a childless marriage with a much older man. Feeling emotionally abandoned and suffocated by her provincial city, Ana seeks to escape dullness and depression first by cultivating a spiritual friendship with an ambitious priest Fermín de Pas and later by accepting the overtures of a provincial casanova, Álvaro Mesía.

It might be tempting to see the adulteries in these novels as rebellions against the social order. In a well-known study, Tony Tanner interpreted the adultery plot in the nineteenth-century novel as a subversion of the bourgeois social contract, which was predicated on marriage.[3] Nevertheless, the adulteries in these novels do not liberate the heroines from convention, but rather plunge them further into banality and cliché. The novel on which we will focus, *Anna Karenina*, reflects profoundly on women's role in society. Anna is Tolstoy's main protagonist, but he also portrays two other women, Anna's sister-in-law Dolly and Dolly's youngest sister Kitty, whose existence is confined by nineteenth-century morality.

Text: Lev Tolstoy, Anna Karenina *(1877)*

All happy families are alike; each unhappy family is unhappy in its own way.

All was confusion in the Oblonskys' house. The wife had found out that the husband was having an affair with their former French governess, and had announced to the husband that she could not live in the same house with him. This situation had continued for three days now, and was painfully felt by the couple themselves, as well as by all the members of the family and household. They felt that there was no sense in their living together and that people who meet accidentally at any inn have more connection with each other than they, the members of the family and household of the Oblonskys. The wife would not leave her rooms, the husband was away for the third day. The children were running all over the house as if lost; the English governess quarrelled with the housekeeper and wrote a note to a friend, asking her to find her a new place; the cook had already left the premises the day before, at dinner-time; the kitchen-maid and coachman had given notice.[4]

As the opening chapter of *Anna Karenina* implies, adultery leads to domestic misery and upheaval. The first sentence of the novel, which has been paraphrased various times in several languages, is one of the best known in nineteenth-century fiction. Stiva Oblonsky has had an extramarital affair with his children's French governess. Dolly, Stiva's wife, is inconsolable and never wants to see him again. Perhaps without the inattentive reader realising it, Tolstoy emphatically foregrounds the importance of family life, showing how this ideal becomes threatened by adultery. The first paragraph contains a number of phrases which underscore the "the cult of domesticity", such as "Family", "families", "husband", "wife", "couple", "children", "house", "household" and "housekeeper". In the narrative, these terms are, however, surrounded by upheaval and vulnerability when one of the parties involved breaches the marriage contract: the children are running about aimlessly, their mother confines herself to her room, their father stays away from home for three days, and the domestic staff are bickering and even resigning.

Anna Karenina, *bon-vivant* Stiva Oblonsky's sister, lives in St. Petersburg with her husband and son. At the request of her brother, she travels to Moscow, in an attempt to reconcile him to Dolly. When Stiva picks Anna up from the station, he introduces her to the young count Alexei Vronsky, who has come to collect his mother. Meanwhile, the young landlord Konstantin Levin has also arrived in Moscow: he is enamoured with Dolly's sister Kitty and intends to propose to her. Anna successfully mediates between her brother and Dolly, but her sojourn in Moscow has serious consequences for Vronsky, for Kitty, for Levin, but above all, for Anna's marriage with the upright but rigid Karenin.

Anna Karenina interweaves two plots: the storyline about the emerging passion between Anna and Vronsky and the responses to their affair which gradually becomes public knowledge; and the story of Levin's intellectual and emotional development. Levin's offer of marriage is initially rejected by Kitty – leading to a situation in which both suffer from heartbreak – but eventually a happy union ensues. It takes Tolstoy more than eight hundred pages to work out these plotlines*. He shows his seven protagonists (Stiva, Dolly, Levin, Kitty, Anna, Vronsky and Karenin) and their circle of family, friends and antagonists during discussions about life and death, as well as debates about social and political reform, agriculture, urban life, commerce, spiritism, art, religion*, woman's role as a wife and mother, and good versus evil. Directed by an omniscient narrator*, who renders the thoughts and feelings of the main and minor characters, readers become acquainted with an entire spectrum of ideas at a time when Russia was subject to new legislation and great societal transformations.

Tolstoy can be considered a moralist as well as a person who questioned developments. Family life and motherhood were sacred to him, he was very critical about industrialization and he saw the introduction of railways as a morally degenerate, undesirable innovation that Western Europe had launched in Russia. The train is a recurrent narrative motif with negative connotations: it features at several stages of the novel: first in the scene where Anna encounters Vronsky, and where a railway worker is accidentally run over by the vehicle; and towards the end when Anna commits suicide on the railways. However, Tolstoy does not give readers access to his personal views through the omniscient narrator. Rather, he presents different perspectives on subjects through the characters and their discussions. According to the customs of the age, it is primarily the male characters who voice their visions on society, by discussing agricultural reform, philosophy and administrative hierarchies during meetings and in the salons. It is in the writer's alter ego, Levin (a name which reminds one of *Lev* Tolstoy), that Tolstoy's personal opinions and his inquisitive nature become most visible.

In the fourth part of the novel, which consists of eight parts altogether, Stiva Oblonsky hosts a dinner for family and invited guests. The novel's core themes, adultery and woman's position, are discussed during these get-togethers. This is somewhat painful for some of those present who have or had to deal with these issues directly in their lives. Among those present are Dolly, her sister Kitty and Stiva's father-in-law, who is accompanied by his young nephew. The guests also include Konstantin Levin, who suspects that he will meet Kitty again, and his half-brother, the philosopher Sergei Ivanovich Koznyshev. Additionally, Stiva has invited "the well-known eccentric and enthusiast Pestsov, a liberal, a talker, a musician, a historian, and the dearest fifty-year-old boy,"[5] and the company also includes Turovtsyn, a family friend. Meanwhile, Anna is in St. Petersburg, pregnant with Vronsky's child, and, after disturbing scenes between her and her husband Karenin, the marriage appears to collapse. Karenin, who finds himself in a difficult position due to rumours about his private life, is also present at the dinner party, albeit against his will. While he had been determined to decline the invitation, Oblonsky had persuaded him to come after all. Earlier that day, Karenin had given Oblonsky an update of the present situation, stating that he is filing for divorce and wants to break all ties with his spouse's brother and her family. Oblonsky had urged him not to overhaste matters, and talk to Dolly first. This is one of the many moments in the novel in which scenes mirror earlier plot developments: in part one Anna travelled to Moscow to help save Stiva and Dolly's marriage; now Stiva wants Karenin to talk with Dolly in order to avert divorce.

During dinner, conversation touches upon what kind of education is preferable: classical learning or knowledge of natural sciences. Proponents and opponents exchange thoughts, and Karenin, who supports traditional education, asserts that this kind of upbringing guarantees spiritual and moral development. By contrast, Karenin believes that a modern education, focusing on natural sciences, may introduce people to harmful, revolutionary ideas. Soon afterwards, the discussion turns to the subject of women's education:

> Stepan Arkadyich [Oblonsky] had made no mistake in inviting Pestsov. With Pestsov intelligent conversation could not die down even for a moment. No sooner had Sergei Ivanovich ended the conversation with a joke than Pestsov started up a new one.
>
> "One cannot even agree," he said, "that the government has such a goal. The government is obviously guided by general considerations and remains indifferent to the influences its measures may have. For instance, the question of women's education ought to be considered as pernicious, yet the government opens courses and universities for women."
>
> And the conversation at once jumped over to the new subject of women's education.
>
> Alexei Alexandrovich [Karenin] expressed the thought that women's education was usually confused with the question of women's emancipation and could be considered pernicious only on that account.
>
> "I would suppose, on the contrary, that these two questions are inseparably connected," said Pestsov. "It's a vicious circle. Women are deprived of rights because of their lack of education, and their lack of education comes from having no rights. We mustn't forget that the subject of women is so great and so old that we often refuse to comprehend the abyss that separates them from us," he said.[6]

As the passage reveals, Pestsov assumes a liberal point of view in the debate. The philosopher Koznyshev looks for nuance by weighing arguments and counterarguments, while Karenin again expresses a conservative opinion. Karenin rejects women's education, as this opens up routes to women's emancipation. After dinner, all the gentlemen continue their discussion, and address legal inequality within marriage:

> In the conversation begun about the rights of women there were questions about the rights in marriage that it was ticklish to discuss in front of ladies. During dinner Pestsov had taken a fling at these questions several times, but Sergei Ivanovich and Stepan Arkadyich had carefully deflected him.
>
> However when they got up from the table and the ladies left, Pestsov did not follow them, but turned to Alexei Alexandrovich and began to explain the main cause of the

inequality. The inequality of the spouses, in his opinion, consisted in the fact that the unfaithfulness of a wife and the unfaithfulness of a husband were punished unequally by the law and public opinion.[7]

Karenin responds to Pestsov, observing that this inequality is the essence of the whole issue. Oblonsky once again tries to switch to another topic, realizing that the discussion about women's rights and duties in marriage must be very unpleasant to his brother-in-law. The chapter ends on a conversation between Dolly and Karenin in which the former tries to dissuade her brother-in-law from divorce. Initially, she will not believe that Anna is guilty of adultery, and even chooses her side. Karenin, however, presents her with the facts, arguing that he learned these from Anna herself:

> "It is rather difficult to be mistaken, when the wife herself announces it to her husband. Announces that eight years of life and a son – that it was all a mistake and that she wants to live over again," he said, sniffing angrily.[8]

Dolly by then acknowledges that an intolerable situation has emerged, and that reconciliation has become impossible. She thinks back of Stiva's adultery and her own grief about this. Nonetheless, she will not give up, insisting to Karenin: "But wait! You're a Christian. Think of her! What will become of her if you leave her?"[9] Karenin, however, will not be moved by Dolly's supplications and arguments. He remains determined to seek a divorce.

Through Oblonsky's manoeuvre, Kitty and Levin are sitting together at dinner. They do not participate in the discussions, but are entirely wrapped up into each other. After dinner, they hold an intimate conversation, in which women's position is also touched upon: "they resumed the conversation that had gone on at dinner about the freedom and occupations of women."[10] By the end of the evening, the misunderstandings that had come to stand between them a year previously have disappeared, and nothing seems to stand in the way of marriage. They have confessed their love for one another through a secret exchange of messages. One of them would chalk down the first letters of words that the other has to guess: "In their conversation everything had been said – that she loved him, that she would tell her father and mother, that he would come tomorrow in the morning."[11]

In the second half of the nineteenth century, everywhere across Europe women's rights were addressed in one way or another. Governments issued laws that turned the Woman Question into a political affair, and that implied social change. Philosophers, such as the previously mentioned John Stuart Mill, drew attention to the inequality between the sexes in pamphlets, and Tolstoy's *Anna Karenina* contributed to nuanced perspectives on the Woman Question by presenting a variety of viewpoints. Anna, Dolly and Kitty all struggle in their own way with ruling conventions. However, it is Anna who openly defies these conventions by abandoning her husband and son, and by living together with her lover. She thus places herself in an untenable position. While social circles in Moscow and St. Petersburg find her conduct scandalous and turn their back on her, Dolly remains loyal to her sister-in-law until the very end. Sergei Ivanovich Koznyshev, Levin's half-brother, also expresses more moderate views about Anna's chosen path. Anna, however, becomes socially isolated and paranoid, and fears that Vronsky's love of her may diminish. She is afraid of being abandoned by him, is jealous of his public contacts, makes scenes and gets entangled in her own delusions. After a series of dramatic clashes with Vronsky, she sees no other option than suicide. Tolstoy shows an adulterous woman in total despair at the end of part seven, but the omniscient narrator refrains from condemning her choices.

Beyond marriage

Other texts adopt a more radical stance, rejecting marriage altogether. In her 1888 essay 'Marriage', Mona Caird condemned the inequalities between husbands and wives, which made the institution a "vexatious failure."[12] This critique is represented in some works by women who abandon their marriages. In Victoria Benedictsson's semi-autobiographical *Pengar* ('Money', 1885), the talented Selma Berg, a girl with wilful "boyish" ways who longs to attend art school, is persuaded instead to marry the old, rich and stout squire Kristerson. Although she leads a life of luxury, she gradually comes to realize that marriage is no better than prostitution: in both cases, women are "sold." Unlike Emma Bovary, however, Selma decides against an adulterous affair with her cousin Richard and instead travels abroad to develop herself. While Benedictsson's narrative does not allow its heroine sexual fulfilment, it does suggest the possibility of achieving freedom and self-knowledge.

Henrik Ibsen's play* *Et Dukkehjem* ('A Doll's House', 1879), which premiered in Copenhagen in December 1879, similarly criticizes traditional roles and women's lack of legal autonomy. Years before the beginning of the play, Nora Helmer forges her father's signature to take out a loan for a stay in Italy for her husband Torvald who has suffered a mental collapse. In the opening scenes, an employee threatens to reveal her secret. When Torvald finds out about the loan, he becomes enraged and accuses Nora of being unfit to raise their children. Realizing that Torvald treats her merely as his doll, a plaything, Nora decides to leave him and their children to find out who she is. The ending of Ibsen's play, with Nora closing the family home's door behind her back, provoked scandal abroad. It was not performed in its original form until 1889 in England and 1894 in France, and in Germany the leading actress Hedwig Niemann-Raabe refused to play the role of a mother who deserted her family. Ibsen was forced to write an alternative ending in which Nora, confronted by her children, decides to reconcile with Torvald and return to his "doll's house."

The possibility of women's independence is explored not only through wives who leave their husbands but also through women who opt not to marry at all – the so-called "spinsters" or "odd women".[13] With a surplus of daughters on the marriage market, many middle-class women educated to be wives and mothers had to look for other modes of fulfilment and, in some cases, subsistence. A number of treatises, such as William Rathbone Greg's 'Why Are Women Redundant?' (1862) and August Bebel's *Die Frau in Vergangenheit, Gegenwart und Zukunft* ('The Woman in the Past, Present and Future', 1881), drew attention to the difficult social and economic position of these unmarried women. In literature, the issue was addressed in novels such as Gabriele Reuter's *Aus guter Familie* ('From a Good Family', 1896), which portrays a German woman from a well-to-do family who is unable to find a man who satisfies both her romantic sensibilities and her bourgeois moral principles. At first, she seeks fulfilment in art and amateur science but is eventually recruited to take care of her retired father and uncle. In the end, her emotional and intellectual needs are never truly satisfied. In its representation of the Madden sisters, George Gissing's *The Odd Women* (1893) offers an even bleaker vision of the austere lives of unmarried middle-class women who have not been educated to work. After their father's death, one sister becomes an alcoholic, while another slaves away at a boarding school until she suffers from "brain trouble and melancholia";[14] ultimately, she commits suicide.

New women

In the 1890s, however, a somewhat different vision of the unmarried woman emerged across Europe: the New Woman*. Generally from a middle- or upper-class background, this figure was well-educated and made her living in the professional world. Reactions to the type were somewhat mixed. In the popular press, the New Woman was often ridiculed as in the 1894 *Punch* cartoon "Donna Quixote", which depicts a proud and unattractive bluestocking whose incessant studying has deranged her mind. A more ambivalent treatment of the figure appears in George Bernard Shaw's play *Mrs. Warren's Profession* (1894). Determined to work hard as a teacher, Vivie Warren rejects "the romance and beauty of life" and vows to remain "permanently single."[15] While the play is not unsympathetic to her determination, her emotional coldness and lack of empathy towards her mother, a former prostitute, are disturbing. Gissing's *The Odd Women*, in contrast, offers a more positive representation of the New Woman in Rhoda Nunn, a single woman who sets up an institution to teach middle-class women professional skills so that marriage will not be their only option. Nevertheless, as in Benedictsson's novel, the emancipated woman never achieves sexual gratification: when Rhoda becomes engaged to the womanizing Everard, she is overcome by jealousy when she hears rumours of his infidelity. Although they prove to be false, Rhoda realizes that she would lose herself in a formal marriage and breaks off her engagement.

Shaw's and Gissing's works represent New Women as characters, but the term was also applied to late nineteenth-century women writers* who dedicated themselves to their craft and who addressed women's issues in their writing. The semi-autobiographical novel *The Beth Book* (1897), by Irish novelist Sarah Grand, focuses on the sexual awakening of its heroine Elizabeth who, after marrying the local doctor, quickly becomes disillusioned with the ideal of feminine sacrifice that she has grown up with. Not only does her husband cheat on her, but he is also involved in the confinement of prostitutes suffering from venereal diseases. Openly addressing taboo subjects such as brothels and sexually transmitted diseases, *The Beth Book* reveals the double standard of Victorian society. In *Hilda van Suylenburg* (1897), the Dutch author Cecile de Jong-Van Beek en Donk critiques the legal position of women in marriage and their limited educational and professional opportunities. Hilda, who has received an unconventional education from her father, decides to study law in Amsterdam and eventually achieves professional fulfilment defending lower-class women. At the same time, she enters into a satisfying relationship with the broad-minded Maarten. The novel not only offers a unique representation of a woman who does not have to sacrifice love for ambition, but it also advocates free love, professional autonomy for women and a reform of divorce laws and of women's education.

The plight of the lower classes

Many emancipated women writers undertook the defence not only of their sex but also of the lower classes, which often lived and worked in squalid conditions. In England, the Fabian society (1884), which aimed to advance equal access to wealth, power and opportunity, included among its members early feminists such as Annie Besant, Emmeline Pankhurst and Karl Marx's daughter Eleanor. In Germany, Clara Eissner Zetkin participated in the Marxist French Workers Party, edited the women's journal *Die Gleichheit* ('Equality') and participated in internationalist socialist congresses, where she drew attention to the situation of women workers.

In literature, the conditions of the poor would be one of the main themes of literary naturalism*, a movement that continued the exploration of social reality in realism (see Chapter 19) but that placed particular emphasis on the ways in which an individual's character and fate were determined by his or her biological inheritance and social environment (*milieu*). The shift towards naturalism in the 1860s can be explained by various developments in society. On the one hand, new scientific ideas and methods shaped the way writers analysed society. Influenced by the theories of Darwin, naturalist authors began to focus on the way inherited traits shape characters' lives, and the French novelist Émile Zola applied the experimental approach of Claude Bernard's *Introduction à l'étude de la médecine expérimentale* ('Introduction to the Study of Experimental Medicine', 1865) to his novels, which he viewed as laboratories in which the influence of social factors on individuals could be neutrally and scientifically observed. On the other hand, the rise of slum journalism and works such as Pierre-Jules Hetzel's *Le Diable à Paris* ('The Devil in Paris', 1845–6) and Henry Mayhew's *London Labour and the London Poor* (1851) drew attention to the misery of the working classes and the overpopulated, unsanitary neighbourhoods in which they lived.

Many naturalist novels explore the impact of these slum conditions on the lives of their inhabitants. The Goncourt brothers' *Germinie Lacerteux* (1865), for example, depicts the "underbelly" of Paris to which the orphan Germinie is sent at the age of fourteen. At the café where she waits tables, she is raped and impregnated by one of her colleagues. After her baby is born dead, she works as a domestic servant. Eventually, she becomes an alcoholic and dies of consumption. William Somerset Maugham's *Liza of Lambeth* (1897) similarly shocked readers with its detailed portrayals of the domestic violence, alcoholism and drudgery that characterized life in a London slum. After turning down a marriage proposal from a co-worker at the factory, Liza is impregnated by a married man whose wife brutally beats her. When she returns to the room she shares with her alcoholic mother, Liza gets drunk and suffers a miscarriage, which leads to her death.

With the rise of Socialist movements throughout Europe and the foundation of the International Workingmen's Association in London in 1864, the struggle of the working classes to overcome poverty became a recurrent topic in European literature. In Zola's *Germinal* (1885), the young migrant Étienne Lantier works at a mine in Northern France where he reads socialist literature and befriends the Russian émigré Souvarine. When the working conditions become unbearable, the miners go on strike and are brutally repressed by the police. After a riot breaks out, the anarchist Souvarine sabotages one of the mine shafts and inadvertently traps Étienne and several others. Although the miners' revolt is beaten down, the novel offers an optimistic vision of the solidarity of the workers, who put aside their grievances and rush to rescue the buried miners. The novel evokes the germination of a unified working-class spirit and thus holds out the promise of future change. These hopes for future reform were not conveyed by all European authors of the time. However, while conservatism ruled, writers increasingly liberated themselves from confining societal concepts.

Notes

1 See Mary Poovey, *Uneven Developments: The Ideological Work of Gender in Mid-Victorian England* (Chicago, IL: University of Chicago Press, 1989), 59.
2 George Eliot, *Middlemarch* (New York: Harper and Brothers, 1874), 287.
3 Tony Tanner, *Adultery in the Novel: Contract and Transgression* (Baltimore, MD: Johns Hopkins University Press, 1979).

4   Lev Tolstoy, *Anna Karenina: A Novel in Eight Parts*, trans. Richard Pevear and Larissa Volokhonsky, preface by John Bailey (London: Penguin Classics, 2000), 1.
5   Tolstoy, *Anna Karenina*, 374.
6   Tolstoy, *Anna Karenina*, 387–88.
7   Tolstoy, *Anna Karenina*, 391.
8   Tolstoy, *Anna Karenina*, 393.
9   Tolstoy, *Anna Karenina*, 394.
10 Tolstoy, *Anna Karenina*, 396.
11 Tolstoy, *Anna Karenina*, 398.
12 Mona Caird, "Marriage," in *The Fin de Siecle: A Reader in Cultural History, c. 1880–1900*, ed. Sally Ledger and Lyn Luckhurst (Oxford: Oxford University Press, 2000), 77.
13 See Elaine Showalter, *Sexual Anarchy: Gender and Culture at the Fin-de-Siecle* (New York:Virago, 1992), 19–25.
14 George Gissing, *The Odd Women*, ed. Arlene Young (Toronto: Broadview Press, 1998), 41.
15 George Bernard Shaw, *Mrs Warren's Profession*, ed. L.W. Conolly (Toronto: Broadview Press, 2005), 160.

Further reading

Byerlie, Alison. *Realism, Representation and the Arts in Nineteenth-Century Literature*. Cambridge: Cambridge University Press, 1997.

Foster, John Burt Jr. *Transnational Tolstoy: Between the West and the World*. New York/London: Bloomsbury Academic, 2013.

Leckie, Barbara. *Culture and Adultery: The Novel, the Newspaper and the Law, 1857–1914*. Philadelphia, PA: University of Pennsylvania Press, 1999.

Ledger, Sally. *The New Woman: Fiction and Feminism at the Fin de Siecle*. Manchester: Manchester University Press, 1997.

Morson, Gary Saul. *Anna Karenina in Our Time: Seeing More Wisely*. New Haven/London:Yale University Press, 2007.

Part V

The modern era

25 Introduction

Helleke van den Braber, Sophie Levie and Mathijs Sanders

Figure 25.1 Nikola Tesla in his laboratory in Colorado Springs around 1899, supposedly sitting reading next to his giant "magnifying transmitter" high voltage generator while the machine produced huge bolts of electricity. Inscription: "To my illustrious friend Sir William Crookes of whom I always think and whose kind letters I never answer! Nikola Tesla June 17, 1901"

Source: Public domain, image adapted by W. Piron.

The twentieth century was the century of the sexual revolution, of women's suffrage and of decolonization. It was also the age of nuclear weapons, digitalization* and the invention of the e-book. It was the century in which virtually all emperors as well as many kings lost their thrones and the century which saw the advent of radio, television and the internet. Means of communication became faster and more accessible than ever before, the rules of art were repeatedly smashed to pieces and high and low started dancing to the rhythm of the American Charleston, rock 'n' roll and house music. But more than any of this, the twentieth century saw an overwhelming number of conflicts fought on European soil. While many of these were caused by a population turning against an oppressive regime and its representatives, in some cases national or regional tensions which had been simmering under the surface for years reached the boiling point. A number of these conflicts turned into wars which gripped the entire continent or even spread out beyond European borders. The following is a long – though by no means exhaustive – list of conflicts which led to important political and social shifts across Europe: the two Russian revolutions (1905, 1917); the Balkan Wars (1912–1913); two World Wars (1914–1918, 1939–1945); the Spanish Civil War (1936–1939); the Hungarian Uprising (1956); the Prague Spring (1968); the Paris student protests, which caused great civil unrest and inspired a following in several European countries (1968); the activities of the Baader-Meinhof group in Germany and those of the Red Brigades ('Brigate Rosse') in Italy; the fall of the Berlin Wall (1989) and the consequent reforms in the Soviet Union; and the Yugoslav Wars (1991–2001). In their own way, each of these conflicts had a serious impact on the lives of ordinary civilians, both on a national and international level. For millions they brought years of terror, starvation, uncertainty, imprisonment and exile, and in the process many lost their possessions, their country or their language.

The chaos and upheaval of the twentieth century left its mark on all European literatures, albeit in different ways, both formally and stylistically speaking. In Russia, for example, the social and political struggles brought by the rise and eventual fall of Communism resonate in the works of its authors throughout the century. In his poems, Vladimir Mayakovsky reflects on the hardships endured by the Russian population in the 1920s, interwoven with reflections on private heartache and his search for a new poetic rhythm capable of representing life in the modern city. Isaac Babel, who as a special wartime correspondent experienced the battle of the Red Army on the Polish Front in 1920, captured his experiences in a series of stories collected in *Konarmiya* ('Red Cavalry', 1926). These stories of cruelty consist of prose fragments, observations by a Jewish first-person narrator on the differences between the Cossacks, the supporters of Communism, and their Catholic Polish adversaries. The violent confrontation between different traditions and beliefs depicted by Babel in *Red Cavalry* captures twentieth-century Europe's volatile political climate. Both these Russian authors bore witness, and eventually fell victim, to the transition from the Tsarist regime to Soviet rule: Mayakovsky took his own life in 1930, and Babel was executed in 1940 after a show trial in which the Military Court declared him guilty of conspiracy and anti-Soviet activities.

The collections of poems written by Anna Akhmatova in the first two decades of the century dealt with themes of love in an everyday language unusual for its time. In her later work, most notably in the poem cycle *Requiem* (1935–1940), she recounts her personal experiences and those of the Russian populace under the terror of the Stalinist purges. The explicit way in which she called the regime to account for her nation's troubles would lead to a publication ban and all-out expulsion from official circles. Unofficially, and in complete secret, she kept on writing, and in the epic* *Poema bez geroya* ('Poem without a Hero', 1940–63) she chronicles the horrors of the nine-hundred-day-long siege of Leningrad by German forces. Akhmatova stayed in Russia, somehow managing to survive the years of isolation and terror. Unlike many other writers of her generation, such as Vladimir Nabokov, she never fled to the West to join the Russian intellectual diaspora.

In 2015, the Belarusian author and journalist Svetlana Alexievich received the Nobel Prize for literature. Her book *Vremja Sekond Khend* ('Second-Hand Time', 2013) collects the stories of hundreds of men and women who lived through the Cold War and who after the fall of Soviet Russia feel forced to reconsider their view of the recent past. The publication of *U vojny ne zhenskoe litso* ('The Unwomanly Face of War', 1983) had gotten Alexievich in trouble with censors* and some years later she sought refuge in the West. Since 2011, she again resides in Belarus. Her narratives typically consist of a collage of individual people's stories presented as one uninterrupted sequence, seemingly without intervention from a narrator*. So the course of Russia's history in the twentieth century can be traced through the writings of these and other authors. In their own way, each of these four writers experimented with autobiographical subject matter and invented new forms in which to capture their experiences. Although they did so in their own language, through translation* their works reached every corner of Europe.

Similar paths can be traced through the literary expression of twentieth-century history in Germany, Spain or Hungary. From the fascist rule of the Nazis or General Franco to the Soviet domination of the Eastern Bloc, all have left their traces in European literature.

Europe

In his memoir* *Die Welt von Gestern* ('The World of Yesterday', 1942), the Austrian-Hungarian-born writer Stefan Zweig paints a nostalgic portrait of his younger days in Vienna and the disintegration of what he calls "the world of security". That world had been irrevocably destroyed by the outbreak of the First World War.

> I was born in 1881 in a great and mighty empire, in the monarchy of the Habsburgs. But do not look for it on the map; it has been swept away without trace. I grew up in Vienna, the two-thousand-year-old supranational metropolis, and was forced to leave it like a criminal before it was degraded to a German provincial city. My literary work, in the language in which I wrote it, was burned to ashes in the same land where my books made friends of millions of readers. And so I belong nowhere, and everywhere am a stranger, a guest at best. Europe, the homeland of my heart's choice, is lost to me, since it has torn itself apart suicidally a second time in a war of brother against brother.[1]

Zweig considered Europe to be his true homeland. Europeans should desire peace and mutual acceptance above all. Since the outbreak of war, however, European cultural values had become ever more threatened. The old continent was in danger of being torn apart, like the multilingual Austrian-Hungarian Empire, "the monarchy of the Habsburgs", had been after the First World War. By the 1930s, when Europe was again facing destruction, Zweig – whose books were indeed publicly burned – was facing a very real threat to his life. After rising during the 1910s and 1920s to become one of the most successful German-writing authors of his time, he now stood to lose his entire readership*. In the last years of his life, he witnessed his beloved metropolis of Vienna fall into the hands of political extremists playing on popular nationalist sentiment.

Would Europe self-destruct, or would it decide to unite after all? Should artists and intellectuals serve their respective fatherlands, or a European ideal? At the start of the First World War, quite a lot of writers chose the first option. Precious few proved immune to the hunger for war which swept the continent like a fever. But after the resulting years of conflict left many feeling disillusioned, authors began to renew international acquaintances and forge new transnational* connections. Like Zweig, many of them sought to define themselves as Europeans. The Spanish philosopher and writer José Ortega y Gasset, for example, who is best known for his *La rebelión de las masas* ('The Revolt of the Masses', 1930), made an impassioned appeal for a United States of Europe, based on a shared culture, so that Europe could once again play a leading role in world affairs. Ortega may have been naïvely optimistic when he wrote:

> There is now coming for Europeans the time when *Europe* can convert itself into a national idea. And it is much less Utopian to believe this today than it would have been to prophesy in the eleventh century the unity of Spain. The more faithful the national State of the West remains to its genuine inspiration, the more surely will it perfect itself in a gigantic continental State.[2]

Both Zweig and Ortega y Gasset longed for the recovery of the ideal of a European civilization, as did many of their writing contemporaries. They believed that literature could act as a binding force between readers and authors with different languages and nationalities. For a short time after the First World War, intellectuals and artists entertained the hope of a renewed European fervour, which found expression in magazine* titles like *L'Europe Nouvelle* (founded in 1918) and *Europäische Revue* (1925), the first issue of which contained a quote by Hugo von Hofmannsthal: "Wherever a great idea is conceived, Europe is" (*Wo ein grosser Gedanke gedacht wird, ist Europa*).[3] As the twentieth century took its course, the European "republic of letters"* grew to a colourful miscellany of voices. Going over the winners and nominees of its important literary awards*, such as the Man Booker Prize and the Prix Goncourt, it becomes evident that "new Europeans", too, have emerged at the centre of this republic. In 2015, the Algerian writer Kamel Daoud won the Prix Goncourt du Premier Roman for his novel *Meursault, contre-enquête* ('The Meursault Investigation', 2013) a re-imagining of Albert Camus's *L'étranger* ('The Stranger', 1942) from a postcolonial* perspective. By telling the story from the point of view of the brother of the nameless Arab who is murdered in Camus's novel, Daoud brings a new perspective to both the French colonial past and one of the classics of European literature.

Context

The twentieth century is the century of the city; the great cities of Europe provided a lively atmosphere of new ideas, new art and new literature. We have grown used to speaking of Proust's Paris, Italo Svevo's Trieste, Fernando Pessoa's Lisbon, and more recently of the multicultural London of Zadie Smith. Other writers led a more nomadic existence, settling somewhere for a time and then moving on. This is particularly true of some of the American writers-in-exile, like Ezra Pound, who first surfaced in the literary circles of London then stayed in Paris before setting off for Italy. Many German writers in 1930s found themselves forced to flee Nazi persecution and seek refuge elsewhere in Europe. Joseph Roth left Berlin in 1933 and spent the rest of his life until his death in 1939 living exclusively in hotels in Vienna, Paris, Brussels and Amsterdam. He used local cafés to write and meet fellow writers in exile. Not only did many Central and Eastern European émigrés settle in these cities, they also attracted American writers with an affinity for the old world, such as T.S. Eliot, Ernest Hemingway, Ezra Pound and Gertrude Stein. In the first half of the twentieth century, Vienna (around 1900), Paris (around 1910), Berlin (around 1920) and after the rise of Hitler again Paris and London (around 1930) successively attracted writers, artists and intellectuals. In and between these capital cities countless networks* sprung up of those who did not want to limit their activities to a single nation or language but sought to create an international public sphere.

Not only were these cities foci of creativity, they were also backdrops of intellectual debate. This duality shows itself in twentieth-century literature: although many writers found inspiration in the energy of modern city life, they also show the tensions inherent in the fast-paced melting pot of modern existence. The push and pull of the city, in its nature both fascinating and terrifying, drew in many young writers and artists. Some of them set their works against the background of the city they inhabited. But the big European cities provided more than just the opportunity for inspiration and accidental encounters. They also had a hand in producing new literature. The city – with its cafés, cabarets and theatres – provided a wealth of gathering places where writers and artists could meet to talk about their work. Much of the literary innovation for which this century is famous was the product of – sometimes heated – intellectual exchange. In the city, the magazines, publishers, bookstores, journalists, TV producers and internet editors necessary to disseminate literary works are within arm's reach – not to mention a large, informed readership to appreciate them. Often in the case of innovative literature, few appreciative readers could be found at first, and the response came largely from fellow writers, whose familiarity with the contemporary literary scene enabled them to evaluate the more experimental works. Only afterwards, and often in small numbers, they found their way to an outside readership, and from there (in some cases) to a mass audience*. The digital and media revolution at the end of the twentieth century helped to speed this journey from obscurity to fame along, but also meant that the popularity of particular writers and their works became more effervescent as the rate of turnover increased.

Twentieth-century literature has been called the literature of technology*. Technological advances have brought drastic changes in the pace of life, and writers have acknowledged and dealt with this quickening pace in various ways. The appearance of cars and busses at the start of the century did not only transform city life and transportation, but also the experience of distance, time and space. When the successive arrivals of radio, television and digital technology revolutionized the way in which people exchanged information, it also changed their experience of communication and human contact. On top of this, the early twentieth century saw the dawn of "the electrical age", as in many homes electric lighting was replacing the old gas lamps. Electricity altered the way in which people lived, worked and spent their free time. Whereas before, many households filled the evening hours by reading books together, now they tuned in to the wireless, watched television or spent time on other, more individual forms of media use. And so with the birth of technology, the notion of a shared, communal reality was being dismantled.

This dismantling was the result of more than just technological progress. At the start of the twentieth century, Friedrich Nietzsche had rocked the foundations of the conventional Christian worldview. He announced the death of God and urged people not to rely on a higher power. It was time people started to follow their own strong "will to power" and create their own set of values, not collectively, but individually, for themselves. To Nietzsche, the new European is a cosmopolitan individual who supersedes one nation, one culture or one belief system. Creating new values meant to take an active interest in other cultures, to expose oneself to other values and immerse oneself in the unfamiliar. But embracing the "will to power" was not necessarily an easy task: Nietzsche believed that reality was ruled by a dark, chaotic force, a destructive energy intent on thwarting any attempt at order, including man's attempts to contain it and incorporate it into a rational worldview. Many writers saw Nietzsche's ideas as a powerful antidote to old conceptual frameworks, and his ideas had an enormous influence on the way in which they experienced and wrote about reality.

Around the same time, Viennese psychiatrist Sigmund Freud was alerting writers to the fact that there is much more to reality, and writing, than the rational and the outwardly visible. Freud's discovery was that psychical processes happen mostly subconsciously, and that our passions and hidden motives control most of our actions. Still, most people adjust themselves to society's expectations by blocking their subconscious desires. Freud's ideas about the workings of the human mind became very influential, as well.

Meanwhile, the philosopher Henri Bergson was exploring the question of our experience of the passage of time, and concluded that this experience, too, varied depending on our perspective. He pleaded for a view of time and reality as flexible, almost fluid. Humanity should get rid of rigid, received notions and intractable ideas, and instead come up with versatile concepts which would be capable of grasping reality in all its meanderings and attune with the movements of the inner life of things. While all this might seem abstract, in his own time these ideas brought Bergson a great deal of fame. In Paris, he lectured before sold-out halls. So great was the enthusiasm that queuing admirers caused traffic jams in the streets.

Early twentieth century authors took inspiration from the revolutionary developments in philosophy and from the budding science of psychology*. Bergson's reflections on the experience of time, Nietzsche's precarious balance of chaos and individually imposed order, and Freud's duality of an intuitive, uncontrollable interior and a rational, adjusted, social exterior gave rise to, among others, the "perspectivist" novel*, in which events are shown through the limited points of view of its characters, generating different perspectives on the same reality.

After the Second World War, writers and philosophers continued to question the possibility of a common experience of reality. The omnipresence of technology, the ever-more-dominant presence of information sharing systems (digitalization*) and the explosive rise in the mobility of people and goods (globalization*) only added to the urgency of the question. Building on the theories of Nietzsche and Freud, philosophers came to the radical conclusion that it is impossible for language, and therefore literature, to render a universal view or theory of the world. Postmodernist* thinkers like Roland Barthes and Michel Foucault believed the world to be at its heart torn and fragmented, and rejected the notion of a single guiding principle or ideal underlying existence. Barthes concluded that the text should no longer be considered as a linear string of words revealing a single unambiguous meaning or intent (the writer's "message"). Instead he spoke of "the death of the author"*, meaning the creator of a text was no longer in complete control of what his words conveyed. In Barthes's view, what had instead developed was a kind of multidimensional textual space, in which the work of different authors from different time periods interacts and collides. The reader's role in this process is as important, if not more so, than that of the author himself.

As the twentieth century drew to a close, this idea of permeability and exchange (and its problematic nature) gained new relevancy in a different context. Under the influence of globalization and migration, the literary stage expanded and stretched ever further. Writers from different parts of the world, especially from former colonies, settled all over Europe. The borders between Europe and the rest of the world started to blur, not least of all in its literature. The work of new Europeans such as these has prompted readers and critics to re-examine existing ideas about what makes literature "European".

Literature

Twentieth-century literature has been governed by the interplay of breakaway and continuation. In prose, the realists* and naturalists* of the nineteenth century (Scott, Balzac, Tolstoy) strove for an objective representation of contemporary or historical social realities and of the laws and mechanisms which formed the basis of those realities, laws derived from historical science and evolution theory. This style of writing would be challenged in the twentieth century. Virginia Woolf claimed that her immediate predecessors like Arnold Bennett limited themselves too much to the representation of an outward reality and neglected what she called "the dark places of psychology": the hard-to-reach inner world of the human mind.[4] It was this hidden world of passions and desires that Sigmund Freud sought to expose in his study *Die Traumdeutung* ('The Interpretation of Dreams', 1900). In her essay *Modern Fiction* (1919), Woolf wrote that modern authors should not limit themselves to an anecdotal account of the everyday, but should try to register "the flickerings of that innermost flame which flashes its messages through the brain."[5] At this juncture of tradition and innovation French author Marcel Proust was writing his seminal work *A la recherche du temps perdu* ('In Search of Lost Time'), the first volume of which appeared in 1913 and the last one (posthumously) in 1927. Proust's *roman-fleuve** sparked important stylistic and thematic changes and its influence on readers and other writers should not be underestimated. Never before had a character's stream of consciousness* been represented with such nuance and precision as in this novel*. Proust also successfully amalgamated different genres: his way of registering states of consciousness and his description of intensely lived experiences and moments gave his prose a strong lyrical quality. He paints the social reality of the early twentieth century as a dazzling panorama and describes with great attention to detail the aristocratic and bourgeois circles in which the protagonist Marcel moves. Besides this, the novel contains a wealth of historical and cultural references, from technological innovations and gay culture to the terrors of the First World War in the final volume. But unlike Dickens, or Balzac in his novel sequence* *La Comédie humaine* ('The Human Comedy', 1830–1856), Proust does not limit himself to the world outside. He also offers the reader insight into his characters' inner worlds, and in a language capable of capturing the transient movements of consciousness. Because of this, Proust's writings do not make for an easy reading experience, and his works demand a very different kind of effort from readers than the novels of the nineteenth century.

In the ironically titled manifesto* *Gebruiksaanwijzing der lyriek* ('Manual for Poetry', 1927) the Belgian writer Paul van Ostaijen claims that the poet, too, is someone who speaks "difficultly."[6] In the nineteenth century, many poets still strove for ease and clarity. Acting as interpreters of collective ideas on religion* and patriotism, they aimed to reach the widest possible audience. By contrast, the new poetry of the twentieth century, like Proust's prose, often demanded the utmost of the reader's readiness to decipher its difficult language. There were still plenty of poets who strove to make themselves understood by the general public, but literary innovation expressed itself mostly through experiments with form* and content*. Influenced by the developments outlined previously, many modern poets realized that the complex and rapidly changing world could not be described by language and literature in the traditional sense. A new language was needed to capture the new age. The disappearance of old certainties, so typical of the changing way of thinking around 1900, also manifested itself in a rejection of literary traditions*. For centuries, poetry had been ruled by "laws" laid down by authoritative poets and critics concerning the nature, form and function of literature. Whoever sought a fitting form or style to treat a chosen theme in verse could refer themself to handbooks on poetry and the decrees of famous predecessors. In the twentieth century, these poetic principles lost their authority. But the relinquishment of old laws did not mean that modern writers rejected the past wholesale. Though "laws" had lost their former power, "tradition" remained an important reference point for many poets and critics. In his 1919 essay *Tradition and the Individual Talent*, T.S. Eliot writes that the true poet should commit himself to something far greater and more universal than his personal feelings, to tradition, consisting of "the whole of the literature of Europe from Homer and within it the whole of the literature of his own country."[7] The poet should always be aware of the vital presence of this tradition – which Eliot calls "the mind of Europe" – to be able to create new work within it. The polar impulses of the need for renewal and the awareness of tradition would continue to steer poetry's development during the twentieth century.

Twentieth-century theatre* would put all kinds of heretofore unquestioned relationships to the test. One example is the relationship between performers and their audiences. Throughout the century, dramatists* would experiment with the interaction between actors and audiences. This experimentation started with the naturalists, who at the end of the nineteenth century forced their audiences to fully immerse themselves in their plays. The advent of electricity made it possible for the first time in the history of the stage to dim the lights in the theatre, leaving audiences sitting in the dark and changing the experience of attending a play from a mainly social event to an intense and intimate personal experience. Later on in the century, expressionist* dramatists would also benefit from the greater power provided to actors to engage their audience. They chose to confront audiences even more directly, compelling viewers through raw, primitive imagery and writing to introspection and emotional involvement. Expressionists like the Austrian Oscar Kokoschka made the audience's imaginations work in order to make them question their values and expectations. French playwright Antonin Artaud appealed for a "Theatre of Cruelty" (*théâtre de la cruauté*), a painful sensory experience without spoken lines, completely immersing the viewer. German playwright and director Bertolt Brecht experimented in a very different way with defying the audience's expectations. Before and (especially) after the Second World War, he would inspire generations of dramatists with what he called the V-effect or *Verfremdungs*-effect*. Brecht taught his actors to play their characters so as to make it purposefully difficult for audiences to identify with them. By breaking character, engaging in routines and asides, and unemotional and distant acting, they created enough distance between audience and character to allow audience members to judge the play in an objective, critical manner. One of the playwrights inspired by this approach was Peter Handke, who would open his play *Publikumsbeschimpfung* ('Offending the Audience', 1966) with the now famous words "You will not be watching a play. No viewing pleasure will be granted to you. There will be no play to watch. We will not be playing" ("*Sie werden kein Schauspiel sehen. Ihre Schaulust wird nicht befriedigt werden. Sie werden kein Spiel sehen. Hier wird nicht gespielt werden.*")[8] Handke is questioning what theatre really is, and what the audience can expect from it. His play features no action at all, only words, and the audience is not beguiled and enchanted, but antagonized and insulted. This type of theatre aims to confront, a direction taken by more and more dramatists of the post-war generation, like the Irishman Samuel Beckett for example, who provokes his audience with minimalist plays in which action, lines and setting are reduced to the bare minimum, and actors and audiences are made to deal with long uncomfortable pauses and silences.

As the twentieth century wore on, the focus in theatrical pieces shifted from the written text to other ways of conveying meaning. Towards the end of the century, the balance between text and performance* had radically changed. Another language now prevailed, a "performative language" of action, movement and space. The playwright had lost his former power and his role as "author" of a play had been taken over by the director. It is no coincidence that theatre after 1980 is known as "director's theatre". In the 1980s and 1990s, directors like the Russian-Frenchwoman Ariane Mnouchkine and the Briton Peter Brooke helped shape a poetic and many-layered multicultural theatre, while Polish director Jan Kott rose to fame with his politically engaged, topical Shakespeare adaptations. Mnouchkine and Brooke took their plays around the world, paving the way for a new type of cross-border global theatre. In its wake, it became possible for talented directors at the start of the twenty-first century to attain a kind of international stardom, not limiting themselves to one theatrical company in one country, but directing several internationally operating companies and festivals simultaneously.

From the 1970s onwards, literature evolved into a performative art*. Poetry became an important part of literary festivals, for example in the form of poetry slams. Nineteenth- and twentieth-century novels were adapted for the screen (e.g. Jane Austen, *Pride and Prejudice*, 1940, 1995, 2005) and for the stage (e.g. Albert Camus, *The Stranger*, 2014) or rewritten from the point of view of those who had originally been secondary characters (e.g. Robin Lippincott, *Mr. Dalloway*, 1999). Graphic novels* opened up a new audience for classic works (e.g. Marcel Proust/Stéphane Heuet, *In Search of Lost Time*, 2003–2016). Authors became public figures thanks to television and internet exposure, allowing them to interact directly with audiences. And so in the course of a few decades, literature entered media culture*.

Notes

1 Stefan Zweig, *The World of Yesterday: An Autobiography* (London: Cassell and Company Ltd., 1943), 5–6.
2 José Ortega y Gasset, *The Revolt of the Masses* (London: Unwin Books, 1972), 136.
3 Hugo von Hofmannsthal, *Natur und Erkenntnis* (Berlin: Deutsche Buch-Gemeinschaft, 1957) [full text web edition; no page given].
4 Virginia Woolf, "Modern Fiction," in *The Common Reader*, ed. Virginia Woolf (London: Penguin Books, 2012), 151.
5 Woolf, "Modern Fiction," 149.
6 Paul van Ostaijen, *Gebruiksaanwijzing der lyriek* (Rimburg: Huis Clos, 2012), 34.
7 T.S. Eliot, "Tradition and the Individual Talent," in *Selected Essays* (London: Faber & Faber, 1999), 14.
8 Peter Handke, "Publikumsbeschimpfung," in *Stücke 1*, ed. Peter Handke (Frankfurt am Main: Suhrkamp, 1972), 19.

Further reading

Blom, Philipp. *The Wars Within: Life and Culture in the West, 1918–1938*. London: Atlantic Books, 2014.
Bradbury, Malcolm and James McFarlane. *Modernism 1890–1930*. Harmondsworth: Penguin Books, 1981.
Watson, Peter. *A Terrible Beauty: The People and Ideas That Shaped the Modern Mind: A History*. London: Weidenfeld and Nicolson, 2000.

26 Breaking boundaries

Sophie Levie

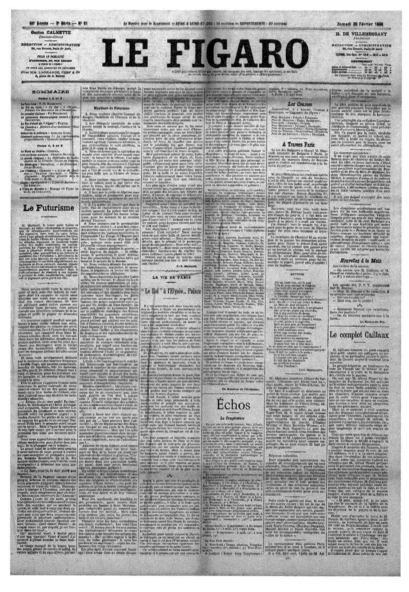

Figure 26.1 Front page of Le Figaro with the first manifesto of Futurism by Filippo Tommaso Marinetti
published February 20, 1909, article circled in blue by Marinetti

The first novel* by Italian author Gabriele d'Annunzio, *Il Piacere* (1899) opens with the description of a late wintry afternoon in Rome.

Text: Gabriele d'Annunzio, Il Piacere *('Pleasure') (1899)*

The year was ebbing away, very gently. The New Year's Eve sun radiated almost imperceptible veiled warmth, infinitely soft, golden, almost vernal, in the sky above Rome. All the roads were crowded, as on Sundays in May. On Piazza Barberini, on Piazza di Spagna, a multitude of carriages were rushing back and forth; and from the two squares the mingled and constant noise, rising up Trinità de' Monti to Via Sistina, reached the rooms of Palazzo Zuccari somewhat dulled.

The rooms were slowly filling with the scent emanating from fresh flowers in vases. Thick, fat roses were immersed in crystal goblets that rose, slender from a sort of gilded stem, widening into the shape of a diamond lily, similar to those that appear behind the Virgin in the tondo by Sandro Botticelli at the Galleria Borghese. No other form of goblet equals in elegance such a form: the flowers in that diaphanous prison seem almost to become spiritual, resembling rather a religious or loving offering.

Andrea Sperelli was awaiting a lover in his rooms. Everything around him revealed special loving care. Juniper wood burned in the fireplace and the small tea table was ready, set with majolica cups and saucers from Castel Durante decorated with mythological scenes by Luzio Dolci, ancient forms of inimitable grace, with Ovidian hexameters written in blue-black cobalt italic script below the figures. Light entered the room softened by curtains of red brocade with pomegranates, leaves and mottos embossed in spun silver. As the afternoon sun struck the windowpanes, the flowered design of the lace curtains cast its shadow on the carpet.

The clock of Trinità de' Monti sounded three thirty. There was still half an hour to wait.[1]

This fragment from the novel *Pleasure* draws heavily upon the literary tradition* from antiquity to Romanticism*. Its main character, Andrea Sperelli, is a romantically doomed, utterly egocentric hero who likes quoting from classical and Renaissance* sources. A range of sensory impressions (sounds, sights, even smells) is evoked by the narrator*, who seems to function as a camera zooming in and out of a variety of scenes. The description starts off in the neighbourhood around Piazza di Spagna before focusing on the rooms of Palazzo Zuccari, where Sperelli awaits his lover, Elena Muti. Veiled eroticism, gender play and blasphemy mark out the novel as an example of Decadentism*. It is precisely this kind of literature which the next generation of writers, the futurists* and their followers wanted to wipe out completely. D'Annunzio's literary work, which besides a number of novels consists of short stories*, poetry and plays*, is on the one hand heavily indebted to both French Symbolism and the cult of beauty pre-eminently foregrounded by Decadentism; on the other hand, his narrative style introduces twentieth-century techniques like the mixing of genres, formal experimentation and montage*. Because of the controversial content of his work and his provocative behaviour d'Annunzio soon developed a problematic relationship with the Italian State, the Catholic Church and the artistic establishment in both Italy and France. In all these respects he may be considered an important forerunner of the futurists, dadaists and surrealists as well as more moderate modernists like Joyce, a fervent admirer of his work. Moreover, his many public appearances, his interest in mass media* and his international literary and political connections make d'Annunzio the perfect example of the twentieth-century author, who is well-aware of his value on the literary market*. With its perverse interest in religion, in sexuality and its – occasional –

hints at societal upheaval, *Pleasure* seems to foreshadow the change in human relations and "the change in religion, conduct, politics, and literature" which according to Virginia Woolf took place "in, or about December, 1910."[2] How did the avant-gardists and modernists respond to this change and what were the literary fruits of their endeavours?

On 20 February 1909, readers of the French newspaper *Le Figaro* were left puzzled by an unusual front-page feature: the French version of Italian author Filippo Tommaso Marinetti's first manifesto*, *The Founding and the Manifesto of Futurism*. In a peculiarly rushed, provocative style, the author put into words the radical changes the futurists championed: a complete rejection of the literary tradition and its representatives, a search for new forms and a new aesthetic posture embracing speed, revolution and violence. In eleven articles, preceded and followed by elaborate, bewildering explications, Marinetti outlines the programme of Futurism*. The first three articles run as follows:

1.   We want to sing about the love of danger, about the use of energy and recklessness as common daily practice.
2.   Courage, boldness and rebellion will be essential elements in our poetry.
3.   Up to now, literature has extolled a contemplative stillness, rapture and reverie. We intend to glorify aggressive action, a restive wakefulness, life at the double, the slap and the punching fist.[3]

Traditional themes like beauty, time and space are obsolete; museums, libraries and similar institutions are to be destroyed; and from now on poetry is to glorify war, militarism and patriotism; these and other statements indicate the manifesto's general tone. For Marinetti, who started his career in the 1880s publishing lyric poetry in French symbolist magazines*, it marked a turn away from his literary beginnings. His call for radical renewal did not go unanswered. He followed up his *Futurist Manifesto* with a series of pamphlets* like *Let's Kill the Moonlight* (1909), *Down with the Tango and Parsifal* (1909) and *Futurist Synthesis of the War* (1914), sometimes signed only by Marinetti, sometimes also by others, which advocated literary and artistic renewal in an energetic, aggressive language and greeted the threat of war with enthusiasm. To connect with a larger audience*, Futurism took to the streets. Among Marinetti's allies were painters, dramatists and composers, with whom he organised a number of futurist manifestations across several Italian cities. These performances regularly erupted into riots. Marinetti's attitude stands in stark contrast to that of the symbolists and decadents, who strove towards a complete amalgamation of art and life in which social realities played no real part. The decadent hero, like Andrea Sperelli, the main character in d'Annunzio's *Pleasure*, has no interest in separating art from real life, but rather strives to elevate life to the level of art. Consequently, everyday realities appear to him troublesome and ultimately futile. The Italian futurists, on the other hand, aimed to integrate art into society. Rather than attempting to rise above the everyday, they insisted art should be both visible and accessible to the larger public.

Marinetti's radical call to arms is perhaps best understood in the context of this larger goal. Futurist painters succeeded in capturing the speed and energy of a cycle race in progress or a wheel spinning, the vibrant noise of machines entered into the repertoire of composers, and poets started to experiment with linguistic innovation, street slang (neologisms*, vulgarisms*) and onomatopoeia* to capture the sounds of the modern city. Traditional metre and poetic form belonging to established genres such as the sonnet* were rejected in favour of an experimental approach in which poets attempted to render the fixed meanings of words flexible again. Futurist poets aimed to surprise the reader with texts constructed according to Marinetti's theory of the *parole in libertà** ('words in free-dom'). Texts constructed according to this principle consisted of a miscellany of disparate cries and fragments seemingly randomly distributed across the page, without punctuation or regard for syntactic coherence. One of the more famous examples is Marinetti's own *Zang Tumb Tuum*, in which he draws the reader into a battle fought during the Italian-Turkish war of 1911–1912, a battle which he had experienced first-hand as a reporter. By mimicking the sounds of the battlefield in language through irregular typography, the experience of war is rendered visible to the Italian public. This strong iconic element, appealing not only to our hearing but to all of our senses, is characteristic of poetry writ-ten according to the principles outlined by Marinetti. Although d'Annunzio's novel, as we have already observed, appeals to the senses in a similar way, Marinetti's text differs radically from *Pleasure*, both in terms of its language as well as the ease and luxury which surrounds its protagonist.

The Russian futurist movement, unlike the Italian, knows not one but several starting points. From 1910 onwards, a variety of groups formed and fell apart again in quick suc-cession, entering into artistic rivalries during their short existence and continually recon-stituting themselves in changing formations. As in Italy, the painters, writers and composers participated in public manifestations, all ultimately striving towards the same main goal: rendering the rapidly changing world visible in art through new techniques and formal innovation. The manifesto *A Slap in the Face of Public Taste*, published in December 1912, would set the tone for the movement's literary exponents. In it the signatories David Burliuk, Alexander Kruchenykh, Vladimir Mayakovsky and Victor Khlebnikov distanced themselves in no uncertain terms from the literature of the nineteenth century, declar-ing Pushkin, Tolstoy and Dostoyevsky outdated and suggesting that the symbolist poets, who had lifted Russian poetry to such great heights since the 1890s, retire to their *dachas* ('country houses').[4] They turned away from language as it had existed before, rejected everything considered to belong to the realm of "good taste", and looked to expand the vocabulary through the use of derivations and neologisms. These were the essential points of their programme. At that time a number of poetry books and collections were already in circulation, allowing the public to become acquainted with the new literature. The poem *Incantation by Laughter* by the poet Velimir Khlebnikov, written in 1910, is a well-known example; it is entirely built up of newly invented nouns, adjectives and verbs such as "laughathons", "laughish" and "overlaugh", all formed by the addition of a prefix or suffix to the stem of the Russian word *smekh* ('laugh').[5] The Russian futurists, too, experimented with genre conventions* and incorporated visual as well as auditive elements into their poetry. The theoretical foundation for their poetic vision was laid in their essays, in which they introduced the key concepts of *ostranenie* ('defamiliariza-tion'*), *slovo kak takoe* ('the word as such') and *zaumnyj jazyk* ('transrational language'). In these writings, they demonstrated how the practical application of these concepts could change poetry forever.[6] We have seen how Marinetti tried to liberate the word from its nineteenth-century shackles through his theory of the *parole in libertà*. In a similar move, the Russian poets turned against earlier traditions from Pushkin to Symbolism, which they considered weak, adulterated and effeminate, advocating instead linguistic innovation and experimentation, concrete language and new possibilities for free poetic expression. In reality this gave rise to a plethora of experiments, not all equally accessible or coherent and not always getting past the level of accumulating random sounds on paper. The most internationally renowned of the experimental poets is probably Vladimir Mayakovsky. In his poem "Kindness to Horses" (1918), an old, worn-down horse slips and is ridiculed by a gathering crowd of onlookers. In the first stanza, Mayakovsky mimics the sound of horses' hooves over the Kuznetsky bridge in Moscow:

"Kindness to horses"

The hooves stooped faster,
Singing as they trod:
– Grib
Grab
Grob
Grub–.
Wind–fostered,
Ice–shod,
The street is skidded.
Onto its side, a horse
toppled,
and immediately,
the loafers gathered,
as crowds of trousers assembled up close
on the Kuznetsky,
and laughter snickered and spluttered.
– A horse tumbled!
It tumbled that horse! –
The Kuznetsky cackled,
and only I
did not mix my voice with the hooting.
I came up
and looked into
the horse's eye . . .[7]

In the following two stanzas, the "I" attempts to talk some courage into the horse, which unexpectedly rallies and sets off on its way back to the stable. Because of the way Mayakovsky has the speaker and the horse communicate, this poem stands as an example of the use of "defamiliarisation", a literary device* typical of formalist texts. Although many of the innovative literary devices found in the source text, such as unusual collocations, the oscillation between everyday language and metaphor*, and the use of half–rhyme*, are largely absent in this translation*, one has to imagine that to a Russian audience in 1918 this poem was extremely shocking, both because of its formal characteristics and its subject matter. Written shortly after the Russian revolution of 1917, with the country still in a state of chaos and people and animals starving on the streets, this poem directly addresses contemporary social troubles. A supporter of the new regime, Mayakovsky tried throughout the 1920s to meet the demands made on literary works by the political leadership, but like so many other artists and intellectuals of his day, he finally grew disenchanted with the new order; artistic freedom and Russian cultural politics proved impossible to reconcile.

In 1914, Marinetti journeyed to Russia. By this time the Russian public was not unacquainted with Italian Futurism. As early as 1909, the Russian newspaper *Vecher* ('Evening') had published an article on Marinetti's manifesto. Several exchanges had taken place between the Italian and Russian avant–garde. Starting in 1910, the magazine* *Apollon*

published a series of "Letters from Italy" informing its readership* of the latest developments regarding the Italian futurist movement. Three years later, the Italian poet Sibilla
Aleramo published an article on Italian Futurism in the renowned magazine *Russkaya
Mysl* ('Russian Thought'). In turn, the Italian futurist magazine *Poesia* published several
poems by Valery Bryusov (who may be considered to belong to the generation directly
preceding the futurists).[8] During his public appearances in Moscow and Saint Petersburg,
Marinetti behaved wholly in line with the futurist code of conduct. The Russian newspapers kept close tabs on the Western visitor and reported every detail of his controversial
speeches. He called the Kremlin absurd and spoke disparagingly of the figureheads of
nineteenth-century Realism*, calling Tolstoy a hypocrite and Dostoyevsky a hysteric.[9]
Marinetti liked to think of the Russians as his followers, but his Russian hosts deigned to
disagree. Their differences aside, Futurism in its many shades formed the first stage of a
wave of artistic innovation to hit Europe, a wave now commonly known as the "historical
avant-garde*". Apart from Futurism, the historical avant-garde is considered to include
Dadaism* (first developed in Zürich in 1916) and Surrealism* (first developed in Paris in
1919), movements which both share a number of tenets with Futurism, though there are
also plenty of differences between them. What the various avant-garde movements have
in common is a desire to rid themselves of tradition – out of tactical considerations, not
ideological ones – their participation in collective manifestations, a tendency towards formal and linguistic experimentation, and the ambition to revolutionise art in order to bring
art and society closer together. This last point finally brings us back around to d'Annunzio,
the literary forerunner of both the futurists and the high modernists, whose mixture of
decadent description with a preference for fast cars is echoed by Marinetti in his *Futurist Manifesto*. With his self-styled image and provocative public appearances, d'Annunzio
exercised a formative influence on Marinetti.[10]

Modernism

Unlike the avant-gardists, who all worked in groups, provoked their audiences with their
anti-bourgeois behaviour and openly took political stances, the more moderate authors
did not manifest themselves as a movement and never drew up a joint literary programme.
Writers like Virginia Woolf, T.S. Eliot, James Joyce, Thomas Mann, Marcel Proust and Italo
Svevo did not disseminate their ideas about literary innovation* through manifestoes,
but instead worked individually on their novels, short stories and essays. Like the avant-
gardists, they were dissatisfied with the representation of reality in the work of their predecessors and searched for new ways to capture a changing world. In their writings, they
exploit the unreliability of linguistic communication while at the same time exploring
the depth of human consciousness, the passing of time and the subconscious impulses that
move every individual. Also like the avant-gardists, they were influenced by the theories
of Nietzsche, Freud, Einstein and Bergson, and the technological and scientific advances
of the late nineteenth century. Any efforts on their part to form a separate group of their
own, however, would have been obstructed by the fact that these writers not only came
from different national traditions but also wrote in their own mother tongues. This is
not to say that they did not keep up with the latest literary developments, both national
and international. A lively exchange sprung up in newspapers and magazines, publishing both critical and original work by the new authors. The little magazines* especially
played an important role as a platform for the dissemination of and discussion on the new
style in prose and poetry. T.S. Eliot's correspondence – as well as the letters, diaries and

critical writings of Virginia Woolf, Rainer Maria Rilke and Thomas Mann, to name but a few examples – show the rapidly increasing internationalisation of literature during the interbellum and the way in which authors influenced each other across national boundaries. Poets and writers such as Eliot and Woolf did more than just correspond; they also reviewed each other's works and published their writings in German and French magazines. Through his writings on his British and Italian contemporaries, the French author Valery Larbaud kept fellow authors and the French public informed. Eliot, an American by birth, worked as British literary correspondent for *La Nouvelle Revue Française*, a magazine founded in 1909 by André Gide, among others. The German-language poet and novelist Rilke, whose extensive travels across Europe brought him into contact with like-minded authors from Scandinavia to Spain, visited Paris several times before and after World War I. The city and his many contacts in the French literary world became a source of inspiration for his work. In turn, André Gide translated selected passages from Rilke's modernist novel *Malte Laurids Brigge* (1910) and published them in the *NRF*.

From the late 1940s onwards, literary historians have successfully propagated the view that these writers should be considered as part of a movement, in spite of their strongly diverging presence on the literary stage. "Modernism" became the commonly accepted but after-the-fact designation for this movement. The authors belonging to it are referred to as the high modernists. Since the mid-1950s, a wave of reception* has resulted in an abundance of critical studies on the period 1910–1940, with interest especially strong in Great Britain and North America. The strong critical interest generated in Anglo-Saxon nations may be explained by the fact that the majority of modernist authors belonged to the English-speaking world. But elsewhere in Europe, too, there were many authors besides those already mentioned whose works contain elements associated with Modernism: Paul Valéry in France, Robert Musil in the German-speaking world, and Italo Svevo and Luigi Pirandello in Italy. Those studies not limited to British-American Modernism – those which adopt a comparative perspective – demonstrate the truly European nature of Modernism.[11]

Modernist prose

In 1922, Irish author James Joyce's novel *Ulysses* was published in Paris by Sylvia Beach. In the heart of Europe's cultural capital, the American-born Beach owned and ran a bookstore and lending library called Shakespeare and Company, which after its opening in November 1919 quickly became a literary meeting place for the many British and American authors who had stayed on in the city after World War I or who had sought refuge there in previous years. Together with its French counterpart *La Maison des Amis du Livre*, operated across the street by her close companion Adrienne Monnier, the bookstore became an international place of exchange. Lectures were held, authors read from their latest works, and books and magazines were available for sale or on loan. Joyce, who had left Ireland in 1904 because of its oppressive intellectual and artistic climate, had for a short time studied medicine in Paris and had subsequently lived in Trieste, Zurich and Rome, finally took up residence in the French capital again in 1920. At this time, Joyce was approaching his forties and had a history of unpleasant experiences with British and American censorship* due to the controversial nature of his prose works. The publication history of *Ulysses*, which like his other works focuses on the lives of ordinary Dubliners, provides a telling example. Publication in the United Kingdom was out of the question due to strict censorship laws which held printers personally accountable for the contents of printed materials. Initial plans to publish the novel in instalments, set to appear simultaneously in *The Little Review* and the British magazine *The Egoist*, were doomed to fail because of Joyce's unambiguous choice of words and the novel's explicit scenes. Only a few selected passages would eventually appear in *The Egoist*. Similar problems ultimately led to a publication ban in the United States that was only lifted in 1933. In the United Kingdom, the first legal copies would appear as late as 1936.

The events in the novel span exactly one day, 16 June 1904. In this limited time span, the novel follows the wanderings through the city of Leopold Bloom, a Jewish advertising salesman. The day starts with his preparations for his and his wife Molly's breakfast, followed by a detailed account of his morning bowel movement on the outside toilet ("cuckstool"), during which he reads a story in an old magazine before putting the pages to other use: "He tore away half the prize story sharply and wiped himself with it."[12] These events start off the novel's fourth episode. During the previous three episodes the reader has been introduced to the much younger male protagonist Stephen Dedalus, whose life story shows remarkable similarities to Joyce's own (his studies in Paris, his mother's recent passing and his career as a teacher) and who is commonly thought to serve as Joyce's literary alter ego. During the day Bloom attends a funeral; encounters several acquaintances; unsuccessfully tries to sell advertisements; has a sandwich in a pub; contemplates his marriage to Molly, a concert singer who he knows is cheating on him with her agent Blazes Boylan; and has several near meetings with Stephen Dedalus before finally running into him in a pub and later in a brothel where Stephen gets himself into trouble. Bloom takes him to his house and makes him a cup of hot chocolate, after which Stephen leaves and Bloom crawls into bed with Molly. The final pages of the novel are given over to a lengthy interior monologue*, noticeable for its lack of punctuation, in which Molly Bloom contemplates her lovers and her marriage. Her thoughts finally take her back to the moment of Bloom's marriage proposal:

> and then he asked me would I yes to say yes my mountain flower and first I put my arms around him yes and drew him down to me so he could feel my breasts all perfume yes and his heart was going like mad and yes I said yes I will Yes.[13]

If anything, these final lines demonstrate that, when dealing with the prose style of *Ulysses*, the term Realism seems less than applicable. What cannot be gleaned from a plot summary, however, is precisely what makes *Ulysses* such a groundbreaking work and to what it owes its worldwide status as one of the key texts of Modernism. One of the most revolutionary aspects of the text is the never-before-seen openness in its treatment of subjects like adultery, bodily functions, lèse-majesté, blasphemy and antisemitism. A second innovative aspect is the use of a wide range of registers, from biblical language and legal terminology to word games, musical intermezzos, street noise, newspaper headlines, sexual fantasies, daydreams and historical references. But arguably the most important innovation is Joyce's development of a narrative style which allows him to directly represent the thoughts, impressions, words, feelings and dreams of his characters, without the mediating influence of a narrator filtering the unrestricted flow of consciousness. A narrator may be present in *Ulysses*, but – unlike in nineteenth-century novels – rarely intervenes, leaving the reader to interpret the voices of the characters. The resulting loss of narrative cohesion is to some extent compensated for by the structural analogy between the novel and Homer's great epic*, the *Odyssey* (see Chapter 2). There are notable similarities between Bloom's wanderings and those of the ancient hero Odysseus; Bloom, too, is an exile of sorts, driven from his home by the knowledge of his wife's amorous escapade. Like Odysseus, he encounters a host of strange characters and faces many obstacles before finally returning home to Molly, his Penelope. Bloom, however, is no classical hero who avenges himself on his wife's lover; instead, he responds to her infidelity with resignation. During one of his encounters the reader is introduced to Gerty McDowell, a seventeen-year-old girl, who is enjoying the evening light on the rocks of Sandymount Beach with her young companions. They squabble and tease each other while Gerty sits apart from the playing children, meditating – in the style of a candlelight romance – on her hopes and expectations of love and married life. The reader follows her inner deliberations on make-up, perfume and undergarments, told in her own words:

> she had four dinky sets, with awfully pretty stitchery, three garments and nighties extra, and each set slotted with different coloured ribbons, rosepink, pale blue, mauve and peagreen and she aired them herself and blued them when they came home from the wash and ironed them and she had a brickbat to keep the iron on because she wouldn't trust those washerwomen as far as she'd seen them scorching the things.[14]

Gerty's romantic reveries are interspersed with sounds emanating from the church of Mary, Star of the Sea, which sits at the edge of the beach overlooking the bay:

> And then there came out upon the air the sound of voices and the pealing anthem of the organ. It was the men's temperance retreat conducted by the missioner, the reverend John Hughes S.J., rosary, sermon and benediction of the Most Blessed Sacrament.[15]

A fitting service, because Gerty's father has a drink problem and the "demon drink" has long been a source of misery to the McDowell family. Joyce interlaces passages from the murmured supplications with Gerty's naive girlish fantasies, demanding the utmost of the reader's flexibility in keeping up with the rapid alternation of registers. The effect of mixing up high and low registers is intensified by Joyce ascribing features and qualities to Gerty traditionally associated with the Virgin Mary, suggesting a parallel between the two. Bloom is present on the beach and notices Gerty. Aware that she is being watched, Gerty starts fantasizing about the gentleman in black: "and while she gazed her heart went pitapat. Yes, it was her he was looking at and there was meaning in his look."[16] In her daydream, Bloom becomes her "dreamhusband". While the others run off to watch a fireworks display, crippled Gerty stays put. She leans back and exposes her legs and while the fireworks go off in the sky above, the masturbating Bloom climaxes. This scene runs parallel to Odysseus's encounter with "Nausicaa" in the *Odyssey*, in which the shipwrecked hero washes up on a beach to find Nausicaa and her companions playing a ball game. To show on which Homeric figures his characters are based, Joyce drew up an explanatory schema. Apart from titles referring to Homeric character names, the schema ties every episode in the novel to a location, an hour of the day, an organ, a colour, a symbol, an art and a style or technique. For instance, the scene in which Bloom is preparing breakfast at eight in the morning is given the title "Calypso", the name of the nymph who holds Odysseus captive on her island home, and the organ is the kidney. In the episode titled "Nausicaa", the time is eight o'clock in the evening, the eye and nose are the key organs, and the art of painting is referenced throughout. The schema, drawn up by Joyce as an aid to critics and early translators of his novel, does not predate the novel itself, but rather materialised in the course of the writing process, sometime during the appearance of the first fourteen episodes in the American magazine *The Little Review* between 1918 and 1920.[17]

In her biography of d'Annunzio, Lucy Hughes-Hallett compares *Ulysses* to *Maia*, a verse novel by the Italian author published in 1903. D'Annunzio, like Joyce, used Homer's epic to provide a structural and thematic foundation for his text, a semi-autobiographical account of a sea journey.[18] Joyce was highly familiar with d'Annunzio's work. He attended performances of his plays and closely studied his prose works, such as the novels *Pleasure* and *Il Fuoco* ('The Flame', 1900). He is known to have spoken highly of d'Annunzio's work on several occasions; in 1909, he went as far as to say he hoped his own writings would one day measure up to those of d'Annunzio. Of course, there is a world of difference between the way in which Joyce depicts the many aspects of life and love in *Ulysses*, and the decadent style d'Annunzio adopts in *Pleasure*. What in the Italian's work is largely left over to suggestion, Joyce describes in colourful and explicit detail. If d'Annunzio pushed the boundaries in his descriptions, landing him in trouble with censors and with the Church, Joyce broke them altogether. The consequences of this would be felt throughout his writing career, culminating in the destruction of his manuscripts* and burning of his books. It was the price he would have to pay for his candid treatment of the daily habits and activities of ordinary men and women, his ironic portrayal of the Church and its representatives, and his efforts to capture the meanderings of human consciousness, even of its most secret and hidden parts, in writing. Together with Mann, Proust, Woolf and other European and non-European authors, Joyce's modernist prose marks a break between the literature of the nineteenth and that of the twentieth century. Like the representatives of the Historical Avant-Garde, what motivated the modernists was their recognition of the change in religion*, conduct, politics and literature brought about by social upheaval and by the investigations of Nietzsche, Freud and Bergson. They made it their mission to express this change through literary means.

Critical reception

The publication of a large part of *Ulysses* in *The Little Review* between 1918 and 1920 had already done much to heighten the anticipation among English-speaking readers and fellow authors in the time leading up to the novel's appearance. French readers, too, would have the opportunity to learn about Joyce's new work ahead of publication. Valery Larbaud, who met Joyce for the first time in Paris near the end of 1920, held a lecture on *Ulysses* in Adrienne Monnier's packed bookstore. Several weeks before, Joyce had sent him his schema as part of the preparation for his lecture. In his introduction, Larbaud stated that Joyce was to lovers of literature what Freud and Einstein were to science. Apart from Larbaud's lecture, the event included a reading of selected passages from the text, translated into French by one of Joyce's young admirers at the request of Beach and Monnier. The expectant crowd was swept away by Larbaud's enthusiasm, and many of the attendees purchased subscriptions to the English version of the novel, set to appear several months later. The first integral French translation would be published in 1929 by Adrienne Monnier.

A quarter of a century later, in 1946, in Bern, Switzerland, a study appeared titled *Mimesis, the Representation of Reality in Western Literature*. The author, a German-born Jewish philologist named Erich Auerbach, had been forced to give up his post at the University of Marburg in 1935. Exiled from Nazi Germany, he spent World War II in Istanbul, writing what was to become his magnum opus. Every chapter in *Mimesis* starts with a passage from a primary text which Auerbach then analyses and puts into context. He takes the reader on an exploratory journey through a European literary canon*, commencing with the *Odyssey* and the Bible and finishing with the prose written during the first decades of the twentieth century. The representation of reality (also known as mimesis) forms the common thread connecting the analyses. The final chapter examines what sets the works of Woolf, Proust and Joyce apart from the realist and naturalist prose of their predecessors. In this, Auerbach's study represents one of the first times Modernism was recognised as a European literary movement. What makes this early example of critical reception* the more interesting is Auerbach's own hesitance in formulating his observations, an indication of the pioneering nature of his work. Auerbach observes that the works of the early twentieth-century authors exhibit certain shared characteristics and – as one of the first critics to do so – sets out to define these characteristics. The first of "the distinguishing stylistic features" identified by Auerbach is the fact that in the works of these authors "the writer as narrator of objective facts has almost completely vanished." Instead of an omniscient narrator interpreting the fictional world, "numerous subjective impressions received by various individuals (and at various times)" serve to suggest an objective reality. A second technical innovation mentioned by Auerbach is the generous amount of freedom taken by the authors in representing the workings of consciousness. A third characteristic is the way in which the authors draw attention to the difference between objective ("exterior") and subjective ("interior") time.[19] Auerbach does not yet attach a name to the new style, but prefers to speak of "the modern technique". It was not until fifteen years later that the prose of the interwar period became known under the common appellation of Modernism.

Notes

1   Gabriele d'Annunzio, *Pleasure*, translation with a foreword and notes by Lara Gochin Raffaelli, introduction by Alexander Stille (New York/London: Penguin Books, 2013), 7.

2   Virginia Woolf, "Mr. Bennet and Mrs. Brown," in *The Captain's Death Bed and Other Essays*, ed. Leonard Woolf (New York: Harcourt Brace Janovich, 1950), 94–119.

3   Alex Danchev, *100 Artists' Manifestos: From the Futurists to the Stuckists* (London: Penguin Modern Classics, 2011), 4.

4   Vladimir Markov, *Russian Futurism: A History* (Berkeley/Los Angeles: University of California Press, 1985), 45, 46.

5   Markov, *Russian Futurism*, 7, 8.

6   Aleksei Kruchenykh and Velimir Khlebnikhov, *Slovo kak takovoe* ('The Word as Such') (Moscow, 1913).

7   Translation by Andrey Kneller. "Russian Poetry in English," accessed March 3, 2016, https://sites.google.com/site/poetryandtranslations/vladimir-mayakovsky/kindness-to-horses

8   Markov, *Russian Futurism*, 148, 400 (notes).

9   Markov, *Russian Futurism*, 150, 151.

10 Lucy Hughes-Hallett, *The Pike: Gabriele D'Annunzio: Poet, Seducer and Preacher of War* (London: Fourth Estate/HarperCollins Publishers, 2013), 306–9.

11 Ricardo Quinones's study *Mapping Literary Modernism* is a good example. In his book Quinones analyzes the ways in which Thomas Mann, Franz Kafka, James Joyce, T.S. Eliot, Marcel Proust and Virginia Woolf responded to the ideas of Bergson, Freud and Nietzsche in their works.

12 James Joyce, *Ulysses* (London: Modern Penguin Classics, 2000), 85.

13 Joyce, *Ulysses*, 933.

14 Joyce, *Ulysses*, 456.

15 Joyce, *Ulysses*, 460.

16 Joyce, *Ulysses*, 465.

17 Gaipa, Mark, Sean Latham and Robert Scholes, *The Little Review "Ulysses": James Joyce* (New Haven/London: Yale University Press, 2015), xvii, xviii.

18 Hughes-Hallett, *The Pike*, 585.
19 Erich Auerbach, *Mimesis: The Representation of Reality in Western Literature*, trans. Willard R. Trask (Princeton, NJ/Oxford: Princeton University Press, 2003), 534, 536, 538.

Further reading

Berman, Art. *Preface to Modernism*. Urbana/Chicago, IL: University of Illinois Press, 1994.
Birmingham, Kevin. *The Most Dangerous Book: The Battle for James Joyce's* Ulysses. New York: The Penguin Press, 2014.
Bradbury, Malcolm and James McFarlane, eds. *Modernism: A Guide to European Literature 1890–1930*. Harmondsworth: Penguin Books, 1991.
Marek, Jayne E. *Women Editing Modernism: "Little" Magazines and Literary History*. Lexington: University of Kentucky Press, 1995.
Rainey, Lawrence, ed. *Modernism: An Anthology*. Malden/Oxford/Carlton: Wiley-Blackwell, 2005.

27 Ordering chaos

Kai Evers

Figure 27.1 Franz Kafka, *In the Penal Colony*

Illustration: "In the Penal Colony" Copyright © Robert Crumb. From *Introducing Kafka* by David Zane Mairowitz and Robert Crumb. Used with permission.

The first decades of the twentieth century were deeply impacted by war, violence, and revolution, but such shared experience led to widely varying and conflicting positions and approaches among literary authors. Modernist writers who explored new ways of capturing modern times and new modes of writing between the 1890s and the 1930s responded to these experiences in both an intellectual and a literary way. Realism proved inadequate as a means to understand a rapidly changing and often hostile world. With the French poet Charles Baudelaire and the German philosopher Friedrich Nietzsche, early representatives of modernist literature and thought emerged after the failed European revolutions of 1848 and after the Franco-Prussian War of 1870–1871. The final phase of the modernist period coincides with the success of revolutionary fascist and national socialist movements in Europe, the Second World War, and the Holocaust. While its precise beginning and end remain up for debate, consensus exists that European literary Modernism* reached its peak in the time between the First World War and the early 1930s with such masterpieces as Kafka's *The Metamorphosis* (1915), Proust's *A la recherche du temps perdu* ('In Search of Lost Time', 1913–27), Joyce's *Ulysses* (1922), Eliot's *The Waste Land* (1922), Döblin's *Berlin Alexanderplatz* (1929), Musil's *Der Mann ohne Eigenschaften* ('The Man without Qualities', 1930–43), and Céline's *Voyage au bout de la nuit* ('Journey to the End of the Night', 1932).

Considering the violent historical context of literary Modernism, it comes as no surprise that war and violence were a preoccupation shared by many modernist works. Rarely has the literary representation of violence been more varied, complex, and ambiguous than in these writings. A more direct relationship between violence and literature has been established for the literary avant-gardes of the militant right and the revolutionary left. These movements embraced violence as an instrument to purify decadent society through warfare (Futurism*), or as a means to fully revolutionize the social order and bring about a "new man". While these militant avant-gardes have been singled out for their ability to confront the violent historical changes of their time directly, European modernists were often disparaged as too delicate to look more closely at twentieth-century violence. But influential literary modernists questioned repeatedly the reductionist approach to violence prevalent in writings of the literary avant-garde*. Rather than reducing violence to a mere means fully justified by its end, a future just society, modernists like Woolf, Babel, and Kafka reflected on the relationship between modernity and violence in all of its ambiguity and contradictions. Instead of dreaming of the next war as the war to end all wars or denouncing violence as modernity's barbaric other, they acknowledged the phenomena of war and violence as inherent to modernity itself.

In August 1914, the overwhelming majority of poets and philosophers supported the war effort of their respective countries. Writers from Guillaume Apollinaire and Henri Barbusse to Georg Trakl and Ludwig Wittgenstein volunteered to fight in the war. Rather than naming all of the literary war enthusiasts, it is more efficient to mention the few – often publically reviled – exceptions to the war euphoria: George Bernard Shaw in Great Britain, Romain Rolland in France, and Karl Kraus in the Habsburg Empire. It took years of warfare until a wider group of European intellectuals and writers came to question central assumptions of Western modernity, assumptions of linear social and political progress and continuous modernization. Sigmund Freud analyzed his deep disappointment with his fellow Europeans in *Zeitgemässes über Krieg und Tod* ('Thoughts for the Times on War and Death') as early as 1915, well before tanks, machine guns, airplanes, and poison gas attacks became emblematic of the new horrors of warfare. The return of warfare to Europe and especially the "brutality shown by individuals whom, as participants in the highest human civilization, one would not have thought capable of such behaviour" provoked his profound disillusionment.[1] Until the eve of war, his contemporaries had lived outwardly well within socially expected norms. Their wartime actions demonstrated, however, that they never fully internalized the norms of civilized interaction. With social prohibitions against violent behavior lifted during wartime, Freud explained, soldiers of all nations lived out their unconscious fantasies of murder and destruction.

Among the central works of literary Modernism, Louis-Ferdinand Céline's *Journey to the End of the Night* stands out in its unflinching representation of warfare. Upon joining the war, Ferdinand Bardamu, the novel's protagonist, witnesses on the battlefield the new wartime liberties Freud had spoken of:

> So there was no mistake? So there was no law against people shooting at people they couldn't even see! It was one of the things you could do without anybody reading you the riot act. In fact, it was recognized and probably encouraged by upstanding citizens, like the draft, or marriage, or hunting![2]

Unlike Freud, Céline's protagonist harbours no deeply held beliefs in human progress and experiences no fundamental disillusionment during the war. Instead, Bardamu registers with curiosity and some fear how quickly social expectations are turned upside down: "there I was, caught up in a mass flight into collective murder. . . . Something had come up from the depths, and this is what happened."[3] Respectable citizens transform themselves into a band of murderers, right before Bardamu's eyes:

> Could I, I thought, be the last coward on earth? How terrifying! . . . All alone with two million stark raving, heroic madmen, armed to the eyeballs? With and with-out helmets, without horses, on motorcycles, bellowing, in cars, screeching, shooting, plotting, flying, kneeling, digging, taking cover, bounding over trails, root-toot-toot-ing, shut up on earth as if it were a looney bin, ready to demolish everything on it, Germany, France, whole continents, everything that breathes, destroy, destroy, madder than mad dogs, worshiping their madness (which dogs don't) a hundred, a thousand times madder than a thousand dogs, and a lot more vicious![4]

Bardamu's language explodes into fragments but his worldview stays the same. As "the last coward on earth," he keeps an observational distance from the war, stays in control of himself, and manages to make sense of his perceptions.

In his way, Bardamu achieved what the poet and critic T.S. Eliot demanded of modern literature in the essay 'Ulysses, Order, Myth' (1923). The central task of literature should be the search for new literary methods to order a modern world in disarray, to keep artistic control while representing the world's chaos. Eliot praised Joyce's use of the *Odyssey* in *Ulysses* as an achievement equal to any scientific discovery. By using myth* to structure the novel*, Joyce found "a way of controlling, of ordering, of giving a shape and a signifi-cance to the immense panorama of futility and anarchy which is contemporary history."[5]

Representing openness: modernist literature and the unpredictability of history

Not all works of modernist literature offer such compensatory aesthetic order to a vio-lently disrupted world. Joyce's *Finnegans Wake* (1939) and Paul Celan's late poetry pose to their readers* almost insurmountable challenges for comprehension. Other major works, including Kafka's novels, remained incomplete. In *The Man without Qualities* (1943), the Austrian novelist Robert Musil presents a project almost designed to fail Eliot's ambition for modern literature. Beginning in August 1913, the novel's plot follows a large set of characters living in the Habsburg Empire as they advance ever closer to August 1914. This historical setup suggests a narrative structure* of linear development and orderly progression. The novel's essayism, its method of approaching the world with a sense of possibility, subverts, however, the belief in predictable historical development. *The Man without Qualities* considers moments of the past to preserve the multiplicity of their potential futures. Narrating the past with a sense of possibility and not with historical hindsight, an outbreak of war in August 1914 seems to become only one of several conceivable endings for Musil's novel.

Looking back in 1922 at the changes his generation had lived through, Musil recalled events that defied conventional notions of continuous experience, development, and storytelling:

> For the past ten years we have doubtless been making world history in the most strident fashion, but without actually being able to see it. We haven't really changed much – a little presumptuous before, a little hung over afterwards. First we were bustling good citizens, then we became murderers, killers, thieves, arsonists, and the like, but without really experiencing anything. . . . So we have been many things, but we haven't changed; we have seen a lot and perceived nothing.[6]

These observations resemble those of Freud and Bardamu, but Musil draws very different conclusions from them to understand history, the self, and the task of modern literature. The strange malleability and plasticity of the human self, its dependence on and openness to rapidly changing historical situations, its limits of experience and perception, and its inability to fit its discontinuous life experiences into the shape of traditional storytelling led Musil to write an unprecedented work of European Modernism. Rather than adjusting expectations and finding explanations, like Freud, or becoming a misanthropic observer of the world around him, like Céline's Bardamu, or finding in myth a parallel structure to order the chaos of contemporary society, as Eliot claimed for Joyce's *Ulysses*, Musil's novel stays radically open. It seeks to fracture the reader's rigid patterns of perception and reality construction to enable a more flexible and malleable understanding of history, modernity, and what it means to be human in times of rapid and often violent transformation. *The Man without Qualities* remained perhaps too open. Musil died in 1942 before he could complete the novel. But this novel might have been inherently unfinishable. Instead of working on a compensatory aesthetic order of the past, Musil's novel follows an aesthetic project that attempts to subvert and disrupt for its readers the "few dozen cake molds of which reality consists."[7] Rather than delivering an otherwise lacking order and meaning to the reader's world, the task of literature was to break up traditional patterns of perception and allow for an awareness of the radical malleability of history, society, and the human self.

War, violence, and Modernism

Modernist theorists and writers analyzed modernization and modernity in terms of war and violence. With their essays on metropolitan life, modernity, and the end of storytelling, the philosopher Georg Simmel, the psychoanalyst Freud, and the cultural critic Walter Benjamin introduced the concepts of shock, trauma, mourning, and melancholia as

central to the study of contemporary life and modernist literature. Developed to comprehend violent disruptions of memory and narrative, these concepts were deemed appropriate to fathom the experience of modernity in all of its aspects. Sociological, political,
and historical discourses conceptualized these transformations under headings like industrialization, urbanization, secularization, rationalization, bureaucratization, or globalization, terms referring to an unsettling process of modernization that affects all facets of
modern society. Central modernist representations of metropolitan life established close
relations between urban experience and war. Subjected to an onslaught of sounds, smells,
images, and touches, the protagonists of Joyce's *Ulysses*, Döblin's *Berlin Alexanderplatz*,
and Céline's *Journey to the End of the Night* are at risk of perceiving too much in Dublin,
Berlin, and New York. An overwhelming amount of experiential data threatens to defeat
their capacity to make sense of the world around them. Taking place during and after
the First World War, Céline's Bardamu and Döblin's Biberkopf experience New York and
Berlin as shaped by their war memories. In postwar Berlin, Döblin's protagonist remains
caught in a state of war. Walking on his city's streets, Biberkopf feels as if he marches once
again on a battlefield with grenades exploding and bullets flying all around him. While
the central characters of these novels are often overwhelmed by their experiences, several
modernist works create for their readers such intricate linguistic networks of echoes and
potential meanings that not even visions of total destruction disrupt the pleasure derived
from their artistic virtuosity. Admired by Joyce, Italo Svevo's *La coscienza di Zeno* ('Zeno's
Conscience', 1923) remains a comic masterpiece even though it ends with predicting
global self-destruction:

> When poison gases no longer suffice, an ordinary man, in the secrecy of a room in this
> world, will invent an incomparable explosive, compared to which the explosives cur-
> rently in existence will be considered harmless toys. And another man, also ordinary,
> but a bit sicker than others, will steal this explosive and will climb up at the centre of
> the earth, to set it on the spot where it can have the maximum effect. There will be
> an enormous explosion that no one will hear, and the earth, once again a nebula, will
> wander through the heavens, freed of parasites and sickness.[8]

Reading Kafka on war, violence, and the ambiguities of communication

Modernists from Céline to Svevo responded in vastly different ways to the central modern
experience of war and violence. A closer look at one writer in particular, Franz Kafka,
will help to appreciate the variance and complexity of modernist responses to violence.
Rather than subscribing to Ezra Pound's modernist motto "make it new", Kafka followed
a motto one might summarize as "make it painful". In 1904, he insisted: "I think we ought
to read only the kind of books that wound and stab us."[9] Six years later, he described the
process of writing as one of self-harming: "I'll jump into my story even though it should
cut my face to pieces."[10] In 1916, he praised a novel for cutting its reader like a knife. Kafka's interest in literature was fuelled not by masochistic desire but by a search for truth in
pain and pain in truth. As he told Milena Jesenská, his friend, lover, and translator in 1920,
"Yes, torture is extremely important to me – my sole occupation is torturing and being
tortured. Why? . . . to get the dammed word out of the dammed mouth."[11] Even though

he acknowledged in the same letter the futility of the entire enterprise, Kafka did not let go of his interest in an assumed link between violence, truth, and justice.

Kafka interrogated the ambivalent relationship between violence, truth, and justice nowhere more daringly than in *In der Strafkolonie* ('In the Penal Colony', 1919). In the story, a European explorer visits a tropical island that serves as a penal colony. He hears from a military officer, the colony's judge and executioner, about the island's past and present legal system. At its center stands a peculiar execution apparatus, a machine that inflicts the utmost pain and suffering before it kills its victims. The officer credits the twelve-hour-long procedure with an unerring ability to produce a visible sign of true justice on the face of the condemned. As the explorer comes to understand, the officer is the last outspoken supporter of these executions. The colony's new commandant, a modernizer, seems intent to abolish the penal system his predecessor had introduced. Having failed to win the explorer as an ally in the defense of the machine, the officer sentences himself to death. Instead of making the truth and justice of his decision slowly visible, however, the apparatus kills the officer quickly while it self-destructs in front of the explorer. Incapable to comprehend the penal colony's truth, the explorer flees the island. He is last seen standing on a small boat, holding a knotted rope to fend off others hoping to join his escape.

Kafka wrote most of *In the Penal Colony* in October 1914. His publisher received the manuscript* two years later, objecting to the story's painfulness. In his reply, Kafka related its painfulness to current events: "By way of clarifying this last story, I need only add that the painfulness is not peculiar to it alone but that our times and my own time as well have been painful."[12] As pained as Kafka felt, he was immensely productive during the first five months of the war. He worked on his first novel *Amerika. Der Verschollene* ('Amerika: The Man Who Disappeared', 1927), wrote several chapters of *Der Prozess* ('The Trial', 1925), as well as stories, including *In the Penal Colony*. Kafka's burst of creativity occurred at a moment of deep ambivalence towards the outside world. Unlike his famed fellow writers, he never glorified the war. Nor did he publically oppose the war, or stay indifferent to it, as the often-cited diary entry of August 2, 1914, seemed to suggest: "Germany has declared war on Russia. Swimming in the afternoon."[13] His response to the war remained fluid and contradictory. Dismayed by the public displays of war euphoria, he felt no sympathies for the jubilant crowds or for the young men they sent off to the front. But in 1915, Kafka tried without success to become a soldier. While he wished everything evil to departing soldiers in August 1914, he was recommended in 1918 to receive a medal for his service to war veterans.

War and violence surrounded Kafka while writing *In the Penal Colony*. Instead of addressing the war directly, however, he examined the ambiguous relationship between violence and truth in modernity. A traveller arrives on an island to explore a French-speaking penal colony. During the reception in his honor, the colony's recently appointed new commandant invites the traveller to observe the following day the execution of a "soldier condemned to death for disobeying and insulting his superior officer."[14] Kafka's narrative begins on this second day. An unnamed officer who serves the colony as judge and executioner explains to the traveller what is going to happen during the execution. In the following excerpt, taken from the story's very center, the officer dwells on his memories of past executions, executions prepared and conducted under the supervision of the island's previous commandant, the old commandant. While he talks to the traveller, the condemned man is being strapped inside the apparatus, incapable to understand the French speaking officer.

Text: Franz Kafka, In der Strafkolonie *('In the Penal Colony') (1919)*

And so the execution would begin! No discordant note disturbed the work of the machine. Many people had stopped watching and lay in the sand, their eyes closed; everyone knew: Now justice is being done. In the silence you only heard the condemned man's moans, muted by the felt plug. Today the machine no longer manages to squeeze a moan out of the condemned man louder than the felt can stifle, but in those days the writing needles dripped an acid fluid that we are no longer allowed to use. Well, and then the sixth hour would come around! It was impossible to grant everyone's request to watch from up close. In his wisdom the commandant ordered that children should be given priority; I, of course, by virtue of my office, was always allowed to stay. I would often be squatting there, with two little children in my arms, right and left. How we all took in the expression of transfiguration from his martyred face, how we bathed our cheeks in the radiance of this justice finally achieved and already vanishing! What times these were, my comrade!" The officer had evidently forgotten who was standing before him; he had embraced the traveller and laid his head on his shoulder. The traveller was completely at a loss; he looked impatiently past the officer. The soldier had finished cleaning up and was now pouring congee from a can into the bowl. The condemned man, who seemed to have recovered completely, had hardly noticed this than he began to snap at the porridge with his tongue. Again and again the soldier shoved him away, since the porridge was meant for later, but it was certainly highly irregular, too, that the soldier should stick his filthy hands into the basin and eat out of it in front of the ravenous condemned man. The officer quickly recovered his composure. "I wasn't trying to play on your emotions," he said. "I know, it's impossible to make those times comprehensible today. In any case, the machine still works and is effective in its own way. It is effective even when it stands by itself in this valley. And at the end the corpse still drops into the pit in an incomprehensively gentle glide even if hundreds of people no longer congregate as they did then, like flies around the pit.[15]

Remembering past executions, the officer speaks for the penal colony. The traveller and Kafka's reader receive almost all of their information about the colony from him. Throughout the story, the officer presents himself as the unbending defender of the colony's old order, especially with regard to its dependence on the painful execution procedure that establishes truth and justice for the community.

Critical reception

Most of the critical reception* accepts the officer's account as reliable since he is "unequivocally committed to the form of justice [the penal machine] dispenses."[16] Readers subscribing to this near consensus have moved from there into radically different directions and theoretical discourses. *In the Penal Colony* has been placed into the historical contexts of deportation, colonialism*, and post-colonialism*, but also read as a story prophetic of the Holocaust. It has been read as a tale of sadism or of masochism but also as an allegory* of military justice. Additional allegorical readings focused on a clash between Western and non-Western cultures, or between Judaism and Christianity, or between the orders of the Old and the New Testaments. Other interpreters, Gilles Deleuze and Stanley Corngold among them, read the workings of the execution machine in relation to the acts of writing, reading, or listening. As different and irreconcilable as these approaches to a single story appear, many of them have shed new light on Kafka's writings. With the possible exception of Samuel Beckett, no other modernist writer has inspired so many equally sophisticated but dissimilar interpretations*, substantiating Theodor W. Adorno's comment about Kafka's writings that "[e]ach sentence says 'interpret me,' and none will permit it."[17]

None permits it because each aspect of Kafka's stories remains open for reinterpretation. Even the near consensus that considers the officer as a true believer of the old order turns deceptive upon inspection. This line of inquiry leads quickly to a re-evaluation of the relationship between violence, truth, and communication in Kafka's works. It becomes apparent that the officer adheres to no single belief system, has no single identity. His speech is riddled with inconsistencies and irreconcilable contradictions that point to deeply ambiguous thoughts and feelings about the new and the old order. Rather than confirming his position as the last defender of the old order, the officer's speech indicates that he no longer trusts the old system of punishment and its method of making justice visible to everyone. He knows, however, of no other way to get the dammed word out of the dammed mouth, as Kafka called it in his letter to Milena Jesenská, of no other path to establish truth beyond any doubt.

According to Kafka, language does not communicate the truth a speaker intends to communicate. A speaker reveals a different truth, the truth of human self-deception. The fault does not lie with language as a means of communication but with its users:

> I am not of the opinion that one can ever lack the power to express perfectly what one wants to write or say. . . . What is clear within is bound to become so in words as well. This is why one need never worry about language, but at sight of words may often worry about oneself. After all, who knows within himself how things really are with him? This tempestuous or floundering or morass-like inner self is what we really are, but by the secret process by which words are forced out of us our self-knowledge is brought to light, and though it may still be veiled, yet it is there before us, wonderful or terrible to behold.[18]

Unlike other modernists from Nietzsche to Hugo von Hofmannsthal, Kafka was less concerned with a crisis of language and more with a crisis of the self. Not language as a distortive medium stands in the way of representing inner and outer reality, but the subject and its incoherent and malleable self.

In Kafka's story, the officer's morass-like inner self transpires within his speech and through his gestures. Only at first sight he identifies fully with the old order. When he reminisces about its past glories, he embraces the traveller happily, completely forgetting to whom he is speaking. If one follows Kafka's suggestion and takes a closer look at his words and gestures, however, a very different image of the officer comes to the fore. One moment he describes the past as a harmonically ordered society with children bathing in the radiance of justice achieved, but in the next moment he dismisses past audiences as having hovered "like flies" around the execution pit. Rather than assembling to see justice done, they attended the executions for the procedure's repulsive-attractive excrement, the sight of a torn corpse in the pit.

The officer is not the unequivocal defender of the old order he claims to be, but a figure of conflicting loyalties and contradictions. He presents himself at first as a mere member of a collective "we", the followers of the old commandant, but then he never stops saying

"I" while talking to the traveller. When he refers to the penal colony's legal system, he claims personal ownership and refers to "my court", "my jurisdiction", "my procedure", and "my plan".[19] His uniform signals not one but three different political alliances. Sweating in a uniform too heavy for a tropical island, he keeps wearing it as a reminder of "our homeland and we don't want to lose touch with our homeland."[20] Besides representing his European fatherland, the uniform signals his rapid advancement to the position of judge and executioner under the old commandant's rule in the penal colony. The way he wears the uniform suggests, however, that he long succumbed to the softening pleasures of the new order. Throughout the story, the officer hailed the old commandant's society as a masculine order, while the new order was falling under the despised softening influence of the "ladies".[21] Rather than wearing the uniform as issued, he has "stuffed two delicate ladies' handkerchiefs under his uniform collar", indicating a preference for the new commandant's gentle, less rigid ways.[22] The officer's speech and uniform reveal his heroic self-portrayal as "the only one who defends the old commandant's legacy" as what it is: more wishful thinking than accurate representation.[23]

The officer's appearance and speech reveal what he cannot admit to himself. He trusts no longer the old order's reliance on physical violence to produce a vision of truth and justice. As the old order's unequivocal representative, he should let the execution machine act for itself and let it produce the sight of justice in complete silence. In the quoted excerpt, the officer stressed two aspects of past executions. First, the machine was perfectly reliable in its workings. Always at the sixth hour, every spectator could see on the condemned man's face the growing understanding that justice was being done to him. Second, the apparatus produced its visual proof in complete silence. The machine itself made no sound. The condemned man's groans were audible only during the first hours of the execution. Speaking incessantly to the explorer, the officer reveals unwittingly that he does not believe anymore in the silently brutal and purely visual regime of the old commandant.

Instead of presenting how the machine delivers justice, the officer delivers a protracted oral defense. With his lengthy oration, he fits far better the colony's new order of deliberation than its past order of silent observation. The officer never comments on his performative contradiction. Instead, he extols how his legal system avoids all direct communication with the accused and with the public at large. Speaking would invite falsehood into his juridical procedure. The accused is never charged with a crime. He is never allowed to speak in his defense. Even judgment is reached in absentia and without knowledge of the accused. As the officer proudly explains:

> If I had first summoned the man, and interrogated him, it would only have led to confusion. He would have lied; if I had succeeded in refuting these lies, he would have substituted new lies for them, and so forth.[24]

For the officer, it seems self-evident that truth cannot be established in spoken words. Truth, justice, and self-knowledge are made visible through physical pain while verbal communication would pervert the course of justice. Consequently, the apparatus is designed to render all speech superfluous. The officer, however, talks and talks to the traveller.

So far, one could conclude that Kafka's story reveals the officer as a false representative of the old visual order. But the officer's speech might as well serve as evidence for his voiced distrust against all verbal communication. The more he speaks, the more he muddles up the basic facts of past events. Early on, the reader learned that the new commandant invited the arriving traveller to attend the next day the execution of an insubordinate soldier. On this next day, the officer asserts, however, that the crime happened hours after the traveller had been invited to witness the execution. The insubordination occurred at 2 a.m., long after the evening reception ended. And the death sentence was decided only an hour before the officer scheduled the beginning of the execution. As the officer tells the traveller, "The captain came to me an hour ago; I took down his statement and immediately added the judgment. Then I had the man put in chains. That was all very simple."[25]

Nothing is ever simple in Kafka's story, not the least because the traveller never takes notice of these inconsistencies. The reader is tasked with perceiving them and to recognize the officer as a figure of ambivalence and contradiction. The officer belongs to the new and the old order. He defends and mistrusts the apparatus. Neither the expectation to establish truth and justice with physical violence nor the frustration of this expectation should be taken as the story's meaning. Kafka's story does not resolve but reveals the ambivalence between violence and truth, description and storytelling, silence and communication. Like the machine in its last run, the story empties itself out without deciding or ending anything. Violence and verbal communication reveal deceptions, not truth. The story moves back and forth between the promise of disclosing truth and justice through pain and violence and the renunciation of any such possibility. *In the Penal Colony* demonstrates the dual impossibility of adhering to a visual regime of absolute immediacy (the officer's ideology) or a politics of deliberation (the new commandant's ideology). Its constant back-and-forth movement, the movement of radical ambivalence, never comes to an end, and Kafka's story disintegrates like the apparatus without renouncing or fulfilling the promise of violence. Rather than dismissing violence as modernity's barbaric other, *In the Penal Colony* acknowledges violence as integral part of modernity and modernization.

Kafka's Modernist poetics* finds its limit in showing how words reveal more truth about their speakers than the speaker can accept if he wishes to live. Kafka's story addresses self-deceptions at the core of modern self-representation without offering recipes against them.

As the reading of *In the Penal Colony* indicates, representations of violence in literary Modernism could avoid the shortcomings of most modern approaches to violence. Unlike proponents of a progressive civilizing process in human history, these representations do not relegate acts of violence to a barbaric other or dismiss them as pathological aberrations inside modern society. Instead, modernist texts by Svevo, Joyce, or Döblin do not reduce acts of violence to predictable and controllable means for the achievement of a higher end. Unlike writings of the militant avant-garde on the right and on the left, from the Futurist manifesto to Agitprop Theatre, Modernist texts like Kafka's story avoid the glorification of yet another war as the war to end all wars and avoid the claim of revolutionary violence to cleanse and purify modern society from all decay. Instead, Kafka's *In the Penal Colony* exposes such instrumental approaches to violence as equally tempting and dangerous modern fantasies. Kafka's story continues to disturb its readers, and this might be its greatest achievement. A modernist representation of violence like Kafka's provides the reader no superior and safe position from its violence. It keeps the question of violence in modernity disturbingly open.

Notes

1 Sigmund Freud, "Thoughts for the Times on War and Death," in *'On the History of the Post Psychoanalytic Movement', 'Papers on Metapsychology' and Other Works*, ed., trans. James Strachey (London: Hogarth Press, 1957), 280.

2 Louis-Ferdinand Céline, *Journey to the End of the Night*, trans. Ralph Manheim (New York: New Directions, 2006), 10.

3 Céline, *Journey to the End of the Night*, 9.

4 Céline, *Journey to the End of the Night*, 9.

5 T.S. Eliot, "Ulysses, Order, and Myth," in *Modernism and Literature: An Introduction and Reader*, eds. Mia Carter and Warren Friedman (New York: Routledge, 2013), 505.

6 Robert Musil, *Precision and Soul*, trans. Burton Pike and David S. Luft (Chicago, IL: University of Chicago Press, 1990), 116–17.

7 Robert Musil, *The Man Without Qualities*, trans. Burton Pike and Sophie Wilkins (New York: Alfred Knopf, 1995), 645.

8 Italo Svevo, *Zeno's Conscience*, trans. William Weaver (New York: Knopf, 2001), 436–7.

9 Franz Kafka, *Letters to Friends, Family, and Editors*, trans. Phillip Boehm (New York City: Schocken, 1990), 16.

10 Franz Kafka, *Diaries 1910–1923*, trans. Joseph Kresh (New York: Schocken, 1988), 28.

11 Franz Kafka, *Letters to Milena*, trans. Phillip Boehm (New York City: Schocken, 1990), 214–15.

12 Kafka, *Letters to Friends, Family, and Editors*, 127.

13 Kafka, *Diaries*, 301.

14 Franz Kafka, "In the Penal Colony," in *Kafka's Selected Stories*, ed. Stanley Corngold, trans. Stanley Corngold (New York: Norton, 2007), 36.

15 Kafka, "In the Penal Colony," 48–9.

16 Richard T. Gray, Ruth V. Gross, Rolf J. Goebel, and Clayton Koelb, *A Franz Kafka Encyclopedia* (Westport: Greenwood, 2005), 135.

17 Theodor W. Adorno, "Notes on Kafka," in *Can One Live After Auschwitz? A Philosophical Reader*, trans. Samuel Weber and Shierry Weber Nicholsen, ed. Rolf Tiedemann (Stanford, CA: Stanford University Press, 2003), 212.

18 Franz Kafka, *Letters to Felice*, eds. Erich Heller and Jürgen Born, trans. James Stern and Elisabeth Duckworth (New York: Schocken, 1973), 198.

19 Kafka, "In the Penal Colony," 40, 47, 49, 50, 51, 52.

20 Kafka, "In the Penal Colony," 36.

21 Kafka, "In the Penal Colony," 50.

22 Kafka, "In the Penal Colony," 50.

23 Kafka, "In the Penal Colony," 47.

24 Kafka, "In the Penal Colony," 41.

25 Kafka, "In the Penal Colony," 41.

Further reading

Carter, Mia and Warren Friedman, eds. *Modernism and Literature: An Introduction and Reader*. New York: Routledge, 2013.

Evers, Kai. *Violent Modernists: The Aesthetics of Deconstruction in Twentieth-Century German Literature*. Evanston: Northwestern University Press, 2013.

Lethen, Helmut. *Cool Conduct: The Culture of Distance in Weimar Germany*. Translated from the German by Don Reneau. Berkeley: University of California Press, 2002.

28 Marketing literature

Helleke van den Braber and Mathijs Sanders

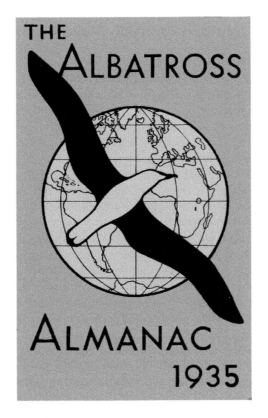

Figure 28.1: The Albatross Almanac for 1935, 1st printing 1934

It is no coincidence that this chapter on marketing literature focuses on the publishing career of D.H. Lawrence. As a writer, he was well known for his fierce independence and his challenging attitude towards his audience. Lawrence wanted to be read widely, but refused to produce literature that was easily digestible. For him, books should not be "all finished and complete," or too "nicely built up of sensations and observations." He felt that his work should engage his readers in ways that could be very direct, confrontational or even aggressive. In 1925 he said:

> I can't bear art that you walk round and admire. A book should either be a bandit or a rebel or a man in a crowd. People should either run for their lives, or come under the colours, or say *how do you do?* . . . An author should be in among the crowd, kicking their shins or cheering them on to some mischief or merriment. . . . Whoever reads me will be in the thick of the scrimmage, and if he doesn't like it − . . . let him read somebody else.[1]

Lawrence's aversion to easily digestible literature shows how much the relationship between writer and audience changed in the twentieth century. The relationship between literature and market changed with it. In order to reach the type of public Lawrence wanted − an audience up to entering the thick of the scrimmage − he had to think very carefully about how to write, for whom and in what form. Thinking about marketing also meant thinking about choosing a publisher. Lawrence's work was distributed by a number of publishing firms, both in England and abroad. From the mid-twenties onwards, they distributed his novels* to an increasingly large audience in mainland Europe, both in translation* and in the original language. In this chapter, we will focus on the publishing options open to a writer like D.H. Lawrence, and we will trace the ways in which publishers* and booksellers* helped his work to reach a European readership*.

Writers, texts, books, publishers, booksellers and readers all participate in forms of exchange, and these exchanges take place on a (partly real, partly imaginary) European literary marketplace*. It can be useful to visualize the contacts between them as a complex "network"*. Book historian Claire Squires emphasises that this international network links not only people, but also objects (books) and activities (writing, distributing, reading).[2] In this network, texts are written and books are designed, produced, distributed, marketed, bought and read, in a constant process of interaction, conflict and alliance. For people participate in the network and enter the market for two reasons: to earn money, and to accrue (or assign) value. Interestingly, authors have always been expected to do either one or the other: if they are out to make money by writing novels, then they should not expect much artistic prestige; if they value their reputation, they should take care not to seem to intent on boosting their market value. In this chapter, we will show that this conflict between economic and artistic value came to a head in the early twentieth century. D.H. Lawrence addressed precisely this theme in his controversial novel *Lady Chatterley's Lover* (1928) − a book proudly and defiantly "kicking the shins" of his audience.

Lady Chatterley's Lover is one of the most controversial books in the history of European literature.[3] In 1960 − more than three decades after the publication of the first edition − a British judge put the matter succinctly:

> Would you approve of your young sons, young daughters − because girls can read as well as boys − reading this book? . . . Is it a book that you would even wish your wife or your servants to read?[4]

While most book reviewers feared the novel's morally undermining effects, critic Edmund Wilson praised its "nobleness":

> Lawrence's theme is a high one: the self-affirmation and triumph of life in the teeth of all the destructive and sterilizing forces − industrialism, physical depletion, dissipation,

careerism and cynicism – of modern England; and in general, he has given a noble account of it.[5]

Still, many readers were shocked by the graphic and frank descriptions of the illegitimate emotional and physical relationship between an upper-class woman, Lady Constance Chatterley, who is married to the minor nobleman Clifford Chatterley, and a working class man, Oliver Mellors, the gamekeeper of their estate Wragby. The explicit descriptions of sex and its use of indecent words ("fuck", "cunt") made the novel unacceptable for the majority of publishers, critics and readers.

The plot* is set against the background of the years following the Great War, as the opening paragraph reveals.

Text: D.H. Lawrence, Lady Chatterley's Lover *(1928)*

> Ours is essentially a tragic age, so we refuse to take it tragically. The cataclysm has happened, we are among the ruins, we start to build up new little habitats, to have new little hopes. It is rather hard work: there is now no smooth road into the future: but we go round, or scramble over the obstacles. We've got to live, no matter how many skies have fallen.[6]

Due to a war injury, Clifford is paralyzed from the waist down and as a result he is impotent. Clifford and Connie gradually drift apart as he neglects her longing for physical love and pursues a literary career* and an intellectual life, a life of the mind. "Of physical life they lived very little."[7] Clifford, who writes and publishes short stories*, becomes more and more obsessed with financial success and literary fame*. In his mansion, he receives successful young authors who, in his view, "had the ear of a few million people, probably."[8] Connie witnesses Clifford making his entrance on a highly commercialized literary marketplace:

> Connie wondered a little over Clifford's blind, imperious necessity to become known: known, that is, to the vast amorphous world he did not himself know, and of which he was uneasily afraid: known as a writer, a first-class modern writer. Connie was aware, from successful old hearty, bluffing Sir Malcolm, that artists did advertise themselves, and exert themselves to put their goods over. But her father used channels ready-made, used by all the other R.A.'s who sold their pictures. Whereas Clifford discovered new channels of publicity, all kinds. He had all kinds of people at Wragby – without exactly lowering himself. But, determined to build himself a monument of a reputation quickly, he used any handy rubble for the making.[9]

One of the guests at Wragby refers to money and success as "the bitch-goddess", luring writers to a worship of fame and popularity. Connie witnesses Clifford making strides into fame.

> There was Clifford's success: the bitch-goddess! It was true, he was almost famous, and his last book brought him in a thousand pounds. His photograph appeared everywhere. . . . His seemed the most modern of modern voices, with his uncanny, lame instinct for publicity he had become, in four or five years, one of the best-known of the young "intellectuals". Where the intellect came in, Connie did not quite see. Clifford was really clever at that slightly humorous analysis of people and motives

which leaves everything in bits at the end. But it was rather like puppies tearing the sofa-cushions to bits: except that it was not young and playful, but curiously old, and almost obscenely conceited.[10]

Clifford is well aware that selling a story to a newspaper or publisher means money, but at the same time he is eager to maintain his status as a literary author, who by modern cultural convention is expected to distance himself from mundanities like wealth and fame. "Clifford seemed to care very much whether his stories were considered first-class literature or not. Strictly, she [Connie] didn't care. Nothing in it! said her father. Twelve hundred pounds, last year! was the retort simple and final."[11]

By exploring the complex relationship between art and commerce, *Lady Chatterley's Lover* mirrors the important preoccupation mentioned earlier: how to be financially and socially successful without losing your reputation as an independent, serious author. This sentiment was shared by many writers in the first half of the twentieth century, including Lawrence, and it is hard to underestimate the influence and authority of this cultural taboo. In this period, being a writer increasingly meant trying to be a professional author. Earlier, writers wrote their novels part-time while holding a day job, or relied on a patron* or on their family capital to keep them in funds. Now, even prickly, non-commercial writers like Lawrence tried to live by their pen. Still, Lawrence was well aware of the fact that professionalism and success meant writing for "a vast amorphous world",[12] that is: a mass audience of unknown readers. Addressing this vast readership meant that authors had to learn to balance cultural and economic interests and develop a keen "instinct for publicity".[13] For publishers, it meant that they had to make use of modern advertising and sales strategies.

The fate and fortune of *Lady Chatterley's Lover* and of its author provide interesting insights into the dynamics of the literary marketplace. David Herbert Lawrence spent his youth in the coal mining town of Eastwood, Nottinghamshire; the son of a miner and a schoolteacher, dreaming of becoming a writer. His determination to write shin-kicking books got him immediately into trouble: his novel *The Rainbow*, published in 1915, was suppressed and prosecuted by the National Purity League for obscenity (the heroine's sexual relations with both men and women) and for its anti-war message. *Sons and Lovers* (1913), *Women in Love* (1920) and *Lady Chatterley's Lover* (1928) were all controversial, but made him famous within and beyond the Anglophone world. His literary success was hindered by his reputation as a "pornographer". By writing serious novels in what seemed like pornographic language he blurred the age-old boundary between pornography and "proper" literature. In his essays as well as in his novels, Lawrence showed himself a fierce cultural critic of an intellectual attitude that underestimated the importance of physical intimacy, of "the peace of fucking,"[14] as a means to escape an industrialized and mechanized society.

Lawrence was well aware of the rapid changes in the literary marketplace. By equating commercial success with "the prostitution to the bitch-goddess", Lawrence's novel bears traces of the ongoing debate about the complex relationship between money and the arts. From the mid-nineteenth century onwards – that is: from the moment a commercial literary mass-market came into being – authors felt the urge to distance themselves from a literary economy in which success was measured by income. When in 1851 a literary friend tried to persuade Gustave Flaubert to publish some fragments in a commercial magazine, the future author of *Madame Bovary* reacted as if hit by fears of contamination. Why should he pursue objectives other than "art itself"?[15] "Fame! Fame! What is fame? It is nothing. A mere noise, the external accompaniment of the joy Art gives us," he wrote to another friend – the successful novelist Louise Colet in 1847.[16] This antagonistic conception of the relationship between art and commerce was a leitmotiv in literary criticism* until at least the 1960s, and dominated debates in the other arts as well.

It is not surprising that so many concerns about the dominance of "the crowd" cropped up in this period. Due to population growth, the extension of secondary education, and an increase in income and leisure time, a growing number of people were able to buy and read books. Moreover, technical developments in the field of book and paper production made it possible to print, reprint and distribute large numbers of relatively cheap paperback books more rapidly than ever before. Authors and publishers responded by producing more books for an increasingly diverse and socially stratified readership, while a growing number of book reviewers – in daily newspapers and magazines*, and on the radio – attempted to guide their readers through the modern literary landscape.

Albatross: literary hierarchies

The changing literary landscape created excellent chances for publishers to pick up on new possibilities and create new markets. Albatross Books, for example, was very successful in forging a new, European readership for contemporary British and American literature. Founded in 1932 in Hamburg, Albatross catered to English-speaking readers across Europe, who would rather read English and American novels in the original language than in translation. Albatross was very international in outlook from the start. It had close ties to Tauchnitz, a longer-standing publishing house* that had been publishing mass market paperbacks* on the European continent since 1841. Tauchnitz had its headquarters in Paris but printed its books in Italy and Germany. By the time Albatross took over Tauchnitz in 1934, it had published reprints of already famous modern books such as Aldous Huxley's *Brave New World* and James Joyce's *Ulysses*. Between 1932 and 1939, Albatross would publish around 400 volumes in the Albatross Modern Continental Library, mixing what we now refer to as the best of English literature from the 1920s and 1930s, and "lighter" and less highbrow titles. The books were read by non-native speakers across the continent. Albatross was very successful in reaching a large European public. In 1937, the editors claimed that four out of five Tauchnitz and Albatross readers were "foreigners".[17]

In the 1930s, the European market for Anglo-American books was divided into three fiercely competing sectors. A German reader interested in the works of Lawrence, for instance, could purchase his work in three different formats. She could buy him in translation (the German Insel Verlag published eleven translations of his books between 1922 and 1934), or, if she was proficient in English, she could buy him in the original language, choosing between either the cheap Tauchnitz or Albatross editions, or the imported original hardcovers British publishers were selling (at lofty prices) through European booksellers. In Germany, Albatross and Tauchnitz offered an attractively large selection of his works: Tauchnitz had produced five Lawrence volumes between 1928 and 1932, Albatross tallied twenty between 1932 and 1939. The availability of cheap and attractive English-language editions hurt translation sales: when, in 1932, Lawrence's *Apocalypse* appeared both in Albatross and in Insel's translation, Albatross easily outsold Insel. The market for imported hardcover editions was virtually destroyed by Albatross as well – even well-heeled and prosperous readers would rather buy their cheap and easily available paperbacks than fork out for costly hardcovers*.

How do these internationally oriented publishers of affordable books work? How do they manage their processes of selecting, marketing, branding and selling authors and texts? It is important to realize that no book is ever published without a large set of pre-liminary decisions – and that for publishers the most important question of all is: who will buy this book? How can it be positioned amid the thousands of other books published each year? And how to convince authors that publishing with this particular publishing firm is going to propel their career? We have seen that for writers like D.H. Lawrence, the decision with whom to publish, in which form, and aimed at which public is crucial. Choosing a publisher (and for publishers: selecting an author) means entering in a form of dialogue and interaction, with the one continually, but not unproblematically, confirming and endorsing the cultural worth of the other. For both parties, succeeding in publishing means finding a balance between economic and artistic gain, between increasing their market value and protecting their cultural prestige.

During the interwar years as well as today, publishers had a whole toolbox of instruments at their disposal to advertise cultural value, their own and the author's, on the literary marketplace. Marketing (the process of targeting an audience and catering to its needs) is one of these instruments. How could makers of books try to persuade readers to attach a certain favourable meaning or value to the books they considered buying? One way to do this was to adapt the exterior of the book to the expectations a buyer might have – and then twist those expectations a little. The publishers of the Albatross series* were remarkably good at this. They successfully influenced buyer's expectations by selling them classic and contemporary novels in modern, bright covers in captivating colours (kelly green, acid yellow, sprightly orange). Earlier series, including its direct predecessor Tauchnitz, tended to look rather staid and solemn; Albatross radiated modernity and flair. This shaped readers' notions of what might be *inside* those covers, and prepared them for the heady mix of modern and traditional texts Albatross had to offer. In order to guide buyers and readers through the rapidly growing supply of new books, Albatross used an advanced "colour system" that was explained on the inside of the paper board back cover in four languages (English, German, French and Italian):

> Red Volumes: stories of adventure and crime
> Blue Volumes: love stories
> Green Volumes: stories of travel and foreign peoples
> Purple Volumes: biographies and historical novels
> Yellow Volumes: psychological novels, essays, etc.
> Orange Volumes: tales and short stories, humorous and satirical works.[18]

A quick look at the covers thus revealed that "Volume 1: James Joyce – *Dubliners*" should be classed among the "psychological novels, essays, etc.", whereas "Volume 2: Aldous Huxley – *The Gioconda Smile*" was to be regarded as a specimen of "tales and short stories, humorous and satirical works" and "Volume 9: Edgar Wallace – *The Man at the Carlton* by Edgar Wallace" as a crime story. By printing a list of future instalments on the final page of each volume, the publisher emphasized the continuity of his series. Retailers across Europe – the owners of bookshops – welcomed Albatross, because the books were instantly recognisable and easy to display and market. The series made the most of what is called "package psychology": readers' inclination to buy new – and similarly packaged – offerings if they liked their earlier purchases. If one bright Albatross cover ended up on their bookshelves, they were inclined to add a few more.

Marketing should be seen as collective effort. Not only authors and publishers played their part, but critics and readers as well – for instance by (not) responding to what was published, by buying or refusing to buy new publications, and by (not) adapting their views and expectations of literature and books along the way. It is important to note that the rapid technical developments and the expanding scope of this period affected the appeal and position of literature in society. Authors, critics and publishers realized that literature was no longer the exclusive preserve of a social elite*, but had become a consumable product for an expanding middle-class public all over Europe. People were increasingly able to build their own private book collections, and had access to books in commercial and public libraries and reading clubs. In order to profit from this market, most publishing companies preferred a mix of both popular fiction (adventure novels and detective stories, for example) and high literature, as well as texts in between these two poles. Most publishing companies relied on cross-subsidization and alternated "difficult" books that sold little with popular fiction and older, canonical texts.

Publishing the best books for the largest audience

The Albatross Press made the most of this mixing and matching of texts, alternating the experimental with the traditional, the controversial with the sedate. Their purpose was to publish literature that would appeal to every kind of reader and to provide the *largest* possible audience with the *best* books, and to balance books that won them cultural capital with those that also promised financial gain. Editor Holroyd-Reece stated in 1934 that:

> the *Albatross* is interested in supplying the best stuff which it can market. The *Albatross* on the whole is particularly fortunate because, so far, broadly speaking, the best stuff has, contrary to the experience of most publishers, found the best market for us.[19]

If we take a look at the first twenty titles published in the series in 1932 (Table 28.1), it becomes clear how diverse and mixed this "best stuff" actually was.

Table 28.1 The first twenty titles published in the Albatross series (1932)

	Title	Author	Genre/style/subject	First published in
1	Dubliners	James Joyce	Naturalistic/ psychological short stories	1914
2	The Gioconda Smile and Other Stories	Aldous Huxley	Ironic representations of modern life	1921
3	Mantrap	Sinclair Lewis	Adventure novel	1926
4	The Bridge of Desire	W. Deeping	Romance	1916
5	Rogue Herries	Hugh Walpole	Historical fiction	1930
6	Night in the Hotel	E. Crawshay-Williams	Psychological novel	1931
7	To the Lighthouse	Virginia Woolf	Psychological novel	1927
8	Two People	E.E. Milne	Psychological novel	1931
9	The Man at the Carlton	Edgar Wallace	Mystery	1931
10	Dodsworth	Sinclair Lewis	Satirical novel	1931
11	Gauntlet	Lord Gorell	Romance	1931

(Continued)

Table 28.1 (Continued)

	Title	Author	Genre/style/subject	First published in
12	*Buttercups and Daisies*	Compton Mackenzie	Comedy	1931
13	*The Limestone Tree*	Joseph Hergesheimer	Historical fiction	1931
14	*The Golden Vase*	Ludwig Lewisohn	Autobiographical psychological novel	1931
15	*The Magic Island*	William Seabrook	Travelogue	1929
16	*The Brothers*	L.A.G. Strong	Romance	1932
17	*The Love of Julie Borel*	Kathleen Norris	Romance	1931
18	*The Bishop Murder Case*	Van Dine	Detective	1928
19	*Ambrose Holt and Family*	Susan Glaspell	Domestic novel	1931
20	*The Maltese Falcon*	Dashiell Hammett	Detective	1930

The first twenty Albatross volumes offer a fascinating cross-section of what publishers thought a European reading public would be interested in around the year 1932. It is obvious that the editors of the press tried to make a statement by putting arch-modernist James Joyce at the head of the list. His *Dubliners*, arguably his most accessible work, had been published sixteen years before; since then, the infamous (and very challenging) *Ulysses* (1922) had catapulted him into literary fame. Still, most Albatross readers in Germany, France, Holland or Italy would have heard *of* him, but wouldn't necessarily have read anything *by* him. *Dubliners*, in a beautiful and cheap Albatross edition, made it easy for aspiring book lovers across Europe to step in. Michele Troy has argued that part of the success of the books was due to their snob appeal: "each book sold, each book seen by fellow passengers on the train, invited Albatross's readers into 'another world,' down the red carpet, past the velvet ropes and into an elite, members only club."[20] Buying modernist masterpieces like *Dubliners* by Joyce or *To the Lighthouse* by Virginia Woolf (number 7 on the list) meant certifying identity and membership; Albatross's serial character ensured that part of this appeal rubbed off on the less challenging books published in the series as well – on page-turners like *The Bishop Murder Case* (number 18) or soppy romances* like *The Bridge of Desire* (number 4).

Albatross took its readers very seriously. Not only by publishing the very latest in British and American literature (as the list above shows, thirteen of the first twenty books were originally published less than two years before), but also by employing a very modern marketing strategy of directly addressing their European public and inviting them to participate. The editor inserted cards inside the books with the following message:

> Dear Reader, If I have not yet chosen that special book you want me to publish, would you care to select it yourself? A free copy is sent of every book published at a reader's suggestion to whoever proposed it first. On receipt of your card you will be informed if the book in question has been suggested already and if not it will be read at once. Hoping yours will be the first suggestion, I remain, Yours sincerely The Albatross.[21]

All this was very new. Publishers always used to work from a *production* perspective*: deciding which texts they wanted to publish first, and thinking about which audience to sell them to afterwards. Here we see Albatross working from a *consumption* perspective*: thinking of ways to target and broaden their audience first, and only then deciding on the texts that would be most suited to this purpose. In this model, marketing becomes a matter of looking at the business through the customers' eyes. At first glance, this seems a symptom of the commercialization* and commodification* of literature ("it's all about selling and money now"), but Albatross claimed that considerations of literary value* and quality were still at the core of any publishing decision. If anything, the shift to a consumption perspective signalled the increasing complexity of the way in which literary value was produced and circulated.

It is an interesting question whether Albatross helped literature to become *more* (or, for that matter, *less*) European in this period. Michele Troy has argued that Albatross "projected a cosmopolitan ethos" and "shaped taste . . . on the continent."[22] The series forged a new readership for English-language books by changing continental readers' access to texts. In this sense, the series unquestionably extended the European reach and reputation of many authors. But on the other hand, the European trade in books was flourishing long before Albatross came into being. Book export exploded at the end of the nineteenth century, with dozens of booksellers in all major European countries specializing in sending out books across borders (see also Chapter 23). In Germany alone, the number of firms catering exclusively to readers outside Germany increased from 64 in 1889 to 134 in 1900, 259 in 1905 and 335 in 1910 – then dropping again to 118 in war-torn 1916.[23] These booksellers had specialized knowledge of the markets abroad and took great care to adjust their supply to the cultural situation in each of the different countries they catered to. Sending out German-language books to a German-speaking minority (mostly expatriates living in the major European cities) must have decreased the sense of geographical and mental distance between countries and cultures.

Germany, with its large number of bookshops and its cultured public, was very important for Albatross. The series sold very well there; the German-speaking countries constituted half of Albatross's markets. It is interesting to note that the works of Lawrence were distributed especially widely there. The writer, who died in 1930, lived to see three of his books published by Tauchnitz and marketed across Europe. This pleased him. Lawrence himself had a lively interest in European culture, and in German culture in particular: throughout his work there are references to German literature and German writers. It gave him pleasure to be published there, first in translation (Insel Verlag published eleven translations of his works) and then in English.[24] After his death, Tauchnitz published another two of Lawrence's books, and Albatross added another twenty between 1934 and 1938. These twenty titles profited from Albatross's wide distribution network in Germany, from the enthusiasm of hundreds of German booksellers and from prominent display positions in their shops. The eye-catching coloured band around Lawrence's books (in bright orange, indicating fiction) helped readers select and distinguish: Albatross used presentational differences like these (in format, design or price) as consciously interlinked presentational strategies. They also served to distinguish the series from the (visually much more subdued) Insel Verlag translations of Lawrence's work, which were also on display in most bookshops.

The marketing of his work was facilitated further by Lawrence's early personal contacts with a number of important gatekeepers in German literary culture. Long articles on his work appeared in prominent reviews like *Die Literatur* ('Literature') and *Die Kolonne: Zeitschrift für Dichtung* ('The Column: Journal for Poetry'). Interestingly, German reviewers hailed him as a truly *European* writer. In 1936, one of them summed up the gist of the German (and even European) reception of his work:

> He was of that rare vitality that affects you for a long time; you find, indeed in every country, followers of his work who speak of him with more than literary warmth, and whoever has read him at all, usually knows the whole of him. His readership is much less numerous than with other celebrities, but it has something of the real nature of a congregation, and this for a good reason, because this poet has touched people in the depth of their view of the world.[25]

This idea of congregation, of the deliberate gathering of a group of like-minded adherents around some cultural phenomenon, tied in especially well with the way in which Albatross saw itself and tried to market its own series in Europe. If Lawrence's titles did not sell especially well (reading and enjoying Lawrence remained something of an acquired taste, both in England and abroad), his reputation as an author for discerning and compassionate readers must have been an important incentive behind Albatross's decision to publish so many of his books in so short a time.

Critical reception

If Lawrence had to think very carefully about what to write for whom, then his publishers faced equally difficult decisions, especially regarding *Lady Chatterley's Lover*. This scandalous novel is an interesting case, because its wide audience and literary reputation were partly a result of the way in which the book was produced, distributed and received. Lawrence wrote three versions of the novel. British and American publishers rejected the manuscript, but rumours about the book spread quickly and the English magazine *John Bull* termed the not yet published novel "A Landmark in Evil".[26] The third version was published in 1928, produced by a private printer in Florence, financed by the author himself, distributed by his friends and available only to subscribers. The print run was 1,000 copies, signed and numbered by the author. The English customs seized copies of the book in order to prevent *Lady Chatterley* from corrupting British morals. The book was banned as obscene, both in the United Kingdom and in the United States. In 1932, two years after Lawrence's death, publishing companies Albert Knopf and Martin Secker issued an abridged and expurgated version of the novel for the American and British book market. This edition would be pirated many times. In January 1933, Frieda Lawrence, who owned the manuscript* of the definitive version, sanctioned the publication of an unexpurgated version of the novel by the Odyssey Press, Paris (an imprint of Albatross Press). The novel was subjected to obscenity trials all over the globe, from the United States and England to Japan.[27] It took until 1961 before an unexpurgated version of the novel was published by Penguin Books, after a controversial obscenity trial in the United Kingdom. The verdict was celebrated as a victory of the freedom of the written word and is still considered a crucial moment in the history of banned books.

As we have seen, Lawrence consciously addressed his books to an international public, and used a wide range of publishing channels to reach it – from private printers to big international firms. Because of its small-scale circulation, the first edition of *Lady Chatterley's Lover* did not receive much public attention. But soon after his death in 1930, the author and his book became well known in Germany, Italy and France, especially after the first translations were issued. Quite a few companies were reluctant to publish a translation, precisely because of the scandalous nature of the story. Tracing the translations and critical reception* in various European countries is one way of looking at the European literary history of this period – and of looking at the "European-ness" of this history. We will limit this section to a few examples.

France would prove to be very important for Lawrence's posthumous reputation, since many influential critics – François Mauriac, Albert Thibaudet, Charles Mauron and André Malraux, among others – wrote about *Lady Chatterley's Lover* and the French translation was read all over Europe. In 1932, publishing company Gallimard issued *L'Amant de Lady Chatterley*, with a preface by the leading writer, critic and left-wing intellectual André Malraux. This introductory essay was immediately reprinted in the authoritative literary periodical* *La Nouvelle Revue Française* (January 1932) under the title "D.H. Lawrence et l'érotisme" and would accompany many reprints of the French translation. Malraux declared that Lawrence was "the leading novelist in his country" and a defender of the value of eroticism and vitality: "Lawrence does not want to be happy or famous; he wants *to be*."[28] In contrast to the Christian tradition, Malraux continues, Lawrence considers women as full human beings, that is: with a sexuality of their own. The novel's libertine purport touched nerves, both in England and abroad. Whereas for many critics this was enough reason to ignore or reject the book, Albert Thibaudet made efforts to relate Lawrence's novel to the tradition of "sensual literature", placing it in line with Montaigne (*Essais*) and Rousseau (*Julie*) and thus legitimizing the novel's literary and cultural value.

> It is perfectly understandable that Lawrence's novel, unhealthy for those who bear the curiosity of the student, and, for the abovementioned reasons, should obviously not be read by young people, seems otherwise perfectly healthy for a normal man or woman of today, who gives sex a place and a normal and serious role.[29]

During the 1930s, critics became more and more interested in Lawrence's critical ideas on the industrialization and of the mechanization of human life. Lawrence's critique of intellectualism and his defence of "physical life" appealed to critics who were in search of moral freedom. In his article on "D.H. Lawrence and eroticism", the Dutch novelist and critic E. du Perron – a friend of Malraux, reviewing the French translation of *Lady Chatterley's Lover* – characterized the book as a testimony of the hatred against the falsification of natural values by both hypocritical intellectuals and ignorant masses. According to Du Perron, the experience of eroticism paved the way for a highly necessary return to primitive, primordial values.[30] These leading critics and their periodicals, who did not fear the novel's contentious themes, played a decisive part in the notorious afterlife of *Lady Chatterley's Lover*.

Notes

1   James T. Boulton and Lindeth Vasey, eds., *The Letters of D.H. Lawrence*, vol. 5: March 1924–March 1927 (Cambridge: Cambridge Universiry Press, 2002), 201.
2   Claire Squires, *Marketing Literature: The Making of Contemporary Writing in Britain* (Basingstoke: Palgrave Macmillan, 2007), 1.
3   D.H. Lawrence, *Lady Chatterley's Lover* (London: Penguin Classics, 2006).
4   C.H. Rolph, *The Trial of Lady Chatterley* (London: Penguin Books, 2005), 1.
5   Edmund Wilson, "The Book That Brought Good Sex Writing to the Masses." *The New Republic*, June 3, 1929, 6.
6   Lawrence, *Lady Chatterley's Lover*, 5.

7 Lawrence, *Lady Chatterley's Lover*, 16.
8 Lawrence, *Lady Chatterley's Lover*, 21.
9 Lawrence, *Lady Chatterley's Lover*, 21.
10 Lawrence, *Lady Chatterley's Lover*, 50.
11 Lawrence, *Lady Chatterley's Lover*, 63.
12 Lawrence, *Lady Chatterley's Lover*, 21.
13 Lawrence, *Lady Chatterley's Lover*, 21.
14 Lawrence, *Lady Chatterley's Lover*, 301.
15 Gustave Flaubert, *The Letters of Gustave Flaubert*, vols. 1 & 2, 1830–1880. Sel., ed., and trans. Francis Steegmuller (London: Picador, 2001), 205.
16 Flaubert, *The Letters*, 133.
17 Michele K.Troy, "Behind the Scenes at the Albatross Press: A Modern Press for Modern Times," in *The Culture of the Publisher's Series*, ed. John Spiers (Basingstoke: Palgrave Macmillan, 2011), 207.
18 Aldous Huxley, *The Gioconda Smile* (Paris/Hamburg/Milan: Albatross, 1932).
19 Troy, "Behind the Scenes," 205.
20 Troy, "Behind the Scenes," 205–6.
21 A card with this text was found inserted in Claude Houghton's *Hudson Rejoins the Herd*, an edition published by The Albatross Library in 1947 (no. 570). See www.worldliteratureforum.com/forum/archive/index.php/t-953.html
22 Troy, "Behind the Scenes," 202–3.
23 Georg Jäger, *Geschichte des deutschen Buchhandels im 19. und 20: Jahrhundert*. Band 1: Das Kaiserreich 1871–1918.Teil 3 (Berlin: De Gruyter, 2003), 467.
24 Christa Jansohn and Dieter Mehl, *The Reception of D.H. Lawrence in Europe* (London: Continuum, 2007), 23.
25 Jansohn and Mehl, *The Reception of D.H. Lawrence*, 38.
26 Quoted in Elisabeth Ladenson, *Dirt for Art's Sake: Books on Trial From* Madame Bovary *to* Lolita (Ithaca/London: Cornell University Press, 2007), 144.
27 Ladenson, *Dirt for Art's Sake*, 131–56.
28 André Malraux, "D.H. Lawrence et l'érotisme," *La Nouvelle Revue Française*, January 1, 1932, 137.
29 Albert Thibaudet, "Langage, Littérature et Sensualité," *La Nouvelle Revue Française*, April 1, 1932, 724.
30 E. du Perron, "D.H. Lawrence en de erotiek," *Forum* 1.6 (1932), 366–79.

Further reading

Baldick, Chris. *The Modern Movement: The Oxford English Literary History*.Vol. 10: 1910–1940. Oxford: Oxford University Press, 2004.
Jaillant, Lise. *Modernism, Middlebrow and the Literary Canon:The Modern Library Series, 1917–1955*. London: Routledge/Taylor & Francis, 2014.
McCleery, Alistair. "Tauchnitz and Albatross: A 'Community of Interests' in English-Language Paperback Publishing, 1934–51." *The Library* 7.3 (2006): 297–316.
Spiers, John. "Introduction: Wondering About 'The Causes of Causes':The Publisher's Series, Its Cultural Work and Meanings." In *The Culture of the Publishers Series*.Vol. 1, edited by John Spiers, 1–61. Basingstoke: Palgrave Macmillan, 2011.

29 Writing the city

László Munteán and Pedro Lange

Figure 29.1 François Schuiten & Benoît Peeters, *"Les Cités Obscures": Brüsel*, Casterman, p. 52

The nineteenth century witnessed substantial changes in European urban life. The advent of industrialization and capitalist economies resulted in unprecedented growth of cities like London, Paris, and Berlin. Not only did they become prominent centres of production, exchange, and consumption of goods, but they also emerged as global cultural and artistic centres. Massive and continuous migration from the countryside to the cities called for new ways of human interactions: crowded streets, new patterns of domestic and public life, new means of transportation, and new architectural and urban planning solutions.

Urban bustle was at once energetic and alienating, inspiring journalists, sociologists, artists, novelists, and poets alike to give expression to this radically new urban experience as well as the characters and social relations that it engendered. Take, for instance, the *flâneur**, the aimless urban stroller who feels at home in the street surveying in his walks the ever-transforming city. This character first takes shape in Edgar Allen Poe's short story* *The Man of the Crowd* (1840), and is further developed in Charles Baudelaire's *Le Peintre de la Vie Moderne* ('The Painter of Modern Life', 1863) and Walter Benjamin's unfinished *Passagenwerk* ('Arcades Project', 1927–1940). The city will be featured as the favoured setting of a great many novels*, a genre that, to a large extent, came to prominence in response to new conditions of living in cities.

This chapter takes the aftermath of World War II as its point of departure. Its arch rests on three thematic pillars: the wounded city, the imagined city, and the multicultural city. These pillars will provide a context to explore thematically some of the urban representations in the vast terrain of city literature*. The section on the wounded city examines literary representations* of architectural and psychological ruination by looking at the urban landscape of post–World War II Europe, including literature written on the Balkan War of the 1990s. Imagined cities entail utopian visions that embody the desire for the reconstruction of Europe after World War II, as well as "corrective" dreams alluding, in one way or another, to the European urban phenomenon. In the last section of this chapter, the multicultural city, resulting from mass migration and globalisation, is explored in novels that address its social and cultural diversity.

The wounded city

By the end of World War II, many of Europe's great cities lay in ruins. Aerial bombardments and subsequent street fights had taken their toll on both the civilian population and the built environment. The bombing of Dresden and the nine-hundred-day siege of Leningrad resulted in a death toll comparable to the nuclear attacks on Hiroshima and Nagasaki. Seventy years on, the names of these cities still echo the unprecedented destruction they suffered during the war. Over time, the old urban fabric had given way to modern designs, new buildings had replaced the ruins, but the psychological wounds of these horrors would linger on for decades. Films such as Wolfgang Staudte's *Die Mörder sind unter uns* ('Murderers Among Us', 1946) and Billy Wilder's *Foreign Affair* (1948) address the hardships of life among ruins, fatigue, efforts to rebuild, and dealing with collective guilt in Germany. A new literary genre, *Trümmerliteratur** (or the 'literature of rubble') emerged in the immediate aftermath of war. It manifested itself in poems, essays, and a few novels, with Heinrich Böll's *Der Engel schwieg* ('The Silent Angel', 1992) as one of its most prominent examples.

Written between 1949 and 1951, the novel was withheld from publication until 1992 because the publisher did not deem readers ready to digest the gloom that pervaded life among the ruins. Written in third person omniscient style, the novel's viewpoint character is Hans Schnitzler, a deserter who returns to his ravaged hometown at war's end, wearing the coat of the lieutenant who was executed in his stead. The reader* is taken on an odyssey in the ruins of a wounded city as Hans attempts to return the coat to the soldier's widow, Elisabeth Gompertz, while also trying to get food, documents of identification, and a place to sleep.

Although the novel's autobiographical elements may suggest that the city is Böll's hometown Cologne, the text does not offer any landmarks to confirm this. Rather, the unnamed city is a metonym* for Germany's war-torn cityscapes, where ruins emerge as new landmarks for navigation and places to live in. With the exception of Frau Gompertz's apartment, everything is severely damaged: the hospital, the church, and the room Hans shares with Regina Unger, who has lost her baby to the war.

On his way to buy bread, Hans sits down amidst the remains of a school and observes the rubble around him.

Text: Heinrich Böll, Der Engel schwieg *('The Silent Angel') (1992)*

The date of the destruction of any particular ruin could be determined by its overgrowth: it was a question of botany. This heap of rubble was naked and barren, raw stone, newly broken masonry piled thickly, violently, with iron beams jutting out, showing scarcely a spot of rust. There wasn't a blade of grass to be seen; while in other places trees were already growing, charming little trees in bedrooms and kitchens, close by the rusty shell of the burned-out stove. Here there was only naked destruction, desolate and terribly empty, as if the breath of the bomb still hung in the air. Only the tiles, those that had survived, gleamed of innocence.[1]

In this passage, the ruins are portrayed as temporal markers of the destruction that "created" them. Focalized through Hans and articulated by a ruthlessly meticulous narrative voice*, the "heap of rubble" is witness to a devastation to which the lingering "breath of the bomb" gives a demonic dimension. The depiction of the bomb as a harrowing monster is coupled by the personification of architecture that, save for a few tiles that remained intact, appears as a ravaged body.

The metaphorical link Böll establishes between bodies and buildings in the previous excerpt recurs in a number of different manifestations throughout the novel. Conveyed in painstaking detail, the material disintegration of the city is reflected in the hunger, fatigue, pain, and psychological trauma that torment Hans, Regina, and Frau Gompertz. Dialogues and events are interspersed with lengthy descriptions of material disintegration as an irreversible process. Regina's fruitless effort to clean the room she shares with Hans is a case in point:

Each time she brought fresh water into the room she stopped in shock: the place she'd mopped had dried in the meantime and shone with a white, ugly roughness, while the floor she had yet to clean was dark and even in tone.[2]

Here, material disintegration manifests itself in the amount of dust that exponentially increases by cleaning but this insurmountable task is also a metaphor* for the incapacity to process personal and collective traumas, as well as bearing witness to a Nazi past that would stain Germans for generations to come.

Yet another aspect of the metaphorical juxtaposition of the architectural and the corporeal comes to the fore in Hans's encounter with damaged statues in a church he used
to frequent as a child:

> He was struck by the demonic grotesqueness. A few faces grimaced like furious crip-
> ples because they lacked an ear or a chin, or because strange cracks deformed them;
> others were headless, and the stone stumps of their necks thrust up horribly from
> their bodies.[3]

Similarly to his personified representation of ruins that bespeak the freshness of destruction, Böll's prose renders the wounds of the statues uncanny ciphers for the deformed
human bodies buried underneath the rubble. The grotesqueness of the statues' appearance, which results from a confluence of the comical and the horrific, is a quality that
Böll describes in relation to the "botany" of ruins. Condensed in a single sentence, the
"charming little trees in bedrooms and kitchens, close by the rusty shell of the burned-out
stove" entails a mixture of war damage with what looks like a misplaced pastoral idyll no
less grotesque than the deformed statues.

Such unlikely juxtapositions are key to Böll's representation of life in the ruined city.
Joy is always imbued with sorrow, like the smile of a stone angel that greets Hans upon his
arrival to the city – a smile that appears to be "one of pain"[4] when he sees it again at the
end of the novel. Likewise, while the growing patches of wet plaster on the ceiling seem
like "eyes staring at them",[5] Hans and Regina find solace in each other's company. The
room, with its falling plaster metaphorically tearing up their psychological wounds, is at
once the crucible of their budding love. But even this ending cannot assuage the heaviness
of material and psychological ruin that transpires from the novel.

The wounded city recurs in literary representations of such recent European conflicts as
the first Balkan War. Steven Galloway's *The Cellist of Sarajevo* (2008) features the infamous
siege of Sarajevo during the Balkan conflict, lasting nearly four years (1992–1996). This
war was precipitated by national sentiments emerging after Marshall Tito's death in 1980
in multi-ethnic Yugoslavia. Orchestrated by the Bosnian Serb state, the siege was one of
the darkest chapters of this war. Thirteen thousand soldiers took to the hills surrounding
the city and sniped at Sarajevo's citizens. Bosnia-Herzegovina, with an ill-equipped army,
was unable to break the siege. A real episode in the history of the siege serves as a dramatic
background to the novel: cellist Vedran Smailović played Albinoni's "Adagio in G minor"
in ruined buildings throughout besieged Sarajevo. For the most part, narration happens in
the present tense to effectively evoke in the reader the vulnerability felt by the inhabitants
of a city under siege. The opening sentences, however, fittingly in the past tense, take us
back to the moment before the explosion:

> It screamed downward, splitting air and sky without effort. A target expanded in size,
> brought into focus by time and velocity. There was a moment before impact that was
> the last time of things as they were. Then the visible world exploded.[6]

These phrases usher the reader into the precarious and frightful world of the three main
characters: Arrow, Kenan, and Dragan.

Kenan lives with his wife and children in a ruinous apartment. He must make regular
trips to the city well to fetch water for his family and for an annoying neighbour, Mrs.
Ristovski. These trips are riddled with the fear of being killed and guilty feelings for being

afraid to join the defence of his city. Dragan is numbed; he is alone and despondent since his family has managed to escape. A fortuitous meeting with Emina, an ex-friend of his wife who risks her life to bring expired pills to strangers, produces in Dragan a moment of awakening. Arrow, the actual hero in the novel, is a renowned sure shot in the resistance. Despite her harshness, it is in Arrow's chapters where the reader can glean images of a pre-war Sarajevo as she reminisces about her life as a girl and ponders what would have become of her had the war not broken out. Because the cellist has become a symbol of Sarajevo's resistance, the snipers want to kill him. Arrow's mission is to protect the cellist. She manages to eliminate the special envoy sent to kill him in a thrilling confrontation of cunning. Only at the end of the novel, before being killed for disobeying orders, does Arrow say her name, Alisa. Various themes braid the experiences of these characters during the siege. One of them is the dislocation and the subsequent remapping which Sarajevo's inhabitants are forced to carry out in order to navigate the wounded city.

But it is the cellist and his music, particularly his interpretation of Albinoni's "Adagio in G minor", that knots the predicament of these three characters. In the prologue, the narrator* reveals the provenance of the music: "In 1945, an Italian musicologist found four bars of a sonata's bass line in the remnants of the firebombed Dresden Music Library."[7] The allusion to Dresden establishes a kinship between Sarajevo and the carpet-bombing of Dresden by the allies in February 1945. Also, the survival of a musical manuscript and the manner it has risen in the interpretation of the cellist to honour Sarajevo's fallen becomes a motif of survival repeated in the main characters. Arrow reconnects with whom she was before the war; Kenan renews his generosity to the uncooperative Mrs Ristovski and makes the point to listen to the cellist each of the days he has played his instrument. And Dragan, inspired by Emina's devotion to the wounded, finds a sense of purpose in the midst of destruction, not unlike the relationship between Hans and Regina in Böll's *The Silent Angel*. The novel ultimately praises the power of music to build bridges among warring factions as suggested by Arrow's realisation: "The sniper had the shot. He had it the whole time. But he didn't shoot, he was listening to the cellist play."[8]

The imagined city

Urban reconstruction in the wake of the destruction left by war provides a fertile ground for the re-imagination of cities and, concomitantly, society as a whole. However, when architects' plans for new urban environments are realised, they are not always to the liking of the people who will inhabit them once they are built. Novels like George Konrád's *A városépítő* ('The City Builder', 1977), Francois Schuiten and Benoit Peeters's series of graphic novels* *Les Cités Obscures* ('Cities of the Fantastic', 1983–2008), and the canonical *Le città invisibili* ('Invisible Cities', 1972) by Italo Calvino, foreground with pathos, humour, and irony how new, grandiose projects that have been drawn up to replace traditional ways of life often have disastrous consequences.

The material, corporeal, and psychological ruination that unfolds from Böll's *The Silent Angel* illustrates what is referred to in German as *Stunde Null* ('zero hour'), which at once marks the end of the Nazi era and the beginning of reconstruction. In both Western and Eastern Europe, reconstruction entailed two parallel processes: the rebuilding of the ruined cities and the reorganization of society. The ideological principles along which reconstruction was to be carried out, were, however, very different on the two sides of the Iron Curtain. In the West, liberation brought the promise of democracy and, with the financial backing of the Marshall Plan, the prospect of economic recovery. In countries liberated by the Soviet Red Army, reconstruction meant the reorganization of society under Communist dictatorship.

Writers in the Eastern Bloc had to face rigorous censorship*. Hungarian writer George Konrád's *The City Builder* is an autobiographical novel* about ill-fated visions of social-ist city planning. Narrated in the first-person singular by an architect of an unnamed city during the early years of Socialism, *The City Builder* is a meditation on the archi-tect's responsibility as an intellectual. Flowing in poetic stream of consciousness*, Konrád's novel paints an ironic portrait of social and architectural reconstruction in Communist Hungary. By no means a surprise, his work was denied publication in Hungarian when he finished it in the late 1960s only to appear first in German and French translations*. The first – heavily censored – Hungarian version came out in 1977, and it was not until after the fall of Communism in 1989 that it was published in full.

The power of the novel lies less in its outright criticism of the regime and more in its presentation of the ethical dilemma of the narrator who, looking back on his career, recog-nizes the naïveté behind his utopian projects and his complicity in a system that granted him the power to realize them. At stake here is a city wounded by the wrecking ball of recon-struction. The disruption of the urban fabric by war damage, which serves as a set for Böll's novel, recurs in Konrád as a "slipshod saturation bombing"[9] that presented an opportunity for the implementation of Socialist city planning. The old city is to be discarded:

> it is cowardly and sentimental to want to spare its undulating and redundant mysteries. This is the eleventh hour, time for major surgery. We managed to rearrange the city down to the last grain of sand. Upheavals of imagination erupted under our fingers.[10]

Reconstruction is framed here as an act of violence against the personified city commit-ted for the sake of its renewal, which the narrator once wholeheartedly embraced.

From the city that he created, however, he finds himself no less alienated than from the autocratic system that it monumentalises. This alienation is conveyed through the narra-tor's confessional tone disclosing his involvement in what he now recognizes as irreversi-ble faults. In his confessional prose, Konrád combines remorse, anger, and satirical humour. In addition, he uses metaphor and metonymy to bring together body, mind, society, and the city. The narrator is inextricably tied to the city that he planned:

> I could go anywhere; in my suitcase and in the furrows of my brow I carry my city with me. Like a character flaw it has become a part of me, and though I may disguise it, I can no longer tell us apart.[11]

Construed metonymically as an ill-fated project, the city becomes an uncanny reminder of the narrator's misguided architectural visions, while in such phrases as "a national char-acter riddled with flaws"[12] the dubious morals of society are framed metaphorically as architectural mistakes. Ultimately, his alienation from the city is reflected in his gradual self-alienation. Haunted by the city he conceived, the paradox of the homeless architect leads to his complete disavowal of his creation, culminating in his effort to disengage him-self from it. At this point, the monotonous stream of consciousness gives way to an all out condemnation of the Socialist city, leading to the declaration of his wish for a "left-wing city"[13] devoid of the shortcomings of Socialist planning.

Utopian visions and their faulty realisations are recurring themes in a number of comic books* and graphic novels. Conceived as a typically American genre and associated with easy entertainment combining images and texts, comics and comic books would feature ever more intricate plotlines. The past few decades have witnessed the rise of the graphic novel as a literary genre developed from comic books. Indeed, graphic novels represent a new kind of literature thriving on both sides of the Atlantic and giving testament to its urban origins. In Europe, graphic novels are particularly popular in France, Belgium, and the Netherlands, where the genre has deep roots in popular culture. Ever since the 1980s, the comic artist Francois Schuiten and writer Benoit Peeters have been working on a series of graphic novels entitled *Les Cités Obscures* ('Cities of the Fantastic'), which has been widely regarded as one of the most elaborate representations of imagined cities in the genre.

The universe Schuiten and Peeters have created is that of independent cities located on Counter-Earth, invisible from our planet. Each city is built in a particular architectural style reminiscent of those in Europe and America. Certain buildings provide passages between the two worlds that allow travellers to explore the cities of Counter-Earth and give account of their experience in much the same way as Marco Polo does in Italo Calvino's *Invisible Cities*. The cities of Counter-Earth constitute a parallel universe where architectural visions are taken to the extreme and in ultimate uniformity. The city of Mylos, for instance, features massive industrial buildings ornate with Victorian glamor, while Xhystos is an art deco city of steel, recalling Fritz Lang's 1927 silent film *Metropolis*. In addition, the cities abound with references to the visions of such writers as Jules Verne, H.G. Wells, Franz Kafka, Jorge Luis Borges, and, most prominently, the Belgian architect, Victor Horta, whose turn-of-the-century art nouveau buildings had earned him world fame.

The graphic novel *Brüsel* (1992) is one of the most popular of the series. The city in the title is a "doppelgänger" of the Brussels of Schuiten and Peeters's childhood in the 1950s and 1960s, when many of the city's old neighbourhoods had fallen victim to new, megalomaniac projects. George Konrád's self-critical portrayal of the brutality of socialist city planning finds its Western counterpart in what Schuiten and Peeters call "brüselization", a radical transformation of the old city into a metropolis of skyscrapers, with traumatic consequences on its inhabitants. Similarly to Konrád's novel, the political and the architectural are inextricably interrelated. The unbridled pursuit of progress is a hubris that by the end of the novel results in the ultimate demise of Brüsel.

Following the immense success of their graphic novels, which earned them the Gaiman Award for best comic in 2012, Schuiten and Peeters have been expanding the world of their graphic novels into an ever-growing universe including CD and DVD supplements, as well as multiple websites with user-generated content. In addition, in 1999, the theme of the systematic demolition of the traditional urban texture dramatized in *Brüsel* resulted in a pseudo-documentary exhibition on brüselization and related conspiracy theories about the destruction of obscure passages, fittingly organized in the Autrique House, an art nouveau building in Brussels designed by Victor Horta.

In Italo Calvino's *Invisible Cities*, the famous Venetian traveller Marco Polo meets regularly with the Kublai Kahn to tell him of his travels and of the many cities in the Khan's vast empire that the emperor will never see – a poignant reflection on the limits of imperial power. Although Marco Polo threads a labyrinthine account of his travels, the aging Kahn discovers in what is perhaps the plausible climax of this unconventional novel (part prose poetry and part travelogue) that Polo's cities are different versions of Venice. "You take delight not in a city's seven or seventy wonders but in the answer it gives to a question of yours,"[14] states Marco Polo early in the novel. This statement, apart from foreshadowing the Kahn's discovery – since, arguably, these cities answer questions Marco Polo might have of his native Venice – also presents an acute reflection on the nature of traveling: to travel is always a return to home.

Indeed, in the whimsical catalogue of cities that structures the book, these cityscapes might come across as utopian and exotic spaces; but a more careful examination will reveal that they contain aspects recognisable in contemporary real cities. Leonia, for instance, is a city that embodies the relationship between consumerism and waste so prevalent in capitalist post-industrial cities: "It is not so much by the things that each day are manu-factured, sold, bought that you can measure Leonia's opulence, but rather by the things that each day are thrown out to make room for the new."[15] The consequence of Leonia's inability to conserve connects this invisible city with current environmental concerns. In the closing lines of the book, the Kahn laments that "the current is drawing us" to the Infernal city. Marco Polo, unveiling once again the grounding in reality of this seemingly magical book, responds:

> The Inferno of the living is not something that will be; if there is one it is what is already here, the inferno where we live every day, that we form by being together. There are two ways to escape suffering it. The first is easy for many: accept the inferno and become such a part of it that you can no longer see it. The second is risky and demands constant vigilance and apprehension: seek and learn to recognize who and what, in the midst of the inferno, are not inferno, then make them endure, give them space.[16]

Literary critic Jonathan Galassi in *The Dreams of Italo Calvino* acknowledges Calvino is "the postwar Italian prose writer who has had the largest and most enduring impact outside his own country."[17] Addressing the relevance of *Invisible Cities*, Galassi refers to Marco Polo's previously quoted closing words ("make them endure, give them space") and interprets Polo's advice as a return to real spaces and a call for social activism. Calvino's cities are invisible to the Khan and require a storyteller (Marco Polo). Similarly, the multi-cultural city – as we shall soon see, at times invisible to the mainstream European city, has also found its storytellers.

The multicultural city

If, in the wounded city, war produces ruination and the material fragmentation of the physical world, literatures about the contemporary moment in Europe show the fragmen-tation of national identities and national narratives along ethnic, linguistic, and cultural pluralities. This fragmentation yields the multicultural city as a result of Europe's history of colonization* and the current pressures of a globalized world. A clear manifestation of these two realities (colonial past and globalization*) is evident in the current refugee crisis affecting European countries. This crisis is partly an exodus caused by wars and partly a massive daily displacement of humans looking for better lives than the ones afforded to them in their home countries – countries in many ways shaped and ruined by the spoils of European empires and colonization. Novels like *Perverzion* (1997) by Ukrainian author Yuri Andrukhovych and *White Teeth* by Zadie Smith (2000) feature the emerging reality of multicultural European cities (see Chapter 30).

Perverzion documents with a satirical tone the last days in the life of Ukrainian poet and cultural icon Stanislav (Stakh) Perfetsky. He is the celebrated guest at "The Post Carnival Absurdity of the World: What's next in the Horizon", a conference organized in Venice.

After traversing European cities that include Budapest, Vienna, Munich, and Berlin, the exuberant Perfetsky reaches the Italian city, where he presumably jumps to his death on March 11, 1993. This is the conceit that triggers the novel's progression and its complicated structure. In the Epilogue, however, Andrukhovych casts doubt on the actual suicide of the outlandish character and the novel ends without resolution. More a slice in the life of Perfetsky than a novel with a storyline, the text agglutinates contradictory perspectives on the character. Throughout a large part of the novel, we hear Perfetsky's voice in diary entries. The tone and writing is assuredly literary and contemplative, but this soulful disposition is at odds with the perspectives offered by other accounts that portray a larger than life, narcissistic, alcoholic, and outrageous man.

The novel features various themes, among which the reader finds a love story: Ada Zitrone falls in love with Perfetsky and in the course of their sexual romance, he will reveal to her his unrelenting love for his deceased wife. There are countless allusions to world literature* including internal dialogues with T.S Eliot, Dante Alighieri, Jorge Luis Borges, and Mihail Bulgakov. Espionage is also present in the novel as an unequivocal echo of the culture of surveillance in the former Soviet Union. But, perhaps, the most salient theme in the novel is the sense of identity of the Eastern European subject *vis-à-vis* Western Europe, shortly after the fall of the Soviet Union.

The critical reception* of the novel has further underscored the divide between Eastern and Western Europe and the issue of Ukrainian identity in the context of Europe. According to Christi Anne Hofland, director of America House in Kyiv, Ukraine, "*Perverzion* illustrates Andrukhovych's opinion of Ukrainian national identity in relation to the West. On one side, he is sarcastic towards a West that he portrays as disinterested and ignorant of Ukraine. On the other side, it appears that Europe is Andrukhovych's ideal."[18] But as Perfetsky crosses the border between Austria and Germany, he is astounded by the sound of German in the voices of refugees realizing that reductive notions of European identity are being effectively contested. In solidarity with the refugees, Perfetsky not only summarizes the maladies created by globalization*, imperialism, and colonialism, but also ponders – in an eloquent and fittingly chaotic enumeration – the gifts and suffering that refugees bring with them to the European cityscape:

> how did they answer – with jazz, with marijuana, with a hundred methods of making love? . . . I walked among the refugees, half poisoned with the aromas, with the green and red flashes, the songs, it's easy to poison me – with everything thought up by these passportless searchers, of the rich German god, . . . to which they managed to force their way through a ship's pier glasses, some through louse-infested benches, through truths and untruths, through bribes, payoffs, killings, pleading, begging, through thrusting out their vaginas, rear ends . . . through eighteen borders and thirty customs checkpoints – as emigrants, musicians, journeyman laborers, sorcerers, sex machines, victims of burned-down houses, dissidents, bandits, rebels, garbagemen, shit carriers, sellers of roses in restaurants, croupiers, communists, Maoists, students of law and philosophy.[19]

Perfetsky's astonishment at the hybrid German spoken by migrants in Munich becomes the stuff of everyday life in the complex image of London that emerges in Zadie Smith's first novel, *White Teeth* (2000). Here, urban space is nuanced by the social forces unleashed by decades of migration to Great Britain, a nation that in its imperial heyday ruled over one-fifth of the world's population. And London, as the capital of the British Empire, has become a cradle of cultures whose influences challenge monolithic ideas about British identity. These influences are captured by Smith's novel in the multilingual and multicultural layers that collide and collude in the city, the vital rhythms that diverse and – at times – conflicting cultures bring to the city, and the hybridity that results from the overlapping of cultures in one space.

Zadie Smith's novel is addressed in detail in Chapter 30. We allude to *White Teeth* here mostly because of the contrast it offers when compared to Andrukhovych's *Perverzion*. If Andrukhovych employs a collage of voices to represent the plurality of an increasingly multicultural world as seen from the more distant and culturally homogenous perspective of an Eastern European visitor in Western Europe, characters in Zadie Smith's novel function not only as microcosms of myriad of cultures and social classes, but also as "Londoners", who nuance the city as a hybrid space. The narrative employs and perhaps exhausts, through an extraordinary proliferation of narratives, the conventions* of realism*.

Although the term is very flexible, realism is a movement in the arts that favours the objective representation of reality. Realistic novels (see Chapter 19) give detailed accounts of everyday life, at times offering profound social insights, as evident in novels by Emile Zola and Charles Dickens, among many others. Realistic narratives are generally entrusted to third person, unobtrusive narrators that implicitly claim that reality can be represented objectively and divorced from subjective influences. Zadie Smith's novel, while employing a rhetoric of realism, also foregrounds realism's limitations when portraying the diverse and multifaceted reality of the multicultural city. It is a realism bursting at the seams.

The reception of the novel has been overwhelmingly positive, but some critics have objected to the novel's proliferating narratives. English-American literary critic James Wood, for instance, has criticized the novel's use of realism on "moral" grounds, calling it hysterical realism:

> It is hysterical realism. . . . Appropriately, then, objections are not made at the level of verisimilitude, but at the level of morality: this style of writing is not to be faulted because it lacks reality – the usual charge against botched realism – but because it seems evasive of reality while borrowing from realism itself.[20]

That the reality of multiculturalism* represented by Smith is redolent of a harmony absent in the grinding relations between cultures existing in today's London is perhaps Smith's wish for multicultural harmony. But, Smith writes fiction*, not journalism*. Without bothering to contest the gender* implications of Wood's characterization of Smith's novel as "hysterical", we should ask the critic what he means by reality. Perhaps the use of the adjective "hysterical", as something uncontrolled and overly emotional, is actually rooted in the difficulty to reckon with the ever-changing plurality of *White Teeth*'s London but also a discomfort with the absence of a single narrative thread conducive to stable identifications. In both novels, Andrukhovych's *Perverzion* and Smith's *White Teeth*, the urban experience resulting from waves of migrants shatters uniform representations of the city.

Conclusion

Understandably not an exhaustive catalogue of urban literature*, the various literary works featured in this chapter were selected because they foreground the imaginative ways in which authors bear witness to the deep wounds left by war, as they affect cityscapes with material and human ruination. The novels that reimagine the reconstruction of European cities through utopian dreams provide a word of caution by exemplifying how quickly utopian dreams can degenerate in urban nightmares; or, ironically, to what extent utopias are riddled with our human–all-too-human realities. Beyond these imagined cityscapes, we have included texts featuring contemporary multicultural cities, centrifugal and always in a process of becoming.

Notes

1 Heinrich Böll, *The Silent Angel*, trans. Breon Mitchell (Bridgend: Andre Deutsch, 1995), 80–1.
2 Böll, *Silent Angel*, 136–7.
3 Böll, *Silent Angel*, 114.
4 Böll, *Silent Angel*, 169.
5 Böll, *Silent Angel*, 139.
6 Steven Galloway, *The Cellist of Sarajevo* (New York: Riverhead Books, 2008), xv.
7 Galloway, *Cellist*, xv.
8 Galloway, *Cellist*, 166.
9 George Konrád, *The City Builder*, trans. Ivan Sanders (New York: Harcourt, 1977), 62.
10 Konrád, *City Builder*, 27.
11 Konrád, *City Builder*, 31.
12 Konrád, *City Builder*, 22.
13 Konrád, *City Builder*, 122.
14 Italo Calvino, *Invisible Cities*, trans. William Weaver (Orlando: Harcourt, 1974), 44.
15 Calvino, *Invisible Cities*, 114.
16 Calvino, *Invisible Cities*, 165.
17 Jonathan Galassi, "The Dreams of Italo Calvino," review of *Invisible Cities*, by Italo Calvino, *The New York Review of Books*, June 20, 2013, www.nybooks.com/articles/2013/06/20/dreams-italo-calvino/
18 Christie Anne Hofland, "Understanding Post-Soviet Ukraine Through Literature," The Ellison Center for Russian, East European and central Asian Studies, University of Washington, http://ellisoncenter. washington.edu/student-spotlight/understanding-post-soviet-ukraine-through-literature/
19 Yuri Andrukhovych, *Perverzion*, trans. Michael M. Nayadan (Evanston: Northwestern University Press, 2005), 27–8.
20 James Wood, "James Wood's Classic Takedown on Faux-Dickensian 'Hysterical Realism'," *New Republic*, July 24, 2000, https://newrepublic.com/article/61361/human-all-too-inhuman

Further reading

Ameel, Lieven, Janson Finch and Markku Salmela, eds. *Literature and the Peripheral City*. New York: Palgrave Macmillan, 2015.
Lehan, Richard. *The City in Literature: An Intellectual and Cultural History*. Berkeley: University of California Press, 1998.
McNamara, Kevin, ed. *The Cambridge Companion to the City in Literature*. Cambridge: Cambridge University Press, 2014.
Varma, Rashmi. *The Postcolonial City and Its Subjects: London, Nairobi, Bombay*. New York: Routledge, 2012.

30 Changing Europe

Theo D'haen

Figure 30.1 Children at sustainable development exhibition "Planète Mode d'Emploi" at Paris, 24
    September 2009

Source: Public domain.

New Europeans

The end of World War II and the subsequent re-adjustment of the borders of many Central and Eastern European countries led to massive migrations, with millions of Germans being forced out of what now became western Poland and millions of Poles from what now became part of the USSR replacing them. In Western Europe, shortages of labour led to first a trickle and then a more massive influx of so-called "guest workers" (from the German term *Gastarbeiter*), first from Italy and Spain, later also from Morocco, Algeria, and Turkey, filling mostly low-skilled jobs in factories in Germany, France, the Netherlands, Belgium, and Scandinavia. In colonial and former colonial powers, there was also growing immigration from the (former) colonies. Many of the latter were Europeans, many of them born in the colonies, such as the more than a million *pieds noirs* from Algeria. But increasingly it was natives from the colonies or former colonies that came to Europe, initially again mainly as immigrant labour. While these migrant labourers were expected to return to their home countries after their contracts expired, many if not most in fact chose to stay. Increasingly joined by their (sometimes) extensive families, this in many Western European countries led to a sizeable proportion, comprising up to 10 percent, of the population being of immigrant labour stock. Finally, since the fall of the Berlin Wall in 1989, the free movement of labour policy of the European Union has caused fairly large streams of labour migration, especially from Central and Eastern Europe to Western Europe. In fact, the very term "Europe" has itself taken on a "new" meaning precisely because of the creation, after WWII, of what through various stages of increased collaboration and enlargement eventually became the European Union. Even more recently, economic and political upheavals in Africa and the wider Middle East have set in motion massive flows of refugees, many of whom find their way to Europe. All these developments once again led to what we might call "new" Europes. What has received most singular attention, though, is how the arrival and establishment of what I will call "the New Europeans" has changed the continent.

New European literature

Just as the early migrants from beyond Europe for a long time continued to be regarded as "foreign", so too with the earliest writings featuring them. This is most strikingly the case with works written in English or French by migrants from the colonies or former colonies. The 492 West Indian men the *SS Windrush* brought to London in 1948 formed the spearhead of what became a steady stream of West Indian migration to the United Kingdom. Most of the immigrants were labourers. However, some were writers. V.S. Naipaul arrived as a student in 1952. The Senegalese hero of Cheikh Hamidou Kane's *L'aventure ambiguë* ('Ambiguous Adventure', 1961) goes to study in France and falls victim to a huge crisis of identity. Regardless of the fact that much or all of the incidents narrated in them took place in Britain or France, all of these works were at least initially classified as "other" than, respectively, part of British or French literature proper. The Anglophone works initially fell under the category of Commonwealth literature*, comprising works written in English in (still or former) British colonies. The corresponding category for works written in French was that of the "francophonie"*. While initially also labelled as a Commonwealth writer, Naipaul later – and especially since the 1980s – has increasingly, though perhaps always still somewhat ambiguously, come to be regarded as a British writer. This change of category happened in parallel with a change in setting of his novels* and stories from his native Caribbean in his early writings such as *The Mystic Masseur* (1957), to

Britain and Europe in (the largely autobiographical) *The Enigma of Arrival* (1987). Writers such as George Lamming and Samuel Selvon in the 1980s and 1990s were seen as typical exponents of "postcolonial"* writing, but since then have come to be included, although again still somewhat ambiguously, under the yet more recent label "Black British Writing". This comprises all writing in English "about" (meaning set in and dealing with issues regarding) domestic Britain, by writers of non-British or non-European "white" stock residing in Britain, in practice all such writers originating from, or descended from ancestors originating from, beyond Europe. The number of such writers by now is legion, with some of the best-known, next to V.S. Naipaul, being Hanif Kureishi, Zadie Smith, Monica Ali, Caryl Phillips, and Salman Rushdie. With the latter two the categories are shifting again, though, as they eventually moved to the US. Thus, they have come to be part of a by now large body of writers, many of them of Indian or Caribbean provenance, who cannot be pinned down to a particular country of residence or "belonging".

Something similar has happened with francophone literature*. Leila Sebbar, in *Parle mon fils, parle à ta mère* ('Silence on the Shores', 1984), describes the dying days of an Algerian immigrant to France. In *Le Thé au harem d'Archimède* ('Tea in the Harem', 1983), Mehdi Charef depicts the life of French teenagers of Algerian immigrant stock in high-rise housing projects in the Paris suburbs. Sebbar and Charef were born in Algeria but moved to France at an early age. Azouz Begag does the same for a Lyon shantytown in *Le Gone du Chaâba* (1986). Begag is of Algerian descent but born in France. All are considered French "Beur" writers, a term referring to second-generation artists, in this case writers, of "Arab" descent, the inversion of the acronym of which, R.B., gave "B.R.", pronounced as "Beur". In one of the earliest articles on "Beur" writing, Tahar Djaout expresses his concern that already in 1990 the term is in danger of retrospectively being applied to all francophone Maghrebian writers and especially to all such writers that for extensive periods have lived or continue to live in France, with as best-known examples Kateb Yacine, Mohammed Dib, Assia Djebar, Driss Chraibi, and Tahar Ben Jelloun. Djaout, however, specifies that the writers just mentioned continue to write "from the Maghreb", even while living in France. "Beur" writers, who belong to a younger generation born in France, "envision their own future in terms of their links with France." Thus:

> they share the worries and preoccupations of all "second generation" young people who hope to find a place for themselves as a unique community capable of becoming integrated in French society and of participating actively in it. . . . Algeria is present, generally as an image associated with the previous generation but occasionally as a dream of the country to which one might someday return.[1]

The definition of "Beur" to a large extent also covers much of what is captured by the term "Black British Writing". In other languages there is no specific term for similar kinds of writing, but it is clear that the work of what in Dutch are labelled "Moroccan-Dutch" authors, the best-known being Hans Sahar (*Hoezo bloedmooi* ['How Do You Mean: Fucking Pretty?'], 1995) and Abdelkader Benali (*Bruiloft aan zee* ['Wedding by the Sea'], 1996), fits the definition. The same thing goes for the much larger category of "Indisch-Nederlandse" (Indonesian-Dutch) literature comprising works by authors of often mixed Dutch-Indonesian descent, and for the comparable categories of "Antillian-Dutch" and "Surinamese-Dutch" literature. All of these touch upon issues related to the former Dutch colonial empire and its aftermath as they affect the lives of natives of the former colonies, or their descendants, living in The Netherlands.

The category of Turkish-German authors by now is already fairly substantial, reflecting the different immigration history of Germany. In fact, authors of Turkish origin, the best-known being Emine Sevgi Özdamar, Feridun Zaimoğlu, and Zafer Şenocak, make up the largest contingent of what in German – in a groping for any appropriate definition – has variously been called, among other terms, "Ausländerliteratur, Gast-, Immigranten-, Emi-grations, Migranten- oder Migrationsliteratur, Minderheitenliteratur" ('Foreign literature, guest-, minority and migrant literature*'), as Sibel Kara puts it in her foreword to a 2009 *Dossier Migrations Literatur: eine neue Deutsche Literatur?* ('File Migration Literature: A New German Literature?')[2]

In the *Dossier*, attention is also paid to authors of Italian, Japanese, Roma and Sinti, African, and various Central and Eastern European origins. What obviously is missing from the definitions listed earlier, Kara writes, is to consider the works of these authors simply "Deutsche Literatur", that is to say, "German literature". Klaus Hübner, in a more recent piece, published on the website of the Goethe Institute in 2013, does just that, but with a twist. Instead of redefining such "hyphenated" literatures as German, he defines all contemporary German literature itself as "interculturally grounded."[3] The same, in fact, may be said of all literatures hitherto mentioned and beyond these of at least all Western European literatures in their contemporary manifestations. In what fol-lows, I will concentrate on three instances of this "new" European literature focusing upon the experiences of three kinds of "New Europeans". Zadie Smith's *White Teeth* (2000) relates to the earliest "New Europeans": those issuing from Europe's, and in this particular case Britain's, colonial past. Emine Sevgi Özdamar details the life of a young Turkish woman migrating to Germany in the 1960s in *Die Brücke vom Goldenen Horn* ('The Bridge of the Golden Horn', 1998). Chika Unigwe's *Fata Morgana*, originally published in Dutch in 2007 and republished in the author's own translation as *On Black Sisters Street* in London in 2009, follows the lives of four African women working as prostitutes in Antwerp.

White Teeth

In *White Teeth*, set in the 1970s–1990s, with flashbacks to the early 1900s as well as the end of WWII, Zadie Smith largely rehearses the story of "black" immigration to Brit-ain.[4] In what is arguably her main character, Irie Jones, Smith creates a distant double of herself. Like Smith herself, Irie is the daughter of a white Englishman and a Jamaican mother. That mother had moved to Britain in her teens, with her mother, to join her father, who had already made the same move fifteen years earlier, part of the first wave of West Indian immigration to the UK. Other characters, though, fill out other parts of the "black" immigration story of Britain. The Iqbal family originates from Bangladesh, but like the Joneses has settled in North London. If we add to this the Jewish Chalfen family, and the various other characters of Arab and other descents, we will get a fair idea of Brit-ain's present-day multicultural* make-up. The interesting part in all this is that the novel revels in the kind of Homi Bhabhian "hybridity"* that usually is flaunted as postcolonial par excellence, but that in this particular instance goes to underscore a very local sense of belonging: to a specific neighbourhood, to a particularly British sense of identity. How-ever, this is a British identity that is marked by the mixed rather than the pure. The "Irish" O'Connell's Pool House, for instance, is run by a Middle Eastern Arab and has as regular customers a pair of octogenarian Jamaicans. It also does not sport any pool tables. Mixed is also what Irie's own daughter will be. The girl is fathered upon Irie by either one of the Bangladeshi-descended Iqbal brothers. Legally, however, the child remains fatherless, as Irie does not marry. Nor does she choose to live with either of the Iqbal boys. Instead, she takes the Jewish Chalfen boy as her partner, effectively turning him into her daughter's substitute father. From Irie – and through her from her maternal grandfather Archie – the girl, however, will inherit the "arch"-English family name of "Jones." In stark contrast to most of his "white" or "native British" compatriots, Archie Jones is a man without racial prejudices. The colonial and imperial heritage of Britain comes through in the passage that provides us with an explanation for the novel's title. On a school-initiated charity outing to the elderly in their neighbourhood Irie Jones and the Iqbal twins Magid and Millat, all of them ten years old, pay a visit to a Mr J.P. Hamilton who after some hesitation invites them to tea. When the children notice him adjusting his set of false teeth, he asks them whether they regularly brush their teeth, and then follows this:

Text: Zadie Smith, White Teeth *(2000)*

Mr Hamilton leant back contemplatively in his chair. "One sometimes forgets the significance of one's teeth. We're not like the lower animals – teeth replaced regularly and all that – we're of the mammals, you see. And mammals only get two chances, with teeth. More sugar?"

The children, mindful of their two chances, declined.

"But like all things, the business has two sides. Clean white teeth are not always wise, now are they? Par exemplum: when I was in the Congo, the only way I could identify the nigger was by the whiteness of his teeth. If you see what I mean. Horrid business. Dark as buggery it was. And they died because of it, you see? Poor bastards. Or rather I survived, to look at it in another way, do you see?"

The children sat silently. And then Irie began to cry, ever so quietly.

Mr Hamilton continued. "Those are the split decisions you make in war. See a flash of white and bang! As it were . . . Dark as buggery. Terrible times. All these beautiful boys lying dead there, right in front of me, right at my feet. Stomachs open, you know, with their guts on my shoes. Like the end of the bloody world. Beautiful men, enlisted by the Krauts, black as the ace of spades; poor fools didn't even know why they were there, what people they were fighting for, who they were shooting at. The decision of the gun. So quick, children. So brutal. Biscuit?"

"I want to go home," whispered Irie.

"My dad was in the war. He played for England," piped up Millat, red-faced and furious.

"Well boy, do you mean the football team or the army?"

"The British army. He drove a tank. A Mr Churchill. With her dad," explained Magid.

"I'm afraid you must be mistaken," said Mr Hamilton, genteel as ever. "There were certainly no wogs as I remember – though you're probably not allowed to say that these days, are you? But no . . . no Pakistanis. . .; what would we have fed them? No, no," he grumbled, assessing the question as if he were being given the opportunity to rewrite history here and now. "Quite out of the question. I could not possibly have stomached that rich food. No Pakistanis. The Pakistanis would have been in the Pakistani army, whatever that was. As for the poor Brits, they had enough on their hands with us old Queens."[5]

A rewriting of history of course is precisely what is going on here, as everything the Iqbal boys are saying is true, and everything Mr Hamilton is saying is wrong, including labelling Samad Iqbal, the boys' father, a Pakistani. And there could not have been any Pakistani army in WWII because Pakistan simply did not yet exist then. It only came into being with Indian independence in 1947. In other words, Mr Hamilton is simply confirming all the colonial stereotypes* that upheld the British Empire. The final sentence, of course, along with his repeated "dark as buggery", indicates that Mr Hamilton is gay, but in his view, that was much more easily accepted in the British army, and by the British public, than that any non-whites should have fought in that same British army.

In *White Teeth*, Smith (and how much closer to "Jones" can you get than "Smith" as a "typical English" name?) casts her characters, and certainly Irie, not as separate from the run of "normal Britishers", but rather as one of them. In the same way, her novel does not profile itself as particularly "Other" than any other British novel; instead, it deliberately inserts itself in the "national" body of British writing. Such, in any case, was the over-whelming feeling in the British literary critical community. Jan Lowe in her 2001 *Small Axe* article 'No More Lonely Londoners', with its tell-tale reference to Selvon's earlier novel, reminds us that "*White Teeth* includes themes of Britain's imperial and colonial relationships with Africa, Asia and the Caribbean, and this gives it a stake in the literatures of those countries", but also finds that "enigmatically, it is also a deeply English novel."[6] And Anita Mathias in *Commonweal* argues that "Zadie Smith, the daughter of a Jamaican immigrant to Britain, continues the enterprise of giving us the view from the margins, as she sweeps Jamaican and Bangladeshi immigrants into mainstream literature in English."[7] Irie's story is one of integration with, not into, and certainly not of assimilation into, Brit-ish society. As such, it is a re-writing of the novels of exile of George Lamming or Sam Selvon. In the process, it also contributes to now retrospectively making the works of these literary ancestors, formerly peripheralized as "Commonwealth" literature, part of "British" literature proper while at the same time turning that literature, on a par with what Hübner argues for German literature, into an "interculturally grounded" one.

The Bridge of the Golden Horn

The Bridge of the Golden Horn of Emine Sevgi Özdamar has as its protagonist a Turkish girl of well-to-do Istanbul stock who in 1966, at the age of eighteen, goes to Germany to work as a *Gastarbeiterin* ('female immigrant labourer') in a factory assembling radios in West Berlin.[8] Like most other women at the factory, she initially lives in a women's hos-tel for migrant workers. Infatuated with the theatre, she wants to become an actress, and mingles with artists, radical socialists, and Turkish political exiles. Eventually, she moves to a small apartment, sharing it with another woman, and to another job, working in a hotel. All along she tries to free herself of all she considers stifling in her Turkish upbringing, seeking sexual as well as social emancipation. The novel, a fiction partially grounded in Özdamar's own experiences, is divided into two parts. The first part is set in Berlin. The second and grimmer part has the protagonist return to Turkey, where she gets almost fatally involved in revolutionary student politics. If the first part rehearses many of the experiences common to the early *Gastarbeiter*, but also much of at least Western Europe's youth in the late 1960s and early 1970s, the second part closely maps onto the much more brutal events of the political struggles in Turkey at the same time. Finally, it is the protagonist's mother that urges her to flee Turkey and return to Germany, there to lead the life she wishes. The scene with which the novel closes perfectly catches both the jaunty style of Özdamar's writing, with its almost theatrical or filmic presentation (Özdamar has worked in theatre and film, both as an actress and a director), and its immersion in wider social and political issues:

> The last night, before I went to Berlin, I cried in bed. My mother heard me, came into my room with her rolled-up bed, lay down beside me and said in the dark: "Flee and live your life. Go, fly". The next day I packed my suitcase and went to the train. A poor man stood in front of the station and showed the soldiers and whores gathered outside the station a bottle in which lay a small, poor snake. The poor man said: "How does a snake smoke?" Then he opened the top of the bottle, drew on his cigarette, blew the smoke into the bottle and closed the top again. And the poor snake lay with the smoke in the bottle. "That's how a snake smokes". A few yards farther on a man had started a fire, on to which he was throwing newspapers. In one newspaper I read: "Watergate Scandal: Nixon faces impeachment", and the newspaper went up in flames. This man had a cockerel with him. He asked the people who had gathered there: "How does a cockerel dance?" and set the cockerel on the burning newspapers, the cockerel's toes burned and it constantly raised its feet, so that they didn't burn up. The man said: "Look, the cockerel is dancing." A poor sesame ring vendor watched and drew on his long filter cigarette, it began to rain. The newspaper fire went out, the train whistled, and I sat down in the train to Berlin. From the train window I saw the Bridge of the Golden Horn. Building workers were dismantling it, because a new bridge was to be built. Their hammers echoed as they struck the bridge. The train to Berlin pulled out, from the window I still saw the Bridge of the Golden Horn. A couple of ships drew the bridge parts behind them, and the seagulls flew after them and cried out and the train cried too, for a long time, and went past the Istanbul houses. Opposite me sat a young man about my age. He opened the CUMHURIYET and I read: "Franco is dead". It was 21 November 1975. The young man who was reading the paper asked me: "Do you want a cigarette?"
> "Yes."[9]

As the narrator-protagonist does not offer any explanation as to how she feels about the various mini-scenes she focalizes or the events chronicled in the newspapers she glimpses, the reader has to draw her own inferences from the associations these juxtapositions suggest. The overall impression is of claustrophobia, suppression, tradition, and the old order, associated with Turkey, being left behind, while the future, at least for the girl on the train, is still uncertain. The symbolic role of the cigarettes is revealing in this regard. Does the girl's acceptance of the cigarette at the end signal rebellion and an accession to freedom on her part, in contrast to the "poor snake"? Or just the opposite? Linking certain elements of this final scene to scenes from the beginning of the novel when in the train carrying her for the first time to Berlin she sits crying for her mother, along with the newspaper events marking the end of what from the revolutionary stance the girl adopts was a reactionary and corrupt US presidency and a fascist dictatorship in Spain, would suggest the former. So does the reference to the workers dismantling the old Golden Horn bridge, even though the new one not yet being in place again leaves us, the girl, and Turkey only on the brink of what may be a better brighter future, but without guarantees. Finally, the very image of the train pulling out of Istanbul is in itself already a powerful indicator of movement, and of at least possible change. Which direction that change should take is suggested by the scene just preceding the one cited, when the narrator-protagonist finds her books, which she had stored in her parents' basement in Istanbul, ruined by dampness and pigeon droppings. That "Karl Marx didn't have an eye anymore" points to her realization that political agitation, such as fostered by leftist Turkish students at the end of the 1960s and early 1970s, and which led to the execution of some of them, but which for some time found favour also with at least part of Western European – and certainly German – leftist youth, and to which she had been exposed during her first Berlin years, does not hold a viable promise after all. On the same occasion, though, she also pulls a volume of Bertolt Brecht's poetry from the same bag of books, and reads:

> Thank the Lord the whole thing's quickly over
> All the loving and the sorrow my dear.
> Where are the teardrops you wept last evening?
> Where are the snows of yesteryear?[10]

That it should be Brecht she reads now and not – as in some early scenes of the novel, and specifically while on the train to Berlin on her first going there – Shakespeare, and particularly *A Midsummer Night's Dream*, as well as the import of the particular Brecht poem cited, signals the narrator-protagonist of *The Bridge of the Golden Horn* having awakened to a more realistic vision of what she may accomplish in the world, through literature, and through the theatre in first instance. Together with the earlier *Das Leben ist eine Karawanserei* ('Life is a Caravanserai', 1992) and the later *Seltsame Sterne starren zur Erde* ('Strange Stars Fall to Earth', 2003), *Die Brücke vom Goldenen Horn* in 2006 was collected into *Sonne auf halben Weg: die Istanbul Berlin Trilogie*. The earlier and later novels each take up different parts of the semi-autobiographical story of the narrator-protagonist of *The Bridge of the Golden Horn*, respectively the period before her first leaving for Germany and that after her return to Berlin in the mid-1970s working at the *Volksbühne* ('People's Stage') in East Berlin while living in West Berlin.

In its mix of the autobiographical and the political, its *Bildungsroman** (see Chapter 18) elements, and its attention to what it means to have to master a foreign language and culture, to bridge the gap between one's native country and one's new abode linguistically, culturally, and mentally, and in its shuttling, also in its settings, between the old and the new country, with all the ambiguities this entails, *The Bridge of the Golden Horn* is symptomatic of much of "immigrant" literature. Especially the issue of language, the memories the mother tongue leaves, and its relationship to a new language to be acquired form the subject of an earlier work of Özdamar, a volume of interlinked stories with which she first gained widespread attention in Germany, *Mutterzunge* ('Mother Tongue', 1990). In 2007, Özdamar for the first time also published a prose work in Turkish.

On Black Sisters Street

The protagonists of *On Black Sisters Street* by Chika Unigwe belong to the most recent wave of immigrants to Europe.[11] Four African women have come to Antwerp to work as prostitutes. All of them have come knowing fully well what it is they have signed up for. They are driven by different motives. Efe at the age of sixteen has given herself to a much older and richer man for the luxuries he can procure her. When she gets pregnant, he dumps her. Now she sends money back to her family to raise her son. Ama at the age of eight was raped by her father, a pillar of the local Christian church. Later he turns out not to be her biological father after all, and Ama is sent away to live with an aunt. Determined to sometime be her own boss, Ama signs up to go to Europe as a whore. Alek at the age of fifteen has her family murdered and is herself gang-raped in the Sudanese civil war. A Nigerian UN soldier whom she falls in love with takes her with him to Lagos. When his family does not approve of her, he arranges for her to go to Europe as a nanny, but she has to change her name to Joyce, as this is easier for white people to pronounce. Once in Antwerp, Joyce is put to work as a prostitute. Sisi has earned a university degree in Nigeria, but without the proper "connections" she cannot get a proper job. Disheartened, and lured by the promise of plenty of money with which she will be free to do whatever she wants, she signs on as a whore. In the Antwerp brothel she functions as the centre of the group of women, and as she is the only one whose thoughts we enter via indirect speech* she also functions as the narrative centre of the novel. All four women are traded by the same pimp, Dele, who parades as a wealthy businessman in Lagos. He provides them to Kate, a light-skinned Nigerian woman with a university degree who has set up as an Antwerp "madam". Gradually the women tell their stories and their dreams for the future to one another. When Sisi meets Luc, a local Antwerp man who wants her to come and live with him, marry him, and become a Belgian citizen, she thinks she can be free at last. Instead, the day she moves in with Luc she is brutally butchered on the order of Dele, who had warned all the women that he would not stand for "insubordination", and most certainly not for the financial loss any girl's defection would cause him. In a magical realist way, Sisi's soul at the moment of her death, recounted on the last pages of the novel, finds its way to Dele's house in Lagos, there to curse the pimp's two little girls, sleeping in an upstairs bedroom:

> Anyone who knew Sisi well might say that she cursed them. They might say that she told them, "May your lives be bad. May you never enjoy love. May your father suffer as much as mine will when he hears I am gone. May you ruin him."[12]

Ironically, the three other women will turn out well afterwards. With their savings from their years in the Antwerp brothel, Efe eventually sets up as a "madam" herself in Antwerp, and Joyce-Alek returns to Nigeria and opens a school there, while Ama opens a boutique.

The original Dutch title of *On Black Sisters Street* was *Fata Morgana*. The latter signals the unrealistic expectations with which many migrants, for whatever reason – but in the case of the four women from the novel in question for what we might call "economic" ones – come to Europe. The former is the actual name of the street on which the brothel in which the women work is situated: Zwartzusterstraat, or "Black Sisters Street," after the nuns' convent located there ever since the fifteenth century – the convent is still there but the last nuns left in 2013. The nuns in question tended to the sick and needy, and the novel's English title plays both on the ironic relationship the African prostitutes' work bears to that of the nuns and on the real sense of sisterhood that grows between the women. At the same time, of course, the novel is a harsh reflection on how especially so-called Third World immigrants are exploited in Europe, often becoming victims of human trafficking, with women as one of the most vulnerable categories. The Dutch title, *Fata Morgana*, not only refers to the delusions the women are under when they first come to Europe, though. It also comes into play when Efe, Ama, and Joyce, upon hearing of Sisi's murder, decide to rebel:

> "We're not happy here. None of us is. We work hard to make somebody else rich. Madam treats us like animals. Why are we doing this? And I don't believe that we

cannot find an honest policeman. I don't believe that for a second! We report Madam, and who knows, maybe we can even get asylum here. There are always people looking for causes to support. They can support us. We can be free. Madam has no right to our bodies, and neither does Dele. I don't want to think that one day I will be dead here and all Madam will do is complain about how bad my death is for business. I don't know what will happen to us, but I want to make sure Madam and Dele get punished." Joyce pulls at the tip of the cloth hanging out from the waist of her trousers.

Ama impatiently lights another cigarette then immediately squashes it into the ashtray. She is crying. "Come here", she says to Joyce and Efe. She stands up and spreads her arms. Joyce gets up and is enclosed in Ama's embrace. Efe stands up too and puts one arm around each woman. Their tears mingle and the only sound in the room is that of them weeping. Time stands still and Ama says, "Now we are sisters." Years later, Ama will tell them that at that moment she knew that they would be friends for ever. They will never go to the police but they do not know that. For now, they believe that they will and that conviction gives them some relief.[13]

Unigwe was born in Nigeria herself, and married a Flemish-Belgian man with whom she has four sons. She lived for many years in Turnhout, a smaller town to the north of Antwerp, but in 2013 emigrated to the US. In fact, *On Black Sisters Street* in its English edition makes no mention at all of its having been published earlier in a Dutch version, and to all intents and purposes is marketed as an English-language original. *Fata Morgana*, however, is firmly part of Flemish literature.

New Europe

The three novels discussed here in some detail address the position of three kinds of "New Europeans". *White Teeth* looks at the multicultural Britain that has resulted from the country's imperial past. *The Bridge of the Golden Horn* highlights a Germany marked by the influx of *Gastarbeiter*. *On Black Sisters Street* sides with Europe's newest immigrants. All three novels in earlier times would have been considered as un-belonging to any "national" European literature. More recently, however, they have been assumed as legitimate branches of, respectively, British, German, and Flemish literature. In fact, all three authors have met with almost immediate success. This is perhaps most obvious with Zadie Smith's *White Teeth*. Smith received an unusually large advance on the strength of a trial chapter she sent out to publishers. Salman Rushdie's almost extravagant praise of the novel was quoted on the book's back cover. Smith almost overnight became an icon of a contemporary multicultural London and Britain. *White Teeth* gained almost all important British literary prizes*. But also *The Bridge of the Golden Horn* and *On Black Sisters Street* have been widely praised, in the original and in translation*. The back cover of the English edition of *On Black Sisters Street*, for instance, quotes the English newspaper *The Independent* as saying that this is "an important and accomplished novel," and that "Unigwe gives voice to those who are voiceless, fleshes out the stories of those who offer themselves as meat for sale, and bestows dignity on those who are stripped of it."

Just as their authors are "New Europeans", then, the three works discussed in this chapter also bring into being a "New Europe" of integration instead of segregation, of inclusion rather than exclusion. The latter is of course fully in line with social and political developments of the last two or three decades. Since the 1960s, Europe has changed from a continent of emigration into one of immigration. European societies have become increasingly diverse and multicultural. The struggles, hopes and deceptions this has brought about with the "New Europeans" is reflected in the literature we have taken a closer look at in this chapter. An even more recent development, a million and more refugees fleeing civil and religious wars in the Middle East, or poverty and unemployment in Africa and elsewhere, may well find its way into the next wave of "New European" literature.

Notes

1 Tahar Djaout and Fatou Mbaye, "Black 'Beur' Writing," *Research in African Literatures* 23.2 *North African Literature* (Summer, 1992): 218. Originally published as "Une écriture au 'Beur' noir," in *Notre Librairie* 103 (1990), Paris: CLEF.
2 Sibel Kara, *Dossier Migrations Literatur: eine neue Deutsche Literatur* (Berlin: Heinrich Böll Stiftung, 2009), 4.
3 "Goethe Institut USA," August 2015, www.goethe.de/ins/us/lp/kul/mag/lit/en10134309.htm accessed 28.11.2017.
4 Zadie Smith, *White Teeth* (London: Penguin, 2000).
5 Smith, *White Teeth*, 171–2.
6 Jan Lowe, "No More Lonely Londoners," *Small Axe* 9 (March 2001): 166.
7 Anita Mathias, "View From the Margins," *Commonweal* (August 11, 2000): 27.
8 Emine Sevgi Özdamar, *The Bridge of the Golden Horn* (London: Serpent's Tail, 2007).
9 Özdamar, *The Bridge of the Golden Horn*, 255–6.
10 Özdamar, *The Bridge of the Golden Horn*, 255.
11 Chika Unigwe, *On Black Sisters Street* (London: Vintage, 2009).
12 Unigwe, *On Black Sisters Street*, 296.
13 Unigwe, *On Black Sisters Street*, 290.

Further reading

Adelson, Leslie. *The Turkish Turn in Contemporary German Literature*. New York: Palgrave Macmillan, 2005.
Behschnitt, Wolfgang, Sarah de Mul and Liesbeth Minnaard, eds., *Literature, Language and Multiculturalism in Scandinavia and the Low Countries*. Amsterdam: Rodopi, 2013.
Gebauer, Mirjam and Pia Schwarz, eds. *Migration and Literature in Contemporary Europe*. Munich: Meidenbauer, 2010.
Procter, James. *Writing Black Britain 1948–1998*. Manchester/New York: Manchester University Press, 2000.
Seyhan, Azade. *Writing Outside the Nation*. Princeton, NJ: Princeton University Press, 2001.
Vlasta, Sandra. *Contemporary Migration Literature in German and English*. Leiden/Boston: Brill/Rodopi, 2015.

Bibliography

Adorno, Theodor W. "Notes on Kafka." In *Can One Live After Auschwitz? A Philosophical Reader*. Translated by Samuel Weber and Shierry Weber Nicholsen, edited by Rolf Tiedemann, 211–39. Stanford, CA: Stanford University Press, 2003.

Albach, Ben. *Langs kermissen en hoven: Ontstaan en kroniek van een Nederlands toneelgezelschap in de 17de eeuw*. Zutphen: De Walburg Pers, 1977.

Allen, Graham. *Shelley's* Frankenstein. London/New York: Continuum, 2008.

Allen, John J. and Domingo Ynduráin. *El gran teatro del mundo*. Barcelona: Crítica, 1997.

Althusser, Mark G. "The Rise and Fall of Walter Scott's Popularity in Russia." In *The Reception of Sir Walter Scott in Europe*, edited by Murray Pittock, 204–40. New York: Continuum, 2006.

Álvarez, Leonor, Frans Blom and Kim Jautze. "Spaans Theater in de Amsterdamse Schouwburg (1638–1672): Kwantitatieve en kwalitatieve analyse van de creatieve industrie van het vertalen." *De Zeventiende Eeuw* 32 (2016): 12-39.

Andrukhovych, Yuri. *Perverzion*. Translated by Michael M. Nayadan. Evanston: Northwestern University Press, 2005.

Anon, "Irish Fairy Tales. Edited, With an Introduction, by W.B. Yeats." *Freeman's Journal* (16 November, 1900).

Appadurai, Arjun. *Modernity at Large: Cultural Dimensions of Globalization*. Minneapolis: University of Minnesota Press, 2000.

Apter, Emily. *Against World Literature: On the Politics of Untranslatability*. London/New York: Verso, 2013.

Auerbach, Berthold. *Schwarzwälder Dorfgeschichte*. 5 vols. Stuttgart: Cotta, 1869.

Auerbach, Erich. *Mimesis: The Representation of Reality in Western Literature*. Translated from the German by Willard R. Trask. With a New Introduction by Edward W. Said. Princeton, NJ/Oxford: Princeton University Press, 2003.

Austin, Colin and Guido Bastianini, eds./trans. *Posidippi Pellaei Quae Supersunt Ominia*. Milan: LED, 2002.

Bancroft, Timothy and David Hopkin, eds. *Folklore and Nationalism in Europe During the Long Nineteenth Century*. Leiden: Brill, 2012.

Barlow, Jane. *Irish Idylls*. New York: Dodd, Mead and Company, 1893.

Benoit-Dusausoy, Annick and Guy Fontaine, eds. *Lettres européennes: Manuel d'histoire de la literature européenne*. Brussels: De Boeck, 2007.

Bernauer, Markus. "Historical Novel and Historical Romance." In *Romantic Prose Fiction*, edited by Gerald Gillespie, Manfred Engel and Bernard Dieterle, 296–324. Amsterdam/Philadelphia, PA: John Benjamins Publishing Company, 2008.

Bernstein, Neil. *Ethos, Identity, and Community in Later Roman Declamation*. Oxford: Oxford University Press, 2013.

Bloomer, W. Martin. "Schooling in Persona: Imagination and Subordination in Roman Antiquity." *Classical Antiquity* 16 (1997): 57–78.

Boccaccio, Giovanni. *Decameron*. The John Payne Translation Revised and Annotated by Charles S. Singleton. 3 vols. Berkeley: University of California Press, 1982.

Böll, Heinrich. *The Silent Angel*. Translated by Breon Mitchell. Bridgend: Andre Deutsch, 1995.

Bonner, Stanley F. *Roman Declamation in the Late Republic and Early Empire*. Liverpool: University Press of Liverpool, 1969 [1949].

Boulding, Maria. *Saint Augustine, The Confessions*. Second edition. New York: New City Press, 2012.

Boulton, James T. and Lindeth Vasey, eds. *The Letters of D.H. Lawrence*. Vol. 5: March 1924–March 1927. Cambridge: Cambridge University Press, 2002.

Breij, Bé. "Dilemmas of *Pietas* in Roman Declamation." In *Sacred Words: Orality, Literacy and Religion: Orality and Literacy in the Ancient World*. Vol. 8, edited by André Lardinois, Josine Blok and Marc G.M. van der Poel, 329–51. Leiden: Brill, 2011.

Brontë, Charlotte. *Jane Eyre*. London: Penguin, 1996.

Brooks, Peter. *Reading for the Plot: Design and Intention in Narrative*. Oxford: Clarendon Press, 1984.

Bruckner, Matilda Tomaryn, Laurie Shepard and Sarah White, eds./trans. *Songs of the Women Troubadours*. New York: Garland, 2000.

Bussels, Stijn. *Spectacle, Rhetoric and Power: The Triumphal Entry of Prince Philip of Spain into Antwerp*. Amsterdam/New York: Rodopi, 2012.

Byron, Lord. "Childe Harold's Pilgrimage." In *The Norton Anthology of English Literature*. Vol. 2, edited by Stephen Greenblatt and Meyer Howard Abrams, 513–37. New York: Norton, 1999.

Byron, Lord. "Sardanapalus: A Tragedy." Accessed March 30, 2016. www.gutenberg.org/files/23475/23475-h/23475-h.htm

Calderón de la Barca, Pedro. *Life's a Dream/ La vida es sueño* (Aris & Phillips Hispanic Classics). Translated by Michael Kidd. Boulder: University Press of Colorado, 2004.

Calvino, Italo. *Invisible Cities*. Translated by William Weaver. Orlando: Harcourt, 1974.

Campbell, David A., ed./trans. *Greek Lyric*. 5 vols. Loeb Classical Library. Cambridge, MA: Harvard University Press, 1982–1993.

Cardwell, Richard A., ed. *The Reception of Byron in Europe*. 2 vols. London/New York: Thoemmes, 2004.

Carleton, William. *Traits and Stories of the Irish Peasantry*. 5 vols. Dublin: William Frederick Wakeman, 1833.

Casanova, Pascale. *The World Republic of Letters*. Translated by M.B. DeBevoise. Cambridge, MA/London: Harvard University Press, 2007.

Céline, Louis-Ferdinand. *Journey to the End of the Night*. Translated from the French by Ralph Manheim. New York: New Directions, 2006.

Cervantes, Miguel de. *Don Quijote*. 2 vols. Edited by J.J. Allen. Madrid: Cátedra, 1977.

Cervantes, Miguel de. *The Ingenious Hidalgo Don Quixote de la Mancha*. Translated and Edited by John Rutherford. New York: Penguin, 2001.

Chateaubriand, François de. "Mémoires d'Outre-Tombe." Translated by A.S. Kline. Accessed April 18, 2016. www.poetryintranslation.com/klineaschateaubriand.htm

Chaucer, Geoffrey. *The Canterbury Tales*. Translated by David Wright. Oxford World's Classics. Oxford: Oxford University Press, 1985.

Chaucer, Geoffrey. *The Riverside Chaucer*. Third edition. Edited by Larry D. Benson. Boston: Houghton Mifflin, 1987.

Chesterton, Gilbert K. *The Crimes of England*. New York: John Lane, 1916.

Cohn, Albert. *Shakespeare in Germany in the Sixteenth and Seventeenth Centuries: An Account of English Actors in Germany and the Netherlands, and of the Plays Performed by Them During the Same Period*. London: Asher & Co, 1865.

Collard, Christopher and Martin Cropp, eds./trans. *Euripides: Fragments*. 2 vols. Loeb Classical Library. Cambridge, MA: Harvard University Press, 2008.

Conti, Alberto. *Il Cesare*. Faenza: G.A. Archi, 1726.

Cornish, Francis W., John P. Postgate and John W. Mackail. *Catullus, Tibullus, Pervigilium Veneris*. Second edition, Revised by George P. Goold. Loeb Classical Library. Cambridge, MA: Harvard University Press, 1988.

Cribiore, Rafaella. *Gymnastics of the Mind: Greek Education in Hellenistic and Roman Egypt*. Princeton, NJ: Princeton University Press, 2001.

Crockett, Samuel Rutherford. "The Minister of Dour." In *Bog-Myrtle and Peat Tales Chiefly of Galloway*, 2–25. London: Bliss, Sands and Foster, 1889.

Csapo, Eric and Margaret C. Miller. *The Origins of Theater in Ancient Greece and Beyond: From Ritual to Drama*. Cambridge: Cambridge University Press, 2007.

Curtius, Ernst Robert. *European Literature and the Latin Middle Ages*. Translated by Willard R. Trask. Princeton, NJ: Princeton University Press, 1990.

D'Annunzio, Gabriele. *Pleasure*. Translated with a Foreword and Notes by Lara Gochin Raffaelli. Introduction by Alexander Stille. New York/London: Penguin Books, 2013.

D'haen, Theo, David Damrosch and Djelal Kadir, eds. *The Routledge Companion to World Literature*. London/New York: Routledge, 2011.

Danchev, Alex, ed. *100 Artists' Manifestos: From the Futurists to the Stuckists*. London: Penguin Modern Classics, 2011.

De Temmerman, Koen. *Crafting Characters: Heroes and Heroines in the Ancient Greek Novel*. Oxford: Oxford University Press, 2014.

Desbordes, Françoise. *La rhétorique antique*. Paris: Hachette, 1996.

Dickens, Charles. "A Preliminary Word." *Household Words* 1 (1850): 1–2.

Djaout, Tahar and Fatou Mbaye. "Black 'Beur' Writing." *Research in African Literatures* 23.2 *North African Literature* (Summer, 1992). Originally published as "Une écriture au 'Beur' noir." In *Notre Librairie* 103 (1990), Paris: CLEF.

Donovan, Josephine. *European Local-Color Literature*. New York: Continuum, 2010.

Engler, Balz. "Constructing Shakespeare in Europe." In *Four Hundred Years of Shakespeare in Europe*, edited by Luis A. Pujante and Ton Hoenselaars, 26–39. London: Rosemont Publishing, 2003.

Eliot, T.S. "Tradition and the Individual Talent." In *Selected Essays*, edited by T.S. Eliot. London: Faber & Faber, 1999.

Eliot, T.S. "Ulysses, Order, and Myth." In *Modernism and Literature: An Introduction and Reader*, edited by Mia Carter and Warren Friedman, 503–5. New York: Routledge, 2013.

Fairclough, H. Rushton. *Horace. Satires, Epistles and Ars Poetica*. Revised edition. Loeb Classical Library. Cambridge, MA: Harvard University Press, 1929.

Fitch, John G. *Seneca. Tragedies*. 2 vols. Loeb Classical Library. Cambridge, MA: Harvard University Press, 2002–2004.

Flaubert, Gustave. *The Letters of Gustave Flaubert*. Vol. 1 & 2, 1830–1880. Selected, Edited and Translated by Francis Steegmuller. London: Picador, 2001.

Foote, Stephanie. *Regional Fictions: Culture and Identity in Nineteenth-Century American Literature*. Madison, WI: University of Wisconsin Press, 2001.

Freud, Sigmund. "Thoughts for the Times on War and Death." In *'On the History of the Post Psychoanalytic Movement', 'Papers on Metapsychology' and Other Works*. Edited and Translated from the German by James Strachey, 273–302. London: Hogarth Press, 1957.

Friedländer, Paul. *Epigrammata: Greek Inscriptions in Verse From the Beginnings to the Persian Wars*. Chicago, IL: Ares, 1948 [1987].

Friedman, Susan Stanford. *Mappings: Feminism and the Cultural Geographies of Encounter*. Princeton, NJ: Princeton University Press, 1998.

Fugard, Athol. *The Township Plays*. Oxford: Oxford University Press, 1993.

Fumaroli, Marc. "L'histoire de la rhétorique dans l'Europe moderne." In *New Chapters in the History of Rhetoric*, edited by Laurent Pernot, 3–15. Leiden: Brill, 2009. (Revised version of chapter in *Histoire de la rhétorique dans l'Europe moderne, 1450–1950*, edited by Marc Fumaroli, 1–16. Paris: Presses Universitaires de France, 1999).

Gaipa, Mark, Sean Latham and Robert Scholes. *The Little Review "Ulysses": James Joyce*. New Haven/London: Yale University Press, 2015.

Galassi, Jonathan. "The Dreams of Italo Calvino." Review of *Invisible Cities*, by Italo Calvino. *The New York Review of Books*. June 20, 2013. www.nybooks.com/articles/2013/06/20/dreams-italo-calvino/

Galloway, Steven. *The Cellist of Sarajevo*. New York: Riverhead Books, 2008.

Geerdink, Nina. "Politics and Aesthetics – Decoding Allegory in *Palamedes* (1625)." In *Joost van den Vondel: Dutch Playwright of the Golden Age*, edited by Jan Bloemendal and Frans-Willem Korsten, 225–48. Leiden: Brill, 2012.

Gerber, Douglas E., ed./trans. *Greek Elegiac Poetry From the Seventh to the Fifth Centuries BC*. Loeb Classical Library. Cambridge, MA: Harvard University Press, 1999.

Gibson, Craig A. "Learning Greek History in the Ancient Classroom: The Evidence of the Treatises on Progymnasmata." *Classical Philology* 99 (2004): 103–29.

Gibson, Craig A. *Libanius's Progymnasmata: Model Exercises in Greek Prose Composition and Rhetoric.* Atlanta: Society of Biblical Literature, 2008.

Gill, Christopher. "The Ethos/Pathos Distinction in Rhetorical and Literary Criticism." *The Classical Quarterly* 34.1 (1984): 149–66.

Goethe, Johann Wolfgang von. "Die Leiden des jungen Werther." In *Goethe Werke: Hamburger Ausgabe.* Vol. 6. *Romane und Novellen,* edited by Erich Trunz. München: DTV, 1986.

Gow, Andrew S.F., trans. *The Greek Bucolic Poets.* Translated with brief notes. Cambridge: Cambridge University Press, 1953. Reprinted by Archon Books, Hamden CT, 1972.

Gray, Richard T., Ruth V. Gross, Rolf J. Goebel and Clayton Koelb. *A Franz Kafka Encyclopedia.* Westport: Greenwood, 2005.

Gunderson, Erik. *Declamation, Paternity and Roman Identity: Authority and the Rhetorical Self.* Cambridge: Cambridge University Press, 2003.

Halliwell, Stephen W. "Aristotle's Poetics." In *The Cambridge History of Literary Criticism. Volume 1: Classical Criticism,* edited by George A. Kennedy, 149–83. Cambridge: Cambridge University Press, 1989.

Halliwell, Stephen W., Hamilton Fyfe and Doreen C. Inness. *Aristotle: Poetics, Longinus: On the Sublime, and Demetrius: On Style.* Corrected Edition. Loeb Classical Library. Cambridge, MA: Harvard University Press, 1999.

Halman, Talat S. *A Millennium of Turkish Literature: A Concise History.* Edited by Jayne L. Warner. New York: Syracuse University Press, 2010.

Håkanson, Lennart, ed. *Declamationes XIX Maiores Quintiliano Falso Ascriptae.* Stuttgart: Teubner, 1982.

Handke, Peter. "Publikumsbeschimpfung." In *Stücke 1,* edited by Peter Handke. Frankfurt am Main: Suhrkamp, 1972.

Hartley, Jenny, ed. *The Selected Letters of Charles Dickens.* Oxford: Oxford University Press, 2012.

Hasenclever, Walter. *Gedichte, Dramen, Prosa.* Reinbek bei Hamburg: Rowolt Verlag, 1963.

Helmers, Helmer. "The Politics of Mobility: Shakespeare's *Titus Andronicus,* Jan Vos' *Aran en Titus* and the Poetics of Empire." In *Politics and Aesthetics in European Baroque Tragedy,* edited by Jan Bloemendal and Nigel Smith, 344–72. Leiden: Brill, 2016.

Henderson, Jeffrey, ed./trans. *Aristophanes.* 4 vols. Loeb Classical Library. Cambridge, MA: Harvard University Press, 1998–2002.

Henke, Robert and Eric Nicholson, eds. *Transnational Mobilities in Early Modern Theater.* Farnham/Burlington: Ashgate, 2014.

Herder, Johann Gottfried. *Briefe Gesamtausgabe.* Edited by Wilhelm Dobbek and Günther Arnold. Weimar: Hermann Böhlaus Nachfolger, 1981–2001.

Heseltine, Michael and William H.D. Rouse. *Petronius. Seneca: Apocolocyntosis.* Loeb Classical Library. Cambridge, MA: Harvard University Press, 1969.

Hicks, Robert D., ed./trans. *Diogenes Laertius: Lives of Eminent Philosophers.* 2 vols. Reprinted with New Introductory Material. Loeb Classical Library. Cambridge, MA: Harvard University Press, 1972.

Hoenselaars, Ton and Helmer Helmers. "*The Spanish Tragedy* and the Tragedy of Revenge in the Low Countries." In *Doing Kyd: A Collection of Articles on the Spanish Tragedy,* edited by Nicoleta Cinpoes. Manchester: Manchester University Press, forthcoming.

Hofland, Christie Anne. "Understanding Post-Soviet Ukraine Through Literature." The Ellison Center for Russian, East European and central Asian Studies, University of Washington. http://ellisoncenter.washington.edu/student-spotlight/understanding-post-soviet-ukraine-through-literature/

Hofmannsthal, Hugo von. *Natur und Erkenntnis.* Berlin: Deutsche Buch-Gemeinschaft, 1957. This edition is full text available at http://gutenberg.spiegel.de/buch/natur-und-erkenntnis-971/22

Hughes-Hallett, Lucy. *The Pike. Gabriele D'Annunzio: Poet, Seducer and Preacher of War.* London: Fourth Estate/HarperCollins Publishers, 2013.

Humpherys, Anne. "Generic Strands and Urban Twists: The Victorian Mysteries Novel." *Victorian Studies* 34 (1991): 455–72.

Hutcheon, Linda and Mario J. Valdés, eds. *Rethinking Literary History: A Dialogue on Theory*. Oxford: Oxford University Press, 2002.

Huxley, Aldous. *The Gioconda Smile*. Paris/Hamburg/Milan: Albatross, 1932.

Ife, Barry W. *Reading and Fiction in Golden-Age Spain: A Platonist Critique and Some Picaresque Replies*. Cambridge: Cambridge University Press, 1985.

Jäger, Georg. *Geschichte des deutschen Buchhandels im 19. und 20: Jahrhundert*. Band 1: Das Kaiserreich 1871–1918. Teil 3. Berlin: De Gruyter, 2010.

Jameson, Frederic. "Third-World Literature in the Era of Multinational Capitalism." *Social Text* 15 (1986): 65–88.

Jansohn, Christa and Dieter Mehl. *The Reception of D.H. Lawrence in Europe*. London: Continuum, 2007.

Jensen, Lotte. "Literature as Access to the Past: The Rise of Historical Genres in the Netherlands, 1800–1850." In *Free Access to the Past: Romanticism, Cultural Heritage and the Nation*, edited by Lotte Jensen, Joep Leerssen and Marita Mathijsen, 127–46. Leiden/Boston: Brill, 2010.

Johns, Adrian. *The Nature of the Book: Print and Knowledge in the Making*. Chicago, IL: University of Chicago Press, 1998.

Jones, Horace L., ed./trans. *Strabo: Geography*. 8 vols. Loeb Classical Library. Cambridge, MA: Harvard University Press, 1917–1932.

Joyce, James. *Ulysses*. With an Introduction by Declan Kiberd. London: Penguin Modern Classics, 2000.

Kafka, Franz. *Letters to Felice*. Edited by Erich Heller and Jürgen Born. Translated from the German by James Stern and Elisabeth Duckworth. New York: Schocken, 1973.

Kafka, Franz. *Letters to Friends, Family, and Editors*. Translated from the German by Richard Winston and Clara Winston. New York: Schocken Books, 1977.

Kafka, Franz. *Diaries, 1910–1923*. Translated from the German by Joseph Kresh. New York: Schocken, 1988.

Kafka, Franz. *Letters to Milena*. Translated from the German by Phillip Boehm. New York City: Schocken, 1990.

Kafka, Franz. "In the Penal Colony." In *Kafka's Selected Stories*, edited by Stanley Corngold. Translated from the German by Stanley Corngold, 35–59. New York: Norton, 2007.

Kara, Sibel. *Dossier Migrations Literatur: eine neue Deutsche Literatur?* Berlin: Heinrich Böll Stiftung, 2009.

Kennedy, George A. *Greek Rhetoric Under Christian Emperors*. Princeton, NJ: Princeton University Press, 1983.

Kennedy, George A. *A New History of Classical Rhetoric*. Princeton, NJ: Princeton University Press, 1994.

Kennedy, George A. *Classical Rhetoric and Its Christian and Secular Tradition From Ancient to Modern Times*. Chapel Hill: The University of North Carolina Press, 1999.

Kennedy, George A. *Progymnasmata: Greek Textbooks of Prose Composition and Rhetoric*. Atlanta: Society of Biblical Literature, 2003.

Konrád, George. *The City Builder*. Translated by Ivan Sanders. New York: Harcourt, 1977.

Kovacs, David, ed./trans. *Euripides*. 6 vols. Loeb Classical Library. Cambridge, MA: Harvard University Press, 1994–2002.

Kraus, Karl. "Heine und die Folgen." (1910). Accessed April 18, 2016. www.uni-due.de/lyriktheorie/texte/1910_kraus.html

Kucich, Greg. "Romance." In *Romanticism: An Oxford Guide*, edited by Nicholas Roe, 463–81. Oxford: Oxford University Press, 1995.

Ladenson, Elisabeth. *Dirt for Art's Sake: Books on Trial From Madame Bovary to Lolita*. Ithaca/London: Cornell University Press, 2007.

Laird, Andrew. "The Ars Poetica." In *The Cambridge Companion to Horace*, edited by Stephen Harrison, 132–43. Cambridge: Cambridge University Press, 2007.

Lardinois, André and M.G.M. van der Poel. "De Letterkunde van de Grieken en Romeinen." In *Cultuurgeschiedenis van de oudheid*, edited by Nathalie de Haan and Stephan Mols, 163–85. Zwolle: W Books, 2011.

Lattimore, Richmond, trans. *The Odyssey of Homer*. New York: HarperCollins, 1965.

Lausberg, Heinrich, David E. Orton and R. Dean Anderson. *Handbook of Literary Rhetoric: A Foundation for Literary Study*. Leiden: Brill, 1998.

Lawrence, D.H. "Why the Novel Matters." In *A Modernist Reader: Modernism in England 1910–1930*, edited by Peter Faulkner, 143–8. London: B.T. Batsford Ltd, 1986.

Lawrence, D.H. *Lady Chatterley's Lover*. London: Penguin Classics, 2006.

Leerssen, Joep. "Literary Historicism: Romanticism, Philologists, and the Presence of the Past." *Modern Language Quarterly* 65.2 (2004): 221–43.

Leerssen, Joep. *National Thought in Europe: A Cultural History*. Amsterdam: Amsterdam University Press, 2008.

Lloyd-Jones, Hugh, ed./trans. *Sophocles*. 3 vols. Loeb Classical Library. Cambridge, MA: Harvard University Press, 1994–1996.

Lowe, Jan. "No More Lonely Londoners." *Small Axe* 9 (March 2001): 166.

Mal-Maeder, Danielle van. *La fiction des déclamations*. Leiden: Brill, 2007.

Malraux, André. "D.H. Lawrence et l'érotisme." *La Nouvelle Revue Française*, January 1, 1932, 136–40.

Markov, Vladimir. *Russian Futurism: A History*. Berkeley/Los Angeles: University of California Press, 1968.

Marmier, Xavier. "Vie d'un Poète." *Revue de Paris* 46 (October 1837): 250–57.

Martin, Josef. *Antike Rhetorik: Technik und Methode*. München: Beck, 1974.

Mathias, Anita. "View From the Margins." In *Commonweal*, August 11, 2000, 27.

May, James M. and Jakob Wisse, trans. *Cicero: On the Ideal Orator*. Translated with introduction, notes, apendixes, glossary and indexes. Oxford: Oxford University Press, 2001.

McNamer, Sarah. "The Literariness of Literature and the History of Emotion." *Publications of the Modern Language Association* 130.5 (2015): 1433–43.

Mellor, Anne K. *Mary Shelley: Her Life, Her Fiction, Her Monsters*. London/New York: Routledge, 1988.

Moi, Toril. *Henrik Ibsen and the Birth of Modernism: Art, Theater, Philosophy*. Oxford: Oxford University Press, 2006.

Montalvo, Garci Rodríguez de. *Amadis de Gaula*. Edited by Juan Manuel Cacho Blecua. Madrid: Cátedra, 2004.Morgan, John R., introduction, trans. and notes. Longus. *Daphnis and Chloe*. Oxford: Aris & Phillips, 2004.

Morgan, Teresa. *Literate Education in the Hellenistic and Roman Worlds*. Cambridge: Cambridge University Press, 1998.

Musil, Robert. *Precision and Soul*. Translated from the German by Burton Pike and David S. Luft. Chicago, IL: University of Chicago Press, 1990.

Musil, Robert. *The Man Without Qualities*. Translated from the German by Burton Pike and Sophie Wilkins. New York: Alfred Knopf, 1995.

Mylius, Johan, de. *The Tales of Hans Christian Andersen*. Copenhagen: Royal Danish Ministry of Foreign Affairs, 1997.

Nolan, Alice. *The Byrnes of Glengoulah*. New York: P. O'Shea, 1868.

Nünlist, René. *The Ancient Critic at Work: Terms and Concepts of Literary Criticism in Greek Scholia*. Cambridge: Cambridge University Press, 2009.

Oliphant, Margaret. "Novels." *Blackwood's Edinburgh Magazine* 102 (1867): 257–80.

Opitz, Martin. *Gesammelte Werke*. Vol. 2. Stuttgart: Hiersemann, 1979.

Ortega y Gasset, José. *The Revolt of the Masses*. London: Unwin Books, 1972.

Ostaijen, Paul van. *Gebruiksaanwijzing der lyriek*. Rimburg: Huis Clos, 2012.

Özdmar, Emine Sevgi. *The Bridge of the Golden Horn*. London: Serpent's Tail, 2007.

Pardo Bazán, Emilia. *Obras Completas*. Madrid: Aguilar, 1973.

Parkes, Malcolm B. and Richard Beadle, eds. *The Poetical Works of Geoffrey Chaucer: A Facsimile of Cambridge University Library MS Gg. 4.27*. Norman, OK: Pilgrim Books, 1980.

Paton, William R., ed./trans. *The Greek Anthology*. 5 vols. Loeb Classical Library. Cambridge, MA: Harvard University Press, 1916–1918.

Pearsall, Derek. *The Canterbury Tales*. London: Allen and Unwin, 1985.

Pearsall, Derek. *The Life of Geoffrey Chaucer*. Oxford: Wiley-Blackwell, 1992.

Penella, Robert J. *Rhetorical Exercises From Late Antiquity: A Translation of Choricius of Gaza's "Preliminary Talks" and "Declamations"*. Cambridge: Cambridge University Press, 2009.

Perkins, David. *Is Literary History Possible?* Baltimore/London: The Johns Hopkins University Press, 1992.

Pernot, Laurent. *La rhétorique dans l'Antiquité*. Paris: Librairie Générale Française, 2000.

Perron, Eduard du. "D.H. Lawrence en de erotiek." *Forum* 1.6 (1932): 366–79.

Picoche, Jean-Louis. "Ramón López Soler, plagiaire et précurseur." *Bulletin Hispanique* 82.1–2 (1980): 81–93.

Pittock, Murray, ed. *The Reception of Sir Walter Scott in Europe*. New York: Continuum, 2006.

Plant, Ian M. *Women Writers of Ancient Greece and Rome: An Anthology*. Norman, OK: University of Oklahoma Press. 2004.

Poovey, Mary. *Uneven Developments: The Ideological Work of Gender in Mid-Victorian England*. Chicago, IL: University of Chicago Press, 1989.

Praag, Andries van. *La comedia espagnole aux Pays-Bas au XVIIe et au XVIIIe siècle*. Amsterdam: A.H. Paris, 1922.

Prendergast, Christopher, ed. *Debating World Literature*. London/New York: Verso, 2004.

Pryse, Marjorie and Judith Fetterley. *Writing Out of Place: Regionalism, Women and American Literary Culture*. Urbana, IL: University Press of Illinois, 2003.

Pujante, A. Luis and Ton Hoenselaars, eds. *Four Hundred Years of Shakespeare in Europe*. London: Rosemont Publishing, 2003.

Quinones, Ricardo. *Mapping Literary Modernism: Time and Development*. Princeton, NJ: Princeton University Press, 1985.

Rabelais, François. "Pantagruel." In *Œuvres Completes*, edited by Mireille Hutchon. Paris: Gallimard (La Pléiade), 1994.

Race, W.H., ed./trans. *Pindar*. 2 vols. Loeb Classical Library. Cambridge, MA: Harvard University Press, 1997.

Rae, W. Fraser. "Sensation Novelists: Miss Braddon." *North British Review* 43 (1865): 180–204.

Rayor, Diane, trans. *Sappho's Lyre: Archaic Lyric and Women Poets of Ancient Greece*. Berkeley: University of California Press, 1991.

Rayor, Diane and André Lardinois. *Sappho: A New Translation of the Complete Works*. Cambridge: Cambridge University Press, 2014.

Reddy, William M. "Against Constructionism: The Historical Ethnography of Emotions." *Current Anthropology* 38.3 (1997): 327–51.

Reddy, William M. *The Navigation of Feeling: A Framework for the History of Emotions*. Cambridge: Cambridge University Press, 2001.

Reynolds, Margaret, ed. *The Sappho Companion*. London: Vintage Publisher, 2000.

Ricks, Christopher, ed. *Alfred Lord Tennyson: Selected Poems*. London: Penguin Books, 2007.

Rigney, Ann. *The Afterlives of Walter Scott: Memory on the Move*. Oxford: Oxford University Press, 2012, 78–126.

Roe, Nicholas, ed. *Romanticism: An Oxford Guide*. Oxford: Oxford University Press, 1995.

Rolph, C.H. *The Trial of Lady Chatterley*. London: Penguin Books, 2005.

Rosenstein, Roy and Yves Leclair, eds./trans. *Jaufre Rudel: Chansons pour un amour lointain*. Gardonne: Fédérop, 2011.

Rousseau, Jean-Jacques. *Julie, ou la nouvelle Héloïse*. Paris: Garnier-Flammaration, 1967.

Rousseau, Jean-Jacques. *Les confessions*. Paris: Pocket, 1996.

Royal Danish Ministry of Foreign Affairs. *Hans Christian Andersen*. Copenhagen: Royal Danish Ministry of Foreign Affairs, 1997.

Ruano de la Haza, José María. "Lope de Vega and the theatre in Madrid." In *A Companion to Lope de Vega*, edited by Alexander Samson and Jonathan Tacker, 29–50. Woodbridge: Tamesis, 2008.

Rubery, Matthew. "*Bleak House* in Real Time." *English Language Notes* 46 (2008): 113–18.

Rubik, Margaret. "Die Furcht der Kritiker vor der Revolution: Der Englische Sensationsroman im Spiegel Deutscher Rezensionen in den *Blättern für Literarische Unterhaltung* und im *Magazin für*

Literatur des Auslandes." In *Beiträge zur Rezeption der Britischen und Irischen Literatur des 19: Jahrhunderts im Deutschsprachigen Raum*, edited by Norbert Bachleitner, 119–36. Amsterdam: Rodopi, 2000.

Russell, David A. "Rhetoric and Criticism." *Greece & Rome* 14 (1967): 130–44.

Russell, David A. *Criticism in Antiquity*. London: G. Duckworth & Co. Ltd, 1981.

Russell, David A. *Greek Declamation*. Cambridge: Cambridge University Press, 1983.

Russell, David A., trans. Libanius, *Imaginary Speeches: A Selection of Declamations*. London: Duckworth, 1996.

Russell, David A. ed./trans., notes. Quintilian. *The Orator's Education*. Cambridge, MA/London: Harvard University Press, 2001.

Russell, David A. "Rhetoric and criticism." In *Ancient Literary Criticism*, edited by Andrew Laird, 267–83. Oxford: Oxford University Press, 2006.

Russell, Donald A. and Michael Winterbottom. *Ancient Literary Criticism: The Principal Texts in New Translations*. Oxford: Oxford University Press, 1972.

Russell, Peter E. "Don Quijote as a Funny Book." *Modern Language Review* 64 (1969): 312–26.

Safranski, Rüdiger. *Goethe: Kunstwerk des Lebens*. München: Carl Hanser, 2013.

Scamell, Geoffrey V. *The First Imperial Age: European Overseas Expansion c. 1400–1715*. London: Routledge, 1989.

Schuiten, Francois and Benoit Peters. *Brüsel*. Doornik: Casterman, 2008.

Sélincourt, Aubrey de, trans. *Herodotus: The Histories*. Revised with Introduction and Notes by John Marincola. London: Penguin Books, 2003.

Shackleton Bailey, David R. *Martial: Epigrams*. 3 vols. Loeb Classical Library. Cambridge, MA: Harvard University Press, 1991/1993.

Shackleton Bailey, David R., ed./trans. notes. Quintilian. *The Lesser Declamations*. Loeb Classical Library. Cambridge, MA: Harvard University Press, 2006.

Showalter, Elaine. *Sexual Anarchy: Gender and Culture at the Fin-de-Siecle*. New York: Virago, 1992.

Smith, Zadie. *White Teeth*. London: Penguin, 2000.

Smits-Veldt, Mieke B. "Vertoningen in opvoeringen van Vondels tragedies 1638–1720: van emblema tot 'sieraad'." *De Zeventiende Eeuw* 11 (1995): 210–18.

Sommerstein, Alan H., ed./trans. *Aeschylus*. 3 vols. Loeb Classical Library. Cambridge, MA: Harvard University Press, 2008.

Spengel, Leonhard. ed. *Rhetores Graeci*. 3 vols. Leipzig: Teubner, 1853, 1854, 1856.

Spiers, John. *The Culture of the Publisher's Series. Vol. 1: Authors, Publishers and the Shaping of Taste*. Basingstoke: Palgrave Macmillan, 2011.

Spivak, Gayatri Chakravorty. *Death of a Discipline*. New York: Columbia University Press, 2003.

Spurgeon, Caroline F.E. *Five Hundred Years of Chaucer Criticism and Allusion*. Cambridge: Cambridge University Press, 1908–1917; reprint: New York: Russell & Russell, 1960.

Squires, Claire. *Marketing Literature: The Making of Contemporary Writing in Britain*. Basingstoke: Palgrave Macmillan, 2007.

Staël, Madame [Germaine] de. *De la littérature considérée dans ses rapports avec les institutions sociales*. Edited by Axel Blaeschke. Paris: Garnier, 1998.

Steiner, Georg. *The Idea of Europe: An Essay*. New York/London: Overlook, 2015.

Stephens, Susan A. and John J. Winkler, eds. *Ancient Greek Novels: The Fragments: Introduction, Text, Translation and Commentary*. Princeton, NJ: Princeton University Press, 1995.

Stipriaan, René van. "Het *theatrum mundi* als ludiek labyrint: De vele gedaanten van het rollenspel in de zeventiende eeuw." *De Zeventiende Eeuw* 15 (1999): 12–23.

Sussman, Lewis, trans. *The Major Declamations Ascribed to Quintilian*. Frankfurt am Main: Peter Lang, 1987.

Sussman, Lewis, ed./trans., comm. *The Declamations of Calpurnius Flaccus*. Leiden: Brill, 1994.

Svevo, Italo. *Zeno's Conscience*. Translated from the Italian by William Weaver. New York: Knopf, 2001.

Tanner, Tony. *Adultery in the Novel: Contract and Transgression*. Baltimore: Johns Hopkins University Press, 1979.

Ten Brink, Jan. *Geschiedenis der Noord-Nederlandsche letteren in de XIXe eeuw: Deel 2*. Amsterdam: Tj. van Holkema, 1888.

Thibaudet, Albert. "Langage, Littérature et Sensualité." *La Nouvelle Revue Française*, April 1, 1932.

Thomas, Julia. *Pictorial Victorians: The Inscription of Values in Word and Image*. Athens, OH: Ohio University Press, 2004.

Tolstoy, Leo. *Anna Karenina: A Novel in Eight Parts*. Translated by Richard Pevear and Larissa Volokhonsky. With a Preface by John Bailey. London: Penguin Classics, 2000.

Trollope, Anthony. "On English Prose Fiction as a Rational Amusement." In *Four Lectures*, edited by Morris L. Parrish, 94–124. London: Constable, 1938.

Troy, Michele K. "Behind the Scenes at the Albatross Press: A Modern Press for Modern Times." In *The Culture of the Publisher's Series. Vol. 1: Authors, Publishers and the Shaping of Taste*, edited by John Spiers, 202–18. Basingstoke: Palgrave Macmillan, 2011.

Unigwe, Chika. *On Black Sisters Street*. London: Vintage, 2009.

Vansina, Jan. *Oral Tradition as History*. Madison, WI: University of Wisconsin Press, 1985.

Vassalo, Peter. "Narrative Poetry." In *Romanticism: An Oxford Guide*, edited by Nicholas Roe, 350–61. Oxford: Oxford University Press, 1995.

Vondel, Joost van den. *Palamedes, oft vermoorde onnooselheyd*. Edited by J.F.M. Sterck. Amsterdam: Wereldbibliotheek, 1929.

Vondel, Joost van den. *Lucifer*. Edited by J.F.M. Sterck. Amsterdam: Wereldbibliotheek, 1931.

Walker, Jeffrey. *Rhetoric and Poetics in Antiquity*. Oxford: Oxford University Press, 2000.

Watson, Nicola J. "Afterlives." In *The Edinburgh Companion to Sir Walter Scott*, edited by Fiona Robertson, 143–55. Edinburgh: Edinburgh University Press, 2012.

Watt, John W. *Rhetoric and Philosophy From Greek into Syriac*. Farnham: Ashgate, 2010.

Webb, Ruth. "The Progymnasmata as Practice." In *Education in Greek and Roman Antiquity*, edited by Yun Lee Too, 289–316. Leiden: Brill, 2001.

West, David, trans. *Horace: The Complete Odes and Epodes*. World's Classics. Oxford: Oxford University Press, 1997.

West, David. *Virgil: The Aeneid: A New Prose Translation*. Revised edition. London: Penguin Books, 2003.

West, Martin L., trans. *Greek Lyric Poetry: A New Translation*. Oxford: Oxford University Press, 1993.

Wilson, Edmund. "The Book That Brought Good Sex Writing to the Masses." *The New Republic*, June 3, 1929.

Winterbottom, Michael, ed./trans., notes. *Seneca the Elder: Declamations*. Loeb Classical Library. Cambridge, MA: Harvard University Press, 1999 [1974].

Wood, James. "James Wood's Classic Takedown on Faux-Dickensian 'Hysterical Realism'." *New Republic*. July 24, 2000. https://newrepublic.com/article/61361/human-all-too-inhuman

Woodford, Charlotte. "Introduction: German Fiction and the Marketplace in the Nineteenth Century." In *The German Bestseller in the Late Nineteenth Century*, edited by Charlotte Woodford and Benedict Schofield, 1–18. Rochester, NY: Camden House, 2012.

Woolf, Virginia. "Mr. Bennet and Mrs. Brown." In *The Captain's Death Bed and Other Essays*. New York: Harcourt Brace Janovich, 1950 [1924].

Woolf, Virginia. "Modern Fiction." In *The Common Reader*. London: Penguin Books, 2012, 145–53.

Worthington, Ian, ed. *Brill's New Jacoby: Fragments of the Greek Historians*. Leiden: Brill, 2006–2017.

Wright, Julia. *Representing the National Landscape in Irish Romanticism*. New York: Syracuse University Press, 2014.

Zeitler, Julius, ed. *Deutsche Freundesbriefe aus sechs Jahrhunderten*. Leipzig: Julius Zeitler, 1909.

Zola, Emile. *Le Roman Expérimental*. Paris: Charpentier, 1880.

Zweig, Stefan. *The World of Yesterday: An Autobiography*. London: Cassell and Company Ltd., 1943.

Index of terms

Index of authors and works